Science Fiction
Criticism

Also available from Bloomsbury

Apocalyptic Fiction, Andrew Tate

Science Fiction: A Guide for the Perplexed, Sherryl Vint

Science Fiction Criticism

An Anthology of Essential Writings

Edited by Rob Latham

Bloomsbury Academic
An imprint of Bloomsbury Publishing Plc

B L O O M S B U R Y
LONDON · OXFORD · NEW YORK · NEW DELHI · SYDNEY

Bloomsbury Academic

An imprint of Bloomsbury Publishing Plc

50 Bedford Square	1385 Broadway
London	New York
WC1B 3DP	NY 10018
UK	USA

www.bloomsbury.com

**BLOOMSBURY and the Diana logo are trademarks
of Bloomsbury Publishing Plc**

British Library Cataloguing-in-Publication Data
A catalogue record for this book is available from the British Library.

ISBN: HB: 978-1-4742-4862-4
             PB: 978-1-4742-4861-7
             ePDF: 978-1-4742-4864-8
             ePub: 978-1-4742-4863-1

Library of Congress Cataloging-in-Publication Data
A catalog record for this book is available from the Library of Congress.

Cover design: Alice Marwick

Typeset by Deanta Global Publishing Services, Chennai, India
Printed and bound in Great Britain

To find out more about our authors and books visit www.bloomsbury.com.
Here you will find extracts, author interviews, details of forthcoming events
and the option to sign up for our newsletters.

Contents

Acknowledgments

Chapter 2: By permission of United Agents LLP.

Chapter 3: By permission of Spectrum Literary Agency.

Chapter 4: By permission of the Estate of Judith Merril and the Virgina Kidd Literary Agency.

Chapters 5, 10, 26, 27, 31, and 35: By permission of the authors.

Chapter 6: By permission of the author and *Mosaic: A Journal for the Interdisciplinary Study of Literature*.

Chapters 7, 8, 12, 18, 19, 20, 28, 30, and 36: By permission of the authors and *Science Fiction Studies*.

Chapter 9: By permission of J.G. Ballard's Estate and the Wylie Agency Ltd.

Chapter 11: By permission of the author and *College English*.

Chapter 13: By permission of the author and *The New York Review of Science Fiction*.

Chapter 14: By permission of the author and Fordham University Press.

Chapter 16: By permission of Farrar, Straus and Giroux.

Chapter 17: By permission of the Diana Finch Literary Agency.

Chapters 21 and 32: By permission of the authors and *Extrapolation*.

Chapter 23: By permission of Penguin Random House LLC and The Philip K. Dick Testamentary Trust/Wylie Agency Ltd.

Chapter 24: By permission of the author and University of Minnesota Press.

Chapter 25: By permission of the author and *October*/MIT Press.

Chapter 29: By permission of the author and Liverpool University Press.

Chapter 33: By permission of the author and *The Yearbook of English Studies*.

Chapter 34: By permission of the author and *MELUS: Multi-Ethnic Literature of the United States*.

Introduction

Over the past two decades, science fiction (SF) literature has moved from the margins to the mainstream of contemporary critical study, as evidenced by the vast number of post-secondary courses that focus on SF and by the proliferation of introductory guidebooks, critical reference works, genre histories, and theoretical studies.[1] Up until the 1960s and 1970s, when the first academic journals devoted to the subject were founded, the bulk of SF criticism was produced by reflective writers and editors, or by highly engaged fans. Indeed, SF is rare among popular genres in having a robust critical discourse that is generated and sustained internally, by its practitioners and consumers, in the pages of fanzines and magazines, in the introductions to literary anthologies, and in memoirs and personal histories. After the 1960s, a scholarly discourse about the genre rapidly blossomed, first within periodicals such as *Extrapolation* and *Science Fiction Studies*, and then in books released by university presses, including dedicated series such as Liverpool's Science Fiction Texts and Studies, established in 1995. A glance at the listings on the selective bibliography of SF criticism maintained on the website of *Science Fiction Studies* shows a remarkable spike in the volume of relevant commentary after the mid-1970s, with the most recent year canvassed—2015—boasting some two-dozen book-length works deemed worthy of attention by scholars and students of the genre.[2]

This anthology brings together a representative selection of the most important critical essays and approaches to SF studies since the inception of the genre in the nineteenth century, combining in one volume essential works in the history of SF criticism, as well as key theoretical statements that have become touchstones in the field. Reflecting the historical development of the discourse, it contains a strong balance of "amateur" and "professional" work, with fourteen pieces produced by SF authors, editors, and fans and twenty-one by academic scholars. The trajectory of coverage is designed to reflect the growth of SF studies as a discipline, moving from the formalist perspectives that dominated early criticism—and that construe SF primarily as a literary genre—to work that reflects contemporary understandings of SF as a mode of analysis, a way of thinking about alterity and difference that has become a useful critical tool for feminist, antiracist, and other political work. The volume canvasses the most important critical methodologies in the history of SF studies, from structuralism to feminism and Marxism to queer theory and critical race studies.

Collecting some of the most indispensable works of SF criticism and theory (including four winners of the Science Fiction Research Association's Pioneer Award for best critical article of the year), this volume is designed to introduce readers to the key developments and statements in SF criticism. The study of SF is now at the center of much contemporary

humanities scholarship, as theoretical paradigms such as cyberculture and posthumanism have raised the critical significance of SF's depictions of nonhuman otherness. At the
same time, the importance of SF to cultural engagements with science and technology
has been widely recognized by scholars. This volume, thus, not only provides guidance
to the most influential methods deployed in the critical study of SF, from formalist/them-
atic criticism concerned with definitions and narrative dynamics to political and cultural
criticism engaged with issues of gender, race, sexuality, and imperialism, it also surveys
the various ways the genre has been configured in relation to discourses of science,
politics, and popular culture.

The book is divided into five sections: "Definitions and Boundaries," "Structure and
Form," "Ideology and Worldview," "The Non-Human," and "Race and the Legacy of
Colonialism." Selections in each section, which are organized chronologically, are
chosen not only to outline the central critical trends in the study of SF but also to show
dialogue and exchange as core concepts have been refined over time. The first section
explores key attempts to delimit the boundaries of SF as a field. While Hugo Gernsback's
editorial for the first issue of the first SF pulp, *Amazing Stories*, sought to articulate a
cohesive corpus, much of the work in this section is concerned with expanding parameters, with Robert A. Heinlein and Judith Merril seeing SF as part of a larger tradition
of "speculative fiction," while Veronica Hollinger connects recent trends in the genre with
postmodern literature and theory. Finally, Roger Luckhurst and John Rieder suggest
ways in which the very impulse to define and delimit SF is historically overdetermined
and theoretically suspect.[3]

Section II examines key interventions in the study of SF as a narrative form. It opens
with J. G. Ballard's polemical call for a surrealist mode of SF writing counterpoised to the
pulp tradition and then moves into classic structuralist analyses of SF's textual dynamics
by Samuel R. Delany, Darko Suvin, and Marc Angenot. Damien Broderick contributes the
key term "megatext" to show how individual works of SF are implicated in a larger body of
shared ideas, images, and tropes. Finally, David Wittenberg examines time-travel stories
as paradigms for narratological operations relating to temporality and subjectivity.

Section III opens a consideration of SF's sociopolitical implications, a theme that, in
various ways, continues through the remaining sections. It begins with a famous early
fan statement of SF's progressive possibilities by John B. Michel, who defends the vision
of the genre as a powerful mode of social criticism. This notion will later be given more
rigorous theoretical formulation by academic Marxist critics such as Fredric Jameson
and Carl Freedman. On the other hand, Susan Sontag and Joanna Russ point to ways
in which the genre is entangled, regressively, with social ideologies. Wendy Pearson's
consideration of SF's queer subtexts is more ambivalent, exploring a dialectic of repression and revelation that structures SF's treatments of nonnormative sexuality, while Lisa
Yaszek shows how the genre has always welcomed perspectives that arraign prevailing
gender norms and values.

Section IV focuses closely on one of the major topics in SF: the representation of
nonhuman others (aliens, robots, cyborgs, etc.), considering the formal and ideological

implications of these depictions. The section opens with Mary Shelley's musings on the origins of SF's first and most famous humanoid creation, *Frankenstein's monster*. Both Philip K. Dick's and Gwyneth Jones's essays examine, from very different perspectives, the ways in which artificial or extraterrestrial beings reflect—and reflect upon—issues of human identity and community, while N. Katherine Hayles and Vernor Vinge consider the emergence of posthuman life forms linked to cybernetic and information technologies. Donna Haraway and Allison de Fren explore how depictions of cyborgs in SF are deeply enmeshed in the politics of gender and sexuality, while Sherryl Vint exposes how SF's many forms of alienness serve as displaced representations of animal otherness.

Finally, Section V gathers key statements about SF's links with imperialist (and neo-imperialist) discourses and the resulting constraints and enablements the genre offers in its engagement with issues of race and ethnicity. Istvan Csicsery-Ronay shows how SF has been historically implicated in the empire-building projects of Western nation states—with the effect of imposing a particular model of technoscientific "progress" that Grace Dillon's essay on indigenous forms of knowledge contests. While Stephen Hong Sohn critiques SF's lingering Orientalism and Nalo Hopkinson its stubborn racism, Kodwo Eshun and Lysa Rivera explore ways in which, despite its colonialist legacy, SF can offer resources for social critique and utopian imagination to peoples of color struggling against repressive histories and racist ideologies. Finally, my own contribution to the volume considers the ways in which imperialist concerns are imbricated with issues of ecological transformation in key works of "eco-catastrophe."

This book has had a long gestation and has benefited from discussions with many scholars and friends. I would particularly like to thank my former colleagues on the editorial board of the journal *Science Fiction Studies*, especially Managing Editor Arthur B. Evans, who has been generous in providing access to key works in the journal's archive, and Sherryl Vint, who helped me cull a basic selection of texts. I am also more indebted than I can possibly express to my former colleague at the University of Iowa, Brooks Landon, whose vision of SF as a literature of change has influenced my own thinking profoundly. My intrepid and gracious research assistant, Brittany Roberts, has done a valiant job tracking down copyright holders and securing permissions for reprint. And my amazing editors at Bloomsbury, David Avital and Mark Richardson, have been both patient and foresightful. Finally, I would like to dedicate this book to all the students in my SF classes who over the years have never failed to inspire me with their insights into the genre's capacity to address important aesthetic, cultural, and sociopolitical concerns.

Notes

1. See the annotated bibliographies contained in this volume for a representative selection.
2. "Chronological Bibliography of Science Fiction History, Theory, and Criticism," *Science Fiction Studies* website at http://depauw.edu/sfs/biblio.htm. See also the four surveys contained in the journal's July 1999 special issue on the "History of Science Fiction Criticism."
3. The introductory headnotes to the five sections offer more in-depth commentary on their specific contents and the interrelationships among them.

Recommended further reading

Bleiler, Everett F. *Science-Fiction: The Early Years*. Kent, OH: Kent State UP, 1990.

Bleiler, Everett F. *Science-Fiction: The Gernsback Years*. Kent, OH: Kent State UP, 1998.

Massive surveys of SF novels and stories from the origins of the genre through 1936 with fully annotated entries and a highly useful critical apparatus, including an extensive thematic index.

Bould, Mark, Andrew M. Butler, Adam Roberts, and Sherryl Vint, eds. *The Routledge Companion to Science Fiction*. New York: Routledge, 2009.

The most thorough and valuable of the recent spate of SF reference works, including fifty-six chapters covering SF in print and other media; includes coverage of historical trends and developments, major themes and authors, and important theoretical issues.

Clute, John, David Langford, Peter Nicholls, and Graham Sleight, eds. *The Encyclopedia of Science Fiction*, at http://www.sf-encyclopedia.com/.

Third (and first online) edition of the most indispensible reference work ever devoted to SF; contains over 16,000 entries, all meticulously cross-referenced, on SF authors, editors, magazines, films, core themes, and much more.

Gunn, James, and Matthew Candelaria, eds. *Speculations on Speculation: Theories of Science Fiction*. Lanham, MD: Scarecrow, 2005.

A critical anthology that gathers twenty-four essays of SF criticism, eschewing high theory in favor of practical considerations of SF history and the dynamics of SF narrative.

Hartwell, David G. *Age of Wonders: Exploring the World of Science Fiction*. 1985. Rev. ed. New York: Tor, 1996.

A superb handbook written by a brilliant SF editor, which examines SF as a vital and ongoing dialogue linking authors, editors, fans, and scholars.

The Internet Speculative Fiction Database at http://www.isfdb.org/.

A highly useful, easily searchable database featuring exhaustive bibliographic information on SF authors, magazines, and publishers, with extensive galleries of cover art.

Latham, Rob, ed. *The Oxford Handbook of Science Fiction*. New York: Oxford UP, 2014.

Gathers forty-four in-depth chapters that consider SF not just as a literary genre, but as a mass-media and cultural phenomenon, as well as a worldview informed by a range of theoretical perspectives, from feminism to libertarianism to Afrofuturism.

Luckhurst, Roger. *Science Fiction*. Cambridge: Polity, 2005.

The best narrative history of the genre, focusing on SF as a technocultural discourse, with roots in the late nineteenth century, that tracks prevailing trends in technoscientific discovery and invention.

The Science Fiction and Fantasy Research Database at http://sffrd.library.tamu.edu/.

The best resource for accessing the critical discourse of science fiction, indexing over 100,000 items by author, title, subject, source, and keyword.

Stableford, Brian. *Science Fiction and Science Fact: An Encyclopedia*. New York: Routledge, 2006.

A magisterial study of the links between science and SF, including 230 alphabetically organized entries offering detailed discussion of the ways SF deploys, distorts, and disputes scientific concepts and phenomena.

Tymn, Marhall, and Mike Ashley, eds., *Science Fiction, Fantasy, and Weird Fiction Magazines*. Westport, CT: Greenwood, 1985.

Critical survey of SF (and related fantastic) magazines, fanzines, and journals, 551 in all, which are canvassed in insightful capsule histories with comprehensive publishing and editing data. Ashley has also authored a useful four-volume history of SF magazines for Liverpool University Press (2000–16).

Wolfe, Gary K. *Critical Terms for Science Fiction and Fantasy: A Glossary and Guide to Scholarship*. Westport, CT: Greenwood, 1986.

Useful, if dated, glossary of critical terms used in the study of SF and fantasy. A more up-to-date reference work is Jeff Prucher's *Brave New Words: The Oxford Dictionary of Science Fiction* (2007), which offers definitions of key terms in SF literature and history, as well as examples of first and subsequent usage.

Part 1

Definitions and boundaries

This section opens with influential early definitions of the genre advanced by two important figures in the field: Hugo Gernsback, editor of the first SF pulp *Amazing Stories*, and H. G. Wells, author of classic scientific romances such as *The Time Machine* (1895) and *The War of the Worlds* (1898). Writing in 1926, Gernsback offered an ostensive definition of what he called "scientifiction": by this term, he meant "the Jules Verne, H. G. Wells, and Edgar Allan Poe type of story . . . a charming romance intermingled with scientific fact and prophetic vision."[1] Such stories, he stressed, were only possible in a world being rapidly transformed by technoscientific change—thus his emphasis on prophesy, the ability of SF to predict futuristic marvels that would eventually come to pass. This focus on prediction, as well as Gernsback's brief for the genre's didactic quality—its "knack of imparting knowledge, and even inspiration, without once making us aware that we are being taught"—would prove highly influential as the specialty SF magazine began to establish itself in the United States.

By contrast, Wells, in the introduction to a 1933 omnibus edition of his most famous SF works, drew a sharp contrast between the "anticipatory inventions" of Verne and his own "scientific fantasies," which (he claims) rely on central premises—time travel, invisibility, anti-gravity—that are logically or scientifically impossible but that, once posited in a narrative, must be extrapolated with the utmost realism. "Touches of prosaic detail," he argues, "are imperative," along with "a rigorous adherence to the hypothesis," however fantastical. Rather than didactically displaying the wonders of scientific progress, as Gernsback suggests SF does, Wells's tales use "magic tricks" to illuminate social life from a fresh angle or to satirize human foibles and pretensions.

This contrast between SF as predictive and didactic on the one hand, fantastic and satirical on the other, runs through much of the criticism of the genre produced in the wake of Gernsback's and Wells's interventions.[2] The third reading in this section, a 1947 essay by American SF author Robert A. Heinlein, directly confronts the division between what he calls "gadget stories" and "human-interest stories," with the latter seen as a richer and more compelling vein of literary exploration. Like Wells, Heinlein argues that an SF story must contain some significant divergence from consensus reality, a speculative postulate that the author works through with great care, showing how human characters learn to "cop[e] with problems arising out of the new situation." Unlike Wells, however,

Heinlein affirms that the element of novelty in the story must be scientifically plausible, not mere fantasy; indeed, premises in SF stories "must *not* be at variance with observed facts." Heinlein's essay is widely credited with coining the phrase "speculative fiction" as a way of registering the genre's imaginative engagement with futuristic possibility.

Subsequent critics—such as SF author-editor Judith Merril, an excerpt from whose 1966 essay "What Do You Mean: Science? Fiction?" follows—have taken up Heinlein's term in order to argue for speculative fiction as a more sophisticated form of writing than what she calls "teaching" and "preaching" stories, whose impulses are more limited in effect. Merril follows Wells and Heinlein in arguing that the best SF introduces "a given set of changes—imaginary or inventive—into the common background of 'known facts,' creating an environment in which the responses and perceptions of the characters will reveal something about the inventions, the characters, or both." She goes further, however, in claiming a prestigious pedigree that transcends the pulp tradition inaugurated by Gernsback's *Amazing Stories*, which was always only a limited subset of a more encompassing tradition that included the *voyages fantastiques* of Cyrano and the *contes philosophiques* of Voltaire. Moreover, true SF, in synch with cutting-edge trends in modern science, is less didactic than speculative in nature: dynamic as opposed to mechanical, relativistic rather than positivist. The best trends in SF will always, according to Merril, move along speculative lines, and her piece concludes with a brief for "a more radical and more exciting" form of writing, then emerging especially in Britain, which would eventually become known as the "New Wave" movement. Indeed, during the 1960s, Merril became an increasingly vocal evangelist for the New Wave as a crucial avant-garde within the field, combating the vestiges of the Gernbackian gadget story with surrealist satire.[3]

Merril's meticulous discussion of the intellectual and commercial milieu within which the genre evolved makes clear that definitions should not be seen as fixed and ahistorical but rather as developing in response to changing cultural and institutional pressures. Indeed, what essentially *counts* as science fiction is perennially revised as new generations of editors, authors and readers contest the genre's scope and boundaries. During the 1980s, the most visible—and voluble—of these groups were the so-called cyberpunks, and the next selection, Bruce Sterling's introduction to his 1986 anthology *Mirrorshades*, addresses how cyberpunk at once continues earlier trends and brings new energy to the field. On the one hand, cyberpunk draws upon the tradition of "hard SF" pioneered by John W. Campbell's magazine *Astounding* during the 1940s, as well as the New Wave's "streetwise" stylishness; on the other hand, it responds to fresh trends in 1980s culture, such as punk music and the ethos of the computer hacker. SF, in short, cannot be defined purely in terms of allegedly timeless formal qualities because the genre is inextricable from the historical influences that shape it at any given moment. Indeed, for Sterling, cyberpunk is merely the "literary incarnation" of a global phenomenon that fuses "the realm of high tech . . . and the modern pop underground."

The final three readings in this section, all written by academic critics rather than front-line genre practitioners, continue even more forcefully the move toward an antiessentialist conception of SF: for these critics, defining science fiction and establishing its bound-aries is inevitably a historical process, and the goals and motives of those doing the defining cannot be ignored in any responsible account of the genre. In her 1990 essay, Veronica Hollinger expressly agrees with Sterling that cyberpunk marks a breakthrough to a new historical form of SF, one that casts aside humanist verities in favor of post-hu-man visions of cyborg possibility. In alignment with trends in postmodern theory and culture, cyberpunk embraces fragmented narratives, mutable subjectivities, and delirious transformations of self and society.[4] Even more provocatively, Hollinger suggests that cyberpunk may augur an epochal breakdown in the boundaries separating the genre from the mainstream of postmodern fiction, though it still remains constrained by the commercial and ideological limitations of its "paraliterary" status. What these two pieces on cyberpunk show, above all, is that SF is always, in Hollinger's words, "The product of a multiplicity of influences from both within and outside of [the] genre," and any attempt to define its features must take this imbrication of factors into account.

Roger Luckhurst's essay, which openly identifies itself as "a polemic," goes even further, attacking the very impulse to draw and police boundaries as a pathological condi-tion endemic to SF history. As he shows, critics—such as Judith Merril, for example—who attempt to legitimate science fiction as literature are impelled to "isolat[e] a central defin-ition through which all other cases can be rejected or shifted to the edges as impure." Thus, so-called "speculative fiction" is elevated as a more genuine form than didactic gadget stories, which are dismissed as atavistic pulp survivals, and the ultimate effect of such proscriptions, according to Luckhurst, is to cast huge swaths of SF into critical oblivion. Yet the ritual impulse to transcend SF's lowly pulp origins only serves, ironically, to reinforce the centrality of Gernback's "initial elaboration of the conditions on which the genre has come to be defined." For Luckhurst, the critical history of SF is a series of quixotic definitional shifts that are largely rhetorical and self-defeating.

The final essay in this section, by John Rieder, offers a magisterial analysis of the contrast between essentialist and what might be called process-based definitions of SF. Rather than seeing genres as "fixed, ahistorical entities," Rieder argues for them as the complex results of decisions and arguments made by particular subjects with identifi-able motives and goals. As he puts it, "Categorization . . . is not a passive registering of qualities intrinsic to what is being categorized, but an active intervention in their dispos-ition." Definitions, thus, are *modes of reading* that connect texts with one another and draw borders between them and other sets of texts; rather than static, they are dynamic and relational. Historically, the key distinctions between SF and other forms of writing were established during the pulp era, with the advent of specialty genre magazines perceived as distinct from so-called "serious" literature. Like Luckhurst, Rieder sees genre attribution as a "rhetorical act" that intervenes in the processes of distribution and reception, though he does not see this intervention as necessarily invidious. Rather, it is simply the way that "communities of practice" pursue reading strategies based on their particular interests and values, and the field that today constitutes science fiction is traversed by multiple such communities, each with its particular vision of the genre's scope and limits. The project of definition is thus not pointless, but it can never be settled once and for all.

Notes

1. The unlovely portmanteau word "scientifiction," which was Gernsback's coinage, did not catch on, being eventually supplanted by the now-common "science fiction" during the 1930s. For a discussion of the consolidation of Gernbackian conceptions of the field, see Gary Westfahl's *The Mechanics of Wonder: The Creation of the Idea of Science Fiction* (Liverpool: Liverpool UP, 1999).
2. Some critics have argued that this contrast highlights a significant difference between the American and British SF traditions, with the former being a gadget-driven writing dominated by "gosh-wow" emotion, while the latter is more philosophical and pessimistic. See, for example, Brian Stableford, *Scientific Romance in Britain, 1890-1950* (New York: St. Martin's, 1985).
3. For a discussion of Merril's role as a passionate advocate for speculative fiction, see my essay "The New Wave" in David Seed's *Companion to Science Fiction* (Malden, MA: Blackwell, 1995), pp. 202–16.
4. Hollinger was one of many critics during the 1980s and 1990s who argued for the convergence of cyberpunk with postmodern literature and culture. See, for example, the essays gathered in Larry McCaffery's *Storming the Reality Studio: A Casebook of Cyberpunk and Postmodern Fiction* (Durham, NC: Duke UP, 1991).

1

Editorial: A new sort of magazine

Hugo Gernsback

Another fiction magazine!

At first thought it does seem impossible that there could be room for another fiction magazine in this country. The reader may well wonder, "Aren't there enough already, with the several hundreds now being published?" True. But this is not "another fiction magazine," *Amazing Stories* is a *new* kind of fiction magazine! It is entirely new—entirely different—something that has never been done before in this country. Therefore, *Amazing Stories* deserves your attention and interest.

There is the usual fiction magazine, the love story and the sex-appeal type of magazine, the adventure type, and so on, but a magazine of "Scientifiction" is a pioneer in its field in America.

By "scientifiction" I mean the Jules Verne, H. G. Wells, and Edgar Allan Poe type of story—a charming romance intermingled with scientific fact and prophetic vision. For many years stories of this nature were published in the sister magazines of *Amazing Stories—Science and Invention* and *Radio News*.

But with the ever increasing demands on us for this sort of story, and more of it, there was only one thing to do—publish a magazine in which the scientific fiction type of story will hold forth exclusively. Toward that end we have laid elaborate plans, sparing neither time nor money.

Edgar Allan Poe may well be called the father of "scientifiction." It was he who really originated the romance, cleverly weaving into and around the story, a scientific thread. Jules Verne, with his amazing romances, also cleverly interwoven with a scientific thread, came next. A little later came H. G. Wells, whose scientifiction stories, like those of his forerunners, have become famous and immortal.

It must be remembered that we live in an entirely new world. Two hundred years ago, stories of this kind were not possible. Science, through its various branches of mechanics, electricity, astronomy, etc., enters so intimately into all our lives today, and we are so much immersed in this science, that we have become rather prone to take new inventions and discoveries for granted. Our entire mode of living has changed with the present progress, and it is little wonder, therefore, that many fantastic situations—impossible 100 years ago—are brought about today. It is in these situations that the new romancers find their great inspiration.

Not only do these amazing tales make tremendously interesting reading—they are also always instructive. They supply knowledge that we might not otherwise obtain—and they supply it in a very palatable form. For the best of these modern writers of scientific-tion have the knack of imparting knowledge, and even inspiration, without once making us aware that we are being taught.

And not only that! Poe, Verne, Wells, Bellamy, and many others have proved themselves real prophets. Prophesies made in many of their most amazing stories are being realized—and have been realized. Take the fantastic submarine of Jules Verne's most famous story, *Twenty Thousand Leagues Under the Sea* for instance. He predicted the present day submarine almost down to the last bolt! New inventions pictured for us in the scientifiction of today are not at all impossible of realization tomorrow. Many great science stories destined to be of an historical interest are still to be written, and *Amazing Stories* magazine will be the medium through which such stories will come to you. Posterity will point to them as having blazed a new trail, not only in literature and fiction, but in progress as well.

We who are publishing *Amazing Stories* realize the great responsibility of this undertaking, and will spare no energy in presenting to you, each month, the very best of this sort of literature there is to offer.

Exclusive arrangements have already been made with the copyright holders of the entire voluminous works of *all* of Jules Verne's immortal stories. Many of these stories are not known to the general American public yet. For the first time they will be within easy reach of every reader through *Amazing Stories*. A number of German, French and English stories of this kind by the best writers in their respective countries have already been contracted for, and we hope very shortly to be able to enlarge the magazine and in that way present always more material to our readers.

How good this magazine will be in the future is up to you. Read *Amazing Stories*—get your friends to read it and then write us what you think of it. We will welcome constructive criticism—for only in this way will we know how to satisfy you.

2

Preface to *The Scientific Romances*

H. G. Wells

Mr. Knopf has asked me to write a preface to this collection of my fantastic stories. They are put in chronological order, but let me say here right at the beginning of the book, that for anyone who does not as yet know anything of my work it will probably be more agreeable to begin with *The Invisible Man* or *The War of the Worlds*. *The Time Machine* is a little bit stiff about the fourth dimension and *The Island of Dr. Moreau* rather painful.

These tales have been compared with the work of Jules Verne and there was a disposition on the part of literary journalists at one time to call me the English Jules Verne. As a matter of fact there is no literary resemblance whatever between the anticipatory inventions of the great Frenchman and these fantasies. His work dealt almost always with actual possibilities of invention and discovery, and he made some remarkable forecasts. The interest he invoked was a practical one; he wrote and believed and told that this or that thing could be done, which was not at that time done. He helped his reader to imagine it done and to realise what fun, excitement or mischief would ensue. Many of his inventions have "come true." But these stories of mine collected here do not pretend to deal with possible things; they are exercises of the imagination in a quite different field. They belong to a class of writing which includes the *Golden Ass of Apuleius*, the *True Histories of Lucian*, *Peter Schlemil* and the story of *Frankenstein*. It includes too some admirable inventions by Mr. David Garnett, *Lady into Fox* for instance. They are all fantasies; they do not aim to project a serious possibility; they aim indeed only at the same amount of conviction as one gets in a good gripping dream. They have to hold the reader to the end by art and illusion and not by proof and argument, and the moment he closes the cover and reflects he wakes up to their impossibility.

In all this type of story the living interest lies in their non-fantastic elements and not in the invention itself. They are appeals for human sympathy quite as much as any "sympathetic" novel, and the fantastic element, the strange property or the strange world, is used only to throw up and intensify our natural reactions of wonder, fear or perplexity. The invention is nothing in itself and when this kind of thing is attempted by clumsy writers who do not understand this elementary principle nothing could be conceived more silly and extravagant. Anyone can invent human beings inside out or worlds like dumbbells or a gravitation that repels. The thing that makes such imaginations interesting is their translation into commonplace terms and a rigid exclusion of other marvels from the story. Then it becomes human. "How would you feel and what might not happen to you," is the typical question, if for instance pigs could fly and one came rocketing over a hedge at you. How would you feel and what might not happen to you if suddenly you were changed into an ass and couldn't tell anyone about it? Or if you became invisible? But no one would think twice about the answer if hedges and houses also began to fly, or if people changed into lions, tigers, cats and dogs left and right, or if everyone could vanish anyhow. Nothing remains interesting where anything may happen.

For the writer of fantastic stories to help the reader to play the game properly, he must help him in every possible unobtrusive way to *domesticate* the impossible hypothesis. He must trick him into an unwary concession to some plausible assumption and get on with his story while the illusion holds. And that is where there was a certain slight novelty in my stories when first they appeared. Hitherto, except in exploration fantasies, the fantastic element was brought in by magic. Frankenstein even, used some jiggery-pokery magic to animate his artificial monster. There was trouble about the thing's soul. But by the end of last century it had become difficult to squeeze even a momentary belief out of magic any longer. It occurred to me that instead of the usual interview with the devil or a magician, an ingenious use of scientific patter might with advantage be substituted. That was no great discovery. I simply brought the fetish stuff up to date, and made it as near actual theory as possible.

As soon as the magic trick has been done the whole business of the fantasy writer is to keep everything else human and real. Touches of prosaic detail are imperative and a rigorous adherence to the hypothesis. Any *extra* fantasy outside the cardinal assumption immediately gives a touch of irresponsible silliness to the invention. So soon as the hypothesis is launched the whole interest becomes the interest of looking at human feelings and human ways, from the new angle that has been acquired. One can keep the story within the bounds of a few individual experiences as Chamisso does in *Peter Schlemil*, or one can expand it to a broad criticism of human institutions and limitations as in *Gulliver's Travels*. My early, profound and lifelong admiration for Swift, appears again and again in this collection, and it is particularly evident in a predisposition to make the stories reflect upon contemporary political and social discussions. It is an incurable habit with literary critics to lament some lost artistry and innocence in my early work and to accuse me of having become polemical in my later years. That habit is of such old standing that the late Mr. Zangwill in a review in 1895 complained that my first book, *The Time Machine,* concerned itself with "our present discontents." *The Time Machine* is indeed quite as philosophical and polemical and critical of life and so forth, as *Men like Gods* written twenty-eight years later. No more and no less. I have never been able to get away from life in the mass and life in general as distinguished from life in the individual experience, in any book I have ever written. I differ from contemporary criticism in finding them inseparable.

For some years I produced one or more of these "scientific fantasies," as they were called, every year. In my student days we were much exercised by talk about a possible fourth dimension of space; the fairly obvious idea that events could be presented in a rigid four dimensional space time framework had occurred to me, and this is used as the magic trick for a glimpse of the future that ran counter to the placid assumption of that time that Evolution was a pro-human force making things better and better for mankind. *The Island of Dr. Moreau* is an exercise in youthful blasphemy. Now and then, though I rarely admit it, the universe projects itself towards me in a hideous grimace. It grimaced that time, and I did my best to express my vision of the aimless torture in creation. *The War of the Worlds* like *The Time Machine* was another assault on human self-satisfaction.

All these three books are consciously grim, under the influence of Swift's tradition. But I am neither a pessimist nor an optimist at bottom. This is an entirely indifferent world in which wilful wisdom seems to have a perfectly fair chance. It is after all rather cheap to get force of presentation by loading the scales on the sinister side. Horror stories are easier to write than gay and exalting stories. In *The First Men in the Moon* I tried an improvement on Jules Verne's shot, in order to look at mankind from a distance and burlesque the effects of specialization. Verne never landed on the moon because he never knew of radio and of the possibility of sending back a message. So it was his shot that came back. But equipped with radio, which had just come out then, I was able to land and even see something of the planet.

The two later books are distinctly on the optimistic side. *The Food of the Gods* is a fantasia on the change of scale in human affairs. Everybody nowadays realises that change of scale; we see the whole world in disorder through it; but in 1904 it was not a very prevalent idea. I had hit upon it while working out the possibilities of the near future in a book of speculations called *Anticipations* (1901). The last story is Utopian. The world is gassed and cleaned up morally by the benevolent tail of a comet.

Men like Gods, written seventeen years after *In the Days of the Comet*, and not included in this volume, was almost the last of my scientific fantasies. It did not horrify or frighten, was not much of a success, and by that time I had tired of talking in playful parables to a world engaged in destroying itself. I was becoming too convinced of the strong probability of very strenuous and painful human experiences in the near future to play about with them much more. But I did two other sarcastic fantasies, not included here, *Mr. Blettsworthy on Rampole Island* and *The Autocracy of Mr. Parham*, in which there is I think a certain gay bitterness, before I desisted altogether.

The Autocracy of Mr. Parham is all about dictators, and dictators are all about us, but it has never struggled through to a really cheap edition. Work of this sort gets so stupidly reviewed nowadays that it has little chance of being properly read. People are simply warned that there are ideas in my books and advised not to read them, and so a fatal suspicion has wrapped about the later ones. "Ware stimulants!" It is no good my saying that they are quite as easy to read as the earlier ones and much more timely.

It becomes a bore doing imaginative books that do not touch imaginations, and at length one stops even planning them. I think I am better employed now nearer reality, trying to make a working analysis of our deepening social perplexities in such labors as *The Work, Wealth and Happiness of Mankind* and *After Democracy*. The world in the presence of cataclysmal realities has no need for fresh cataclysmal fantasies. That game is over. Who wants the invented humors of Mr. Parham in Whitehall, when day by day we can watch Mr. Hitler in Germany? What human invention can pit itself against the fantastic fun of the Fates? I am wrong in grumbling at reviewers. Reality had taken a leaf from my book and set itself to supersede me.

3

On the writing of speculative fiction

Robert A. Heinlein

"There are nine-and-sixty ways

Of constructing tribal lays

And every single one of them is right!"

—Rudyard Kipling

There are at least two principal ways to write speculative fiction—write about people, or write about gadgets. There are other ways; consider Stapleton's *Last and First Men*, recall S. Fowler Wright's *The World Below*. But the gadget story and the human-interest story comprise most of the field. Most science fiction stories are a mixture of the two types, but we will speak as if they were distinct—at which point I will chuck the gadget story aside, dust off my hands, and confine myself to the human-interest story, that being the sort of story I myself write. I have nothing against the gadget story—I read it and enjoy it—it's just not my pidgin. I am told that this is a how-to-do-it symposium; I'll stick to what I know how to do.

The editor suggested that I write on "Science Fiction in the Slicks." I shan't do so because it is not a separate subject. Several years ago Will F. Jenkins said to me, "I'll let you in on a secret, Bob. *Any* story—science fiction, or otherwise—if it is well written, can be sold to the slicks." Will himself has proved this, so have many other writers—Wylie, Wells, Cloete, Doyle, Ertz, Noyes, many others. You may protest that these writers were able to sell science fiction to the high-pay markets because they were already well-known writers. It just ain't so, pal; on the contrary they are well-known writers because they are skilled at their trade. When they have a science fiction story to write, they turn out a well-written story and it sells to a high-pay market. An editor of a successful magazine will bounce a poorly-written story from a "name" writer just as quickly as one from an unknown. Perhaps he will write a long letter of explanation and suggestion, knowing as he does that writers are as touchy as white leghorns, but he will bounce it. At most, prominence of the author's name might decide a borderline case.

A short story stands a much better chance with the slicks if it is not more than 5000 words long. A human-interest story stands a better chance with the slicks than a gadget story, because the human-interest story usually appeals to a wider audience than does a gadget story. But this does not rule out the gadget story. Consider "The Note on Danger B" in a recent *Saturday Evening Post* and Wylie's "The Blunder," which appeared last year in *Collier's.*

Let us consider what a story is and how to write one. (Correction: how *I* write one—remember Mr. Kipling's comment!)

A story is an account which is not necessarily true but which is interesting to read.

There are three main plots for the human interest story: boy-meets-girl, The Little Tailor, and the man-who-learned-better. Credit the last category to L. Ron Hubbard; I had thought for years that there were but two plots—he pointed out to me the third type.

Boy-meets-girl needs no definition. But don't disparage it. It reaches from the *Illiad* to John Taine's *Time Stream*. It's the greatest story of them all and has never been sufficiently exploited in science fiction. To be sure, it appears in most s-f stories, but how often is it dragged in by the hair and how often is it the compelling and necessary element which creates and then solves the problem? It has great variety: boy-fails-to-meet-girl, boy-meets-girl-too-late, boy-meets-too-many-girls, boy-loses-girl, boy-and-girl-renounce-love-for-higher-purpose. Not science fiction? Here is a throw-away plot; you can have it free: Elderly man meets very young girl; they discover that they are perfectly adapted to each other, perfectly in love, "soul mates." (Don't ask me how. It's up to you to make the thesis credible. If I'm going to have to write this story, I want to be paid for it.)

Now to make it a science fiction story. Time travel? Okay, what time theory—probable-times, classic theory, or what? Rejuvenation? Is this mating necessary to some greater end? Or vice versa? Or will you transcend the circumstances, as C. L. Moore did in that tragic masterpiece "Bright Illusion"?

I've used it twice as tragedy and shall probably use it again. Go ahead and use it yourself. I did not invent it; it is a great story which has been kicking around for centuries.

The "Little Tailor"—this is an omnibus for all stories about the little guy who becomes a big shot, or vice versa. The tag is from the fairy story. Examples: "Dick Whittington," all the Alger books, *Little Caesar*, *Galactic Patrol* (but not *Grey Lensman*), *Mein Kampf*, David in the Old Testament. It is the Success story, or, in reverse, the story of tragic failure.

The man-who-learned-better; just what it sounds like—the story of a man who has one opinion, point of view, or evaluation at the beginning of the story, then acquires a new opinion or evaluation as a result of having his nose rubbed in some harsh facts. I had been writing this story for years before Hubbard pointed out to me the structure of it. Examples: my *Universe* and *Logic of Empire*, Jack London's *South of the Slot*, Dickens' *A Christmas Carol*.

The definition of a story as something interesting-but-not-necessarily-true is general enough to cover all writers, all stories—even James Joyce, if you find his stuff interesting. (I don't!) For me, a story of the sort I want to write is still further limited to this recipe: a man finds himself in circumstances which create a problem for him. In coping with this problem, the man is changed in some fashion inside himself. The story is over when the inner change is complete—the external incidents may go on indefinitely.

People changing under stress:

A lonely rich man learns comradeship in a hobo jungle.

A milquetoast gets pushed too far and learns to fight.

A strong man is crippled and has to adjust to it.

A gossip learns to hold her tongue.

A hard-boiled materialist gets acquainted with a ghost.

A shrew is tamed.

This is the story of character, rather than incident. It's not everybody's dish, but for me it has more interest than the most overwhelming pure adventure story. It need not be unadventurous; the stress which produces the change in character can be wildly adventurous, and often is.

But what has all this to do with science fiction? A great deal! Much so-called science fiction is not about human beings and their problems, consisting instead of a fictionized framework, peopled by cardboard figures, on which is hung an essay about the Glorious Future of Technology. With due respect to Mr. Bellamy, *Looking Backward* is a perfect example of the fictionized essay. I've done it myself; "Solution Unsatisfactory" is a fictionized essay, written as such. Knowing that it would have to compete with real *story,* I used every device I could think of, some of them hardly admissible, to make it look like a story.

Another type of fiction alleged to be science fiction is the story laid in the future, or on another planet, or in another dimension, or such, which could just as well have happened on Fifth Avenue, in 1947. Change the costumes back to now, cut out the pseudo-scientific double-talk and the blaster guns, and it turns out to be straight adventure story, suitable, with appropriate facelifting, to any other pulp magazine on the news stand.

There is another type of honest-to-goodness science fiction story which is not usually regarded as science fiction: the story of people dealing with contemporary science or technology. We do not ordinarily mean this sort of story when we say "science fiction"; what we do mean is the speculative story, the story embodying the notion "Just suppose—", or "What would happen if—". In the speculative science fiction story accepted science and established facts are extrapolated to produce a new situation, a new framework for human action. As a result of this new situation, new *human* problems are created—and our story is about how human beings cope with those new problems.

The story is *not* about the new situation; it is about coping with problems arising out of the new situation.

Let's gather up the bits and define the Simon-pure science fiction story:

1. The conditions must be, in some respect, different from here-and-now, although the difference may lie only in an invention made in the course of the story.

2. The new conditions must be an essential part of the story.

3. The problem itself—the "plot"—must be a *human* problem.

4. The human problem must be one which is created by, or indispensably affected by, the new conditions.

5. And lastly, no established fact shall be violated, and, furthermore, when the story requires that a theory contrary to present accepted theory be used, the new theory should be rendered reasonably plausible and it must include and explain established facts as satisfactorily as the one the author saw fit to junk. It may be far-fetched, it may seem fantastic, but it must *not* be at variance with observed facts, i.e., if you are going to assume that the human race descended from Martians, then you've *got* to explain our apparent close relationship to terrestrial anthropoid apes as well.

Pardon me if I go on about this. I love to read science fiction, but violation of that last requirement gets me riled. Rocketships should not make banked turns on empty space the way airplanes bank their turns on air. Lizards can't crossbreed with humans. The term "space warp" does not mean anything without elaborate explanation.

Not everybody talking about heaven is going there—and there are a lot of people trying to write science fiction who haven't bothered to learn anything about science. Nor is there any excuse for them in these days of public libraries. You owe it to your readers (a) to bone up on the field of science you intend to introduce into your story; (b) unless you yourself are well-versed in that field, you should also persuade some expert in that field to read your story and criticize it before you offer it to an unsuspecting public. Unless you are willing to take this much trouble, please, *please* stick to a contemporary background you are familiar with. Paderewski had to practice; Sonja Henie still works on her school figures; a doctor puts in many weary years before they will let him operate—why should you be exempt from preparatory effort?

The Simon-pure science fiction story—examples of human problems arising out of extrapolations of present science:

Biological warfare ruins the farm lands of the United States; how is Joe Doakes, a used-car dealer, to feed his family?

Interplanetary travel puts us in contact with a race able to read our thoughts; is the testimony of such beings admissible as evidence in a murder trial?

Men reach the Moon; what is the attitude of the Security Council of the United Nations? (Watch out for this one—and hold on to your hats!)

A complete technique for ectogenesis is developed; what is the effect on home, family, morals, religion? (Aldous Huxley left lots of this field unplowed—help yourself.)

And so on. I've limited myself to *my* notions about science fiction, but don't forget Mr. Kipling's comment. In any case it isn't necessary to know how—just go ahead and do it. Write what you like to read. If you have a yen for it, if you get a kick out of "Just imagine—", if you love to think up new worlds, then come on in, the water's fine and there is plenty of room.

But don't write to me to point out how I have violated my own rules in this story or that. I've violated all of them and I would much rather try a new story than defend an old one.

I'm told that these articles are supposed to be some use to the reader. I have a guilty feeling that all of the above may have been more for my amusement than for your edification. Therefore I shall chuck in as a bonus a group of practical, tested rules which, if followed meticulously, will prove rewarding to any writer.

I shall assume that you can type, that you know the accepted commercial format or can be trusted to look it up and follow it, and that you always use new ribbons and clean type. Also, that you can spell and punctuate and can use grammar well enough to get by. These things are merely the word-carpenter's sharp tools. He must add to them these business habits:

1. You must *write*.

2. You must *finish* what you start.

3. You must refrain from rewriting except to editorial order.

4. You must put it on the market.

5. You must keep it on the market until sold.

The above five rules really have more to do with how to write speculative fiction than anything said above them. But they are amazingly hard to follow—which is why there are so few profesisonal writers and so many aspirants, and which is why I am not afraid to give away the racket! But, if you will follow them, it matters not how you write, you will find some editor somewhere, sometime, so unwary or so desperate for copy as to buy the worst old dog you, or I, or anybody else, can throw at him.

4

What do you mean: Science? Fiction?

Judith Merril

. . . some notes on the completion of an anthology of the year's best what?

I used to know what "science" meant: at least I understood the word well enough to believe that a statement like, "A revolution is occuring in science," made clear sense. At that time, the distinctions between "physical sciences" and "biological sciences," "theory" and "applica-tion," "research" and "engineering," "experimental" and "clinical," seemed perfectly obvious.

I also used to know what "fiction" meant. I knew the difference between a novel, a novella, a novelette, a short story, and a vignette; between "subjective" and "objective" narrative styles; between "psychological fiction" and the "adventure story"; between "realism" and "fantasy."

I never did know just what "science fiction" meant: in all the nights I stayed awake till dawn debating definitions, I do not recall one that stood up unflinchingly to the light of day. They all relied, in any case, on certain axiomatic assumptions about the meanings of "science" and "fiction."

Actually, when I first became involved in such debates—about twenty-five years ago—there was already a fair amount of honest confusion (among scientists) about the meaning of "science" in the 20th century. As dedicated—*addicted*—s-f readers, we had some awareness of the upheaval in process in scientific philosophy, following on the work of Heisenberg and Schroedinger, Bridgman and de Broglie; but as dedicated—*addicted*—s-f readers, we also made a complete, unconscious, adjustment when we talked stories instead of concepts—"science" in "science fiction" meant (and for most readers—and writers—still does mean) "technology."

What is viable in "science fiction" (whatever *that* may mean) today is coming from a comparatively small group of serious writers—in and out of the specialty field—who are applying the traditions of the genre and the techniques of contemporary literature to the concepts of 20th century science. The first results are already barely discernible. Science fiction is catching up with science. And the genre is returning from its forty years of self-imposed wandering, away from the wellsprings of literature.

The two events could only be simultaneous. Art at any time can achieve validity only if it is rooted in the accumulated human experience of its day, and touches somewhere on the nerve center of the culture from which it springs. The literature of the mid-20th century can be meaningful only in so far as it perceives, and relates itself to, the central reality of our culture: the revolution in scientific thought which has replaced mechanics with dynamics, classification with integration, positivism with relativity, certainties with statistical probabilities, dualism with parity.

If it seems I am saying that there is no adequate literature in existence now—I am. If it further seems I am claiming a special literary validity for science fiction—I would be, except that as it achieves that validity, it ceases to be "science fiction" and becomes simply contemporary literature instead.

I must pause here to establish my lack of credentials. Although, as fellow science fiction readers, our knowledge of scientific history, and contemporary scientific concepts, is probably roughly equatable, and (for many of you at least) arrived at in rather the same manner (elementary courses at school, and wide and presumably intelligent reading since), our knowledge of literature is neither equal nor similar. I learned my definitions of "fiction" from pulp writers and editors initially: their rules were hard-and-fast, and the penalty for breaking them was hunger; or worse yet, working for a living instead of selling stories.

So when I say I knew what fiction was, I mean I really *knew*. Things like: a short story is limited to one main character, who must be involved in a conflict which is resolved before the end of the story; it can be told from only one viewpoint, which must not shift during the story; a novelette is still primarily about one character, though it is possible to develop one or even two subsidiary characters to some degree—the main distinction is that there can be more than one or two incidents involved in developing the conflict before the resolution: if you get good enough, you can occasionally shift viewpoints in a novelette without killing the sale. Things like that.

I found out by a combination of my own dissatisfaction with the rule-book, and by a very slow and extremely erratic catching-up process (still far from complete) in my reading, that the rules I had learned were not only not universal, but not particularly applicable to anything I wanted to do—except *sell*. I also found out that in the upper literary strata, it was possible to break them and sell; and in the way-out literary strata (where nobody gets paid for anything) it was almost required to break them.

I didn't find the rules in other areas any improvement; at least, I kept on enjoying *reading* s-f more than other contemporary work—until a few years ago. What happened, or started to happen, a few years ago, I will come back to. Meantime, let me tell you about my great discoveries, and try to see them through the eyes of a genuine discoverer. Bear with me if I sometimes state the obvious; it was not so to me. And if some things I say are obviously *not* so—remember, I claim no authority: I am speaking only of my own experiences and discoveries.

It is not the Bomb or the Pill (or miracle drugs or synthetic materials or space travel) that are forcing us to re-think the meaning of "science": these, after all, are comparatively mechanical, *technological*, applications of what I have been calling 20th century scientific concepts—although they of course began in the 19th. The reverberations of that conceptual revolution have by now shaken every branch of scientific investigation and human life. Indeed the failure of entrenched, established academic Humanism to comprehend the meaning of the rumblings from cross-campus (the "two-culture" phenomenon) was probably due in part to preoccupation with the local effects of the same conceptual explosion in the arts and social sciences.

It was not James Joyce or Henry Miller or Jack Kerouac or William Burroughs who made it necessary to re-examine the idea of "fiction." They were simply pioneers in the process of re-examination. The seeds of the upheaval, as in the case of the scientific revolution, appeared at the height of Victorian formalist-mechanist complacency—the beginning of modern social science (Darwin, Freud, Boas, Veblen. . .) with a focus on human motivations, rather than surface behavior.

What happened in the various sciences had its almost exact counterpart in literature, and most markedly so in "fiction," that curious prose form which, like physics and chemistry, anthropology and psychology (and their numerous and hybrid offspring), came into existence as a distinct area of human endeavor during the Great Crackup of the 17th century. I will not attempt here to argue the causes. I am inclined to the notion that the voyages of exploration and discovery of America, and the printing press, with its attendant revolution in communications, were major factors. Whatever the chain of causation, the result was as though a figurative planet composed of man's intellect, suddenly acquired so much additional mass, or velocity (or both?), that it flew out of orbit, breaking up and fragmenting under the strain. (Perhaps the settlement of America enlarged the "subjective mass" of the planet in men's minds? Or possibly just the first accumulation of the sheer bulk of paper under which we are nowadays likely to be buried. . .)

One might carry the metaphor further, and assume that the reduced planet, and its severed chunks, would have settled, eventually, into new orbits closer to the source of energy. Some bits would have been drawn into the sun and lost entirely: Divine Right went that way (and with it a substantial part of the certainty of divinity). Other pieces, the largest ones, would have been drawn back into the parent body very quickly, and become attached as discrete territories, no longer part of the amorphous whole: one might conceive of the establishment of national sovereignties this way, or of the broad demarcations of not-yet-"scientific" disciplines as they first appeared—naturalist, mathematician-astronomer, philosopher, and so forth. The intermediate chunks, settling into orbits somewhat closer to the sun at first, absorbed more energy perhaps, and *grew*, moving back closer to the parent body with each increment of mass and velocity.

Take the fancy one bit farther, and picture the return of the pieces (rather as Planetarium lecturers are fond of presenting the image of an eventual falling-back of the Moon). At least one of the first returning bodies would have landed with tremendous impact—Newtonian physics, the laws of motion, gravitation, and the Calculus, containing within them (if anyone had thought to notice, or had energy to spare to think it through) a clear explanatory warning of descents yet to come.

The new literary form, fiction, may be considered to have made its (far less impactful) return as a clearly formed body somewhere about the middle of the 18th century. (Even fancifullier, one might postulate that the date went unnoticed, and is still argued, because it landed in the tropic sea of some enchanted voyage of exploration—quite possibly just out of sight of Alexander Selkirk's lonely island—and that it was in the nourishing warmth of these waters that the solid mass broke somewhat apart, and eventually attached itself to the land mass again as the full-blown novel and incipient short story.)

* * *

All metaphors aside, I believe it is significant that the fiction form took shape and name in the same intellectual-cultural upheaval from which the familiar "scientific disciplines" emerged—that it achieved a discernible form and popularity just about half way between the beginnings of physics and anthropology, and that its later history shows so many parallels with those of nineteenth-century science.

We tend to think of the 19th century in terms of its own popular image of itself: a time of complacency and classification, of rationality, mechanistic philosophy, scientific certainties, technological, literary and artistic polish rather than innovation. Actually, there seem almost to have been two parallel nineteenth centuries: some things about the *other* one we are still finding out. But we do know that the groundwork for modern mathematics—the non-Euclidean geometries of Gauss, Lobachevsky, and Riemann, as well as Boolean algebra and the basis of symbolic logic—had already been worked out in 1850—when Kierkegaard was writing the first Existential works, and Baudelaire was setting forth the principles of the Symbolist movement—all before either the publication of *The Descent of Man*, or the organization of the Periodic Table.

Fifty years later—just at the turn of the century, while Victoria still reigned, and Teddy Roosevelt brandished his Big Stick—Freud and Pavlov, Lorentz and Fitzgerald, Buber and Heidegger, laid the foundations for thought control, space-time cosmology, and even the Ecumenical Council.

The first confused wave of reaction against these innovations came in the form of reinforced mechanism and increasingly "discrete" and complicated "classification"; perhaps it was not so much *reaction* as an honest effort on the part of people trained in the formalisms of the nineteenth century, to cope with the fascinating, staggering, new integrations while still using the familiar methods of separation and analysis.

Thus, the twentieth century opened to a compartmentation and fragmentation of knowledge unprecedented in scope, and probably in attitude. Within the physical sciences, separate but traditional disciplines were splitting and resplitting: chemists became organic or inorganic chemists—then bio-chemists or physical chemists, etc. They devoted themselves to theory or to application. In the "social sciences," the same phenomenon occurred. In both areas, the engineers took over—at least in popular esteem.

The reasons for this are both obvious and subtle, and it would require, I think, a complete separate essay to examine them satisfactorily. All that matters for purposes of this retrospection, is that two completely separate—and for a time increasingly separating—streams of intellectual endeavor proceeded, in dialectical fashion, from the origins of modern thought in the last half of the nineteenth century. The most obvious, and most comprehensible of these was for some time the essentially engineering-type application of bits and pieces of new conceptual discoveries by the best of the old-school mechanicians: the flood of electronic, aeronautic, and biochemical inventions; the sensational discoveries of the behaviorists and early cultural anthropologists; the economic determinists in politics and sociology; and the school of twentieth-century "realism" in fiction.

* * *

I cannot define science fiction, but I can locate it, philosophically and historically:

There is a body of writing of whose general outlines the readers of *Extrapolation* are, by common consent, already aware: that is to say, the "classical antecedents" from Lucian and Plato through, approximately, Kepler and de Bergerac; the "borderline" (both of acceptability and between periods) instances of *Don Quixote* and *Robinson Crusoe*, terminating probably (in general acceptability) with *Gulliver's Travels* and *Micromegas*; the "Gothic" vein which characterizes the first half, or two-thirds, of the nineteenth century, and continues as a major element well into the twentieth; the period generally considered as "modern," beginning with Verne, and achieving general popularity in the last two decades of the nineteenth century; and the specific area of American specialty science fiction starting in the pulp adventure magazines of the 1910's, and being consolidated by Hugo Gernsback as a discrete phenomenon in his specialty publications during the 1920's.

Assuming this to represent some general area of agreement on what we mean when we talk about "science fiction," I believe it is possible to distinguish within the broad area certain distinct and more reasonably definable forms:

1. "Teaching stories": the dramatized essay or disguised treatise, in which the fiction form is utilized to present a new scientific idea, sometimes (as with the *Somnium*, or the works of "John Taine" and other pseudonymous scientists) because of social, political, religious, or academic pressures operating against a direct presentation; sometimes (as with the typical Gernsbackian story, and a fair proportion of late nineteenth-century work) as a means of "popularizing" scientific information or theories, or (hopefully) sugarcoating an educational pill. (This is what used to be called by literary snobs, "pseudoscience," and should have been called "pseudofiction"—although in the hands of an expert it can become reasonably good fiction: Arthur C. Clarke

manages it occasionally, although his best work—*Childhood's End*, for instance—is not of this type.)

2. "Preaching stories": primarily allegories and satires—morality pieces, prophecies, visions, and warnings, more concerned with the conduct of human society than with its techniques. These are the true "pseudoscience" stories: they utilize science (or technology), or a plausible semblance of science (or technology), or at least the language and atmosphere, in just the same way that the scientific treatise in disguise utilizes fiction. And let me point out again (rather more enthusiastically than before) that some first-rate writing has emerged from this sort of forced marriage. (Perhaps the difference between the work of a marriage broker and a shotgun wedding?) Stapledon's *Starmaker* falls into this group, as well as Ray Bradbury's (specifically) science fiction and a large proportion of both Utopian and anti-Utopian novels up through the turn of the century.

3. Speculative fiction: stories whose objective is to explore, to discover, to *learn*, by means of projection, extrapolation, analogue, hypothesis-and-paper-experimentation, something about the nature of the universe, of man, of "reality." Obviously, all fiction worth considering is "speculative" in the sense that it endeavors to reach, or to expose, some aspect of Truth. But it is equally true—and irrelevant—to say that all fiction is imaginative or all fiction is fantasy. I use the term "speculative fiction" here specifically to describe the mode which makes use of the traditional "scientific method" (observation, hypothesis, experimentation) to examine some postulated approximation of reality, by introducing a given set of changes—imaginary or inventive—into the common background of "known facts," creating an environment in which the responses and perceptions of the characters will reveal something about the inventions, the characters, or both.

It is in this last area that the essence of science fiction resides; it covers a great deal of territory, shading at either end into the first two categories. Clearly, there is hybridization all through the groups—as for instance in satire (such as *The Child Buyer*, or *Player Piano*) whose main devil actually is some specific aspect of science or technology.

For purposes of this discussion, I am not considering the space adventure story, the transplanted western or historical, as science fiction at all.

* * *

In his introduction to *Future Perfect*, H. Bruce Franklin points out: "There was no major nineteenth-century American writer of fiction, and indeed few in the second rank, who did not write some science fiction or at least one Utopian romance."

I doubt that a statement quite so all-embracing could be made for all of Western literature, but if you take fiction, for the moment, to include *all* forms of story-telling (other than the documented reportorial), and allow science its broadest (and I think truest) meaning—the conscientious seeking after knowledge of the nature of the universe, the nature of man, and the nature of "reality"—then I believe Franklin's statement can be applied with few exceptions to the major story-tellers of Western civilization, at almost all times in almost all countries.

One of the exceptional times-and-countries was America of the first half of the 20th Century. (There is, frankly, some question in my mind as to whether this period can claim any "major" writers. But within its own framework, it had accepted "greats"—and almost to a man, they shunned anything resembling either science fiction or fantasy—except such fantasy as clearly existed only in the mind of a character.)

My contention is that "realistic" fiction, rather than speculative or science fiction, was the transient oddity—as grotesque a product of nineteenth-century super-rationalism and mechanistic philosophy as Watson babies and the Stakhanovite movement. For nearly a half century, American writers were somehow impelled to choose, not only one *field* of writing (poetry, essays, journalism, drama, fiction, biography), but—within fiction at least—one *area*. "Serious" fiction writers wrote realistic fiction (with Cabell as the exception). "Slick writers" wrote "realistic" stereotypes for the glossy magazines; "pulp writers," for the pulps. (They at least had some variety of subject, if not style, open to them.) Offhand, I can think of four notable names other than Cabell who broke the rules: Philip Wylie, Conrad Aiken, William Saroyan, and Stephen Vincent Benet. (When Santayana published *The Last Puritan*, he added an epilogue explaining that it was really a work of philosophy more than a novel.) But the Name Novelists—with the notable exception of Sinclair Lewis in *It Can't Happen Here*—stuck to realism exclusively; or if they didn't, their realistic work was all we saw. (I used a science-fiction satire of Farrell's in a recent anthology, and met astonishment everywhere; the truth is, Farrell wrote the story almost fifteen years ago, and *wasn't able to sell it*: it wasn't "Farrell"!) Men of scientific or academic or professional standing who suffered from a compulsion to write fiction did so under pen names. Eventually, even the pulp adventure magazines broke up into "categories": detective, western, sea, sports, science fiction, fantasy.

This was the unique—indeed, baroque—situation, when the first magazines devoted exclusively to fantasy and science fiction were published here in the mid-twenties. It was a time for extremes and bizarre combinations. The richest country in the world was enjoying its richest years—in the cities—while mortgages foreclosed and the Big Depression gained its first beachhead on the farms. These were the years of prohibition and gangsterism, Bix Beiderbecke and Isadora Duncan; the Scopes Trial in Tennessee and psychoanalysis in New York; bottle babies and "back to normalcy." Heisenberg published his theories on quantum matrices the year after Coolidge's election, and announced his "uncertainty" principle the year before the Model A replaced the Model T. Alfred Korzybski's first book had been published here in 1921; Ruth Benedict and Margaret Mead were working with Franz Boas in the new field of cultural anthropology; Eugene O'Neill's *The Hairy Ape* and T. S. Eliot's *The Wasteland* had appeared in 1922, as had *Ulysses*, and the big American novel that year was *Babbitt*. In 1926, the "new criticism" was gaining adherents here, but Dali and Surrealism were still almost unknown on this side of the ocean; Goddard tested his first successful liquid fuel rocket; while Lindbergh prepared for his non-stop flight to Paris; Rudolph Valentino died, and the first sound film was made; Hemingway (in Paris) published *The Sun Also Rises*, and became an important writer overnight.

The War to End All War had ended a way of life in Europe; here, we were still clinging desperately to certainties where we could find them, flinging out wildly when we lost hold. If Darwin, Freud, and Einstein had made Our Trust in God less than certain, Edison, Ford, and Marconi had given us back something *solid*. We did our speculating on the stock market—not in our fiction.

"Scientifiction" in its beginnings was a pure extension of the most mechanistic realism: tomorrow's machines today. The early Gernsback magazines were confined almost entirely to the Teaching school of science fiction, and were further confined almost exclusively to technology in particular rather than science in general. (The exceptions tended to be pseudonymous works by scholars and scientists who had no other outlet, in the rigid framework of the academic Establishment, for speculation outside the sharply defined range of their own specialties.) John Taine (Eric Temple Bell) affords perhaps the best, though not only, example.

The others, such as *Amazing*, seem, in retrospect, to have contained endless expositions of technical, technological, technophiliac, and Technocratic ideas, set forth in ponderous prose, illustrated with cardboard figures spouting wooden dialogue—yet at the time, it was exciting stuff indeed. Perhaps it gave us only more hardware, and gave it dressed in olive drab—but it was *tomorrow's* hardware, and it was knowledgeably projected. There was vast scope for the reader's own imagination to operate, in the cities and spaceships and satellites and time machines of the World of Science (Technology) and Progress to Come.

And of course, "scientifiction" was not the only game in town. For those who craved madder music and gaudier lights, there was always *Weird Tales* (established in 1923), where amid warlocks and werewolves one could still find a good supply of mad scientists, mutant plants, Unidentified Alien Objects, mysterious islands, hollow planets, hypnotized beauties, shambling neo-frankensteins, lost civilizations, and all the rest of the gorgeous panoply of Gothic romance—perhaps a bit worn from a century's heavy use by Hawthorne, Poe, Mary Shelley, Wilkie Collins, Stevenson, Doyle, Haggard, Wells, *et al*. At times this Gothicism hardly showed the shabby spots at all in the bright purple and muted mauve lighting effects preferred by Lovecraft and Clark Ashton Smith—and was perhaps no less powerful in its symbolism than when it was first used.

Weird ran heavily to the Preaching school—allegory and fable, not satire—with the idea content almost exclusively limited to the Battle between Good and Evil. Technological or scientific novelties introduced were usually fully exploited by the author; they left comparatively little to the reader's imagination. *But* the rare story (and they were probably no less rare in the fantasy magazines than in science fiction) that did contain some genuine speculative content was much more likely to be equipped with movable-joint characters and appropriate imagery in the background—plus a considerably more colorful and complex prose style. (When they were good they were really quite good, but when they were bad, they were Gothic *awful*.)

What I have described is of course an extreme differentiating characteristic, not so much of two specific magazines as of the prevailing atmospheres associated with "scientifiction" and "weird" as sub-categories of the magazine specialty field of science fiction: Gernsback and Lovecraft (who dominated *Weird Tales*, though he did not edit it) as they look forty years after.

Actually, the near-total polarization imputed here was effective, if at all, only at the starting-point. Science fiction and fantasy of all sorts were still appearing regularly in a number of "all-story" pulp magazines in the twenties, particularly what one might call (absurdly) the "prestige pulps" (*Golden Book, Argosy, Blue Book*). And by 1930, there were two more specialty magazines: Street & Smith's *Astounding*, and Gernsback's *Wonder* (first *Air Wonder* and *Science Wonder*; later, combined in the single title; later yet, *Thrilling Wonder*) In the decade following the first issue of *Amazing*, the admixture of story types, and overlap of authors—and readers—was considerable. Although *Weird* retained its own distinctive flavor, several of its authors (Carl Jacobi, Clark Ashton Smith, C. L. Moore, for instance) adopting their styles somewhat, began to appear in the other magazines; other writers from the general pulp field, like Leinster and Williamson, made themselves at home, particularly in *Astounding* under Tremaine's editorship; and new writers, science fiction specialists from the beginning, established themselves (John W. Campbell, Jr., Harry Bates and Clifford D. Simak and, from England, John Beynon Harris—now John Wyndham—and Eric Frank Russell).

In the thirties, or more precisely in October 1929, it became abruptly apparent, even to the most dedicated believers in Progress as embodied in Free Enterprise and the Survival of the Fittest, that all was not necessarily for the best in this most solid of all possible worlds. Yet inside science fiction, there was no serious questioning of the virtue inherent in machines, or of the inevitability of the accelerated growth of the super-technological civilization. (However blind the first viewpoint may have been, the second was absolutely clear-sighted.) The net effect, was simply to soften the Technocratic tone, and make the evangelical aspect less obvious. The problem-story took over from the treatise: how to *use* the machine, how to *apply* the techniques.

- - -

When John W. Campbell, Jr. took over the editorship of *Astounding* at the end of 1937, the field in general, and *Astounding* in particular, had acquired a solid nucleus of steady contributors of true speculative science fiction: and I do mean "nucleus." The number of thinkers capable of new ideas is never large; the number of those with even those rudimentary insights into human behavior and the story-telling knack that constitute the bare minimum capability of a writer of fiction is much smaller. There has never been any likelihood of *much* genuine speculative science fiction at any time: less so in a low-paid and low-prestige isolated enclave of literature. The *astounding* thing is, not that the quantity was small, but that there was any noticeable quantity at all. Much more astounding was the rapid growth of that nucleus during Campbell's first five years of editorship.

The list of new names in *Astounding* and *Unknown* in 1938 and 1939 alone contains more than half the important bylines of the first book publishing boom of the early 50's: Asimov, De Camp, del Rey, Gold, Heinlein, Hubbard, Jameson, Kuttner, Leiber, Sturgeon, van Vogt. (Boucher, Fredric Brown, Hal Clement, George O. Smith and James H. Schmitz came along in 1941-3.)

Thus the field gained strength; yet John Campbell has taken a good deal of criticism these past years, from fans, writers, and critics inside the field; recently he has been subject to what might better be called abuse, mostly from people too new to the field, or too uninformed (i.e., Amis's churlish comments in *New Maps of Hell*), to comprehend Campbell's role as writer and editor, in the decade 1935-1945—or how much of what has happened since derived from his impact at that time. If he has been a damaging influence on some writers in recent years, the evil he has done is still far outweighed by the good— and one cannot but suspect, particularly considering Campbell's working habits—that those writers who have been trapped in the *Analog* Formula these last years (or intellec- tually raped by Campbell's enthusiasms) solicited the economic haven of the trap, and offered up their thematic honor more eagerly than otherwise. Since 1948, it has been easy for any writer who cared to, to resist Campbell's pressure; before that, *Astounding* dominated the market so completely that a case might be made against the man for liter- ary despoilage at that time—if anyone cared to. Certainly it is true that Asimov, Sturgeon, Heinlein, Leiber, were revivified by the emergence of new and more literarily demanding markets in the fifties. But it is hardly reasonable to condemn Campbell for not improving things *enough*; the fact is, when he took over *Astounding*, the time was ripe for the qual- itative, and quantitative, explosion that occurred. But it is equally true that Campbell was the right man for the right time—and perhaps as true that his peculiar limitations were as useful as his considerable abilities.

After the 1965 Science Fiction Convention in London, the *London Sunday Times Magazine* published a thoughtful profile of Campbell, by Pat Williams, who suggested:

. . . Life to Campbell is a gigantic experiment in form, and earth the forcing-house—an impeccable vision, but one not warmed (in his theories, that is) by a feeling for the pain or personal potential of the individuals in the experiment. That kind of gentleness in expression seemed to disappear with Don A. Stuart.

So that, ironically, as SF becomes increasingly respectable, John Campbell, its acknow- ledged father-figure, can't really claim his throne. He provides the continuity, he shaped much of the thought, he made many reputations. SF narrowed from the vastness of space to the greater complexity of "sociological" SF with him presiding.

But now it is narrowing towards the highly-focused, upside-down detail of "inner space." The tone is personal and subjective, the quality of expression important. . . . None of this is Campbell's style.

I think Mrs. Williams was exceptionally perceptive in her interviewing, and intelligent in her assessment; if she missed a stage between Campbell and "inner space," it is understandable, because British science fiction has not gone through exactly the same development. It was never effectively cut off, as the specialty field was here, from the main streams of literature and scientific philosophy. In England, they had Priestley, Huxley, Collier, Stapledon, Lewis, Heard, Kersh, Russell, through the thirties and forties. Here, we had Campbell—and eventually, Anthony Boucher and H. L. Gold.

It may seem self-contradictory to say that Campbell is the "sociological science fiction" editor, and add that his great limitation is his essentially *engineering* frame of mind: but this is precisely the "useful" limitation I referred to earlier. In the deepest sense, Campbell was the linear and logical successor to Gernsback. He was as technology-minded and application-oriented as the rest of the field in the thirties, with this difference: that he had a broader concept of the scope of "science" (technology and engineering); he wanted to explore the effects of the new technological world on *people*. Cultural anthropology, social psychology, cybernetics, communications, sociology, education, psychometrics— all these, and a dozen intermediate points, were thrown open for examination.

There were two immediately noticeable effects: better stories and more and better speculative development. A third effect came inevitably on their heels: one I do not believe Campbell was looking for, and may not have noticed when it arrived—better writing.

The thinking improved not only because there were vast unworked areas to explore, but because these particular areas attracted writers of somewhat more flexible intellectual inclination—and most of all, because the editor *wanted* clear thinking; he was honestly (at the beginning) interested in learning about human behavior; he genuinely lacked (as yet) any preconceptions, or even strong opinions, about how the answers should look.

The stories improved because they were required to be about things that happened to people, rather than just to have people in them. (Nor could they be *inside* people—and as the "mainstream" has painfully learned, psychiatric introspections make little good fiction.)

The writing gradually improved because the essence of good writing is clear observation, and you cannot project human responses accurately without observing some humans closely first. It also improved, I think, through hybridization: "scientifiction" had been pro-machine; the Lovecraft school, generally, anti-machine. There had been some overlapping before, but now there was fluent admixture of those writers from both areas who were least satisfied with their own sub-genre patterns. Treatise Drab and Poe Purple studied each other with interest, and adapted toward a common center. The general result was not anything that could properly be called literary style; but it approximated a tolerable narrative prose—determinedly matter-of-fact, slangy, colloquial, with a fair balance of color and economy.

There was even the beginning of characterization. In Asimov's robot stories an individual grew out of a prototype: Dr. Susan Calvin became more complex and believable in each story. And of course the robots were individuals: in fact, characterization for aliens, elves, androids and others hit the field awhile before living breathing humans arrived.

Some of Leiber's too-true witches may have marked the transition. Del Rey began to generate character in his protagonists. Simak was perhaps the first to do so with any consistency (in the *City* series). Sturgeon, at that stage, was creating memorable puppets: his characters were cut from no stock on which other authors drew, but the Sturgeon whole-cloth was no more genuine—just brighter colored and better designed.

In those first few years of Campbell's domination of the field, the basic pattern was set for the next twenty years: the application of technological development to human problems; the application of human development to technology.

And, my God, how the stories rolled out! *Beyond This Horizon*, *Gather Darkness*, Asimov's robots, "Microcosmic God," "The Gnarly Man," "Elsewhen," "Helen O'Loy," "Mimsy Were the Borogroves," *Slan*, "Pride," "Smoke Ghost," the *City* stories, "First Contact," *Universe*, "Etaoin Shrdlu," "Nightfall," "Killdozer!," "Opposites—React!," "No Woman Born," "Nerves," "Adam and no Eve". . . One could go on and on, and the sad fact is that with all but a few, remembering them is better than rereading them.

It was in those bright days—in 1941, to be precise—that I discovered the science fiction magazines. Ten years later, I could still re-read every story I've mentioned here, and a good many more, with almost undiminished renewal of experience: *I know* this, because I had cause to reread them, critically, when I began editing "theme anthologies" in 1952 (reading for reprint, you do not allow rosy memories to haze over the actual words). And by that time, there was some impressive new work to compare it with—some of it by the same authors, some by the next flood of new names of the early fifties—generally so much better *written* as to place great strain on the acceptability of the earlier work.

The stories I have mentioned did stand up to—*that*—re-examination. I tried some of them again recently, and will probably not do so again. They were every bit as good as I remembered—but it was not the prose (however good it looked by comparison at the time) or the characters; it was the ideas that were vivid and memorable—and they remain so; re-reading adds nothing. (There is not much of what we now consider good characterization in *Beowulf*, either. Idea-fiction, like pure myth, seems to work as well with solidly constructed prototypes—and there *is* a difference between a player's mask and a cardboard cutout, between Everyman and no-one-at-all. But when did you last *re*-read *Beowulf*?)

By comparison with the new work of the early fifties, the best of the 1940-period stories survived; they still do—on their own terms. But their terms have no more to do with today's science fiction than—let us say, *The Red Badge of Courage* has to do with *Gone with the Wind*.

* * *

I said earlier that Campbell's specific limitation was his "engineering mind," and that I thought this had been useful to him and to s-f. I think it was useful—indeed essential—for the role he played in his first years as editor; I think it was almost as useful—to the field as a whole, though not to his own position in the field—in its second phase.

A few months ago, I participated in a late night radio talk-program, on which John Campbell and two professors of physics from local schools were co-panelists. To everyone's surprise (particularly the M.C.'s) we got into a hot-and-heavy discussion of objective-vs.-subjective reality. In the course of one exchange, I accused Campbell of confusing logic with hardware. He replied that there *is* no logic without hardware.

I do not believe Campbell would have said this twenty years ago. And I offer it here, not in definition of what I mean by "engineering mind," but of what happened to Campbell's attitude—and thus to American science fiction, which, in the late forties, he dominated almost entirely.

An engineer is a man who converts scientific reasoning into functioning technology. (If the word "technology" confuses anyone if applied to the social sciences, I offer my apologies—but I know no more appropriate term. I do *not* mean machines, and I do *not* mean "hardware"—artifacts. I mean useful constructs derived from scientific concepts, but not requiring scientific training or understanding to use. Geometry is part of our technology, and so is algebra—and so is symbolic logic, and so are the "tools" of psychometrics—and the generally less tangible tools of psychoanalysis. Learning theory is part of the body of scientific knowledge and inquiry; teachers' colleges offer education courses consisting of the *technology*, the techniques, and the catalog of matériel, which apply learning theory to the teaching process. It is irrelevant whether the theory is sound or the technology is well-designed; the definitions are the same.)

The way a good engineer works is first to absorb the theory applicable to his job; then to investigate the technology already available for the purpose; determine what is useful to him, and what he needs, to design specifically for the job; try out (as much as possible on paper or in his mind—perhaps in model form) as many ideas as possible *to find out what will work best to do the job*—what offers the best combination of economy, durability, adherence to specifications, ease of operation, etc.; and then construct a pilot model embodying the most of the best of what he has learned. His objective is not learning-for-learning's sake, but the accomplishment of a particular utilitarian goal.

There is today a field called "human engineering," and when the first School of Human Engineering is opened, John W. Campbell will be entitled to the deanship; I doubt that the full extent of his influence, once or twice removed (through his own writing and that of the authors he attracted to what amounted to a "movement" in those early years of *Astounding*-and-*Unknown*), will ever be fully tabulated. Campbell did not originate the ideas; he did not stimulate the emergence of the field; he was one of its earliest and most productive engineers.

And as it happens, the first phases of an engineering job are almost indistinguishable from scientific research; the only significant difference is that side-tracks are less likely to be followed for any length. There may be something interesting at the end of one or another of the by-lanes, but as soon as it becomes apparent that what lies that way does not concern this *particular* job, it is set aside, or referred to the man who is working on that aspect.

Because Campbell thought like an engineer, because there was a specific kind of information he was after, rather than knowledge-in-general, he was able to give shape and direction to the science fiction of the forties, and it was precisely the shape and direction it most needed. Because he was a *good* engineer, he kept his mind entirely open about the nature of the answers he would find, except that he wanted things that *would work in practice*.

Problem: Human nature is such that it has changed the natural environment of humans and is continuing to do so at an accelerating pace. How to adapt human nature to its new environment?

It was when Campbell began to think he had found the answers that the "Golden Age" of *Astounding* was over. (I think, in retrospect, that Dianetics was the line of demarcation. There have been several other Answers since then, but from (at least somewhere about) that time, he has been in the second phase of the engineering job.) He stopped asking questions and examining the available equipment, and started making designs and building models. *Astounding*, quite appropriately, eventually became *Analog*; but long before that, Campbell had lost his real impact on the field. He remains the honored Senior Editor; most of the "big name" s-f writers of today started by selling, or trying to sell, to Campbell. Most of the younger writers, in America at least, grew up on *Astounding* and *Unknown*, and on the reject-overflow into other magazines. Mrs. Williams's characterization of John Campbell as "father-figure" is, I think, exact and precise.

But there is beginning to be—there already is, in England—a body of writers at work who are conscious of no debt at all to Campbell—indeed, know him only as the didactic and "increasingly magisterial" (Mrs. Williams's phrase) figure of the past ten or fifteen years. It is these writers, on the whole, who are making the new science fiction of the sixties, and what they are doing will prove, I think, a more radical and more exciting—intellectually *and* artistically—departure than anything up till now.

What *they* "grew up on" was the specialty s-f of the fifties, and the increasing bulk of s-f writing from "outside" sources.

At the end of World War II, *Astounding* was the only monthly in the field; *Amazing*, *Fantastic*, *Weird*, and *Famous Fantastic Mysteries* were bi-monthlies; *Planet*, *Startling*, and *Thrilling Wonder Stories*, quarterlies—four magazines a month altogether.

Bit by bit, the paper—and author—shortage came to an end. By the summer of 1949, *Amazing* and *Fantastic* were monthly, *Startling* and *TWS* bi-monthly. There were three new titles: *Fantastic Novels* (bi-monthly), *Avon Fantasy Reader* (three issues a year), and Forrest J. Ackerman's "semi-pro" *Fantasy Book* (once or twice a year)—seven magazines a month.

Then the Boom began. It seems appropriate to date it from the first issue of *Fantasy and Science Fiction* (Fall, 1949, as *The Magazine of Fantasy*—bi-monthly from January, 1951, monthly in August, 1952). *Galaxy* started one year later, a monthly from the beginning.

Other Worlds came November, 1949, *Imagination*, October, 1950. *If*, *Infinity*, *Science Fiction Stories*, followed shortly. Through the first half of the decade, new titles kept appearing, old-new ones dropping out. Publishing schedules fluctuated wildly on the second-string regulars; it worked out to between eight and ten magazines a month, on the average. (There were now four s-f magazines in England.)

But the American specialty magazines were no longer an index of the health or popularity of the field. Science fiction was appearing, infrequently, but regularly, in such places as *Collier's*, *The Saturday Evening Post*, *Esquire*, *Blue Book*, *Good Housekeeping*, *Ellery Queen*. Above all, there were books.

Before 1948, there were six anthologies of science fiction in print, all published during the forties: Phil Stong's *Other Worlds*, Wollheim's *Pocket Book of Science Fiction* and *Viking Portable Novels of Science Fiction*, Julius Fast's paperback, *Out of This World*, the Healy-McComas *Adventures in Time and Space*, and Conklin's *The Best of Science-Fiction*. In 1948-49, there were six more, including the first of the Bleiler-Dikty *Best Science Fiction Stories* annuals. There were at least another six in 1950. 1951 was when the Book Boom began. (22 anthologies alone, if memory serves.) The same thing was happening with novels and short story collections. By 1950 or 1951, Doubleday, Simon and Schuster, Pellegrini and Cudahy, as well as most of the paperback houses, were all firmly in the science fiction business, and there were half a dozen specialty houses.

Those were the surface manifestations of a transformation inside s-f which was, within a few years, to make the genre, in the special form in which it had existed for thirty years, moribund.

5

Preface to *Mirrorshades: The Cyberpunk Anthology*

Bruce Sterling

This book showcases writers who have come to prominence within this decade. Their allegiance to Eighties culture has marked them as a group as a new movement in science fiction.

This movement was quickly recognized and given many labels: Radical Hard SF, the Outlaw Technologists, the Eighties Wave, the Neuromantics, the Mirrorshades Group.

But of all the labels pasted on and peeled throughout the early Eighties, one has stuck: cyberpunk.

Scarcely any writer is happy about labels—especially one with the peculiar ring of "cyberpunk." Literary tags carry an odd kind of double obnoxiousness: those with a label feel pigeonholed; those without feel neglected. And, somehow, group labels never quite fit the individual, giving rise to an abiding itchiness. It follows, then, that the "typical cyberpunk writer" does not exist; this person is only a Platonic fiction. For the rest of us, our label is an uneasy bed of Procrustes, where fiendish critics wait to lop and stretch us to fit.

Yet it's possible to make broad statements about cyberpunk and to establish its identifying traits. I'll be doing this too in a moment, for the temptation is far too strong to resist. Critics, myself included, persist in label-mongering, despite all warnings; we must, because it's a valid source of insight—as well as great fun.

Within this book, I hope to present a full overview of the cyberpunk movement, including its early rumblings and the current state of the art. Mirrorshades should give readers new to Movement writing a broad introduction to cyberpunk's tenets themes, and topics. To my mind, these are showcase stories: strong, characteristic examples of each writer's work to date. I've avoided stories widely anthologized elsewhere, so even hardened devotees should find new visions here.

Cyberpunk is a product of the Eighties milieu—in some sense, as I hope to show later, a definitive product. But its roots are deeply sunk in the sixty-year tradition of modem popular SF.

The cyberpunks as a group are steeped in the lore and tradition of the SF field. Their precursors are legion. Individual cyberpunk writers differ in their literary debts; but some older writers, ancestral cyberpunks perhaps, show a clear and striking influence.

From the New Wave: the streetwise edginess of Harlan Ellison. The visionary shimmer of Samuel Delany. The free-wheeling zaniness of Norman Spinrad and the rock esthetic of Michael Moorcock; the intellectual daring of Brian Aldiss; and, always, J. G. Ballard.

From the harder tradition: the cosmic outlook of Olaf Stapledon; the science/politics of H. G. Wells; the steely extrapolation of Larry Niven, Poul Anderson, and Robert Heinlein.

And the cyberpunks treasure a special fondness for SF's native visionaries: the bubbling inventiveness of Philip Jose Farmer; the brio of John Varley, the reality games of Philip K. Dick; the soaring, skipping beatnik tech of Alfred Bester. With a special admiration for a writer whose integration of technology and literature stands unsurpassed: Thomas Pynchon.

Throughout the Sixties and Seventies, the impact of SF's last designated "movement," the New Wave, brought a new concern for literary craftsmanship to SF. Many of the cyberpunks write a quite accomplished and graceful prose; they are in love with style, and are (some say) fashion-conscious to a fault. But, like the punks of '77, they prize their garage-band esthetic. They love to grapple with the raw core of SF: its ideas. This links them strongly to the classic SF tradition. Some critics opine that cyberpunk is disentangling SF from mainstream influence, much as punk stripped rock and roll of the symphonic elegances of Seventies "progressive rock." (And others—hard-line SF traditionalists with a firm distrust of "artiness"—loudly disagree.)

Like punk music, cyberpunk is in some sense a return to roots. The cyberpunks are perhaps the first SF generation to grow up not only within the literary tradition of science fiction but in a truly science-fictional world. For them, the techniques of classical "hard SF"—extrapolation, technological literacy—are not just literary tools but an aid to daily life. They are a means of understanding, and highly valued.

In pop culture, practice comes first; theory follows limping in its tracks. Before the era of labels, cyberpunk was simply "the Movement"—a loose generational nexus of ambitious young writers, who swapped letters, manuscripts, ideas, glowing praise, and blistering criticism. These writers—Gibson, Rucker Shiner, Shirley, Sterling—found a friendly unity in their common outlook, common themes, even in certain oddly common symbols, which seemed to crop up in their work with a life of their own. Mirrorshades, for instance.

Mirrored sunglasses have been a Movement totem since the early days of '82. The reasons for this are not hard to grasp. By hiding the eyes, mirrorshades prevent the forces of normalcy from realizing that one is crazed and possibly dangerous. They are the symbol of the sunstaring visionary, the biker, the rocker, the policeman, and similar outlaws. Mirrorshades, preferably in chrome and matte black, the Movement's totem color appeared in story after story, as a kind of literary badge.

These proto-cyberpunks were briefly dubbed the Mirrorshades Group. Thus this anthology's title, a well-deserved homage to a Movement icon. But other young writers, of equal talent and ambition, were soon producing work that linked them unmistakably to the new SF. They were independent explorers, whose work reflected something inherent in the decade, in the spirit of the times. Something loose in the 1980s.

Thus, "cyberpunk"—a label none of them chose. But the term now seems a fait accompli, and there is a certain justice in it. The term captures something crucial to the work of these writers, something crucial to the decade as a whole: a new kind of integration. The overlapping of worlds that were formerly separate: the realm of high tech, and the modern pop underground.

This integration has become our decade's crucial source of cultural energy. The work of the cyberpunks is paralleled throughout Eighties pop culture: in rock video; in the hacker underground; in the jarring street tech of hip-hop and scratch music; in the synthesizer rock of London and Tokyo. This phenomenon, this dynamic, has a global range; cyberpunk is its literary incarnation.

In another era this combination might have seemed far-fetched and artificial. Traditionally there has been a yawning cultural gulf between the sciences and the humanities: a gulf between literary culture, the formal world of art and politics, and the culture of science, the world of engineering and industry.

But the gap is crumbling in unexpected fashion. Technical culture has gotten out of hand. The advances of the sciences are so deeply radical, so disturbing, upsetting, and revolutionary, that they can no longer be contained. They are surging into culture at large; they are invasive; they are everywhere. The traditional power structure, the traditional institutions, have lost control of the pace of change.

And suddenly a new alliance is becoming evident: an integration of technology and the Eighties counterculture. An unholy alliance of the technical world and the world of organized dissent—the underground world of pop culture, visionary fluidity, and street-level anarchy.

The counterculture of the 1960s was rural, romanticized, anti-science, anti-tech. But there was always a lurking contradiction at its heart, symbolized by the electric guitar. Rock technology was the thin edge of the wedge. As the years have passed, rock tech has grown ever more accomplished, expanding into high-tech recording, satellite video, and computer graphics. Slowly it is turning rebel pop culture inside out, until the artists at pop's cutting edge are now, quite often, cutting-edge technicians in the bargain. They are special effects wizards, mixmasters, tape-effects techs, graphics hackers, emerging through new media to dazzle society with head-trip extravaganzas like FX cinema and the global Live Aid benefit. The contradiction has become an integration.

And now that technology has reached a fever pitch, its influence has slipped control and reached street level. As Alvin Toffler pointed out in *The Third Wave*—a bible to many cyberpunks—the technical revolution reshaping our society is based not in hierarchy but in decentralization, not in rigidity but in fluidity.

The hacker and the rocker are this decade's pop-culture idols, and cyberpunk is very much a pop phenomenon: spontaneous, energetic, close to its roots. Cyberpunk comes from the realm where the computer hacker and the rocker overlap, a cultural Petri dish where writhing gene lines splice. Some find the results bizarre, even monstrous; for others this integration is a powerful source of hope.

Science fiction—at least according to its official dogma—has always been about the impact of technology. But times have changed since the comfortable era of Hugo Gernsback, when Science was safely enshrined—and confined—in an ivory tower. The careless technophilia of those days belongs to a vanished, sluggish era, when authority still had a comfortable margin of control.

For the cyberpunks, by stark contrast, technology is visceral. It is not the bottled genie of remote Big Science boffins; it is pervasive, utterly intimate. Not outside us, but next to us. Under our skin; often, inside our minds.

Technology itself has changed. Not for us the giant steam-snorting wonders of the past: the Hoover Dam, the Empire State Building, the nuclear power plant. Eighties tech sticks to the skin, responds to the touch: the personal computer, the Sony Walkman, the portable telephone, the soft contact lens.

Certain central themes spring up repeatedly in cyberpunk. The theme of body invasion: prosthetic limbs, implanted circuitry, cosmetic surgery, genetic alteration. The even more powerful theme of mind invasion: brain-computer interfaces, artificial intelligence, neurochemistry—techniques radically redefining the nature of humanity, the nature of the self.

As Norman Spinrad pointed out in his essay on cyberpunk, many drugs, like rock and roll, are definitive high-tech products. No counterculture Earth Mother gave us lysergic acid—it came from a Sandoz lab, and when it escaped it ran through society like wildfire. It is not for nothing that Timothy Leary proclaimed personal computers "the LSD of the 1980s"—these are both technologies of frighteningly radical potential. And, as such, they are constant points of reference for cyberpunk.

The cyberpunks, being hybrids themselves, are fascinated by interzones: the areas where, in the words of William Gibson, "the street finds its own uses for things." Roiling, irrepressible street graffiti from that classic industrial artifact, the spray can. The subversive potential of the home printer and the photocopier. Scratch music, whose ghetto innovators turn the phonograph itself into an instrument, producing an archetypal Eighties music where funk meets the Burroughs cut-up method. "It's all in the mix"—this is true of much Eighties art and is as applicable to cyberpunk as it is to punk mix-and-match retro fashion and multitrack digital recording.

The Eighties are an era of reassessment, of integration, of hybridized influences, of old notions shaken loose and reinterpreted with a new sophistication, a broader perspective. The cyberpunks aim for a wide-ranging, global point of view.

William Gibson's *Neuromancer*, surely the quintessential cyberpunk novel, is set in Tokyo, Istanbul, Paris. Lewis Shiner's *Frontera* features scenes in Russia and Mexico—as well as the surface of Mars. John Shirley's *Eclipse* describes Western Europe in turmoil. Greg Bear's *Blood Music* is global, even cosmic in scope.

The tools of global integration—the satellite media net, the multinational corporation—fascinate the cyberpunks and figure constantly in their work. Cyberpunk has little patience with borders. Tokyo's Hayakawa's *SF Magazine* was the first publication ever to produce an "all-cyberpunk" issue, in November 1986. Britain's innovative SF magazine *Interzone* has also been a hotbed of cyberpunk activity, publishing Shirley, Gibson, and Sterling as well as a series of groundbreaking editorials, interviews, and manifestos. Global awareness is more than an article of faith with cyberpunks; it is a deliberate pursuit.

Cyberpunk work is marked by its visionary intensity. Its writers prize the bizarre, the surreal, the formerly unthinkable. They are willing—eager, even—to take an idea and unflinchingly push it past the limits. Like J. G. Ballard—an idolized role model to many cyberpunks—they often use an unblinking, almost clinical objectivity. It is a coldly objective analysis, a technique borrowed from science, then put to literary use for classically punk shock value.

With this intensity of vision comes strong imaginative concentration. Cyberpunk is widely known for its telling use of detail, its carefully constructed intricacy, its willingness to carry extrapolation into the fabric of daily life. It favors "crammed" prose: rapid, dizzying bursts of novel information, sensory overload that submerges the reader in the literary equivalent of the hard-rock "wall of sound."

Cyberpunk is a natural extension of elements already present in science fiction, elements sometimes buried but always seething with potential. Cyberpunk has risen from within the SF genre; it is not an invasion but a modern reform. Because of this, its effect within the genre has been rapid and powerful.

Its future is an open question. Like the artists of punk and New Wave, the cyberpunk writers, as they develop, may soon be galloping in a dozen directions at once.

It seems unlikely that any label will hold them for long. Science fiction today is in a rare state of ferment. The rest of the decade may well see a general plague of movements, led by an increasingly volatile and numerous Eighties generation. The eleven authors here are only a part of this broad wave of writers, and the group as a whole already shows signs of remarkable militancy and fractiousness. Fired by a new sense of SF's potential, writers are debating, rethinking, teaching old dogmas new tricks. Meanwhile, cyberpunk's ripples continue to spread, exciting some, challenging others and outraging a few, whose pained remonstrances are not yet fully heard.

The future remains unwritten, though not from lack of trying.

And this is a final oddity of our generation in SF—that, for us, the literature of the future has a long and honored past. As writers, we owe a debt to those before us, those SF writers whose conviction, commitment, and talent enthralled us and, in all truth, changed our lives. Such debts are never repaid, only acknowledged and—so we hope—passed on as a legacy to those who follow in turn.

Other acknowledgments are due. The Movement owes much to the patient work of today's editors. A brief look at this book's copyright page shows the central role of Ellen Datlow at *Omni*, a shades-packing sister in the vanguard of the ideologically correct, whose help in this anthology has been invaluable. Gardner Dozois was among the first to bring critical attention to the nascent Movement. Along with Shawna McCarthy, he has made *Isaac Asimov's Science Fiction Magazine* a center of energy and controversy in the field. Edward Ferman's *Fantasy and Science Fiction* is always a source of high standards. *Interzone*, the most radical periodical in science fiction today, has already been mentioned; its editorial cadre deserves a second thanks. And a special thanks to Yoshio Kobayashi, our Tokyo liaison, translator of *Schismatrix* and *Blood Music*, for favors too numerous to mention.

Now, on with the show.

6

Cybernetic deconstructions: Cyberpunk and postmodernism

Veronica Hollinger

If, as Fredric Jameson has argued, postmodernism is our contemporary cultural dominant ("Logic" 56), so equally is technology "our historical context, political and personal," according to Teresa de Lauretis: "Technology is now, not only in a distant, science fictional future, an extension of our sensory capacities; it shapes our perceptions and cognitive processes, mediates our relationships with objects of the material and physical world, and our relationships with our own or other bodies" (167). Putting these two aspects of our reality together, Larry McCaffery has recently identified science fiction as "the most significant evolution of a paraliterary form" in contemporary literature (xvii).

Postmodernist texts which rely heavily on science-fiction iconography and themes have proliferated since the 1960s, and it can be argued that some of the most challenging science fiction of recent years has been produced by mainstream and vangardist rather than genre writers. A random survey of postmodernist writing which has been influenced by science fiction—works for which science-fiction writer Bruce Sterling suggests the term "slipstream" ("Slipstream")—might include, for example, Richard Brautigan's *In Watermelon Sugar* (1968), Monique Wittig's *Les Guérillères* (1969), Angela Carter's *Heroes and Villains* (1969), J.G. Ballard's *Crash* (1973), Russell Hoban's *Riddley Walker* (1980), Ted Mooney's *Easy Travel to Other Planets* (1981), Anthony Burgess's *The End of the World News* (1982), and Kathy Acker's *Empire of the Senseless* (1988).

Not surprisingly, however, the specific concerns and esthetic techniques of postmodernism have been slow to appear in genre science fiction, which tends to pride itself on its status as a paraliterary phenomenon. Genre science fiction thrives within an epistemology which privileges the logic of cause-and-effect narrative development, and it usually demonstrates a rather optimistic belief in the progress of human knowledge. Appropriately, the space ship was its representative icon during the 1940s and '50s, the expansionist "golden age" of American science fiction. Equally appropriately, genre science fiction can claim the realist novel as its closest narrative relative; both developed in an atmosphere of nineteenth-century scientific positivism and both rely to a great extent on the mimetic transparency of language as a "window" through which to provide views of a relatively uncomplicated human reality. When science fiction is enlisted by postmodernist fiction, however, it becomes integrated into an esthetic and a world-view whose central tenets are an uncertainty and an indeterminacy which call into question the "causal interpreta-tion of the universe" and the reliance on a "rhetoric of believability" which virtually define it as a generic entity (Ebert 92).

It is within this conflictual framework of realist literary conventions played out in the postmodernist field that I want to look at cyberpunk, a "movement" in science fiction in the 1980s which produced a wide range of fictions exploring the technological ramifica-tions of experience within late-capitalist, post-industrial, media-saturated Western society. "Let's get back to the Cyberpunks," Lucius Shepard recently proposed in the first issue of *Journal Wired* (1989), one of several non-academic periodicals devoted to contempor-ary issues in science fiction and related fields; "Defunct or not, they seem to be the only revolution we've got" (113).

* * *

Cyberpunk was a product of the commercial mass market of "hard" science fiction; concerned on the whole with near-future extrapolation and more or less conventional on the level of narrative technique, it was nevertheless at times brilliantly innovative in its explorations of technology as one of the "multiplicity of structures that intersect to produce that unstable constellation the liberal humanists call the 'self'" (Moi 10). From this perspective, cyberpunk can be situated among a growing (although still relatively small) number of science-fiction projects which can be identified as "anti-humanist." In its various deconstructions of the subject—carried out in terms of a cybernetic breakdown of the classic nature/culture opposition—cyberpunk can be read as one symptom of the postmodern condition of genre science fiction. While science fiction frequently problem-atizes the oppositions between the natural and the artificial, the human and the machine, it generally sustains them in such a way that the human remains securely ensconced in its privileged place at the center of things. Cyberpunk, however, is about the breakdown of these oppositions.

This cybernetic deconstruction is heralded in the opening pages of what is now considered the quintessential cyberpunk novel—we might call it "the c-p limit-text"—William Gibson's *Neuromancer* (1984). Gibson's first sentence—"The sky above the port was the color of television, tuned to a dead channel" (3)—invokes a rhetoric of technology to express the natural world in a metaphor which blurs the distinctions between the organic and the artifi-cial. Soon after, Gibson's computer-cowboy, Case, gazes at "the chrome stars" of shuriken, and imagines these deadly weapons as "the stars under which he voyaged, his destiny spelled out in a constellation of cheap chrome" (12). Human bodies too are absorbed into this rhetorical conflation of organism and machine: on the streets of the postmodern city whose arteries circulate information, Case sees "all around [him] the dance of biz, informa-tion interacting, data made flesh in the mazes of the black market. . ." (16). The human world replicates its own mechanical systems, and the border between the organic and the artificial threatens to blur beyond recuperation.

If we think of science fiction as a genre which typically foregrounds human action *against* a background constituted by its technology, this blurring of once clearly defined boundaries makes cyberpunk a particularly relevant form of science fiction for the post-industrial present. Richard Kadrey, himself a (sometime) cyberpunk writer, recently noted the proliferation of computer-based metaphors—"downtime," "brain dump" and "interface," for example—which are already used to describe human interaction ("Simulations" 75). We can read cyberpunk as an analysis of the postmodern *identification* of human and machine.

Common to most of the texts which have become associated with cyberpunk is an overwhelming fascination, at once celebratory and anxious, with technology and its immediate—that is, *unmediated*—effects upon human being-in-the-world, a fascination which sometimes spills over into the problematizing of "reality" itself. This emphasis on the potential interconnections between the human and the technological, many of which are already gleaming in the eyes of research scientists, is perhaps the central "generic" feature of cyberpunk. Its evocation of popular/street culture and its valorization of the socially marginalized, that is, its "punk" sensibility, have also been recognized as important defining characteristics.

Sterling, one of the most prolific spokespersons for the Movement during its heyday, has described cyberpunk as a reaction to "standard humanist liberalism" because of its interest in exploring the various scenarios of humanity's potential interfaces with the products of its own technology. For Sterling, cyberpunk is "post-humanist" science fiction which believes that "technological destruction of the human condition leads not to futureshocked zombies but to hopeful monsters" ("Letter" 5,4).

Science fiction has traditionally been enchanted with the notion of transcendence, but, as Glenn Grant points out in his discussion of *Neuromancer,* cyberpunk's "preferred method of transcendence is through technology" (43). Themes of transcendence, however, point cyberpunk back to the romantic trappings of the genre at its most conventional, as does its valorization of the (usually male) loner rebel/hacker/punk who appears so frequently as its central character. Even Sterling has recognized this, concluding that "the proper mode of critical attack on cyberpunk has not yet been essayed. Its truly dangerous element is incipient Nietzschean philosophical fascism: the belief in the Overman, and the worship of will-to-power" ("Letter" 5).

It is also important to note that not all the monsters it has produced have been hopeful ones; balanced against the exhilaration of potential technological transcendence is the anxiety and disorientation produced in the self/body in danger of being absorbed into its own technology. Mesmerized by the purity of technology, Gibson's Case at first has only contempt for the "meat" of the human body and yearns to remain "jacked into a custom cyberspace deck that projected his disembodied consciousness into the consensual hallucination that was the matrix" (5). Similarly, the protagonist of K.W. Jeter's *The Glass Hammer* (1987) experiences his very existence as a televised simulation. The postmodern anomie which pervades *The Glass Hammer* demonstrates that Sterling's defense of cyberpunk against charges that it is peopled with "futureshocked zombies" has been less than completely accurate.

* * *

"In virtual reality, the entire universe is your body and physics is your language," according to Jaron Lanier, founder and CEO of VPL Research in California; "we're creating an entire new reality" (qtd. in Ditlea 97-98).

Gibson's *Neuromancer,* the first of a trilogy of novels which includes *Count Zero* (1986) and *Mona Lisa Overdrive* (1988), is set in a near-future trash-culture ruled by multi-national corporations and kept going by black-market economies, all frenetically dedicated to the circulation of computerized data and "the dance of biz" (16) which is played out by Gibson's characters on the streets of the new urban overspill, the Sprawl. The most striking spatial construct in *Neuromancer,* however, is neither the cityscape of the Sprawl nor the artificial environments like the fabulous L-5, Freeside, but "cyberspace," the virtual reality which exists in simulated splendor on the far side of the computer screens which are the real center of technological activity in Gibson's fictional world. Scott Bukatman describes cyberspace as "a new and decentered spatiality . . . which exists parallel to, but outside of, the geographic topography of experiential reality" (45). In a fascinating instance of feedback between science fiction and the "real" world, Autodesk, a firm researching innovations in computerized realities in Sausalito, California, has recently filed for trademark protection of the term "cyberspace" which it may use as the name for its new virtual reality software (Ditlea 99). Jean Baudrillard's apocalyptic commentary seems especially significant here: "It is thus not necessary to write science fiction: we have as of now, here and now, in our societies, with the media, the computers, the circuits, the networks, the acceleration of particles which has definitely broken the referential orbit of things" ("The Year 2000" 36).

Along with the "other" space of cyberspace, *Neuromancer* offers alternatives to conventional modalities of human existence as well: computer hackers have direct mental access to cyberspace, artificial intelligences live and function within it, digitalized constructs are based on the subjectivities of humans whose "personalities" have been downloaded into computer memory, and human bodies are routinely cloned.

This is Sterling's post-humanism with a vengeance, a post-humanism which, in its representation of "monsters"—hopeful or otherwise—produced by the interface of the human and the machine, radically decenters the human body, the sacred icon of the essential self, in the same way that the virtual reality of cyberspace works to decenter conventional humanist notions of an unproblematical "real."

As I have noted, however, cyberpunk is not the only mode in which science fiction has demonstrated an anti-humanist sensibility. Although radically different from cyberpunk—which is written for the most part by a small number of white middle-class men, many of whom, inexplicably, live in Texas—feminist science fiction has also produced an influential body of anti-humanist texts. These would include, for example, Joanna

Russ's *The Female Man* (1975), Jody Scott's *I, Vampire* (1984), and Margaret Atwood's *The Handmaid's Tale* (1985), novels which also participate in the postmodernist revision of conventional science fiction. Given the exigencies of their own particular political agendas, however, these texts demonstrate a very different approach to the construction/deconstruction of the subject than is evident in the technologically-influenced post-humanism of most cyberpunk fiction.

Jane Flax, for example, suggests that "feminists, like other postmodernists, have begun to suspect that all such transcendental claims [those which valorize universal notions of reason, knowledge, and the self] reflect and reify the experience of a few persons—mostly white, Western males. These transhistoric claims seem plausible to us in part because they reflect important aspects of the experience of those who dominate our social world" (626). Flax's comments are well taken, although her conflation of all feminisms with postmodernism tends to oversimplify the very complex and problematical interactions of the two that Bonnie Zimmerman has noted. Moreover, in a forthcoming essay for *Extrapolation,* I have argued that most feminist science fiction rather supports than undermines the tenets of liberal humanism, although "changing the subject" of that humanism, to borrow the title of a recent study by Nancy K. Miller.

We can also include writers like Philip K. Dick, Samuel R. Delany and John Varley within the project of anti-humanist science fiction, although these writers are separated from cyberpunk not only by chronology but also by cyberpunk's increased emphasis on technology as a constitutive factor in the development of postmodern subjectivity. Darko Suvin also notes some of the differences in political extrapolation between cyberpunk and its precursors: "in between Dick's nation-state armies or polices and Delany's Foucauldian micro-politics of bohemian groups, Gibson [for example] has—to my mind more realistically—opted for global economic power-wielders as the arbiters of peoples [sic] lifestyles and lives" (43).

* * *

In "Prometheus as Performer: Toward a Posthumanist Culture?" Ihab Hassan writes: "We need first to understand that the human form—including human desire and all its external representations—may be changing radically, and thus must be re-visioned. We need to understand that five hundred years of humanism may be coming to an end, as humanism transforms itself into something that we must helplessly call posthumanism" (205).

Sterling's *Schismatrix* (1986) is one version of "posthumanity" presented as picaresque epic. Sterling's far-future universe—a rare construction in the cyberpunk "canon"—is one in which countless societies are evolving in countless different directions; the *Schismatrix* is a loose confederation of worlds where the only certainty is the inevitability of change. Sterling writes that "the new multiple humanities hurtled blindly toward their unknown destinations, and the vertigo of acceleration struck deep. Old preconceptions were in tatters, old loyalties were obsolete. Whole societies were paralyzed by the mind-blasting vistas of absolute possibility" (238). Sterling's protagonist, a picaresque hero for the postmodern age, "mourned mankind, and the blindness of men, who thought that the Kosmos had rules and limits that would shelter them from their own freedom. There were no shelters. There were no final purposes. Futility, and freedom, were Absolute" (273).

Schismatrix is a future history different from many science-fiction futures in that what it extrapolates from the present is the all-too-often ignored/denied/repressed idea that human beings will be different in the future and will continue to develop within difference. In this way, *Schismatrix* demonstrates a familiarly post-structuralist sensibility, in its recognition both of the potential anxiety *and* the potential play inherent in a universe where "futility, and freedom, [are] Absolute."

Sterling's interest in and attraction to the play of human possibility appears as early as his first novel, *Involution Ocean* (1977). In this story (which reads in some ways like a kind of drug-culture post-*Moby-Dick*), the protagonist falls into a wonderful vision of an alien civilization, in a passage which, at least temporarily, emphasizes freedom over futility: "There was an incredible throng, members of a race that took a pure hedonistic joy in the possibilities of surgical alteration. They switched bodies, sexes, ages, and races as easily as breathing, and their happy disdain for uniformity was dazzling. . . . It seemed so natural, rainbow people in the rainbow streets; humans seemed drab and antlike in comparison" (154).

This is a far cry from the humanist anxieties which have pervaded science fiction since the nineteenth century. Consider, for example, the anxiety around which H.G. Wells created *The Time Machine* (1895): it is "de-humanization," humanity's loss of its position at the center of creation, which produces the tragedy of the terminal beach, and it is, to a great extent, the absence of the human which results in the "abominable desolation" (91) described by Wells's Time Traveller. Or consider what we might term the "trans-humanism" of Arthur C. Clarke's *Childhood's End* (1953), in which a kind of transcendental mysticism precludes the necessity of envisioning a future based on changing technologies, social conditions and social relations. Greg Bear's more recent *Blood Music* (1985) might be read, from this perspective, as a contemporary version of the same transcendental approach to human transformation, one based on an apocalyptic logic which implies the impossibility of any change in the human condition *within history. Blood Music* is especially interesting in this context, because its action is framed by a rhetoric of science which would seem to repudiate any recourse to metaphysics. Darko Suvin has noted, however, that it functions as "a naïve fairytale relying on popular wishdreams that our loved ones not be dead and that our past mistakes may all be rectified, all of this infused with rather dubious philosophical and political stances" (41).

* * *

"Certain central themes spring up repeatedly in cyberpunk," Sterling points out in his preface to the influential short-fiction collection, *Mirrorshades: The Cyberpunk Anthology.* "The theme of body invasion: prosthetic limbs, implanted circuitry, cosmetic surgery, genetic alteration. The even more powerful theme of mind invasion: brain-computer interfaces, artificial intelligence, neurochemistry—techniques radically redefining the nature of humanity, the nature of the self" (xiii).

The potential in cyberpunk for undermining concepts like "subjectivity" and "identity" derives in part from its production within what has been termed "the technological imagination"; that is, cyberpunk is hard science fiction which recognizes the paradigm-shattering role of technology in post-industrial society. We have to keep in mind here, of course, that the Movement has become (in)famous for the adversarial rhetoric of its ongoing and prolific self-commentary which, in turn, functions as an integral part of its overall production as a "movement." We should be careful, for this reason, not to confuse claims with results. The anti-humanist discourse of cyberpunk's frequent manifestoes, however, strongly supports de Lauretis's contention that "technology is our historical context, political and personal" (167). As I have suggested, this context functions in cyberpunk as one of the most powerful of the multiplicities of structures which combine to produce the postmodern subject.

Thus, for example, the characters in Michael Swanwick's *Vacuum Flowers* (1987) are subjected to constant alterations in personality as the result of programming for different skills or social roles—metaphysical systems grounded on faith in an "inner self" begin to waver. Human bodies in Gibson's stories, and even more so in Sterling's, are subjected to shaping and re-shaping, the human form destined perhaps to become simply one available choice among many; notions of a human nature determined by a "physical essence" of the human begin to lose credibility (for this reason, many behavioral patterns defined by sexual difference become irrelevant in these futures). Thus Rudy Rucker can offer the following as a chapter title in *Wetware:* "Four: in Which Manchile, the First Robot-Built Human, Is Planted in the Womb of Della Taze by Ken Doll, Part of Whose Right Brain Is a Robot Rat."

We must also recognize, however, that "the subject of the subject" at the present time has given rise to as much anxiety as celebration (anxiety from which the postmodernist theorist is by no means exempt). The break-up of the humanist "self" in a media-saturated post-industrial present has produced darker readings which cyberpunk also recognizes. Fredric Jameson, whose stance *vis-à-vis* the postmodern is at once appreciative and skeptical, has suggested that fragmentation of subjectivity may be the postmodern equivalent of the modernist predicament of individual alienation ("Cultural Logic" 63). Pat Cadigan's "Pretty Boy Crossover" (1985), for example, raises questions about the effects of simulated reality upon our human sense of self as complete and inviolable. In her fictional world, physical reality is "less efficient" than computerized simulation, and video stars are literally video programs, having been "distilled. . .to pure information" (89, 88) and downloaded into computer matrices. Cadigan's eponymous Pretty Boy is tempted by the offer of literally eternal life within the matrix and, although he finally chooses "real" life, that reality seems to fade against the guaranteed "presence" of its simulation. Bobby, who has opted for existence as simulation, explains the "economy of the gaze" which guarantees the authenticity of the self in this world: "If you love me, you watch me. If you

don't look, you don't care and if you don't care I don't matter. If I don't matter, I don't exist.
Right?" (91).

* * *

"Pretty Boy Crossover" offers this succinct observation about the seductive power of
simulated reality: "First you see video. Then you wear video. Then you eat video. Then
you *be* video" (82).

In K.W. Jeter's *The Glass Hammer,* being is *defined* by its own simulation. *The
Glass Hammer* is one of the most self-conscious deconstructions of unified subjectivity
produced in recent science fiction, and one which dramatizes (in the neurotic tonalities
familiar to readers of J.G. Ballard) the anxiety and schizophrenia of the (technologic-
ally-produced) postmodern situation. In *The Glass Hammer* the break-up of the "self"
is narrated in a text as fragmented as its subject (subject both as protagonist and as
story). Jeter's novel is a chilling demonstration of the power of simulated re-presentation
to construct "the real" (so that it functions like a cyberpunk simulacrum of the theories
of Jean Baudrillard). It "narrates" episodes in the life of Ross Schuyler, who watches the
creation of this life as a video event in five segments. There is no way to test the accuracy
of the creation, since the self produced by memory is as unreliable a re-presentation as
is a media "bio." As Schuyler realizes: "Just because I was there—that doesn't mean
anything" (59).

The opening sequence of *The Glass Hammer* dramatizes the schizophrenia within the
subjectivity of the protagonist:

Video within video. He watched the monitor screen, seeing himself there, watching.
In the same space. . .that he sat in now. . . .
He watched the screen, waiting for the images to form. Everything would be in the
tapes, if he watched long enough.   (7)

Like Schuyler himself, the reader waits for the images to form as s/he reads the text.
Episodes range over time, some in the past(s), some in the present, some real, some
simulated, many scripted rather than "novelized," until the act of reading/watching
achieves a kind of temporary coherence. It is this same kind of temporary coherence
which formulates itself in Schuyler's consciousness, always threatening to dissolve again
from "something recognizably narrative" into "the jumbled, half-forgotten clutter of his
life" (87).

What takes place in *The Glass Hammer* may also be read as a deconstruction of the
opposition between depth and surface, a dichotomy which is frequently framed as the
familiar conflict between reality and appearance. Jeter reverses this opposition, dramat-
izing the haphazard construction of his character's "inner self" as a response to people
and events, both real and simulated, over time. The displacement of an "originary"
self from the text places the emphasis on the marginal, the contingent, the re-present-
ations (in this case electronically produced) which actually create the sense of "self."

Jeter's technique in *The Glass Hammer* is particularly effective: the reader watches the character, and watches the character watching himself watching, as his past unfolds, not as a series of memories whose logical continuity guarantees the stability of the ego, but as an entertainment series, the logical continuity of which is the artificial re-arrangement of randomness to *simulate* coherence.

* * *

Near the outset of Case's adventures in *Neuromancer,* Gibson's computer cowboy visits the warehouse office of Julius Deane, who "was one hundred and thirty-five years old, his metabolism assiduously warped by a weekly fortune in serums and hormones." In Deane's office, "Neo-Aztec bookcases gathered dust against one wall of the room where Case waited. A pair of bulbous Disney-styled table lamps perched awkwardly on a low Kandinsky-look coffee table in scarlet-lacquered steel. A Dali clock hung on the wall between the bookcases, its distorted face sagging to the bare concrete floor" (12).

In this context, it is significant that the "average" cyberpunk landscape tends to be choked with the debris of both language and objects; as a sign-system, it is overde-termined by a proliferation of surface detail which emphasizes the "outside" over the "inside." Such attention to detail—recall Gibson's nearly compulsive use of brand names, for example, or the claustrophobic clutter of his streets—replaces the more conventional (realist) narrative exercise we might call "getting to the bottom of things"; indeed, the shift in emphasis is from a symbolic to a surface reality.

In a discussion of *Neuromancer,* Gregory Benford observes that "Gibson, like Ballard, concentrates on surfaces as a way of getting at the aesthetic of an age." This observation is a telling one, even as it misses the point. Benford concludes that Gibson's attention to surface detail "goes a long way toward telling us why his work has proved popular in England, where the tide for several decades now has been to relish fiction about surfaces and manners, rather than the more traditional concerns of hard SF: ideas, long perspec-tives, and content" (19).

This reliance on tradition is perhaps what prevents Benford, whose own "hard science fiction" novels and stories are very much a part of science fiction's humanist tradition, from appreciating the approach of writers like Gibson and Jeter. The point may be that, in works like *Neuromancer* and *The Glass Hammer,* surface *is* content, an equation which encapsulates their critique—or at least their awareness—of our contemporary "era of hyperreality" (Baudrillard, "Ecstasy" 128). In this context, the much-quoted opening sentence of *Neuromancer,* with its image of the blank surface of a dead television screen, evokes the anxiety of this new era. Istvan Csicsery-Ronay, for example, sees in cyberpunk the recognition that "with the computer, the problem of identity is moot, and the idea of reflection is transformed in to [sic] the algorithm of replication. SF's computer wipes out the Philosophical God and ushers in the demiurge of thought-as-technique" (273).

Like much anti-humanist science fiction, cyberpunk also displays a certain coolness, a kind of ironically detached approach to its subject matter which precludes nostalgia or sentimentality. This detachment usually discourages any recourse to the logic of the apocalypse, which, whether positive (like Clarke's) or negative (like Wells's), is no longer a favored narrative move. Jameson and Sterling (representatives of "high theory" and "low culture" respectively?) both identify a waning interest in the scenarios of literal apocalypse: Jameson perceives in the postmodern situation what he calls "an inverted millenarianism, in which premonitions of the future. . .have been replaced by the senses of the end of this or that" ("Cultural Logic" 53); in his introduction to Gibson's short-story collection, *Burning Chrome,* Sterling comments that one "distinguishing mark of the emergent new school of Eighties SF [is] its boredom with the Apocalypse" (xi).

This is supported by Douglas Robinson, in his *American Apocalypses,* when he concludes that "antiapocalypse—not apocalypse, as many critics have claimed—is the dominant topos of American postmodernism" (xvi). In a discussion of Derrida's discourse on apocalypse, Robinson argues that "the apocalyptic imagination fascinates Derrida precisely as the 'purest' form, the most mythical expression or the most extreme state-ment of the metaphysics of presence" (251n1).

One reason for this tendency to abandon what has been a traditional science fiction topos may be the conviction, conscious or not, that a kind of philosophical apocalypse has already occurred, precipitating us into the dis-ease of postmodernism. Another reason may be the increased commitment of anti-humanist science fiction to the explora-tion of changes that will occur—to the self, to society and to social relations—in time; that is, they are more engaged with historical processes than attracted by the jump-cuts of apocalyptic scenarios which evade such investment in historical change. Cyberpunk, in particular, has demonstrated a keen interest in the near future, an aspect of its approach to history which discourages resolution-through-apocalypse.

* * *

In a discussion of "the cybernetic (city) state," Scott Bukatman has argued that as a result of the tendency in recent science fiction to posit "a reconception of the human and the ability to interface with the new terminal experience. . .terminal space becomes a legitimate part of human (or post-human) experience" (60). In many cases, however, science-fiction futures are all too often simply representations of contemporary cultural mythologies disguised under heavy layers of futuristic make-up.

The recognition of this fact provides part of the "meaning" of one of the stories in Gibson's *Burning Chrome* collection. "The Gernsback Continuum" humorously ironizes an early twentieth-century futurism which could conceive of no real change in the human condition, a futurism which envisioned changes in "stuff" rather than changes in social relations (historical distance increases the ability to critique such futures, of course). In Gibson's story, the benighted protagonist is subjected to visitations by the "semiotic ghosts" of a future which never took place, the future, to borrow a phrase from Jameson, "of one moment of what is now our own past" ("Progress" 244). At the height of these "hallucinations," he "sees" two figures poised outside a vast city reminiscent of the sets for films like *Metropolis* and *Things to Come*:

> [the man] had his arm around [the woman's] waist and was gesturing toward the city. They were both in white. . . .He was saying something wise and strong, and she was nodding. . . .
> . . .[T]hey were the Heirs to the Dream. They were white, blond, and they probably had blue eyes. They were American. . . .They were smug, happy, and utterly content with themselves and their world. And in the Dream, it was *their* world. . . .
> It had all the sinister fruitiness of Hitler Youth propaganda.   (32-33)

Gibson's protagonist discovers that "only really bad media can exorcise [his] semiotic ghosts" (33) and he recovers with the help of pop culture productions like *Nazi Love Motel*. "The Gernsback Continuum" concludes with the protagonist's realization that his dystopian present could be worse, "it could be perfect" (35).

Gibson's story is not simply an ironization of naive utopianism; it also warns against the limitations, both humorous and dangerous, inherent in any vision of the future which bases itself upon narrowly defined ideological systems which take it upon themselves to speak "universally," or which conceive of themselves as "natural" or "absolute." David Brin's idealistic *The Postman* (1985), for example, is a post-apocalyptic fiction which closes on a metaphorical note "of innocence, unflaggingly optimistic" (321), nostalgically containing itself within the framework of a conventional humanism. Not surprisingly, its penultimate chapter concludes with a re-affirmation of the "natural" roles of men and women:

> And always remember, the moral concluded: Even the best men—the heroes—will sometimes neglect to do their jobs.
> *Women, you must remind them, from time to time. . . .*   (312)

Compare this to Gibson's description of the Magnetic Dog Sisters, peripheral characters in his story, "Johnny Mnemonic" (1981), also collected in *Burning Chrome*: "They were two meters tall and thin as greyhounds. One was black and the other white, but aside from that they were as nearly identical as cosmetic surgery could make them. They'd been lovers for years and were bad news in a tussle. I was never quite sure which one had originally been male" (2).

Another story in the same collection, "Fragments of a Hologram Rose," uses metaphors of the new technology to express the indeterminate and fragmented nature of the self: "A hologram has this quality: Recovered and illuminated, each fragment will reveal the whole image of the rose. Falling toward delta, he sees himself the rose, each of his scattered fragments revealing a whole he'll never know. . . . But each fragment reveals the rose from a different angle. . ." (42).

Gibson's rhetoric of technology finally circumscribes all of reality. In his second novel, *Count Zero* (1986), there is an oblique but pointed rebuttal of humanist essentialization, which implicitly recognizes the artificiality of the Real. Having described cyberspace, the weirdly real "space" that human minds occupy during computer interfacing, as "mankind's unthinkably complex consensual hallucination" (44), he goes on to write the following:

> "Okay," Bobby said, getting the hang of it, "then what's the matrix?. . .[W]hat's cyberspace?"
> "The world," Lucas said.   (131)

It is only by recognizing the consensual nature of socio-cultural reality, which includes within itself our definitions of human nature, that we can begin to perceive the possibility of change. In this sense, as Csicsery-Ronay suggests (although from a very different perspective), cyberpunk is "a paradoxical form of realism" (266).

Csicsery-Ronay also contends that cyberpunk is "a legitimate international artistic style, with profound philosophical and aesthetic premises," a style captured by films such as *Blade Runner* and by philosophers such as Jean Baudrillard; "it even has, in Michael Jackson and Ronald Reagan, its hyperreal icons of the human simulacrum infiltrating reality" (269).

* * *

Lucius Shepard concludes his "requiem for cyberpunk" by quoting two lines from Cavafy's "Waiting for the Barbarians": "What will we do now that the barbarians are gone? / Those people were a kind of solution" (118).

Cyberpunk seemed to erupt in the mid-80s, self-sufficient and full-grown, like Minerva from the forehead of Zeus. From some perspectives, it could be argued that this self-proclaimed Movement was nothing more than the discursive construction of the collective imaginations of science-fiction writers and critics eager for something/anything new in what had become a very conservative and quite predictable field. Now that the rhetorical dust has started to settle, however, we can begin to see cyberpunk as itself the product of a multiplicity of influences from both within and outside of genre science fiction. Its writers readily acknowledge the powerful influence of 1960s and '70s New Wave writers like Samuel R. Delany, John Brunner, Norman Spinrad, J.G. Ballard and Michael Moorcock, as well as the influence of postmodernists like William Burroughs and Thomas Pynchon. The manic fragmentations of Burroughs's *Naked Lunch* and the maximalist apocalypticism of Pynchon's *Gravity's Rainbow* would seem to have been especially important for the development of the cyberpunk "sensibility." Richard Kadrey has even pronounced *Gravity's Rainbow* to be cyberpunk *avant la lettre,* "the best cyberpunk novel ever written by a guy who didn't even know he was writing it" ("Cyberpunk" 83). Equally, Delany has made a strong case for feminist science fiction as cyberpunk's "absent mother," noting that "the feminist explosion—which obviously infiltrates the cyberpunk writers so much—is the one they seem to be the least comfortable with, even though it's one that, much more than the New Wave, has influenced them most strongly, both in progressive and in reactionary ways. . ." (9).

Due in part to the prolific commentaries and manifestoes in which writers like Sterling outlined/analyzed/defended their project(s)—usually at the expense of more traditional science fiction—cyberpunk helped to generate a great deal of very useful controversy about the role of science fiction in the 1980s, a decade in which the resurgence of fantastic literature left much genre science fiction looking rather sheepishly out of date. At best, however, the critique of humanism in these works remains incomplete, due at least in part to the pressures of mass market publishing as well as to the limitations of genre conventions which, more or less faithfully followed, seem (inevitably?) to lure writers back into the power fantasies which are so common to science fiction. A novel like Margaret Atwood's The Handmaid's Tale, for instance, produced as it was outside the genre market, goes further in its deconstruction of individual subjectivity than do any of the works I have been discussing, except perhaps The Glass Hammer.

Gibson's latest novel, Mona Lisa Overdrive, although set in the same universe as Neuromancer and Count Zero, foregrounds character in a way which necessarily mutes the intensity and multiplicity of surface detail which is so marked a characteristic of his earlier work. Sterling's recent and unexpected Islands in the Net (1988) is a kind of international thriller which might be read as the depiction of life after the postmodern condition has been "cured." Set in a future after the "Abolition" (of nuclear warfare), its central character, Laura Webster, dedicates herself to the control of a political crisis situation which threatens to return the world to a global state of fragmentation and disruptive violence which only too clearly recalls our own present bad old days. Sterling's "Net" is the vast information system which underlies and makes possible the unity of this future world and his emphasis is clearly on the necessity for such global unity. Although, in the final analysis, no one is completely innocent—Sterling is too complex a writer to structure his forces on opposite sides of a simple ethical divide—the movement in Islands in the Net is away from the margins toward the center, and the Net, the "global nervous system" (15), remains intact.

As its own creators seem to have realized, cyberpunk—like the punk ethic with which it was identified—was a response to postmodern reality which could go only so far before self-destructing under the weight of its own deconstructive activities (not to mention its appropriation by more conventional and more commercial writers). That final implosion is perhaps what Jeter accomplished in The Glass Hammer, leaving us with the image of a mesmerized Schuyler futilely searching for a self in the videoscreens of the dystopian future. It is clearly this aspect of cyberpunk which leads Csicsery-Ronay to conclude that "by the time we get to cyberpunk, reality has become a case of nerves…. The distance required for reflection is squeezed out as the world implodes: when hallucinations and realia collapse into each other, there is no place from which to reflect" (274). For him, "cyberpunk is. . .the apotheosis of bad faith, apotheosis of the postmodern" (277). This, of course, forecloses any possibility of political engagement within the framework of the postmodern.

Here cyberpunk is theorized as a symptom of the malaise of postmodernism, but, like Baudrillard's apocalyptic discourse on the "condition" itself, Csicsery-Ronay's analysis tends to underplay the positive potential of re-presentation and re-visioning achieved in works like *Neuromancer* and *Schismatrix*. Bukatman, for example, has suggested that the function of cyberpunk "neuromanticism" is one appropriate to science fiction in the post-modern era: the *reinsertion* of the human into the new reality which its technology is in the process of shaping. According to Bukatman, "to dramatize the terminal realm means to somehow insert the figure of the human into that space to experience it *for us*. . . . Much recent science fiction stages and restages a confrontation between figure and ground, finally constructing a new human form to interface with the other space and cybernetic reality" (47-48).

The postmodern condition has required that we revise science fiction's original trope of technological anxiety—the image of a fallen humanity controlled by a technology run amok. Here again we must deconstruct the human/machine opposition and begin to ask new questions about the ways in which we and our technologies "interface" to produce what has become a *mutual* evolution. It may be significant that one of the most brilliant visions of the potential of cybernetic deconstructions is introduced in Donna Haraway's merger of science fiction and feminist theory, "A Manifesto for Cyborgs: Science, Technology, and Socialist Feminism in the 1980s," which takes the rhetoric of technology toward its political limits: "cyborg unities are monstrous and illegitimate," writes Haraway; "in our present political circumstances, we could hardly hope for more potent myths for resistance and recoupling" (179).[1]

Note

1. An earlier version of this essay was presented at the 1988 Conference of the Science Fiction Research Association, Corpus Christi, Texas. I would like to thank the Social Sciences and Humanities Research Council of Canada for their generous support. I would also like to thank Glenn Grant, editor of *Edge Detector: A Magazine of Speculative Fiction,* for making so much information and material available to me during the process of revision.

Works cited

Acker, Kathy. *Empire of the Senseless*. New York: Grove, 1988.

Atwood, Margaret. *The Handmaid's Tale*. Toronto: McClelland, 1986.

Ballard, J.G. *Crash*. 1975. London: Triad/Panther, 1985.

Baudrillard, Jean. "The Year 2000 Has Already Happened." *Body Invaders: Panic Sex in America.* Ed. Arthur Kroker and Marilouise Kroker. Trans. Nai-Fei Ding and Kuan Hsing Chen. Montreal: New World Perspectives, 1987. 35-44.

—. "The Ecstasy of Communication." *The Anti-Aesthetic: Essays on Postmodern Culture.* Ed. Hal Foster. Trans. John Johnston. Port Townsend, WA: Bay, 1983. 126-34.

Bear, Greg. *Blood Music*. New York: Ace, 1985.

Benford, Gregory. "Is Something Going On?" *Mississippi Review* 47/48 (1988): 18-23.

Brautigan, Richard. *In Watermelon Sugar.* New York: Dell, 1968.

Brin, David. *The Postman*. New York: Bantam, 1985.

Bukatman, Scott. "The Cybernetic (City) State: Terminal Space Becomes Phenomenal." *Journal of the Fantastic in the Arts* 2 (1989): 43-63.

Burgess, Anthony. *The End of the World News.* Markham, ON: Penguin, 1982.

Burroughs, William. *Naked Lunch.* New York: Grove, 1959.

Cadigan, Pat. "Pretty Boy Crossover." 1985. *The 1987 Annual World's Best SF.* Ed. Donald A. Wollheim. New York: DAW, 1987. 82-93.

Carter, Angela. *Heroes and Villains.* 1969. London: Pan, 1972.

Clarke, Arthur C. *Childhood's End.* New York: Ballantine, 1953.

Csicsery-Ronay, Istvan. "Cyberpunk and Neuromanticism." *Mississippi Review* 47/48 (1988): 266-78.

Delany, Samuel R. "Some *Real* Mothers: An Interview with Samuel R. Delany by Takayuki Tatsumi." *Science-Fiction Eye* 1 (1988): 5-11.

de Lauretis, Teresa. "Signs of Wo/ander." *The Technological Imagination.* Ed. Teresa de Lauretis, Andreas Huyssen, and Kathleen Woodward. Madison, WI: Coda, 1980. 159-74.

Ditlea, Steve. "Another World: Inside Artificial Reality." *P/C Computing.* November 1989: 90-102.

Ebert, Teresa L. "The Convergence of Postmodern Innovative Fiction and Science Fiction: An Encounter with Samuel R. Delany's Technotopia." *Poetics Today* 1 (1980): 91-104.

Flax, Jane. "Postmodernism and Gender Relations in Feminist Theory." *Signs: Journal of Women in Culture and Society* 12 (1987): 621-43.

Gibson, William. "Fragments of a Hologram Rose." 1977. *Burning Chrome.* New York: Ace, 1987. 36-42.

—. "The Gernsback Continuum." 1981. *Burning Chrome.* 23-35.

—. "Johnny Mnemonic." 1981. *Burning Chrome.* 1-22.

—. *Neuromancer.* New York: Berkley, 1984.

—. *Count Zero.* New York: Arbor House, 1986.

—. *Mona Lisa Overdrive.* New York: Bantam, 1988.

Grant, Glenn. "Transcendence Through Détournement in William Gibson's *Neuromancer.*" *Science-Fiction Studies* 17 (1990): 41-49.

Haraway, Donna. "A Manifesto for Cyborgs: Science, Technology, and Socialist Feminism in the 1980s." 1985. *Coming to Terms: Feminism, Theory, Politics.* Ed. Elizabeth Weed. New York: Routledge, 1989. 173-204.

Hassan, Ihab. "Prometheus as Performer: Toward a Posthumanist Culture?" *Performance in Postmodern Culture.* Ed. Michel Benamou and Charles Caramello. Madison, WI: Coda, 1977. 201-17.

Hoban, Russell. *Riddley Walker.* 1980. London: Pan, 1982.

Hollinger, Veronica. "Feminist Science Fiction: Breaking Up the Subject." *Extrapolation* 31 (1990): forthcoming.

Jameson, Fredric. "Postmodernism, or The Cultural Logic of Late Capitalism." *New Left Review* 146 (1984): 53-94.

—. "Progress versus Utopia, or Can We Imagine the Future?" *Art After Modernism: Rethinking Representation.* Ed. Brian Wallis. New York: The New Museum of Contemporary Art, 1984. 239-52.

Jeter, K.W. *The Glass Hammer.* New York: Signet, 1987.

Kadrey, Richard. "Simulations of Immortality." *Science-Fiction Eye* 1 (1989): 74-76.

—. "Cyberpunk 101 Reading List." *Whole Earth Review* 63 (1989): 83.

McCaffery, Larry. "Introduction." *Postmodern Fiction: A Bio-Bibliographical Guide*. Ed. McCaffery. Westport, CT: Greenwood, 1986. xi-xxviii.

Miller, Nancy K. "Changing the Subject: Authorship, Writing, and the Reader." *Feminist Studies/Critical Studies*. Ed. Teresa de Lauretis. Bloomington: Indiana UP, 1986. 102-20.

Moi, Toril. *Sexual/Textual Politics: Feminist Literary Theory*. New York: Methuen, 1985.

Mooney, Ted. *Easy Travel to Other Planets*. New York: Ballantine, 1981.

Pynchon, Thomas. *Gravity's Rainbow*. 1973. New York: Bantam, 1974.

Robinson, Douglas. *American Apocalypses: The Image of the End of the World in American Literature*. Baltimore, MD: Johns Hopkins UP, 1985.

Rucker, Rudy. *Wetware*. New York: Avon, 1988.

Russ, Joanna. *The Female Man*. New York: Bantam, 1975.

Scott, Jody. *I, Vampire*. New York: Ace, 1984.

Shepard, Lucius. "Waiting for the Barbarians." *Journal Wired* 1 (1989): 107-18.

Sterling, Bruce. "Slipstream." *Science-Fiction Eye* 1 (1989): 77-80.

—. *Islands in the Net*. New York: Arbor House, 1988.

—. Preface to *Mirrorshades: The Cyberpunk Anthology*. New York: Ace, 1988. ix-xvi.

—. Preface to *Burning Chrome*. ix-xii.

—. "Letter from Bruce Sterling." *REM* 7 (1987): 4-7.

—. *Schismatrix*. New York: Ace, 1986.

—. *Involution Ocean*. 1977. New York: Ace, 1988.

Swanwick, Michael. *Vacuum Flowers*. New York: Arbor, 1987.

Suvin, Darko. "On Gibson and Cyberpunk SF." *Foundation* 46 (1989): 40-51.

Wells, H.G. *The Time Machine*. 1895. *The Time Machine and The War of the Worlds*. New York: Fawcett, 1968. 25-98.

Wittig, Monique. *Les Guérillères*. 1969. Trans. David Le Vay. Boston: Beacon, 1985.

Zimmerman, Bonnie. "Feminist Fiction and the Postmodern Challenge." *Postmodern Fiction: A Bio-Bibliographical Guide*. Ed. McCaffery. 175-88.

7

The many deaths of science fiction: A polemic

Roger Luckhurst

How many times can a genre die? How often can the death sentence be passed down, and when do repeated stays of execution cease being moments of salvation and become instead sadistic toying with the condemned?

SF is dying; but then SF has always been dying, it has been dying from the very moment of its constitution. Birth and death become transposable: if Gernsback's pulp genericism produces the "ghetto" and the pogrom of systematic starvation for some, he also *names* the genre and gives birth to it for others. If the pulps eventually give us the "Golden Age," its passing is death for some and re-birth for others. If the New Wave is the life-saving injection, it is also a spiked drug, a perversion, and the onset of a long degeneration towards inevitable death. If the 1970s is a twilight, a long terminal lingering, the feminists come to the rescue. But then the feminists are also partially responsible, Charles Platt argues, for issuing one final vicious twist of the knife. And what of cyberpunk? Dead before it was even born—or rather dead *because* it was named. "Requiem for the Cyberpunks" aims to finally kill the label (5). And what now? Christina Sedgewick asks "Can Science Fiction Survive in Postmodern, Megacorporate America?" A new decline, or rather a circling back: SF dying because of its *re*-commercialization. This is also the thrust of Charles Platt's claim that "we find ourselves wedded to a form that was once provocative and stimulating but is now crippled, corrupt, mentally retarded, and dying for lack of intensive care" (45).

This is a parodic history, no doubt, and yet it seems integral to any putative "history" that SF is haunted by its own death, that it constantly passes through this state of terminal disease. Why? Is this unanswerable? In this I am echoing Derrida's speculation on philosophy at the opening of his essay "Violence and Metaphysics":

> That philosophy died yesterday. . .—and philosophy should still wander towards the meaning of its death—or that it has always lived knowing itself to be dying. . .; that philosophy died *one day, within* history, or that it has always fed on its own agony. . .; that beyond the death, or dying nature of philosophy, thought still has a future, or even, as is said today, is still entirely to come because of what philosophy has held in store. . .—all these are unanswerable questions. (79)

Is SF also only surviving, dwindling in its last days, or paradoxically living on after its death? And is this the fast-fading ghost or the longed-for re-birth? Is it, like "philosophy," *living on,* an "SF" after-living SF? And yet unlike philosophy, there is no determinable phase of "life": its death is there from the beginning. SF indeed seems to be "always feeding on its own agony." In what follows, I want to analyze the narrative of death integral to SF and perhaps attempt to answer the puzzling question of its constant, haunting presence in critical considerations of the genre. It is my polemical proposal that these regularly issued panic narratives, these apocalyptic warnings and calls to arms, in fact conceal the opposite concern: that SF wants to die, that it is ecstatic at the prospect of its own death and desires nothing else.

As a way of entry, let me begin with the work of J.G. Ballard. There has been a systematic re-vision of Ballard's work in recent years. His uneasy relation to the genre was initially figured in terms of his unrelenting pessimism, his perversion of the teleological narrative of scientific progress so central to "hard" SF. Blish objected to the passivity in Ballard's "disaster novels": "you are under absolutely no obligation to do anything about it but sit and worship it" (128). Peter Nicholls condemned Ballard's oeuvre outright: Ballard is "advocating a life style quite likely to involve the sudden death of yourself and those you love" (31). Ballard's nihilism is exemplified by his obsessive representations of mutilation, suicidal passivity, and the embrace, the positive willing, of death. One interpretive possibility remains: that the "disaster novels" focus on "the perverse desires, mad ambitions, and suicidal manias of aberrant personalities now free to fulfill fatal aspirations devoid of any rational motivation" (Barlow 32).

However, the re-vision began with Ballard's dismissal of this "false" reading:

> I don't see my fiction as disaster-oriented. . .they're. . .stories of psychic fulfillment. The geophysical changes which take place in *The Drought, The Drowned World,* and *The Crystal World* are all positive and good changes. . .[that] lead us to our real psychological goals. . . . Really, I'm trying to show a new kind of logic emerging, and this is to be embraced, or at least held in regard. (Pringle and Goddard 40)

Peter Brigg and Warren Wagar have subsequently offered the inverted perspective and "perverse" argument that the literal catastrophe is metaphorically "transvalued" into positive narratives of psychic transcendence: that these are fables of "self-overcoming in perilous confrontation with the world" (Wagar 56). Gregory Stevenson, in *Out of the Night and into the Dream,* has taken this position to its most religiose extreme: all of Ballard's work is to be encoded into a pseudo-Jungian-Christian mish-mash of transcendence. Death as the terminus, as liminal facticity and the problematic of *finitude,* is to be re-figured as the metaphorical transgression of the bounds of the bodily into an ultimate, ecstatic (re-)unification and (re-) integration.

In adjudicating on these competing frames, death is undoubtedly pivotal. The issue comes down to what *form* of death the Ballardian text proposes. Clearly the narrative of transcendence is attempting to shift from the "wrong" (literal) death to the "right" (metaphorical) death. Being-towards-death is replaced by Being-*beyond*-death. But it is not as simple as this straightforward substitution of deaths suggests. There is a certain violence in trying to elide Ballard's oeuvre into a singular narrative, which tends to erase important differences between *The Drowned World* and *The Crystal World,* where textual evidence for transcendence is clear, and *The Drought,* which is more rigorously existential in concentrating on what Jaspers would call the unreadable and unattainable "cipher-script" of the Transcendent.[1] Such a narrative is also uncomfortable with *The Atrocity Exhibition* where the concern for violence and death is displaced onto the figure of the Woman. It is also useful, I think, to retain Ballard's clear debt to Freud's speculations on the literal fact of human aggressivity and violence in *Civilization and Its Discontents,*[2] especially as it is central to the book which so influenced Ballard, Bernard Wolfe's *Limbo.*[3]

It needs re-emphasizing that the literal and figural readings of death are inextricable and intertwined; transcendence of the bodily clearly *depends* on the facticity of the body in order to have any productive meaning. Why is this so important? Because in terms of SF criticism this re-visioning of Ballard forms a kind of meta-commentary on the project of legitimating SF as a whole genre.

Elsewhere I have argued that the attraction of "postmodernism" for SF critics is its apparent transgressive aesthetic, its erasure of the borders between disciplines, discursive regimes, and crucially for SF the boundary between the high and the low. With postmodernism, it would appear, the ghetto walls of the popular can be dismantled and SF can (re)join the "mainstream" of fiction, no longer being equated with the embarrassing and degrading label of popular genre fiction. The longing for (re)entry to the "mainstream" is the enduring central element of SF criticism. Ballard's texts in effect *perform* this desire figured both as literal death (of genre) into a transcendent unity (with the mainstream). In "The Voices of Time," the language of Powers's dissolution is crucial: "he felt his body gradually dissolving, its physical dimensions melting into a vast continuum of the current, which bore him out into the centre of the great channel, sweeping him onward, beyond hope but at last at rest" (39-40). This is the literal entry into the main stream. Indeed, rather than criticism reading Ballard, Ballard's text could be seen to read and expose the fantasy of criticism: release from the bondedness of genre into the undivided stream of Literature. One could read the text's evocative description of the terminal lapse into narcoma as the death throes of generic SF and this final vision as the ecstatic release, the abandonment of generic boundaries. In Derrida's terms, Ballard exposes the "generic law" by *performing that very law*: SF is marked by, and Ballard re-marks, the genre's desire for its own death.

This might seem a provocative and peculiarly perverse argument, but I intend to demonstrate that this fantasy of death is crucial to how SF critics legitimate SF as a genre. It is vital to emphasize that this death-wish is the result of the structure of *legitimation.* The paradigmatic topography of ghetto/mainstream marks a border on which is transposed the evaluations popular/serious, low/high, entertainment/Literature.[4] One might expect SF critics to formulate evaluative criteria specific to the site of SF and the generic. However

SF critics tend to take their criteria from the "high" and then proceed to denigrate SF in its relational, constructed position as "low," as failing to achieve "literary" standards. That this topography is *imposed* by largely invisible and unexamined categories of "worth" (the evaluative designations of "high," as I demonstrate below, are the products of an *historical* moment) is left unquestioned. The only way, it is proposed, to legitimate SF is to smuggle it across the border into the "high." And for the genre as a whole to become legitimate paradoxically involves the very destruction of the genre.

Before the tribunal of the "high," SF legitimates itself in three ways: by the implementation of internal borders; by a certain narrative of its (in/ glorious) history; and by the appeal to the rigor of the scientific. The first two apply for citizenship in Literature, whilst the latter claims partial guilt on the grounds of diminished responsibility. And one could polemically argue that these, in very different ways, all propose a form of death.

SF critics often want to make grand claims for the genre. For Scholes and Rabkin, it "create[s] a modern conscience for the human race" (vii); it fits, indeed supersedes, the great humanistic claims for literature as a whole. At the same time, and on the same page, they are equally aware that SF is constituted out of "trivial, ephemeral works of 'popular' fiction which is barely literate, let alone literary." Most of the subsequent work of their text is dedicated to *affirming* these two contradictory statements by separating them out, divorcing them from each other as distinct and "pure" sites within SF. An internal border is constituted whereby, on the one hand, the "grand claim" is asserted and so entry to Literature can be gained, whilst on the other, SF can, in alliance with the categories of the legitimate, be condemned.

Scholes and Rabkin justify their own critical text on the basis that SF has ceased to be wholly popular now that "a sufficient number of works of genuine merit" have been written from within it (vii). The logic of legitimation through the implementation of internal boundaries can be stated thus: SF is a popular genre which yet contains within it a movement of profundity; in order to secure that "serious" element a mark, a line of division, must be approved, by which the ghetto can be transcended. If, as Darko Suvin insists, "The genre has to be evaluated proceeding from the heights down, applying the standards gained by the analysis of its masterpieces" (*Poetics* 71), and yet these very heights transcend the genre, such texts could be said to *no longer belong* to SF. SF-which-is-not-SF is the apotheosis and judge of SF.

The internal border is usually implemented at the site of the definition. It involves isolating a central definition through which all other cases can be rejected or shifted to the edges as impure. These marginalia are, unsurprisingly, identical with precisely the elements that might mark the genre as popular; their displacement de-contaminates it of the pulp, leaving the "serious" works as the central representatives of the genre. Darko Suvin is the exemplar of this strategy. SF as "cognitive estrangement" defamiliarizes the empirical environment by foregrounding the artificiality of its "natural" norms. This cognitive utility of SF is based on the rigor of applying scientific laws; such worlds must be *possible.* Suvin presents a definition that appeals to the specificity of "hard" SF—which is also asserted by Scholes in *Structural Fabulation,* Charles Platt, and many others. The law of science, however, superimposes on the law of genre; this strict definition is the basis for a wholesale deportation of categories which surround, indeed interpenetrate inextricably, SF. Hence SF "retrogressing into fairy tale. . .is committing creative suicide" (*Poetics* 62); fantasy is a "sub-literature of mystification" (*Poetics* 63). What is truly astonishing in Suvin's system is his dismissal of virtually all, if not *all,* SF in itself. "Narrative Logic, Ideological Domination and the Range of SF" draws a fan-shaped diagram, in which the bottom point, the convergence of the range, is marked as the "optimum" SF. Above it are borderlines marking "good" and "most" SF. This "most" is "debilitating confectionery," and, he asserts, "there is only one ideal optimum" (*Positions* 70). Is the ideal here a Platonic one? Does it imply that the optimum is unattainable in fact? Those falling short of this ideal are discussed under the titles "banal," "incoherent," "dogmatic," and "invalidated": "all uses of SF as prophecy, futurology, program or anything else claiming ontological factuality for the SF image-clusters, are obscurantist and reactionary at the deepest level" (*Positions* 71).

Suvin's final and deathly judgments are proscriptions which result from the desperate desire to decontaminate and inoculate SF. If the rigor of his definitionalism is an attempt to isolate a singular utility for SF, it is also a logic that prescribes a death. The *cordon sanitaire* of legitimacy constricts so far as to annihilate SF.

Suvin's writings on the history of SF are more valuable than this harsh imposition of borders, yet in some senses they are also exemplary of the strategies of legitimation that operate in the histories of SF. SF history serves two functions: that of embedding SF *in* the mainstream (the historical erasure of the boundary) and of serving to eliminate, or at least displace, the illicit site of the *naming* of SF—America. This narrative can be parodically summarized in the following way: once there was an Edenic time when SF swam with the mainstream, was inseparable and unidentifiable from it; then came the Americans who walled it up and issued a proclamation of martial law. This is the self-imposition of the ghetto, the "40 years" (rather than days) in the wilderness (see Merril 54). This narrative ends prophetically: there will come a time when the walls will be demolished, when SF will rejoin the mainstream and cease its disreputable existence. Conclusions to such histories are the sites where the longing for death becomes most explicit.

Historical legitimations can in fact begin in *pre*history; SF is merely a modernized version of the "innately" human need for "mythology" by which to orient experience. The *biological* need for SF is asserted by Scholes, who argues that the desire for narrative, once satisfied by myth, can now be provided by popular forms, given the decadence and abandonment of narrative by the mainstream. This explains why normally respectable readers "resort secretly and guiltily to lesser forms for that narrative fix they cannot do without" ("Roots" 53). SF, it is seemingly argued here, is restoring an imbalance afflicted by the loss of narrative (the language of chemical compulsion is also used by Kingsley Amis, although in a different context: SF is an "addiction" which is "mostly contracted in adolescence or not at all" [16]). The more properly historical mode, however, attempts to embed and entwine SF *into* the mainstream. Legitimation comes from appropriating, say, Swift, Thomas More or Lucian to SF; history saves the illegitimate child by discovering its "true" parentage. This is a fascinating strategy: it is not the attempt to find a fixed identity or essence of SF; it is concerned precisely with constructing a *non*-origin, to disperse it, to deny specificity. SF does not "begin" anywhere as such, and the disreputable generic can be displaced to become a mere bit-part in a larger historical unfolding.

The suppression involved is that of a name: Gernsback. I am not suggesting that the origin of SF lies with him, but his originating of the *site* is crucial. Gernsback is ritually vilified: for Aldiss, he was "one of the worst disasters ever to hit the science fiction field" (63); for Blish, he is solely responsible for ghettoization (118); for Clareson, he initiated the abandonment of literature "to propagandize for technology" (20); for Merril, the 40 years in the wilderness begins in 1926 with *Amazing.* What follows is a movement either backwards to predate a baleful influence, or forward to celebrate his supersession. The attempt at erasure, however, cannot ignore Gernsback's initial elaboration of the conditions on which the genre has come to be defined: "to publish only such stories that have their basis in scientific laws as we know them, or the logical deduction of new laws from what we know" (scientific rigor/extrapolation); that the fictions would "supply knowledge. . .in a very palatable form" (legitimation through educative role—also seen by Janice Radway to be a crucial mode in which women readers of popular romance fiction legitimate their reading); the grand claim for its cultural significance—"Posterity will point to [the SF story] as having blazed a new trail, *not only in literature and fiction,* but progress as well" (my emphasis).[5] These have all been widely used subsequently. *Amazing* was also instrumental in constructing a community through reader participation. Whether seen positively or negatively, SF as a genre can *only* be understood with reference to where its conventions and limits were inscribed, despite the constant attempt to displace it.

It might seem to be the most naive SF historiography to mark Gernsback as the initiator; naming, however, is different from origin. Gernsback did not appear *sui generis.* The constitution of the site of the specific SF magazine in the 1920s was a product of some 40 years of socio-cultural re-alignments around the "literary." H.G. Wells has been cited as both the progenitor of generic SF and the last instance of an "SF" text being accepted into an undifferentiated field of Literature before the ghettoization effected by Gernsback. This is inaccurate, however; the latter decades of the 19th century were the crucial phase of the development of the categories of the "high" and "low" as they now operate institutionally. This is an incredibly complex moment in the construction of cultural value in, as Peter Keating observes, a publishing field that had explosively expanded into a bewildering diversity. The "popular" or "low" was not simply the demonized Other, the defining negative, of an emergent Modernism;[6] moral panic over the links between "penny dreadfuls" and working-class criminality had developed in the 1870s (see Bristow). If Thomas Wright had divided the high from the low in 1881, and 20 years later the *Times Literary Supplement* was set up to distinguish the "better authors" from the "rubbish heap of incompetence,"[7] it should not be forgotten that there was an equally belligerent assertion for the moral superiority of the re-vivified "Romance." Largely in the pages of *The Contemporary Review,* Andrew Lang, Rider Haggard, and others attacked the effete etiolation of the modern "serious" novel and argued for the "muscular" romance or adventure story. Against the diseased interiority of the "analytic novel," the romance "deliberately reverted to the simpler instead of more complicated kind of novel," and, in an inversion that prefigures Scholes's attempt to displace the "mainstream," Saintsbury also argued that "romance is of its nature eternal and preliminary to the novel. The novel is of its nature transitory and parasitic on the romance" (415-16). Literary histories tend to emphasize this late Victorian phase as the construction of the Modernist "Artwork" in opposition to the now degraded "low." It was also, just as significantly, the moment in which the sites (increasingly low priced, increasingly specialized fiction magazines), terminology (Wright entitled his essay "Popular Fiction" in 1881; "bestseller" was coined in 1889), and the very forms and genres of the modern concept of popular literature were founded.

Two things require clarification about this in relation to SF. Firstly, it cannot be said that texts that could be nominated as "SF" at that time existed in an undifferentiated "mainstream"; the very *spaces* in which they found publication were products of a rapidly fragmenting concept of fiction, quickly becoming figured in terms of civilized "high" and degenerate "low."[8] Wells's anxiety to depart from being identified solely with the "scientific romance" and his deference (at least in their letters) to Henry James mark his aware-ness of the emerging equation between the popular and the "degenerate." Secondly, the very use of the term "SF" is already a retrospective extraction of texts out of a mass of "romances." Cross-fertilizations between juvenile adventure stories, imperialist narratives, Gothic revivalism, and the supernatural, as well as pseudo-scientific adventures deriving either from simple technological advance or sociological inflections of Darwin have been traced by Patrick Brantlinger and Judith Wilt. A text like *Jekyll and Hyde* could be said to be premised on a scientific "novum," but it is equally overdetermined by Gothic, melo-dramatic, and imperialist elements; this is no less the case for Wells. Even if this was the moment in which modern popular genres gradually emerged (in the sense of specialist sites, formulated conventions, formulated plots, and reader coteries), SF was a relatively late development in relation to the detective genre, the spy novel, or even the Western. As Andrew Ross notes, even the pulp term "science fiction" had to fight, in the 1920s, for predominance amongst other magazines publishing what were variously termed pseudo-science, weird science, off-trail, or fantascience fiction (415). What must be asserted here concerns two stages: that SF is elaborated as a distinct genre only with Gernsback's and other subsequent specialist magazines, and that its "pre-history" is one of *fundamental impurity.* This impurity, however, does not mark an undifferentiated "mainstream," but is an impurity within the emerging concept of the "popular."

It seems vital that this material production of spaces for the constitution of the modern "popular" be addressed; SF histories, however, either pass over it in the search for legit-imate parentage or mark it as the precarious latency of ghettoization.[9] Notions of impurity also contravene the operation of internal borders. Sources—a historical continuity that would embed SF in the mainstream—are sought that would manipulate an isomorphism of method between the legitimate and the generic: utopic estrangement, say, or extra-polative rigor. And yet it is plain that the attempts to claim Swift or More as SF can only be retrospective ones; they are only "SF" insofar as they intersect with generic conventions. Such histories have to arrive (and then pass over) the moment of the historical consti-tution of the pulps because SF as a demarcation is only comprehensible in relation to them. Even if More and Swift *historically* predate, in the internal temporality of the genre they can only arrive *subsequently* into the arms of an SF genre determined after they were written.

The SF history strenuously seeks to elaborate a fantasy of non-origin, of being indistin-guishable, identical, to the "mainstream": in such narratives of embedding SF into a larger historical unfolding there is clearly a desire to return to an earlier state of things, before the genre divide, before the boundary of high and low. *To restore an earlier stage of things*: this is how Freud formulates the death instinct in *Beyond the Pleasure Principle.* The pleasure principle operates according to an economy of stabilization: excitation causes imbalance and disturbance; this energy is bound and neutralized. Prior to this, Freud hypothesizes, are *instincts* which "do not belong to the type of *bound* nervous processes but of *freely mobile* processes which press towards discharge" (306). The instincts are not concerned with a homeostatic economy, but seek to entirely evacuate from the organism: *"It seems, then, that an instinct is an urge inherent in organic life to restore an earlier state of things"* (308)—that state being the inorganic, the inanimate: death. This "first" instinct is seeking a quick return to the organic state; however, external stimuli keep arriving to disrupt this path of return to the immanent "proper" death. External influences "oblige the still surviv-ing substance to diverge ever more widely from its original course of life and to make ever more complicated *detours* before reaching its aim of death" (311). Life is in fact merely the result of the *detours* enforced by external stimuli, and the threat of "returning to inor-ganic existence other than those which are immanent in the organism itself." Freud can thus state: *"the aim of all life is death"* (311).

Peter Brooks has already proposed Freud's essay as a model for the process of read-ing: for the classic realist text at least, the opening of the novel causes excitation which the text then attempts to expel, to return to zero, at the close. To finish, to complete the text, is to restore an earlier state of things. Narrative is, in effect, the *detour* between two states of quiescence: "The desire of the text (the desire of reading) is hence desire for the end, but desire for the end reached only through the least minimally complicated detour, the intentional deviance, in tension, which is the plot or narrative" (292). But this is also the desire of SF as a genre. Placing generic SF in a historical trajectory, in which there is no origin or name or site of SF, sees the imposition of the "ghetto" as an intolerable blockage to energy which is seeking absolute discharge, the return to zero. The history of the genre is the history of the attempt to die in the *proper* way. This gives a new import-ance to the question of whether it is the "right" or "wrong" death represented in Ballard's

"disaster" novels; it also questions the more Jungian interpretations of his texts as movements towards wholeness and plenitude. That Powers constructs a huge Mandala at the
center of which he finally transcends his body can be taken as a Jungian image; equally
the circular mandala could be seen to draw a zero, a figure which is the precise opposite of plenitude, signalling rather emptiness, nothing, the return of the inorganic. This is
the double-edged death of SF, as literal destruction and metaphorical transcendence: the
return to the mainstream.

The history of SF is a history of ambivalent deaths. The many movements within the
genre—the New Wave, feminist SF, cyberpunk—are marked as both transcendent death-
as-births, finally demolishing the "ghetto" walls, and as degenerescent birth-as-deaths,
perverting the specificity of the genre. To be elevated above the genre is a transcendent
death and the birth of Literature, but as these movements harden, coalesce, are *named,*
they fall back as subgeneric moments of SF. They become detours on the road to the
proper death of SF.

History as the passage between two equivalent states of quiescence displays, evidently, that birth and death become interchangeable. If the projection back, as a fantasy of
non-origin, is SF's past, its complement in the future is the fantasy of non-being. This is
the circular detour back into the mainstream where the fantasy of non-origin had situated
it before the interregnum of the generic. The most enthusiastic claims for approaching
non-being came with the New Wave. The explosion of the New Wave was the explosion
of the genre itself. Aldiss senses a "rapprochement" with the mainstream, the return from
the "ghetto of Retarded Boyhood" and asserts "Science Fiction *per se* does not exist"
(306-07). Scholes and Rabkin end their history with the problematic "place" of Ballard
and Vonnegut: "A writer like Vonnegut forces us to consider the impending disappearance of the category upon which a book like this depends. . . science fiction will not exist"
(98-99). The introduction to Harlan Ellison's *Dangerous Visions* evokes two deaths: that
of the Golden Age being superseded by science itself, and that of the New Wave, which
"has been found, has been termed good by the mainstream, and is now in the process
of being assimilated. . . . Science fiction is dead" (xxii).

That death is so central to the history of SF, that death *propels* the genre is, I must
insist again, the effect of the structure of legitimation: SF is a genre seeking to bury the
generic, attempting to transcend itself so as to destroy itself as the degraded "low." The
third strategy of legitimation, however, that promoting the rigor of the scientific, apparently
refuses this deference to the mainstream. Nevertheless, it posits its own kind of death.

Robert Heinlein's definition of SF as "realistic speculation about possible future
events, based solidly on adequate knowledge of the real world, past and present, and
on a thorough understanding of the nature and significance of the scientific method,"
allows him a "rigorous" future projection, one prediction of which is the disappearance
of "the cult of the phony in art. . . . so-called 'modern art' will be discussed only by
psychiatrists" (*Worlds* 22, 17). Contemporary literature is "sick, written by neurotics. . .sex
maniacs. . .the degraded, the psychotic" ("Science Fiction" 42). The poles are inverted,

as are imputed pathologies. One suspects, however, that this adversarial disrespect is a defensively aggressive response to illegitimacy.

Legitimation by science continually fails by its own allegedly rigorous demands. If Heinlein places a border between SF and fantasy by declaring that fantasy is "any story based on violation of scientific fact, such as space ship stories which ignore ballistics" ("Science Fiction" 19), his point that time-travel stories are legitimate because "we know almost nothing about the nature of time" is exceedingly weak. The depressing litany of rejections and exclusions of certain texts because their science "doesn't work" (as Aldiss chastises Ballard ["Wounded" 128]) insists on a purity that, by the very standards of the science it invokes to judge, fails. The science element of SF is of interest, in fact, *exactly* as it fails, as it "misses" rigor; as Andrew Ross maintains, Gernsback and Campbell's claim to be at the "cutting edge" of science is not so much anachronistic as mediated and ideological. The adherence to a positivistic, technocratic science was scientifically outdated but *politically* current: the populism of technological futurism, the scientist as social engineer. Stableford is right, I think, to assert that the *rhetoric* of scientific rigor was a crucial palliative for early SF: "What seems to have been essential is the *illusion* of fidelity to science and responsibility to the principles of logical extrapolation, probably because it is this illusion that permits. . .the suspension of disbelief which allows the reader to *participate* in the fiction by identifying with its endeavour" (59).

"Science" must miss its mark, because to be accurate is to risk destruction. With a ceaseless regularity in this mode of legitimation, the name of Cleve Cartmill is invoked. Cartmill's atom-bomb story, "Deadline," published in *Astounding* in 1944, was deemed to be so accurate with respect to the research program of the Manhattan Project that the FBI raided *Astounding*'s offices. The frequent appearance of the anecdote indicates its utility for claiming the scientific accuracy and importance of SF. This may be true, but it also marks a death. Cartmill's fiction was overtaken within a year; it survives only as an *anecdote,* not as a read text. There is a sense, in the insistence on scientific rigor, that SF is fighting a limited shelf-life: "one danger threatening science fiction is that the progress of science itself answers so many questions raised by science fiction, thereby removing one idea after another" (de Camp 128-29).

This may be banal, or trivializing of SF's vitality in its consistent confrontations with contemporaneous technological issues. However, the scientific legitimation aims to sidestep the claims of the mainstream on the ownership of the "proper" text through another, far more important strategy: "Even if every work were on the lowest literary level. . .the form would still retain much of its significance—for the significance. . .lies more in its attitudes [the scientific method], in its intention, than in the perfection of its detail" (Bretnor 287). This retreat, this surrender of "fiction" for the claims of science, shifts the emphasis from "science *fiction*" to "*science* fiction": one wonders how SF as such can survive this shift. In Lyotard's model of language games invoked in *The Postmodern Condition,* the scientific statement is a denotative, an assertion of a truth claim on a real referent. Its conditions of acceptance are that it must be open to repetition by others, and that the language of the statement is judged relevant and "good" by the consensual community of experts. Science is, on first glance, a "pure" game in that the conditions of proof can only be established through denotatives. If the legitimation of SF emphasizes *science* such denotative proofs are invoked. As *fiction,* however, this claim is problematic; invoking the "agonistics" of language games, Lyotard says: "This does not necessarily mean that one plays in order to win. A move can be made for the sheer pleasure of its invention: what else is involved in that labour of language harassment undertaken by popular speech and by literature?" (10). The "purity" (or at least minimally determinable conditions) of scientific legitimation murders the fundamentally ludic and "impure" statements of the fictional. How could proofs ever be established for the fictional? For Roland Barthes, having no real referent is something like the "torment" of literature: that it is *"without proofs.* By which it must be understood that it cannot prove, not only *what* it says, but even that it is worth the trouble saying it." However, "at this point, everything turns around, for out of its impotence to prove, which excludes it from the serene heaven of Logic, the Text draws a *flexibility* which is in a sense its essence" (495). The essence of the fictional is its inessence. The insistence on the rigor of the scientific, then, negates the very condition of fiction; another kind of death.

It cannot be so, it will be objected. But, to return to Freud's *Beyond the Pleasure Principle,* this objection can already be found inscribed there: "It cannot be so" (312). *Beyond the Pleasure Principle* is written as a complex shuffling dance—taking one step forward, withdrawing it, stepping forward again. Indeed the essay ends with the image of limping—as if this extension and retraction of "wild" speculations had made Freud footsore.[10] Freud partially withdraws the sole dominance of the death instinct: "the whole path of development to natural death is not trodden by *all* the elementary entities" (312); there is also the question of the sexual instincts. This begins to elaborate the struggle between Eros and Thanatos, the life and death instincts. And once again this leads us to a merry dance:

> It is as though the life of the organism moved with a vacillating rhythm. One group of instincts rushes forward so as to reach the final aim of life as swiftly as possible; but when a particular stage in the advance has been reached, the other group jerks back to a certain point to make a fresh start and so prolong the journey. (313)

It may have been a misreading, then, to have seen the history of SF as the detour between two deaths: who is to say that this continual renewal, these new movements, cycles of regeneration within SF are not a clawing back from the abyss of death rather than a passage towards it? And yet how would it be possible to tell the difference? The death instinct has not been recognized, Freud posits, because it *masquerades* as an apparent propulsion forward, the assertion of life.

The "vacillating rhythm" between instincts, between death and life, recalls the structure of the *fort/da* game that Freud analyzes in an earlier chapter of *Beyond.* The child throws the bobbin out of the cot, shouting *fort,* then reels it back in, shouting *da.* Freud's interpretation is that this stages the absenting and return of the mother: it opens the suggestion of a "beyond" to the pleasure principle because there is more investment in the unpleasurable absenting of the mother than in her pleasurable return. One can see a structurally similar game played by David Pringle with the name of Ballard. Pringle wants to assert that Ballard is a *writer* without that embarrassing pre-modifying "SF" attached to the title. Lists of plaudits, from Graham Greene, Kingsley Amis, Anthony Burgess, and Susan Sontag, are emphasized because "what almost all of these accolades have in common is that they do not refer to Ballard primarily as a SF writer." Ballard has performed the fantasy desire of ecstatic death: he "transcends genre stereotyping" (*Bibliog.* xii). Elsewhere, however, Pringle notes that Ballard's earliest (unpublished) attempts as fiction in the mainstream failed because "Ballard needed science fiction: the pressure of his imagination demanded a freer outlet" (*Alien Planet* 7). Pringle's criticism reveals an anxiety which presents itself as a kind of *fort/da* game, whereby SF reveals its legitimate offspring, who, in the processes of legitimation is orphaned from its parents, and so is reeled back to the hands of SF once more.

Freud's question, the impetus for his "extreme line of thought" (310), is why there is this constant repetition of unpleasure—in the child's game, in traumatic neurosis constantly returning to the traumatic event, in the repetitious "acting out" in transference. And equally it might be wondered why the SF community, so often belligerent in its defense of the genre, nevertheless constantly entertains fantasies of death. For it remains a fantasy. The fatality for this death is that to push towards it is forever to defer it, to perpetuate the detour. In Freud, the detour that is life is in fact *propelled* by death; in a curious way death ceases to be an end, the termination of the system, and becomes inscribed *within* the economy. And if "life" is a transitional state between two deaths, this "ultimately subverts the very notion of beginning and end, suggesting that the idea of the beginning presupposes the end, that the end is a time before the beginning. . . . Analysis, Freud would eventually discover, is inherently interminable, since the dynamics of resistance and the transference can always generate new beginnings in relation to any possible end" (Brooks, 279). The death of SF is that which is endlessly desired and yet endlessly deferred.

What, then, can be said about this death? One can either view it positively as, paradoxically, the very motor of SF. But one can also suggest that such fantasies are produced out of the structure of legitimation, SF's perpetual deference to the criteria of worth elaborated for "mainstream" literature. The death of the genre is the only way in which SF could survive as literature. We have grown used to the language of "crisis" in relation to SF—but the term, as in so many other disciplines, has had its urgency, its punctual (and punctural) immediacy eroded. SF moves from crisis to crisis, but it is not clear that such crises come from outside to threaten a once stable and coherent entity. SF is *produced* from crisis, from its intense self-reflexive anxiety over its status as literature, evidenced partially here by Ballard's re-marking of the law of genre. If the death-wish is to be avoided, we need to install a crisis in "crisis," question the way in which strategies of legitimation induce it. The panic narrative of degeneration might then cease its tediously repetitive appearance, and its inversion, the longing for ecstatic death, might be channeled into more productive writings.

If this is polemic, it rests on a conceit: the analogy of SF criticism's thrust and Freud's hypothesis of the death instinct. This is not, however, as bizarre a linkage as it may at first appear. Just as SF was the "guilty secret," an unanalyzed and repressed element of the fictive, so the institution of psychoanalysis sought to repress Freud's embarrassing speculations. Like the death drive itself, the disruptions caused by *Beyond the Pleasure Principle* had to be reduced to zero, to be excluded, expulsed. Now, for Pefanis at least, the death instinct "forms a major underlying thematic" (108) to much contemporary theory. And perhaps this has an equivalence to the growing visibility of popular literary forms in the academy. There is one more link, then: Freud wrote to Eitingon, "For the *Beyond* I have been punished enough; it is very popular, brings me masses of letters and encomiums. I must have made something very stupid there" (Gay 403). To be popular is somehow to be denied entry to the legitimate—for SF, for Freud. If the economy of such legitimations, the deathly equation of the "popular" and the "stupid," is exposed, perhaps analysis can move into more constructive areas.

Notes

Thanks to Istvan Csicsery-Ronay, Jr. for his advice and support. I would also like to thank the anonymous readers of an earlier draft of this piece for their invigorating hostility; I have tried to meet some of their concerns—to meet them all, however, would have negated the very purpose of a polemic.

1. The long closing section of Jaspers's *Metaphysics* is called "The Reading of Ciphers." It presents a fascinating prospect to read *The Drought,* a text obsessively remarking on the unreadable "ciphers" that litter the desert, against Jaspers. The "cipher-script" is the tremulous evidence of the Transcendent, but it remains only a signifier; to attempt to grasp the meaning of the cipher, to convert it into any form of knowledge, is immediately to see its destruction. In a sense, to "decipher" Ballard's texts in a single explanatory model is to effect a violent de-*cipher*ment. On this, see Roger Luckhurst, "'Between two walls': Postmodernist Theory and the 'Problem' of J.G. Ballard," Ph.D. diss., University of Hull, England, 1993.
2. Ballard has a long citation from this work in the marginal comments to the Re/Search edition of *The Atrocity Exhibition,* ed. Andrea Juno and Vale (Re/Search Publications, 1990), 76.
3. Wolfe, of course, theorizes 20th-century man as "The Masochistic Man," bent on a course of self-destruction.
4. This is of course an overly rigid structure, which is not meant to impose a fixed topography. Passages between are always possible; the border could be determined by the elements which transgress it. However, transgression is meaningful only once an interdiction has been elaborated. The border presupposes transgression just as transgression presupposes the border.
5. Citations from Gernsback from Andrew Ross, "Getting Out of the Gernsback Continuum," *Critical Inquiry* 17:419, Winter 1991, and *The Encyclopedia of Science Fiction,* ed. Peter Nicholls (London, 1979), 159.

6. This is Andreas Huyssen's thesis in "Mass Culture as Woman: Modernism's Other," in his *After the Great Divide* (London, 1986), 44-62. Huyssen is perhaps too formalistic in suggesting that the "low" was *constituted* by the "high"; in Britain, at least, the equation of mass literacy with degenerating literature was part of the antidemocratic discourses of the time, prompted by the 1870 Education Act—some time before a determinable "modernism" could be said to have come into existence.

7. This was in fact the project of the immediate precursor to the *TLS,* the *Literature* journal, set up in 1897. Quoted from Keating, p. 76.

8. The *specific* moment of equating the "low" with the degenerate at this time is effectively established when Keating notes that both Thackeray in the 1830s and Payn in the 1850s looked upon the "Unknown Public" that read "cheap" fiction as laudable and sowing the seeds of a potential democracy of literary taste (401-03).

9. On the latter, see the opening comments in "Introduction to Newer SF History," Suvin's *Metamorphoses of Science Fiction* (New Haven, 1979), 205-07.

10. See Jacques Derrida, "Speculations—on 'Freud,'" in his *The Post Card: From Socrates to Freud and Beyond,* trans. Alan Bass (Chicago, 1987), 257-409.

Works cited

Aldiss, Brian. *Billion Year Spree.* London, 1973.

—. "The Wounded Land: J.G. Ballard." Clareson, ed. (q.v.). 116-29.

Amis, Kingsley. *New Maps of Hell.* London, 1961.

Ballard, J.G. *The Voices of Time.* London, 1974.

Barlow, George. "Ballard." *Twentieth-Century Science-Fiction Writers.* Ed. Curtis C. Smith. 1981. 2nd ed. Chicago & London, 1986.

Blish, James. *More Issues at Hand.* Chicago, 1970.

Barthes, Roland. "Deliberations." Trans. Richard Howard. *Barthes: Selected Writings.* Ed. Susan Sontag. Oxford, 1983.

Brantlinger, Patrick. *Rule of Darkness: British Literature and Imperialism 1830-1914.* Ithaca, NY, 1988.

Bretnor, Reginald. "The Future of Science Fiction. Bretnor, ed. (q.v.). 265-94.

Bretnor, Reginald, ed. *Modern Science Fiction: Its Meaning and Future.* 1953. Rev, ed. Chicago, 1979.

Brigg, Peter. *J.G. Ballard.* Starmont Reader's Guide 26. Mercer Island, WA, 1985.

Brooks, Peter. "Freud's Masterplot." *Yale French Studies* 55-56:280-300, 1977.

Clareson, Thomas, ed. *SF: The Other Side of Realism.* Bowling Green, OH, 1971.

De Camp, L. Sprague. "Imaginative Fiction and Creative Imagination." Bretnor, ed. (q.v.). 119-54.

Derrida, Jacques. "Violence and Metaphysics: An Essay on the Thought of Emmanuel Levinas." *Writing and Difference.* By Derrida. Trans. Alan Bass. London, 1987.

Ellison, Harlan, ed. *Dangerous Visions.* 1967. One-volume ed. London, 1979.

Freud, Sigmund. *Beyond the Pleasure Principle.* 1920. *On Metapsychology.* Trans. James Strachey. Pelican Freud Library, Vol. 11. London, 1988. 269-338.

Gay, Peter. *Freud: A Life for Our Time.* London, 1988.

Haggard, H. Rider. "About Fiction." *Contemporary Review* 51:172-80. Feb 1887.

Heinlein, Robert A. "Science Fiction: Its Nature, Faults, and Virtues." *The Science Fiction Novel: Imagination and Social Criticism.* Ed. Basil Davenport. Chicago, 1959. 17-63.

Keating, Peter. *The Haunted Study: A Social History of the English Novel 1875-1914.* London, 1989.

Luckhurst, Roger. "Border Policing: Postmodernism and Science Fiction." *SFS* 18:358-56, #55, Nov 1991.

Merril, Judith. "What Do You Mean? Science? Fiction?" *SF: The Other Side of Realism.* Ed. Thomas D. Clareson. Bowling Green, OH, 1971.

Nichols, Peter. "Jerry Cornelius at the Atrocity Exhibition: Anarchy and Entropy in New Wave Science Fiction." *Foundation* 9:22-44, Nov 1975.

Pefanis, Julian. *Heterology and the Postmodern.* London, 1991.

Platt, Charles. "The Rape of Science Fiction." *Science Fiction Eye* 1:45-49. July 1989.

Pringle, David. *Earth is the Only Alien Planet.* Milford Series. San Bernardino, CA, 1979.

—. *J.G. Ballard: A Primary and Secondary Bibliography.* Englewood Cliffs, NJ, 1976.

—. and James Goddard. Interview with Ballard. *Vector* 73:24-49, March 1976.

Radway, Janice. *Reading the Romance.* London, 1987.

"Requiem for the Cyberpunks." Editorial statement. *Science Fiction Eye* 1:5, 1987.

Rose, Mark, ed. *Science Fiction: A Collection of Critical Essays.* Englewood, NJ, 1976.

Ross, Andrew. "Getting Out of the Gernsback Continuum." *Critical Inquiry* 17:411-33, Winter 1991.

Saintsbury, George. "The Present State of the Novel," *Fortnightly Review* 49:410-17, Jan 1888.

Scholes, Robert. "The Roots of Science Fiction." Rose, ed. (q.v.). 46-560.

—. and Eric S. Rabkin. *Science Fiction: History, Science, Vision.* London, 1977.

Sedgewick, Christina. "The Fork in the Road: Can Science Fiction Survive in Postmodern, Megacorporate America?" SFS 18:11-52, #53, March 1991.

Stableford, Brian. *The Sociology of Science Fiction.* San Bernardino, CA, 1987.

Stevenson, Gregory. *Out of the Night and Into the Dream.* Westport, CT, 1991.

Suvin, Darko. "On the Poetics of the Science Fiction Genre." Rose, ed. (q.v.). 57-71.

Wagar, Warren. "J.G. Ballard and the Transvaluation of Utopia." *SFS* 18:53-70. #53, March 1991.

Wilt, Judith. "The Imperial Mouth: Imperialism, the Gothic and Science Fiction." *Journal of Popular Culture* 14:618-28, 1981.

On defining sf, or not:
Genre theory, sf, and history

John Rieder

In his groundbreaking 1984 essay, "A Semantic/Syntactic Approach to Film Genre," Rick Altman could accurately state that "genre theory has up to now aimed almost exclusively at the elaboration of a synchronic model approximating the syntactic operation of a specific genre" (12). Only a few years later, in 1991, Ralph Cohen announced that there had been a paradigm shift in genre theory, in the course of which its dominant project had changed from identifying and classifying fixed, ahistorical entities to studying genres as historical processes (85-87). Yet the impact of that paradigm shift on sf studies, while no doubt contributing to the predominantly historical rather than formalist orientation of most scholarly projects these days, has been neither so immediate nor so overpowering as to render entirely clear its implications for conceptualizing the genre and understanding its history. In this essay I aim to help clarify and strengthen the impact of an historical genre theory on sf studies.

I start from the problem of definition because, although constructing generic definitions is a scholarly necessity, an historical approach to genre seems to undermine any fixed definition. The fact that so many books on sf begin with a more or less extended discussion of the problem of definition testifies to its importance in establishing a framework for constructing the history of the genre, specifying its range and extent, locating its principal sites of production and reception, selecting its canon of masterpieces, and so on.[1] Perhaps the scholarly task that best highlights the importance of genre definition is bibliography, where the choice of what titles to include necessarily has to be guided by clearly articulated criteria that often include such definitions.

Yet it seems that the act of definition cannot ever be adequate to the notion of genre as historical process. Altman's 1999 *Film/Genre,* one of the best and fullest elaborations of this approach to genre, argues that "genres are not inert categories shared by all … but discursive claims made by real speakers for particular purposes in specific situations" (101, qtd. Bould and Vint 50). Thus Mark Bould and Sherryl Vint argue in a recent piece, drawing on Altman's work, that "There Is No Such Thing as Science Fiction," by which they mean that "genres are never, as frequently perceived, objects which already exist in the world and which are subsequently studied by genre critics, but fluid and tenuous constructions made by the interaction of various claims and practices by writers, producers, distributors, marketers, readers, fans, critics and other discursive agents" (48). The critical and scholarly act of definition seems reduced, in this conception of the "claims and practices" that constitute the history of the genre, to no more than one among many other "fluid and tenuous constructions." In fact, the only generic definition—if one can call it that—adequate to the historical paradigm would be a kind of tautology, an assertion that the genre is whatever the various discursive agents involved in its production, distribution, and reception say it is. And indeed statements of that kind consistently come up in discussions of the problem of defining sf, the best-known example being Damon Knight's gesture of dismissal toward the very attempt at definition—"Science fiction is what we point to when we say it" (122, qtd. Clute and Nicholls 314).

In his 2003 essay "On the Origin of Genre," Paul Kincaid manages to turn the tautological affirmation of genre identity into a thoughtful position. Basing his argument on the notion of "family resemblance" in Ludwig Wittgenstein's *Philosophical Investigations,* Kincaid proposes that we can neither "extract a unique, common thread" that binds together all science fiction texts, nor identify a "unique, common origin" for the genre (415). He concludes that

> science fiction is not one thing. Rather, it is any number of things—a future setting, a marvelous device, an ideal society, an alien creature, a twist in time, an interstellar journey, a satirical perspective, a particular approach to the matter of story, whatever we are looking for when we look for science fiction, here more overt, here more subtle—which are braided together in an endless variety of combinations. (416-17)

The usefulness of Wittgenstein's concept of family resemblance for genre theory bears further discussion, and I will return to it a bit later. For now, the important theoretical point with regard to Kincaid's argument is not only to agree that, according to an historical theory of genre, sf is "any number of things," but also to note and emphasize that this account of genre definition, like Altman's and Bould and Vint's, involves subjects as well as objects. It is not just a question of the properties of the textual objects referred to as "science fiction," then, but also of the subjects positing the category, and therefore of the motives, the contexts, and the effects of those subjects' more or less consciously and successfully executed projects. To put it another way, the assertion that sf is "whatever we are looking for when we are looking for science fiction" does not mean anything much unless "we" know who "we" are and why "we" are looking for science fiction.

In what follows I propose to offer an account of the current state of genre theory as it applies to the attempt to say what sf is. The first section of the essay will concentrate on conceptualizing what sort of thing a genre is, or is not. The final section will then return to the question of how to understand the collective subjects of genre construction. I am asking, throughout, what does the tautological assertion that sf is what "we" say it is mean if taken as a serious proposition about the nature, not just of sf, but of genre itself? And if the notorious diversity of definitions of the genre is not a sign of confusion, nor the result of a multiplicity of genres being mistaken for a single one, but rather, on the contrary, the identity of sf is constituted by this very web of sometimes inconsistent and competing assertions, what impact should this understanding of genre formation have on the project of writing the history of sf?

Genre as a historical process

I am going to make five propositions about sf, each of which could also be reformulated as a thesis about genre per se, constituting what I take to be a fairly non-controversial but, I hope, useful summary of the current paradigm of genre theory. The sequence leads from the basic position that genres are historical processes to the point where one can effectively address the questions about the uses and users of sf that occupy the final section of this essay. The five propositions are:

1. sf is historical and mutable;
2. sf has no essence, no single unifying characteristic, and no point of origin;
3. sf is not a set of texts, but rather a way of using texts and of drawing relationships among them;
4. sf's identity is a differentially articulated position in an historical and mutable field of genres;
5. attribution of the identity of sf to a text constitutes an active intervention in its distribution and reception.

Let me explain and defend these propositions one at a time.

Sf is historical and mutable

Nearly all twentieth-century genre theorists before 1980 would have agreed that "Theory of genres is a principle of order: it classifies literature and literary history not by time or place (period or national language) but by specifically literary types of organization or structure" (Wellek and Warren 226). The newer paradigm, in contrast, considers generic organizations and structures to be just as messily bound to time and place as other literary-historical phenomena, albeit with patterns of distribution and temporalities of continuity and discontinuity that may differ quite strongly from those of national traditions or "periods" in Wellek and Warren's sense. A newer paradigm is not necessarily a better one, however, and the choice between these two alternatives remains a matter of first principles, where the evidence seems susceptible of logically consistent explanation from either point of view. That is, if one considers sf to designate a formal organization—Darko Suvin's "literature of cognitive estrangement" has of course been by far the most influential formal definition—then it makes just as much sense to find it in classical Greek narratives as in contemporary American ones; and, in addition, it makes sense to say, as

Suvin did, that much of what is conventionally called sf is actually something else. But the newer paradigm holds that the labeling itself is crucial to constructing the genre, and would therefore consider "the literature of cognitive estrangement" a specific, late-twentieth-century, academic genre category that has to be understood partly in the context of its opposition to the commercial genre practices Suvin deplored. Suvin's definition becomes part of the history of sf, not the key to unraveling sf's confusion with other forms.

Strong arguments for the logical superiority of the historical over the formal approach to genre theory have been advanced from the perspective of linguistics and on the grounds provided by the vicissitudes of translation.[2] Beyond that, I would argue, the historical paradigm is to be preferred because it challenges its students to understand genre in a richer and more complex way, within parameters that are social rather than just literary.[3] Confronted, for example, with the controversy over whether such acclaimed pieces as Pamela Zoline's "The Heat Death of the Universe" (1967) or Karen Joy Fowler's "What I Didn't See" (2002) are sf or not, a formal approach can only ask whether the story is or is not a legitimate member of the genre. Does it accomplish "the presence and interaction of estrangement and cognition . . . [in] an imaginative framework alternative to the author's empirical environment" (Suvin, "On the Poetics" 375)? Is it a "realistic speculation about possible future events, based solidly on adequate knowledge of the real world, past and present, and on a thorough understanding of the nature and significance of the scientific method" (Heinlein 9)? Is it "modified by an awareness of the universe as a system of systems, a structure of structures" (Scholes 41)?[4] Does it explore the impact of technology or scientific discovery on lived experience? And so on. An historical approach to genre would ask instead how and why the field is being stretched to include these texts or defended against their inclusion; how the identification of them as sf challenges and perhaps modifies the accepted meaning of the term (so that questions about form also continue to be part of the conversation, but not on the same terms); what tensions and strategies in the writing and publication and reading of sf prepare for this sort of radical intervention; and what interests are put at stake by it.

Sf has no essence, no single unifying characteristic, and no point of origin

That sf has no point of origin or single unifying characteristic is the Wittgensteinian position Kincaid proposes in "On the Origin of Genre." The application of Wittgenstein's thought to the notion of genre that is crucial to Kincaid was first proposed in 1982 in Alistair Fowler's *Kinds of Literature* (41-44), an impressively erudite book whose central thesis is that genres are historical and mutable. As Fowler saw, Wittgenstein's notion of "family resemblance" is enormously suggestive for genre theory because it conceptualizes a grouping not based upon a single shared defining element. In the language game that constructs the category of games, for example, Wittgenstein says, "these phenomena have no one thing in common which makes us use the same word for all—but ... they are *related* to one another in many different ways…. We see a complicated network of similarities overlapping and criss-crossing: sometimes overall similarities, sometimes similarities of detail." We extend the concept "as in spinning a thread we twist fibre on fibre. And the strength of the thread does not reside in the fact that some one fibre runs through its whole length, but in the overlapping of many fibres" (31-32, sections 65-66; emphasis in original).

Another conceptual model for the shape of a genre that has no single unifying characteristic is provided by the notion of the fuzzy set (see Attebery, *Strategies* 12-13). A fuzzy set, in mathematics, is one that, rather than being determined by a single binary principle of inclusion or exclusion, is constituted by a plurality of such operations. The fuzzy set therefore includes elements with any of a range of characteristics, and membership in the set can bear very different levels of intensity, since some elements will have most or all of the required characteristics while others may have only one. In addition, one member of the set may be included by virtue of properties a, b, and c, another by properties d, e, and f, so that any two sufficiently peripheral members of the set need not have any properties in common. It thus results in a very similar conception of the shape of sf as one based on Wittgenstein's concept of family resemblance. Either model allows sf the kind of scope and variety found in John Clute and Peter Nicholls's *Encyclopedia of Science Fiction*.

It seems worth remembering, however, that something like such a fuzzy set was precisely the target of Suvin's influential intervention into the history of definitions of sf. What Suvin opposed to the wide range of texts included in the category of sf was a precise concept of the genre ruled by what Roman Jakobson called a "dominant": "the focusing component of a work of art … [that] rules, determines, and transforms the remaining components" (Jakobson 82). The categorical entity constituted by a fuzzy set or family resemblance, from this point of view, simply allows any number of incompatible versions of the textual dominant to operate silently, side by side, producing in the guise of a narrative genre a motley array of texts with no actual formal integrity. That, according to Suvin, was the state of sf studies when he entered into it his own rigorous formal definition, which directed itself powerfully against the illusion of integrity in a generic field that had allowed itself to be delineated in such a loose manner.

I think that the conceptualization of sf as a fuzzy set generated by a range of definitions remains susceptible to this formalist critique—that it indiscriminately lumps together disparate subgenres under a nominal umbrella—because it is still ruled by the logic of textual determination, albeit in a far more diffuse way than that demanded by Jakobson's notion of the textual dominant. A thoroughgoing theorist of the fuzzy set, rather than being pressed to identify the dominant that commands the operation of inclusion or exclusion from the generic set, would face the daunting task of enumerating the range of characteristics that merit inclusion, including not only textual properties but also intertextual relationships and paratextual functions such as "labeling." Such a task would indeed be encyclopedic in scope, but I want to suggest that it would also be futile, because the quasi-mathematical model of the fuzzy set can never be adequate itself to the open-ended processes of history where genre formation and re-formation is constantly taking place. In this respect, Wittgenstein's thinking is more attuned to the historical approach to genre than is the notion of the fuzzy set, because "the term 'language-*game*' is meant to call into prominence the fact that the *speaking* of language is part of an activity, or of a form of life" (Wittgenstein 11, section 23; emphases in original). Categorization, in this view, is not a passive registering of qualities intrinsic to what is being categorized, but an active intervention in their disposition, and this insistence on agency is what most decisively distinguishes an historical approach to sf from a formalist one.

The term "family resemblance" has its shortcomings, however, when it comes to thinking about the problem of generic origins. Historians of sf are all too fond of proclaiming its moment of birth, whether it be in Mary Shelley's *Frankenstein* (1818), H.G. Wells's *The Time Machine* (1895), Hugo Gernsback's *Amazing Stories* (1926), or elsewhere according to one's geographical and historical emphasis; and the term "family resemblance" encourages the construction of the history of sf as some version of a family tree of descendants from one or more such progenitors.[5] It is not quite enough to argue, as Kincaid does, that there is no "unique, common origin" for the genre (415); the collective and accretive social process by which sf has been constructed does not have the kind of coherent form or causality that allows one to talk about origins at all. Even without reference to Wittgenstein's anti-essentialism, the historical approach to genre proposed in Hans-Robert Jauss's reception theory exposes the logical problem with identifying the moment of origin for a genre insofar as, for Jauss, the notion of genre is based on repetition and is strictly opposed to his notion of originality. In Jauss's reception theory, there cannot be a first example of a genre, because the generic character of a text is precisely what is repeated and conventional in it. A text can violate established generic expectations, but it can only be said to have established new expectations when other texts, in imitating its strategies, solidify them into the features of a genre. In order for a text to be recognized as having generic features, it must allude to a set of strategies, images, or themes that has already emerged into the visibility of a conventional or at least repeatable gesture. Genre, therefore, is always found in the middle of things, never at the beginning of them.[6]

A model that helps to better conceptualize the absence of origins in an historical approach to genre is Gilles Deleuze and Felix Guattari's notion of the rhizomatic assemblage.[7] What Deleuze and Guattari call a "collective assemblage of enunciation" (22) is constituted by "lines of articulation or segmentarity, strata and territories; but also lines of flight, movements of deterritorialization and destratification" (3). It has no center, no "hierarchical modes of communication and preestablished paths, [but rather] the rhizome is an acentered, nonhierarchical, nonsignifying system … without an organizing memory or central automaton, defined solely by a circulation of states" (21). The most important feature of the rhizomatic assemblage in relation to genre theory is that it is an "antigenealogy" that "operates by variation, expansion, conquest, capture, offshoots.… [I]t has neither beginning nor end, but always a middle (*milieu*) from which it grows and which it overspills" (21). The movement of texts and motifs into and through sf does not confer a pedigree on them, then, but instead merely connects one itinerary to another. The paths that connect those itineraries are not given in the "acentered, nonhierarchical, nonsigni-fying" structure of the genre, but rather have been and must be constructed by writers, publishers, and readers out of the conjunctures they occupy and the materials at hand.

   The notion that sf's history is one of "variation, expansion, conquest, capture, offshoots" rather than a lineage of ancestors and descendants is nowhere more important than in the study of what, following the hint in the title of Everett Bleiler's indispensable biblio-graphy, *Science-Fiction: The Early Years* (1990), I would call early science fiction. Studying the beginnings of the genre is not at all a matter of finding its points of origin but rather of observing an accretion of repetitions, echoes, imitations, allusions, identifications, and distinctions that testifies to an emerging sense of a conventional web of resemblances. It is this gradual articulation of generic recognition, not the appearance of a formal type, that constitutes the history of early sf. Thus, rather than sorting out true sf from the genres in its proximity or trying to find its primal ancestors, it is far more useful to take stock of the way that sf gradually comes into visibility in the *milieu* of late nineteenth-century narrative: imperial adventure fiction, the extraordinary voyage, the romance revival of the 1880s and 1890s in England, the boy-scientists of the American dime novel, utopian writing, the future-war motif, and so on.[8] One is not looking for the appearance of a positive entity but rather for a practice of drawing similarities and differences among texts, which is the point further elaborated by the third proposition.

Sf is not a set of texts, but rather a way of using texts and of drawing relationships among them

All those involved in the production, distribution, and consumption of sf—writers, editors, marketing specialists, casual readers, fans, scholars, students—construct the genre not only by acts of definition, categorization, inclusion, and exclusion (all of which are import-ant), but also by their uses of the protocols and the rhetorical strategies that distinguish the genre from other forms of writing and reading. John Frow, at the beginning of his excellent and concise recent summary of the current state of genre theory, writes: "I under-stand genre as a form of symbolic action: the generic organization of language, images, gestures, and sound makes things happen by actively shaping the way we understand the world.... Texts—even the simplest and most formulaic—do not 'belong' to genres but are, rather, uses of them" (*Genre* 2). Genre requires "symbolic action" rather than being inherent in the form or content of a text, illustrated by the way generic difference can reside within verbal identity. Consider the example offered by Samuel R. Delany, who juxtaposes realist and sf readings of the sentence, "He turned on his left side"; the real-ist reading understands that someone has changed the position of his body, but the sf reading might mean that he has activated the left side of his body by turning on a switch (Delany 103). The point of this example is not so much that the sf reading exploits the grammatical and semantic possibilities of the language in a different and richer way, as Delany argued, as that the second reading depends upon the reader's familiarity with and use of sf conventions—in particular, here, the expectation that the distinction between organism and machine is going to be blurred or violated. Both the writer and the reader of the sentence in its sf sense are using the genre to actively shape their understanding of the world—that is, the world depicted in the text in question, and its relation to both an empirical environment and to other generically constructed worlds (the world of fantasy, the world of comedy, and so on).[9]

The distinction between a text's using a genre and its belonging to it also changes the relationship between the individual text and the genre, so that it is no longer one of simple exemplification, where the text stands as a metonym or synecdoche of the genre. The character of genre as "symbolic action" implies that genre is one of the many kinds of codes that, as Roland Barthes pointed out so relentlessly in *S/Z,* a text activates. Generic hybridity is not a special case, then; any narrative longer than a headline or a joke almost inevitably uses multiple generic conventions and strategies. Distinctions between sf and fantasy typically, if tacitly, acknowledge this fact, since they so often turn upon the status afforded to realist conventions in relation to the rest of the narrative. Because of the way that multiple genres play upon and against one another in individual texts, pigeonholing a text as a member of this or that genre is much less useful than understanding the way it positions itself within a field of generic possibilities.[10]

Sf's identity is a differentially articulated position in an historical and mutable field of genres

Frow, after postulating the thesis that texts use genres rather than belong to them, goes on to say that the uses of genre in a text "refer not to 'a' genre but to a field or economy of genres, and [the text's] complexity derives from the complexity of that relation" (*Genre* 2). To speak of an "economy of genres," as Frow does here, is to think of the generic codes activated in a text or by a reader as a matter of making choices with values attached to them by virtue of their difference from other possible choices. Such an economy depends crucially on the system of genres in play at a given time and place. Genres—like phonemes and words in Saussure's lectures on linguistics—are here considered values that signify by virtue of their difference from the other values in their field, and may change or lose their meaning if transposed into a different system. Thus, as Tony Bennett puts it, generic analysis must always take into account "the system of generic differences—conceived as a differentiated field of social uses—prevailing at [a given] time in terms of its influence on both textual strategies and contexts of reception" (108), because every generic choice constitutes what Pierre Bourdieu calls a position-taking with respect to the positions and values that structure the contemporary field of choices. Understanding the dynamics of genre in a given text depends upon being able to understand the field that offers the writer or reader its range of generic possibilities and determines the values attached to them.

Problems of generic economy are absolutely crucial to sf studies in two ways, the first having to do with questions of prestige and the second with writing the genre's history.

Roger Luckhurst has written very entertainingly about sf's "death wish," which is to say its desire to stop being sf and become "literature." The source of that desire is the way positions and values line up in the contemporary economy of genres to produce the negative connotations often attached to "genre fiction:"

> The paradigmatic topography of ghetto/mainstream marks a border on which are transposed the evaluations popular/serious, low/high, entertainment/Literature.... The only way, it is proposed, to legitimate SF is to smuggle it across the border into the "high." And for the genre as a whole to become legitimate paradoxically involves the very destruction of the genre. (Luckhurst, "Many Deaths" 37-38)

The conceit of the death wish actually refers to something rather different than an instinctual drive, of course—the fact that, although one can make choices (in this case, about genre), one can only choose from the options that history makes available. Many scholars (and editors, writers, and readers) of sf would like to have their sf and their literature too, but that is an option that the distinction between high and low culture has tended to foreclose.

The obsession with definite boundaries that once abounded in discussions of genre rested, not on a widespread desire for precision in making genre distinctions, but rather on the effects of prestige attached to positions in the contemporary genre system; and this is the source of the recurrent drawing and redrawing of sf's borders that Luckhurst writes about. The fact that genre boundaries are so frequently described as prescriptive and constricting derives, similarly, not from their really being that way, but rather from the fact that in modern Western artistic practices more prestige accrues to violating these boundaries than to conforming to them. Hence the concept of "literature" as such has repeatedly been formulated as the category where every work constructs its own unique genre (e.g., by Friedrich Schlegel, Benedetto Croce, and Maurice Blanchot; see Frow, *Genre* 26-27, and Altman, *Film/Genre* 4-7). What this understanding of "literature" puts at stake is much less the prescriptive force of generic boundaries than the play of expectation and surprise in a text's handling of them, as in the stark opposition in Jauss's reception theory between innovative strategies and the understanding of genre itself as a set of predictable and eventually worn-out conventions. Yet, although distinctions between high and low modes of narrative can be expected to exist wherever class differences attach themselves to the production and distribution of narratives—which is to say throughout history—the particular way that high and low are connected in contemporary genre practices with innovation versus imitation is a more recent and specific development. The peculiar sense of "literature" as the category whose members defy categorization is an integral part of the history of the sense of "genre" that is one of sf's conditions of existence. Thus writing the history of sf has to involve, at a minimum, attending to the historical change in generic systems that produced that distinction.

The history of sf, then, involves the history of a signal change in the system of genres: that is, the emergence of a genre system associated with mass publication that came to include science fiction alongside the detective story, the modern romance, the Western, horror, fantasy, and other similar genres, and which collectively comprised a practice of genre categorization distinct from and in tension with the pre-existing classical and academic genre system that includes the epic, tragedy, comedy, satire, romance, the lyric, and so on. In this sense, the influence of the great innovators like Shelley, Verne, and Wells takes place within the context of "cultural and historical fluctuations in the composition of generic systems," and close attention to the reception of any of the three authors will show that "the same texts may be subject to different generic classifications in different social and historical contexts" (Bennett 101). But the classical-academic and mass-cultural genre systems also each have a history that has entered into the production, distribution, and reception of texts, and that often forms substantial connections between the systems themselves and the history and significance of a given text. Thus, while it is certainly possible to read the *Oedipus* of Sophocles as a piece of detective fiction, its historical relationship to the genre of tragedy, and to the system of genres and literary values elaborated in relation to classical tragedy, is a good deal more consequential. By the same token, texts that are usually considered science fiction could be read simply as examples of satire, romance, comedy, tragedy, and so on, but doing so, rather than elevating them to the status of "serious" literature, strips them of an important aspect of their historicity.

The way generic terms and choices signify in relation to other terms and choices is constantly in flux. Thus, as Fowler says, "It is neither possible nor even desirable to arrive at a very high degree of precision in using generic terms. The overlapping and mutability of genres means that an 'imprecise' terminology is more efficient" (130). Such overlapping and mutability also makes necessary the practice of retro-labeling in order to trace the lineaments of emerging genre categories (hence, "early science fiction"). Nonetheless, attention to the history of genre systems ought to foreclose the option of transposing the category of sf wholesale onto early modern or classical texts. If Shelley's *Frankenstein* was not sf when it was written (see Rieder, *Colonialism* 19), neither, *a fortiori*, were Swift's *Gulliver's Travels* (1726) or Lucian's *True History.* The important point is that the emergence of sf has to do, not with the first appearance of a certain formal type, nor with when the term "science fiction" was first used or by whom, but rather with the appearance of a system of generic identities that articulates the various terms that cluster around sf (scientific fiction, scientific romance, scientifiction; but also horror fiction, detective fiction, the Western). Clearly Gernsback did not initiate this system of generic identities when he published the first issue of *Amazing Stories* in 1926. But just as clearly, the milieu of mass-marketed periodical publications is one of the historical conditions for sf's emergence as a distinctive genre, and that milieu carries with it its hierarchical opposition to a specific version of the realm of "high" culture.

I propose that understanding the positions and values of sf within past and present economies of genre, or how the history of this shifting and slippery subject fits into the larger context of changes within the system of genres, is the frame in which to put the question, what difference does it make when "we" point to a text and say that it is sf?

The answer to that question from the perspective of genre theory is that *attribution of the identity of sf to a text constitutes an active intervention in its distribution and reception.* Here we should speak of labeling itself as a rhetorical act. One of the most bustling areas of genre theory in recent years has been that explored by rhetoricians focused on the pedagogy of composition, rather than critics and scholars of literature (Frow, "Reproducibles" 1626-27). In an important early contribution to the new rhetorical approach to genre, Carolyn Miller wrote in 1984 that "A theoretically sound definition of genre must be centred not on the substance or the form of discourse but on the action it is used to accomplish" (24). Miller is primarily concerned with "the *'de facto'* genres, the types we have names for in everyday language" because it is these genres that formal-ize "the knowledge that practice creates" (27). Although her analysis is therefore more concerned with analyzing genres such as the letter of recommendation or the inaug-ural speech than with drawing distinctions between different types of storytelling, Miller's approach to genre might well lead one to ask why distinctions between types of story are drawn and insisted upon at all. How can one explain this "mutual construing of objects, events, interests, and purposes that not only links them but makes them what they are: an objectified social need" (30)? What action does it accomplish to attribute the label, sf, to a narrative?

Whatever protocols of interpretation or formal and thematic conventions the label refers to, the labeling itself often serves to position the text within the field of choices offered by the contemporary genre system in quite material ways: how it will be printed, where it will be sold, by whom it is most likely to be read. Generic attribution therefore affects the distribution and reception of texts: that is, the ways that they are put to use. It is a way of telling someone how to read a text, and even more a kind of promise that the text can be usefully, pleasurably, read that way. The attribution does not just classify the text, it promotes its use by a certain group of readers and in certain kinds of ways (e.g., with a high level of seriousness, or a lack of it). When "we" point to a story and say it is sf, therefore, that means not only that it ought to be read using the protocols associated with sf but also that it can and should be read in conversation with other sf texts and readers.

Such acts of labeling, by assigning texts a position and a value within a system of genres, entangle them within both a synchronic web of resemblances and a diachronic history of generic "variation, expansion, conquest, capture, offshoots" (Deleuze and Guattari 21). A history of genre systems attentive to the power that generic attribution exercises upon distribution and reception would not be one structured primarily by the appearance of literary masterpieces, but rather one also punctuated by watersheds in the technology of publication, the distribution of reading materials, and the social production and distribution of literacy itself. Some sense of the contours of such a history might be gleaned from John Guillory's brilliant summary of the forms of the canon from classical times to the present in *Cultural Capital* (55-82); for sf in particular, the list of the conditions for its emergence that Roger Luckhurst gives in his recent history are very much to the point (*Science Fiction* 16-17).[11]

It would be well beyond the scope of the present essay to attempt a comprehensive or even partial account of the history and dynamics of the attribution of sf's various labels to texts, much less an account of the economic and cultural transformation of the production and distribution of literature and literacy that I have been arguing should be its frame. I will turn back, rather, to the questions I raised earlier about the collective subject of sf genre formation. Those questions can now take an expanded form that should make their ramifications clearer. If sf is "whatever [in all its historical mutability and rhizomatic irregularity] we are looking for when we are looking for science fiction," what kind of a collectivity is formed by those who recognize the genre? On what terrain—that is, what system of genres, what regime of the production and distribution of literature and literacy—does the collective endeavor of "looking for science fiction" take place? What in the economy of genres or the dynamics of distribution and reception drives that collectivity to look for sf? And what kind of intervention in that economy is their saying they have found it?

Categorization and communities of practice

Sf history and criticism afford two drastically different versions of the collective subject of genre formation. The list of "writers, producers, distributors, marketers, readers, fans, critics and other discursive agents" in Bould and Vint's "fluid and tenuous" construction of sf indicates an anonymous, disparate, and disunified set of people. The use of the pronominal "we" here would constitute a kind of grammatical mirage imputing collective intentionality to a process without a subject—or, to be more precise, a process involving so many and such disconnected subjects that they share only the nominal common ground of their participation in the production, distribution, and reception of sf. This anonymous and scattered sense of a defining collectivity stands in sharp contrast to the practice of referring the construction and definition of sf to a rather tightly knit community, a folk group who gets to say what sf is by virtue of its shared participation in the project of publishing, reading, conversing, and otherwise interacting with one another about it:

> "Modern" science fiction, generally dated as having begun in late 1937 with the ascent of [John W.] Campbell, was a literature centered around a compact group of people. . . . There could have been no more than fifty core figures who did 90 percent of the writing and editing. All of them knew one another, most knew one another well, lived together, married one another, collaborated, bought each others' material, married each others' wives, and so on. (Malzberg 240)

This sort of usage has the considerable merit of making a concrete history and set of motives underlying sf refreshingly clear. Yet an excessive emphasis on the community of writers, editors, and fans in the early pulp milieu encourages an illusion of voluntary control over genre formation that is certainly exaggerated. Even during the so-called Golden Age of Campbell's editorial influence, sf resided within a larger economy of genres whose shifting values and fluid boundaries no group, much less a single editor or publication, could control. Genre construction is intentional only in fits and starts, only as localized as the circulation of the narratives in question, and even then subject to the pressures of the entire system of publication and circulation in which it takes place.

Even worse, the peculiar situation of the pulps can be taken as normative for genres as such, as Gary Westfahl does in *The Mechanics of Wonder*:

> if we define a genre as consisting of a body of texts related by a shared understand-
> ing of that genre as recorded in contemporary commentary, then a true history of
> science fiction as a genre must begin in 1926, at the time when Gernsback defined
> science fiction, offered a critical theory concerning its nature, purposes, and origins,
> and persuaded many others to accept and extend his ideas. . . . Literary genres appear
> in history for one reason: someone declares that a genre exists and persuades writers,
> publishers, readers and critics that she is correct. (8-12)

If this conception of genre were correct, it could be so only with respect to modern genre practices. Certainly there is no body of contemporary commentary that illustrates a shared generic understanding of the proverb, the riddle, the ballad, or the epic. But even if one stays within the field of genres occupied by Gernsback, one cannot locate a master theorist or "announcer" for the Western, spy fiction, detective fiction, and so on. The more usual case with genres is surely the one described by Michael McKeon in *The Origins of the English Novel,* where he argues that the novel as a generic designation is an abstraction that only came to be formulated when the process of its emergence was complete: "'The novel' must be understood as what Marx calls a 'simple abstraction,' a deceptively monolithic category that encloses a complex historical process" (20).

I suggest that it is possible to articulate the anonymous collectivity of the "complex historical process" of sf's emergence and ongoing construction, maintenance, and revision with the rich particularity of an account like Malzberg's by means of the theorization of categorization and its uses offered by Geoffrey Bowker and Susan Leigh Starr in *Sorting Things Out: Classification and its Consequences* (1999). Bowker and Starr are concerned with the way classifications are constructed within communities of practice, emphasizing the ad hoc supplementation and renegotiation of official or institutional categories by those who make them work: "We need a richer vocabulary than that of standardization or formalization with which to characterize the heterogeneity and the processual nature of information ecologies" (293). They emphasize, too, the "collective forgetting" about "the contingent, messy work" of classification that unites members of a community of practice (299). Full-fledged membership in such a community involves the naturalization of its objects of practice, which "means stripping away the contingencies of an object's creation and its situated nature. A naturalized object has lost its anthropological strange-ness" (299). As a result of its naturalization, it can be pointed to as an example of X with an obviousness that derives, not from the qualities of the object itself, but rather from membership in the relevant community.

Objects and communities of practice do not line up simply and neatly, however, because people come in and out of such communities, operate within them at various levels of familiarity with their categories, and may at the same time be members of different communities with conflicting classification practices. Bowker and Starr therefore emphasize the importance of "boundary objects" as ways of mediating the practices and motives of overlapping communities of practice:

> Boundary objects are those objects that both inhabit several communities of practice and satisfy the informational requirements of each of them. . . . The creation and management of boundary objects is a key process in developing and maintaining coherence across intersecting communities. . . . Boundary objects are the canonical forms of all objects in our built and natural environments. (297-307)

To speak about the common ground that comprises a sense of sf shared by writers, editors, publishers, marketers, fans, general readers, critics, and scholars might mean to identify the boundary objects that these various communities of practice share. The advantage of this conceptualization of classification is that the communities of practice do not disappear into anonymity, nor do the differences and tensions between their practices fall out of view, nor does whatever consensus settles among them embody the essence of the object. Boundary objects—for example, the texts that make up the sf canon—are not by necessity the most important or definitive objects for any given community, but simply the ones that satisfy the requirements of several communities at once.

Using the concepts of communities of practice and boundary objects to sort out the complex agencies constructing sf implies at least three distinct ways of understanding the assertion that sf is "whatever we are looking for when we are looking for science fiction." First, the "we" who are looking for science fiction could refer to the members of the speaker's own community of practice; this is the sense it had when Damon Knight wrote that "Science fiction is what we point to when we say it." Second, however, "we" could be taken to refer to all the different communities of practice who use the category, and "science fiction" to all of the objects all of them collectively point to. Any expectation of coherence here is obviously doomed to disappointment, but nonetheless this encyclopedic sense of the genre has the virtue of pointing toward the broad horizon of social practices where the history of genre systems can come into view. Third, science fiction could be taken as the set of objects the relevant communities of practice point to in common—that is, the boundary objects "we" communities share.

This third reading refers to a shared territory that is not a matter of giving up on arriving at a definition of the genre, but rather is precisely the product of the interaction among different communities of practice using different definitions of sf. The multiplicity of definitions of sf does not reflect widespread confusion about what sf is, but rather results from the variety of motives the definitions express and the many ways of intervening in the genre's production, distribution, and reception that they pursue. A wealth of biographical and paratextual material can be brought to bear here, as in Justine Larbalestier's decision that "letters, reviews, fanzines, and marketing blurbs are as important as the stories themselves" in piecing together her detailed history of a riven and complex sf community in *The Battle of the Sexes in Science Fiction* (1). Brian Attebery's description of the shape of sf in *Decoding Gender in Science Fiction* also attributes it to the interaction of disparate communities:

> Some outgrowths of the genre have so little in common that they hardly seem to consti-tute a single category. Yet if they share few features, all the myriad manifestations of SF may still be analyzed as products of a single process. All result from negotiated exchanges between different segments of culture. (170)

Understanding the relations among its various communities of practice, whether of nego-tiation or conflict or deliberate non-interaction, is among the most important problems that genre theory poses for sf critics and scholars.

Most genre theory has focused on the choices writers make when composing texts or that readers make, or ought to make, in interpreting them. But the practice of generic attribution also clusters heavily in two institutional locations, commercial publishing and the academy, and this pair of institutions bears no accidental resemblance to the oppos-itions between high and low culture referred to earlier. The practice of generic attribution in both places is concerned with constructing and regulating a text's or a genre's public value and significance, and comparing the different forms that publicity takes in these two locations would seem to be a good way to explore large-scale regularities in the contem-porary genre system. The relation between these two institutional locations, however, is a feature of contemporary genre systems upon which much academic theory in the twentieth century simply turned its back, failing to even notice it, much less ask about its significance or implications.[12] Yet in any construction of the history and fortunes of sf, the prominence of commercial sites and motives, from the pulp milieu of Gernsback to the mass market franchises of *Star Wars,* is hard—I would even say, foolish—to ignore.

The contours of an analysis of genre practices in the realm of commercial publishing is suggested by Marxist cultural theory, insofar as much of its best work distinguishes itself precisely by its concern with the pressure of commodification on literary and artistic production, as in Max Horkheimer and Theodor Adorno's arguments in *The Dialectic of Enlightenment* (1947) concerning the "culture industry" (94-136); Fredric Jameson's thesis that the commodity form structures modern artistic production in general, no less in the anti-commodities of high art than in the commercial products of mass culture ("Reification and Utopia" 130-38); or Pierre Bourdieu's thesis that the field of cultural production is structured by an inverse relationship between economic and cultural capital, such that restricted circulation—producing for other producers—enjoys a high level of prestige that is antithetical to, and compensatory for, the high economic rewards of general or mass circulation (312-26). As Horkheimer and Adorno first pointed out, the generic label attached to a narrative by "the culture industry" concerns strategies for identifying and targeting audiences, weighing risks, allocating resources, and capturing profits. Commercial practices, in this line of argument, tend to reify generic classifica-tions, promoting them as instigations to engage in repetitive and predictable habits of consumption. As Bourdieu argues, however, the motives of artistic producers in general cannot be reduced to a simple drive to maximize economic profit. Instead there is a constant struggle for writers and editors to achieve autonomy from the economic imperative. They are doubly, and contradictorily, driven both by the profit motive and by what Bourdieu calls the goal of achieving "consecration" by their peers, the "recognition accorded by those who recognize no other criterion of legitimacy than recognition by those whom they recognize" (320). The different motives and trajectories that appear in the editorial careers of, for example, Hugo Gernsback, John W. Campbell, and Michael Moorcock would richly illustrate these double motives, with the added advantage of distancing the dynamics of "consecration" from an exclusive identification with the avant-garde, high-art practices that Bourdieu tends to emphasize, placing it instead within the communities of practice of sf professionals and fans.

Genre attribution intersects with publicity in a different but perhaps complementary way in academic practices. Genre attribution in the academy has a double articulation that resembles the double motives of economic profit and consecration described by Bourdieu.[13] Thus there is an outward-looking motive by which genres serve as boundary objects that help rationalize curricular regularities in relation to the bureaucratic structure of the educational apparatus. A course on the novel, drama, poetry, creative writing, or science fiction, entered upon a student's transcript, promises his or her exposure to some standardized regime of study that can be measured in credit hours, billed for tuition, used by administrators to determine the allocation of institutional resources, and so on. But there is also an inward-looking side to genre discourse, a dialogue among scholars and critics in which generic labels merely serve as points of departure for exploration and argument. One encounters here a form of publicity that is one of the best contemporary approximations to the public sphere of "rational-critical debate" whose emergence Jürgen Habermas described in eighteenth-century England (57-67, 89-117), in spite of the fact that the demands of bureaucratization continue to exert considerable pressures on academic publishing, the organization of conferences, grant writing and grant giving, and so on. I would venture the hypothesis that the Janus face of genre practice in the academy bears a non-coincidental, structural resemblance to the split in the modern system of genres between practices aimed at aesthetic distinction and crass moneymaking that has been one of its gross features from the time of Alexander Pope's *Dunciad* (1743) to the present. If it seems at all plausible that the tensions between bureaucratic heteronomy and intellectual autonomy within the academy have a structural affinity with the contradictory drives for economic profit and cultural prestige in commercial production, the history of sf is well positioned to contribute importantly to a broader cultural history because, as I argued earlier, it has to involve that second structural transformation of publicity, the emergence of mass culture, that Habermas decried as the dissolution of the promise of social rationality contained in the first (159-74, 181-210).

Thinking of genres as categories wielded by communities of practice has one final advantage that can serve as the conclusion to this discussion. Bowker and Starr's analysis makes all definitions of sf appear in the light of working definitions, provisional conceptualizations suited to the purposes of a particular community of practice and, within that community, to the needs and goals of a specific project. In this way, definitions may be necessary, even indispensable, and yet constructing and adhering to a definition of the genre, far from being the goal of a history of sf, is more likely to be a way to short-circuit it. Definition and classification may be useful points of departure for critical and rhetor-ical analysis, but, if the version of genre theory offered in this essay is valid, the project of comprehending what sf has meant and currently means is one to be accomplished through historical and comparative narrative rather than formal description. I hope to have given some sense of the capaciousness and complexity that a narrative of the formation and maintenance of sf would entail, as well as of the stakes involved in its elaboration.

Notes

1. Examples of this kind of discussion are Freedman (13-23); Luckhurst, *Science Fiction* (6-10); Rieder, *Colonialism and the Emergence of Science Fiction* (15-21); and Roberts (1-20).
2. One of the most notable linguistic arguments is that of Tzvetan Todorov, who, in the opening section of his 1978 *Genres in Discourse,* broke with the emphasis he had earlier placed on the category and properties of "literature" (e.g., in *The Fantastic* 6-7) by arguing that there is no clear distinction between literary and non-literary language. The analysis of literary genres does not have to do with sentences and grammar, he now argued, but rather with discourses composed of "utterances in a given sociocultural context" (9), and therefore genre is a local phenomenon determined by social and cultural practice, not a quasi-grammatical one embed-ded in the deep structures of language. For a strong argument that begins by considering the problems of cultural difference that beset translation, see Owens.
3. Luckhurst makes the same point in a different way in *Science Fiction* (6-10).
4. Suvin and Scholes are quoted in Clute and Nicholls's entry on definitions (310-14).
5. For identification of Shelley's *Frankenstein* as the grand original of sf, see Aldiss and Wingrove (25-52); on the "miraculous birth" of sf in Shelley's *Frankenstein* or Wells's *War of the Worlds* (1898), see Jameson, *Archaeologies* (1, 57); for Gernsback's role as originator, see Westfahl (8).
6. Cf. Altman on "genrification" (*Film/Genre* 49-68).
7. For another discussion of the usefulness of Deleuze and Guattari's conception of rhizomes to genre theory, see Dimock (74).
8. Perhaps the most drastic attempt to sort true sf out from its neighbors is Suvin's (nonetheless very informative) bibliography in *Victorian SF in the UK,* which lists several hundred texts that fail to qualify as sf (most famously, Stevenson's *Dr. Jekyll and Mr. Hyde* [1886]). As Luckhurst comments, Suvin ignores any "sense that the categories of popular literature and notions of what scientific cognition might be were both undergoing transformation in the nineteenth century, and that SF is itself the very product of this change" (*Science Fiction* 8). I would say that the more inclusive and broadly-based bibliographies of Bleiler and Clareson are to be preferred. Examples of the kind of delineation of the emergence of the genre advocated here include Rieder's treatment of the lost-race motif in chapter 2 of *Colonialism and the Emergence of Science Fiction,* and chapters 2 and 3 of Luckhurst's *Science Fiction.*

9. On the way that genres construct worlds, see Frow (*Genre* 86-87).
10. What is usually meant by generic hybridity is perhaps simply that the genres being mixed in a text have not conventionally been considered neighbors (like the combination of philosophical speculation and sword-and-sorcery fantasy in Delany's Nevèrÿon stories [1979-87]), or perhaps that their neighborliness is being foregrounded and exploited in the text rather than allowed a conventionally silent co-presence (as in the explicit use of folkloric material in China Miéville's *King Rat* [1998]). That is, the designation of hybridity has more to do with the way a text positions itself within a system of generic values than with the simple and more or less inevitable fact that it uses a multiplicity of generic strategies.
11. Luckhurst's conditions include:

    1) The extension of literacy and primary education to the majority of the population of England and America, including the working classes; 2) the displacement of the older forms of mass literature, the "penny dreadful" and the "dime novel," with new cheap magazine formats that force formal innovation, and drive the invention of modern genre categories like detective or spy fiction as well as SF; 3) the arrival of scientific and technical institutions that provide a training for a lower-middle-class generation as scientific workers, teachers, and engineers, and that comes to confront traditional loci of cultural authority; and, in a clearly related way, 4) the context of a culture being visibly transformed by technological and scientific innovations. . . . (16)

12. The exception that proves the rule is Altman, *Film/Genre* (90-96, 123-43).
13. I am drawing here on the analysis of the double articulation of academic concepts in Rieder, "Institutional Overdetermination."

Works cited

Aldiss, Brian, with David Wingrove. *Trillion Year Spree: The History of Science Fiction.* London: Gollancz, 1986.

Altman, Rick. *Film/Genre.* London: British Film Institute, 1999.

—. "A Semantic/Syntactic Approach to Film Genre." *Cinema Journal* 23.3 (Spring 1984): 6-18.

Attebery, Brian. *Decoding Gender in Science Fiction.* New York: Routledge, 2002.

—. *Strategies of Fantasy.* Bloomington: Indiana UP, 1992.

Barthes, Roland. *S/Z.* 1970. Trans. Richard Howard. New York: Farrar, Straus, and Giroux, 1974.

Bennett, Tony. *Outside Literature.* London: Routledge, 1990.

Bleiler, Everett F., with Richard J. Bleiler. *Science-Fiction: The Early Years.* Kent, OH: Kent State UP, 1990.

Bould, Mark, and Sherryl Vint. "There Is No Such Thing as Science Fiction." *Reading Science Fiction.* Ed. James Gunn, Marleen Barr, and Matthew Candelaria. New York: Palgrave, 2009. 43-51.

Bourdieu, Pierre. "The Field of Cultural Production, or: The Economic World Reversed." *Poetics* 12 (1983): 311-55.

Bowker, Geoffrey C., and Susan Leigh Starr. *Sorting Things Out: Classification and its Consequences.* Cambridge, MA: MIT, 1999.

Clareson, Thomas. *Science Fiction in America, 1870s-1930s: An Annotated Bibliography of Primary Sources.* Westport, CT: Greenwood, 1984.

Clute, John, and Peter Nicholls, eds. *The Encyclopedia of Science Fiction.* London: Orbit, 1993.

Cohen, Ralph. "Genre Theory, Literary History, and Historical Change." *Theoretical Issues in Literary History.* Ed. David Perkins. Cambridge, MA: Harvard UP, 1991. 85-113.

Delany, Samuel R. "Science Fiction and 'Literature'—or, The Conscience of the King." 1979. *Speculations on Speculation: Theories of Science Fiction.* Ed. James Gunn and Matthew Candelaria. Lanham, MD: Scarecrow, 2005. 95-117.

Deleuze, Gilles, and Felix Guattari. *A Thousand Plateaus: Capitalism and Schizophrenia.* 1980. Trans. and Foreword Brian Massumi. Minneapolis: U of Minnesota P, 1987.

Dimock, Wai Chee. *Through Other Continents: American Literature Across Deep Time.* Princeton, NJ: Princeton UP, 2006.

Fowler, Alistair. *Kinds of Literature: An Introduction to the Theory of Genres and Modes.* Cambridge, MA: Harvard UP, 1982.

Freedman, Carl. *Critical Theory and Science Fiction.* Middletown, CT: Wesleyan UP, 2000.

Frow, John. *Genre.* New York: Routledge, 2006.

—. "'Reproducibles, Rubrics, and Everything You Need': Genre Theory Today." *PMLA* 122.5 (Oct. 2007): 1626-34.

Guillory, John. *Cultural Capital: The Problem of Literary Canon Formation.* Chicago: U of Chicago P, 1993.

Habermas, Jürgen. *The Structural Transformation of the Public Sphere: An Inquiry into a Category of Bourgeois Society.* 1965. Trans. Thomas Burger. Cambridge, MA: MIT, 1991.

Heinlein, Robert A. "Science Fiction: Its Nature, Faults and Virtues." 1959. *Turning Points: Essays on the Art of Science Fiction.* Ed. Damon Knight. New York: Harper, 1977. 3-28.

Horkheimer, Max, and Theodor W. Adorno. *The Dialectic of Enlightenment.* 1947. Trans. Edmund Jephcott. Ed. Gunzelin Schmid Noerr. Stanford: Stanford UP, 2002.

Jakobson, Roman. "The Dominant." Unpublished lecture. 1935. Trans. Herbert Eagle. *Readings in Russian Poetics: Formalist and Structuralist Views.* Ed. Ladislav Matejka and K. Pomorska. Ann Arbor, MI: Michigan Slavic Publications, 1978. 82-87.

Jameson, Fredric. *Archaeologies of the Future: The Desire Called Utopia and Other Science Fictions.* London: Verso, 2005.

—. "Reification and Utopia in Mass Culture." *Social Text* 1 (Winter 1979): 130-48.

Jauss, Hans-Robert. *Toward an Aesthetic of Reception.* Trans. Timothy Bahti. Minneapolis: U of Minnesota P, 1982.

Kincaid, Paul. "On the Origins of Genre." *Extrapolation* 44 (Winter 2003): 409-19.

Larbalestier, Justine. *The Battle of the Sexes in Science Fiction.* Middletown, CT: Wesleyan UP, 2002.

Luckhurst, Roger. "The Many Deaths of Science Fiction: A Polemic." *SFS* 21.1 (Mar. 1994): 35-50.

—. *Science Fiction.* Cambridge: Polity, 2005.

Malzberg, Barry. "Some Notes toward the True and the Terrible." 1982. *Speculations on Speculation: Theories of Science Fiction.* Ed. James Gunn and Matthew Candelaria. Lanham, MD: Scarecrow, 2005. 239-42.

McKeon, Michael. *The Origins of the English Novel, 1600-1740.* Baltimore, MD: Johns Hopkins UP, 1987.

Miller, Carolyn R. "Genre as Social Action." 1984. *Genre and the New Rhetoric.* Ed. Aviva Friedman and Peter Medway. London: Taylor & Francis, 2000. 67-78.

Owen, Stephen. "Genres in Motion." *PMLA* 122.5 (Oct. 2007): 1389-93.

Rieder, John. *Colonialism and the Emergence of Science Fiction.* Middletown, CT: Wesleyan UP, 2008.

—. "The Institutional Overdetermination of the Concept of Romanticism." *Yale Journal of Criticism* 10.1 (Spring 1997): 145-63.

Roberts, Adam. *The History of Science Fiction.* London: Palgrave Macmillan, 2005.

Scholes, Robert. *Structural Fabulation: An Essay on Fiction of the Future.* Notre Dame, IN: Notre Dame UP, 1975.

Suvin, Darko. "On the Poetics of the Science Fiction Genre." *College English* 34.3 (Dec. 1972): 372-82.

—. *Victorian Science Fiction in the UK: The Discourses of Knowledge and of Power.* Boston: G.K. Hall, 1983.

Todorov, Tzvetan. *The Fantastic: A Structural Approach to a Literary Genre.* 1970. Trans. Richard Howard. Ithaca: Cornell UP, 1975.

—. *Genres in Discourse.* 1978. Trans. Catherine Porter. Cambridge: Cambridge UP, 1990.

Wellek, Rene, and Austin Warren. *Theory of Literature.* 3rd. ed. New York: Harcourt Brace Jovanovich, 1977.

Westfahl, Gary. *The Mechanics of Wonder: The Creation of the Idea of Science Fiction.* Liverpool: Liverpool UP, 1998.

Wittgenstein, Ludwig. *Philosophical Investigations.* 1953. Trans. G.E.M. Anscombe. Oxford: Basil Blackwell, 1978.

Recommended further reading

Attebery, Brian, and Veronica Hollinger, eds. *Parabolas of Science Fiction*. Middletown, CT: Wesleyan UP, 2013.

Collection of essays that develops a model for understanding the genre using the figure or metaphor of the parabola, which describes a narrative trajectory that links texts in a larger system based upon their treatment of shared themes.

Clarke, I. F. *The Pattern of Expectation: 1644-2001*. New York: Basic Books, 1979.

Sees the genre as essentially extrapolative, emerging in the early modern period with the advent of predictive futuristic speculation.

Clute, John. *Pardon This Intrusion: Fantastika in the World Storm*. Essex, UK: Beccon, 2011.

Argues that science fiction is part of a broader genre called "fantastika," which also encompasses fantasy and supernatural horror; all of these subgenres are responses to post-Enlightenment scientific discoveries and the emergence of secular history.

Langlet, Irène. *La Science-fiction: Lecture et poétique d'un genre littéraire*. Paris: Armand Colin, 2006.

Defines SF as the literature of "enigma and explanation," highlighting the genre's didactic qualities and its engagement with readers' intellectual curiosity and capacity for ratiocination.

Milner, Andrew. *Locating Science Fiction*. Liverpool: Liverpool UP, 2012.

Argues against formalist or essentialist definitions of SF and in favor of a model of the genre as a constantly contested site, a "selective tradition" that is revised historically as competing accounts set up and challenge putative boundaries.

Roberts, Adam. *The History of Science Fiction*. New York: Palgrave, 2006.

Argues that the genre is centrally defined by the operations of technological rationality and has its roots in narratives of imaginary voyage and discovery.

Rose, Mark. *Alien Encounters: Anatomy of Science Fiction*. Cambridge, MA: Harvard UP, 1981.

Constructs the genre as a hybrid of realist fiction and fantasy, which emerged during the nineteenth century, was consolidated during the pulp era, and self-reflexively reshaped during the postwar period; key categories of analysis include "Space," "Time," "Machine," and "Monster."

Russ, Joanna. "Toward an Aesthetic of Science Fiction." *Science Fiction Studies* 1.4 (1974), pp. 255–69.

Argues that the genre is a didactic form defined primarily by its deployment of plausible science; as a result, categories of aesthetic evaluation appropriate to "literature" fail to grasp SF's core appeal.

Williams, Raymond. "Science Fiction." *The Highway: Journal of the Workers' Educational Association* 48 (December 1956), pp. 41–45.

Defines SF as a subgenre of the fantastic that consists of three basic narrative types: "Putropia" (tales that critique or lampoon the utopian romance), "Doomsday" (tales of apocalypse and post-apocalypse), and "Space Anthropology" (tales of extra-planetary adventure and exploration).

Wolfe, Gary K. *Evaporating Genres: Essays on Fantastic Literature*. Middletown, CT: Wesleyan UP, 2011.

Collection of essays arguing that the boundaries separating genres into distinct categories have begun to dissolve in the contemporary marketplace, while the boundaries between popular and "high" literature have also collapsed.

Part 2

Structure and form

This section opens with two famous essays by SF writers—J. G. Ballard and Samuel R. Delany—outlining their respective visions of the formal qualities of science fiction writing. While Delany seeks to sketch the stylistic operations of SF narratives, Ballard polemically calls for a radical new mode of SF: his approach is not descriptive but *prescriptive*, a manifesto rather than an anatomy. Convinced that the pulp tradition is not only outmoded when faced with the realities of the Space Age but also "invariably juvenile" and "too narrow" in its appeal, Ballard insists that the genre needs to adopt more of the "experimental enthusiasm which has characterized painting, music and the cinema during the last four or five decades." Specifically, he advocates a shift away from extraterrestrial locales because the "only truly alien planet is Earth" and "it is *inner* space, not outer, that needs to be explored." By contrast with the linear storytelling and workmanlike prose of the early pulps, contemporary SF, according to Ballard, needs to develop narrative forms and styles adequate to postwar realities—indeed, "a complete speculative poetry and fantasy of science." Ballard's essay, with its pugnacious attack on old-school SF, is widely seen as the first clear statement of the aesthetic agenda of the 1960s "New Wave."[1]

While himself often identified as a New Wave writer, Delany's approach is considerably less oppositional. The problem for him is not that SF's narrative techniques are outdated or puerile, but rather that we do not fully appreciate the complexity of their function. Unlike Ballard, Delany sees SF as already quite radical, especially linguistically, since its prose is never straightforwardly referential, in the mode of realist fiction, but always contains a significant degree of "subjunctivity." In other words, SF encompasses descriptions that point not toward things as they are but *as they might be*, in other times and places. "The particular subjunctive level of SF expands the freedom of the choice of words that can follow another group of words meaningfully": for example, the sentence "The red sun is high, the blue low" is meaningless in a realist narrative, but in an SF text it orients the reader toward an entirely different universe of reference, a world not here or not yet. The linguistic resources of SF are thus much richer than they have usually been credited for being.

The next selection, a hugely influential 1972 essay by Darko Suvin, implicitly expands Delany's notion of the genre's subjunctivity into a theory of SF as a "literature of cognitive estrangement." An SF story, by deploying a speculative postulate—in Suvin's term, a "novum"—such as time travel or alien contact, constructs a world *estranged* from every-day reality in a way that activates cognition in the reader, who is compelled to reconstruct, in imagination, the conditions and parameters of this strange narrative world. The effect is to defamiliarize the given through "dynamic transformation" and thus open up hori-zons of possibility, utopian or dystopian, that can serve a critical function by satirically arraigning present-day reality. Yet Suvin admits that this function is only visible in the very best SF, and that "95% of printed matter claiming the name" of science fiction does not properly belong to the genre. While scholars have found Suvin's analysis of SF's narrative dynamics deeply insightful and provocative, his proscriptive hostility to large swaths of work, especially stories emanating from the pulp tradition, has been criticized in some quarters.[2]

Marc Angenot's essay, which follows, is one of the most important—and sadly neglected—formalist analyses of SF ever published. In conformity with Suvin, Angenot sees SF as a genre that constructs estranged worlds, and like Delany, he sees that estrangement operating at the level of signification. For Angenot, what an SF text says is ultimately less important than what it leaves unsaid: the unspoken parameters of the unfamiliar narrative world, which the reader is compelled to reconstruct via linguistic clues and oblique references. Neologisms, for example, are powerful indices to the novelty of the fictional semblance evoked in the text, and the reader is compelled to puzzle out their meaning, in the process fleshing out the contours of the futuristic or alien land-scape in which the tale is set. SF, in short, enforces a mode of "conjectural reading," in which the "absent paradigm" governing the operation of the estranged world of the story is gradually unveiled. Delany's subjunctivity, Suvin's cognitive estrangement, and Angenot's absent paradigm are three of the most powerful tools of formal analysis in the SF critical canon.

In his 1992 essay, Damien Broderick added another key term to the critical lexicon: the "megatext." Like the absent paradigm, the megatext is a mechanism, not directly present in the story but accessible to readers via an activity of decipherment and reconstruction, that gives the text's unfamiliar world shape and coherence. But the megatext exceeds any given text since it is the hypothetical repository of all existing SF themes, tropes, and icons—the "collective intertext" whose web of inference helps readers negotiate the perplexities of individual works. Wells's time machine is one such icon or idea, progenitor of all manner of subsequent time-travel stories, all of which contribute their particular emphases to the evolving megatext. These recurring themes and icons function as "discursive attractors" that help to "account for the specificity and idiosyncratic coding" of all SF texts. Experienced SF readers are particularly attuned to megatextual elements in the stories they read, the lines of connection and differentiation that link individual stories with the larger corpus of the genre.

This section concludes with an excerpt from David Wittenberg's 2013 book on time travel, one of the most compelling recent studies of SF as a narrative system.[3] According to Wittenberg, time-travel fictions literalize, at the level of their plots, basic narratological issues of "temporality, history, and subjectivity" that characterize stories generally. More specifically, time-travel texts thematize the relationship, identified by Viktor Shklovsky as fundamental to all narrative fictions, between *fabula* (the linear chronology underlying a story's events) and *syuzhet* (the specific sequence of its narrated incidents), invoking plot paradoxes that raise significant philosophical, historiographic, and psychological questions regarding how these two factors of the storytelling process relate to one another. Time-travel fictions thus constitute a "popular philosophy of narrative": they are not just illustrations of theoretical ideas but "exercises in narratology" themselves. While Wittenberg focuses on just one subgenre of SF, his insights into how time-travel stories activate connections linking literary history and philosophy of science might productively extrapolated to the genre as a whole.

Notes

1. For a discussion of the development of the New Wave in Britain and the role of Ballard as a major polemicist for the movement, see my "*New Worlds* and the New Wave in Fandom: Fan Culture and the Reshaping of Science Fiction in the Sixties," *Extrapolation* 47.2 (Summer 2006), pp. 296–314.
2. Suvin developed the argument of his 1972 essay into his book *Metamorphoses of Science Fiction: On the Poetics and History of a Literary Genre* (New Haven, CT: Yale UP, 1979). A powerful summary and critique of Suvin's contributions to SF criticism can be found in Istvan Csicsery-Ronay, Jr.'s *The Seven Beauties of Science Fiction* (Middletown, CT: Wesleyan UP, 2008), pp. 47–75.
3. David Wittenberg, *Time Travel: The Popular Philosophy of Narrative* (New York: Fordham UP, 2013).

9

Which way to inner space?

J. G. Ballard

One unfortunate by-product of the Russian-American space race is likely to be an even closer identification, in the mind of the general public, of science fiction with the rocket ships and ray guns of Buck Rogers. If science fiction ever had a chance of escaping this identification—from which most of its present ills derive—that chance will soon be gone, and the successful landing of a manned vehicle on the Moon will fix this image conclusively. Instead of greeting the appearance of the space-suited hero with a deep groan, most general readers will be disappointed if the standard paraphernalia of robot brains and hyper-drives is *not* present, just as most cinema-goers are bored stiff if a western doesn't contain at least one major gun-battle. A few westerns without guns have been attempted, but they seem to turn into dog and timberland stories, and as a reader of science fiction one of my fears is that unless the medium drastically reinvigorates itself in the near future the serious fringe material, at present its only justification, will be relegated to the same limbo occupied by other withering literary forms such as the ghost and detective stories.

There are several reasons why I believe space fiction can no longer provide the main wellspring of ideas for s-f. Firstly, the bulk of it is invariably juvenile, though this is not entirely the fault of the writers. Mort Sahl has referred to the missile-testing site at Cape Canaveral as "Disneyland East," and like it or not this sums up the attitude of most people towards science fiction, and underlines the narrow imaginative limits imposed by the background of rocket ships and planet-hopping.

A poet such as Ray Bradbury can accept the current magazine conventions and transform even so hackneyed a subject as Mars into an enthralling private world, but science fiction can't rely for its survival on the continued emergence of writers of Bradbury's calibre. The degree of interest inherent in the rocket and planet story—with its confined physical and psychological dimensions and its limited human relationships—is so slight as to make a self-sufficient fictional form based on it almost impossible. If anything, however, the success of the manned satellites will only tend to establish the limited psychological experiences of their crews—on the whole accurately anticipated, though unintentionally, by s-f writers—as the model of those to be found in science fiction.

Visually, of course, nothing can equal space fiction for its vast perspectives and cold beauty, as any s-f film or comic-strip demonstrates, but a literary form requires more complex ideas to sustain it. The spaceship simply doesn't provide these. (Curiously enough, in the light of the present roster of astronauts, the one authentic element in old-style space opera is its wooden, one-dimensional dialogue. But if one can't altogether blame Commander Shepard for his "Boy, what a ride," Major Titov's dreamless sleep after the first night in space was the biggest let-down since the fall of Icarus—how many s-f writers must wish they had been writing his script!)

But my real objection to the central role now occupied by the space story is that its appeal is too narrow. Unlike the western, science fiction can't rely for its existence upon the casual intermittent pleasure it may give to a wide non-specialist audience if it is to hold its ground and continue to develop. As with most specialized media, it needs a faithful and discriminating audience who will go to it for specific pleasures, similar to the audience for abstract painting or serial music. The old-guard space opera fans, although they probably form the solid backbone of present s-f readership, won't be able to keep the medium alive on their own. Like most purists, they prefer their diet unchanged, and unless s-f evolves, sooner or later other media are going to step in and take away its main distinction, the right to be the shop window of tomorrow.

Too often recently, when I've wanted to stimulate my imagination, I've found myself turning to music or painting rather than to science fiction, and surely this is the chief thing wrong with it at present. To attract a critical readership science fiction needs to alter completely its present content and approach. Magazine s-f was born in the 1930s and like the pseudo-streamlined architecture of the thirties, it is beginning to look old-fashioned to the general reader. It's not simply that time travel, psionics and teleporting (which have nothing to do with science anyway and are so breath-taking in their implications that they require genius to do them justice) date science fiction. The general reader is intelligent enough to realize that the majority of the stories are based on the most minor variations on these themes, rather than on any fresh imaginative leaps.

Historically, this type of virtuosity is a sure sign of decline, and it may well be that the real role science fiction has to play is that of a minor eclectic pastime, its few magazines sustained by opportunist editorial swerves after the latest popular-science fad.

Rejecting this view, however, and believing that s-f has a continuing and expanding role as an imaginative interpreter of the future, how can one find a new wellspring of ideas? First, I think science fiction should turn its back on space, on interstellar travel, extraterrestrial life forms, galactic wars and the overlap of these ideas that spreads across the margins of nine-tenths of magazine s-f. Great writer though he was, H. G. Wells has had a disastrous influence on the subsequent course of science fiction. Not only did he provide it with a repertory of ideas that have virtually monopolized the medium for the last fifty years, but he established the conventions of its style and form, with its simple plots, journalistic narrative, and standard range of situation and character. It is these, whether they realize it or not, that s-f readers are so bored with now, and which are beginning to look increasingly outdated by comparison with the developments in other literary fields.

I've often wondered why s-f shows so little of the experimental enthusiasm which has characterized painting, music and the cinema during the last four or five decades, particularly as these have become wholeheartedly speculative, more and more concerned with the creation of new states of mind, constructing fresh symbols and languages where the old cease to be valid. Similarly, I think science fiction must jettison its present narrative forms and plots. Most of these are far too explicit to express any subtle interplay of character and theme. Devices such as time travel and telepathy, for example, save the writer the trouble of describing the interrelationships of time and space indirectly. And by a curious paradox they prevent him from using his imagination at all, giving him very little true freedom of movement within the narrow limits set by the device.

The biggest developments of the immediate future will take place, not on the Moon or Mars, but on Earth, and it is *inner* space, not outer, that needs to be explored. The only truly alien planet is Earth. In the past the scientific bias of s-f has been towards the physical sciences—rocketry, electronics, cybernetics—and the emphasis should switch to the biological sciences. Accuracy, that last refuge of the unimaginative, doesn't matter a hoot. What we need is not science fact but more science fiction, and the introduction of so-called science fact articles is merely an attempt to dress up the old Buck Rogers material in more respectable garb.

More precisely, I'd like to see s-f becoming abstract and "cool," inventing fresh situations and contexts that illustrate its theme obliquely. For example, instead of treating time like a sort of glorified scenic railway, I'd like to see it used for what it is, one of the perspectives of the personality, and the elaboration of concepts such as the time zone, deep time and archaeopsychic time. I'd like to see more psycho-literary ideas, more meta-biological and meta-chemical concepts, private time-systems, synthetic psychologies and space-times, more of the sombre half-worlds one glimpses in the paintings of schizophrenics, all in all a complete speculative poetry and fantasy of science.

I firmly believe that only science fiction is fully equipped to become the literature of tomorrow, and that it is the only medium with an adequate vocabulary of ideas and situations. By and large, the standards it sets for itself are higher than those of any other specialist literary genre, and from now on, I think, most of the hard work will fall, not on the writer and editor, but on the readers. The onus is on them to accept a more oblique narrative style, understated themes, private symbols and vocabularies. The first true s-f story, and one I intend to write myself if no one else will, is about a man with amnesia lying on a beach and looking at a rusty bicycle wheel, trying to work out the absolute essence of the relationship between them. If this sounds off-beat and abstract, so much the better, for science fiction could use a big dose of the experimental; and if it sounds boring, well at least it will be a new kind of boredom.

As a final text, I'm reminded of the diving suit in which Salvador Dali delivered a lecture some years ago in London. The workman sent along to supervise the suit asked how deep Dali proposed to descend, and with a flourish the maestro exclaimed: "To the Unconscious!" to which the workman replied sagely: "I'm afraid we don't go down that deep." Five minutes later, sure enough, Dali nearly suffocated inside the helmet.

It is that *inner* space-suit which is still needed, and it is up to science fiction to build it!

10

About 5,750 words

Samuel R. Delany

Every generation some critic states the frighteningly obvious in the *style/content* conflict. Most readers are bewildered by it. Most commercial writers (not to say, editors) first become uncomfortable, then blustery; finally, they put the whole business out of their heads and go back to what they were doing all along. And it remains for someone in another generation to repeat:

Put in opposition to "style," there is no such thing as "content."

Now, speculative fiction is still basically a field of commercial writing. Isn't it obvious that what makes a given story SF *is* its speculative content? As well, in the middle and late sixties there was much argument about Old Wave and New Wave SF. The argument was occasionally fruitful, at times vicious, more often just silly. But the critical vocabulary at both ends of the beach included ". . . old style . . . new style . . . old content . . . new content . . ." The questions raised were always: "Is the content meaningful?" and "Is the style compatible with it?" Again, I have to say, "content" does not exist. The two new questions that arise then are: (1), How is this possible, and (2), What is gained by atomizing content into its stylistic elements?

The words *content*, *meaning*, and *information* are all metaphors for an abstract quality of a word or group of words. The one I would like to concentrate on is: *information*.

Is content real?

Another way to ask this question is: Is there such a thing as verbal information apart from the words used to inform?

Most of the vocabulary of criticism is set up to imply there is. Information is carried by/with/in words. People are carried by/with/in cars. It should be as easy to separate the information from the word as it is to open the door of a Ford Mustang: *Content* means something that is *contained*.

But let us go back to *information*, and by a rather devious route. Follow me:

red

As the above letters sit alone on the paper, the reader has no way to know what they mean. Do they indicate political tendencies or the sound made once you pass the *b* in *bread*? The word generates no significant information until it is put in *formal relation* with something else. This formal relation can be with a real object ("Red" written on the label of a sealed tin of paint) or with other words ("The breeze through the car window was refreshing. Whoops—red! He hit the brake").[1]

The idea of *meaning*, *information*, or *content* as something contained by words is a misleading visualization. Here is a more apt one:

Consider meaning to be a thread (or better yet, the path) that connects a sound or configuration of letters called a "word" with a given object or group of objects (or better, memories of those objects). To know the meaning of a word is to be able to follow this thread from the sound to the proper recollections of objects, emotions, or situations—more accurately, to various image-modes of these objects/emotions/situations in your mind. Put more pompously, meanings (*content* or *information*) are the *formal relations* between sounds and images of the objective world.[2]

Any clever logic student, from this point, can construct a proof for the etymological tautology, "All information is formal," as well as its corollary, "It is impossible to vary the form without varying the information." I will not try and reproduce it in detail. I would like to say in place of it, however, that "content" can be a useful word; but, again, it becomes invalid when it is held up to oppose style. Content is the illusion myriad stylistic factors create when viewed at a certain distance.

When I say it is impossible to vary the form without varying the information, I do not mean any *formal change* (e.g., the shuffling of a few words in a novel) must completely obviate the entire informational experience of a given work. Some formal changes are minimal; their effect on a particular collection of words may be unimportant simply because it is undetectable. But I am trying to leave open the possibility that the change of a single word in a novel may be all important.

"Tell me, Martha, *did* you really kill him?"

"Yes."

But in the paperback edition, the second line of type was accidentally dropped. Why should this deletion of a single word hurt the reader's enjoyment of the remaining 59,999 words of the novel . . .

In my second published novel I recall the key sentence in the opening exposition described the lines of communication between two cities as ". . . now lost for good." A printer's error rendered the line "not lost for good," and practically destroyed the rest of the story.

But the simplicity of my examples sabotages my point more than it supports it. Here is another, more relevant:

I put some things on the desk.
I put some books on the desk.
I put three books on the desk.
I put three poetry books on the desk.
I put Hacker's *Presentation Piece*, Ebbe Borregaard's *Sketches for Thirteen Sonnets*, and Wakoski's *Inside the Blood Factory* on the desk.

The variations here are closer to the type people arguing for the chimera of content call meaningless. The information generated by each sentence is clearly different. But what we know about what was put on the desk is only the most obvious difference. Let's assume these are the opening sentences of five different stories. Five tones of voice are generated by the varying specificity. The tone will be heard—if not consciously noted—by whoever reads. And the different tones give different information about the personality of the speaker as well as the speaker's state of mind. That is to say, the *I* generated by each sentence is different.

As a writer utilizes this information about the individual speaker, his story seems more dense, more real. And he is a better artist than the writer who dismisses the variations in these sentences as minimal. This is what makes Heinlein a better writer than Van Vogt.

But we have not exhausted the differences in the information in these sentences when we have explored the differences in the "I . . . ." As we know something about the personality of the various speakers, and something about what the speaker is placing down, ranges of possibility are opened up about the desk (and the room around it) itself—five different ranges. This information is much harder to specify, because many other factors will influence it: does the desk belong to the speaker or someone about whom the speaker feels strongly; or has she only seen the desk for the first time moments before laying the books on it? Indeed, there is no way to say that any subsequent description of the desk is wrong because it contradicts specific information generated by those opening sentences. But once those other factors have been cleared up, one description may certainly seem "righter" than another, because it is reinforced by that admittedly vague information, different for each of the examples, that has been generated. And the ability to utilize effectively this refinement in generated information is what makes Sturgeon a better writer than Heinlein.

In each of those sentences the only apparent *formal* variation is the specificity of what *I* put on *the desk*. But by this change, the *I* and *the desk* change as well. Both the fictive subject and the equally complex (and equally important for science fiction) fictive object are rendered differently by these supposedly minimally different details. The illusion of reality, the sense of veracity in all fiction, is controlled by the author's sensitivity to these distinctions.

A story is not a replacement of one set of words by another—plot-synopsis, detailed recounting, or analysis. The story is what happens in the reader's mind as his eyes move from the first word to the second, the second to the third, and so on to the end of the tale.

Let's look more closely at what happens in this visual journey. How, for example, does the work of reading a narrative differ from watching a film? In a film the illusion of reality comes from a series of pictures each slightly different. The difference represents a fixed chronological relation which the eye and the mind together render as motion.

Words in a narrative generate tones of voice, syntactic expectations, memories of other words, and pictures. But rather than a fixed chronological relation, they sit in numerous inter- and overweaving relations. The process as we move our eyes from word to word is corrective and revisionary rather than progressive. Each new word revises the complex picture we had a moment before.

Around the meaning of any word is a certain margin in which to correct the image of the object we arrive at (in the old grammatical terms, to modify).

I say:

dog

and an image jumps in your mind (as it did with "red"), but because I have not put it in a formal relation with anything else, you have no way to know whether the specific image in your mind has anything to do with what I want to communicate. Hence that leeway. I can correct it:

Collie dog, and you will agree. I can correct it into a *big dog* or a *shaggy dog*, and you will still concur. But a *Chevrolet dog?* An *oxymoronic dog?* A *turgidly cardiac dog?* For the purposes of ordinary speech, and naturalistic fiction, these corrections are outside acceptable boundaries: they distort in much too unusual a way the various images that we have attached to the sound "dog." On the other hand, there is something to be enjoyed in the distortions, a freshness that may be quite entertaining, even though they lack the inevitablity of our big, shaggy collie.

A sixty-thousand word novel is one picture corrected fifty-nine thousand, nine hundred and ninety-nine times. The total experience must have the same feeling of freshness as this turgidly cardiac creature as well as the inevitability of Big and Shaggy here.

Now let's atomize the correction process itself. A story begins:

The

What is the image thrown on your mind? Whatever it is, it is going to be changed many, many times before the tale is over. My own, unmodified, rather whimsical *The* is a grayish ellipsoid about four feet high that balances on the floor perhaps a yard away. Yours is no doubt different. But it is there, has a specific size, shape, color, and bears a particular relation to you. My *a*, for example, differs from my *the* in that it is about the same shape and color—a bit paler, perhaps—but is either much farther away, or much smaller and nearer. In either case, I am going to be either much less, or much more, interested in it than I am in *The*. Now we come to the second word in the story and the first correction:

The red

My four-foot ellipsoid just changed color. It is still about the same distance away. It has become more interesting. In fact, even at this point I feel vaguely that the increased interest may be outside the leeway I allow for a *The*. I feel a strain here that would be absent if the first two words had been *A red* . . . My eye goes on to the third word while my mind prepares for the second correction:

The red sun

The original *The* has now been replaced by a luminous disc. The color has lightened considerably. The disk is above me. An indistinct landscape has formed about me. And I am even more aware, now that the object has been placed at such a distance, of the tension between my own interest level in *red sun* and the ordinary attention I accord a *The*: for the intensity of interest is all that is left with me of the original image.

Less clearly, in terms of future corrections, is a feeling that in this landscape it is either dawn, sunset, or, if it is another time, smog of some sort must be hazing the air (. . . *red sun* . . .); but I hold all for the next correction:

The red sun is

A sudden sense of intimacy. I am being asked to pay even greater attention, in a way that *was* would not demand, as *was* in the form of the traditional historical narrative. But *is*? . . . There is a speaker here! That focus in attention I felt between the first two words is not my attention, but the attention of the speaker. It resolves into a tone of voice: "The *red* sun is . . ." And I listen to this voice, in the midst of this still vague landscape, registering its concern for the red sun. Between *The* and *red* information was generated that between *sun* and *is* resolved into a meaningful correction in my vision. This is my first aesthetic pleasure from the tale—a small one, as we have only progressed four words into the story. Nevertheless, it becomes one drop in the total enjoyment to come from the telling. Watching and listening to my speaker, I proceed to the next correction:

The red sun is high,

Noon and slightly overcast; this is merely a confirmation of something previously suspected, nowhere near as major a correction as the one before. It allows a slight sense of warmth into the landscape, and the light has been fixed at a specific point. I attempt to visualize that landscape more clearly, but no object, including the speaker, has been cleared enough to resolve. The comma tells me that a thought group is complete. In the pause it occurs to me that the redness of the sun may not be a clue to smog at all, but merely the speaker falling into literary-ism; or at best, the redness is a projection of his consciousness, which as yet I don't understand. And for a moment I notice that from where I'm standing the sun indeed appears its customary, blind-white gold. Next correction:

The red sun is high, the

In this strange landscape (lit by its somewhat untrustworthily described sun) the speaker has turned his attention to another gray, four-foot ellipsoid, equidistant from himself and me. Again, it is too indistinct to take highlighting. But there have been two corrections with not much tension, and the reality of the speaker himself is beginning to slip. What will this become?

The red sun is high, the blue

The ellipsoid has changed hue. But the repetition in the syntactic arrangement of the description momentarily threatens to dissolve all reality, landscape, speaker, and sun, into a mannered listing of bucolica. The whole scene dims. And the final correction?

The red sun is high, the blue low.

Look! We are worlds and worlds away. The first sun is huge; and how accurate the description of its color turns out to have been. The repetition that predicted mannerism now fixes both big and little sun to the sky. The landscape crawls with long red shadows and stubby blue ones, joined by purple triangles. Look at the speaker himself. Can you see him? You have seen his doubled shadow . . .

Though it ordinarily takes only a quarter of a second and is largely unconscious, this is the process.

When the corrections as we move from word to word produce a muddy picture, when unclear bits of information do not resolve to even greater clarity as we progress, we call the writer a poor stylist. As the story goes on, and the pictures become more complicated as they develop through time, if even greater anomalies appear as we continue correcting, we say he can't plot. But it is the same quality error committed on a grosser level, even though a reader must be a third or three-quarters of the way through the book to spot one, while the first may glare out from the opening sentence.

In any commercial field of writing, like SF, the argument of writers and editors who feel *content* can be opposed to *style* runs, at its most articulate:

"Basically we are writing adventure fiction. We are writing it very fast. We do not have time to be concerned about any but the grosser errors. More important, you are talking about subtleties too refined for the vast majority of our readers who are basically neither literary nor sophisticated."

The internal contradictions here could make a book. Let me outline two.

The basis of any adventure novel, SF or otherwise, what gives it its entertainment value—escape value if you will—what sets it apart from the psychological novel, what names it an adventure, is the intensity with which the real actions of the story impinge on the protagonist's consciousness. The simplest way to generate that sense of adventure is to increase the intensity with which the real actions impinge on the reader's. And fictional intensity is almost entirely the province of those refinements of which I have been speaking.

The story of an infant's first toddle across the kitchen floor will be an adventure if the writer can generate the infantile wonder at new muscles, new efforts, obstacles, and detours. I would like to read such a story.

We have all read, many too many times, the heroic attempts of John Smith to save the lives of seven orphans in the face of fire, flood, and avalanche.

I am sure it was an adventure for Smith.

For the reader it was dull as dull could be.

"The Doors of His Face, the Lamps of His Mouth" by Roger Zelazny has been described as "all speed and adventure" by Theodore Sturgeon, and indeed it is one of the most exciting adventure tales SF has produced. Let me change one word in every grammatical unit of every sentence, replacing it with a word that "means more or less the same thing" and I can diminish the excitement by half and expunge every trace of wit. Let me change one word and *add* one word, and I can make it so dull as to be practically unreadable. Yet a paragraph by paragraph synopsis of the "content" will be the same.

An experience I find painful (though it happens with increasing frequency) occurs when I must listen to a literate person who has just become enchanted by some hacked-out space-boiler begin to rhapsodize about the way the blunt, imprecise, leaden language reflects the hairy-chested hero's alienation from reality. He usually goes on to explain how the "SF content" itself reflects our whole society's divorce from the real. The experience is painful because he is right as far as he goes. Badly written adventure fiction is our true antiliterature. Its protagonists are our real antiheroes. They move through unreal worlds amid all sorts of noise and manage to perceive nothing meaningful or meaningfully.

Author's intention or no, that is what badly written SF *is* about. But anyone who reads or writes SF seriously knows that its particular excellence is in another area altogether: in all the brouhaha clanging about these unreal worlds, chords are sounded in total sympathy with the real.

"You are talking about subtleties too refined for the vast majority of our readers who are basically neither literary nor sophisticated."

This part of the argument always throws me back to an incident from the summer I taught a remedial English class at my Neighborhood Community Center. The voluntary nature of the class automatically restricted enrollment to people who wanted to learn; still, I had sixteen- and seventeen-year-olds who had never had any formal education in either Spanish or English continually joining my lessons. Regardless, after a student had been in the class six months, I would throw at him a full five-hundred-and-fifty-page novel to read: Dmitri Merezhkovsky's *The Romance of Leonardo da Vinci*. The book is full of Renaissance history, as well as swordplay, magic, and dissertations on art and science. It is an extremely literary novel with several levels of interpretation. It was a favorite of Sigmund Freud (Rilke, in a letter, found it loathsome) and inspired him to write his own *Leonardo da Vinci: A Study in Psychosexuality*. My students loved it, and with it, lost a good deal of their fear of Literature and Long Books.

Shortly before I had to leave the class, *Leonardo* appeared in paperback, translated by Hubert Trench. Till then it had only been available in a Modern Library edition translated by Bernard Gilbert Gurney. To save my latest two students a trip to the Barnes and Noble basement, as well as a dollar fifty, I suggested they buy the paperback. Two days later one had struggled through forty pages and the other had given up after ten. Both thought the book dull, had no idea what it was about, and begged me for something shorter and more exciting.

Bewildered, I bought a copy of the Trench translation myself that afternoon. I do not have either book at hand as I write, so I'm sure a comparison with the actual texts will prove me an exaggerator. But I recall one description of a little house in Florence:

Gurney: "Gray smoke rose and curled from the slate chimney."
Trench: "Billows of smoke, gray and gloomy, elevated and contorted up from the slates of the chimney."

By the same process that differentiated the five examples of putting books on a desk, these two sentences do not refer to the same smoke, chimney, house, time of day; nor do any of the other houses within sight remain the same; nor do any possible inhabitants. One sentence has nine words, the other fifteen. But atomize both as a series of corrected images and you will find the mental energy expended on the latter is greater by a factor of six or seven! And over seven-eighths of it leaves that uncomfortable feeling of loose-en-dedness, unutilized and unresolved. Sadly, it is the less skilled, less sophisticated reader who is most injured by bad writing. Bad prose requires more mental energy to correct your image from word to word, and the corrections themselves are less rewarding. That is what makes it bad. The sophisticated, literary reader may give the words the benefit of the doubt and question whether a seeming clumsiness is more fruitfully interpreted as an intentional ambiguity.

For what it is worth, when I write I often try to say several things at the same time—from a regard for economy that sits contiguous with any concern for skillful expression. I have certainly failed to say many of the things I intended. But ambiguity marks the failure, not the intent.

But how does all this relate to those particular series of corrected images we label *SF*? To answer that, we must first look at what distinguishes these particular word series from other word series that get labeled *naturalistic fiction*, *reportage*, *fantasy*.

A distinct level of subjunctivity informs all the words in an SF story at a level that is different from that which informs naturalistic fiction, fantasy, or reportage.

Subjunctivity is the tension on the thread of meaning that runs between (to borrow Saussure's term for "word":) sound-image and sound-image. Suppose a series of words is presented to us as a piece of reportage. A blanket indicative tension (or mood) informs the whole series: *this happened*. That is the particular level of subjunctivity at which journalism takes place. Any word, even the metaphorical ones, must go straight back to a real object, or a real thought on the part of the reporter.

The subjunctivity level for a series of words labeled naturalistic fiction is defined by: *could have happened*. (While various levels of subjunctivity can be defined by words, those words themselves define nothing. They are not definitions of certain modes of fiction, only more or less useful functional *descriptions* of different modes of narrative.) Note that the level of subjunctivity makes certain dictates and allows certain freedoms as to what word can follow another. Consider this word series: "For one second, as she stood alone on the desert, her world shattered and she watched the fragments bury themselves in the dunes." This is practically meaningless at the subjunctive level of reportage. But it might be a perfectly adequate, if not brilliant, word series for a piece of naturalistic fiction.

Fantasy takes the subjunctivity of naturalistic fiction and throws it into reverse. At the appearance of elves, witches, or magic in a non-metaphorical position, or at some correction of image too bizarre to be explained by other than the supernatural, the level of subjunctivity becomes: *could not have happened*. And immediately it informs *all* the words in the series. No matter how naturalistic the setting, once the witch has taken off on her broomstick the most realistic of trees, cats, night clouds, or the moon behind them become infected with this reverse subjunctivity.

But when spaceships, ray guns, or more accurately any correction of images that indicates the future appears in a series of words and mark it as SF, the subjunctivity level is changed once more: These objects, these convocations of objects into situations and events, are blanketly defined by: *have not happened*.

Events that have not happened are very different from the fictional events that *could have happened*, or the fantastic events that *could not have happened*.

Events that have not happened include several subcategories. These subcategories describe the subcategories of SF. *Events that have not happened* include those events that *might happen*: these are your technological and sociological predictive tales. Another category includes *events that will not happen*: these are your science-fantasy stories. They include *events that have not happened yet* (Can you hear the implied tone of warning?): there are your cautionary dystopias, *Brave New World* and *1984*. Were English a language with a more detailed tense system, it would be easier to see that *events that have not happened* include past events as well as future ones. *Events that have not happened in the past* compose that SF specialty, the parallel-world story, whose outstanding example is Philip K. Dick's *The Man in the High Castle*.

The particular subjunctive level of SF expands the freedom of the choice of words that can follow another group of words meaningfully; but it limits the way we employ the corrective process as we move between them.

At the subjunctive level of naturalistic fiction, "The red sun is high, the blue low," is meaningless. In naturalistic fiction our corrections in our images must be made in accordance with what we know of the personally observable—this includes our own observations or others' that have been reported to us at the subjunctive level of journalism.

Considered at the subjunctive level of fantasy, "The red sun is high, the blue low," fares a little better. But the corrective process in fantasy is limited too: when we are given a correction that is not meaningful in terms of the personally observable world, we *must* accept any pseudoexplanation we are given. If there is no pseudoexplanation, it must remain mysterious. As fantasy, one suspects that the red sun is the "realer" one; but what sorcerer, to what purpose, shunted up that second, azure, orb, we cannot know and must wait for the rest of the tale.

As we have seen, that sentence makes very good SF. The subjunctive level of SF says that we must make our correction process in accord with what we know of the physically explainable universe. And the physically explainable has a much wider range than the personally observable.[3] The particular verbal freedom of SF, coupled with the corrective process that allows the whole range of the physically explainable universe, can produce the most violent leaps of imagery. For not only does it throw us worlds away, it specifies how we got there.

Let us examine what happens between the following two words:

winged dog

As naturalistic fiction it is meaningless. As fantasy it is merely a visual correction. At the subjunctive level of SF, however, one must momentarily consider, as one makes that visual correction, an entire track of evolution: whether the dog has forelegs or not. The visual correction must include modification of breastbone and musculature if the wings are to be functional, as well as a whole slew of other factors from hollow bones to heart rate; or if we subsequently learn as the series of words goes on that grafting was the cause, there are all the implications (to consider) of a technology capable of such an operation. All of this information hovers tacitly about and between those two words in the same manner that the information about *I* and *the desk* hovered around the statements about placing down the books. The best SF writer will utilize this information just as she utilizes the information generated by any verbal juxtapositioning.

I quote Harlan Ellison describing his own reaction to this verbal process:

> . . . Heinlein has always managed to indicate the greater strangeness of a culture with the most casually dropped-in reference: the first time in a novel, I believe it was in *Beyond This Horizon*, that a character came through a door that . . . dilated. And no discussion. Just: "The door dilated." I read across it, and was two lines down before I realized what the image had been, what the words had called forth. A *dilating* door. It didn't open, it *irised*! Dear God, now I knew I was in a future world . . .

"The door dilated," is meaningless as naturalistic fiction, and practically meaningless as fantasy. As SF—as an event that hasn't happened, yet still must be interpreted in terms of the physically explainable—it is quite as wondrous as Ellison feels it.

As well, the luminosity of Heinlein's particular vision was supported by all sorts of other information, stated and unstated, generated by the novel's other words.

Through this discussion, I have tried to keep away from what motivates the construction of these violent nets of wonder called speculative fiction. The more basic the discussion, the greater is our obligation to stay with the reader in *front* of the page. But at the mention of the author's "vision" the subject is already broached. The vision (sense of wonder, if you will) that SF tries for seems to me very close to the vision of poetry, particularly poetry as it concerned the nineteenth century Symbolists. No matter how disciplined its creation, to move into "unreal" worlds demands a brush with mysticism.

Virtually all the classics of speculative fiction are mystical.

In Isaac Asimov's *Foundation* trilogy, one man, dead on page thirty-seven, achieves nothing less than the redemption of mankind from twenty-nine thousand years of suffering simply by his heightened consciousness of the human condition. (Read "consciousness of the human condition" for "science of psychohistory.")

In Robert Heinlein's *Stranger in a Strange Land* the appearance of God Incarnate creates a world of love and cannibalism.

Clarke's *Childhood's End* and Sturgeon's *More Than Human* detail vastly differing processes by which man becomes more than man.

Alfred Bester's *The Stars My Destination* (or *Tiger, Tiger!* its original title) is considered by many readers and writers, both in and outside the field, to be the greatest single SF novel. In this book, man, intensely human yet more than human, becomes, through greater acceptance of his humanity, something even more. It chronicles a social educa-tion, but within a society which, from our point of view, has gone mad. In the climactic scene, the protagonist, burning in the ruins of a collapsing cathedral, has his senses confused by synesthesia. Terrified, he begins to oscillate insanely in time and space. Through this experience, with the help of his worst enemy transformed by time into his savior, he saves himself and attains a state of innocence and rebirth.

This is the stuff of mysticism.

It is also a very powerful dramatization of Rimbaud's theory of the systematic derangement of the senses to achieve the unknown. And the Rimbaud reference is as conscious as the book's earlier references to Joyce, Blake, and Swift. (I would like to see the relation between the Symbolists and modern American speculative fiction examined more thoroughly. The French Symbolists' particular problems of vision have been explored repeatedly not only by writers like Bester and Sturgeon, but also newer writers like Roger Zelazny, who brings both erudition and word magic to strange creations generated from the tension between suicide and immortality. And the answers they discover are all unique.) To recapitulate: whatever the inspiration or vision, whether it arrives in a flash or has been meticulously worked out over years, the only way a writer can present it is by what he can make happen in the reader's mind between one word and another, by the way he can maneuver the existing tensions between words and associated images.

I have read many descriptions of "mystical experiences"—many in SF stories and novels. Very, very few have generated any *feel* of the mystical—which is to say that as the writers went about setting correction after correction, the images were too untrustworthy to call up any personal feelings about such experiences. The Symbolists have a lesson here: the only thing that we will trust enough to let it generate in us any real sense of the mystical is a resonant aesthetic form.

The sense of mystical horror, for example, in Thomas M. Disch's extraordinary novella, *The Asian Shore*, does not come from its study of a particularly insidious type of racism, incisive though the study is; nor does it come from the final incidents set frustratingly between the supernatural and the insane. It generates rather in the formal parallels

between the protagonist's concepts of Byzantine architecture and the obvious architecture of his own personality.

Aesthetic form . . . I am going to leave this discussion at this undefined term. For many
people it borders on the meaningless. I hope there is enough tension between the words
to proliferate with what has gone before. To summarize, however: any serious discussion
of speculative fiction must first get away from the distracting concept of SF content and
examine precisely what sort of word-beast sits before us. We must explore both the level
of subjunctivity at which speculative fiction takes place and the particular intensity and
range of images this level affords. Readers must do this if they want to fully understand
what has already been written, Writers must do this if the field is to mature to the potential
so frequently cited for it.

Notes

1. I am purposely not using the word "symbol" in this discussion. The vocabulary that must
   accompany it generates too much confusion.
2. Words also have "phonic presence" or "voice" as well as meaning. And certainly all writers must
   work with sound to vary the rhythm of a phrase or sentence, as well as to control the meaning.
   But this discussion is going to veer close enough to poetry. To consider the musical, as well
   as the ritual, value of language in SF would make poetry and prose indistinguishable. That is
   absolutely not my intention.
3. I throw out this notion for its worth as intellectual play. It is not too difficult to see that as *events
   that have not happened* include the subgroup of *events that have not happened in the past*, they
   include the subsubgroup of *events that could have happened* with an implied *but didn't*. That is
   to say, the level of subjunctivity of SF includes the level of subjunctivity of naturalistic fiction.

   As well, the personally observable world is a subcategory of the physically explainable
   universe. That is, the laws of the first can all be explained in terms of the laws of the second,
   while the situation is not necessarily reversible. So much for the two levels of subjunctivity and
   the limitations on the corrective processes that go with them.

   What of the respective freedoms in the choice of word to follow word?

   I can think of no series of words that could appear in a piece of naturalistic fiction that could
   not also appear in the same order in a piece of speculative fiction. I can, however, think of many
   series of words that, while fine for speculative fiction, would be meaningless as naturalism.
   Which then is the major and which the subcategory?

   Consider: naturalistic fictions are parallel-world stories in which the divergence from the real
   is too slight for historical verification.

11

On the poetics of the science fiction genre[1]

Darko Suvin

Science fiction as fiction (Estrangement)

The importance of science fiction (SF) in our time is on the increase. First, there are strong indications that its popularity in the leading industrial nations (USA, USSR, UK, Japan) has risen sharply over the last 100 years, regardless of local and short-range fluctuations. SF has particularly affected some key strata of modern society such as the college graduates, young writers, and general readers appreciative of new sets of values. This is a significant cultural effect which goes beyond any merely quantitative census. Second, if one takes as differentiae of SF either *radically different figures* (dramatis personae) or a *radically different context* of the story, it will be found to have an interesting and close kinship with other literary sub-genres, which flourished at different times and places of literary history: the Greek and Hellenistic "blessed island" stories, the "fabulous voyage" from Antiquity on, the Renaissance and Baroque "utopia" and "planetary novel," the Enlightenment "state (political) novel," the modern "anticipation," "anti-utopia," etc. Moreover, although SF shares with myth, fantasy, fairy tale and pastoral an opposition to naturalistic or empiricist literary genres, it differs very significantly in approach and social function from such adjoining non-naturalistic or meta-empirical genres. Both of these complementary aspects, the sociological and the methodological, are being vigorously debated among writers and critics in several countries; both testify to the relevance of this genre and the need of scholarly discussion too.

In the following paper I shall argue for a definition of SF as the *literature of cognitive estrangement*. This definition seems to possess the unique advantage of rendering justice to a literary tradition which is coherent through the ages and within itself, and yet distinct from non-fictional utopianism, from naturalistic literature, and from other non-naturalistic fiction. It thus permits us to lay the basis of a coherent poetics of SF.

I should like to approach such a discussion, and this field of discourse, by postulating a spectrum or spread of literary subject-matter, running from the ideal extreme of exact recreation of the author's empirical environment[2] to exclusive interest in a strange newness, a *novum*. From the 18th to the 20th century, the literary mainstream of our civilization has been nearer to the first of the two above-mentioned extremes. However, at the beginnings of a literature, the concern with a domestication of the amazing is very strong. Early tale-tellers tell about amazing voyages into the next valley where they found dog-headed people, also good rock salt which could be stolen or at the worst bartered for. Their stories are a syncretic travelog and *voyage imaginaire*, daydream and intelligence report. This implies a curiosity about the unknown beyond the next mountain range (sea, ocean, solar system . . .), where the thrill of knowledge joined the thrill of adventure.

An island in the far-off ocean is the paradigm of the aesthetically most satisfying goal of the SF voyage, from Iambulus and Euhemerus through the classical utopia to Verne's island of Captain Nemo and Wells's island of Dr. Moreau, especially if we subsume under this the planetary island in the aether ocean—usually the Moon—from Lucian through Cyrano and Swift's mini-Moon of Laputa to the 19th century. Yet the parallel paradigm of the valley, "over the range"[3] which shuts it in as a wall, is perhaps as revealing. It recurs almost as frequently, from the earliest folk tales about the sparkling valley of Terrestrial Paradise and the dark valley of the Dead, both already in *Gilgamesh*. Eden is the mythological localization of utopian longing, just as Wells's valley in the *Country of the Blind* is still within the liberating tradition which contends that the world is not necessarily the way our present empirical valley happens to be, and that whoever thinks his valley is the world, is blind. Whether island or valley, whether in space or (from the industrial and bourgeois revolutions on) in time, the new framework is correlative to the new inhabitants. The aliens—utopians, monsters or simply differing strangers—are a mirror to man just as the differing country is a mirror for his world. But the mirror is not only a reflecting one, it is also a transforming one, virgin womb and alchemical dynamo: the mirror is a crucible.

Thus, it is not only the basic human and humanizing curiosity that gives birth to SF. Beside an undirected inquisitiveness, a semantic game without clear referent, this genre has always been wedded to a hope of finding in the unknown the ideal environment, tribe, state, intelligence or other aspect of the Supreme Good (or to a fear of and revulsion from its contrary). At all events, the *possibility* of other strange, co-variant coordinate systems and semantic fields is assumed.

The approach to the imaginary locality, or localized daydream, practiced by the genre of SF is a supposedly factual one. Columbus's (technically or genologically non-fictional) letter on the Eden he glimpsed beyond the Orinoco mouth, and Swift's (technically non-factual) voyage to "Laputa, Balnibarbi, Glubbdubbdrib, Luggnagg *and Japan*," stand at the opposite ends of a ban between imaginary and factual possibilities. Thus SF takes off from a fictional ("literary") hypothesis and develops it with extrapolating and totalizing ("scientific") rigor—in genre, Columbus and Swift are more alike than different. The effect of such factual reporting of fictions is one of confronting a set normative system—a Ptolemaic-type closed world picture—with a point of view or glance implying a new set of norms; in literary theory, this is known as the attitude of *estrangement*.

This concept was first developed on non-natural-(*ostranenie*, Viktor Shklovsky, 1917), and most successfully underpinned by an anthropological and historical approach in the opus of Bertolt Brecht, who wanted to write "plays for a scientific age." While working on a play about the prototype scientist Galileo, he defined this attitude (*Verfremdungseffekt*) in his *Short Organon for the Theatre* (1948): "A representation which estranges is one which allows us to recognize its subject, but at the same time makes it seem unfamiliar." And further: for somebody to see all normal happenings in a dubious light, "he would need to develop that detached eye with which the great Galileo observed a swinging chandelier. He was amazed by the pendulum motion as if he had not expected it and could not understand its occurring, and this enabled him to come at the rules by which it was governed." Thus, the look of estrangement is both cognitive and creative; and as Brecht goes on to say: "one cannot simply exclaim that such an attitude pertains to science, but not to art. Why should not art, in its own way, try to serve the great social task of mastering Life?"[4] (Later, Brecht was also to note it might be time to stop speaking in terms of masters and servants altogether.)

In SF, the attitude of estrangement—used by Brecht in a different way, within a still predominantly "realistic" context—has grown into the *formal framework* of the genre.

Science fiction as cognition (critique and science)

The use of estrangement both as underlying attitude and dominant formal device is found also in the *myth,* a ritual and religious approach looking in its own way beneath the empiric surface. However, SF sees the norms of any age, including emphatically its own, as unique, changeable, and therefore subject to *cognitive* glance. The myth is diametrically opposed to the cognitive approach since it conceives human relations as fixed, and supernaturally determined, emphatically denying Montaigne's: "*la constance même n'est qu'un branle plus languissant.*" The myth absolutizes and even personifies apparently constant motifs from the sluggish periods with low social dynamics. Conversely, SF, which is organized by extrapolating the variable and future-bearing elements from the empirical environment, clusters in the great whirlpool periods of history, such as the 16-17th and 19-20th centuries. Where the myth claims to explain once and for all the essence of phenomena, SF posits them first as problems and then explores where they lead to; it sees the mythical static identity as an illusion, usually as fraud, in the best case only as a temporary realization of potentially limitless contingencies. It does not ask about The Man or The World, but which man?: in which kind of world?: and why such a man in such a kind of world? As a literary genre, SF is just as opposed to supernatural estrangement as to empiricism (naturalism).

SF is, then a literary genre whose necessary and sufficient conditions are the presence and interaction of estrangement and cognition, and whose main formal device is an imaginative framework alternative to the author's empirical environment.

The estrangement differentiates it from the "realistic" literary mainstream of 18th to 20th century. The cognition differentiates it not only from myth, but also from the fairy tale and the fantasy. The *fairy tale* also doubts the laws of the author's empirical world, but it escapes out of its horizons and into a closed collateral world indifferent toward cognitive possibilities. It does not use imagination as a means to understand the tendencies in reality, but as an end sufficient unto itself and cut off from the real contingencies. The stock fairy-tale accessory, such as the flying carpet, evades the empirical law of physical gravity—as the hero evades social gravity—by imagining its opposite. The wishfulfilling element is its strength and weakness, for it never pretends that a carpet could be expected to fly—that a humble third son could be expected to become a king—while there is gravity. It just posits another world beside yours where some carpets do, magically, fly, and some paupers do, magically, become princes, and into which you cross purely by an act of faith and fancy. Anything is possible in a fairy tale, because a fairy tale is manifestly impossible. Therefore, SF retrogressing into fairytale (e.g. "space opera" with a hero-princess-monster triangle in astronautic costume) is committing creative suicide.

Even less congenial to SF is the *fantasy* (ghost, horror, Gothic, weird) tale, a genre committed to the interposition of anti-cognitive laws into the empirical environment. Where the fairy tale was indifferent, the fantasy is inimical to the empirical world and its laws. The thesis could be defended that the fantasy is significant insofar as it is impure and fails to establish a super-ordinated maleficent world of its own, causing a grotesque tension between arbitrary supernatural phenomena and the empirical norms they infiltrate.[5] Gogol's Nose is so interesting because it is walking down the Nevski Prospect, with a certain rank in the civil service, etc.; if the Nose were in a completely fantastic world—say H.P. Love-craft's—it would be just another ghoulish thrill. When fantasy does not make for such a tension between its norms and the author's empirical environment, its reduction of all possible horizons to Death makes of it just a sub-literature of mystification. Commercial lumping of it into the same category as SF is thus a grave disservice.

The *pastoral* is essentially closer to SF. Its imaginary framework of a world without money economy, state apparatus, and depersonalizing urbanization allows it to isolate, as in the laboratory, two human motivations—erotics and power-hunger. This approach relates to SF as alchemy does to chemistry and nuclear physics: an early try in the right direction with insufficient sophistication. SF has thus much to learn from the pastoral tradition, primarily from its directly sensual relationships without class alienation. It has in fact often done so, whenever it has sounded the theme of the triumph of the humble (Restif, Morris, etc. up to Simak, Christopher, Yefremov . . .). Unfortunately, the baroque pastoral abandoned this theme and jelled into a sentimental convention, discrediting the genre; but when the pastoral escapes preciosity, its hope can fertilize the SF field as an antidote to pragmatism, commercialism, other-directedness and technocracy.

Claiming a Galilean or Brunoan estrangement for SF does not at all mean committing it to scientfic vulgarization or even technological prognostication, which it was engaged in at various times (Verne, U.S. in the 1920's-1930's, U.S.S.R. under Stalinism). The needful and meritorious task of popularization can be a useful element of the SF works at a juvenile level. But even the *roman scientifique* such as Verne's *From the Earth to the Moon*—or the surface level of Wells's *Invisible Man*—though a legitimate SF form, is a lower stage in its development. It is very popular with audiences just approaching SF, such as the juvenile, because it introduces into the old empirical context only *one* easily digestible new techno- logical variable (Moon missile, or rays which lower the refractive index of organic matter).[6] The euphoria provoked by this approach is real but limited, better suited to the short story and a new audience. It evaporates much quicker as the positivistic natural science loses prestige in the humanistic sphere after the World Wars (cf. Nemo's as against the U.S. Navy's atomic "Nautilus"), and surges back with prestigious peace-time applications in new methodologies (astronautics, cybernetics). Even in Verne, the structure of the "science novel" is that of a pond after a stone has been thrown into it: there is a moment- ary commotion, the waves go from impact point to periphery and back, then the system settles down as before. The only difference is that one positivistic fact—usually an item of hardware—has been added, like the stone to the pond bottom. This structure of transient estrangement is specific to murder mysteries, not to a mature SF.

After such delimitations, it is perhaps possible at least to indicate some differenti- ations within the concept of "cognitiveness" or "cognition". As used here, this term does not imply only a reflecting *of* but also *on* reality. It implies a creative approach tending toward a dynamic transformation rather than toward a static mirroring of the author's environment. Such typical methodology of SF—from Lucian, More, Rabelais, Cyrano, and Swift to Wells, London, Zamiatin, and the last decades—is a *critical* one, often satir- ical, combining a belief in the potentialities of reason with methodical doubt in the most significant cases. The kinship of this cognitive critique with the philosophical basis of modern science is evident.

Science fiction as a literary genre (functions and models)

As a full-fledged literary genre, SF has its own repertory of functions, conventions and devices. Many of them are highly interesting and significant for literary theory and history, but their range can scarcely be discussed in a brief approach as it is properly the subject for a book-length work. However, it might be possible to sketch some determining para- meters of the genre.

In a typology of literary genres for our cognitive age, one basic parameter would take into account the relationship of the world(s) each genre presents and the "zero world" of empirically verifiable properties around the author (this being "zero" in the sense of a central reference point in a coordinate system, or of the control group in an experiment). Let us call this empirical world *naturalistic.* In it, and in the corresponding naturalistic or "realistic" literature, ethics are in no significant relation to physics. Modern mainstream literature is forbidden the pathetic fallacy of earthquakes announcing the assassination of rulers or drizzles accompanying the sadness of the heroine. It is the activity of the protagonists, interacting with other, physically equally unprivileged figures, that determines the outcome. However superior technologically or sociologically one side in the conflict may be, any predetermination as to its outcome is felt as an ideological imposition and genological impurity: the basic rule of naturalistic literature is that man's destiny is man, i.e. other humans.[7] On the contrary, in non-naturalistic, *metaphysical* literary genres discussed above, circumstances around the hero are neither passive nor neutral. The fairy-tale world is oriented positively toward its protagonist. A fairy-tale is defined by the hero's triumph: magic weapons and helpers are, with necessary narrative retardations, at his beck and call. Inversely, the world of the tragic myth is oriented negatively toward its protagonist. Oedipus, Attis or Christ are predestined to empirical failure by the nature of their world— but the failure is then ethically exalted and put to religious use. The fantasy—a derivation of the tragic myth just as the fairy-tale derives from the victorious hero myth—is defined by the hero's horrible helplessness: it can be thought of as tragic mythemes without metaphysical compensations. Thus, in the fairy-tale and the fantasy ethics coincide with (positive or negative) physics, in the tragic myth they compensate the physics, in the "optimistic" myth they supply the coincidence with a systematic framework.

The world of a work of SF is not *a priori* intentionally oriented toward its protagonists, either positively or negatively; the protagonists may succeed or fail in their objectives, but nothing in the basic contract with the reader, in the physical laws of their worlds, guarantees either. SF is thus (possibly with the exception of some prefigurations in the pastoral) the only meta-empirical genre which is not at the same time metaphysical; it shares with the dominant literature of our civilization a mature approach analogous to that of modern science and philosophy. Furthermore, it shares the omnitemporal horizons of such an approach. The myth is located above time, the fairy-tale in a conventional grammatical past which is really outside time, and the fantasy in the hero's abnormally disturbed present. The naturalistic literary mainstream and SF can range through all times: empirical ones in the first, non-empirical ones in the latter case. The naturalistic mainstream concentrates on the present, but it can deal with the historical past, and even to some degree with the future in the form of hopes, fears, premonitions, dreams, *et sim.* SF concentrates on possible futures and their spatial equivalents, but it can deal with the present and the past as special cases of a possible historical sequence seen from an estranged point of view (by a figure from another time and/or space). SF can thus use the creative potentialities of an approach not limited by a consuming concern with empirical surfaces and relationships.

As a matter of historical record, SF has started from a pre-scientific or protoscientific approach of debunking satire and naive social critique, and moved closer to the increasingly sophisticated natural and human sciences. The natural sciences caught up and surpassed the literary imagination in the 19th century, the sciences dealing with human relationships might be argued to have caught up with it in their highest theoretical achievements but have certainly not done so in their alienated social practice. In the 20th century,

SF has moved into the sphere of anthropological and cosmological thought, becoming a diagnosis, a warning, a call to understanding and action, and—most important—a mapping of possible alternatives. This historical movement of SF can be envisaged as an enrichment of and shift from a basic direct or extropolative model to an indirect or analogic model.

The earlier dominant model of SF from the 19th century on (though not necessarily in preceding epochs) was one which started from certain cognitive hypotheses and ideas incarnated in the fictional framework and nucleus of the fable. This *extrapolative* model—e.g., of London's *Iron Heel,* Wells's *The Sleeper Wakes* and *Men Like Gods,* Zamiatin's *We,* Stapledon's *Last and First Men,* Pohl and Kornbluth's *Space Merchants,* or Yefremov's *Andromeda*—is based on direct, temporal extrapolation and centered on sociological (i.e., utopian and anti-utopian) modelling. This is where the great majority of the "new maps of hell" belongs for which postwar SF is justly famous, in all its manifold combinations of socio-technological scientific cognition and social oppression (global catastrophes, cybernetics, dictatorships). Yet already in Wells's *Time Machine* and in Stapledon, this extrapolation transcended the sociological spectrum (from everyday practice through economics to erotics) and spilled into biology and cosmology. Nonetheless, whatever its ostensible location (future, "fourth dimension", other planets, alternate universes), "extrapolative modelling" is oriented futurologically. Its values and standards are to be found in the cognitive import of the fable's premises and the consistency with which such premises (usually one or very few in number) are narratively developed to its logical end, to a cognitively significant conclusion.

SF can thus be used as a hand-maiden of futurological foresight in technology, ecology, sociology, etc. Whereas this may be a legitimate secondary function the genre can be made to bear, any oblivion of its strict secondariness may lead to confusion and indeed danger. Ontologically, art is not pragmatic truth nor fiction fact. To expect from SF more than a stimulus for independent thinking, more than a system of stylized narrative devices understandable only in their mutual relationships within a fictional whole and not as isolated realities, leads insensibly to critical demand for and of scientific accuracy in the extrapolated *realia.* Editors and publishers of such "hard" persuasion have, from the U.S. pulp magazines to the Soviet agitprop, been inclined to turn the handmaiden of SF into the slavey of the reigning theology of the day (technocratic, psionic, utopian, catastrophic, or whatever). Yet this fundamentally subversive genre languishes in strait-jackets more quickly than most other ones, responding with atrophy, escapism, or both. Laying no claim to prophecies except for its statistically to be expected share, SF should not be treated as a prophet: neither enthroned when apparently successful, nor beheaded when apparently unsuccessful. As Plato found out in the court of Dionysus and Hythloday at cardinal Morton's, SF figures better devote themselves to their own literary republics, which, to be sure, lead back—but in their own way—to the Republic of Man. SF is finally concerned with the tensions between *Civitas Dei* and *Civitas Terrena,* and it cannot be uncritically committed to any mundane City.

The *analogic model* in SF is based on analogy rather than extrapolation. Its figures may but do not have to be anthropomorphic or its localities geomorphic. The objects, figures, and up to a point the relationships from which this indirectly modelled world starts can be quite fantastic (in the sense of empirically unverifiable) as long as they are logically, philosophically and mutually consistent. Again, as in all distinctions of this essay, one should think of a continuum at whose extremes there is pure extrapolation and analogy, and of two fields grouped around the poles and shading into each other on a wide front in the middle.

The lowest form of analogic modelling goes back to a region where distinction between a crude analogy and an extrapolation backwards are not yet distinguishable: it is the analogy to Earth past, from geological through biological to ethnological and historical. The worlds more or less openly modelled on the Carboniferous Age, on tribal prehistory, on barbaric and feudal empires—in fact modelled on handbooks of geology and anthropology, on Spengler and *The Three Musketeers*—are unfortunately abundant in the foothills of SF. Some of them may be useful adolescent leisure reading, which one should not begrudge; however, their uneasy coexistence with a superscience in the story framework or around the protagonist, which is supposed to provide an SF alibi, brings them close to or over the brink of minimum cognitive standards required. The Burroughs-to-Asimov space-opera, cropping up in almost all U.S. writers right down to Samuel Delany belongs here, i.e., into the uneasy borderline between inferior SF and non-SF (forms mimicking SF scenery but modelled on the structures of the Western and other avatars of fairy-tale and fantasy).

The highest form of analogic modelling would be the analogy to a mathematical model, such as the fairly primary one explicated in Abbott's *Flatland*, as well as the ontological analogies found in a compressed overview form in some stories by Borges and the Polish writer Lem, and in a somewhat more humane narration with a suffering protagonist in some stories by Kafka (*The Metamorphosis* or *In the Penal Colony*) and novels by Lem (*Solaris*). Such highly sophisticated philosophico-anthropological analogies are today perhaps the most significant region of SF, indistinguishable in quality from best mainstream writing. Situated between Borges and the upper reaches into which shade the best utopias, anti-satires and satires, this semantic field is a modern variant of the *conte philosophique* of the 18th century. Similar to Swift, Voltaire, or Diderot, these *modern parables* fuse new visions of the world with an applicability—usually satirical and grotesque—to the shortcomings of our workaday world. As different from the older Rationalism, a modern parable must be open-ended by analogy to modern cosmology, epistemology, and philosophy of science.[8]

The indirect models of SF fall, however, still clearly within its cognitive horizons insofar as their conclusions or import is concerned. The cognition gained may not be immediately applicable, it may be simply the enabling of the mind to receive new wavelengths, but it eventually contributes to the understanding of the most mundane matters. This is testified by the works of Kafka and Lem, of Karel Čapek and Anatole France, as well as of the best of Wells and the "SF reservation" writers.

For a poetics of science fiction (summation and anticipation)

The above sketch should, no doubt, be supplemented by a sociological analysis of the "inner environment" of SF, exiled since the beginning of 20th century into a reservation or ghetto which was protective and is now constrictive, cutting off new developments from healthy competition and the highest critical standards. Such a sociological discussion would enable us to point out the important differences between the highest reaches of the genre, glanced at in this essay in order to define functions and standards of SF, and the 80% or more of debilitating confectionery. Yet it should be stressed that, as different from many other para-literary genres, the criteria for the insufficiency of most SF is to be found in the genre itself. This makes SF in principle, if not yet in practice, equivalent to any other "major" literary genre.

If the whole above argumentation is found acceptable, it will be possible to supplement it also by a survey of forms and sub-genres. Beside some which recur in an updated form—such as the utopia and fabulous voyage—the anticipation, the superman story, the artificial intelligence story (robots, androids, etc.), time-travel, catastrophe, the meeting with aliens, etc., would have to be analyzed. The various forms and sub-genres of SF could then be checked for their relationships to other literary genres, to each other, and to various sciences. For example, the utopias are—whatever else they may be—clearly sociological fictions or social-science-fiction, whereas modern SF is analogous to modern polycentric cosmology, uniting time and space in Einsteinian worlds with different but co-variant dimensions and time scales. Significant modern SF, with deeper and more lasting sources of enjoyment, also presupposes more complex and wider cognitions: it discusses primarily the political, psychological, anthropological *use and effect of sciences, and philosophy of science*, and the becoming or failure of new realities as a result of it. The consistency of extrapolation, precision of analogy and width of reference in such a cognitive discussion turn into aesthetic factors. (That is why the "scientific novel" discussed above is not felt as completely satisfactory—it is aesthetically poor because it is scientifically meager.) Once the elastic criteria of literary structuring have been met, *a cognitive—in most cases strictly scientific—element becomes a measure of aesthetic quality, of the specific pleasure to be sought in SF.* In other words, the cognitive nucleus of the plot co-determines the fictional estrangement in SF. This works on all literary levels: e.g., purely aesthetic, story-telling reasons led modern SF to the cognitive assumption of a hyperspace where flight speed is not limited by the speed of light.

Finally, it might be possible to sketch the basic premises of a significant criticism, history and theory of this literary genre. From Edgar Allan Poe to Damon Knight, including some notable work on the older sub-genres from the utopia to Wells, and some general approaches to literature by people awake to methodological interest, much spadework has been done.[9] In the work of Lem (see note 1) we may even possess some cornerstones for a needed critical home. If one may speculate on some fundamental features or indeed axioms of such criticism, the first might be the already mentioned one that the genre has to be evaluated proceeding from its heights down, applying the standards gained by the analysis of its masterpieces. The second axiom might be to demand of SF a level of cognition higher than that of its average reader: the strange novelty is its *raison d'être*. As a minimum, we must demand from SF that it be wiser from the world it speaks to.

In other words, this is an educational literature, hopefully less deadening than most compulsory education in our split national and class societies, but irreversibly shaped by the pathos of preaching the good word of human curiosity, fear, and hope. Significant SF (to which, as in all genres—but somewhat disappointingly so—at least 95% of printed matter claiming the name does not belong) denies thus the "two-cultures gap" more efficiently than any other literary genre I know of. Even more importantly, it demands from the author and reader, teacher and critic, not merely specialized, quantified positivistic knowledge (*scientia*) but a social imagination whose quality, whose wisdom (*sapientia*), testifies to the maturity of his critical and creative thought.

Notes

1. The first version of this essay crystallized out of a lecture given in the seminar on fantastic literature in the Yale University Slavic Department in Spring 1968. It was presented at Temple University, Philadelphia, at the University of Toronto, and at the 1970 conference of the Science Fiction Research Association at Queens-borough Community College, New York. I am grateful for the opportunity of discussing it in these places. In particular I have derived much profit from personal discussion with Professor David Porter at the University of Massachusetts, J. Michael Holquist and Jacques Ehrmann at Yale, with Mr. James Blish and Miss Judy Merril, and with my colleagues at McGill University, Michael Bristol, Irwin Gopnik, Myrna Gopnik, and Donald F. Theall. This final version owes much to Stanislaw Lem's *Fantastyka i futurologia,* undoubtedly the most significant full-scale morphological, philosophical, and sociological survey of modern SF so far, which has considerably emboldened me in the further pursuit of this elusive field, even where I differed from some of its conclusions. I am also much indebted to the stimulus given by members of my graduate seminar on SF in the Department of English at McGill University. The final responsibility for the structure and conclusions of the essay cannot be shifted onto any other shoulders than mine, however little I may believe in private property over ideas. "Literature" and "literary" are in this essay synonymous with "fiction(al)".

2. A virtue of discussing this seemingly peripheral subject of "science fiction" and its "utopian" tradition is that one has to go back to first principles, one cannot really assume them as given— such as in this case what is literature. Usually, when discussing literature one determines what it says (its subject matter) and how it says what is says (the approach to its themes). If we are talking about literature in the sense of significant works possessing certain minimal aesthetic qualities rather than in the sociological sense of everything that gets published at a certain time or the ideological sense of all the writings on certain themes, this principle can more precisely be formulated as a double question. First, epistemologically, what possibility for aesthetic qual- ities is offered by different thematic fields ("subjects")? The answer of dominant aesthetics at

the moment is—an absolutely equal possibility, and with this answer our aesthetics kicks the question out of its field into the lap of ideologists who pick it up by default and proceed to bungle it. Second, historically, how has such a possibility in fact been used? Once you begin with such considerations you come quickly up against the rather unclear concept of *realism* (not the prose literary movement in the 19th century but a meta-historical stylistic principle), since the SF genre is often pigeonholded as non-realistic. I would not object but would heartily welcome such labels if one had first persuasively defined what is "real" and what is "reality". True, this genre raises basic philosophical issues; but is perhaps not necessary to face them in a first approach. Therefore I shall here substitute for "realism" and "reality" the concept of "the author's empirical environment", which seems as immediately clear as any.

3. Subtitle of Samuel Butler's SF novel *Erewhon*.

4. Viktor Shklovsky, "*Iskusstvo kak priem,*" in *Poètika*, Petrograd 1919. In the English translation of this essay "Art as Technique," in Lee T. Lemon and Marion J. Reis eds., *Russian Formalist Criticism: Four Essays,* Lincoln Nebraska 1965, *ostranenie* is rendered somewhat clumsily as "defamiliarization." Cf. also the classical survey of Victor Erlich, *Russian Formalism: History-Doctrine,* The Hague 1955.

> Bertolt Brecht, "*Kleines Organon für das Theater*", in his *Schriften zum Theater* 7, Franfort a.M. 1964, translated in John Willett ed., *Brecht On Theatre,* New York 1964. My quotation is from p. 192 and 96 of this translation, in which I have changed Mr. Willett's translation of *Verfremdung* as "alienation" into my "estrangement," since alienation evokes incorrect, indeed opposite connotations: estrangement was for Brecht an approach militating directly against social and cognitive alienation.

5. Since my first penning these lines, such a thesis has been ably developed in Tzvetan Todorov, *Introduction à la littérature fantastique,* Paris 1970.

6. Note the functional difference to the anti-gravity metal in Wells's *First Man on the Moon* which is an introductory gadget and not the be-all of a much richer novel.

7. In cases such as some novels of Hardy and plays by Ibsen, or some of the more doctrinaire works of the historical school of Naturalism, where determinism strongly stresses circumstances at the expense of the main figures' activity, we have underneath a surface appearance of "realism" obviously to do with an approach to tragic myth using a shamefaced motivation in an unbelieving age. As contrary to Shakespeare and the Romantics, in this case ethics follow physics in a supposedly causal chain (most often through biology). An analogous approach to fairy-tale is to be found in, say, the mimicry of "realism" found in the Hollywood happy-end movies.

8. I have tried to analyze one such representative work in my afterword to Lem's *Solaris,* New York 1970, entitled "The Open-Ended Parables of Stanislaw Lem and *Solaris.*"

9. On this continent, one ought to mention in the first place Northrop Frye's *Anatomy of Criticism,* New York 1966, and Angus Fletcher's *Allegory,* Ithaca, 1964.

Selected bibliography: Theory and general surveys of SF after Wells

Kingsley Amis, *New Maps of Hell,* New York 1960.

"William Atheling Jr." (James Blish), *The Issues at Hand,* Chicago 1970.

—, *More Issues at Hand,* Chicago 1970.

James O. Bailey, *Pilgrims Through Space and Time,* New York 1947.

Henri Baudin, *La Science-fiction,* Paris-Montreal 1971.

Reginald Bretnor ed., *Modern Science Fiction*, New York 1953.

Jean-Jacques Bridenne, *La littérature francaise d'imagination scientifique,* Paris 1950.

Anatolii Britikov, *Russkii sovetskii nauchnofantasticheskii roman,* Leningrad 1970.

Roger Caillois, *Images, images . . .* , Paris 1966.

Thomas Clareson ed., *The Other Side of Realism,* Bowling Green, Ohio 1971.

I. F. Clarke, *Voices Prophesying War 1163-1984,* London-New York-Toronto 1966.

Basil Davenport ed., *The Science Fiction Novel,* Chicago 1964.

Richard Gerber, *Utopian Fantasy,* London 1955.

Georgii Gurevich, *Karta Strany Fantaziy,* Moscow 1967.

Ryszard Handke, *Polska proza fantasztycznonaukowa,* Wroclaw 1969.

Mark R. Hillegas, *The Future as Nightmare,* New York 1967.

Damon Knight, *In Search of Wonder,* Chicago 1967.

Hans-Jürgen Krysmansky, *Die utopische Methode,* Köln 1967.

Stanislaw Lern, *Fantastyka i futurologia I-II,* Cracow 1970.

Sam Moskowitz, *Explorers of the Infinite,* Cleveland 1963.

—, *Seekers of Tomorrow,* New York 1967.

Alexei Panshin, *Heinlein in Dimension,* Chicago 1968.

Michael Pehlke and Norbert Lingfeld, *Roboter und Gartenlaube,* Munich 1970.

Martin Schwonke, *Vom Staatsroman zur Science Fiction,* Stuttgart 1957.

Darko Suvin ed., *Other Worlds, Other Seas,* New York 1970.

Leon Trotsky, *Literature and Revolution,* Ann Arbor 1960 (ch. 6).

Donald A. Wollheim, *The Universe Makers,* New York 1971.

The best available anthology is Robert Silverberg ed., *The Mirror of Infinity,* San Francisco 1970, with critical introductions by various hands to each story.

12

The absent paradigm:
An introduction to the
semiotics of science fiction[1]

Marc Angenot

My aim in this essay is to describe SF as a semiotic practice. That is, I will attempt to provide the kind of theoretical groundwork that seems to me an indispensable preliminary for any consideration of the meaning of SF relative to its social context.

The modem reader can immediately identify an SF text as such. This implies that there exist certain simple yet essential rules and criteria for doing so. Semiotics can be thought of as the formalization of those rules or criteria. Just as the modern linguist deals methodically with the sort of knowledge that every speaker of a language possesses (albeit unconsciously) by the age of four, so the semiotician endeavors to organize the prior knowledge of literary discourse that the ability to read (or write) necessarily presupposes. SF criticism, however, has persistently ignored the semiotic approach: either because semiotic problems are seen as being too simplistic or (what is more likely) because critics of SF generally have a penchant for philosophical idealism rather than materialism.

Hoping eventually to arrive at fundamental hypotheses relevant to a semiotic definition of the genre, I shall begin with some remarks on what distinguishes "realistic" from SF discourse. By way of illustration, I have chosen more or less arbitrarily the following fragments:

1. "A young lady with a blue merino dress trimmed with three rows of frills came to the doorstep. She introduced Mr. Bovary in the kitchen, where a big fire had been kindled." (Gustave Flaubert, *Madame Bovary [1856], 1: 2)*

2. "Around the swimming pool were strangely shaped chairs made of blentox . . . . Over her driscoll she was wearing an iridescent gown fashioned of vovax and adorned with bernital inlays." (B.-R. Bruss, *Complot Vénus Terre* [1963], chapt. 1).[2]

Obviously the second fragment belongs to SF. The presence of four "neologisms" enables the reader to come to that conclusion unhesitatingly. But can these made-up words really be considered as neologisms? If not, what are they? How is the sentence intelligible through their opacity and "meaninglessness"? What type of message does the text convey, if it is not totally intelligible? What type of *reading pleasure is* invested here that is different from the one experienced with Flaubert?

Underlying these questions is another more basic one. The quotation from Bruss, it is true, exemplifies the most mediocre SF (more complex examples will be discussed in the pages to follow). But with its clumsy attempt at estrangement ("strangely shaped"), it serves for the purpose, of comparison. The question, then, is how to differentiate a "blue merino dress trimmed with three rows of frills" from "an iridescent gown fashioned of vovax and adorned with bernital inlays."

A reader not versed in the frivolities of fashion in the first half of the nineteenth century would have some trouble in making any distinction. He might find words like "merino" and "frills" just as queer as "vovax" and "bernital." But this does not mean that an apprehension of the realistic character of a narrative is totally subjective. It only shows that reading requires a *code*. Which brings me to the crux of my argument.

1 Sign/referent/paradigm

The fact that an SF story is by definition void of referent—e.g., that the planets Gethen, Fomalhaut, Hain, Urras, and Anarres (to mention a few from Ursula Le Guin's opus) do not exist—this fact does not in any way help us to characterize SF. After all, "Madame Bovary, " "Monsieur Homais," and "Yonville l'Abbaye" are also signs without a referent. The co-presence of such "fictional" signs with others, likewise supposedly deictical or referential, is at the very core of the problem of specifying the meaning of "mimesis" and "credibility" in realistic narratives.

In contrast to realistic fiction, SF is a *conjectural* genre in two respects. Its aesthetic goal consists in creating a remote, estranged, and yet intelligible "world." The narrative about such a world itself requires a conjectural reading. It does not call for the reader to apply the norms, rules, conventions, and so forth of his empirical world, but instead assumes a paradigmatic intelligibility that is both delusive and necessary. The reader, in the act of cognitively coming to terms with the text, shifts from the unfolding (syntagmatic) sequence of the plot to an "elsewhere"—to the semantic paradigms, and hence to the immanent practical or theoretical models, which are supposed to confer meaning on the discourse. From a semiotic point of view, then, SF characteristically is fictional discourse based on intelligible *syntagmatic* rules which also govern, and are governed by, delusive *missing paradigms*. This is what I shall try to clarify and demonstrate.

But before going on, I should stress that the concept of *paradigm* twinned with *syntagm* in European functional semiotics, does not carry the meaning usually given to that word in English. In order to clarify this concept as it is understood in Saussurean general linguistics, it might prove useful to illustrate the basic axioms of the "structuralist" school.

The sign "horse," for example, does not in itself immediately refer to any empirical being. As a sign, it forms a class in a semantic field; and its extension and comprehension varies according to other complementary classes with which it is associated. We can thus construct the following paradigm:

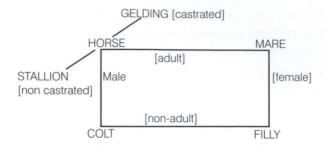

In this paradigm, six signs are disposed on several axes with six "semes" (units of significa-tion) in binary opposition: male vs. female, adult vs. non-adult, castrated vs non-castrated. Each sign is meaningful only because it is different from all the others. As a sign, "filly," while it contains the semic core of "horseness" common to the whole paradigm, is defined in contrast to "horse," "mare," and "colt." It is worth noting that in any paradigm one element can be neutralized, i.e. it can subsume the whole set of oppositions: "horse" may mean /horseness plus male plus adult/, or by neutralization/either male or female, either adult or not/ - /either castrated or not/.

This amounts to saying that in the linguistic code there are no contents but only contrasts. Each sign is constituted out of a common semantic articulation. Meaning is therefore always "in relation to" other elements. The value of a term depends on the pres-ence or the absence of a contiguous element. The English word "mutton," for instance, does not have the extension of the French "mouton," since it is contrasted on a given axis to "sheep," an articulation which French does not possess.

"The sign itself (the link between the signifier and the signified) is nothing but the coun-terpart of all the other signs in language."[3] Therefore—and this axiom is essential to our discussion – paradigmatic and syntagmatic structures imply one another: syntagmatic structures are defined as the rules that combine signs *in praesentia* in a linear sequence of utterance. These two types of functions (syntagmatic and paradigmatic) are interde-pendent. The linguistic system which is by definition paradigmatic, exists only through syntagmatic conjunctions.

If on an unfamiliar beach I notice a yellow flag, a little dirty and faded, and if I identify it as a signal, I do not know offhand its meaning. In order to assign meaning to it, I have to asso-ciate the concrete object with an abstract class of "Yellow Flags" (and from then on, the dirtiness or ragginess of the flag becomes irrelevant). I must learn afterwards that the class of Red Flag is contrasted in the paradigm with the classes of Yellow Flags and Green Flags, and that each and every one of them corresponds to a class of messages: "Swimming forbidden" (Red Flag), "Unsupervised swimming" (Yellow Flag), "Swimming supervised and permitted" (Green Flag). I can now make something out of this—namely, that I can swim today, although it might be dangerous since no lifeguards are at their posts. The collection of possible signifieds, the semantic paradigms, determine the extent of possible messages. Nothing in the messages transmitted by these flags (in their "universe of discourse") will tell me whether the water is warm or cold, deep or shallow. Semiotic phenomena, of course, do not exist in a vacuum. In everyday life they are transmitted together with other symbols, indexes, and clues of a different nature. If huge dark clouds are collecting or if a harsh wind blows, I do not need a red flag (that the wind has anyway probably torn off) to warn me of the danger. If the flag is up, and if everyone is swimming just the same, I may think that the sender of the message was overly cautious and decide to follow the crowd.[4]

The reader of SF is in the same situation as the swimmer on an unfamiliar beach. He can only reconstitute the meaning of some signs in the texts if he knows the paradigm, i.e. the full array of classes complementary to a given sign. In any fictional text, some signals are lures that do not refer to an empirical phenomenon. Moreover, in SF the semantic paradigms, hypothesized as being much more complex than in my example of the flags, are always partially missing and therefore delusive since they do not integrally exist in the text.

My aim, then, is to show how SF functions in its semiotic axioms as a paradigmatic "phantasm," shifting the reader's attention from the syntagmatic structure of the text to a delusion which is an important element of the reader's pleasure. In this regard, SF is a u-topia (no-place) both through its ideological influence and in its mode of decipherment: As in a utopia, the reader is transported from a locus or place—the actual syntagmatic sequence to a non-locus or no-place, the paradigmatic "mirage" which presumably regulates the message. I therefore hold that SF is not determined by any direct relationship between its fictional given and the empirical world, but by the relations inherent to the fictional discourse between syntagm and paradigm.

2 Neologisms and fictive words

Words created by SF writers to convey a feeling of estrangement are not at all neologisms but "fictive words." Such words represent one of the most obvious characteristics of the genre. They can be divided into two categories: a) words that supposedly anticipate forms of language from the future or from "parallel" universes; b) words that are supposedly taken from extraterrestrial languages—related to what Myra Barnes has termed exolinguistics.[5]

Despite these differences in chimerical status, the semiotic impact of these utterances is much the same. Every "fictive word," no matter what its "etymology," will be read in a particular context. Surrounding elements irradiate virtual meanings on the opaque signs. The use of the same fictive word in different contexts enables the reader to form a more and more "accurate" idea of its meaning.

> Hiero had thought he was familiar with many types of leemutes, the Man-rats and Hairy Howlers, the werebears (which were not bears at all), the stimers and several others besides. (Sterling E. Lanier, *Hiero's Journey*, chapt. 1).

Lewis Carroll's lexical creations may cast light on the similar practice in SF:

> 'Just the place for a Snark,' the Bellman cried,
> As he landed his crew with care;
> Supporting each man on the top of the tide
> by a finger entwined in his hair. (*The Hunting of the Snark*).

For Carroll, it is not a matter of describing the Snark as an "extralinguistic being," but of attributing to it a set of predicates intended to produce a stable paradigm. Of course, Carroll is amusing himself at our expense: he launches into a maelstrom of associations which, although they are not totally incompatible, lead nowhere. The SF writer does not lead the reader to a semantic dead end as Carroll does: he leads the reader to believe in the possibility of reconstituting consistent paradigms—whose semantic structures are supposedly homologous to those in the fictive textual "world."

It is however the *syntagm* that actualizes the virtual meaning of the signs. Words are not stable "entities": only their syntagmatic surroundings imprint a meaning on them. The word "duck." for instance, is out of context so ambiguous as to be virtually meaning-less. In one sentence, it may signify "a swimming bird," in another "a darling," in another "an instance of duckling," or "a durable closely woven cotton fabric," or "an amphibious truck."[6] Nevertheless, the user has the impression that the meaning of the word *precedes* its use: syntagmatic consistency leads to a belief in the pre-existence of paradigmatic structures.

"An iridescent gown fashioned of vovax, and adorned with bernital inlays": if the reader understands to a certain extent that fragment, he tends to perceive "vovax" and "bernital" as nouns—which in the trivial conception means substitutes for empirical objects. But in that case, he is ignoring the semantic irradiation conveyed by the syntagm. The syntagmatic insertion of the fictive word creates the illusion of a paradigmatic structure, which supposedly corresponds to empirical constructions.

The coined word may sometimes appear to be a creation *ex nihilo.* Often it will seem to have an ascertainable etymology—which both permits an attempt at a definition and gives the reader the impression that the word is a sociolinguistic clue, a symptom of the epoch described. Here again, the reader's attention is shifted from the sign to a diachronic model of lexical creation. Neology implies a number of rules which govern word formation. An example of this can be found in Albert Robida's *Le Vingtième Siècle* (1883) where the author invents the "Tele," short for "telephonoscope"—something later known as "television". "Tele," with its apocope (i.e., omission of syllables at the end of the word), is a clue indicating a society in which advanced technology (implied by the Greek prefixes) is part of everyday life (as indicated by the "colloquiality" of the shortened verbal form).

The reader perceives the contextual meaning of the coined word but he also gets an idea of the type of society he is dealing with through such a word's semantic formation and use. In the nineteenth century, Greco-Latin derivations gave a text a scientific look.

Nowadays, other modes of formation give an impression of "futurism" to the contemporary reader. This is true of portmanteau words, acronyms and heterogeneous compounds regarded by purists as barbaric (e.g. the techno-bureaucratic vocabulary: vertiport, warphan, swimmando, stagflation, transistor, radar, etc.).

SF has, little by little, created its own vocabulary which is to a large degree used in common by different writers and has penetrated everyday language: android, cyborg, robotics, chronolysis. It is quite possible that words such as airship, aeronautics, cosmonaut, and televison were first employed in fiction and only later entered common usage.

3 Exolinguistics

One of the first French space operas *is Les Posthumes (The Posthumous Letters)* written by Restif de la Bretonne in 1802. In a voyage through the galaxy, the Duke of Multipliandre comes across gigantic fleas, intelligent forms of life on a comet. A flea declares his love to his demoiselle in poignant terms: "Amagilego! syni dllia psouheh sgyngllu bouun evintage": which means (says Restif) "Lovely Lady! Do grant me the possession of the ravishing charms that I contemplate on the surface of your seductive and provocative body." (Vol 111, p. 256) Here, early in the history of SF, appears one of the first examples of extraterrestrial languages. This is only one example, since the author also describes the Rondin language of Selenite origin, a language "made of 24 masculine words and 24 feminine, that are sufficient for every circumstance" (Letter 208). The hero is assaulted in these terms by a Martian swamp hippopotamus: "This animal called on Mars Nüsüsümü (with the ü pronounced the French way), jumped on him screaming Mümüarümü,—which means: I want to fuck you."

What is relevant and significant in these strange passages is not so much the Martian linguistic "performance" or utterance as the paradigm it presupposes—the *absent paradigm—i.e. the whole Martian language*, without which no utterance would be possible. The verisimilitude is invested in the presuppositions of the text, in what the text itself *implies* without attempting to show it extensively. A great many things can be evoked in a text set in an alien world, but only its words can be directly reported. The existence of a language, even if represented only by a few queer "quotations," implies the existence of intelligent life and a fictive "referential" world. Georges Mounin has suggested that someone ought to make a study of what—for a given language—represents the utmost strangeness: namely (in phonetic terms), the unpronounceable.[7] The unpronounceable in a paradoxical element that confers authenticity on even the most mediocre SF.

Exolinguistics is as old as conjectural fiction. Make-believe languages are to be found in John Mandeville and Thomas More. The most famous examples of these fabricated languages—George Orwell's Newspeak, Lyon S. De Camp's Uchronical English (*The Wheels of If*, 1948), Anthony Burgess' Nadsat (*A Clockwork Orange*, 1963), Tolkien's Hobbit languages, etc.—have been investigated by Myra Barnes, who made their study the subject of her dissertation. By means of fragments "cited" by these authors, she tried to isolate the characteristics of these forged languages and test their coherence. Whether this attempt was linguistically legitimate or not, it illustrates my point: the reader's cognitive activity, the very possibility of understanding SF, is necessarily interwoven with conjecture. The reader is transported to an illusive "elsewhere" of a semiotic nature, to the paradigms both suggested in and yet absent from the textual message.

4 From the actual syntagm to the missing paradigm

Coined words and forged extraterrestrial languages are only two obvious manifestations on a phenomenon peculiar to SF semiotics as a whole. The SF narrative always assumes a "not-said" that regulates the message. The rhetoric of credibility aims at having the reader believe not so much in what is literally said as in what is assumed or presupposed. Emphasis is not placed primarily on the characters and events of the future or extraterrestrial world but on types, models, norms, and institutions that are only summarily and allusively represented by these characters and events.

In any linguistic performance, a rule is implied, and in any utterance, a semantic paradigm. Any action supposes a model (to which it conforms or not); any category, an inventory; any sample, an overarching structure; any value, an axiology; any group, roles and criteria of conformity. Any events (and narratives of such events) are related to a more global structure.

While reading SF, one slowly drifts from the narrative sequence as such (syntagm) to these illusory general systems (paradigms). The notion of paradigm must here be enlarged to encompass a full array of semiotic configurations, not limited to linguistic structures. For example: SF characters, as Kingsley Amis has rightly observed in his *New Maps of Hell* (New York, 1975), are never individuals but representatives of a group or species.

While the realistic novel should lead the reader to believe in the events it narrates, the SF novel must also have him believe in what it does not and can not show: the complex universe within which such events are supposed to take place. The reader of a realistic novel proceeds from the general (the commonplace, the ideological topos) to the particular (the specific plot governed by this ideological structure). The SF reader follows the reverse path: he induces from the particular some imagined, general rules that prolong the author's fantasies and confer on them plausibility. The reader engages in a conjectural reconstruction which "materializes" the fictional universe.

In A Trap on *Zarkass* (*Piège sur Zarkass*, Paris 1958) by Stefan Wul, for example, the Terran hero looks down on a native Zarkassian:

> One of his arms looked faded pink. The other one was glowing, with a new brown skin - shining as the peel of a fruit. When passing by, Lawrence stepped over a relinquished

piece of epiderm . . . . He yelled: if you go on peeling like this before me, I shall kick your ass." (chapt. 1)

Such a fragment is intelligible only by filling in a "rule of intercom-prehension" that the author takes care not to provide immediately. The Zarkassians, vaguely humanoid beings, slough regularly. The reader's attention is attracted not specifically to the superficial anecdote—the altercation between Terrestrial and Zarkassian—but to what is presupposed and not immediately explained: this queer biological feature of the alien, and also the relations between that aborigine and the colonialist-cum-racist Earthling (here the reader may draw upon the empirical paradigms of his own world to supplement the information given in the text). However, the conjecture does not stop here: other Zarkassian features can be correlated to the biological trait already mentioned. The reader necessarily embarks upon a series of expanding conjectures. At the same time, he elaborates a structure which is not integrated in the plot, a structure through which the narrative sequence seems to run without ever showing it exhaustively.

The linear plot evokes a tabular paradigm, the complexity and limits of which it gives merely a notion. This might become a rhetorical feature peculiar to the kind of "realism" required in SF. In a fiction set on an alien planet, what represents for the "Terran reader" the utmost strangeness must be perfectly trivial and banal for the Alien narrator. It would therefore be totally abnormal for the narrator to stress this obvious feature at the outset. It seems more "realistic" that such data be given *en passant,* late in the narrative, and in a rather indirect way. A number of readers of Ursula Le Guin's *The Dispossessed* may not have noticed that the members of the Cetian race on Urras and Annares have their bodies and faces covered with hair. For why should Shevek, the narrator, state (for him) the obvious? He does so only in a very enigmatic way when meeting the Ambassador from Terra:

The woman's skin was yellow-brown, like ferrous earth, and hairless, except on the scalp; not shaven, but hairless. (chapt. 11)

Even where SF features the first meeting of an Earthling and an Alien, although the latter tries to "explain" as much as he can (if he is supposed to be in a cooperative mood), there are always basic value systems that will slip his mind: they are at the same time too obvious and too complex. And one value judgment in the text is never isolated: it carries with it contiguous hierarchies, institutions, a whole society in capsule form. In this sense, the reading of the text requires a kind of drifting: the semiotics of SF calls forth a centrifugal model.

The author could, of course, try to explain systematically every datum, but this would be tedious and contrary to the "rules" of the genre. SF novels are elaborated in a way that makes them resemble a Hall of Mirrors in an amusement park—a labyrinth of glass which disorients the passers by strolling through it. An immanent aesthetics of SF is implied here: if the mechanical transposition of "this-worldly" paradigms is sufficient to account for every narrative utterance, we have a witless, even infantile, type of SF. If, on the contrary, a maximum distance is maintained between the empirical and the "exotopic" paradigms, although the alien rules tend to organize themselves into a consistent whole, the reader's pleasure increases.

In *The Left Hand of Darkness*, Ursula Le Guin begins the narrative with the following *incipit* (I assume that the *incipit* of a given text contains clues for its decipherment, what French sociocriticism calls its "conditions of readability"):

> From the Archives of Hain. Transcript of Ansible Document 01-01101-934-2 Gethen: To the Stabile on Ollul: Report from Genli Ai, first Mobile on Gethen/Winter, Hainish Cycle 93, Ekumenical Year 1490-97.

The non-aficionado will consider this fragment to be gibberish (and rightly from his point of view). However, all these fictive words do not only convey a feeling of remoteness. Through their eventual repetition in various contexts, they lead to the elaboration of a paradigm: the envoy of the League explores institutional systems more than actual places. Pleasure rests not so much in the final structure extrapolated as in its progressive reconstruction. Summaries never give a good idea of the value of an SF narrative. They cannot take into account the numerous possible meanings hidden in it. What Michel Butor says of *Finnegans Wake* can also be said, mutatis mutandis, of "significant" SF: "Each word will become like a railway switching device, and we will go from one to the other through a multitude of routes."[8]

By virtue of the aims inherent in the genre, the SF writer does not endeavor to thoroughly subvert the production of paradigms; but he does use a technique that may lead to a powerful critique of them. A certain skepticism as to the limits of human knowledge—a skepticism present in contemporary SF, and particularly in the work of Stanislaw Lem—finds expression in *Solaris* (1961) as precisely the fruitless creation of paradigms. The central theme of Lem's fiction concerns the Sisyphean labor of taxonomies and nomenclatures. The object of the story is not so much the mysterious planet Solaris as "Solaristics" itself, the science dealing with it, contained in the thousand-volume series "Solariana." Hundreds of definitions, schemes, hypotheses, models, and taxonomies pass through the text in brief and fragmentary allusions. Here is the missing paradigm. But the author is very careful in judging the relation between this "knowledge" and its object:

> Giese devised a plain descriptive terminology, supplemented by terms of his own invention, and although these were inadequate and sometimes clumsy, it has to be admitted that no semantic system is as yet available to illustrate the behavior of the Ocean. The "tree-mountains," "extensors," "fungoid," "mimoids," "symmetriads" and "asymmetriads," "vertebride" and "agilus" are artificial, linguistically awkward terms, but they do give some impression of Solaris to anyone who has only seen the planet in bluffed photographs and incomplete films. (chapt. 8)

Contemporary SF unfolds in its very structure, as a parabolic double, its own cognitive project. The "realism" of SF resides in a paradigmatic delusion: codes, series, coordinates, systems, are simultaneously absent yet indispensable for the coherence of the syntagm. That is what Lem admits and claims in the above-quoted sentence.

5 The missing paradigm, the empirical paradigm, and the referent

The reader projects onto the text semantic, logical, and anthropological structures taken from his empirical world. This fact does not contradict my general hypothesis.

By analogy, contiguity, or inversion, paradigms of the empirical world will be—have to be—used to interpret the SF text. SF criticism has invested a lot of energy in trying to measure the distance between the empirical and fictive worlds. Such a focus might be quite useful in its place, but it tends to assume that the empirical world is homogenous and that a verbal construction can be compared right away to the empirical reality. This diverts analysis away from the semiotics of textual structures. No doubt, links exist between the worldview of the author's society and the fictive *topoï* since without such links the fictional world would remain arbitrary and unintelligible. Yet the first task of the SF critic is to identify precisely the SF "world" as something estranged from the reader's empirical world and possessing its own rules. Even the question of verisimilitude, as a tacit contract in SF, is strongly related to the metaphorical, metonymical, and other transformations from the empirical cognitive systems to the paradigms of the story.

For the SF writer the "map" and the "ground" are necessarily confused (small wonder Van Vogt and others were fascinated by Korzybski's general semantics). How many maps have been drawn by SF authors, from that of Lincoln Island (Jules Verne) to those of Urras and Anarres (Ursula Le Guin)? The veracity of the story has been implied in the coherence of its codes. This mingling has often been used in eighteenth-century utopias. The European traveller, upon his arrival on the Utopian island, would ask his wise mentor: how do you say "steal," "rape," "murder"? We do not have such words, would be the answer. And the traveller would then conclude with amazement: What? No robberies! No rape! No murder!

At the beginning of this essay, I noted that the linguistic sign does not "hide" or "conceal" anything. If it denotes, it does so through its paradigmatic position, through the semantic universe which as a whole is coextensive with the phenomenal world. "We cannot say that language creates reality (in the literal sense of the word 'create') nor that language makes a copy of reality (in any sense of the word 'copy')."[9] The truthfulness of language is twofold: external (in its reference to the empirical world), and internal (in the operative character of its code). SF takes advantage of this cleavage between the signified and the referent, concepts which are incompatible yet necessarily linked and taken for each other. My intent has been to show that SF produces a paradigmatic mirage, and consequently entails a conjectural mode of reading. The consideration of such traits immanent to SF is an essential step in understanding the genre. Semiotic description is far from being the alpha and omega of literary criticism; but to pass it by is to deal with the text in an idealistic way that greatly increases the chances of being taken in by the semiotic lures which I have tried to identify.

Notes

1. A different version of this article was published in French in *Poétique, 33:* Feb. 1978.
   I am grateful to the Canada Council for a two-year grant for research into SF history and theory.
2. See the list of SF texts quoted above.
3. Ferdinand de Saussure, *Cours de linguistique générale.* (Paris: Payot, 1915) translated as *Course in General Linguistics.* (New York: McGraw Hill, 1966) II, chap. 4, sect. 2.
4. This statement is inspired by Luis Prieto, *Pertinence et pratique* (Paris: Editions de Minuit, 1975), especially chapt. 1.
5. Myra E. Barnes, *Linguistics and Language in SF – Fantasy.* (New York: Arno Press, 1975).
6. From a synchronic point of view the fact that these meanings do not relate to the same etymology is irrelevant.
7. Georges Mounin, "La Communication avec 1'espace," *Introduction à la sémiologie* (Paris: Editions de Minuit, 1970).
8. Michel Butor, *Introduction aux fragments de Finnegans Wake.* (Paris: Gallimard, 1972), p. 12 (My translation).
9. Adam Schaff, "Langage et réalité," *Problèmes du langage.* (Paris: Gallimard, 1966).

SF texts quoted

Félix Bodin. *le Roman de l'avenir.* Paris: Lecointe & Pougin, 1835.
B.R. Bruss. *Complot Vénus-Terre.* Paris: Fleuve noir, 1963. (My translation).
Sterling E. Lanier. *Hiero's Journey.* New York: Bantam, 1973.
Ursula K. Le Guin. *The Left Hand of Darkness.* New York: Ace Books, 1969.
—. *The Dispossessed.* New York: Harper & Row, 1974.
Stanislaw Lem. *Solaris.* New York: Berkeley Publishing Corp., 1970. (original: Warsaw, 1961).
[N. Restif de la Bretonne]. *les Posthumes, lettres reçues apres la mort du Mari par la Femme qui le croit à Florence. Par Feu Cazotte* [forged attribution]. Paris: Duchène, 1802. 4 Vols. (My translation.)
Albert Robida. *le Vingtième Siècle.* Paris: G. Decaux, 1883.
Stefan Wul. "Piège sur Zarkass," *Oeuvres.* Paris: Laffont, 1970. (My translation.)

13

Reading sf as a mega-text

Damien Broderick

There is an apparent paradox at the heart of science fiction's narrative method. Unlike most other literary projects, sf's inventions are alienatingly distanced from any consensual *Weltbild* outside their own very elaborate intertext—yet the mode is carefully mimetic (rather than metaphoric) in address, and explicitly cognitive, centering on systems of knowledge (rather than unchecked or surreal imagination). Sf insists on the literal level.

Nor is the function of estrangement in sf identical with more familiar textual strategies. With Roland Barthes, for example, we can value history "for the strangeness of other epochs and what they can teach us about the present [. . .]. History is interesting and valuable precisely for its otherness."[1] It is an ambiguous project, of course:

> We need to develop the historical sense [. . .] into a real sensual delight. When our theatres perform plays of other periods they like to annihilate distance, fill in the gap, gloss over the differences. But what comes then of our delight in comparisons, in distance, in dissimilarity—which is at the same time a delight in what is close and proper to ourselves? (Bertolt Brecht)[2]

Does sf then, above all else, write the narrative of the other/s? If this suggestion is taken in a spirit of description (though hardly of definition), a negating (perhaps demystifying) alternative is instantly inscribed in its logical shadow: that sf writes, rather, the narrative of the *same,* as other.

Consider Phillip Mann's *The Eye of the Queen,* an extremely effective dramatization of the central sf notion of *alienness:* the quiddity of nonhuman consciousness in three-and-a-half meter tall aliens who shed their skins, reproduce asexually, and spend much of their time patched into the spiritual broadcasts of beings resembling angels (a trope echoed in Card's *Xenocide*). For all their alienness, though, Mann's Pe-Ellians resemble a child's idea of human adults: very large, very mysterious, custodial but selfishly dedicated to the incomprehensible, and (of course and perhaps above all) the focus of enormously confusing thoughts and feelings about gender and sex, usually dealt with at the conscious level (for the child) by repression.

So sf, like fairy tales, clearly transforms and subdues elements of forgotten experi-ence that linger to trouble us, allowing us to articulate these repressed perceptions. In this regard, it familiarizes the estranged. Yet it also allows us to speak (and relish) the unspeakable, to sanitize malign wishes by presenting the known under a new label. Larry Niven and Jerry Pournelle's *Footfall* was palpably a metaphor for US/Soviet nuclear war. Their interstellar invaders are a herd species, a fact gratifying to the commissars before Russia, too, gets pounded. It's a hymn to grit, xenophobia, manifest destiny and the Joy of Nuclear War, capturing the Reagan '80s even more vividly than the *Rambo* movies.

Gregory Renault locates this co-opting move at the core of Darko Suvin's cognitive estrangement model:[3] "The claim is that naturalist fiction portrays the Same (author's empirical environment) by the Same ('exact recreation'), while estranged fiction portrays the Same by the Other [. . .]" (p. 115). But any act of signification "selects from available potential signifiers; the strictest attempt at representation is therefore always an interpret-ation, an artistically mediated re-presentation or re-construction of 'the real' (itself signifier as well as signified)" (p. 116). Sf's special character must therefore be in part to extend the range of potential signifiers. Citing Brian Stableford, Renault observes that sf is reliant on "an ever-changing supply of images which 'gradually change so as always to appear novel while never becoming truly strange'" (p. 136).

For sf's amusing (or shocking) distortions and defamiliarizations of the present consensus world can be merely random, catch-penny. As Kim Stanley Robinson notes: "when this is done regularly, as it was during the 1930s, then the distortions are meaningless individually, and cumulatively they tend to reinforce the assumptions and values of the dominant culture of our time, for assumptions and values survive this sort of distortion and are presented as existing unchanged, thousands of years into the future."[4]

Unsympathetic commentators have regularly advanced this general point with a killing flourish, evidently in the belief that sf criticism has never thought of it. Gerald Graff, in his assault on poststructuralist and postmodernist trends in fiction and theory, is unmistake-ably of this view:

> Might not the effect of radical disorientation and cognitive estrangement be to confuse or disarm critical intelligence rather than to focus it? The question is never asked. [. . .]
>   It does not follow that such a work induces its audience to see things more critic-ally. [Estrangement effects] discovered by recent critics in the conventions of science fiction may result in a dulling of the audience's sense of reality, in shell-shocked accept-ance rather than criticial intransigence. The "models for the future" celebrated by Scholes and other critics of science fiction may stimulate escapist fantasies rather than critical thinking—all the more probably if these models are inserted into an already uncritical, fad-worshipping mass culture. [. . .] Whether fantasy makes us more critical or merely more solipsistic and self-indulgent depends finally on whether it is accountable to some-thing that is not fantasy.[5]

Graff's critique is not without force, the more so today, over a decade later, as paperback racks replace traditional sf with an endless succession of 1500-page Tolkienesque trilogies. (Graff here conflates sf and genre fantasy, and might today add horror; I am prepared to do the same for the sake of the argument and because most sf specialty stores and their customers blur the distinction.) He is quite wrong, however, in supposing that "the question is never asked." Darko Suvin himself, for example, has recently summarized this aporia nicely:

> SF can be grasped as a genre in an unstable equilibrium or dynamic compromise between two factors. The first is its cognitive—philosophical and political—potentiality as a genre that grows out of the subversive, lower-class form of "inverted world," within the horizons of knowledge and liberation. The second is a cluster of powerful upper and middle-class ideologies that has, in the great majority of texts, sterilized such potential horizons by contaminating them with mystifications which preclude significant presentations of truly other relationships, with the horizons of power and repression.[6]

Vulgar manifestations of the sf mode are even more one-sided than this portrait of a narrative field struggling with internal tensions and antinomies might suggest. "Sci-fi" ("skiffy") is now more common than sf, for an opportunistic market has forced a return to the 1930s.

For all that, science fiction's "glorious eclecticism," notes the feminist critic Sarah Lefanu, "with its mingling of the rational discourse of science with the pre-rational language of the unconscious—for SF borrows from horror, mythology and fairy tale—offers a means of exploring the myriad ways" in which the social construction of feminine identity is accomplished.[7] What is more, it allows those ways to be put in question.

So it is clear that sf need not inevitably restrict its ambitions to "Instant Whip" whimsy. Implicit in the kinds of stories it tells, and the ways it tells them, is the clue we seek for the specific ways in which science fictions codes and transcodes the discourses from which it springs: the rhetorics and practices of the sciences and the humane arts, of wishful compensation fantasies which disclose the lacunae of our lives and the social order within which we live those lives, and of elaborated speculations which sometimes go beyond wish into aspiration and artistry. Geoff Ryman's wonderful *The Child Garden,* say, with its rich reverberations of *The Divine Comedy,* dystopian tradition, and hard sf usages alike, comes close to genuine sf that is simultaneously literature, as do John Crowley's late fictions (poised uncertainly between hermeticism, sf, and fantasy).

There have been abundant attempts to define sf in terms of mimeticism in the service of imagination, which suggests that sf operates metaphoric strategies via metonymic tactics. In its very structure, sf thus constitutes a break from literature's cycle of formal polarities from metaphor to metonymy and back, avoiding the alternative postmodernist traps of unchecked babble and tongue-tied silence.[8]

On this account, the strategy of realism is centrally metonymic. In its attempts to "represent the real world," realist textuality (John Updike is a premier exemplar, as is Robert Stone) enacts an epistemological fragmentation and reconstitution: it builds strings of signifiers which themselves are chosen for their contiguity with interacting elements in the socially/linguistically constructed *Umwelt*. Sf textuality, by contrast (Delany's oeuvre, especially, but really everything from Heinlein's *Beyond This Horizon* to, say, Zindell's *Neverness*), is grounded in a different subjunctivity,[9] one in which metonymy passes first through cascades of suspended paradigm sets, detached and sent aloft from any last vestige of quotidian referentiality.

Yet the process is very far from solipsistic. Christine Brooke-Rose provides a germinal account of its principles of operation in several theoretical discussions of postmodernist sf novels (McElroy's *Plus,* Vonnegut's *Sirens of Titan*), comparing their mechanisms with those of Tolkien's *Lord of the Rings*.[10] Regrettably, she blurs her most telling insight.

Her poetics of the fantastic starts with a modification and compression of Philippe Hamon's 1973 study of the mechanisms of reading,[11] one parameter of which is *the parallel story* or *mega-text:*

> [T]he realistic narrative is hitched to a megastory (history, geography), itself valorized, which doubles and illuminates it, creating expectations on the line of least resistance through a text already known, usually as close as possible to the reader's experience. Exoticism is reduced to the familiar. This gives points of anchorage, allows an economy of description and insures a general effect of the real that transcends any actual decoding since the references are not so much understood as simply recognised as proper names (p. 243).

Most of Hamon's parameters are shared with conventional sf, but the mega-text or parallel story is not, Brooke-Rose believes; or not to any great extent. Her reasoning is deceptively direct.

If the function of the parallel story is to evoke shared verities and commonplaces (however provisional and arbitrary these might be from the standpoint of a deconstructive critic, cultural relativist, or epistemological anarchist), providing behind every item in a syntagm a certified and secure paradigm of references, how could this procedure be mimicked in sf, where many of the lexical items have no "real-world" references? She grants that an sf story or novel "usually creates a fictional historico-geographico-sociological megatext but leaves it relatively vague, concentrating on technical marvels" (p. 243). Thus, Tolkien's fantasy compensates for this lack of external referentiality by providing its own lumbering mega-text:

> [*The Lord of the Rings*], like SF but more so, is particularly interesting in that there is such a megatext, not pre-existent but entirely invented, yet treated with the utmost seriousness and in great detail, thus destroying the element of recognition and hence readability which this feature provides in the realistic novel, and causing on the contrary a plethora of information and the collapse of the referential code. [. . .]
>
> That is to say, it is treated *as if* it existed, except that instead of allowing an economy of description and ensuring a general effect of the real, it needs on the contrary to be constantly explained (since it is unfamiliar) [. . .] (p. 243).

So its function is radically unlike that of any "realist" mega-text. "Since the megatext is not 'already known,' it cannot fulfil the readability requirement, but on the contrary, produces a pseudo-exoticism, much of which can be savoured simply as such, rather than tactically understood [. . .]" (p. 248).

Tolkien fans are not alone in savoring the details of invented worlds and peoples (quite a different pleasure to that found in relishing those invented "realistic" biographies known as "fiction"). *Star Trek* enthusiasts have for years gathered together garbed in the costume of starship crews, complete with weapons and "Beam me up, Scotty" communicators. Manuals showing the design features of starships are purchased and pored over. Members of the Society for Creative Anachronism, who tend to be fans of both sf and genre fantasy, not only dress in mock mediaeval garb but adopt appropriate personae and have at one another with blunt instruments. The extension of sf and fantasy mega-texts into board and computer gaming has developed into a series of virtual cults, whose mega-texts, in a continuous state of communal expansion, are far more ornate than those once-and-for-all histories and genealogies which, in Brooke-Rose's tart words, "have given much infantile happiness to the Tolkien clubs and societies, whose members apparently write to each other in Elvish" (p. 247).

The element in sf which Brooke-Rose appears to have slighted, at a severe cost to her analysis, is the extensive generic mega-text built up over fifty years, even a century, of mutually layered sf texts. Using a similar strategy of *semiological compensation*, or redundancy and over-coding, which Hamon and Brooke-Rose discern in realism, the sf mega-text works by embedding each new work, seen by Delany[12] as a self-structuring web of non-mundane signifiers and syntagms, in an even vaster web of interpenetrating semantic and tropic givens or vectors.

Consider the astonishing amount of tacit detailed knowledge invoked without a moment's thought in decoding the second paragraph of Robert Stone's contemporary *Outerbridge Reach:*

> When the last week of February came in mild and spring-scented as April, Browne decided to deliver a boat to Annapolis. He passed under the Verrazano Bridge shortly after dawn on the last Wednesday in February. With Sandy Hook ahead, he cut his auxiliary and hoisted the mainsail and genoa.

For an Australian, the first remark suggests delusion, since April is early autumn. The place-names aid orientation, and the nautical lexicon (opaque to one who, like me, hasn't a clue what a "genoa" is) conveys authority as well as fact. Above all, the text situates itself within the actual American universe.

Contrast this with Zindell's *Neverness:*

> My ship did not fall out into the center of the moons. Instead, I segued into a jungle-like decision tree . . . Each individual ideoplast was lovely and unique. The representation of the fixed-point theorem, for instance, was like a coiled ruby necklace. As I built my proof, the coil joined with feathery, diamond fibres of the first Lavi mapping lemma.

These star pilots, the sf-trained reader understands via a many-plyed reconstruction from the mega-text, are taking their ships through windows in hyperspace *by proving theorems!* It's an audacious and shivery pleasure to those who know the trick to decoding such sentences is not by way of the conventional dictionary and encyclopedia—although it is true that recognizing the fixed-point theorem (which governs the transformation of one set of points into an isomorphic set) helps you appreciate a sense of recursion in what is being described/constructed.

Some of these have been dubbed "icons" by Gary K. Wolfe;[13] they include the spaceship, the robot and the monster, as well as paradigmatic items shared with the "real" world lexicon, such as the city, the wasteland and the barrier:

> Like a stereotype or a convention, an icon is something we are willing to accept because of our familiarity with the genre, but unlike ordinary conventions, an icon often retains its power even when isolated from the context of conventional narrative structures. (p. 16)

It is, then, to be conceived as more nearly a narrative archetype; not an archaic trace so much as a proleptic one, or at any rate one in a linguistically unprecedented subjunctive state.

While Wolfe's suggestion is provocative, it is important to see what an iconography of sf does *not* propose. None of the candidates (alien, robot, spaceship, etc.) has a single, univocal conventional weight or meaning even within a given generic timeframe or publishing regime. If robots are seen as soulless and threatening in the 1930s, Asimov reconstructs them a decade later as rule-governed and sweet-natured (though not every writer follows his lead; Clarke re-reconstructs them two decades on as murderous (*2001's* HAL) or rather, on second thoughts, baffled by Hofstadterian aporia (the version in *2010*); Lem, in Poland, makes them the allegorical focus of comical but profound parables of "cosmic constructors"; in the 1980s and '90s, Benford (especially the chip-augmented humans and fused organism-machines of his *Great Sky River* and *Tides of Light*) and many cyberpunk authors (especially William Gibson, with his data cowboys jacked into cyberspace), blend human and machine into a disturbing symbiosis; still other writers, like opportunistic Darwinian species, develop and invest every possible modulation.

Yet all these variants bear certain family resemblances, and tend to cohere about a limited number of narrative vectors. Wolfe was not unaware of this dissemination within his schemata:

> such transformations and combinations of the favorite images of the genre become like variations on a theme, with writers working from a relatively limited number of consensual images to create a vast and complex body of fiction that nevertheless often rests upon the assumption of reader familiarity with the fundamental icons of the genre (p. xiv).

But that familiarity, so necessary in alerting trained readers to the appropriate reception codes and strategies for concretizing an sf text, maintains at its heart a *de*-familiarizing impulse absolutely pivotal to the genre's specificity. Basic to the very definition of most genres is stability in characteristic situations, emblems, actions and types of conflict and personality-response—it is why one chooses to discern/construct a category out of a catalogue. Sf is different, being (at least by vocation) grounded in a *novum*. Discussing the literal iconography of sf film, Vivian Sobchack stresses this feature of sf by contrast to the Gangster or the Western genres:

> [B]oth these genres are visually circumscribed by an awareness of history, the Western even more so than the Gangster film. This linkage of situation and character, objects, settings, and costumes to a specific *past* creates visual boundaries to what can be photographed and in what context. This historical awareness, which leads at least to an imaginative if not actual authenticity, demands repetition and creates consistency throughout these genres. This is not true, however, of the SF film, a genre which is unfixed in its dependence on actual time and/or place.[14]

The railroad, for Sobchack, has a quite different iconic weight to the spaceship. "From its first silent chugging to the clangorous present, the railroad in the history of the Western film has not altered in its physical particularity or its specific significance; it is, indeed, an icon" (p. 68). But "there is no *consistent* cluster of meanings provided by the image of a spaceship" (Idem). From the sleek aerofoil Noah's Ark of *When Worlds Collide* to the sublime or celebratory UFO in *Close Encounters of the Third Kind,* from the clinical spinal column of *2001's Discovery* to the adventurous "dog-fighting" modules of the *Star Wars* films which naturalize the future in the image of a glamorous and heroic past, the iconographical weight and density alters radically.[15] The spacecraft is a means of transportation which enables an entire cosmology of narratives, positive, negative and neutral in moral and aesthetic charge.

In what sense, then, can it be an icon? In the minimal sense, at least, that the spaceship is *not* a railroad, nor any other known, assimilated component of the quotidian (except, precisely, in its now-extensive iconicity). A vast range of connotations hang in generic hyperspace above or behind its manifestation in a given text, drawn together by association and practice into certain most-probable-use vectors, but the image or concept of the sf emblem remains parsable as a new noun or verb, a signifier which posts notice to us of an "absent signified," an empirically empty but imaginatively laden paradigm.[16]

Still, there are constraints. Marie Maclean notes: "The reader's development of the missing paradigm may be idiosyncratic, but it remains limited by the syntagmatic aspects of the narrative" (p. 171), as does the use within any given text of any given iconic signifier by the grand exfoliating syntagm of the sf mega-text. At the very least, we can agree with Wolfe that sf's icons

> consolidate the "sense of wonder" and offer readers some word or image that will assure them that what they are reading is in some way connected to the vast body of other science-fiction works.
>
> The use of conventional symbols or icons is one of the most convenient methods for science-fiction writers to make this connection, for they embody not only the dialectic of known and unknown but also the germ of recognizable formulas. They are a

message in code to the initiated reader and an emblem of dissociation to the uninitiated. (Wolfe, p. 27)[17]

It is the creation of such a shared, icon-echoing, redundant and inconsistent mega-text in the collective intertextuality of those works we name "sf" which gives this kind of writing its power, a power verging on obsession or dream and only available elsewhere in other somewhat comparable varieties of textuality (genre fantasy, myth, fairytale, surrealism) and then just because of their resonances with primordial—if often culture constrained—signification nexi (key cultural aporia, in myth; key psychosocial development episodes, in fairytale; dream states, in surrealism).

One is reminded of Bachelard's speculations on the elements (literally) of science and poetry, while reading as well the kinds of objections raised to them. Gaston Bachelard (1884–1962), at one time a tremendously influential historian and philosopher of science, proposed a "psychoanalysis of matter," using a sort of proto-structuralist aesthetic of dream and reverie. He proposed water as wine's binary opposite, for instance (though Roland Barthes argued in *Mythologies* that milk rather than water had become the cultural "other" to wine; in Australia it would, of course, be Foster's beer). Culler has commented wryly on the psychoanalytic motifs Bachelard brought to literary studies "as a way of analyzing not authors but images, whose power is said to derive from their exploitation of a primordial and archetypal experience—not unlike that of a nineteenth-century village childhood of the kind, by a curious coincidence, that Bachelard himself enjoyed.[18] Some of sf's favorite icons clearly work this way—one thinks of recurrent tropes in the sweet pastorales of Clifford Simak[19]—but Culler is not wholly dismissive: Bachelard's doctrine

> has the virtue of falsifiability. We dispute it by showing that the force and significance of images depend more on specific ideological or differential functions within a text than on universal associations: that images of earth are not always 'stables et tranquilles' nor walls and houses welcoming and protective.
>
> Moreover Bachelard's hypothesis leads us to argue that much poetry does not simply evoke or invoke an immediate and "natural" experience of the world but works much as Bachelard claims science does; breaking down immediate intuitions, deconstructing a universe of archetypical clichés, and reinventing the world by giving it an order which is discursive rather than immediately affective. (Idem.)

It is this same fulcrum upon which any theory of sf iconography teeters: icons in a literature of cognitive estrangement must be intrinsically destabilized and multivocal (in a degree which outruns the always-already ruptured dissemination postulated by deconstruction for every act of language; that is, these icons are unstable at a higher level of discursive strategy, as science's always-provisional hypotheses must be, by contrast to the graven doctrinal character of traditional religious claims, for example), yet they undoubtedly exist as discursive attractors, about which narratives orbit in their contained but unpredictable paths. And while it is important to grasp that they are not archetypes in any timeless and universal sense (though their invocation of the known and unknown, stressed by Wolfe, comes close to such a station), this fact does not detract from their salience in helping account for the specificity and idiosyncratic coding of sf texts.

In consequence, only readers inducted into the sf mega-text web or intertext (only "native speakers," as it were) will be competent to retrieve/construct anything like the full semiotic density of a given text, most of which will overflow or escape the "realistic-ally"-sanctioned definitions of the words in the fiction, not to mention their unorthodox schemata of combination. This is certainly not immediately obvious to the inexperienced reader, and helps explain why many capable but uninitiated readers recoil in utter baffle-ment at sf-conventionalized rhetorical moves in the narrative, as well as from a textual surface which seems bizarrely under-determined (a difficulty usually experienced as defective characterization, which, as it happens, is usually the case, though not as a deficiency). Estrangement indeed!

Such obstacles to reception are not, it's true, found in sf alone. The usual way to express rhetorical singularity in a discourse is to define its practice—the text it writes, and the readings it elicits—as a genre. So it is one of the virtues of otherness that sf can exist at all, to the snug pleasure of its inducted readers and the equally snug consternation of those excluded from its codes and mega-texts.

Notes

1. Jonathan Culler, *Barthes,* Fontana, 1983, p. 24.
2. From *Brecht on Theatre,* ed. J. Willett [London, 1964], cited in *Marxism and Literary Criticism* by Terry Eagleton, Methuen, 1976, p. 13.
3. Gregory Renault, "Science Fiction as Cognitive Estrangement: Darko Suvin and the Marxist Critique of Mass Culture," *Discourse* No. 2, 1980.
4. Kim Stanley Robinson, *The Science Fiction of Philip K. Dick*, UMI Research Press, 1984, p. x.
5. Gerald Graff, *Literature Against Itself,* University of Chicago Press, 1989, pp. 74-5, 99-100.
6. Darko Suvin, *Victorian Science Fiction in the UK: The Discourses of Knowledge and of Power*, G. K. Hall: Boston, 1983, p. 419.
7. Sarah Lefanu, *In the Chinks of the World Machine: Feminism and Science Fiction*, The Women's Press, 1988, p. 5.
8. An argument advanced compellingly by David Lodge in *The Modes of Modern Writing: Metaphor, metonymy and the typology of modern literature*, Arnold 1977, and *Working with Structuralism: Essays and reviews on 19th and 20th century literature*, Routledge & Kegan Paul, 1981.
9. A use of the grammatical tool authorized by Samuel R. Delany in an early paper reprinted in *The Jewel-Hinged Jaw: Notes of [sic] the Language of Science Fiction*, [1977] Berkeley Windhover, 1978, p. 31 *et sequ.* Briefly: "A distinct level of subjunctivity informs all the words in an s-f story at a level that is different from that which informs naturalistic fiction, fantasy, or reportage. [. . . Heinlein's] 'the door dilated,' is meaningless as naturalistic fiction, and practically mean-ingless as fantasy." (pp. 31, 34). As sf, it confirms, while enacting, the text's radical "futurity" or "otherness."
10. Christine Brooke-Rose, *A Rhetoric of the Unreal: Studies in narrative and structure, especially of the fantastic*, Cambridge University Press, 1981.

11. Philippe Hamon, "Un discours constraint," *Poétique* 16 [*Le discours réaliste*], 411-45, cited Brooke-Rose, p. 85.

12. Delany, *op. cit.* See my "Reading by Starlight: SF as a Reading Protocol," in *Science Fiction* #32, ed. Van Ikin, pp. 5-16.

13. Gary K. Wolfe, *The Known and the Unknown*, Kent State University Press, 1979.

14. Vivian Sobchack, *Screening Space. The American Science Fiction Film*, [1980] 2nd, enlarged edition, Ungar, 1987, p. 66.

15. I draw these examples from Sobchack's discussion of these films and others in her chapter on sf iconography.

16. See Marie Maclean's useful discussion, influenced by Marc Angenot's "The Absent Paradigm" (*Science-Fiction Studies*, Vol. 6, pp. 9-19), in her "Metamorphoses of the Signifier in 'Unnatural' Languages," *Science-Fiction Studies*, Vol. 11, pp. 166-173.

17. Perhaps one might say "the dialect" as well as the "dialectic," in view of the daunting or off-putting effects of sf-specialized tropes correctly noted here by Wolfe.

18. Jonathan Culler, *Framing the Sign. Criticism and its Institutions*, Blackwell, 1988, p. 101.

19. Amis called him "a kind of science-fiction poet laureate of the countryside" (*New Maps of Hell*, p. 62), a countryside stocked with grouchy but loyal robots, talking dogs, paranormal powers around the cosmic village pump . . .

14

Time travel and the mechanics of narrative

David Wittenberg

"What happened to me?" I whispered to the lady at my side.

"Pardon? Oh, a meteor got you, but you didn't miss a thing, believe me, that duet was absolutely awful. Of course it *was* scandalous; they had to send all the way to Galax for your spare," whispered the pleasant Ardritess.

"What spare?" I asked, suddenly feeling numb.

"Why, yours, of course."

"Then where am I?"

"Where? Here in the theater. Are you all right?"

"Then I am the spare?"

"Certainly."

—Stanislaw Lem, *The Star Diaries*

Anyone who thinks about time travel for a while is likely to encounter something like the following dilemma. On the one hand, time travel stories would seem to constitute a minor and idiosyncratic literature, a subtype of other popular genres such as science fiction, romance, and action-adventure; time travel makes use of improbable devices and extravagant paradoxes, and in general lays claim to only a small share of the plots, topics, or themes that could conceivably interest a reader, writer, or critic of literature. On the other hand, since even the most elementary narratives, whether fictional or nonfictional, set out to modify or manipulate the order, duration, and significance of events in time—that is, since all narratives do something like "travel" through time or construct "alternate" worlds—one could arguably call narrative itself a "time machine," which is to say, a mechanism for revising the arrangements of stories and histories. In this more expansive view, literature itself might be viewed as a subtype of time travel, rather than the other way around, and time traveling might be considered a fundamental condition of storytelling itself, even its very essence.

This book sets out, not exactly to resolve such a dilemma over the significance of time travel stories, but rather to amplify and further complicate it, even to expose some of its more provocative implications. In this respect, the book is polemical as well as analytical.

I contend that there ought to be much more attention paid to the seemingly eccentric genre of time travel fiction by literary, cultural, and film theorists, as well as by readers and scholars interested more broadly in either theories of narrative or philosophies of time. If it eventually turns out that the question of time travel is tantamount to the question of narrative itself, then such a fundamental question will almost certainly have been woefully underconsidered by the very thinkers best positioned to comprehend and answer it.

I argue that time travel fiction is a "narratological laboratory," in which many of the most basic theoretical questions about storytelling, and by extension about the philosophy of temporality, history, and subjectivity, are represented in the form of literal devices and plots, at once both convenient for criticism and fruitfully complex. I wish to suggest not merely that time travel stories are examples or depictions of narratological or philosophical issues, but that these stories are themselves already exercises in narratology and the theorization of temporality—they are in essence "narrative machines," more or less latent, emergent, or full blown. And following the leads they expose, the present book intends to contribute its part to a fundamental reconsideration of the philosophy of time, as well as to a fundamental synthesis of such philosophy with narrative theory, goals in the service of which time travel fiction will be regarded as a philosophical literature *par excellence*.

If it seems brash for an academic critic to make such broad philosophical claims for a popular genre and, moreover, for a genre that has previously garnered only sporadic attention from academic criticism, the brashness may be mitigated by the book's inevitably interdisciplinary focus. By necessity, I borrow and amalgamate a range of insights and information from cultural and film theory, philosophy (both analytic and continental), physics, psychology, and historiography. In each case, interpretations of the literature of time travel, chiefly of popular science fiction, serve as a kind of escort into and around these other fields. Let me begin with a few such interpretations. Each of the following three readings analyzes a single time travel story as a paradigm of a certain form of temporal manipulation, and in turn as an access into crucial aspects of narrative theory. Following these three readings, I briefly outline some of the conceptual and methodological links that such interpretations might suggest between fields of study concerned with problems of time travel—in particular, popular literature and film, literary history and criticism, analytic philosophy, and physics. I also comment on the somewhat counterintuitive history of the genre of time travel fiction that I necessarily construct alongside the specific theoretical considerations time travel stories compel me to pursue.

First reading: Fabula *and* Sjuzhet *in* Up the Line

In Robert Silverberg's 1969 novel *Up the Line,* the following conversation takes place between Jud Elliott, a transtemporal tour guide for researchers and vacationers journeying into the past, and his mentor in the "Time Service," Themistoklis Metaxas. In a side plot, Metaxas is helping Jud get invited to a party in Constantinople in the year 1105, so that Jud can seduce his own "great-great-multi-great-grandmother":

> Metaxas, as always, was glad to help.
> "It'll take a few days," he said. "Communications are slow here. Messengers going back and forth."
> "Should I wait here?"
> "Why bother?" Metaxas asked. "You've got a timer. Jump down three days, and maybe by then everything will be arranged."
> I jumped down three days. Metaxas said, "Everything is arranged."[1]

Here is a seemingly extraordinary narrative event, one peculiar to the temporal manipulations made possible by a time machine: the narrator, Jud, using his "timer," is able instantaneously to skip over three full days of time, meeting up with Metaxas in the same location "down the line."[2] Silverberg constructs the conversation to reflect the unusual temporal elision enabled by the timer, skipping instantaneously between the two disconnected fragments of dialogue and treating them as continuous: "I jumped down three days . . . '[e]verything is arranged.'" The reader's own perspective, which has also been made to "jump" over the same three days, is therefore allied with Jud's experience of the hiatus rather than, for instance, with that of Metaxas, who has presumably been occupied during the entire interval. In turn, Silverberg can joke, via the deadpan substitution of tenses in the phrase "everything will be arranged/is arranged," about the economic convenience the time machine provides for Jud, who now proceeds directly to his tryst, bypassing the labor of preparations undertaken by his colleague Metaxas. For a brief moment, whatever other unusual advantages it may offer, time travel permits the indulgence of an erotic perquisite, one that the reader shares by being positioned all the nearer, in terms of the economy of reading, to the imminent seduction.

Although the most extraordinary element in this fragment of dialogue is surely the presence of the time machine (the timer), it is not easy to determine precisely in what its extraordinariness consists. Consider this slight rewriting of the scene, in which I merely replace the time traveler's technical jargon with some more mundane language:

> Metaxas, as always, was glad to help.
> "It'll take a few days," he said. "Communications are slow here. Messengers going back and forth."
> "Should I wait here?"
> "Why bother?" Metaxas asked. "You've got things to do. Come back in three days, and maybe by then everything will be arranged."
> I came back in three days. Metaxas said, "Everything is arranged."

With all explicit reference to timers and jumping removed, we now have a perfectly ordinary sequence of narrative events, in which the narrator-protagonist also skips, still instantaneously from the reader's viewpoint, three days of time. The vague "things to do" with which I have replaced "a timer" in my new version, and that Metaxas now suggests might account for Jud's missing three days, are, in terms of the progress of the narrative, exactly as nondescript and formally empty as the three days originally "jumped" using time travel. Even the humor entailed by Jud's avoidance of the labor Metaxas has undertaken on his behalf can be retained in the deadpan echo of the final line. Indeed, whether the skipping of three days consists, for Jud, in a physically discontinuous *nothing* enabled by a time machine or whether, instead, he merely expends three days in the background of the narrative doing nothing much, makes very little difference to the structure or coherence of the fiction, even though it may, of course, make considerable difference to the story's genre.

In short, physical time travel and metanarrative juxtaposition are, in narratological if not in generic terms, identical. Whether such identity is an artifact of the way in which specific stories are constructed or whether it has some more profound and wide-ranging narratological or even ontological significance—whether, in other words, the metanarration of time travel is truly a basic feature of the way in which we tell even the most conventional stories—remains an open question, and one that I will pursue in greater detail especially in the book's second half. For now, the apparent structural equivalence of the time travel plot with more conventional plots should at least indicate how a time machine might duplicate some of the fundamental actions of narratives generally. The timer appears to do exactly what plots do already, but in some sense more *literally*.

As Mieke Bal notes, within conventional narratives, temporal discontinuities, dilations, and repetitions occur constantly, "often without being noticed by the reader."[3] Indeed, in most stories, quite drastic manipulations of chronology on the level of form—hiatuses, flashbacks, sudden temporal cuts, overlapping events—are cheerfully tolerated by the story's audience. Even when such manipulations are directly foregrounded, for instance by an explicitly reminiscing chronicler or by a Scheherazadean metanarrator, the reader usually has little difficulty receiving such plotlike narratological exposures as unobtrusive (if that is the author's goal) and, in a word, "normal," or as what Gérard Genette calls "classical."[4]

However, in a time travel story, even the most elementary experience of plot involves an essentially abnormal metanarrative intervention, since the "classical" mechanisms of temporal discontinuity, dilation, or reordering are now introduced directly into the story itself, in the guise of literal devices or mechanisms. They are no longer either tacit or formalistic but rather actual and eventlike—or, in terms of the fiction itself, *real*—a fact that makes time travel fiction already, and inherently, a fiction explicitly about the temporality of literary form. Simply to follow the action of *Up the Line,* the reader must directly relate the two divergent time frames experienced by Jud and Metaxas, and then further compare them against the hypothetical background of a metaframe that leaves entirely open the question of whether the original two time frames might ultimately be reconciled. Indeed, it is this potential irreconcilability—the possibility that, for instance, Metaxas could kill rather than solicit Jud's "great-great-multi-great-grandmother"—that gives the science fiction reader, as well as the consumer of time travel stories in the broader culture, a glimpse of what is known as a paradox story. But even where it doesn't eventuate in paradox, or for that matter in any logical or causal conundrum, the potential irreconcilability of narrative frames within a time travel story still potentially imparts to the reader's experience an unusual and subversive novelty, one that automatically exposes and destabilizes some of the basic conditions of story construction.

In short, the novelty of the time machine is simultaneously *outré* and utterly basic to what we accept as normal or classical storytelling. We are able to see this most clearly in narratological terms, because the time travel plot is essentially a creative abuse of the usual narratological rules, or even a direct mimesis or parody of narrative formation. Narratologists, following the tradition of early formalist criticism, distinguish between "story" and "plot," or what the Russian formalists termed *fabula* and *sjuzhet,* a terminology I will revisit at greater length in Chapter 4.[5] *Fabula* is the ostensible underlying sequence of story events in a narrative, *sjuzhet* its re-formation as a specific plot, the reconstructed montage of story elements arranged by an author within a given set of generic rules or protocols. In conventional narratives, temporal alterations such as changes of order or pace, repetitions, and the skipping of time occur on the level of *sjuzhet,* and the rules governing plot construction within genres allow for considerable and even radical variations in the order or frequency of *sjuzhet* events. So when Clarissa Dalloway is suddenly no longer on Bond Street but rather back at her house, or when we see Charles Foster Kane decrepit and dying in an early scene of *Citizen Kane* and then as a young child in a later scene, such chronological anomalies or "anachronies"[6] are immediately understood to be artifacts of plot manipulation arranged on the level of *sjuzhet,* and not characteristic of the underlying *fabula,* which is presumed to remain linear and chronological. Such a presumption is tantamount to asserting that neither *Mrs. Dalloway* nor *Citizen Kane* is either a supernatural or a time travel story, and that we (readers, writers, audience, and critics) continue to assume that Clarissa "really" takes more or less the usual number of minutes to walk home from Bond Street, and that Charles Foster Kane "really" grows from childhood to old age instead of the reverse. Indeed, the presumption of chronological regularity within the underlying story material is crucial for the coherence of the classical narrative. Otherwise, the potentially extreme temporal variations of the *sjuzhet* would emerge as merely fragmented and anachronic. Indeed, they can easily be made to emerge that way within a variety of experimental fictions, for instance in Jorge Luis Borges's "Garden of Forking Paths," Martin Amis's *Time's Arrow,* or Philip K. Dick's *Time Out of Joint.* We might even preliminarily define the "normal" narrative—so closely related to Genette's "classical"—as one in which divergences from regular chronology occur *only* on the level of the *sjuzhet,* never in the *fabula.*[7]

By contrast, in a time travel fiction, even a relatively normal one, no such underlying coherence in the *fabula* may be assumed. A time machine potentially alters the chronology of story events themselves, making it impossible to presuppose or determine any single consistent relationship between *fabula* and *sjuzhet,* and requiring, therefore, more or less artificial or narratively supplemental mechanisms of coherence. In Silverberg's *Up the Line,* the interval over which Jud jumps using the time machine cannot, in principle, be recovered or reconstructed in the mode of three days that really passed in the *fabula* while only the reader jumped over them in the *sjuzhet.* Here it is no longer possible at all to decide whether these three days have really taken place without first selecting a privileged viewpoint other than Jud's (for instance, that of Metaxas), or without explicitly adopting some further metanarrative frame within which the several actual or potential views of the story's chronology might be contrasted and adjudicated. It would not even be possible to declare that Jud's three days are "gone," excised altogether from the *fabula,* since any time travel story necessarily offers multiple interpretations of the existence or nonexistence of such durations and of the agents who experience or witness them. We must say instead that the ontological status of these three days, as well as their partial or quasi assimilation by the domains of either *fabula* or *sjuzhet,* has been rendered radically ambiguous. Such radical structural ambiguity becomes even more obvious as soon as time travelers begin to do more unusual things, such as relive their own pasts, meet or duplicate themselves, retroactively eliminate slices of history, reexperience those same slices in altered versions or "lines," and so on. What "normal" narratives can bring about only in the form of fantasy, allegory, or formalistic experimentation, time travel narratives accomplish in the mode of unfussy realism, a literal or mimetic description of charac- ters, events, and machines. Hence "anachrony" in a time travel story can never be either dismissed as provisional or finessed as a mere artifact of retelling; it belongs ineluctably to the *fabula* itself, and remains fully present in all its potentially paradoxical provocation.

In this sense, time travel fiction directly represents, on the level of straightforward content, not only the processes by which narratives are formed, but also the experimental conditions under which controlled narratological inquiry might take place, and "normal" or "classical" narrative procedures and techniques be manipulated and productively malformed. Even the naïve reader or audience of a time travel fiction becomes, by default or exigency, a practicing narrative theorist or a practical experimenter in the philosophy of time. As I show in more detail beginning in Chapter 3, all narratives, even "normal" ones, can be read only in a kind of hyper-space or metaverse, a quasi-transcendental "space" in which the relation between always potentially divergent lines of narration is negoti- ated and (usually) brought back to coherence and synchrony. The reader of time travel fiction, even in its most mainstream or adolescent-literary modes, is entirely familiar with this hyperspatial or metaversal realm of narratological negotiation. It is the very medium through which the time-traveling protagonist, who is *de facto* never either fully in or fully outside of the plot, realistically travels. Narratology is the very *mise-en-scène* of time travel fiction, and time travel itself the machinery by which narrative is manufactured.

Second reading: Psychohistoriography in Behold the Man

In my second reading, from Michael Moorcock's 1968 novel *Behold the Man,* the sorts of eccentric plot twists encountered in Silverberg's humorously narcissistic and oedipal adventure are considerably dampened, even as *Behold the Man* contrives to maintain in more polemical tension much of the potentially paradoxical relation between its *fabula* and *sjuzhet.* Indeed, Moorcock inflects this relation with a pathos engendered by the difficulty of interpreting and retelling, with any real precision and consistency, our most elemental or influential stories and histories. Overall, Moorcock is considerably more interested in the underlying psychological motivations of such temporal and historical manipulation, which for Silverberg remain largely a formalistic game.

Moorcock's protagonist, Karl Glogauer, an alienated and melancholic late-modern subject, exhibits an unhealthy obsession with two types of historical questions: first, his own recurring self-destructive relationships with women, and, second, the apparently more objective or pedantic theological question of the divinity of Christ. Being keen to circumvent the former question by way of pursuing the latter, and having become acquainted with the inventor of a time machine, Glogauer offers himself as test subject for a time travel experiment, on condition that he be sent back to A.D. 29 in order to witness the crucifixion of Jesus. Following a crash landing in the desert outside Jerusalem, in which Glogauer's delicate, liquid-filled time machine bursts open and he is stranded in the past, he soon acclimates very nicely to the first century, even given his limited knowledge of the local dialect of Aramaic. He gradually adopts the superstitious and self-mortifying culture of John the Baptist and his sect of Essenes. However, despite a determined search, Glogauer has difficulty turning up any evidence of Jesus of Nazareth, or even of Mary or Joseph. When he finally does track down the "holy family," he discovers that Joseph has deserted his wife, Mary herself is anything but virginal, and, to his greatest disappointment, the adolescent Jesus is misshapen and mentally disabled, an unpromising candidate for a messiah.

However, by the time Glogauer gets around to making these unsettling discoveries, his odd and repeated inquiries about a Nazarene carpenter named Jesus, along with his own anachronistic quirks of character and his apparent ability to predict impending events with uncanny detail, have attracted attention in Nazareth and Bethlehem. The locals begin to consider him a prophet.[8] As the novel proceeds toward its conclusion, Glogauer embraces the prophetic role into which his incongruity has thrust him, and willingly acts the part of Jesus of Nazareth. He then sets about to orchestrate the series of events that he knows, with an ironically detailed retrospect, to have made up the end of Jesus's life. Ultimately, he arranges to have himself crucified by the Romans, all the while scrupulously duplicating Jesus's specific gestures and expressions, which he recalls from the Gospels and histories he had obsessively studied in his "earlier" life two millennia hence.

Unlike Silverberg, Moorcock is not concerned with creating suspense about the paradoxical twists in his plot. Relatively early in the novel, it becomes clear what is going to happen to Karl Glogauer, although, in proportion to the strength of his own delusions, Glogauer himself is slower than the reader to figure it out. Here, for instance, is his initial conversation with John the Baptist just after crashing in the desert and being rescued by the Essenes:

> "So you are from Egypt. That is what we thought. And evidently you are a magus, with your strange clothes and your chariot of iron drawn by spirits. Good. Your name is Jesus, I am told, and you are the Nazarene."
> The other man must have mistaken Glogauer's inquiry as a statement of his own name. He smiled and shook his head.
> "I seek Jesus, the Nazarene," he said.[9]

What Glogauer seeks, however, is both the actual man Jesus and, in a sense that is not yet apparent to him, a more complex amalgam of theological and psychological cathexes, which in a more straightforwardly modern theological vocabulary might be described as the "sense of Christ within" him, or, in a psychoanalytic vocabulary, as an ego-ideal. In short, Glogauer himself now gradually evolves into the person or archetype he seeks, a halting and uncanny change for him because he remains unaware of the full range of his own motivations:

> Karl Glogauer grew his hair long and let his beard come unchecked. His face and body were soon burned dark by the sun. He mortified his flesh and starved himself and chanted his prayers beneath the sun, as [the Essenes] did. But he rarely heard God and only once thought he saw an archangel with wings of fire.
>
> One day they took him to the river and baptized him with the name he had first given John the Baptist. They called him Emmanuel.
>
> The ceremony, with its chanting and its swaying, was very heady and left him completely euphoric and happier than he ever remembered.[10]

In *Behold the Man,* the mechanics of time travel, now in the hands of a more contemplative and psychologically incisive writer than Silverberg, readily permits complex intersections between a number of the book's themes: Glogauer's neurotic obsessions with certain sexual objects (for instance, crucifixes between women's breasts); Glogauer's half-hearted efforts to do away with himself, his "martyr complex"; Glogauer's obsession with the theological problem of Christ's divinity; Glogauer's sense of dislocation or alienation in the present day, his feeling that he would be more at home in the past; the philosophical or psychological significance of Jesus as a paragon of self-sacrifice or self-mortification; the variety of sexual subtexts of Christian doctrine; the question of the relation between Christ's godliness and an individual person's inherent divinity; the psychical and sociological motivations of the actual historical Jesus and his followers; and the significance of fate (e.g., in Jesus's prediction of Judas's betrayal) and its ironic correlation with the "predictions" of the time traveler. Of course, with the exception only of the last one, these are all themes raised in any number of other literary, philosophical, and theological works. However, a time travel narrative, because of the way in which its literal devices bear upon or even directly affect the basic structure of the narrative itself, may be more likely than most popular literary forms to raise several such issues simultaneously. In that sense, presumably, the value of a book such as *Behold the Man* might be its capacity, within a relatively accessible generic medium, to address problems that are usually relegated to "higher" literary types, or at least to more self-consciously experimental and philosophically oriented ones.

But the more substantial difference that the time travel story makes, as I also wished to show in the Silverberg example, is not the specific theoretical or philosophical issue at hand, nor its ostensible or unusual level of complexity, but rather the *mode* in which that issue is woven into the substance of the narrative itself—namely, in the form of literal or realistic plot events. In this sense, the most interesting problem in Moorcock's novel is neither psychological nor theological per se, but rather historiographical or, in a term I promise not to reuse, psychohistoriographical. It concerns the meaning of the individual historical event and its capacity to affect and define the broader historical record, as well as, alternatively, the capacity of that historical record to define and characterize the individual event. In turn, the various psychological issues raised in *Behold the Man* are tethered to a larger, more central historiographical question, as Moorcock himself indicates superficially through his frequent allusions to Jung's theory of archetypes; what tendencies or forces motivate the historical event or are motivated by it? This question of the relationship between event and history is perhaps the central problem of modern historiography, dating back at least to Hegel. It concerns what Hayden White calls the fundamental "ambiguity of the term 'history,'" which "unites the objective with the subjective side" and "comprehends not less what has *happened* than the *narration* of what has happened."[11]

Moorcock, pursuing this historiographical inquiry within the terms of his own narrower interest in Jung, composes a series of subtle jokes about the "inevitability" of the story of Christ and about Glogauer's ironic attempts to co-opt or reinforce that inevitability:

> "There must be twelve," he said to them one day, and he smiled. "There must be a zodiac."
> And he picked them out by their names. "Is there a man here called Peter? Is there one called Judas?"[12]

Later, as Glogauer singles out Judas to help him—foretelling, in some ambiguous sense just as Jesus himself did in the Gospels, which one of the disciples will betray him—the ironic juxtaposition between historical fact and archetype or allegory is perfectly apparent:

> "Judas?" said Glogauer hesitantly.
> There was one called Judas.
> "Yes, master," he said. He was tall and good looking with curly red hair and intelligent eyes. Glogauer believed he was an epileptic.
> Glogauer looked thoughtfully at Judas Iscariot. "I will want you to help me later," he said, "when we have entered Jerusalem."
> "How, master?"
> "You must take a message to the Romans."
> "The Romans?" Judas looked troubled. "Why?"
> "It must be the Romans. It can't be the Jews. They would use stones or a stake or an axe. I'll tell you more when the time comes."[13]

A consideration of the inevitability of the past summons an ambiguity so basic to the problem of history that it cannot be contemplated without opening up, even within the course of the popular fiction, an inquiry into the ontology of the event itself. Is the "must" that accompanies the story of the crucifixion—"it must be the Romans"—constituted by (a) the sheer empirical facticity of the historical event itself (i.e., in the actual past it really was the Romans who crucified Jesus); or (b) the mythological or suprahistorical inexorability of the conflict that the crucifixion represents, a conflict between allegorical figurations of imperial-bureaucratic force and individualistic (or monotheistic) subjectivity; or (c) the weighty exigency of the two millennia of subsequent historical events and trends, in light of which the crucifixion has been ceaselessly, but of course retroactively and even circularly, interpreted as an essential, archetypal cause? We could phrase the trilemma this way: is the historical event, in and of itself, a blankly preliminary cause, an overdetermined revisionist effect, or a mere component or signifier of some even larger story or allegory?[14] Or, yet again, to insert some of the language of time travel back into the three possibilities I have suggested: is the inevitability of the crucifixion the result of the somehow unalterable pastness of that event, the result of the deliberate intervention of the time traveler from out of the present (the historian? the Church?), or the result of a powerful inertia or causelike weight of history itself?

In Chapters 4 through 6, I will have occasions to discuss in greater detail the "conservative" characteristic of time travel fiction, which, perhaps surprisingly, tends to restore histories rather than to destroy or subvert them. This tendency toward historical conservation, like the ambiguity of the relation between present and past more generally, is a fundamental philosophical problem, opening up questions about the tendentiousness of events themselves and of the momentum or inertia of their histories. Most important, the time travel story efficiently conjoins questions of form, psychology, and history within the context of a fundamental historiographical query presented straightforwardly on the level of plot: How, quite literally, is the past event reconstructed by or from the present? How is it discovered, or made, to be "real"? *When* is it caused?

The time travel paradox initiated by Karl Glogauer—that the presence and significance of the story of Jesus within cultural history result from a temporal intervention out of the present—is a tale about how psychological motivations or, more concretely, masochistic and obsessive fixations, cathect, repeat, and continually reestablish the larger historical record, in essence preserving it or rendering it history in the first place. Moorcock's novel thus compels a question about the conditions within the present that drive us toward certain segments of the historical past—that is, to history's ostensibly crucial moments. This is a radical formulation of historiography, a formulation that oversteps any lukewarm inquiry into the present's effect on the past—indeed, shortcuts the whole fraught philosophical question of "presentism"—and advances directly to the basic structure of the past itself, its reality, as well as the connection of that reality to the ways in which stories are retold. In time travel fiction, the fundamental historiographical question—how is the past reconstructed by or within the present?—becomes a literal *topos,* is told as a tale, or is enacted by a real person seated in a vehicle or machine.

Third reading: The ontology of the event in "All the Myriad Ways"

My third reading belongs to the science fiction subgenre sometimes referred to as the alternate universe or alternate history story, in which the time machine transports its rider not into the past or future but rather into alternate timelines—or, to use a term from physics that also works for narrative theory, worldlines. In Larry Niven's 1968 short story "All the Myriad Ways," pilots flying for a company called Crosstime, Inc., take their vehicles to parallel universes, or "branching" worlds, and then return to the primary world of the story, bringing back exotic artifacts and information about alternate histories. Part of the story focuses on the trouble that Crosstime pilots encounter when they must distinguish the innumerable alternate worlds from one another, and their invention of technological controls for accurately determining which worlds they are traveling to or from. "In those first months," Niven writes, "the vehicles had gone off practically at random," but now, since the engineers at Crosstime have improved their machinery and also refined their archival and commercial goals in exploiting alternate timelines, "the pinpointing was better":

> Vehicles could select any branch they preferred. Imperial Russia, Amerindian America, the Catholic Empire, the dead worlds. Some of the dead worlds were hells of radioactive dust and intact but deadly artifacts. From these worlds Crosstime pilots brought strange and beautiful works of art which had to be stored behind leaded glass.[15]

Here, as in many other examples of the alternate universe subgenre, the language of a much older type of speculative romance—"Imperial Russia, Amerindian America, the Catholic Empire"—is directly appended to the generic language of science fiction ("dead worlds," "radioactive dust") in order to form a kind of fable about historical evolution and variation. As I discuss in Chapter 1, in older speculative fiction, especially in utopian or dystopian romance written before the turn of the twentieth century, the scientific machinery of travel itself would more likely have remained incidental or subordinate to the writer's presentation of an alternative sociopolitical milieu. However, in a science fiction alternate universe story such as Niven's, something like the opposite is true: history, culture, politics, religion, and so forth remain the background for a speculation about the specific mechanisms of movement and travel.

Niven's alternate universe story belongs to a class that arises directly from the reception by popular fiction writers of the "many-worlds" interpretation of quantum mechanics first proposed by Hugh Everett III in his 1957 Ph.D. dissertation and floated as a controversial hypothesis among physicists through the 1960s.[16] In Everett's interpretation of quantum theory, as Bryce DeWitt explains it in a 1970 gloss:

> This universe is constantly splitting into a stupendous number of branches, all resulting from the measurementlike interactions between its myriads of components. Moreover, every quantum transition taking place on every star, in every galaxy, in every remote corner of the universe is splitting our local world on earth into myriads of copies of itself.[17]

Consistent with this interpretation, the branching worlds of Niven's story are, as his title suggests, also "myriad," because the pivotal incidents that give rise to them are as indeterminately numerous as the virtually countless number of quantum events. At every moment, this theoretical model suggests—although we cannot take for granted, particularly at the quantum level, that we know even in a general sense what such a "moment" consists of—alternate histories are possible, and if possible then also real. Thus any palpable difference between two nearby branching worlds might be, from the relatively coarse perspective of a Crosstime pilot's perception, vanishingly minute: "The latest vehicles could reach worlds so like this one that it took a week of research to find the difference. In theory they could get even closer."[18] Nothing but another story, for instance another "week of research," would be sufficient to distinguish them.

From a narrative-theoretical viewpoint, it is quite interesting to contemplate two worlds that are declared, theoretically or in the abstract, to be different, but between which no concrete or practical difference can be discovered. The positing of such a pure narrative simulacrum suggests that Niven is interested (even if not fully explicitly) in theorizing the narrative event as such. He is asking, in essence, precisely what are the formal, aesthetic, and/or ontological markers of the event that could constitute a moment of narrative difference—the markers, perhaps, of fictionality, or of what analytic philosophers sometimes call "incompleteness," as a means of distinguishing between the real and its alternates.[19] Niven, in order to allegorize the ambiguity of narrative differences encountered by the Crosstime pilot who tries to return to his own worldline, continues to borrow freely from quantum theory's model of events as uncertain across a probability continuum:

> There was a phenomenon called "the broadening of the bands." . . .
>   When a vehicle left its own present, a signal went on in the hangar, a signal unique to that ship. When the pilot wanted to return, he simply cruised across the appropriate band of probabilities until he found the signal. The signal marked his own unique present.[20]

In a Crosstime ship, the signal that marks the pilot's "unique present" is a clear-cut electronic manifestation, for instance a reading on a meter or gauge, or a visual or audible blip. Thus, in the science-fictional world of vehicles that use this sort of convenient technology, the pilot is able to identify straightforwardly ("simply cruise") his or her own present via the unambiguously legible mechanism of this unique marker, a positive signifier, so to speak, of the continuous and self-identical reality to which he properly belongs, his home world. However, because such signifiers in the non-fictional world are neither so present nor so unique, we are perhaps invited to be suspicious of the very idea of a signal or device that could assure one of a return to one's own reality, especially once the possibility of an infinitely divergent set of alternates has been introduced by the story itself or by the underlying physical theory upon which the story is based. Where, in the real world, could we look for signals that would distinguish an original worldline from some alternate one, or an actual one from a fictional one? Where is the signal for the originality or self-consistency of the real world?

Niven is quite cognizant of the profound problem that his fictional signal exposes concerning the artificiality and arbitrariness of narratives about reality once time travel is given free rein. Indeed, he gives the impression of being appalled by the "horrible multiplicity" that results.[21] In a later preface written for the story, Niven complains, presumably with his tongue half in cheek:

> I spent time, sweat, effort, and agony to become what I am. It irritates me to think that there are Larry Nivens working as second-rate mathematicians or adequate priests or first-rate playboys, who went bust or made their fortunes on the stock market. I even sweated over my mistakes, and I want them to count.[22]

Without presuming that Niven has read Nietzsche's *The Gay Science,* this is nonetheless a close counterpart to Nietzsche's earliest formulation of the doctrine of eternal return, presented as a thought experiment about moral decisions under the burden of an infinite proliferation of real presents: would you still choose precisely the life you are now living, even were it to be repeated throughout eternity, given your knowledge of the myriad possibilities you might have chosen instead—or, in light of such a choice, would the suddenly immense question of your decision cripple you, cause you to "gnash your teeth and curse"?[23] Like Nietzsche, Niven observes the moral crisis into which the scenario of infinitely multiplied choice plunges the conventions of narrative, which appear generally to presume that certain choices are more plausible or acceptable than others, lending themselves to stories that give at least the impression of logical or natural bias. Alternate universe stories, in their role as ontological thought experiments, effectively undercut that presumption, introducing the disturbing possibility that there is no natural criterion for preferring certain lines over others: "[E]very time you've made a decision in your life, you made it all possible ways," Niven writes; "I see anything less than that as a cheat, an attempt to make the idea easier to swallow."[24] Thus at least one ethical upshot of the alternate universe story is the death of narrative significance itself or, at the very least, the exposure of the "cheat" required to keep it alive.[25] If all narrative lines are equally possible, then the logical or naturalistic basis for realism, in the most general sense, can no longer be used to distinguish better from worse narratives, or even to pick out specifically *narrative* lines from mere amalgamations of coincidence.

I will return, at certain moments in my argument, to the question of narrative ethics, if that's what this precipitous opening of narrative possibility really amounts to, as well as to the narrative-theoretical question of fictionality. But to continue first with the more basic epistemological quandary that the apparatus of Niven's story has broached: I have been asking, what would ever correspond to a "unique signal," one that could allow one to identify one's own subjective present, one's "line," as the proper or primary world, as opposed to the branching one? What signal could enable us to call one history real and another a fiction or fantasy, even before we arrive at the apparently ethical question of many possible or plausible narrative sequences? The time travel story permits Niven to pose such questions in an especially elegant fashion. Continuing from the quotation above:

> The signal marked his own unique present.
>   Only it didn't. The pilot always returned to find a clump of signals, a broadened band. The longer he stayed away, the broader was the signal band. His own world had

continued to divide after his departure, in a constant stream of decisions being made
both ways.[26]

This pilot, returning from another cross-time world, encounters, in practical terms,
precisely the same quandary that the narratologist or philosopher encounters in theoretical terms. Confronted with a "clump" of signals, the pilot implicitly asks what remains
of the unique difference that constitutes the identity of *his* world, the one he left, or, more
exactly, the one he is still ostensibly *in,* as a temporally coherent and continuous subject.
At best, he is now living in a world-simulacrum, effectively or pragmatically the same
as his original world only because *he does not yet know how to tell the story that would
distinguish them.*[27] Yet the pilot's quandary represents that of any reader who "travels" to
alternate worlds while remaining a subject within the home world of the drama of reading, and whose reliance upon the spatiotemporal coherence and consistency of that
home world helps him or her to distinguish fact from fiction, reality from mere plot. There
are those of us who don't make these distinctions as easily or automatically, and who
may have trouble either inhabiting or discarding a supplemental story about the act of
interpreting "the real," for instance the small child, the schizophrenic, the psychoanalyst,
the skeptical fact-checker, or the everyday dreamer. For these more incredulous types,
the seemingly natural assumption that either a subjective or objective self-identity—what
Philip K. Dick calls the "inner conviction of oneness [that] is the most cherished opinion of
Western Man"[28]—will survive the act of differentiating between any "real" narrative world
and a hypothetical or fantastical one is not nearly so certain an assumption as we, in our
narratologically coherent waking lives (or fantasies), would generally like to believe.

In essence, Niven's Crosstime pilots disclose a situation in which the arbitrary and
tenuous conditions of the ostensible coherence of our "normal" world are quite literally
exposed:

> Usually it didn't matter. Any signal the pilot chose represented the world he had left. And
> since the pilot himself had a choice, he naturally returned to them all.[29]

The worlds in proximity to the one to which the pilot returns are similar enough to his
home world to render the difference between them—for there *is* always some difference,
or else there would be no question of describing them as "alternates"—pragmatically
indistinguishable.[30] Again one can ask, what is the criterion for this pragmatic indistin-
guishability? That is to say, precisely when would the difference between this and that
narrated world be of *no* pragmatic consequence—like "two worlds that differ by only
the disposition of two grains of sand on a beach," as Keith Laumer suggests, "or of two
molecules within a grain of sand"?[31] We can only use narrative theory, either explicit or
tacit, to answer this question, for the consequence of the difference constituted by a
divergent narrative line is determinable only by the participant within yet another story,
a participant who *notes* that difference and whose own further *narrative* of the history of
difference has therefore altered his or her relation, as subject, to the events in which he
or she participates.

Niven gives a single dramatic instance of such a narrated difference, one of a type that is virtually canonical within time travel literature, for reasons I will have occasion later to discuss:

> There was a pilot by the name of Gary Wilcox. He had been using his vehicle for experiments, to see how close he could get to his own timeline and still leave it. Once, last month, he had returned twice.[32]

Here is a difference sufficiently dramatic to expose a pragmatic narrative discrepancy: two Wilcoxes in the same worldline. We might therefore call the Crosstime pilot Wilcox himself a type of "laboratory narratologist"—and, indeed, Wilcox has been conducting something like field research in narrative theory, using his vehicle to try to determine the precise interval between two different worldlines, the minimum quantum of difference required to establish a pragmatic distinction. In Niven's words, he is trying to find out "how close he could get to his own timeline and still leave it." But what Wilcox seeks is basically what Tzvetan Todorov, summarizing the research of earlier structural narratologists, calls the "smallest narrative unit," or what Eugene Dorfman even more pithily calls "the narreme," the minimum divergence that could be identified as proper narrative variation.[33]

Niven, whose tale is largely premised on his own mistrust both of time travel conventions and of alternate universe stories generally, characteristically recounts Wilcox's experiment with overdramatic bravado: the Wilcox who returns twice commits suicide, as do large numbers of other people after the establishment of Crosstime, Inc. In reality (if we may continue to speak this way), the difference between narrative lines could be dramatized by events much more subtle than the return of two Wilcoxes or their suicides. In fact, it could be dramatized by any minimal event that failed to coincide with the "normal" narrative that keeps coherent, without threat of hypothetical otherness, the thread of a narrating subject. If Wilcox someday discovered, after his return, that his memory of some specific episode differed minutely from his wife's or commander's memory of it, or that some empirical fact he had always assumed to be true was now false, or that some person at the fringes of his acquaintance now failed to recognize him, we would have, in less melodramatic terms than Niven's but in terms no less philosophically significant, the same quandary, the same divergence between a subject's putatively self-identical narrative world (or "band" of indistinguishable "nearby" worlds) and a world in which a new history has been commenced and must now be renarrated. Ultimately, what Niven offers is a description of the epistemological conditions of *any* act of narrative, which commences at the moment in which the divergence between the subject's own world, on the one hand, and the hypothetical or alternate world constituted by a concrete divergence, on the other hand, must itself be renarrated.

It is therefore to his credit that Niven ends his story, not with the rather pallid psychological insight that an infinity of moral choices is equivalent to no choice at all, or is an impetus for suicide, but instead with a narratological complication that casts his plot into a kind of interworld limbo, fundamentally unfixable with respect to the specific worldline it asserts as primary, or with respect to the specific narrative closure for which it therefore opts. At one point in the story, the narrator, Detective-Lieutenant Gene Trimble, recalls that "they've found a world line in which Kennedy the First was assassinated," suggesting, of course, that the history of the *present* story is already an alternate one, in which there exists such a figure as "Kennedy the First."[34] Niven uses this brief reference to alternate political histories in order to engage in some slight humor about the 1960s American fascination with the Kennedys and their pseudoroyal "Camelot," a joke that obliquely alludes again to the prehistory of time travel literature in the sociopolitical fictions of utopian and scientific romance. In the late 1960s of Niven's story, Kennedy (the king, not the president) is still alive, and with tongue in cheek Niven declines to consider whether that alternate set of facts makes any real difference. But the brief reference to "Kennedy the First" alerts the reader to a basic uncertainty in the story concerning the precise relationship between fictional and nonfictional elements. In turn, this uncertainty anticipates a curious denouement in which a series of multiple and logically incompatible narrative lines are offered side by side:

> Casual murder, casual suicide, casual crime. Why not? If alternate universes are a reality, then cause and effect are an illusion. The law of averages is a fraud. You can do anything, and one of you will, or did.
>
> Gene Trimble looked at the clean and loaded gun on his desk. Well, why not? . . .
>
> And he ran out of the office shouting, "Bentley, listen! I've got the answer . . ."
>
> And he stood up slowly and left the office shaking his head. This was the answer, and it wasn't any good. The suicides, murders, casual crimes would continue. . . .
>
> And he suddenly laughed and stood up. Ridiculous! Nobody dies for a philosophical point! . . .
>
> And he reached for the intercom and told the man who answered to bring him a sandwich and some coffee. . . .[35]

Narrative rules, even clichés, govern whatever aesthetic or ethical choices remain to be made between the various lines juxtaposed here, even if, strictly speaking, cause-and-effect does not. For instance, in at least one of the lines, the loaded gun that appeared earlier in the story must be fired; in another, the crime gets solved. So in the story's end—if that's what it is—the criterion that determines the choice of closure is purely a narrative rule or a generic convention, even as the epistemological relationship between narrative lines and worldlines is being radically reinterpreted:

> And picked the gun off the newspapers, looked at it for a long moment, then dropped it in the drawer. His hands began to shake. On a world line very close to this one. . . .
>
> And he picked the gun off the newspapers, put it to his head and
> fired. The hammer fell on an empty chamber.
> fired. The gun jerked up and blasted a hole in the ceiling.
> fired. The bullet tore a furrow in his scalp. took off the top of his head.[36]

With neither epistemological nor ontological grounds for preferring one set of events over the others—because all are equally real within the story's myriad alternatives—we can, finally, rely only on narrative means to select at least one of them or to place them all in a plausible order. The ontological equivalence of several contingent possibilities here comes up against the necessity of positing a sufficient aesthetic reason for preferring one possibility over the others. This is an old philosophical problem. As Leibniz beautifully expresses it, the seeming contingency of such myriad possible events, their apparent equivalence or homogeny, is only an artifact of an observer's continued "confus[ion]" about the full set of causes leading to the single one of them that will, in the end, have remained plausible—which is to say, in a truly "sufficient" world, possible.[37] In any fully determined (and fully transparent) universe, were it only "distinct" to us, one worldline alone would retain sufficient reason to exist, and therefore only one ending could result from the infinitely interwoven arrangements of events and causes that preceded it in the underlying story.

Of course, the question remains open whether, or to what degree, a fictional narrative is a fully determined universe, and whether, either in fiction or reality, any distinct observation of deterministic lines is possible or even imaginable. Such questions are especially pressing within alternate universe stories, which literalize their means (here, a Crosstime ship and a "unique signal" on a gauge) for creating and observing multiplicity and contingency, just as a time travel paradox story like Silverberg's or Moorcock's literalizes its means for creating narrative lacunae or historical precedence. In this sense, Niven's story is very much like a quantum theorist's thought experiment in which hypothetical conditions of observation (or "measurement") are constructed and played out—a "Schrödinger's cat" of narration, literally depicting both the radical epistemological ambiguity of narrative alternates and the aesthetic means of their final collapse into genre.

Let us be quite precise about what is at stake in the ontological game Niven plays here. In one of the responses to Hugh Everett's "relative state" or "many-worlds" thesis, which I mentioned above, John Wheeler notes that Everett's formulation of quantum theory has the effect of eliminating any possibility of a useful "external observer" for whom "probabilities are assigned to the possible outcomes of a measurement," and who could therefore determine which result, or "line," is the most likely consequence of an observed event.[38] The status of observation in quantum theory is of course a matter of extensive analysis, and nothing to be taken for granted. However, as Wheeler suggests, the traditional Copenhagen interpretation does still posit an "ultimate" determination of that outcome "by way of observations of a classical character made from outside the quantum system"[39]—in brief, the system "collapses" onto a definite state when measured. Everett's model differs: "Every attempt," as Wheeler asserts, "to ascribe probabilities to observables is as out of place in the relative state formalism as it would be in any kind of quantum physics to ascribe coordinate and momentum to a particle at the same time."[40] Indeed, Everett's theory has the effect of further exposing the arbitrariness of the imputation of "some super-observer" who is seemingly required, within the more canonical Copenhagen interpretation, to correlate, with one of the myriad possibilities prompted by a quantum event, a *single* measurement of that event in the physical world, taken with "classical" equipment.[41] In a nutshell, Everett's "relative state formalism" or, more broadly, the "many-worlds" interpretation overall, contrives to describe the full range of myriad possible outcomes of an event, but declines ever to offer an ontological basis for adjudic-ating or "collapsing" them[42]—declines, in other words, to offer what Niven offers (at first) his fictional Crosstime pilot, that "unique signal" for separating and distinguishing the various potentially observed lines, and for selecting which of them to narrate as actual. In a sense, Niven's "signal" literalizes what the Copenhagen interpretation demands but Everett's formulation prohibits: a pragmatic means of super-observation, and therefore of finally *deciding* how the story is supposed to go or was supposed to have gone.

Ultimately, therefore, the interesting thing about alternate universe fiction is that, unlike the actual spacetime continuum (or perhaps more like it than we realize), it *does* offer "unique signals" for adjudicating lines of possibility, in the form of conventions of narrative structure. Among these is the vague conglomeration of half-conscious generic rules out of which both writer and reader form the sense of an ending, rules that conventionally call for guns to be fired or crimes to be solved. Although the three final lines of Niven's story are ontologically simultaneous, their specific concrete sequence in the text, and therefore their diachronic order in the plot, is nonetheless fairly strictly constrained by genre. One of the lines, namely the one that appears last on the physical page of the story, is its *de facto* ending: Gene Trimble blows off the top of his head. The sequence of *noir* detective elements that leads to this generically consistent conclusion is in turn governed by broader structural rules that tend to favor melodramatic escalations of viol-ence near the climaxes of detective fictions. The explanation of why this should be the case might require us to traverse the entire oeuvre of structuralist narratology, with a healthy portion of genre history appended. I necessarily touch on only a small, but I hope significant, portion of that literary-theoretical landscape in this book. In a very powerful sense, the story ends as an *illustration* of itself, a visual diagramming rather than a telling of its possible outcomes. In my final two chapters, I discuss at length how and why time travel and alternate universe stories become "visual" in this way, depictions rather than narrations of their own *fabulas*. That discussion will involve, among other things, taking far more seriously and literally than narrative theorists sometimes do the structural and physical attributes of the odd term "viewpoint."

For the moment, given the specific philosophical apparatus of quantum mechanics and observability that Niven's story confronts, we may pursue this question narrowly by inquiring further about the free-indirect narrative observer who *tells* the tale, and whom the text itself exposes for severe critical scrutiny. For the quantum theorist, of course, the matter of who observes, and from what position or frame an observation is made, can never be mere postulate but must enter directly into both the calculations and the theorization of the event itself.[43] In the many-worlds interpretation, an observation remains rigorously *within* the system at hand, never outside of it, which is to say it remains precisely what it is to begin with in the history and aftermath of the quantum event: a physical fact rather than a hypothetical position or act. Hence, within the rigorously physical interpret-ation of quantum formalism provided by Everett and his followers, there is no possibility of a free-indirect viewpoint that could compare and contrast different lines of probable event-histories. Such a viewpoint would be precisely as unphysical as any other posited means of "collapsing" the possibilities onto a single measurement.

The unphysical "super-observer" who would (hypothetically) be capable of determining which event-histories are more probable than others, and, ultimately, which history is the correct description of the event, corresponds to the godlike viewpoint depicted in Leibniz's description of a determined universe: from *its* perspective, only a degree of unclarity about the sufficient reasons for events, an unclarity from which the super-observer alone would be exempt, creates the illusion that more than one line is possible. In the metaworld of all possible worlds, into which presumably only a god has a fully clear vista, the "unique signal" of each worldline shines out with the singular exactitude of logic itself, on an infinitely discernible continuum of possibility. But, to ask a question that anticipates my later discussion, how close is such a god to the entirely mundane position we describe as the narrator's point of view—how necessary, therefore, might such a god's perspective be to the telling or viewing of any story? The fact that the metaworld of the god's-eye view may be unphysical[44]—indeed, the fact that its inhabitation is rigorously excluded by the same philosophical framework that Niven adopts in order to construct a time travel or multi-universe story, the implications of which he finds so "horrible"—does not in the least prevent him from narrating the story *from* the viewpoint of that metaworld, in which the story of all stories, as it were, may be transmitted. "All the Myriad Ways"—and not just it, but finally any story that juxtaposes the fictional to the historical, the alternate to the real—is essentially a "super-observation" of multiple worlds, and (usually) a set of decisions about when and how to collapse them.

Contexts, methods, directions

I wish to mention briefly some of the fields of inquiry in which the problem of time travel has especially been of interest, and at the same time some of the contexts for the cross-disciplinary synthesis I intend to fashion in the chapters to follow.

There are two popular genres in which time travel has long played a significant role, science fiction and the romance novel. In modern romances, the time travel plot is almost exclusively a transportation medium: the hero or heroine is carried to or from a particular future or historical past, or is visited by a counterpart from that other time; some (usually) heterosexual liaison ensues. Because neither technologies of time travel, nor historicity per se, nor problems of narrative, tend to be immediately at stake in this highly regularized fiction, I will have little occasion to discuss it here, despite its considerable theoretical interest in other domains of literary studies.[45] By contrast, science fiction writers—at least after a certain historical point, as I shall detail shortly in Chapter 1—tend much more often to emphasize, over and against a political or erotic agenda, the mechanisms and significance of time travel itself, as well as its psychological, narratological, and historiographical implications. This is the case even though the viability or acceptability of time machines within the genre has been a fraught topic from at least the advent of "hard" science fiction in the late

1930s and early 1940s. Science fiction authors are divided over the generic and/or aesthetic question of whether time travel counts as proper science fiction or as "mere" fantasy, and critics have perhaps too quickly followed suit, continuing to debate whether time travel plots are legitimately "hard" or realistic.[46] Robert Silverberg himself writes in 1967:

> Among some modern science-fiction writers, stories of time-travel are looked upon with faint disdain, because they are not really "scientific." The purists prefer to place such stories in the category of science-*fantasy*, reserved for fiction based in ideas impossible to realize through modern technology.[47]

For reasons that should become clear in my brief mention of current physics to follow, as well as in my longer discussion of the origins of time travel fiction in nineteenth-century utopian romance in Chapter 1, I am not very concerned with debates over the putative hardness of time travel stories, debates that seem to me both inconsequential and obsolete alongside what I perceive to be time travel fiction's potential contribution to narratological study. The essence of time travel fiction, for the purposes of narrative-theoretical work, lies in its specific methods of constructing and juxtaposing narrative registers, layers, or lines. These methods may or may not correspond to the subgeneric or sub-subgeneric classifications of time travel stories and their paradoxes that enthusiasts (I include myself) are inclined to contemplate or dispute. Leaving such debates aside for now, the literary-critical scholarship dealing directly with time travel in science fiction is sufficiently finite to permit a summary here. I am aware of only two comprehensive books on the topic, Bud Foote's *The Connecticut Yankee in the Twentieth Century: Travel to the Past in Science Fiction* and Paul J. Nahin's *Time Machines: Time Travel in Physics, Metaphysics, and Science Fiction*, along with a number of more brief but superbly illuminating discussions by literary and film critics such as Katherine Hayles, Stanislaw Lem, Constance Penley, Brooks Landon, Vivian Sobchack, Garrett Stewart, and several others whom I will mention when their work bears on my analysis.[48]

In general, literary theorists have been relatively indifferent to time travel fiction, even where their interests unmistakably verge on the sorts of narratological questions I have attempted to raise in my three examples above. As I mentioned initially, such a dearth of attention may turn out, in future retrospect, to have been somewhat surprising. For one thing, the basic question of "fictionality," or of storytelling as "world-making," is at least as old as the theory of narrative itself, if not considerably older; similarly inveterate is the poetic conception that narratives, both fictional and nonfictional, recoup or recover past time through a kind of cerebral or conceptual "travel."[49] One might also argue that certain theoretical problems in literary modernism—for instance, Proustian *rechercher* as an immanent theorization of the structure and psychology of storytelling,[50] or Joycean and Woolfian experimentation with the spatial and temporal rearrangement of narrative forms—might have encouraged academic literary theorists to notice generic time travel fiction as an opportunity or a challenge. Of course, such notice would also require a broader shift in the object of academic literary study, from canonical texts to wholly popular and even pulp texts. This type of adjustment is proceeding apace in the academy, particularly in light of the multiplex and ironic temporalities of postmodern fiction, but is still relatively nascent, and more so in literary than in film studies. Nonetheless, it is possible to catalog, at least loosely, a series of contemporary narrative-theoretical problems that touch directly on the question of time travel, even where that question is not yet fully explicit—for instance, the problem of fictionality (Thomas Pavel, Wolfgang Iser), the problem of possible worlds and counterfactuals (Ruth Ronen, Lubomír Doležel), the problem of worldmaking and metafiction (Kendall Walton, Mieke Bal), the problem of modality and virtual reality (Marie-Laure Ryan, Monika Fludernik), and the problem of the relation between textuality and visuality (W. J. T. Mitchell, Garrett Stewart). All the theorists mentioned in these parentheses are allied with longstanding traditions of literary narratology, traditions that are in turn traceable to the formalist and structuralist underpinnings of nearly all contemporary literary theory; a continual benchmark is the work of Gérard Genette, itself grounded in both structuralism and Russian formalism. However, it may be telling that when contemporary narrative theorists refer to specific influences on their theories, such influences are often likely to come not from either literary theory or structural anthropology and linguistics but from analytic philosophy and logic.

In analytic philosophy, time travel has enjoyed a cachet it lacks among literary theorists. Philosophers interested in problems of time, causality, and philosophical realism have very often invoked time travel scenarios as cogent thought experiments. I will have occasion to examine the technics of a few of these experiments, particularly where time travel fiction itself raises philosophical or quasi-philosophical questions of causality or paradox. For now, I will note that analytic philosophers have made use of time travel to elucidate a number of canonical problems in metaphysics and logic: causality and temporal direction (Michael Dummett, Donald Davidson), personal identity or continuity through time (Daniel Dennett, Arthur Danto), causality and realism (W. V. O. Quine, Hilary Putnam), and counterfactuals and possible worlds (Nelson Goodman, David Lewis).

An amenable touchstone for analytic philosophy is, of course, theoretical physics. Particularly with respect to questions of philosophical realism, a number of the philosophers just mentioned are directly concerned with theories of time and causality in quantum mechanics, relativity theory, and thermodynamics. Recently, however, philosophical speculation within physics itself has tended to outstrip strictly disciplinary philosophy, as a result of a burgeoning of speculations about time and causality following the work of Stephen Hawking in the 1980s and continuing with contemporary research into multiverse cosmologies and, among other topics, quantum computing. Thus, within physics itself, the once-benighted "fantasy" of time travel has experienced a surprising renaissance, and is now widely considered to be both a valuable logical exercise and a potential physical experiment. Such legitimacy is in turn reflected in science fiction, to the degree it tends to follow the lead of scientists. Where theoretical physics touches on questions of time travel and narrative, I will reference canonical work by Einstein, Bohr, Gödel, Heisenberg, Everett, and Hawking. And I will also have occasion to refer to certain more current lay depictions of physical theory, written mainly by physicists, that consider time travel both as an immediately pressing issue in itself and as an access to fundamental physical problems, for instance the interpretation of causality and the direction of time (Igor Novikov, Kip Thorne) and the feasibility of parallel universe or multiverse models (Richard Gott, David Deutsch, Brian Greene).

Genre history

I wish briefly to anticipate the unconventional, even slightly eccentric history of time travel fiction that I will be assembling alongside my analyses of specific theoretical problems within time travel stories. The development of time travel fiction has an internal trajectory that proceeds somewhat independently from science fiction overall, in keeping with its relatively iconoclastic relationship with that larger genre. As I have begun to do in this Introduction, throughout the book I will be construing time travel fiction as a certain variety of self-conscious narratological self-depiction—what I will sometimes describe as a literalization of structuring conditions of storytelling, and eventually as a diagramming or even a "filming" of such conditions. In this specific sense, time travel fiction posits or projects its own culmination—which is not the same as saying that it *ends*—at the formal extreme to which such a narratological self-depiction might be pushed. Indeed, in my second "Historical Interval," between Chapters 2 and 3, I suggest that it would already be possible to view the "closed loop" or "time loop" story, a form of paradox fiction that peaks in the early 1940s, as this culmination. I am far less concerned with the strict correctness of this revisionist historical claim, or of the watershed moment it posits, than I am with the assistance it might provide in delineating key theoretical problems within distinct periods or phases of time travel fiction. The configuration of these phases also has consequences for the way I organize my chapters in the book, so I want to sketch it briefly in advance. More detailed discussions of its implications will follow, especially in the first few chapters and "Intervals."

In each of its three phases, time travel fiction is influenced and even defined by specific developments in the popularization of science. The first phase I identify is that of "evolutionary" utopian travel, or of the "macrologue," a term I explicate in the first chapter. It runs from the late 1880s to approximately 1905. This first phase commences with the rapid burgeoning of utopian romance following Edward Bellamy's *Looking Backward,* and concludes with the almost equally abrupt decline of utopianism around the turn of the twentieth century. During this phase, time travel is always a subsidiary narrative device, utilized in reaction to certain aesthetic and conceptual demands placed upon utopian fiction by the widespread popular reception of Darwinist models of social and political development. As I argue in my second "Historical Interval," this subsidiary status is apropos even of the most famous time travel story of the period, H. G. Wells's *The Time Machine.* The prominence of Darwinism, and of biology generally, impels a general shift toward specifically temporal models of sociopolitical extrapolation: plausible utopian futures must be directly "evolved" from actual present-day conditions, not merely envisaged or conjectured as potential replacements. Under such pressures, time travel framing narratives become a valuable, possibly indispensible means for writers to link present and future realistically, and thereby to legitimize social prognostications under the rubric of evolution. In my first chapter, I examine how and why time travel becomes the default frame for evolutionary utopian narratives, and I analyze the peculiar and fruitful narrative pitfalls created in the process.

Only when the first phase of time travel as utopian macrologue is coming to an end, just after the turn of the twentieth century, does the time travel story per se begin to emerge as an autonomous type. Even so, for a long while time travel remains more fallout than innovation, an orphaned remainder of utopianism, stripped of its rationale as a bolster for evolutionary realism in romance fictions. Thus, even with its new independence, time travel fiction persists as a minor, somewhat frivolous adventure story type, often a mere comedic offshoot of scientific romance. In my first "Historical Interval," between Chapters 1 and 2, I suggest an obscure, derivative, and entirely minor work as the exemplar of this somewhat inauspicious generic origin: Harold Steele Mackaye's 1904 novel *The Panchronicon*.[51] And I propose that we consider the early stages of the autonomous time travel story as an "interregnum," awaiting a new governing cultural or scientific paradigm to replace the one lost with the waning of evolutionary utopia.

Such a paradigm arrives with the popularization of "the Einstein theory" of relativity in the 1920s, and hence the beginning of a second phase in the history of time travel fiction. What relativity physics provides, mainly, is a repertoire of new plot possibilities: temporal dilation or reversal, physical access to one's own past or future (or alternate presents), viewpoints encompassing many or all possible worlds, "narcissistic" or "oedipal" meetings, and so on. With such narrative innovations, time travel stories start to focus intensively on the multiplication or recombination of narrative lines and worlds, a focus that was nascent in earlier time travel fiction but hardly ever indulged. Time travel now becomes, above all, a literature about the forms and mechanisms of storytelling itself, or what I have called a narratological laboratory. Noticeably, also, much of the sociopolitical motivation of earlier time travel fictions is sacrificed to this intensive concentration on form and narrative structure.

When time travel writers begin fully to embrace these narratological opportunities, the already self-conscious or quasi-parodic attitude toward plots that had characterized the early genre progresses toward a certain splendid excess. The result is what is sometimes called the "time loop" or "closed causal loop" story, an invention of 1930s pulp writers in which it is impossible to determine whether a cause precedes or follows its effect; such stories become standard fodder in the pulps by the early 1940s. Overall, I identify this second period of time travel fiction as its "paradox story" phase, and discuss some primary examples of its development in the second chapter, from the early use of "the Einstein theory" in G. Peyton Wertenbaker's mid-1920s fiction to its culmination in the loop stories of the 1930s and 1940s.

The third phase of time travel, which is comparatively amorphous, I designate with the deliberately broad term "multiverse/filmic." It encompasses a range of story subtypes that follow upon the advent and triumph of paradox fiction in the midcentury. Some of these subtypes are revisionist or parodic versions of the loop story; others are quite serious forays into the psychological or narratological implications of paradox fiction; still others attempt to pursue more current physical theory, from quantum gravity to ekpyrotic cosmology. The variety of thematic and narrative concerns that occupy time travel writers roughly in the postwar period and up to the present are the subject of the final four chapters of the book, as well as the "Theoretical Interval" between Chapters 4 and 5. Let me only briefly note two of the crucial aspects of this period: first, the growth of popular time travel film and television, which has flourished more than ever in the past couple of decades, and, second, the recent scientific legitimization and popularization of multiverse physics and cosmology, which has revitalized both time travel paradox stories and alternate or multiple universe stories. The second half of my book is substantially concerned with time travel within visual media, and especially with time travel fiction's capacity to represent, or even intrinsically to theorize, problems of visual perspective and viewpoint in narrative fiction and film. Chapters 4, 5, and 6 offer readings of, respectively, an illustrated text of Samuel Delany's novella *Empire Star,* several episodes of the *Star Trek* franchise, and the film *Back to the Future.* The "Theoretical Interval" briefly discusses what I assert is the primacy of the visual in time travel narrative.

Finally, the Conclusion offers a series of suggestions about a possible "last time travel story," intended to hypothesize the trajectory of both time travel fiction itself and the narrative theorizations that follow in its wake. My final reading—a closing complement to the three readings I offer in this Introduction—is of Harlan Ellison's short story "One Life, Furnished in Early Poverty," along with the new exegetical layers generated by its adaptation for the 1980s *Twilight Zone* television series, and by Ellison's own DVD commentary. The fact that time travel fiction lends itself to such hybrid textual/visual reconfigurations is no coincidence; indeed, time travel's inherently intermediated composition is among its most provocative theoretical characteristics.

Notes

1. Robert Silverberg, *Up the Line* (New York: Ballantine, 1969), pp. 186–87.
2. Of course, I am momentarily ignoring the story's other extraordinary event, Jud's liaison with his own ancestor. I will revisit the significance of such oedipal or quasi-oedipal encounters especially in Chapter 6.
3. Mieke Bal, *Narratology: Introduction to the Theory of Narrative* (Toronto: U of Toronto P, 2009), p. 217.
4. Gérard Genette, *Narrative Discourse*, trans, Jane E. Lewin (Ithaca, NY: Cornell UP, 1980), p. 35.
5. Jonathan Culler offers a useful survey of the varieties of this distinction in structuralist theory and narratology, as well as of its basis in Russian formalism (see *The Pursuit of Signs: Semiotics, Literature, Deconstruction* [Ithaca, NY: Cornell UP, 2001], pp. 169–87).
6. Genette, pp. 35–47; see also Bal, pp. 82–88.

7. Genette describes the sacrosanct position of the *fabula* in "classical" narrative, a type that he considers opposed to post-Proustian modern narrative, as "domination" by *fabula*. Speaking of instances in Proust in which "the time of the story ... regains its hold over the narrative," Genette writes, "It is in fact as if the narrative, caught between what it tells (the story) and what tells it (the narrating, led here by memory), had no choice except domination by the former (classical narrative) or domination by the latter (modern narrative, inaugurated with Proust)" (pp. 156, 156n).

8. Note that John Brunner suggests a similar theme in his novel *Times Without Number* (New York: Ace, 1969): "[T]here were three zones of history which had exercised an obsessive fascination on temporal explorers ever since the Society was founded. One, inevitably, was the beginning of the Christian era ... but access to Palestine of that day was severely restricted for fear that even the presence of non-intervening observers should draw the attention of the Roman authorities to the remarkable interest being generated by an unknown holy man, and cause Pilate to act earlier than the Sanhedrin, according to the written record, had desired" (p. 145, Brunner's ellipsis).

9. Michael Moorcock, *Behold the Man* (New York: Avon, 1968), pp. 26–27.

10. Ibid., p. 49.

11. White, "The Question of Narrative in Contemporary Historical Theory," *History and Theory* 23.1 (1984): pp. 1–33; the quotation is from p. 29. White is partly quoting Hegel's *Lectures on the Philosophy of History*.

12. Moorcock, p. 135.

13. Ibid., pp. 145–46.

14. In an earlier book, I discuss a similar historiographical problem in the context of the formation of philosophical canons and histories, and argue that critics and philosophers construct, through revisionist rereading techniques, histories of philosophy that must be seen as simultaneously retroactive and proleptic, essentially texts with "no present." See Wittenberg, *Philosophy, Revision, Critique: Rereading Practices in Heidegger, Nietzsche, and Emerson* (Stanford, CA: Stanford UP, 2001), especially Chapters 3 and 4 and the "Interlude."

15. Laryry Niven, "All the Myriad Ways," in *All the Myriad Ways* (New York: Del Rey, 1971): pp. 1–11; the quotation is from pp. 6–7.

16. See Hugh Everett III, "The Theory of the Universal Wave Function" and "'Relative State' Formulation of Quantum Mechanics," in in *The Many-Worlds Interpretation of Quantum Mechanics*, edited by Bryce S. DeWitt and Neill Graham (Princeton, NJ: Princeton UP, 1973), pp. 3–140 and 141–9.

17. Bryce S. DeWitt, "Quantum Mechanics and Reality," in *Many-Worlds Interpretation*, pp. 155–43; the quotation is from p. 161.

18. Niven, "All the Myriad Ways," p. 7.

19. For an excellent discussion of incompleteness and fictionality, see Ruth Ronen, *Possible Worlds in Narrative Theory* (New York: Cambridge UP, 1994), pp.114–43. Also see Lubomír Doležel, *Heterocosmics: Fiction and Possible Worlds* (Baltimore: Johns Hopkins UP, 1998), who usefully cites a number of sources in analytic philosophy for this definition of fictionality (pp. 22f).

20. Niven, "All the Myriad Ways," p. 7 (Niven's ellipsis and punctuation).

21. Niven, "Preface" (to "All the Myriad Ways"), in *N-Space* (New York: Tor, 1990), pp. 71–80; the quotation is from p. 70.

22. Ibid.

23. Friedrich Nietzsche, *The Gay Science*, trans. Josefine Nauckhoff (New York: Cambridge UP, 2001), p. 194.

24. Niven, "Preface," p. 70.
25. Niven writes elsewhere that "a writer who puts severe limits on his time machine is generally limiting its ability to change the past in order to make his story less incredible" ("The Theory and Practice of Time Travel," in *All the Myriad Ways* [New York: Del Rey, 1971], pp. 110–23; the quotation is from p. 111).
26. Niven, "All the Myriad Ways," p. 7.
27. This question of simulacra is not entirely a common motif in time travel stories, but one that is occasionally invoked both in highly philosophical instances and in highly popular ones—or in some cases both. In the popular vein, compare Michael Crichton's *Timeline* (New York: Ballantine, 2003):

    "The person didn't come from our universe," Gordon said....
    "So she's almost Kate? Sort of Kate? Semi-Kate?"
    "No, she's Kate. As far as we have been able to tell with our testing, she is absolutely identical to our Kate. Because our universe and their universe are almost identical." (p. 180)

28. Philip K. Dick, *A Scanner Darkly* (New York: Vintage, 1991), p. 100.
29. Niven, "All the Myriad Ways," p. 7.
30. This problem is cleverly elaborated in a 1994 episode of *The Simpsons* entitled "Time and Punishment": Homer, upon returning in a time machine to a present that clearly diverges from the one he left—for instance, his family members now all have forked tongues—exclaims, "Ah, close enough."
31. Keith Laumer, *Assignment in Nowhere* (New York: Berkley, 1968), p. 51.
32. Niven, "All the Myriad Ways," p. 7.
33. Tzvetan Todorov discusses the difficulty of establishing any such "smallest narrative unit" (*Introduction to Poetics*, trans. Richard Howard [Minneapolis: U of Minnesota P, 1981], pp. 48f). See also Eugene Dorfman, *The Narreme in the Medieval Romance Epic: An Introduction to Narrative Structrues* (Toronto: U of Toronto P, 1969), passim.
34. Niven, "All the Myriad Ways," p. 10.
35. Ibid. (all ellipses Niven's).
36. Ibid., p. 11 (Niven's ellipsis). In the reprinted version of the story in Niven's collection *N-Space*, the concrete arrangement of these lines on the page is altered:

    And picked the gun off the newspapers, looked at it for a long moment, then dropped it in the drawer. His hands began to shake. On a world line very close to this one ...
    And he picked the gun off the newspapers, put it to his head
    and
    fired. The hammer fell on an empty chamber.
    fired. The gun jerked up and blasted a hole in the ceiling.
    fired.
    The bullet tore a furrow in his scalp.
    took off the top of his head.
    ("All the Myriad Ways," in *N-Space* [New York: Tor, 1990], pp. 71–80; the quotation is from p. 80 [Niven's ellipsis]).

37. See G.W. Leibniz, *Monadology*, in *Philosophical Texts*, trans. R.S. Woodhouse and Richard Francks (New York: Oxford UP, 1998), §60–62 (pp. 276–77).
38. John A. Wheeler, "Assessment of Everet's 'Relative Space' Formulation of Quantum Mechanics," in *Many-Worlds Interpretation*, pp. 151–53; the quotation is from p. 151.

39. Ibid.

40. Ibid, 152.

41. Ibid.

42. Wheeler, responding to Everett, states: "The word 'probability' implies the notion of observation from outside with equipment that will be described typically in classical terms. Neither these classical terms, nor observation from outside, nor a priori probability considerations[,] come into the *foundations* of the relative state form of quantum theory" (p. 152).

43. Again in Wheeler's words: "The model has a place for observations only insofar as they take place within the isolated system. The theory of observation becomes a special case of the theory of correlations between subsystems" (p. 151).

44. There may be interpretations in which the inhabitation of a metaworld is not "unphysical," albeit in precise and limited senses. In Chapters 3 through 5, I allude at greater length to the physical model of a metaverse, which in certain aspects parallels the metaworld imputed within the metaphysics of Leibniz's *Monadology*. In "All the Myriad Ways," Niven calls it a "megauniverse of universes" (p. 1).

45. For instance, see Diane M. Calhoun-French, "Time Travel and Related Phenomena in Contemporary Popular Romance Fiction," in *Romantic Conventions*, edited by Anne K. Kaler and Rosemary Johnson-Kurek (Bowling Green, OH: Bowling Green State UP, 1999), pp. 100–12, on contemporary romance time travel; see Janice Radway, *Reading the Romance: Women, Patriarchy, and Popular Literature* (Chapel Hill: U of North Carolina P, 1991), for a more general discussion of the significance of the romance genre.

46. Paul J. Nahin, in *Time Machines: Time Travel in Physics, Metaphysics, and Science Fiction* (New York: Springer-Verlag, 1993), exhibits such a bias in his book on time travel, which, despite its admirable expansiveness, begins by severely limiting the possible domain of the study of time travel fiction: "In this book we are interested in physical time travel *by machines* that manipulate matter and energy in a *finite* region of space.... In addition, the machine must have a *rational explanation*" (p. 18, Nahin's emphasis). Thus Nahin excludes, for instance, any story that uses "mind travel," "dreams," "drugs," "freezing and sleeping [into the future]," "channeling," "accidents" (as in Twain's *Connecticut Yankee*), "illness" (as in Octavia Butler's *Kindred*), "time portals that look like green fog," "psi powers," any technology lacking an "explanation" or a basis in "rationality and science," and so on. Needless to say, such criteria preclude a great many narratives, time travel or otherwise, from critical scrutiny. Nahin's bias, a quite common one in the context of "hard" science fiction, emerges most clearly in his tendency to equate "interest" with "hardness": "More interesting—that is, more rational..." (p. 16); "...interesting to us because they are rational" (p. 21); "Interesting, yes, but it isn't physics..." (p. 16), and so on. The canonical "hard" science fiction writer Arthur C. Clarke, in *Report on Planet Three, and Other Speculations* (New York: Harper and Row, 1972), makes the point in a similar way, listing and judging the following catalog of "scientific" possibilities for fiction: "immortality, invisibility, time travel, thought transference, levitation, creation of life. For my part, there is only one of these that I feel certain (well, practically certain!) to be impossible, and that is time travel" (p. 173). Gregory Benford, an equally "hard" author who *does* write time travel, claims that "a science fiction writer is—or should be—constrained by what is, or logically might be" ("Exposures," in *In Alien Flesh* [New York: Tor, 1988], pp. 231–47; the quotation is from p. 247). I discuss the applicability and the limitations of a logical constraint on time travel narratives in Chapters 4 and 5. For useful historical discussions of the advent of "hard" science fiction, see Roger Luckhurst,

Science Fiction (Malden, MA: Polity, 2005), pp. 66–91, 99ff; and Mark Bould and Sherryl Vint, *The Routledge Concise History of Science Fiction* (New York: Routledge, 2011), pp. 74–91.

47. Robert Silverberg, "Introduction," in *Voyages in Time*, edited by Silverberg (New York: Tempo, 1970), p. x.

48. See N. Katherine Hayles, *The Cosmic Web: Scientific Field Models and Literary Strategies in the 20th Century* (Ithaca, NY: Cornell UP, 1984), especially pp. 111–37; Stanislaw Lem, "The Time-Travel Story and Related Matters of SF Structuring," *Science Fiction Studies* 1 (Spring 1973), pp. 26–33; Constance Penley, "Time Travel, Primal Scene, and the Critical Dystopia," in *Close Encounters: Film, Feminism, and Science Fiction*, edited by Penley, Elisabeth Lyon, Lynn Spigel, and Janet Bergstrom (Minneapolis: U of Minnesota P, 1991), pp. 63–83; Vivian Sobchack, *Screening Space: The American Science Fiction Film* (New York: Ungar, 1991), pp. 223–305; Brooks Landon, *The Aesthetics of Ambivalence: Rethnking Science Fiction Film in the Age of Electronic (Re)Production* (Westport, CT: Greenwood, 1992), especially 74–83; Garrett Stewart, *Framed Time: Toward a Postfilmic Cinema* (Chicago: U of Chicago P, 2007), pp. 122–63. I can mention in passing that there are, perhaps surprisingly, also a fairly large number of works dealing with supposedly actual time travel, either as something already accomplished or as soon forthcoming—usually with little basis in either science or literary theory, although sometimes with ties to various pseudosciences and to New Age metaphysics. For the most part, I deliberately decline to distinguish subtypes of the genre of science fiction here, for instance "hard" science fiction, new wave, cyberpunk, and so on, with the understanding that the genre of time travel fiction evolves relatively independently of these types, and to a great degree in an uneasy tension with the larger sociocultural history of science fiction. Some sense of this tension may be gleaned by noting the relative absence of discussions of time travel fiction as a distinct story type within excellent critical studies of science fiction such as Bould and Vint's *Concise History of Science Fiction*, Luckhurst's *Science Fiction*, or Istvan Csicsery-Ronay, Jr.'s *The Seven Beauties of Science Fiction* (Middletown, CT: Wesleyan UP, 2008). These critics mention time travel, for instance, as a "framework" for addressing other themes or sociopolitical issues (Luckhurst, p. 195; Luckhurst's approach is relatively consistent with Suvin's foundational understanding of science-fictional structuring as "cognitive estrangement"), or as a narrative means to permit "a conscious mortal being [to] return to its origins" or to imagine "the permeability of history" (Csicsery-Ronay Jr., pp. 99, 100). Such understandings of the usefulness of time travel within science fiction are, of course, compatible with my analysis of its functioning as a narratological laboratory, but they also help explain why time travel has tended to avoid falling into a distinct subgeneric niche within science fiction at large, and has instead cut across more clearly visible delineations of aesthetic, stylistic, and political subtypes.

49. See Richard J. Gerrig, *Experiencing Narrative Worlds: On the Psychological Activities of Reading* (New Have, CT: Westview, 1998), pp. 10–17.

50. This latter problem is Gerard Genette's chief focus in *Narrative Discourse*.

51. During this first period of time travel literature, the single work most often identified as an origin is also written: H. G. Wells's *The Time Machine* (1895). For a number of reasons, which I discuss in the opening chapters, I decline to grant such credit to Wells's book. However, I discuss *The Time Machine* at greater length in my "Historical Interval II."

Recommended further reading

Broderick, Damien. *Reading by Starlight: Postmodern Science Fiction*. New York: Routledge, 1995.

Develops a model for reading SF that draws on Delany's theory of "subjunctivity," arguing that the best SF uses the genre's linguistic resources to fundamentally unsettle ontological categories, in ways that converge with the insights of postmodern theory.

Csicsery-Ronay, Jr., Istvan. *The Seven Beauties of Science Fiction*. Middletown, CT: Wesleyan UP, 2008.

A major study that anatomizes the genre into seven distinct "beauties," each with its own aesthetic logic and history: "Fictive Neology," "Fictive Novums," "Future History," "Imaginary Science," "The Sublime," "The Grotesque," and "The Technologiade" (i.e., the epic construction of the cosmos as a "technological regime").

Delany, Samuel R. *The Jewel-Hinged Jaw: Notes on the Language of Science Fiction*. 1977.
Rev. ed. Middletown, CT: Wesleyan UP, 2009.

Collection of ten essays on the function of language in SF, which contrasts the genre's estranging techniques with the naturalizing rhetoric of realist fiction; includes powerful analyses of works by Thomas M. Disch, Ursula K, Le Guin, Joanna Russ, and Roger Zelazny.

Ferns, Chris. *Narrating Utopia: Ideology, Gender, Form in Utopian Literature*. Liverpool: Liverpool UP, 1999.

One of the most insightful studies of the narrative dynamics of utopian writing, anatomizing the tensions between conservative form and radical content in ways that have significance for the SF genre as well.

Gomel, Elana. *Postmodern Science Fiction and Temporal Imagination*. London: Continuum, 2010.

A study of postmodern SF in terms of its engagement with the narrative logics of temporality, especially the movement beyond linear schemes and mechanistic causality; see also the author's *Narrative Space and Time: Representing Impossible Topologies in Literature* (Routledge, 2014).

Jameson, Fredric. *Archaeologies of the Future: The Desire Called Utopia and Other Science Fictions*. New York: Verso, 2005.

Dense study of the relationship between SF and utopian writing, analyzing the poetic ideologies that structure these genres, both enabling and constraining their powers of social critique.

Malmgren, Carl. *Worlds Apart: Narratology of Science Fiction*. Bloomington: Indiana UP, 1991.

A structuralist anatomy of the genre that divides work into extrapolative and speculative modes, with the former driven by prediction and the latter by visionary projection; offers one of the best analyses of the operations of "science fantasy" available.

Meyers, Walter E. *Aliens and Linguists: Language Study and Science Fiction*. Athens: Georgia UP,
    1980.
    A study of SF in relation to problems of communication, especially with aliens; offers trenchant
analyses of how SF texts both thematize and structurally address these linguistic difficulties.

Scholes, Robert. *Structural Fabulation: An Essay on Fiction of the Future*. Notre Dame, IN: Notre
    Dame UP, 1975.
    Argues for SF as a genre of speculative fabulation, which combines the forms of satire and
romance, and which (following Darko Suvin) engages readers conceptually through a strategy of
defamiliarization.

Stockwell, Peter. *The Poetics of Science Fiction*. Harlow, UK: Longman, 2000.
    Examines how readers decode SF texts, drawing on the discourse of cognitive linguistics to
show the ways that connections are made between imaginary worlds and real-world experience.

Part 3

Ideology and world view

This section opens with a polemical defense of the genre as a potentially radical form of literature, originally delivered as a speech at the 1937 Third Eastern Science Fiction Convention in Philadelphia by John B. Michel on behalf of the Committee for the Political Advancement of Science Fiction. Strongly influenced by Marxist theory and activism, Michel—a member of the left-leaning fan group The Futurians—denounced the political complacency of most of his fellow fans, as well as the "gigantic junk pile of stinking literature and less than puerile achievement" that, he alleged, constituted the bulk of pulp SF. The genre was in danger, Michel argued, of squandering its great potential as a vehicle for evoking utopian futures and thus combatting the forces of "barbarism." His argument for a political awakening of SF can be seen as being aligned with what Michael Denning has called the "Cultural Front" against fascism during the 1930s.[1] Michel's essay ends with a stirring call to arms, urging fans, authors, and fellow travelers to embrace a mission to "lead humanity out of the Valley of the Shadow into the dazzling light of a triumphant future."

Writing almost three decades later, Susan Sontag's arraignment of SF's complicity with facile and reactionary apocalyptic fantasies does not suggest that the genre had taken up Michel's militant leftism. Sontag is addressing SF film rather than literature, a form that, she argues, is in many ways superior because, unlike print SF, it has the "unique strength" of immediacy and representational power. The core theme of SF cinema, according to Sontag, is disaster, featuring multifarious scenarios of catastrophe up to and including "the destruction of humanity itself." In its treatment of this theme, SF cinema is often deeply contradictory, on the one hand longing for peaceful resolutions, while on the other reveling in bellicose paranoia about alien enemies. Like Michel, Sontag argues that most SF constitutes an "*inadequate response*" to contemporary geopolitical threats, its undeniable charms insufficient to counteract the "primitive gratifications" offered by its powerful visions of armageddon.

Like Sontag, SF author Joanna Russ offers a harsh indictment of the political ideologies of science fiction, while still holding out hope, like Michel, that the genre can be redeemed from its worst impulses. While SF, which ostensibly has the whole universe and all of the future in which to operate, ought to be able to summon imagery and ideas far exceeding the status quo, the sad fact, according to Russ, is that the vast majority of work published in the genre regurgitates stereotypes about women without interrogating them. One of the earliest works of feminist SF criticism, Russ's essay attacks SF for constructing a kind of "intergalactic suburbia" in which gender roles and values conform with those prevailing in the present day, rather than critiquing or transcending them. Invidiously misogynistic assumptions about women—for example, that they lack intelligence or should be viewed solely in terms of appearance—are embedded in the fabric of much SF, while some stories—such as works that satirize imagined matriarchal dystopias—are actively anti-feminist, lampooning women's pretensions to social power and autonomy. Russ's essay was hugely influential in impelling the genre to confront its ideological limitations, paving the way for an overtly feminist SF writing in the coming decades.[2]

While Michel and Russ believe that SF has the resources to project alternative realities, resources that have simply not been activated by most authors, Fredric Jameson provides a more sobering perspective, suggesting that the genre can be defined precisely by its *inability* to truly imagine the future. The anticipatory promise of SF can always be shown, in retrospect, to be a failure, with the genre historically mounting a series of fictive projections that never escape the orbit of the prevailing "political unconscious," which both enables and constrains the prophetic imagination. Yet that does not mean the enterprise is pointless or quixotic since the mere fact that SF defamiliarizes present-day reality is a serious political function, potentially reorienting a reader's experience of that reality in important ways. The future, for Jameson, can never be represented in an SF text, because writers are obviously limited to the worlds they know, but the possibility of simply *grasping* the nature of these limitations, however obliquely, is itself a significant political accomplishment of the genre. Since Jameson is a Marxist critic, his goal is the imagination of a world *after* capitalism, but even if SF fails in its attempts to project such a world, the failure itself can be powerfully instructive. At the very least, by purporting to gaze forward in time, SF can restore to readers a sense of their own historicity and of the evanescence and mutability of all "presents," including their own.

An even more optimistic argument for the political potential of SF, in terms of its capacity for critiquing capitalism, is offered by Carl Freedman. Freedman's thesis is at once simple yet sweeping in its theoretical implications: SF as a genre has deep affinities with the tradition of Marxist critical theory. In particular, its mode of representing the future is "profoundly dialectical," showing the historically constructed nature of the most taken-for-granted institutions and values. Building on Jameson, as well as on Darko Suvin's definition of SF as a literature of cognitive estrangement, Freedman argues that SF tends, in its defamiliarization of the actual, to offer, "at least implicitly," a sense of "utopian possibility"; however, like Suvin, Freedman is compelled to admit that the vast bulk of SF fails to live up to this heady promise, acknowledging that "many texts classified as SF make major retreats from the conceptual radicalism of the SF tendency." Nonetheless, SF's capacity to project alternative realities makes it one of the most powerful agencies for the critical demystification of social ideologies in modern popular culture.[3]

Wendy Pearson's essay converges in some ways with Freedman's concerns, arguing that SF can function to denaturalize sexual ideologies in provocative and productive ways. The genre does this not simply by representing alternatives to heteronormative identities, though this strategy itself might be a useful tool for unsettling homophobic assumptions. Rather, its most powerful texts work to "queer" identity as such, "resisting attempts to make sexuality signify in monolithic ways" (e.g., in terms of the binary of gay vs. straight) and moving toward a completely "different understanding of subjectivity and agency." Pearson distinguishes between "queer texts"—that is, stories that either explicitly or covertly challenge naturalized assumptions about sexual identity and desire—and "queer readings," which involve deconstructive reevaluations of tales that, on the surface, may seem deeply heteronormative. Just as Freedman argues for a homology between SF and critical theory, so Pearson suggests that SF shares significant epistemological terrain with contemporary queer theory; in short, both scholars locate, within the genre's representational strategies, a compelling and incisive critical problematic.

The final essay in this section by Lisa Yaszek moves in a different direction, away from large-scale theoretical claims toward a careful historical reconstruction of the sociopolitical valences of science fiction. While Russ dismissed the vast bulk of pulp-era SF as a wasteland of misogyny, Yaszek shows instead that a serious discourse on gender conflict and relationships—spurred by a diverse array of female authors, editors, and fans—had evolved within the genre well before the advent of the women's liberation movement in the 1960s and the emergence of overtly feminist SF in the 1970s. Examining the work of a number of authors who have seldom been seen as part of SF's literary canon, Yaszek shows that the immediate postwar decades, assumed to be a period when women were consigned to domestic roles, featured proto-feminist SF writers who at once challenged this social orthodoxy and pointed toward futures of increasing female empowerment.[4] Yaszek also demonstrates that this sort of subversively critical writing was aligned with nascent forms of women's activism—around issues of civil rights and nuclear disarmament, for example—that potently interrogated and rejected Cold War era ideologies. While several of the critics in this section see political value in only a small subset of genre production, Yaszek's approach is instructive in showing that much SF that is now largely forgotten was, in its time, significantly effective in critiquing prevailing social norms and values.

Notes

1. See Michael Denning, *The Cultural Front: The Laboring of American Culture in the 1930s* (New York: Verso, 2011). For background on the political activities of SF fans during the period, see Damon Knight, *The Futurians* (New York: John Day, 1977) and Frederik Pohl, *The Way the Future Was: A Memoir* (New York: Ballantine, 1978).

2. For discussions of Russ's central role in establishing a feminist critical discourse within the genre, see the essays gathered in Farah Mendlesohn's *On Joanna Russ* (Middletown, CT: Wesleyan UP, 2009).

3. Freedman expanded the argument in this article into a book length treatise, *Critical Theory and Science Fiction* (Middletown, CT: Wesleyan UP, 2000).

4. Yaszek's essay formed the seed for her book, *Galactic Suburbia: Recovering Women's Science Fiction* (Columbus: Ohio State UP, 2002).

15

Mutation or death!

John B. Michel

"Mutation or Death" is a transcript of the speech delivered by Donald A. Wollheim for John B. Michel at the Third Eastern Science Fiction Convention, Philadelphia, October 1937.

Mr. Chairman, Members of the Convention Committee, visitors, and friends:

What I am about to say is the result of much thinking and introspection on my part and on the part of the several of my friends here today who support a new program for the future of science fiction—which shall be the main topic of my talk this afternoon.

To open this discussion it would be well to put forward a statement pregnant with meaning, a statement above all appropriate to the speech, a statement heavily loaded with dynamite and fraught with shaking possibilities.

I hereby make that statement.

The Science Fiction Age, as we have known it during the past few years, is over. Definitely over and done with. Dead, gentlemen, of intellectual bankruptcy.

Unfortunately, for any persons who might still be harboring any thoughts of optimism while moping over the moldering corpse, the decision is entirely final. I am not fooling when I say this. You can take it or leave it. But I believe, in the light of what I shall say further on in this talk, you'll take it.

Naturally such a statement calls for proof, strong, unbending proof guaranteed to stand up under criticism of the most searching nature.

Need I offer any more positive a proof than the conduct of this convention itself?

Gentlemen, we are gathered here this afternoon in solemn conclave—to do what? To do precisely what?

In a few words let me put forth my opinion on what we are doing. My opinion is that we are baloney bending, throwing the bull, indulging in dull flights of fancy, tossing barrels of rhodomontade all over the place.

I see before me fans, writers, editors, and publishers, stf fans all and but a handful really awake to the enormous possibilities inherent in that fragile little thing called science fiction, that potentially mighty force which is rapidly being buried in a deluge of obscure issues, meaningless phrases, stupid interpretations, and aimless goals.

When the first science fiction fan organizations came into existence several years ago, they did so because of a need—a need, however obscure, which nevertheless existed.

That need was expression. We all know the various organizations that were formed. Why recall their history, their mistakes, their stupid, colossal, blundering mistakes of bickering and internal strife and more and still more baloney bending? In reviewing the field in its entirety we would be doing nothing more than adding to the dull, dreary reams upon reams of historical fact, consigned already to the limbo of forgotten things.

The very fact that no single science fiction organization has ever made any lasting impression on anything (except for the single exception of the ISA which did more or less practical research work on rockets before its dissolution) speaks for itself.

It speaks in a resounding question:

Just where has science fiction got to in six or seven years of loosely organized existence?

On a world scale, nowhere. Locally, practically nothing has been done. The great local organizations are gone, their banners furled and tossed on the scrap heap. Internationally, science fiction is but the last gasping beats of a never very strong and young and healthy heart. What remains of it all is a gigantic junk pile of stinking literature and less than puerile achievement.

Just what is this urge to organize, anyway? Why do science fiction fans gather all over the world in local clubs and sit up far in the nights to publish fan magazines and correspond on a scale almost unprecedented in its scope?

Certainly because they like science fiction. And why do they like science fiction? Wherein lies this mysterious attraction which prompts most of them to make a fetish out of a new form of literature, a little tin god, as it were, before which their souls bend and scrape? Is it because of the cadence of the words, the turn of the clever phrases, well constructed paragraphs, a temporary exaltation on reading some powerful descriptive scene? Is it to orate and argue endlessly about the qualities of this or that writer or the shortcomings of this or that writer? We all know that science fiction itself is something different in literature. But what form and shape has it given the ideas of its adherents? Again I repeat, wherein lies this mysterious compelling force which has made science fiction fans accomplish what little practical work they have accomplished?

The answer in great part is that science fiction is the smoothest form of escape literature known. In its infinite depths the lost, the lonesome, the inhibited, the frustrated soul finds understanding and expression, precisely because the world to which they escape is a world of their own fancies and imaginings—a world which they like. In this haven of refuge their creative instincts are given full rein.

I venture to predict that a heavy majority of science fiction fans are escapists. I think I'm right when I say that because I'm a more or less normal type of fan, and I was an escapist and in a certain sense I still am.

But why have the fans stopped at this point, content to revel in a seemingly unending debauch of good fellowship leading to what may seem to be a common end and purpose? As you can see by looking about you in the fan field, what remains of the great directive forces, the organizations proper, is nothing. Fandom has resounded for almost a decade with the hullabaloo and the shouting, and now the hollow shell of a structure stopped suddenly in headlong growth sounds to nothing but a painful silence, sterile on the shores of a lost world.

What are you people looking for, anyway? Do you really intend to go on harping for more and better science fiction? Do you really think that merely asking for more and better science fiction is, in some miraculous way, to lift the field out of the slough? What makes you think that the editors and publishers of the magazines are going to give you their ears? Have they in the past? No. Can it actually be your intended purpose to continue arguing on the pros and cons of the literature of science fiction forever?

Can it? If such is your purpose, you are a pack of fools, content to sit smugly by while the fine talents inherent in your brains, the brains which provided the spark which sent science fiction leaping to a halted youth, stagnate.

But you cannot!

Because, gentlemen, the world is catching up with you and will pass you by.

Because, gentlemen, there is something in each and every one of you fans which places him automatically above the level of the average person; which, in short, gives him a vastly broadened view of things in general. The outlook is there, the brains are there. Yet, nothing has happened!

But why not give science fiction a meaning? Naturally all types of fiction are idealized versions of situations found in everyday life. Science fiction is an idealized type of vision of the life of the future.

What is wrong with science fiction today is that its outlook on the future has changed; or rather, has never existed in a rational sense.

How can science fiction have any rational outlook on the future when today exists the greatest confusion in world affairs since the dawn of recorded history?

What is important to us is what science fiction is going to do about it.

Science fiction has to do something about it because its very life is bound up with the future and today practical events are working to shape the outline of that future in bold, sharp relief.

Today we are face to face, *face to face*, I repeat, with the choice: Civilization or Barbarism—*reason* or *ignorance*.

As idealists, as visionaries, we cannot retreat before this challenge. We must accept it and carry the battle into the enemy's camp. Hitherto, this challenge has not even been recognized, much less accepted.

So come out of your secure cubbyholes of clubrooms and laboratories and meeting places and look at the world before you.

It is swiftly sinking in darkness and chaos. Why? Because the masses are being led by stupid men to a dreary doom.

Dare any of you deny this? Look at the daily newspapers. Look at the authoritative weeklies and monthlies. You see nothing but confusion and the abandonment of every decent instinct left to this mad system under which we live.

As *idealists* we cannot refuse to accept the challenge of the future.

Science fiction has finally come to the parting of the ways with meaningless idealism, and, with that idealism, dies. Science fiction must mutate—must change into a new form of idealism, a fighting, practical idealism, an idealism based on action and not on words, on experience and achievements and not on bombastic and irrelevant swaggerings.

The main point of this whole discussion is that you fans must prepare to incept this new state of things, else nothing is left but a slow, gradual decay of the gaunt corpse of the body stf until it disappears, eaten up by the fiery acid of mighty world events.

Thus today the world of science fiction totters. Even science, its mainstay, wavers increasingly toward the vague and obscure.

It would seem as though science were too secure in its ivory tower to pay much heed to the wails and groans (and pardon me if I use this old bromide) of suffering humanity. In its lofty and utterly pure elevation it squats safely amidst its own escapist atmosphere and does precisely nothing practical in the way of saving itself from the consequences of the coming world smash.

Out of its test tubes and instruments it extracts life and the energy of the atom and with them both it fills up our war machine and vomits death and terror throughout the world.

On one hand we are faced with the sickening spectacle of scientists throughout the world turning their backs on cold logic for the magic tinsel of colored military trappings, of a Pirandello in art and a Marconi in radio stooging for the Fascist dictator and general dirty rat, Benito Mussolini. On our own side of the Atlantic, renowned scientists and savants such as Millikan and others bow hypocritically before a standardized version of a God (of which none of them could possibly conceive) and attend rallies and demonstrations to uphold our military pride and honor.

As the technical brains of the world in their supreme cynicism line up on the side of reaction, the backbone of science fiction itself dies, dies of inaction, of do-nothingness, of an inability to forget for a while its above-it-allness and lead humanity out of the Valley of the Shadow into the dazzling light of a triumphant future.

Why all this? Because we have become stale and we stink in our staleness to the high heavens. Because we are conventional and set in our ways and the old way of life is easier to go on living because it demands little effort on the part of the haves and near-haves. We continue to do the same old things in the same old way and are smug and content in our pipe-dreams of super-scientific smoke. "Why change?" we cry.

Why *not* change? Why in hell not *do* something about it?

Great guns! We have brains, technical brains, introspective brains, thoughts and ideals that would put the greatest minds to shame for scope and insight. Put these brains to work *before it is too late*! The planet is ready for work, for practical work to wipe clean the slate and start anew. We *must* start anew if we have to smash every old superstition and outworn idea to do it.

We fans can do a lot towards the realization of this rational idea. We can do tha. because determination very often means achievement. And how sick we are at base of this dull, unsatisfying world, this stupid asininely organized system of ours which demands that a man brutalize and cynicize himself for the possession of a few dollars in a savage, barbarous, and utterly boring struggle to exist.

We say: "Put a stop to this—*now*!"

We say: "Smash this status quo of ours by smashing the present existing forms of economic and social life!" Boldly, perhaps a bit crudely, we say: "Down with it!" Down with it before the war-lovers clamp on the screws and bind us in submission for who knows how long!

Let humanity swing along in its goalless rut for more hundreds and thousands of years while the universe beckons for our participation in its active life?

Not for us!

Fearlessly and before the entire world we state our platform and beliefs (and I speak for all the visitors here today wearing the red delegate badges of the NYFA).

We come out wholly and completely in support of every force seeking the advancement of civilization along strictly scientific and humanitarian lines.

All help to the democratic forces of the world!

All help to the heroic defenders of Madrid and Shanghai, defenders of democracy!

Death and destruction to all forms of reaction!

The machine that will shatter forever the reactional assault on civilization is already in motion. Let us become part of it.

It is our job to work and plan and prepare, to teach and expound for the coming of that day when the human race shall stand erect as should a man and gaze on the stark, naked cosmos with firm eyes, to feel the solid, inconceivable impact of the grim void, to flood its consciousness with the realization that in the vast emptiness we must stand on our own feet and fight it out!

Therefore:

Be it moved that this, the Third Eastern Science Fiction Convention, shall place itself on record as opposing all forces leading to barbarism, the advancement of pseudo-sciences and militaristic ideologies, and shall further resolve that science fiction should by nature stand for all forces working for a more unified world, a more Utopian existence, the application of science to human happiness, and a saner outlook on life.

imagination of disaster

Susan Sontag

Ours is indeed an age of extremity. For we live under continual threat of two equally fearful, but seemingly opposed, destinies: unremitting banality and inconceivable terror. It is fantasy, served out in large rations by the popular arts, which allows most people to cope with these twin specters. For one job that fantasy can do is to lift us out of the unbearably humdrum and to distract us from terrors, real or anticipated—by an escape into exotic dangerous situations which have last-minute happy endings. But another one of the things that fantasy can do is to normalize what is psychologically unbearable, thereby inuring us to it. In the one case, fantasy beautifies the world. In the other, it neutralizes it.

The fantasy to be discovered in science fiction films does both jobs. These films reflect world-wide anxieties, and they serve to allay them. They inculcate a strange apathy concerning the processes of radiation, contamination, and destruction that I for one find haunting and depressing. The naïve level of the films neatly tempers the sense of otherness, of alien-ness, with the grossly familiar. In particular, the dialogue of most science fiction films, which is generally of a monumental but often touching banality, makes them wonderfully, unintentionally funny. Lines like: "Come quickly, there's a monster in my bathtub"; "We must do something about this"; "Wait, Professor. There's someone on the telephone"; "But that's incredible"; and the old American stand-by (accompanied by brow-wiping), "I hope it works!"—are hilarious in the context of picturesque and deafening holocaust. Yet the films also contain something which is painful and in deadly earnest.

Science fiction films are one of the most accomplished of the popular art forms, and can give a great deal of pleasure to sophisticated film addicts. Part of the pleasure, indeed, comes from the sense in which these movies are in complicity with the abhorrent. It is no more, perhaps, than the way all art draws its audience into a circle of complicity with the thing represented. But in science fiction films we have to do with things which are (quite literally) unthinkable. Here, "thinking about the unthinkable"—not in the way of Herman Kahn, as a subject for calculation, but as a subject for fantasy—becomes, however inadvertently, itself a somewhat questionable act from a moral point of view.

The films perpetuate clichés about identity, volition, power, knowledge, happiness, social consensus, guilt, responsibility which are, to say the least, not serviceable in our present extremity. But collective nightmares cannot be banished by demonstrating that they are, intellectually and morally, fallacious. This nightmare—the one reflected in various registers in the science fiction films—is too close to our reality.

A typical science fiction film has a form as predictable as a Western, and is made up of elements which are as classic as the saloon brawl, the blonde schoolteacher from the East, and the gun duel on the deserted main street.

One model scenario proceeds through five phases:

1. The arrival of the thing. (Emergence of the monsters, landing of the alien space-ship, etc.) This is usually witnessed, or suspected, by just one person, who is a young scientist on a field trip. Nobody, neither his neighbors nor his colleagues, will believe him for some time. The hero is not married, but has a sympathetic though also incredulous girlfriend.

2. Confirmation of the hero's report by a host of witnesses to a great act of destruction. (If the invaders are beings from another planet, a fruitless attempt to parley with them and get them to leave peacefully.) The local police are summoned to deal with the situation and massacred.

3. In the capital of the country, conferences between scientists and the military take place, with the hero lecturing before a chart, map, or blackboard. A national emergency is declared. Reports of further atrocities. Authorities from other countries arrive in black limousines. All international tensions are suspended in view of the planetary emergency. This stage often includes a rapid montage of news broadcasts in various languages, a meeting at the UN, and more conferences between the military and the scientists. Plans are made for destroying the enemy.

4. Further atrocities. At some point the hero's girlfriend is in grave danger. Massive counterattacks by international forces, with brilliant displays of rocketry, rays, and other advanced weapons, are all unsuccessful. Enormous military casualties, usually by incineration. Cities are destroyed and/or evacuated. There is an obligatory scene here of panicked crowds stampeding along a highway or a big bridge, being waved on by numerous policemen who, if the film is Japanese, are immaculately white-gloved, preternaturally calm, and call out in dubbed English, "Keep moving. There is no need to be alarmed."

5. More conferences, whose motif is: "They must be vulnerable to something." Throughout, the hero has been experimenting in his lab on this. The final strategy, upon which all hopes depend, is drawn up; the ultimate weapon—often a super-powerful, as yet untested, nuclear device—is mounted. Countdown. Final repulse of the monster or invaders. Mutual congratulations, while the hero and girlfriend embrace cheek to cheek and scan the skies sturdily. "But have we seen the last of them?"

The film I have just described should be in technicolor and on a wide screen. Another typical scenario is simpler and suited to black-and-white films with a lower budget. It has four phases:

1. The hero (usually, but not always, a scientist) and his girlfriend, or his wife and children, are disporting themselves in some innocent ultra-normal middle-class house in a small town, or on vacation (camping, boating). Suddenly, someone starts behaving strangely or some innocent form of vegetation becomes monstrously enlarged and ambulatory. If a character is pictured driving an automobile, something gruesome looms up in the middle of the road. If it is night, strange lights hurtle across the sky.

2. After following the thing's tracks, or determining that It is radioactive, or poking around a huge crater—in short, conducting some sort of crude investigation—the hero tries to warn the local authorities, without effect; nobody believes anything is amiss. The hero knows better. If the thing is tangible, the house is elaborately barricaded. If the invading alien is an invisible parasite, a doctor or friend is called in, who is himself rather quickly killed or "taken possession of" by the thing.

3. The advice of anyone else who is consulted proves useless. Meanwhile, It continues to claim other victims in the town, which remains implausibly isolated from the rest of the world. General helplessness.

4. One of two possibilities. Either the hero prepares to do battle alone, accidentally discovers the thing's one vulnerable point, and destroys it. Or, he somehow manages to get out of town and succeeds in laying his case before competent authorities. They, along the lines of the first script but abridged, deploy a complex technology which (after initial setbacks) finally prevails against the invaders.

Another version of the second script opens with the scientist-hero in his laboratory, which is located in the basement or on the grounds of his tasteful, prosperous house. Through his experiments, he unwittingly causes a frightful metamorphosis in some class of plants or animals, which turn carnivorous and go on a rampage. Or else, his experiments have caused him to be injured (sometimes irrevocably) or "invaded" himself. Perhaps he has been experimenting with radiation, or has built a machine to communicate with beings from other planets or to transport him to other places or times.

Another version of the first script involves the discovery of some fundamental alteration in the conditions of existence of our planet, brought about by nuclear testing, which will lead to the extinction in a few months of all human life. For example: the temperature of the earth is becoming too high or too low to support life, or the earth is cracking in two, or it is gradually being blanketed by lethal fallout.

A third script, somewhat but not altogether different from the first two, concerns a journey through space—to the moon, or some other planet. What the space-voyagers commonly discover is that the alien terrain is in a state of dire emergency, itself threatened by extra-planetary invaders or nearing extinction through the practice of nuclear warfare.

The terminal dramas of the first and second scripts are played out there, to which is added a final problem of getting away from the doomed and/or hostile planet and back to Earth.

I am aware, of course, that there are thousands of science fiction novels (their heyday was the late 1940's), not to mention the transcriptions of science fiction themes which, more and more, provide the principal subject matter of comic books. But I propose to discuss science fiction films (the present period began in 1950 and continues, considerably abated, to this day) as an independent sub-genre, without reference to the novels from which, in many cases, they were adapted. For while novel and film may share the same plot, the fundamental difference between the resources of the novel and the film makes them quite dissimilar. Anyway, the best science fiction movies are on a far higher level, as examples of the art of the film, than the science fiction books are, as examples of the art of the novel or romance. That the films might be better than the books is an old story. Good novels rarely make good films, but excellent films are often made from poor or trivial novels.

Certainly, compared with the science fiction novels, their film counterparts have unique strengths, one of which is the immediate representation of the extraordinary: physical deformity and mutation, missile and rocket combat, toppling skyscrapers. The movies are, naturally, weak just where the science fiction novels (some of them) are strong—on science. But in place of an intellectual workout, they can supply something the novels can never provide—sensuous elaboration. In the films it is by means of images and sounds, not words that have to be translated by the imagination, that one can participate in the fantasy of living through one's own death and more, the death of cities, the destruction of humanity itself.

Science fiction films are not about science. They are about disaster, which is one of the oldest subjects of art. In science fiction films, disaster is rarely viewed intensively; it is always extensive. It is a matter of quantity and ingenuity. If you will, it is a question of scale. But the scale, particularly in the wide-screen Technicolor films (of which the ones by the Japanese director, Inoshiro Honda, and the American director, George Pal, are technically the most brilliant and convincing, and visually the most exciting), does raise the matter to another level.

Thus, the science fiction film (like a very different contemporary genre, the Happening) is concerned with the aesthetics of destruction, with the peculiar beauties to be found in wreaking havoc, making a mess. And it is in the imagery of destruction that the core of a good science fiction film lies. This is the disadvantage of the cheap film—in which the monster appears or the rocket lands in a small dull-looking town. (Hollywood budget needs usually dictate that the town be in the Arizona or California desert. In *The Thing from Another World* [1951], the rather sleazy and confined set is supposed to be an encampment near the North Pole.) Still, good black-and-white science fiction films have been made. But a bigger budget, which usually means Technicolor, allows a much greater play back and forth among several model environments. There is the populous city. There is the lavish but ascetic interior of the space ship—either the invaders' or ours—replete with streamlined chromium fixtures and dials, and machines whose complexity is indicated by the number of colored lights they flash and strange noises they emit. There is the laboratory crowded with formidable machines and scientific apparatus. There is a comparatively old-fashioned looking conference room, where the scientist brings charts to explain the desperate state of things to the military. And each of these standard locales or backgrounds is subject to two modalities—intact and destroyed. We may, if we are lucky, be treated to a panorama of melting tanks, flying bodies, crashing walls, awesome craters and fissures in the earth, plummeting spacecraft, colorful deadly rays; and to a symphony of screams, weird electronic signals, the noisiest military hardware going, and the leaden tones of the laconic denizens of alien planets and their subjugated earthlings.

Certain of the primitive gratifications of science fiction films—for instance, the depiction of urban disaster on a colossally magnified scale—are shared with other types of films. Visually there is little difference between mass havoc as represented in the old horror and monster films and what we find in science fiction films, except (again) scale. In the old monster films, the monster always headed for the great city where he had to do a fair bit of rampaging, hurling buses off bridges, crumpling trains in his bare hands, toppling buildings, and so forth. The archetype is King Kong, in Schoedsach's great film of 1933, running amok, first in the African village (trampling babies, a bit of footage excised from most prints), then in New York. This is really not any different from Inoshiro Honda's *Rodan* (1957), where two giant reptiles—with a wingspan of five-hundred feet and supersonic speeds—by flapping their wings whip up a cyclone that blows most of Tokyo to smithereens. Or, the tremendous scenes of rampage by the gigantic robot who destroys half of Japan with the great incinerating ray which shoots forth from his eyes, at the beginning of Honda's *The Mysterians* (1959). Or, the destruction, by the rays from a fleet of flying saucers of New York, Paris and Tokyo, in *Battle in Outer Space* (1960). Or, the inundation of New York in *When Worlds Collide* (1951). Or, the end of London in 1968 depicted in George Pal's *The Time Machine* (1960). Neither do these sequences differ in aesthetic intention from the destruction scenes in the big sword, sandal, and orgy color spectaculars set in Biblical and Roman times—the end of Sodom in Aldrich's *Sodom and Gomorrah*, of Gaza in de Mille's *Samson and Delilah*, of Rhodes in *The Colossus of Rhodes*, and of Rome in a dozen Nero movies. D. W. Griffith began it with the Babylon sequence in *Intolerance*, and to this day there is nothing like the thrill of watching all those expensive sets come tumbling down.

In other respects as well, the science fiction films of the 1950's take up familiar themes. The famous movie serials and comics of the 1930's of the adventures of Flash Gordon and Buck Rogers, as well as the more recent spate of comic book super-heroes with extra-terrestrial origins (the most famous is Superman, a foundling from the planet, Krypton, currently described as having been exploded by a nuclear blast) share motifs with more recent science fiction movies. But there is an important difference. The old science fiction films, and most of the comics, still have an essentially innocent relation to disaster. Mainly they offer new versions of the oldest romance of all—of the strong invulnerable hero with the mysterious lineage come to do battle on behalf of good and against evil. Recent science fiction films have a decided grimness, bolstered by their much greater degree of visual credibility, which contrasts strongly with the older films. Modern historical reality has greatly enlarged the imagination of disaster, and the protagonists—perhaps by the very nature of what is visited upon them—no longer seem wholly innocent.

The lure of such generalized disaster as a fantasy is that it releases one from normal obligations. The trump card of the end-of-the-world movies—like *The Day the Earth Caught Fire* (1962)—is that great scene with New York or London or Tokyo discovered empty, its entire population annihilated. Or, as in *The World, the Flesh, and the Devil* (1959), the whole movie can be devoted to the fantasy of occupying the deserted city and starting all over again—*Robinson Crusoe* on a world-wide scale.

   Another kind of satisfaction these films supply is extreme moral simplification—that is to say, a morally acceptable fantasy where one can give outlet to cruel or at least amoral feelings. In this respect, science fiction films partly overlap with horror films. This is the undeniable pleasure we derive from looking at freaks, at beings excluded from the category of the human. The sense of superiority over the freak conjoined in varying proportions with the titillation of fear and aversion makes it possible for moral scruples to be lifted, for cruelty to be enjoyed. The same thing happens in science fiction films. In the figure of the monster from outer space, the freakish, the ugly, and the predatory all converge—and provide a fantasy target for righteous bellicosity to discharge itself, and for the aesthetic enjoyment of suffering and disaster. Science fiction films are one of the purest forms of spectacle; that is, we are rarely inside anyone's feelings. (An exception to this is Jack Arnold's *The Incredible Shrinking Man* [1957].) We are merely spectators; we watch.

   But in science fiction films, unlike horror films, there is not much horror. Suspense, shocks, surprises are mostly abjured in favor of a steady inexorable plot. Science fiction films invite a dispassionate, aesthetic view of destruction and violence—a *technological* view. Things, objects, machinery play a major role in these films. A greater range of ethical values is embodied in the décor of these films than in the people. Things, rather than the helpless humans, are the locus of values because we experience them, rather than people, as the sources of power. According to science fiction films, man is naked without his artifacts. *They* stand for different values, they are potent, they are what gets destroyed, and they are the indispensable tools for the repulse of the alien invaders or the repair of the damaged environment.

   The science fiction films are strongly moralistic. The standard message is the one about the proper, or humane, uses of science, versus the mad, obsessional use of science. This message the science fiction films share in common with the classic horror films of the 1930's, like *Frankenstein, The Mummy, The Island of Doctor Moreau, Dr. Jekyll and Mr. Hyde*. (Georges Franju's brilliant *Les Yeux Sans Visage* [1959], called here *The*

Horror Chamber of Doctor Faustus, is a more recent example.) In the horror films, we have the mad or obsessed or misguided scientist who pursues his experiments against good advice to the contrary, creates a monster or monsters, and is himself destroyed—often recognizing his folly himself, and dying in the successful effort to destroy his own creation. One science fiction equivalent of this is the scientist, usually a member of a team, who defects to the planetary invaders because "their" science is more advanced than "ours."

This is the case in *The Mysterians*, and, true to form, the renegade sees his error in the end, and from within the Mysterian space ship destroys it and himself. In *This Island Earth* (1955), the inhabitants of the beleaguered planet Metaluna propose to conquer Earth, but their project is foiled by a Metalunan scientist named Exeter who, having lived on Earth a while and learned to love Mozart, cannot abide such viciousness. Exeter plunges his space ship into the ocean after returning a glamorous pair (male and female) of American physicists to Earth. Metaluna dies. In *The Fly* (1958), the hero, engrossed in his basement-laboratory experiments on a matter-transmitting machine, uses himself as a subject, accidentally exchanges head and one arm with a housefly which had gotten into the machine, becomes a monster, and with his last shred of human will destroys his laboratory and orders his wife to kill him. His discovery, for the good of mankind, is lost.

Being a clearly labeled species of intellectual, the scientists in science fiction films are always liable to crack up or go off the deep end. In *Conquest of Space* (1955), the scientist-commander of an international expedition to Mars suddenly acquires scruples about the blasphemy involved in the undertaking, and begins reading the Bible mid-journey instead of attending to his duties. The commander's son, who is his junior officer and always addresses his father as "General," is forced to kill the old man when he tries to prevent the ship from landing on Mars. In this film, both sides of the ambivalence toward scientists are given voice. Generally, for a scientific enterprise to be treated entirely sympathetically in these films, it needs the certificate of utility. Science, viewed without ambivalence, means an efficacious response to danger. Disinterested intellectual curiosity rarely appears in any form other than caricature, as a maniacal dementia that cuts one off from normal human relations. But this suspicion is usually directed at the scientist rather than his work. The creative scientist may become a martyr to his own discovery, through an accident or by pushing things too far. The implication remains that other men, less imaginative—in short, technicians—would administer the same scientific discovery better and more safely. The most ingrained contemporary mistrust of the intellect is visited, in these movies, upon the scientist-as-intellectual.

The message that the scientist is one who releases forces which, if not controlled for good, could destroy man himself seems innocuous enough. One of the oldest images of the scientist is Shakespeare's Prospero, the over-detached scholar forcibly retired from society to a desert island, only partly in control of the magic forces in which he dabbles. Equally classic is the figure of the scientist as satanist (*Dr. Faustus*, stories of Poe and Hawthorne). Science is magic, and man has always known that there is black magic as well as white. But it is not enough to remark that contemporary attitudes—as reflected in science fiction films—remain ambivalent, that the scientist is treated both as satanist and savior. The proportions have changed, because of the new context in which the old admiration and fear of the scientist is located. For his sphere of influence is no longer local, himself or his immediate community. It is planetary, cosmic.

One gets the feeling, particularly in the Japanese films, but not only there, that mass trauma exists over the use of nuclear weapons and the possibility of future nuclear wars. Most of the science fiction films bear witness to this trauma, and in a way, attempt to exorcise it.

The accidental awakening of the super-destructive monster who has slept in the earth since prehistory is, often, an obvious metaphor for the Bomb. But there are many explicit references as well. In *The Mysterians*, a probe ship from the planet Mysteroid has landed on earth, near Tokyo. Nuclear warfare having been practiced on Mysteroid for centuries (their civilization is "more advanced than ours"), 90 per cent of those now born on the planet have to be destroyed at birth, because of defects caused by the huge amounts of Strontium 90 in their diet. The Mysterians have come to earth to marry earth women and possibly to take over our relatively uncontaminated planet. . . . In *The Incredible Shrinking Man*, the John Doe hero is the victim of a gust of radiation which blows over the water, while he is out boating with his wife; the radiation causes him to grow smaller and smaller, until at the end of the movie he steps through the fine mesh of a window screen to become "the infinitely small. . . ." In *Rodan*, a horde of monstrous carnivorous prehistoric insects, and finally a pair of giant flying reptiles (the prehistoric Archeopteryx), are hatched from dormant eggs in the depths of a mine shaft by the impact of nuclear test explosions, and go on to destroy a good part of the world before they are felled by the molten lava of a volcanic eruption. . . . In the English film, *The Day the Earth Caught Fire*, two simultaneous hydrogen bomb tests by the U.S. and Russia change by eleven degrees the tilt of the earth on its axis and alter the earth's orbit so that it begins to approach the sun.

Radiation casualties—ultimately, the conception of the whole world as a casualty of nuclear testing and nuclear warfare—is the most ominous of all the notions with which science fiction films deal. Universes become expendable. Worlds become contaminated, burnt out, exhausted, obsolete. In *Rocketship X-M* (1950), explorers from Earth land on Mars, where they learn that atomic warfare has destroyed Martian civilization. In George Pal's *The War of the Worlds* (1953), reddish spindly alligator-skinned creatures from Mars invade Earth because their planet is becoming too cold to be habitable. In *This Island Earth*, also American, the planet Metaluna, whose population has long ago been driven underground by warfare, is dying under the missile attacks of an enemy planet. Stocks of uranium, which power the force-shield shielding Metaluna, have been used up; and an unsuccessful expedition is sent to Earth to enlist earth scientists to devise new sources of nuclear power.

There is a vast amount of wishful thinking in science fiction films, some of it touching, some of it depressing. Again and again, one detects the hunger for a "good war," which poses no moral problems, admits of no moral qualifications. The imagery of science fiction films will satisfy the most bellicose addict of war films, for a lot of the satisfactions of war films pass, untransformed, into science fiction films. Examples: the dogfights between earth "fighter rockets" and alien spacecraft in the *Battle in Outer Space* (1959); the escalating firepower in the successive assaults upon the invaders in *The Mysterians*, which Dan Talbot correctly described as a nonstop holocaust; the spectacular bombardment of the underground fortress in *This Island Earth*.

Yet at the same time the bellicosity of science fiction films is neatly channeled into the yearning for peace, or for at least peaceful coexistence. Some scientist generally takes sententious note of the fact that it took the planetary invasion or cosmic disaster to make the warring nations of the earth come to their senses, and suspend their own conflicts. One of the main themes of many science fiction films—the color ones usually, because they have the budget and resources to develop the military spectacle—is this UN fantasy, a fantasy of united warfare. (The same wishful UN theme cropped up in a recent spectacular which is not science fiction, *Fifty-Five Days at Peking* [1963]. There, topically enough, the Chinese, the Boxers, play the role of Martian invaders who unite the earthmen, in this case the United States, Russia, England, France, Germany, Italy, and Japan.) A great enough disaster cancels all enmities, and calls upon the utmost concentration of the earth's resources.

Science—technology—is conceived of as the great unifier. Thus the science fiction films also project a utopian fantasy. In the classic models of utopian thinking—Plato's Republic, Campanella's City of the Sun, More's Utopia, Swift's land of the Houyhnhnms, Voltaire's Eldorado—society had worked out a perfect consensus. In these societies reasonableness had achieved an unbreakable supremacy over the emotions. Since no disagreement or social conflict was intellectually plausible, none was possible. As in Melville's *Typee*, "they all think the same." The universal rule of reason meant universal agreement. It is interesting, too, that societies in which reason was pictured as totally ascendant were also traditionally pictured as having an ascetic and/or materially frugal and economically simple mode of life. But in the utopian world community projected by science fiction films, totally pacified and ruled by scientific concensus, the demand for simplicity of material existence would be absurd.

But alongside the hopeful fantasy of moral simplification and international unity embodied in the science fiction films, lurk the deepest anxieties about contemporary existence. I don't mean only the very real trauma of the Bomb—that it has been used, that there are enough now to kill everyone on earth many times over, that those new bombs may very well be used. Besides these new anxieties about physical disaster, the prospect of universal mutilation and even annihilation, the science fiction films reflect powerful anxieties about the condition of the individual psyche.

For science fiction films may also be described as a popular mythology for the contemporary *negative* imagination about the impersonal. The other-world creatures which seek to take "us" over, are an "it," not a "they." The planetary invaders are usually zombie-like. Their movements are either cool, mechanical, or lumbering, blobby. But it amounts to the same thing. If they are nonhuman in form, they proceed with an absolutely regular, unalterable movement (unalterable save by destruction). If they are human in form—dressed in space suits, etc.—then they obey the most rigid military discipline, and display no personal characteristics whatsoever. And it is this regime of emotionlessness, of impersonality, of regimentation, which they will impose on the earth if they are successful. "No more love, no more beauty, no more pain," boasts a converted earthling in *The Invasion of the Body Snatchers* (1956). The half earthling-half alien children in *The Children of the Damned* (1960) are absolutely emotionless, move as a group and understand each others' thoughts, and are all prodigious intellects. They are the wave of the future, man in his next stage of development.

These alien invaders practice a crime which is worse than murder. They do not simply kill the person. They obliterate him. In *The War of the Worlds*, the ray which issues from the rocket ship disintegrates all persons and objects in its path, leaving no trace of them but a light ash. In Honda's *The H-Men* (1959), the creeping blob melts all flesh with which it comes in contact. If the blob, which looks like a huge hunk of red jello, and can crawl across floors and up and down walls, so much as touches your bare boot, all that is left of you is a heap of clothes on the floor. (A more articulated, size-multiplying blob is the villain in the English film *The Creeping Unknown* [1956].) In another version of this fantasy, the body is preserved but the person is entirely reconstituted as the automatized servant or agent of the alien powers. This is, of course, the vampire fantasy in new dress. The person is really dead, but he doesn't know it. He's "undead," he has become an "unperson." It happens to a whole California town in *The Invasion of the Body Snatchers*, to several earth scientists in *This Island Earth,* and to assorted innocents in *It Came from Outer Space, Attack of the Puppet People* (1961), and *The Brain Eaters* (1961). As the victim always backs away from the vampire's horrifying embrace, so in science fiction films the person always fights being "taken over"; he wants to retain his humanity. But once the deed has been done, the victim is eminently satisfied with his condition. He has not been converted from human amiability to monstrous "animal" blood-lust (a metaphoric exaggeration of sexual desire), as in the old vampire fantasy. No, he has simply become far more efficient—the very model of technocratic man, purged of emotions, volitionless, tranquil, obedient to all orders. The dark secret behind human nature used to be the upsurge of the animal—as in *King Kong.* The threat to man, his availability to dehumanization, lay in his own animality. Now the danger is understood as residing in man's ability to be turned into a machine.

The rule, of course, is that this horrible and irremediable form of murder can strike anyone in the film except the hero. The hero and his family, while grossly menaced, always escape this fact and by the end of the film the invaders have been repulsed or destroyed. I know of only one exception, *The Day That Mars Invaded Earth* (1963), in which, after all the standard struggles, the scientist-hero, his wife, and their two children are "taken over" by the alien invaders—and that's that. (The last minutes of the film show them being incinerated by the Martians' rays and their ash silhouettes flushed down their empty swimming pool, while their simulacra drive off in the family car.) Another variant but upbeat switch on the rule occurs in *The Creation of the Humanoids* (1964), where the hero discovers at the end of the film that he, too, has been turned into a metal robot, complete with highly efficient and virtually indestructible mechanical insides, although he didn't know it and detected no difference in himself. He learns, however, that he will shortly be upgraded into a "humanoid" having all the properties of a real man.

Of all the standard motifs of science fiction films, this theme of dehumanization is perhaps the most fascinating. For, as I have indicated, it is scarcely a black-and-white situation, as in the vampire films. The attitude of the science fiction films toward depersonalization is mixed. On the one hand, they deplore it as the ultimate horror. On the other hand, certain characteristics of the dehumanized invaders, modulated and disguised—such as the ascendancy of reason over feelings, the idealization of teamwork and the consensus-creating activities of science, a marked degree of moral simplification—are precisely traits of the savior-scientists. For it is interesting that when the scientist in these films is treated negatively, it is usually done through the portrayal of an individual scientist who holes up in his laboratory and neglects his fiancée or his loving wife and children, obsessed by his daring and dangerous experiments. The scientist as a loyal member of a team, and therefore considerably less individualized, is treated quite respectfully.

There is absolutely no social criticism, of even the most implicit kind, in science fiction films. No criticism, for example, of the conditions of our society which create the impersonality and dehumanization which science fiction fantasies displace onto the influence of an alien It. Also, the notion of science as a social activity, interlocking with social and political interests, is unacknowledged. Science is simply either adventure (for good or evil) or a technical response to danger. And, typically, when the fear of science is paramount—when science is conceived of as black magic rather than white—the evil has no attribution beyond that of the perverse will of an individual scientist. In science fiction films the antithesis of black magic and white is drawn as a split between technology, which is beneficent, and the errant individual will of a lone intellectual.

Thus, science fiction films can be looked at as thematically central allegory, replete with standard modern attitudes. The theme of depersonalization (being "taken over") which I have been talking about is a new allegory reflecting the age-old awareness of man that, sane, he is always perilously close to insanity and unreason. But there is something more here than just a recent, popular image which expresses man's perennial, but largely unconscious, anxiety about his sanity. The image derives most of its power from a supplementary and historical anxiety, also not experienced *consciously* by most people, about the depersonalizing conditions of modern urban society. Similarly, it is not enough to note that science fiction allegories are one of the new myths about—that is, ways of accommodating to and negating—the perennial human anxiety about death. (Myths of heaven and hell, and of ghosts, had the same function.) Again, there is a historically specifiable twist which intensifies the anxiety, or better, the trauma suffered by everyone in the middle of the 20th century when it became clear that from now on to the end of human history, every person would spend his individual life not only under the threat of individual death, which is certain, but of something almost unsupportable psychologically—collective incineration and extinction which could come any time, virtually without warning.

From a psychological point of view, the imagination of disaster does not greatly differ from one period in history to another. But from a political and moral point of view, it does. The expectation of the apocalypse may be the occasion for a radical disaffiliation from society, as when thousands of Eastern European Jews in the 17th century gave up their homes and businesses and began to trek to Palestine upon hearing that Shabbethai Zevi had been proclaimed Messiah and that the end of the world was imminent. But peoples learn the news of their own end in diverse ways. It is reported that in 1945 the populace of Berlin received without great agitation the news that Hitler had decided to kill them all, before the Allies arrived, because they had not been worthy enough to win the war. We are, alas, more in the position of the Berliners than of the Jews of 17th-century Eastern Europe; and our response is closer to theirs, too. What I am suggesting is that the imagery of disaster in science fiction films is above all the emblem of an *inadequate response*. I do not mean to bear down on the films for this. They themselves are only a sampling, stripped of sophistication, of the inadequacy of most people's response to the unassimilable terrors that infect their consciousness. The interest of the films, aside from their considerable amount of cinematic charm, consists in this intersection between a naïvely and largely debased commercial art product and the most profound dilemmas of the contemporary situation.

The image of women in science fiction

Joanna Russ

Science fiction is *What If* literature. All sorts of definitions have been proposed by people in the field, but they all contain both The What If and The Serious Explanation; that is, science fiction shows things not as they characteristically or habitually are but as they might be, and for this "might be" the author must offer a rational, serious, consistent explanation, one that does not (in Samuel Delany's phrase) offend against what is known to be known.[1] Science fiction writers can't be experts in all disciplines, but they ought at least to be up to the level of the *New York Times* Sunday science page. If the author offers marvels and does not explain them, or if he explains them playfully and not seriously, or if the explanation offends against what the author knows to be true, you are dealing with fantasy and not science fiction. True, the fields tend to blur into each other and the borderland is a pleasant and gleeful place, but generally you can tell where you are. Examples:

J. R. R. Tolkien writes fantasy. He offends against all sorts of archaeological, geological, paleontological, and linguistic evidence which he undoubtedly knows as well as anyone else does.

Edgar Rice Burroughs wrote science fiction. He explained his marvels seriously and he explained them as well as he could. At the time he wrote, his stories did in fact conflict with what was known to be known, but he didn't know that. He wrote *bad* science fiction.

Ray Bradbury writes both science fiction and fantasy, often in the same story. He doesn't seem to care.

Science fiction comprises a grand variety of common properties: the fourth dimension, hyperspace (whatever that is), the colonization of other worlds, nuclear catastrophe, time travel (now out of fashion), interstellar exploration, mutated supermen, alien races, and so on. The sciences treated range from the "hard" or exact sciences (astronomy, physics) through the life sciences (biology, biochemistry, neurology) through the "soft" or inexact sciences (ethology, ecology) to disciplines that are still in the descriptive or philosophical stage and may never become exact (history, for example).[2] I would go beyond these last to include what some writers call "para-sciences"—extra-sensory perception, psionics, or even magic—as long as the "discipline" in question is treated as it would have to be if it were real, that is rigorously, logically, and in detail.[3]

Fantasy, says Samuel Delany, treats what cannot happen, science fiction what has not happened.[4] One would think science fiction the perfect literary mode in which to explore (and explode) our assumptions about "innate" values and "natural" social arrangements, in short our ideas about Human Nature, Which Never Changes. Some of this has been done. But speculation about the innate personality differences between men and women, about family structure, about sex, in short about gender roles, hardly exists. And why not?

What is the image of women in science fiction?

We can begin by dismissing fiction set in the very near future (such as *On the Beach*) for most science fiction is not like this; most science fiction is set far in the future, some of it *very* far in the future, hundreds of thousands of years sometimes. One would think that by then human society, family life, personal relations, child-rearing, in fact anything one can name, would have altered beyond recognition. This is not the case. The more intelligent, literate fiction carries today's values and standards into its future Galactic Empires. What may politely be called the less sophisticated fiction returns to the past—not even a real past, in most cases, but an idealized and exaggerated past.[5]

Intergalactic suburbia

In general, the authors who write reasonably sophisticated and literate science fiction (Clarke, Asimov, for choice) see the relations between the sexes as those of present-day, white, middle-class suburbia. Mummy and Daddy may live inside a huge amoeba and Daddy's job may be to test psychedelic drugs or cultivate yeast-vats, but the world inside their heads is the world of Westport and Rahway *and that world is never questioned.* Not that the authors are obvious about it; Fred Pohl's recent satire, *The Age of the Pussyfoot*, is a good case in point.[6] In this witty and imaginative future world, death is reversible, production is completely automated, the world population is enormous, robots do most of the repetitive work, the pharmacopoeia of psychoactive drugs is very, very large, and society has become so complicated that people must carry personal computers to make their everyday decisions for them. I haven't even mentioned the change in people's clothing, in their jobs, their slang, their hobbies, and so on. But it you look more closely at this weird world you find that it practices a laissez-faire capitalism, one even freer than our own; that men make more money than women; that men have the better jobs (the book's heroine is the equivalent of a consumer-research guinea pig); and that children are raised at home by their mothers.

In short, the American middle class with a little window dressing.

In science fiction, speculation about social institutions and individual psychology has always lagged far behind speculation about technology, possibly because technology is easier to understand than people. But this is not the whole story.[7] I have been talking about intelligent, literate science fiction. Concerning this sort of work one might simply speak of a failure of imagination outside the exact sciences, but there are other kinds of science fiction, and when you look at them, something turns up that makes you wonder if failure of imagination is what is at fault.

I ought to make it dear here that American science fiction and British science fiction have evolved very differently and that what I am going to talk about is—in origin—an American phenomenon. In Britain science fiction not only was always respectable, it still is, and there is a continuity in the field that the American tradition does not have. British fiction is not, on the whole, better written than American science fiction but it continues to attract first-rate writers from outside the field (Kipling, Shaw, C. S. Lewis, Orwell, Golding) and it continues to be reviewed seriously and well.[8]

American science fiction developed out of the pulps and stayed outside the tradition of serious literature for at least three decades; it is still not really respectable.[9] American science fiction originated in the adventure-story-*cum*-fairy-tale which most people think of (erroneously) as "science fiction." It has been called a great many things, most of them uncomplimentary, but the usual name is "space opera". There are good writers working in this field who do not deserve the public notoriety bred by this kind of science fiction. But their values usually belong to the same imaginative world and they participate in many of the same assumptions.[10] I will not, therefore, name names, but will pick on something inoffensive—think of Flash Gordon and read on.

Down among the he-men

If most literate science fiction takes for its gender-role models the ones which actually exist (or are assumed as ideals) in middle-class America, space opera returns to the past for *its* models, and not even the real past, but an idealized and simplified one. These stories are not realistic. They are primitive, sometimes bizarre, and often magnificently bald in their fantasy. Some common themes:

A *feudal economic and social structure*—usually paired with advanced technology and inadequate to the complexities of a seventh-century European mud hut.

Women are important as prizes or motives—i.e. we must rescue the heroine or win the hand of the beautiful Princess. Many fairy-tale motifs turn up here.

Active or ambitious women are evil—this literature is chockfull of cruel dowager empresses, sadistic matriarchs, evil ladies maddened by jealousy, domineering villainesses, and so on.

Women are supernaturally beautiful—all of them.

Women are weak and/or kept off stage—this genre is full of scientists' beautiful daughters who know just enough to be brought along by Daddy as his research assistant, but not enough to be of any help to anyone.

Women's powers are passive and involuntary—an odd idea that turns up again and again, not only in space opera. If female characters are given abilities, these are often innate abilities which cannot be developed or controlled, e.g. clairvoyance, telepathy, hysterical strength, unconscious psi power, eidetic memory, perfect pitch, lightning calculation, or (more baldly) magic. The power is somehow *in* the woman, but she does not really possess it. Often realistic science fiction employs the same device.[11]

The real focus of interest is not on women at all—but on the cosmic rivalries between strong, rugged, virile he-men. It is no accident that space opera and horse opera bear similar names.[12] Most of the readers of science fiction are male and most of them are young; people seem to quit reading the stuff in their middle twenties and the hard-core readers who form fan clubs and go to conventions are even younger and even more likely to be male.[13] Such readers as I have met (the addicts?) are overwhelmingly likely to be nervous, shy, pleasant boys, sensitive, intelligent, and very awkward with people. They also talk too much. It does not take a clairvoyant to see why such people would be attracted to space opera, with its absence of real women and its tremendous over-rating of the "real he-man." In the March 1969 issue of *Amazing* one James Koval wrote to the editor as follows:[14]

> Your October issue was superb; better than that, it was uniquely original . . . Why do I think it so worthy of such compliments? Because of the short stories *Conqueror* and *Mu Panther*, mainly. They were, in every visual and emotional sense, stories about real men whose rugged actions and keen thinking bring back a genuine feeling of masculinity, a thing sorely missed by the long-haired and soft-eyed generation of my time, of which I am a part . . . aiming entertainment at the virile and imaginative male of today is the best kind of business . . . I sincerely hope you keep your man-versus-animal type format going, especially with stories like *Mu Panther.* That was exceptionally unique.

The editor's response was "GROAN!"

But even if readers are adolescents, the writers are not. I know quite a few grown-up men who should know better, but who nonetheless fall into what I would like to call the he-man ethic. And they do it over and over again. In November 1968, a speaker at the Philadelphia Science Fiction Convention[15] described the heroes such writers create:

> The only real He-Man is Master of the Universe . . . The real He-Man is invulnerable. He has no weaknesses. Sexually he is super-potent. He does exactly what he pleases, everywhere and at all times. He is absolutely self-sufficient. He depends on nobody, for this would be a weakness. Toward women he is possessive, protective, and patronizing; to men he gives orders. He is never frightened by anything or for any reason; he is never indecisive and he always wins.

In short, masculinity equals power and femininity equals powerlessness. This is a cultural stereotype that can be found in much popular literature, but science fiction writers have no business employing stereotypes, let alone swallowing them goggle-eyed.

Equal is as equal does

In the last decade or so, science fiction has begun to attempt the serious presentation of men and women as equals, usually by showing them at work together. Even a popular television show like *Star Trek* shows a spaceship with a mixed crew; fifteen years ago this was unthinkable.[16] *Forbidden Planet*, a witty and charming film made in the 1950s, takes it for granted that the crew of a spaceship will all be red-blooded, crew-cut, woman-hungry men, rather like the cast of *South Pacific* before the nurses arrive. And within the memory of living adolescent, John W. Campbell, Jr., the editor of *Analog*, proposed that "nice girls" be sent on spaceships as prostitutes because married women would only clutter everything up with washing and babies. But Campbell is a coelacanth.

At any rate, many recent stories do show a two-sexed world in which women as well as men work competently and well. But this is a reflection of present reality, not genuine speculation. And what is most striking about these stories is what they leave out: the characters' personal and erotic relations are not described; child-rearing arrangements (to my knowledge) are never described; and the women who appear in these stories are either young and childless or middle-aged, with their children safely grown up. That is, the real problems of a society without gender-role differentiation are not faced. It is my impression that most of these stories are colorless and schematic; the authors want to be progressive, God bless them, but they don't know how. Exceptions:

Mack Reynolds, who also presents a version of future socialism called "the Ultra-Welfare State." (Is there a connection?) He has written novels about two-sexed societies of which one is a kind of mild gynocracy. He does not describe child-rearing arrangements, though.

Samuel Delany, who often depicts group marriages and communal child-rearing, "triplet" marriages (not polygamy or polyandry, for each person is understood to have sexual relations with the other two) *und so weiter*, all with no differentiation of gender roles, all with an affectionate, East Village, Berkeley-Bohemian air to them, and all with the advanced technology that would make such things work. His people have the rare virtue of fitting the institutions under which they live. Robert Heinlein, who also goes in for odd arrangements (e.g the "line marriage" in *The Moon Is a Harsh Mistress* in which everybody is married to everybody, but there are seniority rights in sex), peoples his different societies with individualistic, possessive, competitive, pre-World War II Americans—just the people who could not live under the cooperative or communal arrangements he describes. Heinlein, for all his virtues, seems to me to exemplify science fiction's failure of imagination in the human sphere. He is superb at work but out of his element elsewhere. *Stranger in a Strange Land* seems to me a particular failure. I have heard Heinlein's women called "boy scouts with breasts"—but the subject takes more discussion than I can give it here. Alexei Panshin's critical study, *Heinlein in Dimension*, undertakes a thorough investigation of Heinlein vs. Sex. Heinlein loses.[17]

Matriarchy

The strangest and most fascinating oddities in science fiction occur not in the stories that try to abolish differences in gender roles but in those which attempt to reverse the roles themselves. Unfortunately, only a handful of writers have treated this theme seriously. Space opera abounds, but in space opera the reversal is always cut to the same pattern.

Into a world of cold, cruel, domineering women who are openly contemptuous of their cringing, servile men ("gutless" is a favorite word here) arrive(s) men (a man) from our present world. With a minimum of trouble, these normal men succeed in overthrowing the matriarchy, which although strong and warlike, is also completely inefficient. At this point the now dominant men experience a joyful return of victorious manhood and the women (after initial reluctance) declare that they too are much happier. Everything is (to quote S. J. Perelman) leeches and cream.[18] Two interesting themes occur:

1. the women are far more vicious, sadistic, *and openly contemptuous* of men than comparable dominant men are of comparable subordinate women in the usual space opera.

2. the women are dominant because they are taller and stronger than the men (1).

Sometimes the story is played out among the members of an alien species modeled on insects or microscopic sea-creatures, so that tiny males are eaten or engulfed by huge females. I remember one in which a tiny male was eaten by a female who was not only forty feet tall but maddened to boot.[19] There are times when science fiction leaves the domain of literature altogether. Least said, soonest mended.

I remember three British accounts of future matriarchies that could be called serious studies. In one the matriarchy is incidental. The society is presented as good because it embodies the traditionally feminine virtues of serenity, tolerance, love, and pacifism.[20] In John Wyndham's "Consider Her Ways" there are no men at all; the society is a static, hierarchical one which (like the first) is good because of its traditionally feminine virtues, which are taken as innate in the female character. There is something about matriarchy that makes science fiction writers think of two things: biological engineering and social insects; whether women are considered naturally chitinous or the softness of the female body is equated with the softness of the "soft" sciences I don't know, but the point is often made that "women are conservative by nature" and from there it seems an easy jump to bees or ants. Science fiction stories often make the point that a matriarchy will be static and hierarchical, like Byzantium or Egypt. (It should be remembered here that the absolute value of progress is one of the commonest shibboleths of science fiction.) The third story I remember—technically it's a "post-Bomb" story—was written by an author whose version of matriarchy sounds like Robert Graves's.[21] The story makes the explicit point that while what is needed is static endurance, the Mother rules; when exploration and initiative again become necessary, the Father will return. The Great Mother is a real, supernatural character in this tale and the people in it are very real people. The matriarchy—again, the women rule by supernatural knowledge—is vividly realized and there is genuine exploration of what personal relations would be like in such a society. There is a kind of uncompromising horror (the hero is hunted by "the hounds of the Mother"—women whose minds have been taken over by the Magna Mater) which expresses a man's fear of such a world much more effectively than all the maddened, forty-foot-tall male-gulpers ever invented.

So far I've been discussing fiction written by men and largely for men.[22] What about fiction written by women?

Women's fiction: Potpourri

Most science fiction writers are men, but some are women, and there are more women writing the stuff than there used to be. The women's work falls into four rough categories:

1. *Ladies' magazine fiction*—in which the sweet, gentle, intuitive little heroine solves an interstellar crisis by mending her slip or doing something equally domestic after her big, heroic husband has failed. Zenna Henderson sometimes writes like this. *Fantasy and Science Fiction*, which carries more of this kind of writing than any of the other magazines, once earned a deserved slap over the knuckles from reviewer James Blish.[23]

2. *Galactic suburbia*—very often written by women. Sometimes the characters are all male, especially if the story is set at work. Most women writing in the field (like so many of the men) write this kind of fiction.

3. *Space opera*—strange but true. Leigh Brackett is one example. Very rarely the protagonist turns out to be a sword-wielding, muscular, aggressive *woman*—but the he-man ethos of the world does not change, nor do the stereotyped personalities assigned to the secondary characters, particularly the female ones.

4. *Avant-garde fiction*—part of the recent rapprochement between the most experimental of the science fiction community and the most avant-garde of what is called "the mainstream." This takes us out of the field of science fiction altogether.[24]

In general, stories by women tend to contain more active and lively female characters than do stories by men, and more often than men writers, women writers try to invent worlds in which men and women will be equals. But the usual faults show up just as often. The conventional idea that women are second-class people is a hard idea to shake; and while it is easy enough to show women doing men's work, or active in society, it is in the family scenes and the love scenes that one must look for the author's real freedom from our most destructive prejudices.

An odd equality

I would like to close with a few words about *The Left Hand of Darkness*, a fine book that won the Science Fiction Writers of American Nebula Award for 1969 as the best novel of that year.[25] The book was written by a woman and it is about sex—I don't mean copulation; I mean what sexual identity means to people and what human identity means to them, and what kind of love can cross the barriers of culture and custom. It's a beautifully written book. Ursula K. Le Guin, the author, has imagined a world of human hermaphrodites— an experimental colony abandoned by its creators long ago and rediscovered by other human beings. The adults of this glacial world of Winter go through an oestrus cycle modeled on the human menstrual cycle: every four weeks the individual experiences a few days of sexual potency and obsessive interest in sex during which "he" becomes either male or female. The rest of the time "he" has no sex at all, or rather, only the potential of either. The cycle is involuntary, though it can be affected by drugs, and there is no choice of sex—except that the presence of someone already into the cycle and therefore of one sex will stimulate others in oestrus to become of the opposite sex. You would imagine that such a people's culture and institutions would be very different from ours and so they are; everything is finely realized, from their household implements to their customs to their creation myths. Again, however (and I'm very sorry to see it), family structure is not fully explained. Worse than that, child-rearing is left completely in the dark, although the human author herself is married and the mother of three children. Moreover, there is a human observer on Winter and he is male; and there is a native hero and *he is* male—at least "he" is *masculine in gender, if not in sex.* The native hero has a former spouse who is long-suffering, mild and gentle, while he himself is fiery, tough, self-sufficient, and proud. There is the Byronesque memory of a past incestuous affair; his lover and sibling is dead. There is an attempted seduction by a kind of Mata Hari *who is female* (so that the hero, of course, becomes male). It is, I must admit, a deficiency in the English language that these people must be called "he" throughout, but put that together with the native hero's personal encounters in the book, the absolute lack of interest in child-raising, the concen- tration on work, and what you have is a world of men. Thus the great love scene in the book is between two men: the human observer (who is a real man) and the native hero (who is a female man). The scene is nominally homosexual, but I think what lies at the bottom of it (and what has moved men and women readers alike) is that it is a love scene between a man and a woman, with the label "male: high status" pasted on the woman's forehead. Perhaps, with the straitjacket of our gender roles, with women automatically regarded as second-class, intelligent and active women *feel* as if they were female men or hermaph- rodites. Or perhaps the only way a woman (even in a love scene) can be made a man's equal and the love scene therefore deeply moving, is to make her *nominally* male. That is, female in sex but male in gender. Here is the human narrator describing the alien hero:

> to ignore the abstraction, to hold fast to the thing. There was in this attitude something feminine, a refusal of the abstract ideal, a submissiveness to the given . . .[26]

Very conventional, although the story is set far, far in the future and the narrator is supposed to be a trained observer, a kind of anthropologist. Here is the narrator again, describing human women (he has been asked if they are "like a different species"):

> No. Yes. No, of course not, not really. But the difference is very important, I suppose the most important thing, the heaviest single factor in one's life, is whether one's born male or female . . . Even where women participate equally with men in the society, *they still after all do all the child-bearing and so most of the child-rearing* . . .

And when asked "Are they mentally inferior?":

> I don't know. They don't often seem to turn up mathematicians, or composers of music, or inventors, or abstract thinkers. But it isn't that they're stupid . . .[27]

Let me remind you that this is centuries in the future. And again:

> The boy . . . had a girl's quick delicacy in his looks and movements, but no girl could keep so grim a silence as he did . . .[28]

It's the whole difficulty of science fiction, of genuine speculation: how to get away from traditional assumptions which are nothing more than traditional straitjackets.[29] Miss Le Guin seems to be aiming at some kind of equality between the sexes, but she certainly goes the long way around to get it; a whole new biology has to be invented, a whole society, a whole imagined world, so that finally she may bring together two persons of different sexes who will nonetheless be equals.[30]

The title I chose for this essay was "The Image of Women in Science Fiction." I hesitated between that and "Women in Science Fiction" but if I had chosen the latter, there would have been very little to say.

There are plenty of images of women in science fiction.

There are hardly any women.

Notes

1. In conversation and in his discussion of "Speculative Fiction" given at the MLA Seminar on Science Fiction in New York City, December 27, 1968.
2. Basil Davenport, *Inquiry Into Science Fiction*, Longmans, Green and Co., New York, London, Toronto, 1955, pp. 39ff.
3. A recent novel by James Blish, *Black Easter*, published by Doubleday, Garden City, N.Y. in 1968, does exactly this. See in particular the Introduction, pp. 7–8.
4. Samuel Delany, "About Five Thousand One Hundred and Seventy Five Words," in *Extrapolation: the Newsletter of the Conference on Science Fiction of the MLA*, ed. Thomas D. Clareson, College of Wooster, Wooster, Ohio, Vol. X, No. 2, May 1969, pp. 61–63.
5. There have been exceptions, e.g. Olaf Stapledon, George Bernard Shaw. And of course Philip Wylie's *The Disappearance*. Wylie's novel really ranks as a near-future story, though.
6. Frederik Pohl, *The Age of the Pussyfoot*, Trident Press, New York, 1968.
7. I don't want to adduce further examples, but most well-known science fiction is of this kind. It suffices to read *Childhood's End* for example (Arthur C. Clarke), and ask about the Utopian society of the middle: What do the men do? What do the women do? Who raises the children? And so on.

8. See William Atheling, Jr. (James Blish), *The Issue at Hand*, Advent Press, Chicago, 1964, pp. 117–19. I ought to make it clear that I am talking here of science fiction as a literary/cultural phenomenon, e.g., nobody can accuse George Bernard Shaw of suffering from the he-man ethos. But Shaw's ventures into science fiction have had little influence on the American tradition.

9. The American pioneer was Hugo Gernsback, whose name adorns the "Hugo," the yearly fan awards for best novel of the year, best short story, etc. In 1908 Gernsback founded a magazine called *Modern Electrics*, the world's first radio magazine. In 1911 he published a serial of his own writing called "Ralph 124C41+." Gernsback founded *Amazing Stories* in 1926 and by common consent, real science entered the field with John W. Campbell, Jr., in the late 1930s.

10. Some of the better writers in this genre are Keith Laumer, Gordon Dickson, and Poul Anderson. Most magazine fiction is at least tainted with space opera.

11. In *Age of the Pussyfoot* the heroine makes her living by trying out consumer products. She is so ordinary (or statistically extraordinary) that if she likes the products, the majority of the world's consumers will also like them. A prominent character in John Brunner's recent novel, *Stand on Zanzibar*, is a clairvoyant.

12. Also "soap opera"—the roles of the sexes are reversed.

13. I would put the ratio of male to female readers at about five to one. It might very well be higher.

14. I *think* March and I think it was *Amazing*; it is either *Amazing* or *Worlds of If* for 1968 or 1969. Sorry!

15. Me.

16. It is noteworthy, however, that the ladies of the crew spend their time as nurses, stewardesses and telephone operators.

17. See Alexei Panshin's *Heinlein in Dimension*, Advent Press, Chicago, 1968, especially Chapter VI.

18. Entertaining use can be made of this form. Keith Laumer's delightfully tongue-in-cheek "The War With the Yukks" is a case in point. You will now complain that I don't tell you where to find it, but trying to find uncollected stories or novellas is a dreadful task. I don't know where it is. I read it in a magazine publication; magazines vanish.

19. Again, vanished without a trace. It's an oldie and I suspect it appeared in one of Groff Conklin's fat anthologies of *The Best S.F.* for (fill in year). It was a lovely story.

20. This one may be American. A Russian (or American) and a Red Chinese, both from our present, are somehow transported into the future. They kill each other at a party in a xenophobic rage which their hostesses find tragic and obsolete. I remember that the ladies in the story shave their heads (that is, the ladies' own heads). Not exactly a matriarchy but a semi-reversal of gender roles occurs in Philip Wylie's *The Disappearance*, a brilliant argument to the effect that gender roles are learned and can be unlearned.

21. Again I find myself with distinct memories of the story and none of the author's name. I would appreciate any information. Science fiction is in a dreadful state bibliographically.

22. This is perhaps too sweeping a statement; Isaac Asimov certainly writes for everybody, to give one example only. But male readers do outnumber female readers, and there is a definite bias in the field toward what I have called the he-man ethos. I think the generalization can stand as a generalization.

23. See William Atheling, Jr. (James Blish), *The Issue at Hand*, Advent Press, Chicago, 1964, p. 112.

24. Carol Emshwiller is a good example, See the *Orbit* series of anthologies edited by Damon Knight (Putnam's in hardcover, Berkley in paperback).

25. Ursula K. Le Guin, *The Left Hand of Darkness*, Ace Books, New York, N.Y. 1969 (paperback). As of this writing it has also received the Hugo, a comparable fan award.

26. *Ibid.*, p. 201.

27. *Ibid.*, p. 223.

28. *Ibid.*, p. 281.

29. I am too hard on the book; the narrator isn't quite that positive and one could make out a good case that the author is trying to criticize his viewpoint. There is also a technical problem: we are led to equate the human narrator's world (which we never see) with our own, simply because handling *two* unknowns in one novel would present insuperable difficulties. Moreover, Le Guin wishes us to contrast Winter with our own world, not with some hypothetical, different society which would then have to be shown in detail. However, her earlier novel, *City of Illusions*, also published by Ace, is surprisingly close to the space opera, he-man ethos—either anti-feminism or resentment at being feminine, depending on how you look at it.

30. There is an old legend (or a new one—I heard it read several years ago on WBAIFM) concerning Merlin and some sorceress who was his sworn enemy. Each had resolved to destroy the other utterly, but they met and—each not knowing who the other was—fell in love. The problem was solved by Merlin's transforming her into him and she transforming him into herself. Thus both destroyed and reconstituted in the other sex, they lived happily ever after (one assumes). Or as Shaw was supposed to have said, he conceived of his female characters as being himself in different circumstances.

Progress versus Utopia; or, can we imagine the future?

Fredric Jameson

It will then turn out that the world has long dreamt of that of which it had only to have a clear idea to possess it really.

—Karl Marx to Arnold Ruge (1843)

A storm is blowing from Paradise; it has got caught in his wings with such violence that the angel can no longer close them. The storm irresistibly propels him into the future to which his back is turned, while the pile of debris before him grows skyward. This storm is what we call progress.

—Walter Benjamin, *Theses on the Philosophy of History* (1939)

What if the "idea" of progress were not an idea at all but rather the symptom of something else? This is the perspective suggested, not merely by the interrogation of cultural texts, such as SF, but by the contemporary discovery of the Symbolic in general. Indeed, following the emergence of psychoanalysis, of structuralism in linguistics and anthropology, of semiotics together with its new field of "narratology," of communications theory, and even of such events as the emergence of a politics of "surplus consciousness" (Rudolf Bahro) in the 1960s, we have come to feel that abstract ideas and concepts are not necessarily intelligible entities in their own right. This was of course already the thrust of Marx's discovery of the dynamics of ideology; but while the older terms in which that discovery was traditionally formulated—"false consciousness" versus "science"—remain generally true, the Marxian approach to ideology, itself fed by all the discoveries enumerated above, has also become a far more sophisticated and non-reductive form of analysis than the classical opposition tends to suggest.

From the older standpoint of a traditional "history of ideas," however, ideology was essentially grasped as so many *opinions* vehiculated by a narrative text such as an SF novel, from which, as Lionel Trilling once put it, like so many raisins and currants they are picked out and exhibited in isolation. Thus Verne is thought to have "believed" progress,[1] while the originality of Wells was to have entertained an ambivalent and agonizing love-hate relationship with this "value," now affirmed and now denounced in the course of his complex artistic trajectory.[2]

The discovery of the Symbolic, however, suggests that for the individual subject as well as for groups, collectivities, and social classes, abstract opinion is, but a symptom or an index of some vaster *pensée sauvage* about history itself, whether personal or collective. This thinking, in which a particular conceptual enunciation such as the "idea" of progress finds its structural intelligibility, may be said to be of a more properly *narrative* kind, analogous in that respect to the constitutive role played by master-fantasies in the Freudian model to the Unconscious. Nevertheless, the analogy is misleading to the degree to which it may awaken older attitudes about objective truth and subjective or psychological "projection," which are explicitly overcome and transcended by the notion of the Symbolic itself. In other words, we must resist the reflex which concludes that the narrative fantasies which a collectivity entertains about its past and its future are "merely" mythical, archetypal, and projective, as opposed to "concepts" like progress or cyclical return, which can somehow be tested for their objective or even scientific validity. This reflex is itself the last symptom of that dissociation of the private and the public, the subject and the object, the personal and the political, which has characterized the social life of capitalism. A theory of some narrative *pensée sauvage*—what I have elsewhere termed the political unconscious[3]—will, on the contrary, want to affirm the epistemological priority of such "fantasy" in theory and praxis alike.

The task of such analysis would then be to detect and to reveal— behind such written *traces* of the political unconscious as the narrative texts of high or mass culture, but also behind those other symptoms or traces which are opinion, ideology, and even philosophical systems—the outlines of some deeper and vaster narrative movement in which the groups of a given collectivity at a certain historical conjuncture anxiously interrogate their fate, and explore it with hope or dread. Yet the nature of this vaster collective subtext, with its specific structural limits and permutations, will he registered above all in terms of properly narrative categories: closure, recontainment, the production of episodes, and the like. Once again, a crude analogy with the dynamics of the individual unconscious may be useful. Proust's restriction to the windless cork-lined room, for instance, the emblematic eclipse of his own possible relationships to any concrete personal or historical future, determines the formal innovations and wondrous structural subterfuges of his now exclusively retrospective narrative production. Yet such narrative categories are themselves fraught with contradiction: in order for narrative to project some sense of a totality of experience in space and time, it must surely know some closure (a narrative must have an ending, even if it is ingeniously organized around the structural repression of endings as such). At the same time, however, closure or the narrative ending is the mark of that boundary or limit beyond which thought cannot go. The merit of SF is to dramatize this contradiction on the level of plot itself, since the vision of future history cannot know any punctual ending of this kind, at the same time that its novelistic expression demands some such ending. Thus Asimov has consistently refused to complete or terminate his *Foundation* series; while the most obvious ways in which an SF novel can wrap its story up—as in an atomic explosion that destroys the universe, or the static image of some future totalitarian world-state—are also clearly the places in which our own ideological limits are the most surely inscribed.

It will, I trust, already have become clear that this ultimate "text" or object of study—the master-narratives of the political unconscious—is a *construct*: it exists nowhere in "empirical" form, and therefore must be re-constructed on the basis of empirical "texts" of all sorts, in much the same way that the master-fantasies of the individual unconscious are reconstructed through the fragmentary and symptomatic "texts" of dreams, values, behavior, verbal free-association, and the like. This is to say that we must necessarily make a place for the formal and textual *mediations* through which such deeper narratives find a partial articulation. No serious literary critic today would suggest that content—whether social or psychoanalytic—inscribes itself immediately and transparently on the works of "high" literature: instead, the latter find themselves inserted in a complex and semi-autonomous dynamic of their own—the history of forms—which has its own logic and whose relationship to content per se is necessarily mediated, complex, and indirect (and takes very different structural paths at different moments of formal as well as social development). It is perhaps less widely accepted that the forms and texts of mass culture are fully as mediated as this: and that here too, collective and political fantasies do not find some simple transparent expression in this or that film or TV show. It would in my opinion be a mistake to make the "apologia" for SF in terms of specifically "high" literary values—to try, in other words, to recuperate this or that major text as exceptional, in much the same way as some literary critics have tried to recuperate Hammett or Chandler for the lineage of Dostoyevsky, say, or Faulkner. SF is a sub-genre with a complex and interesting formal history of its own, and with its own dynamic, which is not that of high culture, But which stands in a complementary and dialectical relationship to high culture or modernism as such. We must therefore first make a detour through the dynamics of this specific form, with a view to grasping its emergence as a formal and historical event.

1. Whatever its illustrious precursors, it is a commonplace of the history of SF that it emerged, virtually full-blown, with Jules Verne and H.G. Wells, during the second half of the 19th century, a period also characterized by the production of a host of utopias of a more classical type. It would seem appropriate to register this generic emergence as the symptom of a mutation in our relationship to historical time itself: but this is a more complex proposition than it may seem, and demands to be argued in a more theoretical way.

I will suggest that the model for this kind of analysis, which grasps an entire genre as a symptom and reflex of historical change, may be found in Georg Lukács' classical study, *The Historical Novel* (1936). Lukács began with an observation that should not have been particularly surprising: it was no accident, he said, that the period which knew the emergence of historical thinking, of historicism in its peculiarly modern sense—the late 18th and early 19th century—should also have witnessed, in the work of Sir Walter Scott, the emergence of a narrative form peculiarly restructured to express that new consciousness. Just as modern historical consciousness was preceded by other, for us now archaic, forms of historiography—the chronicle or the annals—so the historical novel in its modern sense was certainly preceded by literary works which evoked the past and recreated historical settings of one kind or another: the history plays of Shakespeare or Corneille, *La Princesse de Clèves*, even Arthurian romance: yet all these works in their various ways affirm the past as being essentially the same as the present, and do not yet confront the great discovery of the modern historical sensibility, that the past, the various pasts, are culturally original, and radically distinct from our own experience of the object-world of the present. That discovery may now be seen as part of what may in the largest sense be called the *bourgeois cultural revolution*, the process whereby the definitive establishment of a properly capitalist mode of production as it were reprograms and utterly restructures the values, life rhythms, cultural habits, and temporal sense of its subjects. Capitalism demands in this sense a different experience of temporality from that which was appropriate to a feudal or tribal system, to the polls or to the forbidden city of the sacred despot: it demands a *memory* of qualitative social change, a concrete vision of the past which we may expect to find completed by that far more abstract and empty conception of some future terminus which we sometimes call "progress." Sir Walter Scott can in retrospect be seen to have been uniquely positioned for the creative opening of literary and narrative form to this new experience: on the very meeting place between two modes of production, the commercial activity of the Lowlands and the archaic, virtually tribal system of the surviving Highlanders, he is able to take a distanced and marginal view of the emergent dynamics of capitalism in the neighboring nation-state from the vantage point of a national experience—that of Scotland—which was the last arrival to capitalism and the first semi-peripheral zone of a foreign capitalism all at once.[4]

What is original about Lukács' book is not merely this sense of the historical meaning of the emergence of this new genre, but also and above all a more difficult perception: namely, of the profound historicity of the genre itself, its increasing incapacity to register its content, the way in which, with Flaubert's *Salammbô* in the mid-19th century, it becomes emptied of its vitality and survives as a dead form, a museum piece, as "archeological" as its own raw materials, yet resplendent with technical virtuosity. A contemporary example may dramatize this curious destiny: Stanley Kubrick's *Barry Lyndon*, with its remarkable reconstruction of a whole vanished 18th-century past. The paradox, the historical mystery of the Revitalization of form, will be felt by those for whom this film, with its brilliant images and extraordinary acting, is somehow profoundly *gratuitous*, an object floating in the void which could just as easily not have existed, its technical intensities far too great for any merely formal exercise, yet somehow profoundly and disturbingly unmotivated. This is to say something rather different from impugning the content of the Kubrick film: it would be easy to imagine any number of discussions of the vivid picture of 18th-century war, for example, or of the grisly instrumentality of human relationships, which might establish the relevance and the claims of this narrative on us today. It is rather the relationship to the past which is at issue, and the feeling that any other moment of the past would have done just as well. The sense that this determinate moment of history is, of organic necessity, precursor to the present has vanished into the pluralism of the Imaginary Museum, the wealth and endless variety of culturally or temporally distinct forms, all of which are now rigorously equivalent. Flaubert's Carthage and Kubrick's 18th century, but also the industrial turn of the century or the nostalgic 1930s or '50s of the American experience, find themselves emptied of their necessity, and reduced to pretexts for so many glossy images. In its (post-) contemporary form, this replacement of the historical by the nostalgic, this volatilization of what was once a *national* past, in the moment of emergence of the nation-states and of nationalism itself, is of course at one with the disappearance of historicity from consumer society today, with its rapid media exhaustion of yesterday's events and of the day-before-yesterday's star players (who was Hitler anyway? who was Kennedy? who, finally, was Nixon?).

The moment of Flaubert, which Lukács saw as the beginning of this process, and the moment in which the historical novel as a genre ceases to be functional, is also the moment of the emergence of SF, with the first novels of Jules Verne. We are therefore entitled to complete Lukács' account of the historical novel with the counter-panel of its opposite number, the emergence of the new genre of SF as a form which now registers some nascent sense of the future, and does so in the space on which a sense of the past had once been inscribed. It is time to examine more closely the seemingly transparent ways in which SF registers fantasies about the future.

2. The common-sense position on the anticipatory nature of SF as a genre is what we would today call a *representational* one. These narratives are evidently for the most part not modernizing, not reflexive and self-undermining and deconstructing affairs. They go about their business with, the full baggage and paraphernalia of a conventional realism, with this one difference: that the full "presence"—the settings and actions to be "rendered"—are the merely possible and conceivable ones of a near or far future. Whence the canonical defense of the genre: in a moment in which technological change has reached a dizzying tempo, in which so-called "future shock" is a daily experience, such narratives have the social function of accustoming their readers to rapid innovation, of preparing our consciousness and our habits for the otherwise demoralizing impact of change itself. They train our organisms to expect the unexpected and thereby insulate us, in much the same way that, for Walter Benjamin, the big city modernism of Baudelaire provided an elaborate shock-absorbing mechanism for the otherwise bewildered visitor to the new world of the great 19th-century industrial city.

If I cannot accept this account of SF, it is at least in part because it seems to me that, for all kinds of reasons, we no longer entertain such visions of wonder-working, properly "S-F" futures of technological automation. These visions are themselves now historical and dated—streamlined cities of the future on peeling murals our lived experience of our greatest metropolises is one of urban decay and blight. That particular Utopian future has in other words turned out to have been merely the future of one moment of what is now our own past. Yet, even if this is the case, it might at best signal a transformation in the historical function of present-day SF.

In reality, the relationship of this form of representation, this specific narrative apparatus, to its ostensible content—the future—has always been more complex than this. For the apparent realism, or representationality, of SF has concealed another, far more complex temporal structure: not to give us "images" of the future—whatever such images might mean for a reader who will necessarily predecease their "materialization"—but rather to defamiliarize and restructure our experience of our own *present*, and to do so in specific ways distinct from all other forms of defamiliarization. From the great intergalactic empires of an Asimov, or the devastated and sterile Earth of the post-catastrophe novels of a John Wyndham, all the way back in time to the nearer future of the organ banks and space miners of a Larry Niven, or the conapts, autofabs, or psycho-suitcases of the universe of Philip K. Dick, all such apparently full representations function in a process of distraction and displacement, repression and lateral perceptual renewal, which has its analogies in other forms of contemporary culture. Proust was only the most monumental "high" literary expression of this discovery: that the present—in this society, and in the physical and psychic dissociation of the human subjects who inhabit it—is inaccessible directly, is numb, habituated, empty of affect. Elaborate strategies of indirection are therefore necessary if we are somehow to break through our monadic insulation and to "experience," for some first and real time, this "present," which is after all all we have. In Proust, the retrospective fiction of memory and rewriting after the fact is mobilized in order for the intensity of a now merely remembered present to be experienced in some time-released and utterly unexpected posthumous actuality.

Elsewhere, with reference to another sub-genre or mass-cultural form, the detective story, I have tried to show that at its most original, in writers like Raymond Chandler, the ostensible plots of this peculiar form have an analogous function.[5] What interested Chandler was the here-and-now of the daily experience of the now historical Los Angeles: the stucco dwellings, cracked sidewalks, tarnished sunlight, and roadsters in which the curiously isolated yet typical specimens of an unimaginable Southern Californian social flora and fauna ride in the monadic half-light of their dashboards. Chandler's problem was that his readers—ourselves—desperately needed not to see that reality: humankind, as T.S. Eliot's magical bird sang, is able to bear very little of the unmediated, unfiltered experience of the daily life of capitalism. So, by a dialectical sleight-of-hand, Chandler formally mobilized an "entertainment" genre to distract us in a very special sense: not from the real life of private and public worries in general, but very precisely from our own defense mechanisms against that reality. The excitement of the mystery story plot is, then, a blind, fixing our attention on its own ostensible but in reality quite trivial puzzles and suspense in such a way that the intolerable space of Southern California can enter the eye laterally, with its intensity undiminished.

It is an analogous strategy of indirection that SF now brings to bear on the ultimate object and ground of all human life, History itself. How to fix this intolerable present of history with the naked eye? We have seen that in the moment of the emergence of capitalism the present could be intensified, and prepared for individual perception, by the construction of a historical past from which as a process it could be felt to issue slowly forth, like the growth of an organism. But today the past is dead, transformed into a packet of well-worn and thumbed glossy images. As for the future, which may still be alive in some small heroic collectivities on the Earth's surface, it is for us either irrelevant or unthinkable. Let the Wagnerian and Spenglerian world-dissolutions of J.G. Ballard stand as exemplary illustrations of the ways in which the imagination of a dying class—in this case the cancelled future of a vanished colonial and imperial destiny—seeks to intoxicate itself with images of death that range from the destruction of the world by fire, water, and ice to lengthening sleep or the berserk orgies of high-rise buildings or superhighways reverting to barbarism.

Ballard's work—so rich and corrupt—testifies powerfully to the contradictions of a properly representational attempt to grasp the future directly. I would argue, however, that the most characteristic SF does not seriously attempt to imagine the "real" future of our social system. Rather, its multiple mock futures serve the quite different function of transforming our own present into the determinate past of something yet to come. It is this present moment—unavailable to us for contemplation in its own right because the sheer quantitative immensity of objects and individual lives it comprises is untotalizable and hence unimaginable, and also because it is occluded by the density of our private fantasies as well as of the proliferating stereotypes of a media culture that penetrates every remote zone of our existence—that upon our return from the imaginary constructs of SF is offered to us in the form of some future world's remote past, as if posthumous and as though collectively remembered. Nor is this only an exercise in historical melancholy: there is, indeed, something also at least vaguely comforting and reassuring in the renewed sense that the great supermarkets and shopping centers, the garish fast-food stores and ever more swiftly remodelled shops and store-front businesses of the near future of Chandler's now historic Los Angeles, the burnt-out-center cities of small mid-Western towns, nay even the Pentagon itself and the vast underground networks of rocket-launching pads in the picture-post-card isolation of once characteristic North American "natural" splendor, along with the already cracked and crumbling futuristic architecture of newly built atomic power plants—that all these things are not seized, immobile forever, in some "end of history," but move steadily in time towards some unimaginable yet inevitable "real" future. SF thus enacts and enables a structurally unique "method" for apprehending the present as history, and this is so irrespective of the "pessimism" or "optimism" of the imaginary future world which is the pretext for that defamiliarization. The present is in fact no less a past if its destination prove to be the technological marvels of Verne or, on the contrary, the shabby and maimed automata of P.K. Dick's near future.

We must therefore now return to the relationship of SF and future history and reverse the stereotypical description of this genre: what is indeed authentic about it, as a mode of narrative and a form of knowledge, is not at all its capacity to keep the future alive, even in imagination. On the contrary, its deepest vocation is over and over again to demonstrate and to dramatize our incapacity to imagine the future, to body forth, through apparently full representations which prove on closer inspection to be structurally and constitutively impoverished, the atrophy in our time of what Marcuse has called the *utopian imagination*, the imagination of otherness and radical difference; to succeed by failure, and to serve as unwitting and even unwilling vehicles for a meditation, which, setting forth for the unknown, finds itself irrevocably mired in the all-too-familiar, and thereby becomes unexpectedly transformed into a contemplation of our own absolute limits.

This is indeed, since I have pronounced the word, the unexpected rediscovery of the nature of utopia as a genre in our own time.[6] The overt utopian text or discourse has been seen as a sub-variety of SF in general. What is paradoxical is that at the very moment in which utopias were supposed to have come to an end, and in which that asphyxiation of the utopian impulse alluded to above is everywhere more and more tangible. SF has in recent years rediscovered its own utopian vocation, and given rise to a whole series of powerful new works—utopian and S-F all at once—of which Ursula Le Guin's *The Dispossessed*, Joanna Russ' *The Female Man*, Marge Piercy's *Woman on the Edge of Time*, and Samuel Delany's *Triton* are only the most remarkable monuments. A few final remarks are necessary, therefore, on the proper use of these texts, and the ways in which their relationship to social history is to be interrogated and decoded.

3. After what has been said about SF in general, the related proposition on the nature and the political function of the utopian genre will come as no particular surprise: namely, that its deepest vocation is to bring home, in local and determinate ways, and with a fullness of concrete detail, our constitutional inability to imagine Utopia itself, and this, not owing to any individual failure of imagination but as the result of the systemic, cultural, and ideological closure of which we are all in one way or another prisoners. This proposition, however, now needs to be demonstrated in a more concrete analytical way, with reference to the texts themselves.

It is fitting that such a demonstration should take as its occasion not American SF, whose affinities with the dystopia rather than the utopia, with fantasies of cyclical regression or totalitarian empires of the future, have until recently been marked (for all the obvious political reasons); but rather Soviet SF, whose dignity as a "high" literary genre and whose social functionality within a socialist system have been, in contrast, equally predictable and no less ideological. The renewal of the twin Soviet traditions of Utopia and SF may very precisely be dated from the publication of Efremov's *Andromeda* (1958), and from the ensuing public debate over a work which surely, for all its naïveté, is one of the most single-minded and extreme attempts to produce a full representation of a future, classless, harmonious, world-wide utopian society. We may measure our own resistance to the utopian impulse by means of the boredom the sophisticated American reader instinctively feels for Efremov's culturally alien "libidinal apparatus":

"We began," continued the beautiful historian, "with the complete redistribution of Earth's surface into dwelling and industrial zones.

"The brown stripes running between thirty and forty degrees of North and South latitude represent an unbroken chain of urban settlements built on the shores of warm seas with a mild climate and no winters. Mankind no longer spends huge quantities of energy warming houses in winter and making himself clumsy clothing. The greatest concentration of people is around the cradle of human civilization, the Mediterranean Sea. The subtropical belt was doubled in breadth after the ice on the polar caps had melted. To the north of the zone of habitation lie prairies and meadows where countless herds of domestic animals graze. . . .

"One of man's greatest pleasures is travel, an urge to move from place to place that we have inherited from our distant forefathers, the wandering hunters and gatherers of scanty food. Today the entire planet is encircled by the Spiral Way whose gigantic bridges link all the continents. . . . Electric trains move along the Spiral Way all the time and hundreds of thousands of people can leave the inhabited zone very speedily for the prairies, open fields, mountains or forests."[7]

The question one must address to such a work—the analytical way into the utopian text in general from Thomas More all the way down to this historically significant Soviet novel— turns on the status of the *negative* in what is given as an effort to imagine a world without negativity. The repression of the negative, the place of that repression, will then allow us to formulate the essential contradiction of such texts, which we have expressed in a more abstract fashion above, as the dialectical reversal of intent, the inversion of representation, the "ruse of history" whereby the effort to imagine utopia ends up betraying the impossibility of doing so. The content of such repressed "semes" of negativity will then serve as an indicator of the ways in which a narrative's contradiction or antinomy is to be formulated and reconstructed.

Efremov's novel is predictably enough organized around the most obvious dilemma the negative poses for a utopian vision: namely, the irreducible fact of death. But equally characteristically, the anxiety of individual death is here "recontained" as a collective destiny, the loss of the starship *Parvus,* easily assimilable to a whole rhetoric of collective sacrifice in the service of mankind. I would suggest that this facile *topos* functions to displace two other, more acute and disturbing, forms of negativity. One is the emotional fatigue and deep psychic depression of the administrator Darr Veter, "cured" by a period of physical labor in the isolation of an ocean laboratory; the other is the *hubris* and crime of his successor, Mven Mass, whose personal involvement with an ambitious new energy program results in a catastrophic accident and loss of life. Even Mass is "rehabilitated" after a stay on "the island of oblivion," a kind of idyllic Ceylonese Gulag on which deviants and anti-socials are released to work out their salvation in any way they choose. We will

say that these two episodes are the nodal points or symptoms at which the deeper contradictions of the *psychiatric* and the *penal,* respectively, interrupt the narrative functioning
of the Soviet Utopian Imagination. Nor is it any accident that these narrative symptoms
take spatial and geographical form. Already in Thomas More, the imagining of Utopia is
constitutively related to the possibility of establishing some spatial *closure* (the digging
of the great trench which turns "Utopia" into a self-contained island).[8] The lonely oceano-
graphic station and the penal island thus mark the return of devices of spatial closure and
separation which, formally required for the establishment of some "pure" and positive
utopian space, thus always tend to betray the ultimate contradictions in the production of
utopian figures and narratives.

Other people's ideologies always being more "self-evident" than our own, it is not hard
to grasp the ideological function of this kind of nonconflictual utopia in a Soviet Union
in which, according to Stalin's canonical formula, class struggle was at the moment of
"socialism" supposed to have come to an end. Is it necessary to add that no intelligent
Marxist today can believe such a thing, and that the process of class struggle is if anything
exacerbated precisely in the moment of socialist construction, with its "primacy of the
political"? I will nevertheless complicate this diagnosis with the suggestion that what is
ideological for the Soviet reader may well be Utopian for us. We may indeed want to take
into account the possibility that alongside the obvious qualitative differences between
our own First World culture (with its dialectic of modernism and mass culture) and that
of the Third World, we may want to make a place for a specific and original culture of the
Second World, whose artifacts (generally in the form of Soviet and East European novels
and films) have generally produced the unformulated and disquieting impression on the
Western reader or spectator of a simplicity indistinguishable from naive sentimentalism.
Such a renewed confrontation with Second World culture would have to take into account
something it is hard for us to remember within the ahistorical closure of our own "*société
de consommation*": the radical strangeness and freshness of human existence and of
its object world in a non-commodity atmosphere, in a space from which that prodigious
saturation of messages, advertisements, and packaged libidinal fantasies of all kinds,
which characterizes our own daily experience, is suddenly and unexpectedly stilled. We
receive this culture with all the perplexed exasperation of the city dweller condemned to
insomnia by the oppressive silence of the countryside at night; for us, then, it can serve
the defamiliarizing function of those wondrous words which William Morris inscribed
under the title of his own great Utopia, "an epoch of rest."

All of this can be said in another way by showing that, if Soviet images of Utopia
are ideological, our own characteristically Western images of *dystopia* are no less so,
and fraught with equally virulent contradictions.[9] George Orwell's classical and virtually inaugural work in this sub-genre, *1984,* can serve as a text-book exhibit for this
proposition, even if we leave aside its more obviously pathological features. Orwell's
novel, indeed, set out explicitly to dramatize the tyrannical omnipotence of a bureaucratic elite, with its perfected and omnipresent technological control. Yet the narrative,

seeking to reinforce this already oppressive closure, subsequently overstates its case in a manner which specifically undermines its first ideological proposition. For, drawing on another topos of counterrevolutionary ideology, Orwell then sets out to show how, without freedom of thought, no science or scientific progress is possible, a thesis vividly reinforced by images of squalor and decaying buildings. The contradiction lies of course in the logical impossibility of reconciling these two propositions: if science and techno-logical mastery are now hampered by the lack of freedom, the absolute technological power of the dystopian bureaucracy vanishes along with it and "totalitarianism" ceases to be a dystopia in Orwell's sense. Or the reverse: if these Stalinist masters dispose of some perfected scientific and technological power, then genuine freedom of inquiry must exist *somewhere* within this state, which was precisely what was not to have been demonstrated.

4. The thesis concerning the structural impossibility of utopian representation outlined above now suggests some unexpected consequences in the aesthetic realm. It is by now, I hope, a commonplace that the very thrust of literary modernism—with its *public introuvable* and the breakdown of traditional cultural institutions, in particular the social "contract" between writer and reader—has had as one significant structural consequence the transformation of the cultural text into an *auto-referential* discourse, whose content is a perpetual interrogation of its own conditions of possibility.[10] We may now show that this is no less the case with the utopian text. Indeed, in the light of everything that has been said, it will not be surprising to discover that as the true vocation of the utopian narrative begins to rise to the surface—to confront us with our incapacity to imagine Utopia—the center of gravity of such narratives shifts towards an auto-referentiality of a specific, but far more concrete type: such texts then explicitly or implicitly, and as it were against their own will, find their deepest "subjects" in the possibility of their own production, in the interrogation of the dilemmas involved in their own emergence as utopian texts.

Ursula Le Guin's only "contemporary" SF novel, the underrated *Lathe of Heaven* (1971), may serve as documentation for this more general proposition. In this novel, which establishes Le Guin's home city of Portland, Oregon, alongside Berkeley and Los Angeles, as one of the legendary spaces of contemporary SF, a hapless young man finds himself tormented by the unwanted power to dream "effective dreams," those which in other words change external reality itself, and reconstruct the latter's historical past in such a way that the previous "reality" disappears without a trace. He places himself in the hands of an ambitious psychiatrist, who then sets out to use his enormous proxy power to change the world for the benefit of mankind. But reality is a seamless web: change one detail and unexpected, sometimes monstrous transformations occur in other apparently unrelated zones of life, as in the classical time-travel stories where one contemporary artifact, left behind by accident in a trip to the Jurassic age, transforms human history like a thunderclap. The other archetypal reference is the dialectic of "wishes" in fairy tales, where one gratification is accompanied with a most unwanted secondary effect, which must then be wished away in its turn (its removal bringing yet another undesirable consequence, and so forth).

The ideological content of Le Guin's novel is clear, although its political resonance is ambiguous: from the central position of her mystical Taoism, the effort to "reform" and to ameliorate, to transform society in a liberal or revolutionary way is seen, after the fashion of Edmund Burke, as a dangerous expression of individual *hubris* and a destructive tamper-ing with the rhythms of "nature." Politically, of course, this ideological message may be read either as the liberal's anxiety in the face of a genuinely revolutionary transformation of society or as the expression of more conservative misgivings about the New-Deal type reformism and do-goodism of the welfare state.[11]

On the aesthetic level, however—which is what concerns us here—the deeper subject of this fascinating work can only be the dangers of imagining Utopia and more specific-ally of writing the utopian text itself. More transparently than much other SF, this book is "about" its own process of production, which is recognized as impossible: George Orr cannot dream Utopia; yet in the very process of exploring the contradictions of that production, the narrative gets written, and "Utopia" is "produced" in the very movement by which we are shown that an "achieved" Utopia—a full representation—is a contradic-tion in terms. We may thus apply to *The Lathe of Heaven* those prophetic words of Roland Barthes about the dynamics of modernism generally, that the latter's monuments "linger as long as possible, in a sort of miraculous suspension, on the threshold of Literature itself 1 read, in this context: Utopial, in this anticipatory situation in which the density of life is given and developed without yet being destroyed through its consecration as an [institutionalized] sign system."[12]

It is, however, more fitting to close this discussion with another SF-Utopian text from the Second World today, one of the most glorious of all contemporary Utopias, the Strugatsky Brothers' astonishing *Roadside Picnic* (1977; first serialized in 1972).[13] This text moves in a space beyond the facile and obligatory references to the two rival social systems; and it cannot be coherently decoded as yet another *samizdat* message or expression of liberal political protest by Soviet dissidents.[14] Nor, although its figural material is accessible and rewritable in a way familiar to readers who live within the rather different constraints of either of the two industrial and bureaucratic systems, is it an affirmation or demonstration of what is today called "convergence" theory. Finally, while the narrative turns on the mixed blessings of wonder-working technology, this novel does not seem to me to be programmed by the category of "technological determinism" in either the Western or the Eastern style: that is, it is locked neither into a Western notion of infinite industrial progress of a non-political type, nor into the Stalinist notion of socialism as the "development of the forces of production."

On the contrary, the "zone"—a geographical space in which, as the result of some inexplicable alien contact, artifacts can be found whose powers transcend the explanatory capacities of human science—is at one and the same time the object of the most vicious bootlegging and military-industrial Greed, and of the purest religious—I would like to say Utopian—Hope. The "quest for narrative," to use Todorov's expression,[15] is here very specifically the quest for the Grail; and the Strugatskys' deviant hero—marginal, and as "antisocial" as one likes; the Soviet equivalent of the ghetto or countercultural anti-heroes of our own tradition—is perhaps a more sympathetic and human figure for us than Le Guin's passive-contemplative and mystical innocent. No less than *The Lathe of Heaven,* then, *Roadside Picnic* is self-referential, its narrative production determined by the structural impossibility of producing that Utopian text which it nonetheless miraculously becomes. Yet what we must cherish in this text—a formally ingenious collage of documents, an enigmatic cross-cutting between unrelated characters in social and temporal space, a desolate reconfirmation of the inextricable relationship of the utopian quest to crime and suffering, with its climax in the simultaneous revenge-murder of an idealistic and guiltless youth and the apparition of the Grail itself—is the unexpected emergence, as it were, beyond "the nightmare of History" and from out of the most archaic longings of the human race, of the impossible and inexpressible Utopian impulse here none the less briefly glimpsed: "Happiness for everybody! . . . Free! . . . As much as you want! . . . Everybody come here! . . . HAPPINESS FOR EVERYBODY, FREE, AND NO ONE WILL GO AWAY UNSATISFIED!"

Notes

1. See, on Verne, Pierre Macherey's stimulating chapter in *Pour une théorie de la production littéraire* (Paris, 1966).
2. The literature on Wells is enormous: see, for an introduction and select bibliography, Darko Suvin, *Metamorphoses of Science Fiction* (New Haven, 1979). This work is a pioneering theoretical and structural analysis of the genre to which I owe a great deal.
3. See *The Political Unconscious* (Ithaca, NY: 1981).
4. An important discussion of Scotland's unique place in the development of capitalism can be found in Tom Nairn, *The Break-Up of Britain* (London: New Left Books, 1977).
5. Fredric Jameson, "On Raymond Chandler," *Southern Review*, 6 (Summer 1970): 624–50.
6. A fuller discussion of these propositions and some closer analyses of More's *Utopia* in particular, will be found in my review-article of Louis Marin's *Utopiques* (which also see!), "Of Islands and Trenches," *Diacritics,* 7 (June 1977): 2–21. See also the related discussion in "World Reduction in Le Cuin: The Emergence of Utopian Narrative," *SFS*, 2 (1975): 221–30.
7. Ivan Efremov, *Andromeda* (Moscow: Foreign Languages Publishing House, 1959), pp. 54–55.
8. Compare "Of Islands and Trenches" (see note 6).
9. In other words, to adapt Claudel's favorite proverb, *le pire n'est pas toujours sûr, non plus!*
10. See my *The Prison-House of Language* (Princeton, 1972), pp. 203–05.
11. That the author of *The Dispossessed* is also capable of indulging in a classical Dostoyevskian and counterrevolutionary anti-utopianism may be documented by her nasty little fable,

"The Ones Who Walk Away from Omelas," in *The Wind's Twelve Quarters* (NY: Harper & Row, 1975), pp. 275–84.

12. Roland Barthes, *Writing Degree Zero*, trans. Annette Lavers and Colin Smith (London, 1967), p. 39.

13. Arkady and Boris Strugatsky, *Roadside Picnic*, trans. A.W. Bouis (NY: Macmillan, 1977).

14. This is not to say that the Strugatskys have not had their share of personal and publishing problems.

15. Tzvetan Todorov, *Poétique de la prose* (Paris, 1971).

19

Science fiction and critical theory

Carl Freedman

To change the world is not to explore the moon. It is to make the revolution and build socialism without regressing back to capitalism.

The rest, including the moon, will be given to us in addition.

—Louis Althusser

1 Definitions

If by *theory* is meant an intellectual framework, a problematic which, by the structure of its questions even more than by the content of its answers, defines a certain conceptual terrain, then all thought whatever is theoretical; and it may be added that few theories are more narrow and dogmatic than those, like commonsense empiricism, which attempt to deny their own theoretical status. Keynes's aphorism about his colleagues—that those economists who think they dislike theory are simply attached to an older theory—is generally true as well. By *critical* theory, however, I mean something far more specific: something broader than Critical Theory in the Frankfurt School sense, but not unrelated to it. Indeed, a key passage from the founding text of the Frankfurt usage, Horkheimer's "Traditional and Critical Theory," is quite pertinent here:

> Critical thinking is the function neither of the isolated individual nor of a sumtotal of individuals. Its subject is rather a definite individual in his real relation to other individuals and groups, in his conflict with a particular class, and, finally, in the resultant web of relationships with the social totality and with nature. The subject is no mathematical point like the ego of bourgeois philosophy; his activity is the construction of the social present. Furthermore, the thinking subject is not the place where knowledge and object coincide, nor consequently the starting-point for attaining absolute knowledge. Such an illusion about the thinking subject, under which idealism has lived since Descartes, is ideology in the strict sense, for in it the limited freedom of the bourgeois individual puts on the illusory form of perfect freedom and independence. (Horkheimer 210-11)

Horkheimer also suggests the social and political ramifications of critical theory:

> The hostility to theory as such which prevails in contemporary public life is really directed
> against the transformative activity associated with critical thinking. Opposition starts as
> soon as theorists fail to limit themselves to verification and classification by means of
> categories which are as neutral as possible, that is, categories which are indispensable
> to inherited ways of life. (Horkheimer 232)

Critical theory, then, may be defined as dialectical thought: that is, thought which (in principle) can take nothing less than the totality of the social field for its object, and yet which
not only regards the social field as a *historical* process, constantly in material flux, but which
also conceptualizes its own methodology as deeply imbricated in that flux rather than as
a passive intellectual instrument by means of which an unproblematic Cartesian subject
extracts absolute knowledge from pre-given objects; and which, furthermore, by dissolving
the reified static categories of the ideological status quo, constantly shows that things are
not what they seem to be—but also that things need not eternally be as they are—and thus
maintains a cutting edge of social subversion even at its most rarefied and abstract.

The central instance of critical theory is, of course, the Marxist tradition, of which
Horkheimer himself was primarily thinking. But I would widen the term so as to include
Freudian psychoanalysis—for such fundamental concepts of the latter as the unconscious, the drives, transference, and the Oedipus and castration complexes are
profoundly dialectical categories—and also, given some qualifications, what might be
called the post-dialectical theories of thinkers like Foucault and Derrida. In what follows
I will be concerned with critical theory mainly in its cultural and, still more, its literary
contexts: but any procrustean disciplinary division is of course profoundly contrary to the
spirit of critical theory itself.

Any serious attempt to define SF must begin by considering Suvin's already classic formulation: "SF is. . .a literary genre whose necessary and sufficient conditions are
the presence and interaction of estrangement and cognition, and whose main formal
device is an imaginative framework alternative to the author's empirical environment."
He usefully adds:

> Estrangement differentiates SF from the 'realistic' literary mainstream extending from
> the eighteenth century into the twentieth. Cognition differentiates it not only from myth,
> but also from the folk (fairy) tale and the fantasy. (Suvin 7-8)

This definition seems to suffer, however, from a sacrifice of descriptive to eulogistic force.
Can we accept a definition by the logic of which the *Star Wars* films, or most of the pulp SF
of an earlier age, are *not* SF, but the plays of Brecht are? The latter objection is perhaps
met if we recall that for Brecht historical materialism was not only cognitive but positively
scientific in the strongest sense, and Marx fully as much the founder of a science as Galileo.
But Suvin does, in fact, seem to find Brecht a difficult case: well aware of the latter's status
as the major theorist and practitioner of literary estrangement *(Verfremdung),* he remarks
that estrangement is "used by Brecht in a different way, within a still predominantly

'realistic' context" (Suvin 7). The assertion is surely false, for Brecht is in no sense a literary realist, not even in inverted commas—as Lukacs angrily charged and as Brecht himself proudly admitted.[1] The apparent problems with Suvin's fundamentally sound definition may be resolved, however, by clarifying the nature of genre criticism itself: specifically, by displacing the category of genre from a static and classificatory to a dialectical sense. A literary genre—SF or any other—ought to be understood not as a pigeon-hole into which certain texts may be filed and certain others may not, but rather as an element or, still better, a tendency, which is active to a greater or lesser degree within a literary text which is itself conceptualized as a complexly structured whole.

Accordingly, there is probably no text which is a perfect and pure embodiment of SF but, on the other hand, there are perhaps relatively few texts which lack the SF tendency altogether. Brecht might be seen as an author in whose work the SF tendency is strong, but who lacks interest in the specifically *technological* version of cognition that has usually figured (though today it figures to a decreasing degree) in those works commonly called SF. *Star Wars* might be described as a work in which the SF tendency is visually strong but conceptually weak. It follows that, in the strictest sense, it is incorrect to say that any given text "is" or "is not" SF. But it is nonetheless justifiable to make an at least provisional discrimination on the basis of whether, in any actual text, the SF tendency is sufficiently strong to be considered dominant—just as no one but a pedant would object to describing the US as a capitalist nation, even though capitalism is not the only mode of production operative within the US socio-economic formation.

Given these definitions of SF and of critical theory, I will now attempt, in the remainder of this essay, to bring the two categories together. My aim is not to read SF "in the light of" critical theory (itself a suspiciously positivistic metaphor) but to articulate certain structural affinities between the two terms. As I will try to show, the conjunction of critical theory and SF is not fortuitous but fundamental.

2 Articulations

The process of reading, though by no means always critical, is inevitably theoretical; and no better illustration of this point can be cited than the frequently noticed tendency of any mode of reading (critical or precritical) to privilege, whether implicitly or explicitly, a particular area of the literary terrain. Two examples may be noted. Lukacsian criticism, which is certainly a critical theory, is overwhelmingly oriented toward the novel of classical realism. Balzac and Tolstoy provide Lukacs with his essential models, and, despite the immense range of his empirical erudition, he seldom strays far from them in any conceptual sense. His intense admiration for Thomas Mann is based on his ability to theoretically (re)construct Mann as the authentic successor of the 19th-century realists. On the other hand, literary modernism seldom figures in his work save as an object of denunciation—or, as with his late recognition of Brecht, an object assimilable after all to the basic principles of realism. Lyric poetry scarcely even exists for Lukacs. But lyric poetry, especially that of T.S. Eliot and his 17th-century precursors, is the central genre for American New Criticism, a precritical school, though one of considerable technical soph-istication. Engaged in working out pedagogically convenient styles of "close reading" on short and highly-wrought poetic artifacts, the New Critics have far less to say about fiction and would be hopelessly at sea with a work like *Finnegans Wake* or Trotsky's *History of the Russian Revolution.* There is, of course, a major difference between Lukacs and the New Critics: whereas he knows what he is doing—he is constructing a theory of realism for determinate philosophical and political ends—they seem to imagine that they are simply and innocently "reading." But it is noteworthy how both posit a privileged generic space, and it would be easy to show how equivalent spaces are assumed or stated by many other schools as well: organicist English fiction, especially that of Lawrence, by the *Scrutiny* school; symbolist poetry tending toward self-referentiality by Derridean Reconstruction; modernist drama and fiction by the Frankfurt School and by Althusserian Marxism; Spenserian and Shakespearian romance (and the Prophetic Books of Blake) by the myth criticism of Northrop Frye; Romantic and neo-Romantic poetry by the influence criticism of Harold Bloom; etc. SF, it may be noted, has been overtly privileged by relat-ively few readers; Suvin and Delany are perhaps the most important examples.

How do we account for such wide discrepancies of privileged reading material? The problem cannot be resolved by lapsing into pluralism, where we happily agree to maintain some sympathy for and some distance from *all* competing schools, availing ourselves of particular insights and freeing ourselves from particular limitations and blind spots. Instead, it is necessary to recall that the category of literature (in sharp distinction to that of genre) has no meaning other than a purely *functional* one. As Eagleton has argued with great cogency (pp. 1-16), those works are literature which are called literature by the minority of readers who, in a given time and place, possess the social and institutional power which allows their views on the matter to prevail. In our present historical situation, these authoritative readers include academic critics and teachers, publishing executives, librarians, editors of journals and reviews, and others. Such agents, acting in a determ-inate social context and toward determinate (if often unconscious) ends, decide that a certain relatively small number of texts, out of the much vaster number which actually exist, shall be canonized. They judge, for instance, that the poems, essays, and some of the letters written by Wallace Stevens are literature, while the insurance policies and office memoranda also written by him are not. But, of course, such judgments vary greatly in various historical situations, as the most cursory acquaintance with literary history reveals. Though it might be difficult for us to imagine a circumstance in which the Homeric poems would not be literature or in which our daily shopping lists would be, variations almost as wide have actually taken place;[2] for which reason, the attempt to construct an essential or transhistorically substantive definition of literature is vain. Whereas genre is a substantive property of discourse and its context, literature is a formally arbitrary and socially determ-inate category. In this sense, reading does not merely respond to literature: reading (of a certain sort) *creates* literature.

But, if it is vain to try to define literature other than functionally, it is not vain to describe the process by which the category "literature" is constructed. Though the process is fundamentally ideological, in its primary phase it is ideological not in any straightforward or obvious sense, but, for the most part, as mediated by generic considerations. So it is that the business memoranda of so conservative and respectable an author as Stevens are denied the title of literature, while, on the other hand, a poem by a militant and unknown slumd-weller, if it obeyed a few simple conventions, would probably not be denied the title. Indeed, generic determination operates so functionally on this level that the same verbal construction may be literary or non-literary depending upon the material context: the sentence, "Walk with light," would be literature in a book of spiritual aphorisms but not on a metal sign at a street intersection. Most works of literature, however—like the slum-dweller's poem—are generally considered bad or negligible literature, and are relegated to near-invisibility at the periphery of the canon. There is, then, a secondary phase of the canon-constructing process, which is devoted to distinguishing "good" literature, literature worth studying and teaching and writing articles about. Though directly ideological considerations are more important here than in the primary phase of the process, the power of genre is still strong. Shakespeare's contemporaries were generally convinced of his personal genius, but they doubted that the scripts of English stage plays could be considered literature in the same eulogistic sense that applied to ancient drama or even to English odes and sonnets; similarly, in our own time academic critics seem to be deciding that autobiography belongs more centrally to the literary canon than they would have allowed only a generation ago. Finally, there is a tertiary phase of canon-formation as well: this is precisely the tendency, discussed above, of every distinct school of reading to privilege a distinct kind of reading matter. This phase of the process, which distinguishes not merely literature or even "good" literature but the "best," the most important literature, is, as we have seen, also largely governed by generic factors, though no doubt more crudely ideological forces are here stronger. SF is certainly literature in the primary sense, but often not in the secondary and—in any explicit fashion—very rarely in the tertiary sense.

Two conclusions may, then, be drawn. In the first place, it is evident that the affinity which a mode of reading has for a particular literary object is by no means a matter of taste or judgment within an unproblematically predetermined field of literature. Rather, it is the most subtle moment within the project of constructing literature itself, of determining, out of all the verbal material extant, which works possess the peculiar power which all respecters of literature from Plato to Paul de Man have attributed to the object of their devotion or fear: which is to say, furthermore, that it is, like the primary phase of the same process, a functional act involving, in the long run, determinate social ends. Though genre plays a large role in all phases of the canon-forming process, genre is, as we shall see, not in the least an ideologically innocent factor. Accordingly, if SF has rarely been a privileged genre—despite the fact that much of it clearly possesses the kind of purely *formal* attributes (intellectual complexity, stylistic felicity, narrative sophistication, and the like) generally held to characterize "great" literature—this only means that the literary powers-that-be have not wished SF to function with the social prestige that literature in the stronger senses enjoys. Some plausible reasons for the general disinclination to eulogize SF will become clear later in the present argument.

The second conclusion involves the fact that, at least in the most rarefied or what I have called the tertiary phase of the canon-forming process, the operative judgments may be implicit rather than explicit. Usually, this distinction is relevant when considering the negative choices of pre-critical schools of reading: the Leavisites, for instance, would have hotly denied that they had any special—and certainly any *ideological*—attachment to the sort of fiction produced by George Eliot or D.H. Lawrence, except insofar as such a preference expressed an innocent recognition of what was worth reading (and favorable to "life") at all. But what I want to maintain here is that critical theory itself—especially in its most central, Marxian version— does implicitly privilege a certain genre, and that this genre is SF. This may seem a large claim. But it should, at least, be clear from the forego-ing analysis that I am not trying to "revalue" any particular canon in order to beg admission for SF. Instead, I have tried to describe canon-formation itself and am now maintaining that the most conceptually advanced forms of criticism unconsciously privilege a genre that has been generally despised and ghettoized.

Such an assertion raises two difficult questions. Why and how does critical theory privilege SF? And, if it does, why have most critical theorists been unaware of the fact? To these questions I now turn.

The affinity of critical theory for SF may be micrologically examined in the following passage, which opens a well-known SF novel:

> A merry little surge of electricity piped by automatic alarm from the mood organ beside his bed awakened Rick Deckard.
> Surprised—it always surprised him to find himself awake without prior notice—he rose from the bed, stood up in his multicolored pajamas, and stretched. Now, in her bed, his wife Iran opened her gray, unmerry eyes, blinked, then groaned and shut her eyes again. (*Do Androids. . .* 1:1)

To some degree, the passage could be the straightforward opening of a mundane novel: a married man awakes and is, presumably, about to start the day. But the linguistic register of the paragraph marks it as unmistakably SF. The key factor here is the refer-ence to the mood organ—evidently a technical device somehow connected to emotional states and one which, though unknown in our own empirical environment, is an ordinary accoutrement of everyday life in the world of the text. In fact, the mood organ does figure as an important motif in Dick's novel as a whole. But in the context of the opening para-graph, its chief function is to signal the SF character of the language, and thus to impel us to read the latter differently than we would read the language of mundane fiction.[3] Since technology and emotions are apparently connected in ways unfamiliar to us—though not *wholly*, unfamiliar or unpredictable, because we do know of mood-altering drugs—the adjective *merry*, as applied to a surge of electricity, may have a sense other than the expected metaphorical one. What does it mean to be "awake without prior notice"? We understand the difference between being jerked from deep sleep to full consciousness and gradually passing through intermediate stages; but the context suggests that a more specific meaning may be operative. Nor is the grammatically simple phrase "his wife Iran" free of ambiguities. Are we here in a world where a man can be married to an entire country'? And what of the fact that Rick and Iran seem to sleep in different beds? As in mundane fiction, it may be a detail without profound significance, or it may signify certain sexual problems between the couple; but it might also signify some completely novel arrangement of sexual relations that is normal in the society portrayed. In any case, the whole topic of human feelings, sexual and otherwise, is estranged, and the question of a technology of emotion is posed. A few lines after the above paragraph is this bit of conversation:

> 'Get your crude cop's hand away,' Iran said.
>   'I'm not a cop.' He felt irritable now, although he hadn't dialed for it. (*Do Androids.* . . 1:1)

This exchange might be completely mundane, until the final clause. But that clause, though formally subordinate, makes the salient SF point.

It would be possible, in a full-scale reading of the novel, to show how the first paragraph does function as an appropriate overture. Of course, not all of the possibilities raised there are actually developed. But the relations between technology and emotion do constitute the principal focus of the text, not only with regard to such household appliances as the mood organ, but also in connection with the state of virtual war between human authorities and androids, the latter presumed—though one cannot be quite certain—to have no emotions at all. But the opening of the novel may also stand alone, on the molecular level, as paradigmatic of the SF generic tendency. The point to be stressed about the language is its profoundly dialectical character. For undialectical theory, the most familiar emotions—love, affection, hatred, anger, *et alia*—tend to be unproblematic categories, assumed to be much the same in all times and places, and to exist on an irreducibly subjective level. They may of course occur in a practically infinite number of permutations, and the undialectical reader may relish such psychological fiction as that of Dostoevsky or Flaubert for the subtlety and acuteness with which those authors portray the varieties of affective experience. A dialectical approach, on the other hand, would adopt the kind of perspective suggested by Dick. As the paragraph shows an emotional dynamic of a future age operating, at least in some respects, quite differently from what we ourselves empirically experience, the question of the *historicity* of feelings is raised and the possibility of a historical periodization of emotion in co-ordination with other aspects of human development (such as technology) is at least implied. The technical emphasis of the paragraph also tends to remove emotion from idealist notions of spirituality or the unproblematically individual, and to suggest that psychic states may be reducible to concrete and trans-individual material realities—a reduction which Freud held to be the ultimate conceptual goal of psychoanalysis and which Lacan claims to have achieved through the mediation of structural linguistics. We may also note that, if the phrase I used above, "technology of emotion," has a strongly Foucauldian ring, it is not by chance: for Dick's paragraph does indeed resonate with Foucault's concern to show that power does not merely repress individual subjectivity but actually constitutes subjectivity in historically variable ways.

Historical materialism, psychoanalysis, Foucauldian archeology—I do not mean to suggest that such elaborate theoretical structures are actually present, even embryonic- ally, in the short and unpretentious paragraph which opens *Do Androids Dream of Electric Sheep?* It is, rather, a matter of the shared perspectives between SF and critical theory, of the dialectical standpoint of the SF tendency, with its insistence upon historical mutability, material reducibility, and, at least implicitly, Utopian possibility. In a sense, SF is of all genres the one most devoted to historical specificity: for the SF world is not only one different in time or place from our own, but one whose chief interest is precisely the difference that such difference makes, and, in addition, one whose difference is nonetheless contained within a cognitive continuum with the actual (thus sharply distinguishing SF from the irrationalist estrangements of fantasy or Gothic literature, which secretly work to ratify the mundane status quo by presenting no alternative to the latter other than inexplicable discontinuities).

It may appear, then, that SF is an inverted or paradoxical version of historical fiction, and that the affinity for which I argue between it and critical theory is a rewriting of the privileged relationship maintained by Lukacs between Marxism and the historical novel. The analogy is valid, but the comparison cuts in both directions at once. On the one hand, much SF, especially of the more conformist sort, is a kind of historical fiction in disguise: witness the nostalgic reconstructions of entrepreneurial capitalism in Heinlein's novella *The Man Who Sold the Moon* or in the section on the merchant traders in Asimov's *Foundation*, both classic works of "Golden Age" SF which, however liberal in overt ideo- logy, do find Utopian traces in the entrepreneurialism which the monopoly capitalism of the postwar US was, at the time of writing, rendering more and more obsolete. On the other hand, it might also be argued that some historical novels contain an SF tendency: consider the estranging but rational reconstruction of the Jacobite rebellion of 1745 in Scott's *Waverley*, a reconstruction quite different in method from that of normative middle- class historiography. But if SF shares with historical fiction the dialectic of difference and identity celebrated by Lukacs, there is nonetheless reason to grant the critical superi- ority to SF. For historical fiction, paradoxically, is the more vulnerable to an unhistorical fetishism of the past, a fetishism in which the merely aesthetic relish of costume and exoticism triumphs over the genuinely conceptual issues of historical specificity and difference; and this danger is of course amply illustrated in the post-Tolstoyan histor- ical novels which regularly figure in current best-seller lists. Though SF is not immune to equivalent temptations—Heinlein's apotheosis of early-20th-century America as the apogee of human civilization is a notorious case in point—its general tendency is essen- tially anti-nostalgic and more conducive to a Marxian "poetry of the future."

The matter may be put in another way—concentrating on the macrocosm of SF narrative structure rather than the microcosm of SF language—by considering the virtual identity of the SF and the utopian fictional traditions. The most genuinely critical element in Thomas More's pioneering text lies not in the empirical content of his fictional country but in the neo-Greek coinage that produces his title. Though not completely unprecedented, the mere act of writing an entire work about no *place*—that is, no place actually locatable—was an immensely liberating act, as the huge success of More's coinage might suggest.[4] The freedom from the actual thus attained—a rational and hence true, as opposed to a fantastic and therefore false, freedom—opened up new literary possibilities, which, perhaps, could only first become visible in the bright morning of mercantile capitalism when, for the first time in history, the efforts of human beings were not only leading to the discovery of new worlds but were being seen to restructure social life in fundamental ways. These new possibilities are coterminous with the SF tendency. For every work of SF is a utopia, a text whose initial act (however severely the act may ultimately be compromised) is to refuse the status quo in favor of a social alternative which is not ours but which, for better or worse, could, at least in principle, become ours. Like critical theory, SF, generically considered, can never limit itself to "verification and classification by means of categories which are as neutral as possible, that is, categories which are indispensable to inherited ways of life." Indeed, though many texts classified as SF make major retreats from the conceptual radicalism of the SF tendency, a surprising amount even of "Golden Age" SF, if read with adequate historical perspective, does display something of the oppositional cutting edge which Horkheimer's words attribute to the Frankfurt inflection of Marxist philosophy. The flat Skinnerian rationalism of Asimov's "Foundation" trilogy and of his robot stories, or the synthesis of romantic technologism with vulgar Nietzschean evolutionism in Clarke's major works, however unacceptable in themselves, gain considerably if they are understood as refusals to join in the Cold War anti-Communism predominant in postwar America and (though to a lesser degree) Britain: in that impoverished intellectual culture, merely to insist that a manichaean struggle between a diabolical Moscow and an angelic Washington was not the only or most important factor shaping human affairs in itself constituted a significantly critical act.

The early career of the more fully subversive talent of Dick tells a similar story. Beginning in the early 1950s with no special ambition to become an SF author, he found that SF magazines were usually the only outlets willing to publish his work—a circumstance which owes less to overt radicalism among SF editors than to generically intrinsic potentialities. We need, of course, to distinguish between utopia and Utopia: that is, between. an SF generic tendency and a Marxian-Blochian hermeneutic which construes fragmentary prefigurations of an unalienated future in the cultural artifacts of the past and present. But even mere negativity is an indispensable moment in the dialectical process, and utopian narrative is a particularly fertile field for Utopian speculation.

Such speculation, and the concomitant "transformative activity associated with critical thinking" of which Horkheimer writes, is the *telos* of critical theory: the elaborate and powerful demystifying apparatus of Marxist (and Freudian) thought exist, ultimately, in order to clear space upon which positive alternatives to the existent can be constructed. No doubt SF authors, like critical theorists, have been more extensively occupied with the negative or demystifying aspect of the dialectic. But this aspect, the aspect of *critique* in the strict sense, contains its own implicit positivity; and, for overtly Utopian work, one would today turn, for the most part, to such self-consciously SF narratives as Sturgeon's *Venus Plus X*, Le Guin's *The Dispossessed*, Piercy's *Woman on the Edge of Time*, or perhaps Delany's *Stars in My Pocket Like Grains of Sand*—to name but a few examples.

It would be possible to detail the affinity between SF and critical theory at much greater length than is feasible here: I have only attempted to sketch the major lines of conceptual force. But an unavoidable question, mentioned earlier, remains. Though the continued marginalization of SF by the literary governing class is explicable in terms of the hostility which all genuine criticism can expect, it is less clear why critical theorists themselves, committed to dialectics and radical transformation, should have done so little to resist this marginalization. To be sure, the oversight is far from total. In addition to Suvin and Delany, both vocationally tied to SF and both critical theorists of considerable sophistication, one could also cite, for example, the importance ascribed to SF by Jameson, the most note-worthy critical theorist active in the US today and not, in the professional sense, primarily an SF critic—not to mention a large number of younger critical theorists who are more and more finding SF a crucial field in which to work. Yet it is nonetheless true that, in the voluminous pages emanating from the great names in critical theory, overt references to SF tend to be few and far between. If SF has the importance for critical theory which I have maintained it has, the neglect seems astonishing.

To some degree, the explanation is historical in a quite specific way. It was hardly possible to define clearly what I have called the SF tendency until it was strongly embod-ied in a large amount of work explicitly published and marketed as SF: that is, the work, all of comparatively recent vintage, of such writers as Lem, Dick, Le Guin, Disch, Delany, Russ, Ballard, *et alit.* Though writers like Beckett and Kafka certainly belong more to SF than to any other genre; though the Joycean method, especially in *Finnegans Wake*, incorporates something of the SF tendency in its radical estrangement of the appar-ently smooth surface of everyday perception and consciousness; though the "theoretical fictions" of Freud, such as the description of drives in *Beyond the Pleasure Principle*, are in a real sense SF; yet it would have been extremely difficult to produce such formulations before the era of the British New Wave and *Dangerous Visions*. Even so, the comparat-ive belatedness of radical conceptualization in overt SF, itself explicable in terms of the internal sociology and political economy of the SF industry, cannot fully explain the critical ignorance of SF. For one thing, it does not explain the neglect of such individual authors, integral to the SF tradition, as Wells and Stapledon and even Mary Shelley, nor, for that matter, of the Bester of *The Demolished Man* and the Sturgeon of *More Than Human*. If critical theorists have on the whole been more at home with Sophocles or Shakespeare or Balzac, the reason also partly lies in the nature of canonization itself.

It ought to be clear from my earlier discussion that canon-formation is an essentially *conservative* process, though not in a wholly evil sense. To conserve what seems of value from a particular point of view is, at least, a practical necessity, for no individual has the time to read all the texts available, and no library has the money to buy them. But the conservatism of canon-formation, whose first and most decisively conservative phase is to separate the literary from the non-literary, is, if to some degree necessary, also something which critical theory must be wary and skeptical of. The procedure is intrinsically repressive, and, given the inevitable hegemony of precritical thought in class society, the repressions involved are by no means unselective.

Unfortunately, critical theorists have not, on the whole, been sufficiently alert to this danger. Swayed, no doubt, by the socially normative conservatism into which the most rigorously critical mind is bound at times to lapse (and which is not completely separable even from the basic constitution of individuals as subjects of a repressive society), they have tended to work with the received literary canon, though with the proviso that canonical texts need not be read in received ways. To be sure, the Benjaminian project of rereading the cultural monuments of the past is, in itself, perfectly legitimate. But it becomes illegitimate to the extent that it leads theorists to neglect the ideological function of canon-formation and the ways in which the latter is wont to stigmatize those texts distributed from marginalized sectors of the literary market or even denied direct access to the market altogether; for, *pace* Adorno, such texts may, as in the case of SF, contain much material of the highest importance from a critical-theoretical point of view. Accordingly, though the canonization of SF and the construction of canons within SF are certainly to some degree implicit in the present essay, it must be stressed that these (practically unavoidable) processes are potentially in conflict with the most radical intent of my argument. If SF is read seriously, then SF will inevitably have its internal canons and its place within the general canon as a whole: but the danger will always exist that SF-canonizing may repress much that is genuinely new and critical within and beyond the genre. There is, indeed, a certain correct sense, as well as a good deal of reactionary anti-intellectualism, in the alarm that many older SF writers and editors, especially survivors of the Campbell era, express at the currently increasing though still slight academic respectability which SF enjoys. For the cutting edge of SF may well be blunted to the extent that the genre becomes at all official.

3 Excursuses

In the following section, I will offer brief analyses of several SF novels. My aim is to demonstrate, with more detail than has heretofore been feasible, the (different) ways in which each of them resonates strongly with concerns proper to critical theory. I do not offer exhaustive readings, partly for reasons of economy, but also in order to warn against the empiricism which the notion of "practical criticism" often implies and the concomitant naivete which holds the minute examination of particular texts to be the ultimate test or *telos* of literary theory. These readings are not proposed precisely as examples of the argument in the foregoing section, still less as proof of it. Rather, I am continuing the argument in a somewhat different register.

It may be convenient to begin with Lem's *Solaris*, a novel in which cognition and estrangement figure not only as conceptual qualities but as overt themes. Though the novel can boast an exciting plot, a protagonist of some depth and complexity, and a remarkable pseudo-naturalistic mode of representation which is characteristic of Lem (one thinks of *Return from the Stars*, a closely observed and unsensational tale "about" advanced space travel and the radical reconstitution of humanity), the chief interest of *Solaris* lies less in action or psychology than in epistemology. Indeed, one of the features that marks Lem's work in general as strongly S-F is its unblushing devotion to philosophical speculation, a novelistic element that can be found in George Eliot and Tolstoy but which has become largely extinct in the European and Anglo-American mundane fiction of today. The central subject-matter of *Solaris* is dialectical thought itself or, more specifically, the dialectical nature of even the physical or "hard" sciences. Though Lem's invented science of Solaristics—the focus of which is the attempt to establish communication with the immense sentient ocean of Solaris—is presented with such pseudofactual solidity that one almost believes the research articles and academic controversies "really" to exist, this presentation is primarily the vehicle of an elaborate theoretical fable.

It is indicative only of the widespread confusion of science with positivism that some readers have interpreted the novel as an attack on, or at least a demystification of, science. The text does indeed mention the work of the anti-Solarist Muntius—who has denounced Solaristics as a religious faith camouflaged as science and who implicitly would deconstruct the distinction between religion and science in general—but his views, while seriously and somewhat sympathetically considered, are decisively rejected. Lem's purpose is quite different and considerably more complicated: namely, to demonstrate the ever-provisional rigors of science in all its dialectical complexity. The second chapter of the novel, in which the protagonist Kris Kelvin summarizes for himself (and the reader) the history and current state of Solarist studies, insinuates a mood of weighty frustration, a frustration motivated partly by the occasional degeneration of science into dogma as different schools of Solarists establish varying degrees of institutional hegemony, but more fundamentally by the refusal of genuine science to yield definite onto-theological answers:

> The situation seemed much worse now than in the time of the pioneers, since the assiduous efforts of so many years had not resulted in a single indisputable conclusion. The sum total of known facts was strictly negative. (*Solaris* 2:29)

As in all dialectics, much depends upon the position of the theoretical investigator, and Solarists with different methodological leanings—mathematical, cybernetic, biological, and others—frame the problem in different ways. At the same time, the various special-ized endeavors are haunted by a more basic conceptual problem which constitutes the major crux of the novel: given that all known models of communication derive from the relations among humans, does the category of communication itself have any meaning when dealing with nonhuman intelligence? In more general terms, is the radically Other a concept perhaps *intrinsically* beyond the power of the human mind to grasp?

The text offers no final answer, but it does suggest that any positivistic form of thought is utterly inadequate to the task. For one sort of "communication" between the ocean and the scientists does take place, and it foregrounds the necessary involvement of the latter: most of the plot concerns the creation by the ocean of phantom humans, each a simulacrum of someone remembered from the erotic past of each of the Solarists in the experimental station suspended above the planet. These phantoms, though products of the ocean, attain some degree of autonomy from it and seem progressively more human: but, of course, it is just at this point that the overfamiliar category of the "human" is estranged and problematized.[5] The issues with which Lem deals—the nature of commu-nication, of humanity, of thought—are thus fundamental; and it is in this regard that his careful attention to pseudo-mundane detail is most crucial. For the device of phantoms created from memory is, after all, more common in fantasy than in SF, and may easily resolve into mysticism. Lem avoids such irrationalism not only by the general cognitive structure of the text, not only by attention to the technical mechanism of phantom-cre-ation (for instance, the use of neutrinos instead of atoms), but also (and perhaps most importantly for the texture of the novel) by the deliberately understated tone and mode of representation. The most staggering phenomena are, in one sense, all in the day's work—think, in contrast, of what a fantasy writer like Lovecraft would have made of such a theme. The novel ends by suggesting that the largest questions of the universe may time and again defeat the best efforts of dialectical reason, but also that only dialectical reason is capable of genuinely posing such questions at all.

Epistemological issues also figure in Le Guin's *The Dispossessed*. The narrative structure of the novel—with its alternating chapters relating Shevek's past on Anarres and his present visit to Urras—is designed to mimic both the controversy in physics between the competing theories of sequency and simultaneity, and Shevek's insight into the resol-ution of the problem as well: "The fundamental unity of the Sequence and Simultaneity points of view became plain; the concept of interval served to connect the static and the dynamic aspect of the universe" (9:225). But Le Guin's main stress, as compared with Lem's, is much more directly political; and Shevek's dialectical approach to physics, his synthesis of diachrony and synchrony, reflects the dialectical view of political theory which the text is most centrally concerned to uphold.

Much of the force of the novel is based on its estranging and near-Marxist critique of our own world, particularly the consumer capitalism of the US as satirically represented by the invented nation of A-lo. Seldom in modern fiction has the sheerly *unnatural* char-acter of the economic system which we most take for granted been portrayed more powerfully than, for instance, in the scene where Shevek (functioning as an inverted version of the usual mundane Everyman—the Raphael Hythloday or Gulliver—of utopian fiction) wanders through an ordinary shopping district and is nearly driven to a nervous breakdown by what he sees:

> And the strangest thing about the nightmare street was that none of the millions of things for sale were made there. They were only sold there. Where were the workshops, the factories, where were the farmers, the draftsmen, the miners, the weavers, the chemists, the carvers, the dyers, the designers, the machinists, where were the hands, the people who made'? Out of sight, somewhere else. Behind walls. All the people in all the shops were either buyers or sellers. They had no relation to the things but that of possession. (5:107)

On Urras, the bourgeois culture of A-Io is challenged, structurally, by the Stalinist communism of Thu. whose representative, Chifoilisk, offers accurate critiques of capitalist society but whose own system is almost equally unacceptable. The Iotic ethos is also challenged, idiosyncratically, by the aristocratic ethic of blood and military glory upheld by Shevek's colleague Atro. But the major alternative which Le Guin offers to American actuality is of course the anarchist society of Odonian Anarres.

The finest dialectical subtlety of her intelligence, however, lies in the fact that in producing a positive alternative to existing society—a utopia in a strong and self-conscious sense—she incorporates a critique of her own production. Despite her clear sympathy with the basic Odonian principles—the abolition of law, of government, of private property, of the division of labor to the maximum extent possible; even the weakening of the very concept of possession to the point that possessive adjectives are dropped from the language—Le Guin's outlook remains strictly critical, forcing a rigorous self-examination. Anarres is a harsh world, poor in natural resources and desperately underdeveloped, and the violence and regimentation (the latter substantive though not formal) which erupt during periods of extreme scarcity recall Marx's and Trotsky's doubts as to whether a genuinely egalitarian society can ever be achieved except in the context of overwhelming material abundance. Anarres is also an insular world: determined to insulate itself as completely as possible from Urrasti corruption and injustice, it eventually becomes chauvinistic to the point that it denies entry to a group of latter-day Odonians from a "Third World" nation on Urras. Here again a specifically Trotskyist dialectic is at work, for the question is whether Socialism in One Country (or one planet) may not be, in the long run, a contradiction in terms. But the worst features of Anarres are those which seem most intrinsic to its anarchistic premises. The elimination of all governmental and legal systems opens the way to an elaborate tyranny of public opinion and informal pressure, a tyranny which is all the more difficult to fight precisely because it is officially nonexistent. Shevek himself, always something of a misfit on Anarres, suffers considerably from conformist pressures and quasibureaucratic stupidity; and the text suggests that anarchism may be not only difficult to implement but, at least to some degree, internally destructive of its own stated goals. There is here a complex recognition that, although law in class society ultimately functions as an instrument of class coercion (law in Alo is devoted mainly to the sanctity of private property), law also works to offer some measure of protection from arbitrary power. For all its criticisms of Anarres, however, the text by no means resolves itself into a stance of liberal neutrality. The general superiority that anarchistic socialism (with all its faults) has over capitalism is rarely in doubt and is firmly vindicated by the novel's end. The text's dialectical interrogation of its own official ideology finally strengthens rather than weakens the cognitive integrity of its utopian and Utopian project.

One secondary feature of Odonianism concerns the breakdown of middle-class norms governing gender roles and sexual preferences. But *The Dispossessed is* in fact only very moderately feminist (even in comparison to the same author's *The Left Hand of Darkness*). Though Shevek is appalled by the sexism in A-Io, he (and his own society) are, as Delany has persuasively argued (pp. 218-83), considerably less free from sexism than Shevek and the novel itself seem to think. For a more radically feminist inflection of SF—for a more rigorous examination of the dialectic of sex—we may turn to Russ's *The Two of Them.* Indeed, the fusion of SF with radical feminism is the dominant project of Russ's work in general. But the term *fusion* is perhaps misleading here. The viability of Russ's project depends upon certain potentialities always intrinsic to SF, but rarely exploited until recently, and largely occluded by the almost exclusively masculine and sexless ethos which dominated magazine SF from the Gernsback through the Campbell eras. SF, however, is a uniquely appropriate vehicle for feminism. Because of the peculiar nature of the social contradiction which it addresses—women being the only subaltern group whose members typically live with members of the corresponding hegemonic group—feminism is, of all forms of critical theory, the most concerned with the ideological inscriptions of everyday life, with the imbrication of the political in the personal. Unfortunately, everyday life remains perhaps the least satisfactorily theorized moment of the social field, and current feminist theory has only partially made up the deficiency. Furthermore, it may be the case that concrete narration, with its necessary attention to the details of living, is capable of a more adequate critique of everyday life than can ever be attained, even in principle, by discursive theory. SF narration, then, with its special resources for estranging the familiar and suggesting alternatives to the given, is particularly well equipped to deal with the penetration of sexism into the quotidian world.

Such is the achievement of *The Two of Them.* The novel is structured on two theoretical moments: first, liberal feminism, and, second, the sublation of the latter into dialectical or radical feminism. The liberal moment is represented primarily by the encounter of the Trans Temp agents Irene Waskiewicz and Ernst Neumann with the society of Ka'abah, the economically important but culturally regressive planet to which they are dispatched on a secret mission, and the dominant sexual ideologies and general accoutrements of which are based upon those of the Islamic, especially the Arab, world. Irene is effortlessly appalled (as the reader is meant to be) by the oppression of women on Ka'abah, and, in particular, by the desperate plight of the young would-be poet Zubeydeh, whom the novel presents as a kind of typical case-study of victimization by overtly brutal sexism: but Irene's outrage and sympathy are initially framed by the secure sense of superiority with which liberal First World feminism typically regards the gender relations of Third World—especially Middle Eastern—societies. The text shifts gears when Irene—acting against Ernst's gentle cautions, against his general "yes, but—"response to Irene's anger at Ka'abah misogyny— moves beyond attitudinal sympathy and takes action to rescue Zubeydeh. After this break, not only does Irene's relationship with Zubeydeh (the nature of which is never wholly clear in any familiar terms) become more interesting and important to her than her well-defined relationship with Ernst, her lover, partner, and professional superior (and thus the significance of Russ's title is shifted). Even more importantly, though not unrelatedly, Ka'abah begins to function not as a locus of opaque otherness and evil, but as a negative utopia which effects a cognitive estrangement of the much more subtle but equally widespread sexism that dominates Irene's own sphere of Trans Temp (whose general cultural ethos recalls that of the Western middleclass professional world inhabited by Russ herself and by most of her readers). Irene's bond with Ernst becomes increasingly unsatisfactory, as the condescending and fundamentally oppressive character of many small turns of phrase, tones of voice, and unspoken assumptions becomes clear to her for the first time; the text even suggests an analogy between the domination of Zubeydeh by her father and the domination of Irene by Ernst (a good many years her senior). Finally Irene is moved not only to leave Trans Temp but, in a scene of grisly violence characteristic of Russ, to murder Ernst.

The attitude of the novel towards the killing is deliberately ambiguous. Irene may be seen either as a feminist heroine battling for freedom or as a psychotic killer; but such a binary opposition is just what the text aims to deconstruct. Irene herself, as her rage towards Ernst grows, questions her own sanity, but also, in a kind of Foucauldian feminism, questions her own questioning:

> It occurs to her that they may even be right, that nothing in her life accounts for the intensity of her anger, that Center [the Trans Temp headquarters] is not Ka'abah, that Ernst is a man who loves and respects women. He has good judgment; once he judged her worthy and now he judges her mad. *The gentlemen always think the ladies have gone mad.* (p. 147)

The thrust of the text is political rather than moral, and to ask whether Ernst's murder is morally justifiable (which it obviously is not) is somewhat beside the point. The point of *The Two of Them is*, rather, to demonstrate the complex gender relations that link social power, everyday details of routine and intimacy, and the formation and deformation of psychic balance.

I have attempted to demonstrate, then, that, in each of the SF novels which I have considered, a major conceptual topic—the structure of theoretical knowledge; the contradictions of capitalism and of anarchistic socialism; the variety of gender oppression—is subjected to critical, dialectical interrogation. In concluding this section, I will discuss

Dick's *The Man in the High Castle*, a metageneric text whose aim, *inter alia*, is both implicitly and explicitly to interrogate the structure of SF itself.

The Man in the High Castle was not originally marketed as SF and probably never would have been if the author had not previously established a reputation in the field; for the setting is the apparently mundane one of postwar America, and no technological marvels are prominent. The difference, of course, is that the Second World War is supposed to have been lost by the Allies, and the US has been conquered and dismembered by the victorious Axis nations. Germany and Japan are now the superpowers, and the status they enjoy subtly estranges the character of victory and world dominance. The post-Hitler Nazi hierarchy has remained intact and preserved its essential nature, but it commands the respect and respectability which winners normally possess. The genocide of the Jews has been nearly completed, and has been followed, against equally little opposition or outrage, by the even more enormous project of depopulating Africa. Germany is pursuing a vigorous space program, and is widely admired as the world's technological leader. Tensions have developed, however, between the wartime partners, and by the end of the novel we learn that Germany is planning to attack Japan and exterminate the Japanese. It is the difference between Germany and Japan—which figures, for Dick, partly as a difference between Western and Eastern philosophies, and which evidently seems to him more fundamental than the actual difference between the historical victors of the war, the US and the USSR—that the text exploits in its main critical cutting edge.

In part, the critical power lies simply in the foregrounding of historical mutability. The outcome of the Second World War remains the largest fact of the postwar era, and, in American ideology, has generally been represented as inevitable and almost metaphysically sanctioned. It is therefore salutary to be reminded that the Allied victory was the result of quite specific sociohistorical forces and that the evil of Nazism in no way guaranteed Germany's defeat. But *The Man in the High Castle* also has more specific aims in view. The eastern part of America is pointed to as living under a Nazi terror similar to that which many European countries actually experienced, while, in the western US, life under Japanese rule is comparatively tolerable. There is a certain austere discipline, inevitable given the presence of an occupying foreign power, but the Japanese officials—especially the one who appears most prominently, Mr Tagomi—are on the whole cultivated and humane individuals, with considerable private contempt for their German counterparts and even with a measure of sympathy for the victims of Nazism (whose offense, after all, was to be, like the Japanese, non-Aryan). This contrast between the Axis nations resolves less into a difference of political system than into one of culture and philosophy. The Oriental approach, with its stress on enduring values, on fate, on received non-utilitarian wisdom (typified in the novel by the *I Ching*),[6] is represented as naturally moderate. On the other hand, Nazi atrocity is seen as the logical extension of the typically Western valorization of incessant activity, of achievement, of expansion and acquisition. But these latter are, of course, precisely the values which characterize the actual postwar US. If there is a certain uncritical (and in the long run unconsciously racist) romanticism in Dick's attitude towards Asia, it may be understood as an estranging device to highlight the implicit fili-ations between German fascism and the imperialistic activism of American monopoly capitalism (it is not accidental that the novel was first published in the early days of the American assault on Vietnam).

The structural device of an alternative present is complicated by the presence of a novel-within-the-novel, an immensely popular though partly banned work called *The Grasshopper Lies Heavy*. Written by the title character of Dick's novel, it is a precise equi-valent of *The Man in the High Castle* itself, and presents in fictional form an America which did *not* lose the war (though its details are not precisely the same as those of actual history). At one point, a young Japanese couple, over dinner with a visitor, discuss the book's generic status:

> "Not a mystery," Paul said. "On the contrary, interesting form of fiction possibly within genre of science fiction."
>
> "Oh no," Betty disagreed. "No science in it. Nor set in future. Science fiction deals with future, in particular future where science has advanced over now. Book fits neither premise."
>
> "But," Paul said, "it deals with alternative present. Many well-known science fiction novels of that sort." To Robert he explained, "Pardon my insistence in this, but as my wife knows, I was for a long time a science fiction enthusiast." (7:108)

Betty presents the ordinary Philistine view, Paul a more critical one. Betty sees SF exclus-ively as narratives of the future (a widespread view in Germany, as it happens), and takes a progressivist and positivistic view of "science" (i.e., the physical sciences). Paul, on the other hand, understands—what Dick himself implicitly suggests throughout the novel—that the identity of the genre lies neither in chronology nor in technological hardware, but in the cognitive presentation of *alternatives* to actuality and the status quo. Though it may seem ironic that Dick won his only major SF award for a novel that its original publisher did not even consider SF, the irony is in fact much finer: namely, that Dick won his Hugo for a novel which demonstrates how the essential conceptual structure of the genre may be preserved while discarding the comparatively superficial trappings with which Hugo Gernsback tried to identify it. In its critical estrangement of Dick's own America, *The Man in the High Castle* is certainly SF.

4 Conclusions

If SF and, in the last quarter century or so, overt SF has the critical importance which I have argued it has, then it must compare favorably (to put the matter gently) with most other literature currently being produced in the West. The historical context of this liter-ary situation is not difficult to understand. Since the Second World War, the societies of Western Europe and North America have been on the whole frozen: domestically, in vari-ous forms of (usually) democratic capitalism; geopolitically, within the anti-Communist

Cold War alliance. Such stasis, with its inevitable pressure to eternalize the status quo and to minimize awareness of historical difference, is hardly conducive to the production of genuinely critical literature—as the actual literary trends of the era, in all their mundane narcissism, generally attest. Where exceptions have emerged, it has usually been in works by authors from groups marginalized within the West, or, as with SF, in works whose generic determinants tend to discourage conformism and the uncritical acceptance of actuality. But the achievement in SF, it seems to me, remains unmatched even by the rich traditions of Jewish-American or Afro-American fiction (though there is indeed some overlap here).

There is, however, a world beyond the West. In order to suggest a more global contextualization of SF and critical theory, I will, in a kind of coda to this essay, briefly consider the situation of Third World literature. The critical importance of the latter is beyond dispute. In Africa and Latin America especially, literature is today being produced which possesses a conceptual sophistication and critical acuteness far beyond the "mainstream" literature of the West. Analysis could easily show that a work such as (for instance) *One Hundred Years of Solitude is* imbricated in the concerns proper to critical and dialectical thought in a way similar to that which I have tried to demonstrate in the case of SF. Yet the Third World has produced little or no SF, which is still the domain of the West (and the Soviet bloc). How is this apparent paradox to be explained?

I am tempted to say that, if the Third World has no SF—i.e., no work explicitly and self-consciously in the SF tradition—it is because the Third World has no need of SF. Admittedly, the very phrase "Third World" is deeply problematic, conflating as it does a great many vastly different nations. But if the term is understood to mean those social formations on the increasingly integrated periphery of the multinational capitalist system whose centers lie in the West, and which stand to the metropolitan economies of the West somewhat as proletariat stands to bourgeoisie in classical 19th-century capitalism, then at least one important generalization may be ventured: that in the Third World, historical difference and specificity are not abstruse concepts but urgent and unavoidable facts of life. From the perspective of San Salvador or Kampala, First World life—not only as it exists in Paris or New York, but, more importantly, as the First World commodity structure penetrates the social field of El Salvador or Uganda—must seem as radically different and estranging as the imagined planets and futures of SF seem to readers in the West. And yet, as with the worlds of SF, the differences, however complex, are not ultimately mysterious: they are dialectically explicable in the critical terms of political economy and geopolitics. It may be added that Third World authors presumably feel little temptation to universalize empirical actuality, which for their nations means grinding misery and oppression. We might say, then, that in the Third World realism itself is, as it were, *naturally* SF. It is not mundane because the mundane, in the First World sense, does not exist. It is no accident that "cognitive estrangement," the Suvinian term for SF, finds its precise counterpart in "magical realism," Márquez's term for his own literary practice and that of many of his colleagues. From the Latin American coign of vantage, North American commodity capitalism appears on the scene with the immensely estranging force of magic, and "magic" not as a matter of irrationalist fantasy, but understood in cognitive and (in that sense) "realistic" terms. To live in the Third World is virtually to live in an SF situation, and this obviates the need to write what we in the West would immediately recognize as SF—just as in a genuinely classless society there will be no need for Marxism in any currently understood sense.

But if Third World literature can be conceptualized in terms of SF, the reverse formulation is also viable and perhaps more powerful: SF is the Third World literature of the First World (and, to some degree, of the Second World—the Soviet bloc—as well). Once the affinity is recognized, a number of useful analogies suggest themselves; for instance, it is noteworthy that the familiar post-Romantic "alienation" between author and audience is considerably smaller in the Third World and in the SF community. But the most important analogy is the most political. Whereas most literary practice and study in the First World is generally regarded as a trivial game by nearly all those not professionally involved in it (and even by many who are), the situation is much different in the Third World, where the political importance of cultural practice is widely recognized. Revolutionary movements and governments generally place literary culture high on their agenda of priorities, while subfascist regimes tend to murder left-wing cultural workers with a special thoroughness and glee. Nor is it by chance that so many of the major literary figures of the Third World (Neruda, Neto, Cesaire, among many others) have been major political figures as well. Though one can hardly claim that a comparable situation actually exists as regards First World SF, this entire essay has been devoted to maintaining that SF does possess the critical potentiality to play a role in our own liberation. That is why SF is worth writing about.

Notes

1. The terminological situation here is complicated, since Brecht, when arguing *against* Lukács, did occasionally call himself a realist; but he used the term tactically. and meant it not in any literary sense but in the sense of one concerned with reality. For a useful summary of the Brecht-Lukács controversy, see Henri Arvon, *Marxist Esthetics*, trans. Helen Lane (Ithaca, NY: 1973), pp. 100-12. Some of the relevant documents in this controversy are collected, along with some related material and an important retrospective analysis by Fredric Jameson, in *Aesthetics and Politics*, ed. Ronald Taylor (London, 1977).

2. A nice illustrative anecdote concerns the Bodleian Library of Oxford University, which was presented with a copy of the First Folio of Shakespeare upon publication but discarded it shortly thereafter during routine house-cleaning: a book of English scripts was hardly considered appropriate for a proper university library. In more recent years, however, the prevailing Oxford attitude towards Shakespeare has changed.

3. Samuel Delany is probably the critic who has dealt most interestingly with SF language, and my own discussion here is indebted to him. See especially Delany's *The Jewel-Hinged Jaw.* See also the interview with him in Charles Platt, *Dream Makers* (NY, 1980), pp. 69-75. Interesting

work in the same area may also be found in Kathleen L. Spencer's "'The Red Sun is High, the Blue Low': Towards a Stylistic Description of Science Fiction," *SFS*, 10 (1983): 35-49.

4. Perhaps the most important work on More's innovative utopianism is Louis Marin's *Utopiques: jeux d'espaces* (Paris, 1973). A convenient discussion of Marin's argument may be found in Fredric Jameson's "Of Islands and Trenches: Naturalization [*sic*—the term ought to read "Neutralization"] and the Production of Utopian Discourse," *Diacritics* (June 1977), pp. 2-21.

5. For a useful discussion of humanity and Otherness in Lem's novel, see Istvan Csicsery-Ronay's "The Book is the Alien: On Certain and Uncertain Readings of Lem's *Solaris*," *SFS*, 12 (1985): 6–21. See also Mark Rose, *Alien Encounters* (Cambridge, MA: 1981), pp. 82-95; and Darko Suvin, "The Open-Ended Parables of Stanislaw Lem and *Solaris*," in *Solaris*, *ed. cit.*, pp. 212-23.

6. One of the few critics to stress the role of the I *Ching* and Oriental philosophy in Dick's novel is Patricia Warrick, "The Encounter of Taoism and Fascism in Philip K. Dick's *The Man in the High Castle*," *SFS*, 7 (1980): 174-90.

Works cited

Delany, Samuel R. *The Jewel-Hinged Jaw: Notes on the Language of Science Fiction*. NY: Berkley Windhover Books, 1978.

Dick, Philip K. *Do Androids Dream of Electric Sheep?* 1968; rpt. NY: Ballantine Books, 1982.

—. *The Man in the High Castle*. 1962; rpt. NY: Berkley Medallion Books, 1974.

Eagleton, Terry. *Literary Theory: An Introduction*. Oxford: Basil Blackwell, 1983.

Horkheimer, Max. *Critical Theory: Selected Essays*, trans. Matthew J. O'Connell *et al*. NY: Herder & Herder, 1972.

Le Guin, Ursula K. *The Dispossessed*. 1974; rpt. NY: Avon Books, 1975.

Lem, Stanislaw. *Solaris* [1961], trans. Joanna Kilmartin & Steve Cox. NY: Berkley Books, 1971.

Russ, Joanna. *The Two of Them*. 1978; rpt. NY: Berkley Books, 1979.

Suvin, Darko. *Metamorphoses of Science Fiction*. New Haven: Yale UP, 1979.

20

Alien cryptographies: The view from queer

Wendy Pearson

Fiction, then, can be divided according to the manner in which men's relationships to other men and their surroundings are illuminated. If this is accomplished by endeavoring faithfully to reproduce empirical surfaces and textures vouched for by human senses and common sense, I propose to call it *naturalistic fiction*. If, on the contrary, an endeavor is made to illuminate such relations by creating a radically or significantly different formal framework. . . I propose to call it *estranged fiction*.

—Darko Suvin, *Metamorphoses of Science Fiction* (18)

1 Introduction: Fear of a queer galaxy

On November 25, 1998, the memberships of the U.S.S. Harvey Milk and the Voyager Visibility Project (offshoots of the lesbian and gay sf group, the Gaylaxians) issued a call for a boycott of the then soon-to-be-released *Star Trek: Insurrection*. After nearly two decades of lobbying the producers of the various *Star Trek* shows and movies for the inclusion of a lesbian or gay character[1] in a cast intended to represent all types of humans (including a variety of racial and ethnic types, as well as both sexes[2]) and quite a miscellany of aliens, the group's membership has finally, it seems, had enough. Curious as it might seem at first glance, sf shows seem to be the last hold-outs in a medium that is rapidly accommodating itself to the idea that there really are lesbian and gay people in the "real" world that television claims, however peculiarly, to reflect (in precisely that mode that Suvin labels "naturalistic").

Spokespeople for the Voyager Visibility Project note, trenchantly enough, that despite the addition of visible lesbian and gay characters to non-sf television shows, "it is just as important as ever to show that gays and lesbians will exist and will be accepted in the future." The heteronormative assumptions behind much science fiction, both cinematic and literary, are very neatly exposed by the circular reasoning with which the producers of *Star Trek* refute demands for visibly non-straight characters: homophobia, they say, does not exist in the future as it is shown on *Star Trek*; gay characters therefore cannot be shown, since to introduce the issue of homosexuality is to turn it back into a problem: in order for *Star Trek* to depict a non-homophobic view of the future, it must depict a universe with no homosexuals in it.[3] Clearly, logic is not a pre-requisite for would-be television gurus.

Nevertheless, while I certainly acknowledge that a visible gay or lesbian character on the cast of a *Star Trek* show would be a politically astute move for those whose day-to-day politics are focused on an inclusionary, rights-based approach to ameliorating the conditions in which lesbian and gay people live, it's worth asking whether the inclusion of a gay character on a show that presupposes an already heteronormative view of the human future can be said to "queer" that future in any significant way. If a lesbian officer is shown on the bridge, for instance, or a gay male couple is shown holding hands on the holodeck, either might certainly be an instance of "cognitive estrangement" (to borrow Suvin's term) for many audience members, but neither instance would necessarily be queer. Of course, the producers will have to use a little—and one might suggest that it would only take a very little—imagination in showing us that their new lieutenant, shall we say, is lesbian, without making her sexuality into a "problem."

Moving from a consideration of *Star Trek* to sf in general, I suggest that the presence of a lesbian or gay character, while not *per se* a radical or subversive strategy, may change one thing, for a particular reader, the reader who is unused to—and is perhaps searching for—a gay/lesbian presence within sf. In this case, the naturalization of a lesbian or gay character within a plot that has nothing explicitly to do with sexuality may, temporarily, function as a *novum* for this reader, just as the incidental revelation in Heinlein's *Starship Troopers* of Johnny Rico's blackness did for Samuel Delany.[4] In this case it is not so much the character as the character's environment that produces cognitive estrangement, since the character goes unremarked within his world and is not marked as different, either racially in the case of Rico or sexually in the case of our putative gay/lesbian character. It is precisely this revelation that the Voyager Visibility Project wishes the producers of *Star Trek* to provide for its viewers: the vision of a future in which queerness is neither hidden nor revealed *as difference*, but is simply there. Given the ubiquity of political, religious, and social commitment to the continual reinscription of hetero-normative "family values," this strategy may be queerer and more subversive than one might at first think.[5]

For the remainder of this essay, I want to explore what might be implied when one combines the terms "queer theory" and "science fiction." This contemplation will circulate around two quite different strategic interventions of "queer" into the world of sf—one is the performance of a "queer reading" and the other is the recognition of a "queer text." In speaking of queer readings, I want to make it clear that this is not necessarily a strategy most usefully applied to already queer texts; similarly, I want to suggest that the inclusion of gay and lesbian characters or issues does not make a text queer. The answer to my earlier question—what *would* queer *Star Trek*?—presumes, then, a movement beyond the inclusionary towards a radical re-writing of the assumption within the show of the naturalness, endurance, and fixity of our current understandings of sexuality and its relationship both to the sex/gender dyad and to sociocultural institutions. To return to my *Star Trek* example one final time, the portrayal of a marriage between, say, Lieutenant Tom Paris and Ensign Harry Kim would certainly be gay—likely in both senses of the word—but it would not necessarily be queer.

What, exactly, do I mean by "queer?" Or, as an esteemed elderly colleague of mine was heard to say, after reading my partner's M.A. thesis proposal, "Isn't queer a bad word?" Of course, queer *is* a bad word. Despite the particular joy with which both academics[6] and activists (often they are the same people) have reappropriated it, for the majority of gays and lesbians "queer" is still an insult, too often accompanied by bottles, fists, or the blows of a baseball bat. Because queer theory is a politically engaged form of academic work, most people immersed in the field are only too conscious of the ethical implications of this reappropriation. Queer resonates not only with its pejorative usage, but also with its mundane connotations—odd, strange, eccentric. In fact, the first defini-tion in my dictionary explains it as "deviating from the expected or normal." Any attempt to define "queer" within a postmodernist theoretical milieu must take into account the context through which we come to understand this deviation: is the deviation itself a misunderstanding by society at large of the fact that we are all human, that lesbians and gays deviate from the normal *only* in terms of our choice of romantic and sexual partners, a difference which is itself understood in this formulation as minor, even inconsequential? Or does queer deviate from the "normal" in ways that are radical and subversive, dedic-ated to exposing and challenging an ideologized teleology that reaches beyond sexual attraction to reveal the deeply un-natural and constructed nature of our understandings of biological sex, the performative nature of gender roles, and the sociocultural institutions founded upon this ideology? Or, to put it in its simplest possible terms, is queer a politics of identity or a politics of difference?[7]

My answer to this question is dependent on my own sense of where queer comes from: a dissatisfaction with both the universalizing (all gays are alike) *and* the segregating (gay men and lesbians are different) style of "identity politics" influenced by an ethnic model of gayness; the late twentieth century's intellectual shift to a more contingent, discursive, and localized understanding of the production of knowledge; and AIDS. The construction in the West of AIDS as a disease identified with homosexuality and the concomitant rise of an overt and death-dealing homophobic has discourse reinforced the existing tend-encies towards political engagement and consciousness on the part of those theorists, critics, and activists whose work has been gathered under the rubric of queer—even when that term has not always been used by the individuals themselves. Nevertheless, queer remains, both within the academy and among gays and lesbians in general, very much a contested term. As Annamarie Jagose points out in her survey of queer theory's origins and meanings: "Given the extent of its commitment to denaturalization, queer itself can have neither a foundational logic nor a consistent set of characteristics" (96). Queer's very slipperiness, however, its tendency towards instability and its pleasure in resisting attempts to make sexuality signify in monolithic ways, are all parts of its appeal.

Furthermore, queer suggests a move towards not just a different conception of sexuality, but also towards a different understanding of subjectivity and agency. Lee Edelman notes, in "The Mirror and the Tank," that

> To the extent that we are capable of identifying those junctures where the gay subjectivity we seek to produce recapitulates the oppressive logic of the culture that necessitated its emergence, we have the chance to displace that logic and begin to articulate the range of options for what might *become* a postmodern subject; we have the chance, in other words, to challenge, as Andreas Huyssen suggests postmodernism must, "*the ideology of the subject* (as male, white, and middle-class [and we must add, as he does not, heterosexual]) by developing alternate and different notions of subjectivity." (111)

How, we might ask, does sf allow us to develop alternate notions of subjectivity? What practices of representation have developed within the genre to allow for the expression of a subject who is not male, white, middle-class, and heterosexual? To see the potential within the genre for postmodern and, specifically, queer subjects, we need only look at the works of Samuel R. Delany and Joanna Russ. As with each of these writers, sf provides for the potential queer author more than a possible field in which to represent an alternative subjectivity. Its very popularity, its resistance to interpellation within the "mundane" field of literature, provides tools for the author who wishes to avoid the dangers of mimesis that have typically hampered gay and lesbian writing in the naturalist mode. The Cartesian subject of realist fiction always risks reincorporation back into a naturalized and faithful reproduction of "empirical surfaces and textures vouched for by human senses and common sense" (Suvin 18).

Furthermore, sf has a long history, dating back at least to Mary Shelley's *Frankenstein*, of questioning systems of thought, particularly those we now label metanarratives (science, history, and so on), even as it appears to—and sometimes does—valorize notions of scientific method, objectivity, and progress. Queer, with its denaturalization of master narratives and its movement towards subcultural and subaltern understandings of texts, operates, by analogy, on some of the same levels as sf. As Earl Jackson points out, "*Science fiction* offers a tradition of representational formalization of a worldview in which the subject is not the cause but the effect of the system that sustains it" (102). This insistence that the subject is the effect of the system neatly recapitulates the imbrication of alternate narrative strategies with dissident subjectivities, with a refusal of the Cartesian subject. This resonates for me with precisely the strategic rationale behind Samuel Delany's call to resist attempts to reclaim sf as "literature." In Jackson's words,

> Delany's theoretical blueprints for and his own examples of the kind of critical fiction that the science fiction writer can achieve revalorizes the "fictive." The specific importance Delany places on the paraliterary differences of the genre at once constitute a challenge . . . to the dominant obfuscating obsession with "authenticity," while providing eloquent theoretical grounding for that challenge as well as for textual practices that prioritize specification over referentiality, the production of meaning over the repetition

of "Truth." It is science fiction's foundational infidelity to the "real world" that affords the fictive world the status of a critical model. (125)[8]

In the remainder of this essay—which is literally *un essai*, an attempt, to see how sf and queer may illuminate each other—I hope to bring some of this "theoretical grounding" to bear on the actual practice of sf as it has evolved over this century. In so doing, I am going to suggest a variety of models for understanding the intersections of queer with sf at the level of the text. These may include, first, the sf narrative that is not overtly queer, but that can be read analogically within a specific historical context and sensibility; second, what one might call the "proto-queer" text that, although not queer itself, effects a kind of discursive challenge to the naturalized understanding of sexuality and its concomitant sociocultural surround; third, the text that is coded as queer, but in such a way as to hide in plain sight—this is the narrative equivalent of the "open secret," the one which everybody knows, but no one wishes to call attention to, at least not within the specific historico-cultural milieu in which it was written; and finally, the overtly queer text, the text which questions the "naturalist fiction" that sex and gender and sexuality are matters of "human senses and common sense."

While this list may have the appearance of being categorical and complete, I want to insist that these "categories" are nothing more than tentative and temporary attempts, readings-in-process of a subject (and subject matter) that is itself in process. None of these readings, then, are necessarily authoritative nor can they take place outside a historical and cultural context, since what is hidden from one audience is plainly visible to another, and what can easily be seen from one perspective is indecipherable from another viewpoint. Like "queer" itself, my discursive strategy in this essay will require movement backwards as well as forwards, will prove on occasion slippery and even fractured in its attempt at narrative, and will remain, no doubt, contestatory and contested.

2 (E)strange(d) fictions: Who goes there?

> Each of us with an eye on the other to make sure he doesn't do something—peculiar. Man, aren't we going to be a trusting bunch! Each man eyeing his neighbors with the grandest exhibition of faith and trust—I'm beginning to know what Connant meant by 'I wish you could see your eyes.' Every now and then we all have it, I guess. One of you looks around with a sort of 'I-wonder-if-the-other-*three*-are-look.'—John W. Campbell, Jr., "Who Goes There?" (108)

I once asked my science-fiction class, during a seminar discussion of *The Left Hand of Darkness*, whether they could draw any parallels between the construction in the novel of Estraven as a traitor[9] and the history, recent at the time Ursula Le Guin wrote the novel, of the House Committee for Un-American Activities. What, they responded, was a House Committee for Un-American Activities? I asked if any of them knew who Joseph McCarthy was—and received eighteen perfectly blank looks. What did the phrase "commie pinko queer" mean? Well, they could parse parts of it—"commie" was a communist and "queer" was, well, you know—but they couldn't put the parts together. What could being communist possibly have to do with being gay, or vice versa? And what did either have to do with *The Left Hand of Darkness*?

Queer how things have changed, isn't it? And now—belatedly—I should warn you that discussions like this, of sexuality and particularly of sexuality in the context of the fluidity and semantic sensitivity of queer theory, inevitably lead to bad puns and worse jokes. The stories invoked within the complex field of attempting to understand how we exist in the world as sexual beings are fraught with *double entendres*, contradictions, misapprehensions, and (un)faithful reiterations—so much so that one might, in fact, be tempted to agree with Leo Bersani when he argues that, at heart, most people really don't like sex (95). Certainly we fear its power, just as we fear being exposed as different. But unlike the differences of race and biological sex, sexual difference is often invisible.[10]

I would like to offer, as my first example of a possible application of queer theory to sf, a reading of John W. Campbell's classic "Who Goes There?"(1938) against the cultural anxiety that enveloped ideas about homosexuality in the era surrounding WWII. At its height, this anxiety was related to a widespread desire to return to a vision of pre-war morality and lifestyle,[11] in part by persuading women to return to the home, and in part by repudiating a practice of unspoken but official tolerance—within fairly strict limits—for gays and lesbians in the military and in government service.[12] The backlash was spectacular, exacerbated as it was in most of the Western world both by xenophobia and anti-communist propaganda. It is also one of those historical events that exhibits particularly well the imbrication of misogyny and homophobia: both the women and the queers had to be put back in their place. At the same time, the need to reassert heteronormativity was reflected in cultural production by a proliferation, particularly within sf, of both stories and movies which demonized the Other—already a prevalent theme within the genre. While these sf tales are normally viewed as allegories of the dangers of communism, they can also be read as warnings of the dangers of homosexuality to the emergent nuclear family: whereas in Nazi Germany, the Jew and the homosexual were metonymically the same person,[13] in the US and Canada, the communist and the homosexual were seen as representing so clear and present a danger to the American way of life as to render them virtually indistinguishable.[14]

However, in order to carry out such a policy, or to police it, one must be able to identify "the enemy." Women, except for the occasional passing butch, were relatively easily identified. But how does one recognize a "homosexual"? The problem of how to identify the alien in our midst, the queer who could pass, remained fraught both for governmental institutions and for "ordinary" people. Lee Edelman, in his study of the discursive contradictions underwriting the conceptualization of sexuality in this time period, points to the ways in which, on the one hand, queerness was envisioned as always already written on the body, while, at the same time, queers were feared in part because of their ability to "pass" ("Tearooms and Sympathy" 151-156).

Under these circumstances, it is hardly surprising to find a proliferation of stories and films fixated on the danger of the alien who is able to assume human guise and travel unseen amongst us, wreaking havoc on the nation and destroying the family. Among films, *Invasion of the Body Snatchers* (1956) is probably the best known, although the film version of Campbell's story, *The Thing* (1951), certainly merits an honorable mention. Just as *Frankenstein*'s tale of the monster created from within can be read in a multitude of ways that focus on the revelation of different kinds of monstrous births—in at least one of which it can be read as an originary story about the parent's, especially the father's, fear of producing a queer child (queer as different serving always synecdochically to bring into view queer as *sexually* different)—so "Who Goes There?" serves as a near perfect example of the way in which the story of the alien who passes as human derives from the precise confluence of anxieties that serve to claim, *at the same time*, that homosexuality is always written on the body and that it is always able to pass.

In "Who Goes There?" the alien—and a very nasty alien it is, too, with an immutable drive to conquest that may be part guilty imperialist conscience and part fear of the Other—has been frozen into the ice of Antarctica for twenty thousand years. A team of researchers finds the alien ship, retrieves the solitary frozen specimen, and sets out to thaw and study the apparent corpse. That the alien is not innocently dead is presaged by the dreams of various members of the all-male team; even frozen, it appears to be able to exert some sort of telepathic and perhaps suggestive pressure on the human mind, luring men into unconsciously betraying both themselves and their species.

The revived alien takes over the bodies of other species, merging with them and consuming their physical being, so that each in turn becomes the Other. The alien imitation of the "normal" man is so perfect, however, that it remains undetectable by all the tests that the men are initially able to devise. They know that some of them have become monsters, but they do not know which. The threat is internalized, as all of these apparently human males are involved, one way or another, in a race to discover a test that will reveal (that is, make visible) the monstrosity lurking in the guise of human before the alien is able to muster enough strength to escape Antarctica and conquer the remainder of the planet. The tone throughout the story is minatory, every scene replete with the unseen but omnipresent threat: "An air of crushing menace entered into every man's body, sharply they looked at each other. More keenly than ever before—*is that man next to me an inhuman monster?*" (118).

The conversion from human to alien is figured in bodily terms that are reminiscent of the sexual act. The men, caught in the monster's gaze, are passive victims of its alien seductions—Connant, for example, stares into the living red eyes of what is supposed to be a corpse but it seems to him "of no more importance than the labored, slow motion of the tentacular things that sprouted from the base of the scrawny, slowly pulsing neck" (95); he puts up no resistance, psychological or physical, to his absorption by the alien. The actual moment of alien takeover is never shown to us, taking place discreetly "off camera"; yet it is figured in terms of both consumption and consummation: the alien inserts a part of its substance into the men, taking them over complelely. Contacts with identifiable versions of the alien are depicted in terms of violence of very specific types: the men burn it with a fiery probe, they fall upon it and virtually tear it to pieces which they then cauterize, and they attack Blair—the first convert and last survivor—with yet another equivalent of the red-hot poker:[15]

> The huge blowtorch McReady had brought coughed solemnly. Abruptly it rumbled disapproval throatily. Then it laughed gurglingly, and thrust out a blue-white, three-foot tongue. The Thing on the floor shrieked, flailed out blindly . . . crawled and howled. (123)

The alien seduces men into submission to its will and then uses their appropriated bodies as the means by which to assimilate the remaining men. The men, some of whom are already aliens in disguise, argue about its imitative abilities, concluding that a perfect imitation "would take a superhuman skill" (102):

> "It would do no good," said Dr. Cooper, softly as though thinking out loud, "to merely look like something it was trying to imitate; it would have to understand its feelings, its reactions. It *is* unhuman; it has powers of imitation beyond any conception of man . . . no [human] actor could imitate so perfectly as to deceive men who had been living with the imitated one in the complete lack of privacy of an antarctic camp." (102)

The fear of the perfect imitation, undetectable even within an environment as intimate as the camp, resonates with the fear that the gay male can imitate "real" men so perfectly as to pass undetected in the most masculine of environments. The imitation should be detectable—written on the body of the gay man pretending to be straight—yet he remains undetectable within the military, the government, and—most frightening of all— the family.[16]

The alien is also unable to reproduce and is portrayed as having, by necessity, to recruit its forces by converting the normal in literally physical ways—consumption and appropriation—into the monstrous. In addition, what gives the monstrous alien away in the end is its selfishness, the one thing that distinguishes it from the valorous altruism of real humans. McReady explains that every part of the alien is a whole—even its blood once it's split off—with the result that, being too selfish to sacrifice itself for the good of the species, the new part will strive to preserve itself: "the *blood* will live—and try to crawl away from a hot needle."[17] There is a resonance here with the populist conception of the gay man as selfish, a conception which may have arisen, in part, because he's seen as refusing to share his genes and perform his male role in perpetuating the species, but which may also be partially a bowdlerization of Freud's theories of the role of narcissism in the psychosocial construction of the male homosexual.

Not only is there an extremely dark homoerotic tone underwriting both the construction of and the threat against this closed all-male society (traditionally the one environment in which homosexual activity is most likely to take place among men who do not define themselves as gay), but the threat is also conceived in terms that replicate the particular rhetoric with which the heteronormative forces of the political and religious right have chosen to characterize the threat of the (male) homosexual: he is endlessly but inexplicably seductive; he cannot reproduce and so must convert in order to continue his species; he is the monster who comes from within, since he is, by necessity, produced by apparently normal heterosexuals; and he is able to vanish and to remain nearly undetectable, free to work his wiles against all of those institutions Americans hold most dear.[18]

There are powerful resonances between the historical understanding of dissident sexuality, particularly homosexuality, from the turn of the century through to the beginning of the gay liberation movement and the construction of the alien in this story. Nevertheless, I do not mean to suggest that this reading of the story is necessarily more authoritative than or precludes other potential readings. It does serve, I think, as a useful example of how that peculiar, imprecise thing we have come to call "queer theory" can illuminate the connections between, on the one hand, a particular perspective on our sexual ontology and its origins and, on the other, a science-fiction story about the dangers of aliens who can pass invisibly in the midst of "normal" people. Not surprisingly, it is Blair, the first alien convert, who argues for a viewpoint not based on an attempt to naturalize a normative ideological formation, when he tells the other men that they "are displaying that childish human weakness of hating the different" (94). Given the events of the story, "hating the different" would appear to be just what the doctor ordered.

3 Alien nation: Visualizing the (in)visible

> . . . it is a central purpose of art, in conjunction with criticism, to expand the realm of conscious choice and enlarge the domain of the ego. It does this by making manifest what was latent, a process that can be resisted, but not easily reversed. And so even those who dislike what I have had to say may yet find it useful as a warning of how things appear to other eyes . . . . Thomas M. Disch, "The Embarrassments of Science Fiction" (155)

Cultural constructions of visibility operate like magic: they make certain things disappear, or appear only in very particular contexts. Let me tell you a story. Once, about a decade ago, on a long and boring car ride with a young woman I scarcely knew, I found myself running out of topics of conversation. It was all too obvious that everything that interested me bored her. Her descriptions of her fiancé, on the other hand, bored me, but might, I thought, at least give us some commonality on an aesthetic level. So, as we waited at a stop light, I pointed out a particularly lovely young man. She perked up, gazed in the direction of my pointing finger, and finally said, with much puzzlement, "Where?"

"Right there," I said, "at the bus stop."

"I don't see anyone."

"Sure you do—that good-looking black guy. . . ." And at that moment I looked at her blonde hair and contemplated the story of her Norwegian husband-to-be and finally figured it out.

You see, now I've told you a story. It's one that functions—as sf itself often does—on the level of analogy. On an academic and intellectual level, we are generally conscious—I hope—of race and racial issues. It's no longer completely improbable to us that a young white woman, someone who probably would describe herself as not at all racist, would be unable to see a young black man in this context.[19] We understand this story. It is less clear to me that we—that is, all of us—understand the other story, the one by which queer people in plain sight escape the heterosexual or, perhaps more precisely, the hetero-normative gaze. This is the other half of the story: while "Who Goes There?" replicates the concern with the gay man (or lesbian) who "passes" invisibly within the larger society, other queer people, their history and their cultural production, remain invisible and unre-cognized, even when that invisibility comes at the cost of a willful act of blindness.

Now I can theorize this peculiarity of the heteronormative gaze in reference to feminist theorizing of the gaze[20] itself or—in a useful analogy to heteronormativity—to work by people like Richard Dyer on the visual and cultural meanings of whiteness, or to the larger discursive strategies of post-colonial theory. Furthermore, I can also explain the invisibility of queerness within the text, specifically, by reference to the work of critics and theorists such as Alan Sinfield, who have labored to make visible the invisible and to demonstrate the usefulness and importance of reading from a subcultural position, whether it be queer or racial, ethnic or gendered, a matter of class or location. Such theoretical constructions are useful, perhaps essential, to what I'm calling queer theory, since they help to explain the seemingly quixotic inability of heteronormative institutions (which largely includes academia itself and also, I'm sorry to say, often includes sf, both readers and critics) to see anything queer in a text, an image, or the world itself.

Thus, on the one hand, a queer reading can be a reading against the grain, where one looks at a text from what is clearly a subcultural position: often that involves read-ing the text through the cultural and historical milieu in which it is written; that milieu is not, however, understood in hegemonic terms, but rather through the historical and sociocultural perspectives afforded by the reader's subculture. On the other hand, a queer reading may set out either to reveal or to recuperate what is already in some sense a queer text, usually a product of a history in which writing as a gay man or as a lesbian was impossible or dangerous. Such queer readings also provide alternative understandings of texts that cannot be labelled gay or lesbian, since those subject posi-tions were not available to their creators. Thus, for example, we queer certain, indeed many, Renaissance texts. This does not, however, imply that their authors are "queer" or gay/lesbian or even homosexual, since those categories are all modern; it does imply, though, that we can recognize within the texts the traces of an alternative or dissident sexual subjectivity that may be revealed through close and careful reading within both a historical context and a theoretical framework. Such a reading is delineated, for example, by Earl Jackson when he attempts to map the strategies by which deviant subjectivities can be represented within the text. Jackson notes the necessity for a decoding practice, a cryptography of the text, which is historically contingent:

> Like the Renaissance sodomite, the nineteenth-century "Uranian" relied on phallocentric mythographs of masculine self-overestimation to disguise his fantasies—he sought a visibility through which he could remain unseen. This defense allowed the writers or artists to elude surveillance while conveying their hidden meanings to those whose desires enabled them to read the codes. (51)

While it is possible to argue both that such subterfuge was historically necessary—and may still be necessary for those desiring to have their work commercially published, at least in some fields—and that it was a self-defeating strategy in terms of a nascent homosexual identity politics, such encrypting of meaning should not be understood as necessarily subversive. Both Sinfield and Jackson note the containment by hegemonic forces of coded texts: one can be a little subversive so long as one remains below the synaptic threshold at which the dominant regime is forced to take notice. Furthermore, as Jackson notes, "Although the perverse resignification of dominant masculine iconography provided a cryptography for an 'outlaw' community, its mimesis of patriarchal autoaffection was too well executed to disturb the dominant meanings of those expressions" (51).

The mimetic reproduction of a hegemonic vision of the world is itself a historically contingent process, in the sense that codes that are indecipherable to one decade or age or to one set of people may become obvious to another. Thus, for example, we have masculinist readings of the stories of James Tiptree. Jr—Alice Sheldon's male pseudonym and alter ego—that are wholly lacking in irony. Tiptree was praised for "his" understanding of the male psyche, and texts that, to us, are not only obviously but almost paradigmatically feminist were understood totally within the domain of a reading practice that rendered women invisible. Tiptree's works were not only not read as feminist but were defined—and not only by Robert Silverberg, although he seems to have been the only person unfortunate enough to put what appear to have been widely held opinions in print—as arising from a clearly masculine understanding of the world. Not only does Silverberg refer to Tiptree's prose (having, ironically, just cited "The Women Men Don't See") as "lean, muscular, supple," he adds that

> there is, too, that prevailing masculinity about both [Hemingway and Tiptree]—that preoccupation with questions of courage, with absolute values, with the mysteries and passions of life and death as revealed by extreme physical tests, by pain and suffering and loss. (xv)

Men, it seems, did not see *any* of the women in "The Women Men Don't See."

In a not dissimilar way, purely feminist readings of "Houston, Houston, Do You Read?" may not account for, or have any interest in, either the necessary lesbianism of these future women or the construction of the Andys as transgendered. Andy is variously described, mostly by Bud, the sexually aggressive male (of the three, one of the others is figured as a patriarch—literally, the name of the father—and the other, the narrator, is likely homosexual), as "a boy," as having "no balls at all," as "a dyke," and as a woman with excess androgen (thus the name). Yet a reading that foregrounds only the gender relations within the story is one that, in a sense, makes *men* central once again. The story is then read as a sad parable of the impossibility of heterosexual women and men being able to create a viable world together, since Tiptree, it seems, has already damned the men as innately violent, domineering, patriarchal, and sexually aggressive (although none of those constructions explain the narrator). The positive, loving, and intimate relationships between the women, the fact that they have survived and prospered, that they have, in fact, become "humanity," are seen as less important, in such a reading, than the failure to repatriate heterosexuality. Yet demonstrating the viability of a successful, happy, and entirely non-heteronormative world seems quite queer to me. Surely the story's assertion that heteronormative relationships are irredeemable argues not so much for a feminist uprising in which all men will be slaughtered as for a rethinking of the ideological and sociocultural presuppositions that make it impossible to imagine relationships across the sexes outside the limited regime of what one might call the "heterosexual imaginary"?[21] Is it then possible to consider "Houston, Houston, Do You Read?" as a queer text, as well as a feminist one? Can it be both? I raise these questions not to answer them, but to suggest to the reader some of the potential ways by which one might perform a queer reading of this text.

4 Becoming alien, becoming homosexual: From cyptography to cartography

> "Under the Hollywood Sign," I think, is a perfect example of that one quadruple somersault from the highest bars that Tom could manage again and again, but which Reamy-clones never seem able to pull off. In this piece, as I say, we can hear the singular voice of Tom Reamy, singing a dangerous song of primal fears so deep and yet so commonplace that we automatically reject them, precisely because they may be universally shared. No one likes to imagine him- or herself as a potential point-beast ready to run with the slavering pack.—Harlan Ellison, "Introduction" to *San Diego Lightfoot Sue*. (xiii)

I want to turn in this section of my essay to a story that was first published in 1975 and that was not, I suspect, read at the time as primarily a gay text or a text about either homosexuals or homosexuality, Tom Reamy's "Under the Hollywood Sign." Reamy died in 1977, at the age of 42, having published only a handful of sf stories and one novel, *Blind Voices* (1978), that is more horror than sf. Reading between the lines of Harlan Ellison's introduction to the posthumous collection of Reamy's short stories, *San Diego Lightfoot Sue and Other Stories*, I deduce that Reamy was probably gay himself. If not, it is evident in the stories—especially "Under the Hollywood Sign" and "San Diego Lightfoot Sue" (which won the 1975 Nebula Award for best novelette)—that he was remarkably familiar with the gay idiom of the time. Either way, it doesn't matter a great deal, since a text's queerness cannot be said to reside in the sexual identity of its author. Yet having said this, I am aware of having, yet again, opened up the question of the ways in which "queer" can be construed variously as belonging to, being seen in, or being read into the text, the author, or the reading. "Under the Hollywood Sign," for all its being, I suspect, relatively unknown within the world of sf criticism, may prove a particularly fruitful (and, yes, the pun is deliberate) example of the ways in which queer theory can effect a re-reading—and not just of the text, but also, perhaps, of the heteronormative reading protocols that have constrained earlier readings. In this case, I will be reading "Under the Hollywood Sign" in part for its peculiarly (un)faithful reiteration of the trope of the invisible alien; as such, I will be reading it against the ghosts of earlier readings—difficult as those traces are to discern—both of the story itself and of that other story I have set up here as exemplary of the trope, Campbell's "Who Goes There?"

"Under the Hollywood Sign" tells the story, in first person narration, of a self-identified heterosexual LA cop, Lou Rankin, who sees and becomes obsessed with a group of near-identical and extraordinarily beautiful redheaded young men who lurk in the back-ground of vehicle crashes and other sites of lethal violence (and who are, in the end, revealed as aliens who feed on the life energies of dying humans). Invisible to everyone else, the young men exert a peculiar fascination on Rankin, to the extent that he even-tually kidnaps one of them and takes him to a borrowed cabin in the foothills. There he chains the young man up and attempts to make some sort of contact with him. These attempts consist at first of highly unsatisfactory question and answer sessions; after three weeks, the narrator resorts to a violence that quickly becomes sexualized. It soon becomes apparent, however, even to the narrator, that the young man is not remotely what he seems. In fact, the narrator has interrupted some form of alien life cycle, which results in the stillbirth of a winged creature described (as the young man had earlier been) in terms reminiscent of traditional depictions of angels. After the death, the narrator returns to LA, where he finds his partner's wife, whose sexual attentions he's been trying to avoid, hiding in his apartment. The partner, Carnehan, turns up while they're having (reluctant, on the narrator's part) sex, kills the wife, knocks out the narrator, drives him to the Hollywood Hills, and eventually dumps him out on the hillside under the Hollywood sign, shoots him in the gut, and leaves him to die. Unable to acknowledge that he's dying, the narrator attempts to crawl to safety—only to look up and find himself surrounded by four more of the beautiful red-headed young men who "look at [him] the same way Carnehan looks at an apple he's been saving for a special occasion" (66).

From the very first sentence—"I can't pinpoint the exact moment I noticed him" (40)—the story foregrounds the paradox that these exceptionally beautiful, and therefore one would think noticeable, young men are visible only to the narrator. Part of the crowd of gawkers around the site of a nasty traffic accident, the young man is seen, apparently, only by Rankin. The narrator makes three specific observations: first, that he has been seeing but not seeing the young man: "I suppose I had been subliminally aware of him for some time" (40). Then, he notes that the young man does not react the same way as the rest of the crowd: "That's one of the reasons I noticed him in particular. He wasn't wearing that horrified, fascinated expression they all seem to have. He might have been watching anything—or nothing" (40). And finally, the narrator makes an observation that situates the story firmly within the realm of the sexual, although he does so by denying that very interpellation: "Don't get the wrong idea—my crotch doesn't get tight at the sight of an attractive young man. But there's only one word to describe him—beautiful" (41).

The story thus circulates from the beginning around three related issues: the question of visibility, as it is expressed through the narrator's ability to see the aliens; the sexual identity of the narrator, who, although self-identified as heterosexual, has an immediate and overwhelming sexual response to the aliens; and the identity of the aliens themselves, which is only slowly unveiled, as the objects of the narrator's gaze slip from an initial identification as beautiful young men to a sense that there is something profoundly different about them to the final revelation that they are, in fact, an entirely alien lifeform—or, to be more precise, that they represent a stage, a kind of chrysalis, in a profoundly alien life-cycle that has nothing at all to do with human wants, desires, or identities. Because the aliens are never explained—never even overtly identified within the story *as aliens*—the story hesitates on the borderline between sf and fantasy/horror: a scientific explanation would tip it one way, a supernatural one would tip it the other. Furthermore, there is a marked refusal within the text to make a definitive pronouncement on the issue of the narrator's sexual identity. Instead, the text plays with conventional notions of homosexual/heterosexual difference, never fully locating the narrator at a specific point on the psycho-sexual map of the homo-hetero divide. It does so, furthermore, within the framework of an outlaw cryptography, a series of codings, of in-jokes, that are only indeterminately available to the presumed heterosexual audience of sf. How many straight readers, I wonder, were familiar in the late 70s with *The Advocate*, the US national gay magazine in which, among other things, Pat Califia gave explicit sexual advice to gay men?

In 1984, on the only occasion that I have taught "Under the Hollywood Sign" to my science fiction course—it has since gone out of print—I found my students divided into two distinct camps: on the one hand, the majority, who saw only the most obvious signs of queerness in the text, assumed that, had the story really been about homosexuality, it would have been expressed by some other metaphor; on the other hand, I had several students from the nearby Bible College in the class, for whom the story was, it appeared, perfectly clear. Fundamentalists to the core, these particular students objected vehemently to the story's inclusion on the syllabus, claiming that it was both pornographic and blasphemous. Both responses exemplify particular cultural assumptions about the representation of homosexuality in literature—the one, used to a reading protocol founded on assumptions of universality and "Truth," finds the homosexuality in the story insufficient in itself, so that it must be about something more "universal," which is inevitably then something more heterosexual; the other, used to a reading protocol that weighs everything against the "literal Truth" of the Bible, reads (and judges) the story against both a particular moral standard and a particular iconography, in which an angel, for example, can only be an angel and a homosexual can only be evil. Both interpretations locate the story at specific, albeit different, positions on the cultural map, positions which say a great deal about our sociocultural beliefs about queerness, if very little about queerness itself—or about the text.

As an intervention into or a rewriting of the story that reveals the menace of the alien passing invisibly amongst us, "Under the Hollywood Sign" reverses many of the standard tropes that inform "Who Goes There?" The monstrosity of these aliens, if it exists at all, resides not in their deformity, their ugliness, or their insatiable appetite for conquest; however, although these aliens are, by human standards, extraordinarily beautiful—"all the artists for the last thousand years have been trying to paint that face on angels, but their fumbling attempts never came close" (54)—they are not necessarily "good." As it becomes clear that the aliens need to feed on the life-energy of dying creatures in order to complete their metamorphosis (into winged beings who are even more obviously angel-like than their "human" forms), it becomes equally clear that they are somehow causing the sudden increase in human deaths. As Cunningham, the pretty cop who is normally on "Pansy Patrol," says to the narrator: "What got into people last night, anyway? Seems like everybody was trying to get themselves killed" (52). Thus, while the alien of "Who Goes There?" is never figured as anything but monstrous evil, the aliens in Reamy's story are much more morally ambiguous. Furthermore, because, on the one hand, they are marked as "queer" by the text—compared with the "pretty boys" in the gay bars, as well as to Cunningham and even to Rankin's partner, Carnehan, in a reproduction of the stereotype that certain men are too beautiful to be straight—and, on the other hand, they are marked as angelic and described in terms of a kind of beautiful neutrality, as if they are above the pettiness of human concerns, these aliens are only ambiguously interpellated as either monsters or angels. Metonymically, they fail to serve as warnings of the invisible "passing" Other, whether communist or homosexual, since not only does the text provide the reader with no clear way to judge the relative value of a human life against the birth of an alien/angel, but the narrator's remorse at the winged creature's death and his comparison of the angelic disinterested beauty of the alien with the fleshy demands of Carnehan's wife suggest that the aliens/Others may be the true norm against whom humans, the not-Other, are revealed as lacking.

In addition, the text's refusal to disambiguate Rankin's overt sexual attraction to the apparently male aliens (they have penises, but use them neither to urinate nor for sex) and his repeated assertion of himself as a heterosexual man, call into question the very heterosexual/homosexual dyad by which our century has come to understand and to differentiate forms of sexual attraction.[22] At the same time, both the style of narration, reminiscent both of hard-boiled detective stories and of the "lean, muscular, supple" prose of Tiptree, and Rankin's position as a cop mark him as clearly male, disrupting the presupposition that effeminacy is a prerequisite for the experience of masculine same-sex desire. The text does not disallow the reading that suggests that Rankin has been, all along, a repressed homosexual; however, by making the discourse of repression overt in the conversations between the cops, and specifically between Cunningham, of "Pansy Patrol" fame, and the police psychologist, the text suggests both that such a repression is universal—Cunningham suggests the psychologist is gay, Carnehan reads *The Advocate*, the narrator concludes that Cunningham probably *is* gay—and that it is inadequate to explain either the specificity of the narrator's desire for the aliens or the extent of his obsession. In constructing Rankin as the most masculine of men, the cop, the story also reveals the curious imbrication of the police, especially the vice squad, with their prey—pretty Cunningham goes out on "Pansy Patrol" with a padded crotch, Carnehan chuckles over an anti-cop joke in a gay magazine, both Cunningham and the narrator reveal an obsession with penis size, and all of them are familiar with the bars and restaurants, with the gestures and idiom of the gay subculture. Masculinity, it would seem, does not automatically equate to heterosexuality. Furthermore, the very location of the story in LA, where everyone's first reaction, when the narrator asks if they've seen the aliens, is to talk about actors, grounds the story within a notion of performance: under the Hollywood sign, masculinity is most obviously a role played with varying degrees of verisimilitude. Or, as Judith Butler notes in "Critically Queer":

> [i]nsofar as heterosexual gender norms produce inapproximable ideals, heterosexuality can be said to operate through the regulated production of hyperbolic versions of 'man' and 'woman.' These are for the most part compulsory performances, ones which none of us choose, but which each of us is forced to negotiate. (22)

As with "Who Goes There?," the construction of the masculine as the object of the gaze creates a profound uneasiness. Rankin's ability to *see* the aliens is nearly indecipherable from his desire for them, a desire which is figured nearly as much in terms of wanting to see and to be seen, to be acknowledged, as it is in overtly sexual terms. After he rapes the alien for the first time, Rankin holds the alien's face and forces him to respond, to be present:

> "Don't hide from me. It doesn't do any good. I can see you. I can see you!" He swam to the surface and looked at me. "Did you enjoy it? Did you even feel it?"
> "Yes."
> "Did it feel good? Did it hurt?"
> "Yes." (60)

The alien's responses to the narrator's questions, as to his actions, settle nothing. On the one hand, they can be interpreted within the standard conventions of pornographic writing, in which the description of anal penetration in terms of "hurts so good" has become a cliché; on the other hand, they indicate the alien's near-complete disengagement with anything human, as he strives to complete his birth. The alien's transformation, the end of his life cycle, produces a moment of cognitive dissonance that resonates both in terms of sf and in terms of the deconstruction of our assumptions about gender and sexuality, as this apparent male quite literally attempts to give birth, an attempt that fails only because the narrator has prevented the alien from gathering enough life energy—an intervention which the narrator sees as tragic, but which, ironically, has no doubt saved the lives of humans.

It is possible then to read "Under the Hollywood Sign" as a text in the process of becoming queer; initially accessible through a kind of outlaw cryptography, the signs by which its queerness are produced have become more familiar to the "general population" through the proliferation of a visible gay and lesbian subject. It has become harder for the reader, however attached ideologically to a heteronormative reading protocol, to dismiss anything queer within texts as "a rag of extraneous meaning that had got stuck onto them" (Sinfield 63).[23] Consequently, a queer reading of Reamy's story might chart the movement from cryptography to cartography, from decoding a text whose signification is only apparent to the chosen few to locating its insights into the sexual epistemology of the culture on the map of our own sexual ontologies. Thus, both the narrator and the object of his obsession remain, in a sense, indeterminate within the text itself: it is through our reading that the narrator becomes homosexual (or not), just as it is through our reading that the beautiful young men become either aliens or angels. The quality of their otherness can only be understood as a doubling effect, just as the queerness of the text depends on the reader's particular subject position and willingness to indulge in different reading protocols. The alien/Others are both ineluctably masculine and, like Tiptree him/herself, not masculine at all, since the mere fact of their otherness equates them synecdochically with the female, the black, the queer. As Jackson suggests, the subject of the sf story is "not the cause but the effect of the system that sustains it" (102); in "Under the Hollywood Sign," the narrator's subjectivity is an identity-in-process, an effect of a system that can be variously understood, depending on one's worldview. In the end then, I locate the text's queerness not in a determination that the narrator *is* gay, because he desires and finally rapes the alien, but rather because the text itself calls into question the very system which effects the narrator as a gay subject.

5 Conclusion: An alien cartography

A text's subversive potential is not dependent upon its generic innovation, but on how it maps and motivates the antagonisms constituting the subject(s) of representation, and on how it transfigures and recathects the available forms of cultural expression. . . . This rewriting is coextensive to the articulation of gay male identities-in-process as these deviant subjects confront culture and enter into representational agency within it. The most radical representational practices of deviant subjects not only challenge the official versions of their lives, but also transvalue the notion of deviance, and interrogate the mechanisms and meanings of representational practices—including their own.—Earl Jackson, Jr., *Strategies of Deviance* (44)

I have argued in this essay that a queer reading is performative in itself and that it is, in the long run, less about content—we have already considered the lack of queerness of gay and lesbian content within mimetic representations—than about worldview. Queer readings are informed by a desire to understand the text both in terms of its potential for representing dissident sexual subjectivities outside of a Cartesian understanding of the

subject and in terms of the text's engagement with a specific historico-cultural understanding of dissident sexualities and of the place of such sexualities within the sex/gender
system that regulates and constructs normative—and thus also non-normative—ways
of being-in-the-world as a sexed and sexual subject. When the questions raised by the
formulations "queer reading" and "queer text" are brought to bear on sf, what is revealed
is a complex and contradictory fictional arena. On the one hand, there is the particular
aptness of sf, as a non-mimetic form of writing, to produce stories in which sexuality does
not need to be understood in ways "vouched for by human senses and common sense"
and to interrogate the ways in which sexual subjectivities are created as effects of the
system that sustains them. On the other hand, there are also the variety of ways in which
most sf texts, regardless of their identification as "estranged fictions," are completely
unselfconscious in their reproduction of the heteronormative environment in which they
were written.

A queer reading may then work through a range of different strategies—from decoding
the outlaw cryptographies that have hidden—and may still hide—issues of sexual difference (often in plain sight) to delineating the specifics that may make a particular text queer,
to disinterring the many and peculiar ways through which the dominant twentieth-century
Western conception of sexuality underlies, is implicated in, and sometimes collides with
sf's attempt to envision alternative ways of being-in-the-world, ways which are always, no
matter how deeply their signs are hidden, already about being-in-the-world as a person
with a sex, a gender, and a sexuality. The subversive potential of sf as a mode through
which non-Cartesian subjectivities can be represented is a function precisely of sf's ability to create a "radically or significantly different formal framework" (Suvin 18), of its very
estrangement from the mimetic attempt of naturalistic—or mundane—fiction to reiterate
faithfully a teleological understanding of humanity's being-in-the-world, to represent the
subject as the cause rather than the effect of the system. Thus, sf's "foundational infidelity" (Jackson 125) to the world "vouched for by human senses and common sense"
at one and the same time makes it possible—although obviously not inevitable—for sf
to tell alternative stories—other stories, alien stories—of both sexual ontologies and the
systems that sustain and create them. Sf narratives may, seen from a queer viewpoint(s),
provide a map or chart of those alien spaces—whether inner or outer—in which queers
do, have, and will exist. Queer sf provides spaces to go beyond simply writing gay men
and lesbians into uninterrogated heteronormative visions of both present and future and
may, at its best, answer Eve Kosofsky Sedgwick's call to bypass the old familiar routes
"across the misleadingly symmetrical map . . . fractured in a particular historical situation
by the profound asymmetries of gender oppression and heterosexist oppression" and,
instead, to engage in

> the more promising project [which] would seem to be a study of the incoherent dispens-
> ation itself, the indisseverable girdle of incongruities under whose discomfiting span,
> for most of a century, have unfolded both the most generative and the most murderous
> plots of our culture. (90)

Notes

1. Henry Jenkins has a useful discussion of this movement in the final chapter ("'Out of the Closet and Into the Universe': Queers and Star Trek") of *Science Fiction Audiences*; the history of the involvement of the Gaylaxians with *Star Trek* and the formation of the Voyager Visibility Project can be found online at the following url: http://www.gaytrek.com/history.html>.

2. There is, of course, some argument as to whether humans do indeed come in only two biological sexes. For a comprehensive discussion of this issue, see Marianne van den Wijngaard's *Reinventing the Sexes: The Biomedical Construction of Masculinity and Femininity*. (Bloomington: Indiana UP, 1997).

3. These arguments can be found online in copies of the correspondence between the producers of *Star Trek* and the Voyager Visibility Project that are documented at the Gaytrek web page (http://www.gaytrek.com).

4. This now well-known story is told by Delany in "Shadows":

    What remains with me, nearly ten years after my first reading of the book, is the knowledge that I have experienced a world in which the *placement* of the information about the narrator's face is *proof* that in such a world much of the race problem, at least, has disappeared. The book as text . . . became, for a moment, the symbol of that world. (94-5)

5. As Lauren Berlant and Michael Warner have pointed out with reference to the political climate in the US, this reinscription is not merely the policy of right-wing fundamentalists but reflects a broader sociopolitical climate "whose highest aspirations are marriage, military patriotism, and protected domesticity." They add that

    It is no accident that queer commentary—on mass media, on texts of all kinds, on discourse environments from science to camp—has emerged at a time when United States culture increasingly fetishizes the normal. A fantasized mainstream has been invested with normative force by leaders of both major political parties. (345)

6. There is sometimes a tendency among people whose only exposure to queer theory is through academia to forget that, like earlier theorizations of same-sex and/or dissident sexualities, "queer" is not merely about playfulness and fluidity, but also about an active political engagement in the realpolitik of queer people's lives. One might think, to take only one example, of the two major threads of political engagement that run through Eve Kosofsky Sedgwick's work—the need to create a world that's safe for queer kids and the desire for an ethical, humane, and sex-positive response to AIDS. See, for example, *The Epistemology of the Closet* (Berkeley: U of California P, 1990) and "How to Bring Your Kids up Gay," in *Fear of a Queer Planet: Queer Politics and Social Theory* (ed. Michael Warner. Minneapolis: U of Minnesota P, 1993): 69-81. The fact that queer theory is so heavily imbricated in the study, theorization, and practical and political response to AIDS is itself an indication of the extent to which "queer" does not and, I think, should not exist purely as an intellectual construct whose primary feature is its *jouissance*.

7. Annamarie Jagose has a useful discussion of the meanings and contestations of "queer" in chapters 7 and 8 (72-126) of *Queer Theory*, as does Michael Warner in his "Introduction" to *Fear of a Queer Planet* (vii-xxxi).

8. Delany has frequently argued this position. See, for example, "Science Fiction and 'Literature.'" *Analog* 99 (May 1979): 59-78, and "The Semiology of Silence: The *Science-Fiction Studies* Interview," in *Silent Interviews: On Language, Race, Sex, Science Fiction, and Some Comics* (Hanover: Wesleyan UP, 1994): 21-58.

9. For an examination of this construction in both *The Left Hand of Darkness* and Eleanor Arnason's *Ring of Swords*, see my "Queer as Traitor, Traitor as Queer: Denaturalizing Sexuality, Gender and Nationhood" (in *Flashes of the Fantastic: Selected Essays from the Nineteenth International Conference on the Fantastic in the Arts*, ed. David Ketterer [Westport, CT: Greewood Press, forthcoming]).

10. The difficulty of ascertaining who is and who isn't homosexual, within a conceptual framework that renders the homosexual/heterosexual dyad as *the* axis of difference, preoccupies science, which seeks "objective" proof of this difference, first through psychoanalysis, then through a variety of supposedly accurate physiological tests (such as the RCMP's infamous "fruit machine"), and most recently through the drive to discover the "gay gene."

11. Like all "Golden Age" narratives, this one also imagines an era that never did exist; one might trace several genealogies for this particular cultural anxiety—one, at least, that tracks back to the Bolshevik Revolution of 1917, and another that recalls that WWI also had its Rosie the Riveter and her equivalents, whose labor freed men for military service. Yet another trace might chart much the same territory as Christopher Isherwood's *I Am A Camera* and its cinematic offspring, *Cabaret*.

12. For a discussion of gays and lesbians in the military during WWII, see Allen Bérubé's "Marching to a Different Drummer: Lesbian and Gay GIs in World War II," in *Hidden from History: Reclaiming the Gay and Lesbian Past* (eds. Martin Bauml Duberman, Martha Vicinus, and George Chauncey Jr. New York: New American Library, 1989): 383-94.

13. I do not, obviously, mean this literally, although the rhetoric of the time (from the early 1930s to the late 1950s) suggests that some of the people persecuting Jews, communists, and homosexuals saw them as being literally the same and not just as occupying the same structural position as threats to the white (Aryan), male-dominant, and heterosexual social structure.

14. See both chapter 4 of Sinfield (60-82) and Lee Edelman's "Tearooms and Sympathy."

15. Think of Marlowe's *Edward II*.

16. See Lee Edelman's "Tearooms and Sympathy" for a discussion of this formation.

17. Today it is impossible not to think of AIDS in the context of the role that blood plays in determining who is human and who (what) is the alien Other; in the West, where AIDS has been popularly conflated with the figure of the homosexual, "bad blood" becomes a marker not of one's HIV status but of one's queerness (which, as an aside, explains why lesbians, who have a very small incidence of AIDS, are widely presumed to be as much at risk—and as much a danger—as are gay men).

18. We can see how the figure of the vampire might also serve to carry the same burden of monstrosity in this context. See, for instance, Ellis Hanson's "Undead" for a critical discussion of the ways in which AIDS and vampirism have become conflated in popular discourses since the onset of the AIDS epidemic (Ellis Hansen, "Undead," in *Inside/Out: Lesbian Theories, Gay Theories*, ed. Diana Fuss [New York: Routledge, 1991]: 324-340).

19. There is, of course, that other improbability to be taken into account: that I, as a self-described dyke or queer, should recognize a beautiful young man when I see one. For some people, including some gay people, that, too, defies explanation.

20. It is interesting to note, in regards to the gaze, the unease generated among the male characters in "Who Goes There?" once they become the objects of each other's gaze; they spend a huge amount of time staring at each other, and even talking about the way in which they look at

each other ("Your eyes—Lord, I wish you could see your eyes staring—" [104]). Theoretically, of course, the object of the gaze is always a sexual object—and cannot be a (heterosexual) man. To quote Laura Mulvey, "[a]ccording to the principles of the ruling ideology and the psychical structures that back it up, the male figure cannot bear the burden of sexual objectification" (27-28). See Laura Mulvey, "Visual Pleasure and Narrative Cinema," in *The Sexual Subject: A Screen Reader in Sexuality*. (London: Routledge, 1992): 22-34.

21. I first encountered this useful phrase in an eponymously named article by sociologist Chrys Ingraham; it indicates a worldview that cannot imagine certain relationships as "heterosexual," even when they occur between two people of opposite sexes. At its most heteronormative, the heterosexual imaginary cannot conceive of either a sexually aggressive woman or a sexually passive man, still less of a heterosexual man who wishes to be the receptive partner in anal sex. Anything outside of the heterosexual imaginary is thus conceived as either a perversion or a fetish.

22. Eve Kosofsky Sedgwick's introduction to *Epistemology of the Closet* gives a good historical overview of contemporary understandings of this development:

It is a rather amazing fact that, of the very many dimensions along which the genital activity of one person can be differentiated from that of another . . ., precisely one, the gender of object choice, emerged from the turn of the century, and has remained, as *the* dimension denoted by the now ubiquitous category of "sexual orientation." (8)

23. The quote is part of Laurence Lerner's response to the idea that gay readers might read W.H. Auden's poems for some sort of gay meaning. Sinfield notes that

Lerner allows that there will have been gay readers. "That Auden was a homosexual is well known, and it is perfectly possible, even likely that some of his friends winked when they read his love poems and gave an extra smirk . . . But in doing this they were not reading the poems; they were noticing a rag of extraneous meaning that had got stuck onto them . . . They, like Sinfield, were unwriting them" (Sinfield 62-63).

Works cited

Berlant, Lauren, and Michael Warner. "What Does Queer Theory Teach Us About *X*?" *PMLA* 110.3 (May 1995): 343-49.

Bersani, Leo. "Is the Rectum a Grave?" In *AIDS: Cultural Analysis/Cultural Activism*, ed. Douglas Crimp. Cambridge, MA: MIT Press, 1988. 197-222.

Butler, Judith. "Critically Queer." In *Playing with Fire: Queer Politics, Queer Theories*, ed. Shane Phelan. New York: Routledge, 1997. 11-29.

Delany, Samuel R. "Shadows." In *The Jewel-Hinged Jaw: Notes on the Language of Science Fiction*. New York: Dragon, 1977. 51-134.

Disch, Thomas. "Embarassments of Science Fiction." In *Science Fiction at Large*, ed. Peter Nicholls. London: Gollancz, 1976. 141-55.

Edelman, Lee. "The Mirror and the Tank: 'AIDS,' Subjectivity, and the Rhetoric of Activism." In *Homographesis: Essays in Gay Literary and Cultural Theory*. New York: Routledge, 1994. 93-117.

—. "Seeing Things: Representation, the Scene of Surveillance, and the Spectacle of Gay Male Sex." In *Inside/Out: Lesbian Theories, Gay Theories*, ed. Diana Fuss. New York: Routledge, 1991. 93-116.

—. "Tearooms and Sympathy: Or, the Epistemology of the Water Closet." In *Homographesis: Essays in Gay Literary and Cultural Theory*. New York: Routledge, 1994. 148-70.

Ellison, Harlan. "Introduction." In *San Diego Lightfoot Sue and Other Stories*. New York: Ace, 1983. ix-xxviii.

Heinlein, Robert A. *Starship Troopers*. 1959. New York: Ace, 1987.

Ingraham, Chrys. "The Heterosexual Imaginary: Feminist Sociology and Theories of Gender." *Sociological Theory* 12.2 (July 1994): 203-19.

Jackson, Earl. *Strategies of Deviance: Studies in Gay Male Representation*. Bloomington: Indiana UP, 1995.

Jagose, Annamarie. *Queer Theory: An Introduction*. New York: New York UP, 1996.

Kinsman, Gary. *The Regulation of Desire: Homo and Hetero Sexualities*. Montreal: Black Rose, 1996.

Le Guin, Ursula K. *The Left Hand of Darkness*. New York: Ace, 1969. Reamy, Tom. *Blind Voices*. 1978. New York: Berkley, 1979.

—. "San Diego Lightfoot Sue." 1975. In *San Diego Lightfoot Sue and Other Stories*. New York: Ace, 1983. 40-66.

—. "Under the Hollywood Sign." 1975. In *San Diego Lightfoot Sue and Other Stories*. New York: Ace, 1983. 40-66.

Sedgwick, Eve Kosofsky. *The Epistemology of the Closet*. Berkeley: U of California P, 1990.

Silverberg, Robert. "Who is Tiptree? What is He?" In *Warm Worlds and Otherwise*. New York: Ballantine, 1975. ix-xviii.

Sinfield, Alan. *Cultural Politics—Queer Reading*. Philadelphia: U of Pennsylvania P, 1994.

Stuart, Donald A. [John W. Campbell, Jr.]. "Who Goes There?" 1938. In *Science Fiction: The Science Fiction Research Association Anthology*, eds. Patricia S. Waugh, Charles G. Waugh, and Martin H. Greenberg. New York: HarperCollins, 1988. 84-124.

Suvin, Darko. *Metamorphoses of Science Fiction: On the Poetics and History of a Literary Genre*. New Haven, CT: Yale UP, 1979.

Tiptree, Jr., James [Alice Sheldon]. "Houston, Houston, Do You Read?" 1976. In *Science Fiction: The Science Fiction Research Association Anthology*, eds. Patricia S. Waugh, Charles G. Waugh, and Martin H. Greenberg. New York: HarperCollins, 1988. 434-74.

—. "The Women Men Don't See." 1973. In *Warm Worlds and Otherwise*. New York: Ballantine, 1975. 131-64.

Tulloch, John and Henry Jenkins. *Science Fiction Audiences: Watching* Doctor Who *and* Star Trek. New York: Routledge, 1995.

21

The women history doesn't see: Recovering midcentury women's sf as a literature of social critique

Lisa Yaszek

In last year's Wiscon issue of *Extrapolation* I argued for the importance of reclaiming midcentury women's SF in relation to the history of the genre as a whole. Conventionally speaking, postwar authors such as Judith Merril, Mildred Clingerman, and Zenna Henderson have been relegated to the sidelines of SF history because their depictions of love and life in "galactic suburbia" do not seem to have anything like the critical edge of later feminist science fictions (Russ 88). Although I certainly agree that most of the stories written by midcentury SF authors are not overtly feminist ones, that does not mean that they are not deeply enmeshed in the culture and politics of their historical moment. Instead, these authors often mobilized some of cold war America's most dearly-held beliefs about domesticity and motherhood in the framework of the SF narrative to create powerful interrogations of the new scientific and social arrangements emerging at that time. As such, they are very much a part of SF history.

The argument I make in this essay is that because it often forges strong parallels between interpersonal relations in the private home and broad social relations in the larger public arena, midcentury women's SF must be seen as important to feminist history as well. One of the oldest—and arguably still most important—tasks of feminist scholarship is to recover women's histories in all their complexities. This includes women's political practices outside those eras marked by overtly feminist activity. The decades between the end of World War II in 1945 and the beginning of second-wave feminism in the mid-1960s, often referred to as the domestic decades, are an ideal place to begin this kind of inquiry. As I demonstrate in the following pages, women participated in some of the most progressive political movements of these decades. Of course, courtrooms and city streets were not the only places where they expressed their political convictions. They also took their stands on issues such as antiwar and civil rights activism in the pages of those science fiction magazines that seemed to be, as Judith Merril recollects, "virtually the only vehicle[s] of political dissent" available to authors of the period ("What Do

You Mean" 74). To demonstrate this point I first examine how authors Judith Merril, Alice Eleanor Jones, and Carol Emshwiller used one of the most then-fashionable SF story types, the nuclear war narrative, to interrogate the cold war status quo and champion the newly-resurrected peace movement. I then consider how Margaret St. Clair, Kay Rogers, and Mildred Clingerman adapted one of the oldest SF tropes, the encounter with the alien other, to advocate the cause of civil rights in America. Taken together, this group of stories provide a powerful demonstration of how midcentury women's literary practices both anticipated and extended the politics of their activist counterparts.

Recovering the domestic decades in feminist history and feminist science fiction studies

The domestic decades are usually depicted as a low point in feminist history, a period when women were encouraged to become "domestic patriots" by exchanging their jobs in the public sphere for the more important work of raising children and tending their new suburban homes.[1] Over the past two decades, however, a growing number of scholars have suggested a more complex picture of women's lives at midcentury.[2] Women may have shied away from feminism in this period, but they did not abandon politics altogether. Instead, they channeled their energies into those causes that seemed most pressing at the dawn of the atomic era. Such activists usually made their arguments for progressive social change by invoking (and subtly revising) some of postwar America's most dearly-held beliefs about motherhood in particular and femininity in general. For instance, as Harriet Hyman Alonso has persuasively demonstrated, antiwar activists portrayed themselves as mothers reluctantly moved to action in the public arena by fear for the fate of all children born in the shadow of the mushroom cloud (131). In a similar vein, Susan Lynn argues that women in the civil rights movement made persuasive arguments for the logical connection between women's private duties as the primary facilitators of communication between family members and their public roles as mediators between members of different races (106). Thus activists positioned themselves as a new and more progressive breed of domestic patriots who translated their private-sphere skills into public-sphere action.

Unfortunately, new feminist histories of midcentury women's political praxis rarely involve an extended consideration of these same women's literary endeavors. For instance, in her otherwise comprehensive monograph *Mothers and More: American Women in the 1950s*, historian Eugenia Kaledin carefully chronicles the extensive aesthetic achievements of postwar women in a variety of canonical literary genres including fiction, poetry, and drama as well as popular genres including horror, romance, and detective fiction. Although she acknowledges that these authors often used fiction writing to "assert their individuality and their social imagination," she ultimately concludes that they almost never "attempted in any fictional way to comment on the real political anxieties of the time" (125, 136).

I find it significant that Kaledin did not include science fiction in her survey of midcentury women's writing, nor have many other historians done so since then.[3] This oversight is perhaps to be expected. As feminist SF scholars have long noted, our counterparts outside the SF community tend to dismiss SF as an aggressively masculine genre that had little to offer women readers and writers before the advent of second-wave feminism in the 1970s.[4] I suspect that this dismissal has been compounded by the enduring legacy of Betty Friedan's classic study, *The Feminine Mystique* (1963). As Joanne Meyerowitz notes, historians have questioned some of Friedan's claims about women's experience with domesticity at midcentury, but most have accepted her argument that women's magazine fiction uncritically glorified conservative notions of proper femininity (230). According to Meyerowitz, this has led to a nearly total silence about how women might have written differently—and more progressively—in other kinds of magazines or popular literary venues (231).

While it is certainly true that midcentury SF was dominated by men, over the past few years SF scholars have demonstrated that a significant number of women were actively involved in the genre at that time.[5] In contrast to a few well-known authors like Leigh Brackett, C.L. Moore, and Andre Norton, who are remembered primarily for having written stories that were "as ungendered as their names" (Clute and Nicholls 1344), authors including Judith Merril, Mildred Clingerman, and Zenna Henderson produced tales that clearly addressed women's concerns with life in a high-tech era—and that were, as their bylines indicated, clearly written by women. In doing so, as Justine Larbalestier suggests, they paved the way for the more radical critiques of patriarchy launched by later feminist authors (172).

As these brief histories of feminist history and feminist SF scholarship might suggest, academics in both fields seem to be moving toward similar conclusions about women's political and literary praxis at midcentury. To date, however, there has been very little discussion of how the two areas of inquiry might productively inform one another. Accordingly, the rest of this essay is devoted to just that kind of discussion. In the following pages, I draw upon new research in both fields to show how postwar activists and authors alike engaged in the kind of future-oriented, extrapolative thinking most commonly associated with science fiction writing. I also show how they both deployed rhetorical strategies common to the progressive activism of the time, appealing to women as political subjects based on their common situation as wives and mothers (or potential wives and mothers) and advocating a feminine ethos of social reformation through interpersonal dialogue between members of different races and genders.

Midcentury peace activism and SF's nuclear holocaust narrative

Although the peace movements of the 1950s and 1960s were modest compared to their Vietnam-era counterparts, they were nonetheless a significant outlet for women's political energies. At first, it might seem surprising that women raised on the twin rhetorics of cold war patriotism and the feminine mystique might have joined such movements at all. As Elaine Tyler May points out, the dominant professional and popular discourses of this time told American women that they could best serve their country as cold war patriots by carefully tending their suburban homes (105). Thus women were encouraged to embrace the feminine mystique not just because it was the natural thing to do, but because it was essential to the proper workings of national defense.

Of course, not all women were persuaded by this logic, and the more active of these dissenters were drawn into peace organizations such as the Women's International League for Peace and Freedom (WILPF), the Catholic Workers and War Resistors' League (WRL), and Women Strike for Peace (WSP). These organizations also invoked specific equations between patriotism and domesticity, but to radically different ends than their governmental counterparts. For instance, throughout the 1950s WILPF recruited new members by appealing to common feminine experience, arguing that it was only by joining together in the peace movement that "you and I—and all the mothers in the world—can go to sleep without thinking about the terrors of the Atomic Bomb" (in Alonso 131). For WIPLF, it was the American woman's civic duty to protest against—rather than acquiesce to—the cold war status quo.

Peace organizations also justified their activities by aligning maternal instinct with scientific knowledge. Throughout the 1950s and 1960s WSP distributed educational pamphlets quoting Albert Einstein, Linus Pauling, the Atomic Energy Commission, the U.S. Public Health Service, and the Federal Radiation Council on topics ranging from the dangers of irradiated milk to the futility of preparing for life after nuclear war. Thus WSP activists positioned themselves as rational beings reluctantly driven to public action by an understanding of nuclear weapons similar to that of the experts themselves.[6]

Similar political sensibilities and rhetorical strategies informed many of the nuclear war stories written by women in the midcentury SF community. As Edward James notes, SF authors of the 1940s and 1950s often used nuclear war stories to explore "how societies decline into tribalism or barbarism. . . or develop from barbarism to civilization" (90). In the hands of writers like Judith Merril, Carol Emshwiller, and Alice Eleanor Jones, these stories showed readers how nuclear-age civilization inherently tended toward barbarism, especially for women and their families.[7] Indeed, these authors made their appeals to readers precisely by describing in sometimes grisly detail the nightmare fates of forced marriage, reproductive mutation, and familial destruction that inevitably awaited those women who managed to survive World War III. Writ large upon the postnuclear future, such stories were also clearly in dialogue with the progressive sensibilities of the midcentury peace movement. Indeed, as we shall see, they provided women writers with an ideal narrative space in which to make concrete those "terrors of the Atomic Bomb" that could only be hinted at in peace activist literature.

As a self-identified leftist and feminist at a time when it was unfashionable to be either of those things, it is appropriate that Judith Merril produced one of the earliest and best-known of these domestic nuclear war stories. Published in 1948, "That Only a Mother" brings together two of the primary fears of the early atomic age: the possibility of mutation from radioactive materials and the probability that an international nuclear war would effectively destroy all humanity (Trachtenberg 355). Set in a near future where exposure to radiation from an on-going nuclear war has produced a generation of radically mutated children, Merril's tale depicts an insane world where mothers struggle to protect their children against fathers who commit infanticide, juries who acquit the men of any wrongdoing, and journalists who report the whole process with tacit approval. Although such events are initially presented as part of a terrible new moral and social order located specifically in postwar Japan, the land of the enemy other, Merril ultimately suggests that this new world order—much like radioactivity itself—has no respect for national borders. The majority of "That Only a Mother" follows the story of Margaret and Hank, an American couple who give birth to Henrietta, a "flower-faced child" whose stunning intelligence is offset by her limbless body (349). Margaret responds to her child's deformity by retreating into her own insanity and insisting that "*my baby's fine. Precocious, but normal*" (345, 351), while Hank—equally horrified by both his child and Margaret's response to her—seems destined to repeat the insanity of his Japanese counterparts as he prepares to kill his child at the close of the story. Thus Merril's story effectively anticipates the kind of warning that peace groups like WILPF would issue in the 1950s: that "a bomb doesn't care in the least whether you are wearing a soldier's uniform or a housewife's apron" (in Alonso 130).

Alice Eleanor Jones's "Created He Them" (1955) also merges contemporary under-standings of nuclear war with the maternalist sensibilities of women's peace activism. By the mid-1950s many Americans had exchanged their earlier convictions about the apocalyptic nature of the bomb for the new belief that a limited nuclear war was fightable and that society would simply have to adjust to this new reality (Trachtenberg 355). At the same time public concern about nuclear fallout continued to grow, especially as reports about unexpected illnesses filtered in from the Nevada Test Site and from the Marshall Islands, where the first H-bomb tests were performed in 1954 (Hafemeister 437-38). It should come as no surprise, then, that in Jones's story families do indeed survive World War III—but only because the government creates a ruthless breeding program that forces the few remaining healthy men and women into loveless marriages. When the offspring of these unions reach the age of three, they are taken away to mysterious Centers where "if any child were ever unhappy, or were taken ill, or died, nobody knew it" (132). Although the children produced by this breeding program are indeed physically healthy, family relations are anything but that. Instead, men like Henry Crothers treat their children as mere commodities to be exchanged for government bonuses. Meanwhile, women like Ann Crothers are forced to "lend" their babies to childless neighbors in exchange for black-market goods including eggs, cigarettes, and the Seconal they so desperately need to endure their husbands' nightly embraces (129-30). Much like Merril, then, Jones insists that the brave new world of the nuclear age will inevitably affect the soldier and the housewife alike in terrible—and terribly unexpected—ways.

Carol Emshwiller's story "Day at the Beach" (1959) literalizes the terrors of nuclear war in more subtle but equally tragic ways. Although expert discourses and public polls of the late 1950s continued to reflect the belief that America could (and should) fight a limited nuclear war if the situation arose (Trachtenberg 354), this period also saw the publication of numerous books that suggested otherwise (Stone 192). Popular novels such as Nevil Shute's *On the Beach* (1957) and Walter Miller's *A Canticle for Leibowitz* (1959) both insisted that even the most limited of nuclear wars would affect all peoples across space and time. Emshwiller's story offers readers a similar, if more specific, warning. At first, the family depicted in "Day at the Beach" seems to have survived World War III fairly successfully. Although Myra and Ben are bald and toothless and their child, Little Boy, is a feral creature who can only communicate through physical violence, the couple remain deeply in love with one another and struggle to give their child a reasonably normal life. This includes outings such as the one that gives the story its name; indeed, the beach feels so safe compared to the rest of war-torn America that it leads Ben to dream that the couple might resume the sexual relations they have refrained from since Little Boy's birth. Myra, however, quickly negates this dream, pointing out that "I don't even know a doctor since Press Smith was killed by those robbing kids and I'd be scared"(280). Herein lies the tragedy of Emshwiller's story: in a postholocaust world the family can only survive by avoiding normal reproductive activities since the birth of a new child might well mean the death of its mother. And yet, without more children, there can be no more family whatsoever. Thus Emshwiller appeals specifically to women readers as potential mothers and potential antiwar activists by insisting that there can be no future for children in a world where nuclear war (or at least its immanent possibility) has become one of the central facts of life.

As all of the above stories demonstrate, SF—especially in its short story form—provided midcentury women writers with a powerful narrative form through which to explore what might happen to women and their families if America continued down the path it seemed to have set for itself at the beginning of the cold war. But how might women prevent these nightmare futures from happening? What other futures might be available, given the then-current scientific and social situation?

Full-length novels like Judith Merril's *Shadow on the Hearth* (1950) suggest one answer that anticipates the maternalist politics of peace organizations like WSP: women can prevent these scenarios from occurring in the real world by allying themselves with other women and with scientists to build an anti-war community. *Shadow on the Hearth* begins much like its short-story counterparts by establishing a nightmare future designed specifically to hail women readers based on their common situation as mothers haunted by the possibility of nuclear war. The novel follows the story of Gladys Mitchell, a Westchester housewife and mother who is the epitome of domesticity, dispensing nuggets of wisdom about the effects of French toast on ill-tempered children while struggling with her conscience about whether or not she can abandon the laundry to attend a neighborhood luncheon (87). With the advent of World War III Gladys's life turns upside-down: her husband Jon is presumed dead in New York City, her daughters Barbara and Ginny are exposed to radioactive rain at school, and her son Tom, a freshman at Texas Tech, seems to have vanished off the face of the planet. In this brave new world, even the most familiar aspects of suburban life become terrifyingly strange: basic utilities fail and men become monsters who abuse their power as civil defense officers to harass the women and children they are meant to protect.

Of course, this is only the beginning of *Shadow on the Hearth*. The majority of Merril's novel follows Gladys's transformation from helpless housewife to activist mother who helps to prevent this world from becoming the kind of full-blown dystopia imagined elsewhere in midcentury short stories. First, Gladys allies herself with the other women populating her world, by rescuing her housekeeper Veda Klopak from the local civil defense officials who believe she is a Communist spy and by giving shelter to her neighbor Edie Crowell, a self-absorbed, aristocratic woman who fears being trapped alone in her home when the American government declares martial law. In turn, Veda quickly adapts the Mitchell household to the rhythms of its new circumstances (a good thing, since Gladys is a lackadaisical housekeeper at best), while Edie uses her sharp tongue to fend off the civil defense officers who hope to break up the household and regain control over the women. Thus Veda, Gladys, and Edie create a quasi-utopian community of women who work together—however temporarily—to protect themselves and their children from the dangerous new social and moral orders that threaten them.[8]

Much like her counterparts in the peace movement, Merril also suggests that women can most effectively challenge the new social and moral order of the cold war status quo by forging alliances with another group of like-minded people, namely scientists. The potential effectiveness of such alliances are made clear in Merril's novel through her depiction of the growing friendship between Gladys and Garson Levy, the local nuclear physicist-turned-high school math teacher who has been under surveillance by the government for years due to his antiwar activities. Gladys first meets Levy when he defies his house arrest and comes to warn her about the radioactive rain that her daughters have been exposed to at school; impressed by his concern for her children, Gladys invites him to stay with her and the other women. Significantly, it is by working together that Gladys and Levy manage to ensure the future well-being of the Mitchell household, pooling Levy's scientific knowledge with Gladys's social skills to secure medical attention for the Mitchell girls and to prevent the civil defense officials from evacuating (and thus breaking up) the household on what turn out to be rather dubious grounds.

Of course, it is important to note that for Merril, this alliance between mothers and scientists is at best an only partial solution to the problems posed by the threat of nuclear war. At the end of the novel the family unit is preserved, but its survival is far from guaranteed: Gladys's son Tom is located but much to her horror has been drafted into the army; her husband Jon returns from New York City but is wracked with radiation burns and gunshot wounds that prevent him from asserting his place as the head of the family; and Levy himself is diagnosed with a potentially fatal strain of radiation poisoning.[9]

This ambivalence is key to Merril's project: if she depicts a postholocaust future where scientists can solve all the problems of nuclear war, then there would be no reason to protest that kind of war in the first place. But that is not her project. Instead, by demonstrating how even the natural sympathies of mothers and scientists might not be enough to guarantee survival in the future, she makes a strong case for the necessity of peace activism in the present.

The civil rights movement and SF's "encounter with the alien other"

Although nuclear weapons might have been the most pressing *technological* issue for women involved in midcentury political activism, it was certainly not the only one that captured their interest. Many turned their attention to what was undoubtedly the most pressing *social* issue of the day: the struggle for racial integration in America. In contrast to the antiwar movement, which continually had to justify its existence in an era when cold war politics seemed to necessitate the development and stockpiling of nuclear weapons, civil rights organizations such as the National Association for the Advancement of Colored People (NAACP) and the Congress of Racial Equality (CORE) were able to position themselves as a necessary part of America's effort to spread democracy and social justice throughout the world (Lynn 108).

In practice, overturning nearly 300 years of American prejudice was a much more complex task. Civil rights organizations took a two-pronged approach to this task, working to secure integration at the levels of both the state and the neighborhood. The efforts that occurred at the first level are those that have been most thoroughly recorded by history: the struggle to integrate public schools as mandated by the Supreme Court's landmark 1954 decision in *Brown v. Board of Education of Topeka, Kansas* (which firmly rejected the "separate but equal" doctrine that had governed U.S. policymaking since the 1890s); the year-long Montgomery bus boycott organized by Martin Luther King, Jr. after Rosa Parks was arrested for refusing to give up her bus seat to a white man in 1955; and, of course, the massive, nonviolent demonstrations initiated by King and other black leaders in the late 1950s and early 1960s (Kaledin 150-155). All these activities were carefully aligned with the liberal humanist ethos of the time as planned efforts to secure the rights of all individuals through the regular channels of participatory and representative democracy.[10]

But this is, as feminist historians have pointed out, quite literally only half the story. Efforts to ensure integration in public institutions were accompanied by efforts to do much the same in the realm of private relations as well. As Susan Lynn notes, progressive interracial women's organizations such as the Young Women's Christian Organization (YWCA) were certainly instrumental in lobbies for civil rights legislation. What has been less often recognized, however, is they were also central in developing new strategies for integration that "emphasized a female ethic as central to creating social change, particularly by building friendships across racial lines" (112). These strategies included the development of antiracist literature, lecture series, and, most centrally, summer conferences where black and white girls worked and lived together for months at a time. Hundreds of girls attended these conferences, and hundreds left testimonials reporting that the most important part of the conferences for them was the realization that "in hundreds of little ways we felt the same whether our skin was dark or light" (in Lynn 113). It should come as no surprise, then, that many of the girls who attended these conferences in the 1950s grew up to participate in the women's liberation movement of the 1960s and 70s, since both emphasized the connections between personal and political relations.

These connections were further demonstrated by women's activities on other fronts of the civil rights struggle. Throughout the 1950s women allied with the American Friends Service Committee (AFSC, a mixed-sex group originally founded by Quaker activists in 1917) worked closely with local NAACP leaders to ensure that the *Brown v. Board of Education* decision would be enacted as smoothly as possible. These women enacted the feminine ethos of social change through interpersonal dialogue by facilitating meetings between black and white parents, students, school boards, and community leaders (Lynn 116-17). More than mere auxiliary to the rest of the civil rights movement, then, this new mode of social change became central to the daily implementation of civil rights legislation.[11]

Of course, the battle to integrate girls' associations and public schools was hardly the stuff of midcentury SF—or at least not at any immediately obvious level. However, the clash between two cultures most certainly was. John Clute and Peter Nicholls note that "encounter with the alien other" stories are as old as SF itself. Influenced by Darwinian theory, early science fiction stories ranging from H.G. Wells's *The Time Machine* (1895) to Edmond Hamilton's "Thundering Worlds" (1934) depicted alien others as the natural enemies of mankind. By the middle of the twentieth century, however, most SF authors had forsaken such crude depictions for more nuanced investigations of "the problems of establishing fruitful communications with alien races" (16). Women writing SF at that time were no exception to this rule. Authors including Margaret St. Clair, Kay Rogers, and Mildred Clingerman all inflected the new alien encounter narrative with an ethos of social change through interpersonal communication much like that deployed by their counterparts in the civil rights movement. In doing so, they created stories that explored the very real problems of establishing fruitful communications with *human* races on the American homefront.

Significantly, midcentury women's alien encounter narratives tend to focus on communication not between like-minded people working together in the public sphere, but between star-crossed lovers who can only flourish in the private worlds they create for themselves in the face of a hostile society. As such, these stories function much like the nuclear war ones written by Merril, Emshwiller, and Jones: as warnings about the nightmare future America might create for itself given present-day scientific and social arrangements. Midcentury women's alien encounter narratives also resemble their nuclear war counterparts in that both refuse the apolitical, ahistorical "love conquers all" mentality that dominated so many other forms of midcentury popular culture (and that continue to do so today). Instead, they show how private relations between individuals are always already conditioned by historical and material factors, and how reformation of these relations can only be meaningful if accompanied by a similar reformation of their institutional counterparts.

Women's alien encounter narratives from the early 1950s reflect much of the hesitation and pessimism attending the early years of the civil rights struggle. Although President Harry Truman established the first Civil Rights Commission in 1946 and then ordered the desegregation of the American military in 1948, he restrained from enforcing any more specific legislation at the time for fear of alienating white Southern voters (Chafe 91). It is not surprising, then, that stories such as Margaret St. Clair's "Brightness Falls from the Air" (1951) imagined that even the most wildly successful examples of interracial communication would inevitably fail in the face of an entrenched bureaucracy. St. Clair's story depicts a far future where humans have ruthlessly taken over every habitable planet they can find, leaving indigenous peoples to starve and die unless they are willing to participate in the deadly "battle sports" that have become the conquering race's favorite distraction. Kerr is a minor human bureaucrat who acknowledges his people's wrong-doings but shrugs them off as "a particular instance of the general cruelty and stupidity" that he believes characterizes all peoples in all times (162). He is forced to revise this opinion when he meets Rhysha, a beautiful bird-woman with whom he promptly falls in love. Rhysha is also intrigued by Kerr and the two exchange life stories. When Kerr learns that the battle sports are a perversion of the dignified leadership rituals that once structured life on Rhysha's world, Kerr vows to help her people escape extinction by sponsoring their immigration to a new world. But all is for naught: Kerr's petitions are denied and the young man falls gravely ill from his exertions; when he recovers, it is only to learn that Rhysha has sacrificed herself in the battle sports arena to secure food for her family. Thus the love between individuals from different races is rendered meaningless precisely because the new social perspectives engendered by this love are negated by the intransigency of public institutions.

A similar pessimism informs Kay Roger's short story "Experiment" (1952), where humans have been enslaved by the snake-like Venusians, a cold-blooded race with limited emotional capabilities. Intrigued by the human concept of love, one particular Venusian, Cobr, decides to perform an experiment in which he rescues a human woman from the slave pens and installs her in his own household with all the comforts that his people usually accord one another. In return, Cobr asks the woman (a professional performer who remains unnamed throughout the story) to help with his experiment by singing her people's love songs to him. Inevitably, Cobr becomes enchanted with the singer and is delighted when she learns the forms of courteous expression that pass for affection between members of his race. Before the relationship can progress further, however, the singer dies of a sudden illness and Cobr finds himself in a surprising position: alone and far too heartsick to continue the experiment with another human. Once again, then, love fails to conquer all—indeed, this love, such as it is, cannot even be named by the individual who experiences it.

Published at the height of the midcentury civil rights movement—three years after *Brown v. Board of Education* and two years after the Montgomery bus boycott—Mildred Clingerman's "Mr. Sakrison's Halt" (1957) treats the problem of racial justice in America in a more direct and complex manner than its predecessors. Here, the encounter with the alien other takes the form of a romantic encounter between the southern belle Mattie Compton and the northern liberal Mr. Sakrison. Although she initially dismisses him as a "Yankee beast" (39), Miss Mattie soon falls in love with the gentle man and his vision for a better world: "I'd never heard anybody speak so sadly about the nigras. . . .He put words to the little sick feelings I'd had at times, and I began to catch his vision" (40). The young couple decide to migrate north and marry, but their plans collapse when their train makes an unexpected stop in an unnamed town where beautifully-dressed people of all races live together in prosperity and harmony. Mr. Sakrison immediately gets off the train and is welcomed by a distinguished-looking black man; Miss Mattie, overcome by a flash of prejudicial anger and fear, hangs back—and promptly looses her chance for happiness when the train starts up and barrels on without her fiancé. As a kind of penance, Miss Mattie spends the next forty years of her life riding the Jim Crow cars of the same train, desperately searching for the mysterious town where her beloved vanished. Much like St. Clair and Rogers, then, Clingerman suggests that interpersonal communication in the guise of romantic love may indeed be the first important step toward the elimination of racial prejudice in America but it is by no means necessarily enough to eliminate prejudice altogether.

This is not, however, the whole of Clingerman's story. "Mr. Sakrison's Halt" is narrated by an anonymous young woman born in Miss Mattie's hometown but raised in the north. To counteract the hostility she feels as an outsider when visiting her birth-town, the narrator makes friends with the only other person in town who does "too much traveling around": Miss Mattie (38). In contrast to the other townsfolk, Clingerman's narrator does not simply dismiss Miss Mattie's tale as the product of a lovesick mind; accordingly, she is given the privilege of witnessing its final act. During their last train ride together the narrator spots the mysterious stop that Miss Mattie has described so many times before. This time Miss Mattie does not hesitate to get off the train, where she is rewarded with the return of both her youth and Mr. Sakrison. Thus it would seem that with patience and continued communication between sympathetic individuals, there might be a future in which love—between individuals and between races—could prevail.

Again, however, this is not the entire story. Miss Mattie and her lover are only reunited in a magical, alternative America that the narrator glimpses but can never find for herself again, trapped as she is in a world of "firey crosses" and white supremacist rage (43). The narrator's closing observation underscores the difference between these two worlds:

> the Katy local was retired years ago. There's a fine highway now to the city. . . . I hear everything has changed. But I read in my newspaper last week how they've locked the

doors to the schoolhouse and barred with guns and flaring anger the way to the hill, and I realize how terribly far [my birth-town] still is from Mr. Sakrison's halt. (43-44)

More than mere apocalyptic imagination, this final image encapsulates some of the most dreadful newspaper headlines of Clingerman's day: after all, "Mr. Sakrison's Halt" appeared in print the very same year that President Dwight Eisenhower sent out the National Guard to ensure the integration of Little Rock Central High School (and Alabama's governor shut down the entire state school system in retaliation). And much the same thing can be said of Clingerman's entire story. With all its twists and turns, the narrative structure of "Mr. Sakrison's Halt" closely mirrors the complex and some-times contradictory hopes and fears attending the dream of racial justice in America. Although Clingerman's narrator—and by extension, Clingerman's readers—might have been able to catch glimpses of the brave new world imagined by civil rights activists and their sympathizers, in the American South of 1957 it might well have felt like that dream was still almost impossibly far away.

Conclusion: Feminist history and feminist SF studies reconsidered

As Helen Merrick notes in her essay "'Fantastic Dialogues': Critical Stories About Feminism and Science Fiction," feminist SF has received a certain amount of critical attention from the feminist literary community, but "for the most part, dialogue across the genre-mainstream border has been rare" (52). This kind of dialogue is important to all feminist scholars interested in the recovery of women's diverse authorial activities throughout the modern era. More specifically, it is important to feminist SF scholars inter-ested in establishing women's SF as more than a mere appendage to their more serious or canonical literary efforts.

As feminist SF scholars we are uniquely positioned to enable this kind of dialogue because we have access to literary histories and analytic tools that are neither apparent nor available to our counterparts elsewhere in academia. As I have argued in this over-view of women's political and literary praxis at midcentury, women writing SF in the cold war era may not have endorsed an explicitly feminist agenda, but they did invoke cultur-ally-specific ideas about gender to interrogate the predominantly patriarchal scientific and social arrangements of their day. By invoking these ideas in science fiction narratives, they both made concrete and in many cases directly anticipated the hopes and fears of their activist counterparts. For instance, nuclear war narratives enabled authors like Judith Merril, Carol Emshwiller, and Alice Eleanor Jones to show how cold war America's national security policies threatened the very same families they were designed to protect. Meanwhile, stories about the problems of communicating with alien races were, as authors like Margaret St. Clair, Kay Rogers, and Mildred Clingerman demonstrate, easily adapted to explorations of the problems attending communication between human races on the American homefront.

In the beginning of this essay I suggested that midcentury women's SF has been marginalized by SF scholarship because longstanding assumptions about its trivial nature have, until recently, precluded serious study of its relation to the development of science fiction as a whole. If this history has been "lost" to the SF community, we can hardly be surprised that the larger feminist community never even knew it existed in the first place. And this is precisely where we as feminist SF scholars can give something back to the discipline which has inspired so much of our own work. By continuing to recover the history of women's science fiction in all its diversity, and by continuing to talk about it amongst ourselves and with our colleagues from other fields of inquiry, we can make important strides toward the larger feminist effort to remember those women that history doesn't see.

Notes

1. For one of the most influential discussions of this trend in midcentury political and cultural discourse, see Elaine Tyler May's *Homeward Bound: American Families in the Cold War Era*.
2. See Dee Garrison, "'Our Skirts Gave Them Courage': The Civil Defense Protest Movement in New York City, 1955-1961"; Harriet Hyman Alonso, "Mayhem and Moderation: Women Peace Activists During the McCarthy Era"; Eugenia Kaledin, *Mothers and More: American Women in the 1950s*; Susan Lynn, *Progressive Women in Conservative Times: Racial Justice, Peace, and Feminism, 1945 to the 1960s*; and Amy Swerdlow, *Women Strike For Peace: Traditional Motherhood and Radical Politics in the 1960s*.
3. This tendency is not limited to feminist scholarship; science fiction is one of the few areas of midcentury popular culture that historians and cultural critics rarely examine. Consider, for instance, two of the most prominent anthologies published on this subject in the past fifteen years: Lary May's *Recasting America: Culture and Politics in the Age of Cold War* and Joel Foreman's *The Other Fifties: Interrogating Midcentury American Icons*. Both offer essays that examine the political radicalism of midcentury art forms ranging from painting and social journalism to postmodern literature and film noir. Not once, however, do they reflect on science fiction.
4. For discussions of this omission, see Helen Merrick's essays "Fantastic Dialogues: Critical Stories about Feminism and Science Fiction" and "The Readers Feminism Doesn't See: Feminist Fans, Critics and Science Fiction"; Robin Roberts's "It's Still Science Fiction: Strategies of Feminist Science Fiction Criticism"; and Jenny Wolmark's "Science Fiction and Feminism."
5. Recent explorations of midcentury women's SF have taken a variety of forms. For discussions of how individual authors mobilized midcentury beliefs about gender relations to critique Cold War politics, see Farah Mendlesohn, "Gender. Power, and Conflict Resolution: 'Subcommittee" by Zenna Henderson" and David Seed, *American Science Fiction and the Cold War: Literature and Film*; for an exploration of how these strategies circulated throughout a range of women's SF texts, see my essay "Unhappy Housewife Heroines, Galactica Suburbia, and Nuclear War".

For an examination of how women revised midcentury SF conventions to present readers with female-friendly futures, see Brian Attebery's *Decoding Gender in Science Fiction*. For arguments concerning the relationship between midcentury women's SF and its relation to feminist narrative strategies, see Jane Donawerth's *Frankenstein's Daughters*. And finally, for discussion of how midcentury women's "sweet little domestic stories" marked the emergence of a literary sensibility that would inform the feminist SF community of the 1970s, see Justine Larbalestier, *Battle of the Sexes in Science Fiction* and her essay co-authored with Helen Merrick, "The Revolting Housewife: Women and Science Fiction in the 1950s."

6. For an excellent discussion of how women became scientific experts in their own right during the midcentury peace movement, see Amy Swerdlow's *Women Strike for Peace: Traditional Motherhood and Radical Politics in the 1960s*.

7. Some readers may recognize that I have discussed these short stories elsewhere, in "Unhappy Housewife Heroines, Galactica Suburbia, and Nuclear War." I am briefly reviewing them again in this article to show how my thinking about midcentury women's science fiction has developed over the past year: in the first essay, I provide readers with relatively lengthy analyses of these stories in relation to science fiction history; here, I discuss them in relation to the history of women's political and literary practice at midcentury (and in relation to other kinds of midcentury women's SF as well). In doing so, I hope to demonstrate the complexity of these rich cultural texts.

8. This household utopia is temporary, of course, because Merril refuses romantic notions of rugged individualism. No suburban household can be magically transformed into a self-sustaining fiefdom, and the women must maintain contact with the outside world to get food and medical attention for Gladys's daughters and Edie Crowell (all of whom have been exposed to radioactive dust and rain). Nonetheless, Merril insists that the tenor of her characters' dealings with the outside world does change radically once the women realize that they can rely on themselves to take care of many of the problems they have traditionally delegated to their men, like fixing gas leaks and defending themselves against burglars.

9. The original ending of the novel—which Doubleday refused to publish—was even more pessimistic. In Merril's final draft, Gladys's husband survives the horrors of postwar New York only to be shot to death by civil defense officials in his own backyard (Merril and Pohl-Weary, 100).

10. Although men like Thurgood Marshall (who represented the NAACP in *Brown v. Board of Education*) and Martin Luther King, Jr., are the people most commonly associated with the midcentury civil rights movement, black women were also important leaders in efforts to secure civil rights legislation. For further discussion, see Jacqueline Jones's essay "The Political Implications of Black and White Southern Women's Work in the South, 1890-1965" and Eugenia Kaledin's *Mothers and More: American Women in the 1950s*.

11. Susan Lynn's essay "Gender and Progressive Politics: A Bridge to Social Activism of the 1960s" and her book-length study *Progressive Women in Conservative Times: Racial Justice, Peace, and Feminism, 1945 to the 1960s* are the definitive works in this subject. For other discussions about race relations and progressive politics, see Jacqueline Jones, "The Political Implications of Black and White Southern Women's Work in the South, 1890-1965" and Leila J. Rupp and Verta Taylor, *Survival in the Doldrums: The American Women's Rights Movement, 1945 to the 1960s*.

Works cited

Alonso, Harriet Hyman. "Mayhem and Moderation: Women Peace Activists During the McCarthy
    Era." *Not June Cleaver: Women and Gender in Postwar America, 1945–1960*, Ed. Joanne
    Meyerowitz. Philadelphia: Temple UP, 1994. 128–50.

Attebery, Brian. *Decoding Gender in Science Fiction*. New York and London: Routledge, 2002.

Clingerman, Mildred. "Mr. Sakrison's Halt." 1956. Reprinted in *Best from Fantasy & Science Fiction*,
    6th series. Ed. Anthony Boucher. New York: Doubleday, 1957. 36–44.

Clute, John, and Peter Nicholls, Eds. *The Encyclopedia of Science Fiction*. New York:
    St. Martin's, 1995.

Donawerth, Jane. *Frankenstein's Daughters: Women Writing Science Fiction*. Syracuse: Syracuse
    UP, 1997.

Emshwiller, Carol. "Day at the Beach." 1959. Reprinted in *SF: The Best of the Best*. Ed. Judith
    Merril. New York: Delacourt, 1967. 274–284.

Foreman, Joel. *The Other Fifties: Interrogating Midcentury American Icons*. Urbana and Chicago:
    U Chicago P, 1997.

Garrison, Dec. "'Our Skirts Gave Them Courage': The Civil Defense Protest Movement in New York
    City, 1955–1961." *Not June Cleaver: Women and Gender in Postwar America, 1945–1960*, Ed.
    Joanne Meyerowitz. Philadelphia: Temple UP, 1994. 201–26.

Hafemeister, D.W. "A Chronology of the Nuclear Arms Race." *Nuclear Arms Technologies in the
    1990s*. Eds. Dietrich Schroeer and David Hafemeister. New York: American Institute of Physics,
    1988. 435–43.

James, Edward. *Science Fiction in the Twentieth Century*. Oxford: Oxford UP, 1994.

Jones, Alice Eleanor. "Created He Them." 1955. *Best from Fantasy & Science Fiction*, 5th series.
    Ed. Anthony Boucher. New York: Doubleday, 1956. 125–136.

Jones, Jacqueline. "The Political Implications of Black and White Southern Women's Work in the
    South, 1890–1965." *Women and Political Change*. Eds. Louise A. Tilley and Patricia Gurin.
    New York: Russell Sage Foundation, 1992. 108–29.

Kaledin, Eugenia. *Mothers and More: American Women in the 1950s*. Boston: Twayne
    Publishers, 1984.

Larbalestier, Justine. *The Battle of the Sexes in Science Fiction*. Middletown, CN: Wesleyan
    UP, 2002.

Larbalestier, Justine and Helen Merrick. "The Revolting Housewife: Women and Science Fiction in
    the 1950s." *Paradoxa* 18 (2003): 136–156.

Lynn, Susan. "Gender and Progressive Politics: A Bridge to the Social Activism of the 1960s.
    Not June Cleaver: Women and Gender in Postwar America, 1945–1960. Ed. Joanne Meyerowitz.
    Philadelphia: Temple University Press, 1994. 103–27.

—. *Progressive Women in Conservative Times: Racial Justice, Peace, and Feminism, 1945 to the
    1960s*. New Brunswick, NJ: Rutgers UP, 1992.

May, Elaine Tyler. *Homeward Bound: American Families in the Cold War Era*. New York: Basic
    Books, 1988.

May, Lary. *Recasting America: Culture and Politics in the Age of Cold War*. Chicago and London:
    U Chicago P, 1989.

Mendlesohn, Farah. "Gender, Power, and Conflict Resolution: 'Subcommittee' by Zenna
    Henderson." *Extrapolation* 35.2 (1994): 120–129.

Merrick, Helen. "Fantastic Dialogues: Critical Stories about Feminism and Science Fiction." *Speaking Science Fiction: Dialogues and Intepretations*. Eds. Andy Walker and David Seed. Liverpool: Liverpool UP, 2000. 52–68.

—. "The Readers Feminism Doesn't See: Feminist Fans, Critics and Science Fiction." *Trash Aesthetics: Popular Culture and Its Audience*. Ed. Deborah Cartmell et al. London and Chicago: Pluto Press, 1997. 48–65.

Merril, Judith. *Shadow on the Hearth*. Garden City, NY: Doubleday & Co., 1950.

—. "That Only a Mother." 1948. Reprinted in *Science Fiction Hall of Fame*. Ed. Robert Silverberg. New York: Avon, 1970. 344–354.

—. "What Do You Mean: Science? Fiction?" *SF: The Other Side of Realism*. Ed. Thomas D. Clarenson. Bowling Green: Bowling Green U Popular P, 1971. 53–95.

Merril, Judith, and Emily Pohl–Weary. *Better to Have Loved: The Life of Judith Merril*. Toronto: Between the Lines, 2002.

Meyerowitz, Joanne. "Beyond the Feminine Mystique: A Reassessment of Postwar Mass Culture, 1946–1958. *Not June Cleaver: Women and Gender in Postwar America, 1945–1960*. Ed. Joanne Meyerowitz. Philadelphia: Temple University Press, 1994. 229–262.

Roberts, Robin. "It's Still Science Fiction: Strategies of Feminist Science Fiction Criticism." *Extrapolation* 36.3 (1995): 184–197.

Rogers, Kay. "Experiment." 1953. Reprinted in *Best from Fantasy & Science Fiction*, 3rd series. Ed. Anthony Boucher. New York: Doubleday, 1954. 96–99.

Rupp, Leila J., and Verta Taylor, *Survival in the Doldrums: The American Women's Rights Movement, 1945 to the 1960s*. New York and Oxford: Oxford UP, 1987.

Russ, Joanna. "The Image of Women in Science Fiction." 1971. Reprinted in *Images of Women in Fiction: Feminist Perspectives*. Ed. Susan Koppleman Cornillion. Bowling Green: Bowling Green U Popular P, 1972. 79–94.

St. Clair, Margaret. "Brightness Falls from the Air." 1951. *The Science Fiction Century*. Ed. David G. Hartwell. New York: Tor, 1997. 161–165.

Stone, Albert E. *Literary Aftershocks: American Writers, Readers, and the Bomb*, New York: Twayne Publishers, 1994.

Swerdlow, Amy. *Women Strike For Peace: Traditional Motherhood and Radical Politics in the 1960s*. Chicago and London: U Chicago P, 1993.

Trachtenberg, Mark. "American Thinking on Nuclear War." Strategic Power: USA/USSR. Ed. Carl G. Jacobsen. New York: St. Martin's, 1990. 355–369.

Wolmark, Jenny. "Science Fiction and Feminism." *Foundation* 37 (1986): 48–51.

Yaszek, Lisa. "Unhappy Housewife Heroines, Galactic Suburbia, and Nuclear War: A History of Midcentury Women's Science Fiction." *Extrapolation* 44.1 (2003): 97–111.

Recommended further reading

Attebery, Brian. *Decoding Gender in Science Fiction*. New York: Routledge, 2002.
　　Compellingly analyzes a range of pulp-era and contemporary SF in terms of its depictions of gender difference; includes excellent chapters on masculinity and androgyny in SF.

Bould, Mark, and China Miéville, eds. *Red Planets: Marxism and Science Fiction*. Middletown, CT: Wesleyan UP, 2009.
　　A collection gathering essays that consider the ways in which SF mobilizes or actuates the perspectives of Marxist critical theory, including issues of class stratification, bourgeois scientism, and activist struggle.

Huntington, John. *Rationalizing Genius: Ideological Strategies in the Classic American Science Fiction Short Story*. New Brunswick, NJ: Rutgers UP, 1989.
　　A trenchant study of the social ideologies informing pulp-era SF, including technology worship and the cult of the (masculine) genius.

Larbalestier, Justine. *The Battle of the Sexes in Science Fiction*. Middletown, CT: Wesleyan UP, 2002.
　　A searching historical study of how pulp-era SF dealt with gender ideologies, restoring the centrality of the contribution of female authors and fans to proto-feminist criticism of the genre.

Moylan, Tom. *Demand the Impossible: Science Fiction and the Utopian Imagination*. New York: Metheun, 1986.
　　An influential study of the "critical utopias" of modern SF, especially the work of Samuel R. Delany, Ursula K. Le Guin, Marge Piercy, and Joanna Russ, focusing on their critiques of social ideologies.

Parrinder, Patrick, ed. *Learning from Other Worlds: Estrangement, Cognition and the Politics of Science Fiction and Utopia*. Liverpool: Liverpool UP, 2000.
　　A festschrift for Darko Suvin that offers reassessments, revisions, and extensions of his model of "cognitive estrangement," especially as the concept defines the genre as a mechanism for the critique of sociopolitical ideologies.

Pearson, Wendy, Veronica Hollinger, and Joan Gordon, eds. *Queer Universes: Sexualities in Science Fiction*. Liverpool: Liverpool UP, 2008.
　　A collection of essays on the representation of sexuality in SF, exploring the ways the genre reinforces heteronormative ideologies and offers the resources to "queer" them at the same time.

Ross, Andrew. *Strange Weather: Culture, Science and Technology in the Age of Limits*. New York:
   Verso, 1991.
   Examines a range of technological subcultures—including Gernsbackian pulp SF and cyberpunk—in terms of their engagement with left-wing causes and populist values, especially the
critique of the technocratic domination of nature.

Seed, David. *American Science Fiction and the Cold War: Literature and Film*. Chicago: Fitzroy
   Dearborn, 1999.
   The first in a series of studies by Seed—also including *Brainwashing: The Fictions of Mind Control*
(Kent State UP, 2004) and *Under the Shadow: The Atomic Bomb and Cold War Narratives* (Kent State
UP, 2013)—that focus on how the ideologies of the Cold War (e.g., nuclear paranoia) have been
expressed in postwar SF.

Wolmark, Jenny. *Aliens and Others: Science Fiction, Feminism and Postmodernism*. Iowa City:
   U of Iowa P, 1994.
   Carefully examines the links among the terms in the book's subtitle, using the figure of the alien
as a way to interrogate "gendered subjectivity" in SF.

Part 4

The nonhuman

This section opens with Mary Shelley's introduction to the 1831 edition of her classic novel *Frankenstein* (1818), often claimed to be the first ever work of science fiction.[1] It is certainly one of the most sophisticated attempts in the early history of the genre to imagine the creation of artificial life using the methods of modern science. Shelley outlines the sensational circumstances for her initial conception of the novel during sessions of reading ghost stories with Lord Byron and her late husband, Percy Shelley—thus linking her depiction of the Creature with the fantastic reveries of the Gothic tradition. She admits that she sought a subject that would "speak to the mysterious fears of our nature, and awaken thrilling horror," but she also acknowledges that discussions of contemporary scientific discoveries such as galvanism exerted a significant influence. Striking a moral tone that would forever haunt subsequent stories of artificial beings, such as H. G. Wells's *The Island of Dr. Moreau* (1897), Shelley identifies the theme of her work as blasphemous and overreaching, with Victor Frankenstein "endeavor[ing] to mock the stupendous mechanism of the Creator of the world" by endowing lifeless matter with animation and sentience. Of course, critics and readers over the past two centuries have found in her novel a much more complex and ambivalent portrait of the "monster" than this negative verdict suggests.

   Almost 150 years later, another SF writer celebrated for his depictions of humanoid creatures, Philip K. Dick, meditated on his own interest in the topic of "androids"—mechanically produced entities eerily indistinguishable, on the surface, from human beings. Building on the insights of Norbert Wiener, the founder of cybernetics, Dick argues that "machines are becoming more human," mimicking functions traditionally assumed to be beyond their capacities and, in the process, laying claims to autonomy and personhood usually reserved for their creators. Meanwhile, as machines seem to be attaining human sentience, human beings themselves have begun to appear increasingly machinelike, driven by programmed reflexes rather than conscious volition—a situation reinforced by powerful contemporary discourses of persuasion and manipulation, especially those emanating from the mass media. While we might assume that androids are mere simulacra of humanity, Dick asserts that they are fundamentally no different than "schizoid" human beings, whose affectless literal-mindedness has "a mechanical, reflex quality." For Shelley, the distinction between humans and their replicas was categorically precise, but Dick has much less confidence that such a distinction can hold any longer.

This assumption of the growing convergence between humans and machines governs the next two readings in this section; influential academic essays on the implic- ations of cybernetics discourse for definitions of personhood. Donna Haraway's widely cited and hugely influential "Cyborg Manifesto" takes a position at least as extreme as Dick's: categorical divisions between humans and machines have collapsed in the figure of the "cyborg," which has emerged as a powerful ethical-political agent. For Haraway, the challenge is not to recover some essential core of humanity—or even to mourn its loss—but rather to embrace and celebrate the cyborg as a social vector for critique and liberation. Liberal-humanist conceptions of the self can no longer provide a basis for self-understanding or political praxis in a world where biology can be recoded by genetic engineers and subjectivity can be extended and reconfigured by computer networks. In such a world, "forms of political organization and participation"—in particular, Haraway asserts, the politics of gender and race—have to be radically rethought based on tech- nosocial affiliations rather than essential identities. While the cyborg historically emerges within discourses of power and domination, the concept contains the seeds of a protean, subversive agency, the implications of which are visible in the writings of SF authors, especially the work of women and people of color.

Building on Haraway's insights, N. Katherine Hayles argues that the very definition of the embodied self is under erasure in cybernetics discourse, a situation particularly visible within the SF subgenre of cyberpunk. Just as information technology portends "unexpected metamorphoses, attenuations, and dispersions" of the humanist self, so these epochal changes are powerfully materialized in SF texts that portray "virtual bodies," entities that emerge at the interface with computer technologies. In cyberpunk SF, personhood can be synthetically simulated and agency dispersed throughout a cyberspatial matrix, resulting in depictions that at once diminish the substance of human bodies, while at the same time amplifying and extending their powers virtually. Cyberpunk thus "presents a vision of the posthuman future" that operates at the representational level of the text itself: characters are reduced to "flickering signifiers" circulating as coded information within the narratives. Unlike Haraway, Hayles is ultimately disturbed by the implications of this cyborgized selfhood, especially the "systematic devaluation of materiality and embodiment" that it seems to express. The tension between Haraway's qualified embrace of, and Hayles's hesitant warnings about, posthumanist possibility has informed the discourse of cyberculture to which they are both such significant contrib- utors, as well as the critical discourse of science fiction, which has drawn upon their insights in compelling ways.[2]

A further extrapolation of the cyborgization of humanity is offered in Vernor Vinge's essay on the "Singularity," defined as "a point where our old models must be discarded and a new reality rules."[3] According to Vinge, the snowballing effects of rapid techno- logical change will eventually lead both to the creation of artificial intelligence (A.I.) and to projects for "intelligence amplification" (I.A.), with the former producing intelligent machines and the latter superhuman intelligence. Beyond this threshold, scientific progress will accelerate exponentially, with humans and machines beginning to network, symbiotically fuse, and coevolve toward some momentous cyborg synthesis. Vinge seems much more sanguine about this development than Hayles or even Haraway, carefully laying out—as befits this celebrated author of hard SF—the nuts and bolts of what a posthuman future might look like, citing several prominent works of SF as exemplars. Indeed, Vinge's essay—like Haraway's manifesto—can itself be seen as a kind of science fiction, an imaginative projection of futuristic possibility.

Most of the readings in this section examine forms of artificial personhood, but the essay by Gwyneth Jones, a major British SF author, shows that the depiction of extraterrestrial beings in SF has much to say about the scope and limits of human agency as well. As Jones points out, traditional SF depictions of aliens tend to anthropomorphize them, emphasizing their similarities with humanity, rather than attempting to create "an *authentically incomprehensible* other." Moreover, unconsciously recapitulating the historical dynamics of colonialism, many "first contact" stories operate with the knee-jerk assumption that aliens will be hostile to humanity, with the characteristic narrative featuring an invasion and occupation (as in H. G. Wells's classic *The War of the Worlds* [1898]). Jones discusses her own practice as an SF writer: when crafting aliens, she believes it is essential to be aware of these historical and ideological echoes, rather than permitting them to govern a story unconsciously. Describing in particular the thinking that went into her brilliant trilogy of "Aleutian" novels, which commenced with *The White Queen* (1991), Jones outlines how she used aliens to obliquely explore the fraught nature of communication and interaction across lines of difference in a way that evoked without being simplistically reducible to allegories of racial and sexual politics. Jones's essay is one of the most powerful accounts of the difficult art of world-building ever written by a practicing SF author.

One of the issues Jones explored in her work involved the possibility of inter-species desire, a theme Allison de Fren's essay on "technofetishism" echoes in her provocative discussion of human-robot erotics. While Dick's essay had jokingly suggested the possibility of sexual relations between humans and machines, De Fren analyzes both real-world and science-fictional depictions of precisely such relationships. Focusing on famous SF texts that have treated the theme of mechanical female love objects as well as on "technosexual" communities that literally fetishize robots as prospective partners, De Fren deploys classic theories of sexology, especially Freudian psychoanalysis, to analyze the implications of this strange variant of technophilia. As she shows, the heady possibilities of "cyborg sex," while seemingly spawned by the growing intimacy of interaction between humans and machines in the contemporary world, has deep roots in longstanding discourses about desire and technology. Wide-ranging and provocative, De Fren's essay suggests that the attraction toward nonhuman otherness, so pronounced throughout the genre's history, may activate complex psychosexual dynamics in SF readers and viewers.

De Fren's essay concludes with a citation of both Haraway's "Cyborg Manifesto" and her later "Companion Species Manifesto" (2003) as pioneering studies of the ways in which the nonhuman others that surround us are deeply implicated in our own self-understanding.[4] The latter work by Haraway developed an idea mentioned in the former: that boundaries between humans and animals are breaking down as rapidly as those between humans and machines. The interdisciplinary discourse of "human-animal studies" has emerged to explore this topic, and the final reading in this section, an excerpt from Sherryl Vint's book *Animal Alterity: Science Fiction and the Question of the Animal* (2010), develops the relevance of this area of inquiry for SF studies. As Vint shows, an implicit relationship to animal life and consciousness runs throughout the genre's multifarious depictions of aliens and artificial persons. We have, she asserts, "always-already been living with 'alien' beings," and these relationships form the "material history" from which fictional projections of extraterrestrial creatures have emerged. SF has also, Vint argues, often deployed iconic animal-machine hybrids in ways that allow readers to consider the nature of their own connections with technology and the natural environment.[5] Vint's essay suggests that even the strangest depictions of alien alterity in SF may be rooted in our mundane daily interactions with the creatures who share our planet.

Notes

1. The most famous argument for Shelley as the "mother of science fiction" can be found in Brian W. Aldiss (with David Wingrove), *Trillion Year Spree: The History of Science Fiction* (New York: Atheneum, 1986).
2. Cyberculture studies has exploded since the mid-1980s, when Haraway's manifesto appeared coevally with the major works of cyberpunk SF. An excellent anthology that draws together the major threads of this discourse is Barbara M. Kennedy and David Bell's *The Cybercultures Reader* (New York: Routledge, 2000).
3. For critical treatments of the concept of Singularity, see the essays by Brooks Landon, Neil Easterbrook, and myself gathered in the special section on the topic in the March 2012 issue of *Science Fiction Studies*.
4. A solid discussion of the field of animal studies that clearly situates Haraway's work within the discourse is Dawne McCance, *Critical Animal Studies: An Introduction* (New York: SUNY P, 2013).
5. Joan Gordon has coined the term "amborg" to describe these fusions of animal and machine: see her "Gazing Across the Abyss: The Amborg Gaze in Sheri S. Tepper's *Six Moon Dance*," *Science Fiction Studies* 35.2 (2008), pp. 189–206.

22

Author's introduction to *Frankenstein*

Mary Shelley

The Publishers of the Standard Novels, in selecting "Frankenstein" for one of their series, expressed a wish that I should furnish them with some account of the origin of the story. I am the more willing to comply, because I shall thus give a general answer to the question, so frequently asked me—"How I, then a young girl, came to think of, and to dilate upon, so very hideous an idea?" It is true that I am very averse to bringing myself forward in print; but as my account will only appear as an appendage to a former production, and as it will be confined to such topics as have connection with my authorship alone, I can scarcely accuse myself of a personal intrusion.

It is not singular that, as the daughter of two persons of distinguished literary celebrity, I should very early in life have thought of writing. As a child I scribbled; and my favourite pastime, during the hours given me for recreation, was to "write stories." Still I had a dearer pleasure than this, which was the formation of castles in the air—the indulging in waking dreams—the following up trains of thought, which had for their subject the formation of a succession of imaginary incidents. My dreams were at once more fantastic and agreeable than my writings. In the latter I was a close imitator—rather doing as others had done, than putting down the suggestions of my own mind. What I wrote was intended at least for one other eye—my childhood's companion and friend; but my dreams were all my own; I accounted for them to nobody; they were my refuge when annoyed—my dearest pleasure when free.

I lived principally in the country as a girl, and passed a considerable time in Scotland. I made occasional visits to the more picturesque parts; but my habitual residence was on the blank and dreary northern shores of the Tay, near Dundee. Blank and dreary on retrospection I call them; they were not so to me then. They were the eyry of freedom, and the pleasant region where unheeded I could commune with the creatures of my fancy. I wrote then—but in a most common-place style. It was beneath the trees of the grounds belonging to our house, or on the bleak sides of the woodless mountains near, that my true compositions, the airy flights of my imagination, were born and fostered. I did not make myself the heroine of my tales. Life appeared to me too common-place an affair as regarded myself. I could not figure to myself that romantic woes or wonderful events would ever be my lot; but I was not confined to my own identity, and I could people the hours with creations far more interesting to me at that age, than my own sensations.

After this my life became busier, and reality stood in place of fiction. My husband, however, was from the first, very anxious that I should prove myself worthy of my parentage, and enrol myself on the page of fame. He was for ever inciting me to obtain literary reputation, which even on my own part I cared for then, though since I have become infinitely indifferent to it. At this time he desired that I should write, not so much with the idea that I could produce any thing worthy of notice, but that he might himself judge how far I possessed the promise of better things hereafter. Still I did nothing. Travelling, and the cares of a family, occupied my time; and study, in the way of reading, or improving my ideas in communication with his far more cultivated mind, was all of literary employment that engaged my attention.

In the summer of 1816, we visited Switzerland, and became the neighbors of Lord Byron. At first we spent our pleasant hours on the lake, or wandering on its shores; and Lord Byron, who was writing the third canto of Childe Harold, was the only one among us who put his thoughts upon paper. These, as he brought them successively to us, clothed in all the light and harmony of poetry, seemed to stamp as divine the glories of heaven and earth, whose influences we partook with him.

But it proved a wet, ungenial summer, and incessant rain often confined us for days to the house. Some volumes of ghost stories, translated from the German into French, fell into our hands. There was the History of the Inconstant Lover, who, when he thought to clasp the bride to whom he had pledged his vows, found himself in the arms of the pale ghost of her whom he had deserted. There was the tale of the sinful founder of his race, whose miserable doom it was to bestow the kiss of death on all the younger sons of his fated house, just when they reached the age of promise. His gigantic, shadowy form, clothed like the ghost in Hamlet, in complete armor, but with the beaver up, was seen at midnight, by the moon's fitful beams, to advance slowly along the gloomy avenue. The shape was lost beneath the shadow of the castle walls; but soon a gate swung back, a step was heard, the door of the chamber opened, and he advanced to the couch of the blooming youths, cradled in healthy sleep. Eternal sorrow sat upon his face as he bent down and kissed the forehead of the boys, who from that hour withered like flowers snapt upon the stalk. I have not seen these stories since then; but their incidents are as fresh in my mind as if I had read them yesterday.

"We will each write a ghost story," said Lord Byron; and his proposition was acceded to. There were four of us. The noble author began a tale, a fragment of which he printed at the end of his poem of Mazeppa. Shelley, more apt to embody ideas and sentiments in the radiance of brilliant imagery, commenced one founded on the experiences of his early life. Poor Polidori had some terrible idea about a skull-headed lady, who was so punished for peeping through a key-hole—what to see I forget—something very shocking and wrong of course; but when she was reduced to a worse condition than the renowned Tom of Coventry, he did not know what to do with her, and was obliged to despatch her to the tomb of the Capulets, the only place for which she was fitted. The illustrious poets also, annoyed by the platitude of prose, speedily relinquished the uncongenial task.

I busied myself *to think of a story*, —a story to rival those which had excited us to this task. One which would speak to the mysterious fears of our nature, and awaken thrilling horror—one to make the reader dread to look round, to curdle the blood, and quicken the beatings of the heart. If I did not accomplish these things, my ghost story would be unworthy of its name. I thought and pondered—vainly. I felt that blank incapability of invention which is the greatest misery of authorship, when dull Nothing replies to our anxious invocations. *Have you thought of a story?* I was asked each morning, and each morning I was forced to reply with a mortifying negative.

Every thing must have a beginning, to speak in Sanchean phrase; and that beginning must be linked to something that went before. The Hindoos give the world an elephant to support it, but they make the elephant stand upon a tortoise. Invention, it must be humbly admitted, does not consist in creating out of void, but out of chaos; the materials must, in the first place, be afforded: it can give form to dark, shapeless substances, but cannot bring into being the substance itself. In all matters of discovery and invention, even of those that appertain to the imagination, we are continually reminded of the story of Columbus and his egg. Invention consists in the capacity of seizing on the capabilities of a subject, and in the power of moulding and fashioning ideas suggested to it.

Many and long were the conversations between Lord Byron and Shelley, to which I was a devout but nearly silent listener. During one of these, various philosophical doctrines were discussed, and among others the nature of the principle of life, and whether there was any probability of its ever being discovered and communicated. They talked of the experiments of Dr. Darwin (I speak not of what the Doctor really did, or said that he did, but, as more to my purpose, of what was then spoken of as having been done by him), who preserved a piece of vermicelli in a glass case, till by some extraordinary means it began to move with voluntary motion. Not thus, after all, would life be given. Perhaps a corpse would be re-animated; galvanism had given token of such things: perhaps the component parts of a creature might be manufactured, brought together, and endued with vital warmth.

Night waned upon this talk, and even the witching hour had gone by, before we retired to rest. When I placed my head on my pillow, I did not sleep, nor could I be said to think. My imagination, unbidden, possessed and guided me, gifting the successive images that arose in my mind with a vividness far beyond the usual bounds of reverie. I saw—with shut eyes, but acute mental vision, —I saw the pale student of unhallowed arts kneeling beside the thing he had put together. I saw the hideous phantasm of a man stretched out, and then, on the working of some powerful engine, show signs of life, and stir with an uneasy, half vital motion. Frightful must it be; for supremely frightful would be the effect of any human endeavor to mock the stupendous mechanism of the Creator of the world. His success would terrify the artist; he would rush away from his odious handywork, horror-stricken. He would hope that, left to itself, the slight spark of life which he had communicated would fade; that this thing, which had received such imperfect animation, would subside into dead matter; and he might sleep in the belief that the silence of the grave would quench for ever the transient existence of the hideous corpse which he had looked upon as the cradle of life. He sleeps; but he is awakened; he opens his eyes; behold the horrid thing stands at his bedside, opening his curtains, and looking on him with yellow, watery, but speculative eyes.

I opened mine in terror. The idea so possessed my mind, that a thrill of fear ran through me, and I wished to exchange the ghastly image of my fancy for the realities around. I see them still; the very room, the dark *parquet*, the closed shutters, with the moonlight struggling through, and the sense I had that the glassy lake and white high Alps were beyond. I could not so easily get rid of my hideous phantom; still it haunted me. I must try to think of something else. I recurred to my ghost story, my tiresome unlucky ghost story! O! if I could only contrive one which would frighten my reader as I myself had been frightened that night!

Swift as light and as cheering was the idea that broke in upon me. "I have found it! What terrified me will terrify others; and I need only describe the spectre which had haunted my midnight pillow." On the morrow I announced that I had *thought of a story*. I began that day with the words, *It was on a dreary night of November*, making only a transcript of the grim terrors of my waking dream.

At first I thought but of a few pages of a short tale; but Shelley urged me to develope the idea at greater length. I certainly did not owe the suggestion of one incident, nor scarcely of one train of feeling, to my husband, and yet but for his incitement, it would never have taken the form in which it was presented. From this declaration I must except the preface. As far as I can recollect, it was entirely written by him.

And now, once again, I bid my hideous progeny go forth and prosper. I have an affection for it, for it was the offspring of happy days, when death and grief were but words, which found no true echo in my heart. Its several pages speak of many a walk, many a drive, and many a conversation, when I was not alone; and my companion was one who, in this world, I shall never see more. But this is for myself; my readers have nothing to do with these associations.

I will add but one word as to the alterations I have made. They are principally those of style. I have changed no portion of the story, nor introduced any new ideas or circumstances. I have mended the language where it was so bald as to interfere with the interest of the narrative; and these changes occur almost exclusively in the beginning of the first volume. Throughout they are entirely confined to such parts as are mere adjuncts to the story, leaving the core and substance of it untouched.

23

The android and the human

Philip K. Dick

It is the tendency of the so-called primitive mind to animate its environment. Modern depth psychology has requested us for years to withdraw these anthropomorphic projections from what is actually inanimate reality, to introject—that is, bring back into our own heads—the living quality that we, in ignorance, cast out onto the inert things surrounding us. Such introjection is said to be the mark of true maturity in the individual, and the authentic mark of civilization in contrast to mere social culture, such as one finds in a tribe. A native of Africa is said to view his surroundings as pulsing with a purpose, a life, that is actually within himself; once these childish projections are withdrawn, he sees that the world is dead and that life resides solely within himself. When he reaches this sophisticated point he is said to be either mature or sane. Or scientific. But one wonders: Has he not also, in this process, reified—that is, made into a thing—other people? Stones and rocks and trees may now be inanimate for him, but what about his friends? Has he now made them into stones, too?

This is, really, a psychological problem. And its solution, I think, is of less importance in any case than one might think, because, within the past decade, we have seen a trend not anticipated by our earnest psychologists—or by anyone else—that dwarfs that issue; our environment, and I mean our man-made world of machines, artificial constructs, computers, electronic systems, interlinking homeostatic components—all of this is in fact beginning more and more to possess what the earnest psychologists fear the primitive *sees* in his environment: animation. In a very real sense our environment is becoming alive, or at least quasi-alive, and in ways specifically and fundamentally analogous to ourselves. Cybernetics, a valuable recent scientific discipline, articulated by the late Norbert Wiener, saw valid comparisons between the behavior of machines and humans—with the view that a study of machines would yield valuable insights into the nature of our own behavior. By studying what goes wrong with a machine—for example, when two mutually exclusive tropisms function simultaneously in one of Grey Walter's synthetic turtles, producing fascinatingly intricate behavior in the befuddled turtles—one learns perhaps, a new, more fruitful insight into what in humans was previously called "neurotic" behavior. But suppose the use of this analogy is turned the other way. Suppose—and I don't believe Wiener anticipated this—suppose a study of ourselves, our own nature, enables us to gain insight into the now extraordinary complex functioning and malfunctioning of mechanical and electronic constructs? In other words—and this is what I wish to stress in what I am saying here—it is now possible that we can learn about the artificial external environment around us, how it behaves, why, what it is up to, by analogizing from what we know about ourselves.

Machines are becoming more human, so to speak—at least in the sense that, as Wiener indicated, some meaningful comparison exists between human and mechanical behavior. But is it ourselves that we know first and foremost? Rather than learning about ourselves by studying our constructs, perhaps we should make the attempt to comprehend what our constructs are up to by looking into what we ourselves are up to.

Perhaps, really, what we are seeing is a gradual merging of the general nature of human activity and function into the activity and function of what we humans have built and surround[ed] ourselves with. A hundred years ago such a thought would have been absurd, rather than merely anthropomorphic. What could a man living in 1750 have learned about himself by observing the behavior of a donkey steam engine? Could he have watched it huffing and puffing and then extrapolated from its labor an insight into why he himself continually fell in love with one certain type of pretty young girl? This would not have been primitive thinking on his part; it would have been pathological. But now we find ourselves immersed in a world of our own making so intricate, so mysterious, that as Stanislaw Lem the eminent Polish science fiction writer theorizes, the time may come when, for example, a man may have to be restrained from attempting to rape a sewing machine. Let us hope, if that time comes, that it is a female sewing machine he fastens his intentions on. And one over the age of seventeen-hopefully, a very old treddle-operated Singer although possibly, regrettably, past menopause.

I have, in some of my stories and novels, written about androids or robots or simulacra—the name doesn't matter; what is meant is artificial constructs masquerading as humans. Usually with a sinister purpose in mind. I suppose I took it for granted that if such a construct, a robot, for example, had a benign or anyhow decent purpose in mind, it would not need to so disguise itself. Now, to me, that then seems obsolete. The constructs do not mimic humans; they are, in many deep ways, *actually* human already. They are not trying to fool us, for a purpose of any sort; they merely follow lines we follow, in order that they, too, may overcome such common problems as the breakdown of vital parts, loss of power source, attack by such foes as storms, short-circuits—and I'm sure any one of us here can testify that a short-circuit, especially in our power supply, can ruin our entire day and make us utterly unable to get to our daily job, or, once at the office, useless as far as doing the work set forth on our desk.

What would occur to me now as a recasting of the robot-appearing-ashuman theme would be a gleaming robot with a telescan lens and a helium-battery power pack, who, when jostled, bleeds. Underneath the metal hull is a heart such as we ourselves have. Perhaps I will write that. Or, as in stories already in print, a computer, when asked some ultimate question such as "Why is there water?" prints out 1 Corinthians. One story I wrote, which I'm afraid I failed to take seriously enough, dealt with a computer that, when able to answer a question put to it, ate the questioner. Presumably—I failed to go into this—had the computer been unable to answer a question, the human questioner would have eaten *it*. Anyhow, inadvertently I blended the human and the construct and didn't notice that such a blend might, in time, actually begin to become part of our reality. Like Lem, I think this will be so, more and more. But to project past Lem's idea: A time may come when, if a man tries to rape a sewing machine, the sewing machine will have him arrested and testify, perhaps even a little hysterically, against him in court. This leads to all sorts of spin-off ideas: false testimony by suborned sewing machines who accuse innocent men unfairly; paternity tests; and, of course, abortions for sewing machines that have become pregnant against their will. And would there be birth control pills for sewing machines? Probably, like one of my previous wives, certain sewing machines would complain that the pills made them overweight—or rather, in their case, that it made them sew irregular stitches. And there would be unreliable sewing machines that would forget to take their birth control pills. And, last but not least, there would have to be Planned Parenthood clinics at which sewing machines just off the assembly lines would be counseled as to the dangers of promiscuity, with severe warnings of venereal diseases visited on such immoral machines by an outraged God—Himself, no doubt, able to sew buttonholes and fancy needlework at a rate that would dazzle the credulous merely metal and plastic sewing machines, always ready, like ourselves, to kowtow before divine miracles.

I am being facetious about this, I suppose, but the point is not merely a humorous one. Our electronic constructs are becoming so complex that to comprehend them we must now reverse the analogizing of cybernetics and try to reason from our own mentation and behavior to theirs—although I suppose to assign motive or purpose to them would be to enter the realm of paranoia; what machines *do* may resemble what we do, but certainly they do not have intent in the sense that we have; they have tropisms, they have purpose in the sense that we build them to accomplish certain ends and to react to certain stimuli. A pistol, for example, is built with the purpose of firing a metal slug that will damage, incapacitate, or kill someone, but this does not mean that the pistol *wants* to do this. And yet there we are entering the philosophical realm of Spinoza when he saw, and I think with great profundity, that if a falling stone could reason, it would think, "I *want* to fall at the rate of thirty-two feet per second per second." Free will for us—that is when we feel desire, when we are conscious of wanting to do what we do—may be even for us an illusion; and depth psychology seems to substantiate this: Many of our drives in life originate from an unconscious that is beyond our control. We are as driven as are insects, although the term "instinct" is perhaps not applicable for us. Whatever the term, much of our behavior that we feel is the result of our will, may control us to the extent that for all practical purposes we are falling stones, doomed to drop at a rate prescribed by nature, as rigid and predictable as the force that creates a crystal. Each of us may feel himself unique, with an intrinsic destiny never before seen in the universe . . . and yet to God we may be millions of crystals, identical in the eyes of the Cosmic Scientist.

And—here is a thought not too pleasing—as the external world becomes more animate, we may find that we—the so-called humans—are becoming, and may to a great extent always have been, inanimate in the sense that we are led, directed by built-in tropisms, rather than leading. So we and our elaborately evolving computers may meet each other halfway. Someday a human being, named perhaps Fred White, may shoot a robot named Pete Something-or-Other, which has come out of a General Electric factory, and to his surprise see it weep and bleed. And the dying robot may shoot back and, to its surprise, see a wisp of gray smoke arise from the electric pump that it supposed was Mr. White's beating heart. It would be rather a great moment of truth for both of them.

I would like, then, to ask this: What is it, in our behavior, that we can call specifically human? That is special to us as a living species? And what is it that, at least up to now, we can consign as merely machine behavior, or, by extension, insect behavior, or reflex behavior? And I would include in this the kind of pseudohuman behavior exhibited by what were once living men-creatures who have, in ways I wish to discuss next, become instruments, means, rather than ends, and hence to me analogues of machines in the *bad* sense, in the sense that although biological life continues, metabolism goes on, the soul—for lack of a better term—is no longer there or is at least no longer active. And such does exist in our world—it always did, but the production of such inauthentic human activity has become a science of government and suchlike agencies now. The reduction of humans to mere use—men made into machines, serving a purpose that although "good" in the abstract sense has, for its accomplishment, employed what I regard as the greatest evil imaginable: the placing on what was a free man who laughed and cried and made mistakes and wandered off into foolishness and play a restriction that limits him, despite what he may imagine or think, to the fulfilling of an aim outside of his own personal—however puny—destiny. As if, so to speak, history has made him into its instrument. History, and men skilled in—and trained in—the use of manipulative techniques, equipped with devices, ideologically oriented themselves, in such a way that the use of these devices strikes them as a necessary, or at least desirable, method of bringing about some ultimately desired goal.

I think, at this point, of Tom Paine's comment about one or another party of the Europe of his time, "They admired the feathers and forgot the dying bird." And it is the "dying bird" that I am concerned with. The dying—and yet, I think, beginning once again to revive in the hearts of the new generation of kids coming into maturity—the dying bird of authentic humanness…. [W]e are merging by degrees into homogeneity with our mechanical constructs, step by step, month by month, until a time will perhaps come when a writer, for example, will not stop writing because someone unplugged his electric typewriter but because someone unplugged *him.* But there are kids *now* who cannot be unplugged because no electric cord links them to any external power sources. Their hearts beat with an interior, private meaning…. Back in California, where I came from, I have been living with such kids, participating, to the extent I can, in their emerging world. I would like to tell you about their world because—if we are lucky—something of that world, those values, that way of life, will shape the future of our total society, our utopia or anti-utopia of the fu ture. As a science fiction writer, I must, of course, look continually ahead, always at the future…. If you are interested in the world of tomorrow you may learn something about it, or at least read about possibilities that may emerge to fashion it, in the pages of *Analog* and *F&SF* and *Amazing,* but actually, to find it in its authentic form, you will discover it as you observe a sixteen- or seventeen-year-old kid as he goes about his natural peregrinations, his normal day…. These kids that I have known, lived with, still know, in California, are my science fiction stories of tomorrow, my summation, at this point of my life as a person and a writer; they are what I look ahead to—and so keenly desire to see prevail. What, more than anything else I have ever encountered, I believe in….

It would … be rather dismaying, if the first two-legged entity to emerge on the surface of Mars from a Terran spacecraft were to declare, "Thanks be to God for letting me, letting me, click, letting, click, click … this is a recording." And then catch fire and explode as a couple of wires got crossed somewhere within its plastic chest And probably even more dismaying to this construct would be the discovery when it returned to Earth that its "children" had been recycled along with the aluminum beer cans and Coca-Cola bottles as fragments of the urban pollution problem. And, finally, when this astronaut made of plastic and wiring and relays went down to the City Hall officials to complain, it would discover that its three-year guarantee had run out, and, since parts were no longer available to keep it functioning, its birth certificate had been canceled.

Of course, literally, we should not take this seriously. But as a metaphor—in some broad sense maybe we should scrutinize more closely the two-legged entities we plan to send up, for example, to man the orbiting space station. We do not want to learn three years from now that the alleged human crew had all married portions of the space station and had settled down to whirr happily forever after in connubial bliss…. The *absence* of something vital—that is the horrific part, the apocalyptic vision of a nightmare future….

Becoming what I call, for lack of a better term, an android, means, as I said, to allow oneself to become a means, or to be pounded down, manipulated, made into a means without one's knowledge or consent—the results are the same. But you cannot turn a human into an android if that human is going to break laws every chance he gets. Androidization requires obedience. And, most of all, *predictability.* It is precisely when a given person's response to any given situation can be predicted with scientific accuracy that the gates are open for the wholesale production of the android life form. What good is a flashlight if the bulb lights up only now and then when you press the button? Any machine must always work to be reliable. The android, like any other machine, must perform on cue. But our youth cannot be counted on to do this; it is unreliable. Either through laziness, short attention span, perversity, criminal tendencies whatever label you wish to pin on the kid to explain his unreliability is fine. Each merely means: We can tell him and tell him what to do, but when the time comes for him to perform, all the subliminal instruction, all the ideological briefing, all the tranquilizing drugs, all the psychotherapy are a waste. He just plain will not jump when the whip is cracked….

What has happened is that there has been too much persuasion. The television set, the newspapers—all the so-called mass media—have overdone it. Words have ceased to mean much to these kids; they have had to listen to too many. They cannot be taught because there has been too great an eagerness, too conspicuous a motive, to make them learn. The anti-utopia science fiction writers of fifteen years ago, and I was one of them, foresaw the mass communications propaganda machinery grinding everyone down into mediocrity and uniformity. But it is not coming out this way.... The totalitarian society envisioned by George Orwell in *1984* should have arrived by now. The electronic gadgets are here. The government is here, ready to do what Orwell anticipated. So the power exists, the motive and the electronic hardware. But these mean nothing, because, progressively more and more so, no one is listening.... The absolutely horrible technological society—that was our dream, our vision of the future. We could foresee nothing equipped with enough power, guile, or whatever to impede the coming of that dreadful, nightmare society. It never occurred to us that the delinquent kids might abort it out of the sheer perverse malice of their little individual souls, God bless them....

Speaking in science fiction terms, I now foresee an anarchistic, totalitarian state ahead.... If, as it seems, we are in the process of becoming a totalitarian society in which the state apparatus is all-powerful, the ethics most important for the survival of the true, human individual would be: Cheat, lie, evade, fake it, be elsewhere, forge documents, build improved electronic gadgets in your garage that'll outwit the gadgets used by the authorities. If the television screen is going to watch you, rewire it late at night when you're permitted to turn it off—rewire it in such a way that the police flunky monitoring the transmission from your living room mirrors back *his* house.

I wonder if you recall the "brain mapping" developed by Penfield recently; he was able to locate the exact centers of the brain from which each sensation, emotion, and response came. By stimulating one minute area with an electrode, a laboratory rat was transfigured into a state of perpetual bliss. "They'll be doing that to all of us, too, soon," a pessimistic friend said to me regarding that. "Once the electrodes have been implanted, they can get us to feel, think, do anything they want." Well, to do this, the government would have to let out a contract for the manufacture of a billion sets of electrodes, and in their customary way, they would award the contract to the lowest bidder, who would build substandard electrodes out of secondhand parts.

The technicians implanting the electrodes in the brains of millions upon millions of people would become bored and careless, and, when the switch would be pressed for the total population to feel profound grief at the death of some government official—probably the minister of the interior, in charge of the slave-labor rehabilitation camps—it would all get folded up, and the population, like that laboratory rat, would go into collective seizures of merriment. Or the substandard wiring connecting the brains of the population with the Washington, D.C., thought control center would overload, and a surge of electricity would roll backward over the lines and set fire to the White House.

Or is this just wishful thinking on my part? A little fantasy about a future society we should really feel apprehensive about?

The continued elaboration of state tyranny such as we in science fiction circles anticipate in the world of tomorrow—our whole preoccupation with what we call the "anti-utopian" society—this growth of state invasion into the privacy of the individual, its knowing too much about him, and then, when it knows, or thinks it knows, something it frowns on, its power and capacity to squash the individual—as we thoroughly comprehend, this evil process utilizes technology as its instrument. The inventions of applied science, such as the almost miraculously sophisticated sensor devices right now traveling back from war use in Vietnam for adaptation to civilian use here—these passive infrared scanners, sniperscopes, these chrome boxes with dials and gauges that can penetrate brick and stone, can tell the user what is being said and done a mile away within a tightly sealed building, be it concrete bunker or apartment building, can, like the weapons before them, fall into what the authorities would call "the wrong hands"—that is, into the hands of the very people being monitored. Like all machines, these universal transmitters, recording devices, heat-pattern discriminators, don't in themselves care who they're used by or against....

At one time—you may have read this in biographical material accompanying my stories and novels—I was interested in experimenting with psychedelic drugs. That is over for me. Too many suicides, psychoses, organic—irreversible—damage to both heart and brain. But there are other drugs, not illegal, not street drugs, not cut with flash powder or milk sugar, and not mislabeled, that worry me even more. These are reputable, establish-ment drugs prescribed by reputable doctors or given in reputable hospitals, especially psychiatric hospitals. These are pacification drugs. I mention this in order to return to my main preoccupation, here: the human versus the android, and how the former can become—can, in fact, be made to become—the latter. The calculated, widespread, and thoroughly sanctioned use of specific tranquilizing drugs such as the phenothiazines may not, like certain illegal street drugs, produce permanent brain damage, but they can—and, God forbid, they'd—produce what I am afraid I must call "soul" damage. Let me amplify.

It has been discovered recently that what we call mental illness or mental disturb-ance—such syndromes as the schizophrenias and the cy clothemic phenomena of manic-depression—may have to do with faulty brain metabolism, the failure of certain brain catalysts such as serotonin and noradrenaline to act properly. One theory holds that, under stress, too much amine oxidase production causes hallucinations, disorient-ation, and general mentational breakdown. Sudden shock, especially at random, and grief-producing, such as loss of someone or something dear, or the loss of something vital and taken for granted—this starts an overproduction of noradrenaline flowing down generally unused neural pathways, overloading brain circuits and producing behavior that we call psychotic. Mental illness, then, is a biochemical phenomenon. If certain drugs, such as the phenothiazines, are introduced, brain metabolism regains normal balance;

the catalyst serotonin is utilized properly, and the patient recovers. Or if the MAOI drug is introduced—a monoamine oxidase inhibitor—response to stress becomes viable and the person is able to function normally. Or—and this right now is the Prince Charming hope of the medical profession—lithium carbonate, if taken by the disturbed patient, will limit an otherwise overabundant production or release of the hormone noradrenaline, which, most of all, acts to cause irrational thoughts and behavior of a socially unaccept-able sort. The entire amplitude of feelings, wild grief, anger, fear, and all intense feelings will be reduced to proper measure by the presence of the lithium carbonate in the brain tissue. The person will become stable, predictable, not a menace to others. He will feel the same and think the same pretty much all day long, day after day. The authorities will not be greeted by any more sudden surprises emanating from him.

In the field of abnormal psychology, the schizoid personality structure is well defined; in it there is a continual paucity of feeling. The person thinks rather than feels his way through life. And as the great Swiss psychiatrist Carl Jung showed, this cannot be successfully maintained; one must meet most of crucial reality with a feeling response. Anyhow, there is a certain parallel between what I call the "android" personality and the schizoid. Both have a mechanical, reflex quality.

Once I heard a schizoid person express himself—in all seriousness—this way: "I receive signals from others. But I can't generate any of my own until I get recharged. By an injection." I am, I swear, quoting exactly. Imagine viewing oneself and others this way. Signals. As if from another star. The person has reified himself entirely, along with everyone around him. How awful. Here, clearly, the soul is dead or never lived.

Another quality of the android mind is an inability to make exceptions. Perhaps this is the essence of it: the failure to drop a response when it fails to accomplish results, but rather to repeat it, over and over again. Lower life forms are skillful in offering the same response continually, as are flashlights. An attempt was made once to use a pigeon as a qualitycontrol technician on an assembly line. Part after part, endless thousands of them, passed by the pigeon hour after hour, and the keen eye of the pigeon viewed them for deviations from the acceptable tolerance. The pigeon could discern a deviation smaller than that which a human, doing the same quality control, could. When the pigeon saw a part that was mismade, it pecked a button, which rejected the part, and at the same time dropped a grain of corn to the pigeon as a reward. The pigeon could go eighteen hours without fatigue and loved its work. Even when the grain of corn failed—due to the supply running out, I guess—the pigeon continued eagerly to reject the substandard parts. It had to be forcibly removed from its perch, finally.

Now, if I had been that pigeon, I would have cheated. When I felt hungry, I would have pecked the button and rejected a part, just to get my grain of corn. That would have occurred to me after a long period passed in which I discerned no faulty parts. Because what would happen to the pigeon if, God forbid, *no* parts ever were faulty? The pigeon would starve. Integrity, under such circumstances, would be suicidal. Really, the pigeon had a life-and-death interest in finding faulty parts. What would you do, were you the pigeon, and, after say four days, you'd discovered no faulty parts and were becoming only feathers and bone? Would ethics win out? Or the need to survive? To me, the life of the pigeon would be worth more than the accuracy of the quality control. If I were the pigeon—but the android mind, "I may be dying of hunger," the android would say, "but I'll be damned if I'll reject a perfectly good part." Anyhow, to me, the authentically human mind would get bored and reject a part now and then at random, just to break the monotony. And no amount of circuit testing would reestablish its reliability….

I have never had too high a regard for what is generally called "reality." Reality, to me, is not so much something that you perceive, but something you make. You create it more rapidly than it creates you. Man is the reality God created out of dust; God is the reality man creates con tinually out of his own passions, his own determination. "Good," for example—that is not a quality or even a force in the world or above the world, but what you do with the bits and pieces of meaningless, puzzling, disappointing, even cruel and crushing fragments all around us that seem to be pieces left over, discarded, from another world entirely that did, maybe, make sense.

The world of the future, to me, is not a place but an event. A construct, not by one author in the form of words written to make up a novel or story that other persons sit in front of, outside of, and read—but a construct in which there is no author and no readers but a great many characters in search of a plot. Well, there is no plot. There is only themselves and what they do and say to each other, what they build to sustain all of them individually and collectively, like a huge umbrella that lets in light and shuts out the darkness at the same instant. When the characters die, the novel ends. And the book falls back into dust…. And a new cycle begins; … and the story, or another story, perhaps different, even better, starts up. A story told by the characters to one another. "A tale of sound and fury"—signifying very much. The best we have….

In my novel *The Three Stigmata of Palmer Eldritch*, which is a study of absolute evil, the protagonist, after his encounter with Eldritch, returns to Earth and dictates a memo. This little section appears ahead of the text of the novel. It *is* the novel, actually, this paragraph; the rest is a sort of postmortem, or rather, a flashback in which all that came to produce the one-paragraph book is presented. Seventy-five thousand words, which I labored over many months, merely explains, is merely there to provide background to the one small statement in the book that matters. (It is, by the way, missing from the German edition.) This statement is for me my credo—not so much in God, either a good god or a bad god or both—but in ourselves. It goes as follows, and this is all I actually have to say or want ever to say:

I mean, after all; you have to consider, we're only made out of dust. That's admittedly not much to go on and we shouldn't forget that. But even considering, I mean it's a sort of bad beginning, we're not doing too bad. So I personally have faith that even in this lousy situation we're faced with we can make it. You get me?

This tosses a bizarre thought up into my mind: Perhaps someday a giant automated machine will roar and clank out, "From rust we are come." And another machine, sick of

dying, cradled in the arms of its woman, may sigh back, "And to rust we are returned."
And peace will fall over the barren, anxiety-stricken landscape.

Our field, science fiction, deals with that portion of the life cycle of our species that
extends ahead of us…. I, myself, can't envision that far; … our total environment, a *living*,
external environment as animate as ourselves—that is what I see and no farther. Not yet,
anyhow…. "We see as through a glass darkly," Paul in 1 Corinthians—will this someday
be rewritten as, "We see as into a passive infrared scanner darkly?" A scanner that, as in
Orwell's *1984*, is watching us all the time? Our TV tube watching back at us as we watch
it, as amused, or bored, or anyhow somewhat as entertained by what we do as we are by
what we see on its implacable face?

This, for me, is too pessimistic, too paranoid. I believe 1 Corinthians will be rewritten
this way: "The passive infrared scanner sees into *us* darkly"—that is, not well enough
really to figure us out. Not that we ourselves can really figure each other out, or even our
own selves. Which, perhaps, too, is good; it means we are still in for sudden surprises
and unlike the authorities, who don't like that sort of thing, we may find these chance
happenings acting on our behalf, to our favor.

Sudden surprises, by the way—and this thought may be in itself a sudden surprise to
you—are a sort of antidote to the paranoid … or, to be accurate about it, to live in such a
way as to encounter sudden surprises quite often or even now and then as an indication
that you are not paranoid, because to the paranoid, nothing is a surprise; everything
happens exactly as he expected, and sometimes even more so. It all fits into his system.
For us, though, there can be no system; maybe *all* systems—that is, any theoretical,
verbal, symbolic, semantic, etc., formulation that attempts to act as an all-encompassing,
all-explaining hypothesis of what the universe is about—are manifestations of paranoia. We should be content with the mysterious, the meaningless, the contradictory, the
hostile, and most of all the unexplainably warm and giving—total so-called inanimate
environment, in other words very much like a person, like the behavior of one intricate,
subtle, half-veiled, deep, perplexing, and much-to-be-loved human being to another. To
be feared a little, too, sometimes. And perpetually misunderstood. About which we can
neither know nor be sure; and we must only trust and make guesses toward. Not being
what you thought, not doing right by you, not being just, but then sustaining you as by
momentary caprice, but then abandoning you, or at least seeming to. What it is actually
up to we may never know. But at least this is better, is it not, than to possess the self-defeating, life-defeating spurious certitude of the paranoid—expressed, by a friend of mine,
humorously, I *guess*, like this: "Doctor, someone is putting something in my food it make
me paranoid." The doctor should have asked, was that person putting it in his food free,
or charging him for it?

To refer back a final time to an early science fiction work with which we are all familiar,
the Bible: A number of stories in our field have been written in which computers print out
portions of that august book. I now herewith suggest this idea for a future society; that a
computer print out a man.

Or, if it can't get that together, then, as a second choice, a very poor one in comparison, a condensed version of the Bible, "In the beginning was the end." Or should it go the other way? "In the end was the beginning." Whichever. Randomness, in time, will sort out which it is to be. Fortunately, I am not required to make that choice.

Perhaps, when a computer is ready to churn forth one or the other of these two statements, an android, operating the computer, will make the decision- although, if I am correct about the android mentality, it will be unable to decide and will print out both at once, creating a self-canceling nothing, which will not even serve as a primordial chaos. An android might, however, be able to handle this; capable of some sort of decision making power, it might conceivably pick one statement or the other as quote "correct." But no android—and you will recall and realize that by this term I am summing up that which is not human—no android would think to do what a bright-eyed little girl I know did, something a little bizarre, certainly ethically questionable in several ways, at least in any traditional sense, but to me truly human in that it shows, to me, a spirit of merry defiance, of spirited, although not spiritual, bravery and uniqueness:

One day while driving along in her car she found herself following a truck carrying cases of Coca-Cola bottles, case after case, stacks of them. And when the truck parked, she parked behind it and loaded the back of her own car with cases, as many cases, of bottles of Coca-Cola as she could get in. So, for weeks afterward, she and her friends had all the Coca Cola they could drink, free—and then, when the bottles were empty, she carried them to the store and turned them in for the deposit refund.

To that, I say this: God bless her. May she live forever. And the Coca Cola Company and the phone company and all the rest of it, with their passing infrared scanners and sniperscopes and suchlike—may they be gone long ago. Metal and stone and wire and thread did never live. But she and her friends—they, our human future, are our little song. "Who knows if the spirit of man travels up, and the breath of beasts travels down under the Earth?" the Bible asks. Someday it, in a later revision, may wonder, "Who knows if the spirit of men travels up, and the breath of *androids* travels down?" Where do the souls of androids go after their death? But—if they do not live, then they cannot die. And if they cannot die, then they will always be with us. Do they have souls at all? Or, for that matter, do we?

I think, as the Bible says, we all go to a common place. But it is not the grave; it is into life beyond. The world of the future.

24

A cyborg manifesto: Science, technology, and socialist-feminism in the late twentieth century

Donna Haraway

An ironic dream of a common language for women in the integrated circuit

This essay is an effort to build an ironic political myth faithful to feminism, socialism, and materialism. Perhaps more faithful as blasphemy is faithful, than as reverent worship and identification. Blasphemy has always seemed to require taking things very seriously. I know no better stance to adopt from within the secular-religious, evangelical traditions of United States politics, including the politics of socialist feminism. Blasphemy protects one from the moral majority within, while still insisting on the need for community. Blasphemy is not apostasy. Irony is about contradictions that do not resolve into larger wholes, even dialectically, about the tension of holding incompatible things together because both or all are necessary and true. Irony is about humor and serious play. It is also a rhetorical strategy and a political method, one I would like to see more honored within socialist-feminism. At the center of my ironic faith, my blasphemy, is the image of the cyborg.

A cyborg is a cybernetic organism, a hybrid of machine and organism, a creature of social reality as well as a creature of fiction. Social reality is lived social relations, our most important political construction, a world-changing fiction. The international women's movements have constructed "women's experience," as well as uncovered or discovered this crucial collective object. This experience is a fiction and fact of the most crucial, political kind. Liberation rests on the construction of the consciousness, the imaginative apprehension, of oppression, and so of possibility. The cyborg is a matter of fiction and lived experience that changes what counts as women's experience in the late twentieth century. This is a struggle over life and death, but the boundary between science fiction and social reality is an optical illusion.

Contemporary science fiction is full of cyborgs—creatures simultaneously animal and machine, who populate worlds ambiguously natural and crafted. Modern medicine is also full of cyborgs, of couplings between organism and machine, each conceived as coded devices, in an intimacy and with a power that was not generated in the history of sexuality. Cyborg "sex" restores some of the lovely replicative baroque of ferns and invertebrates (such nice organic prophylactics against heterosexism). Cyborg replication is uncoupled from organic reproduction. Modern production seems like a dream of cyborg colonization work, a dream that makes the nightmare of Taylorism seem idyllic. And modern war is a cyborg orgy, coded by C3I, command-control-communication-intelligence, an $84 billion item in 1984's US defence budget. I am making an argument for the cyborg as a fiction mapping our social and bodily reality and as an imaginative resource suggesting some very fruitful couplings. Michael Foucault's biopolitics is a flaccid premonition of cyborg politics, a very open field.

By the late twentieth century, our time, a mythic time, we are all chimeras, theorized and fabricated hybrids of machine and organism; in short, we are cyborgs. The cyborg is our ontology; it gives us our politics. The cyborg is a condensed image of both imagination and material reality, the two joined centers structuring any possibility of historical transformation. In the traditions of "Western" science and politics—the tradition of racist, male-dominant capitalism; the tradition of progress; the tradition of the appropriation of nature as resource for the productions of culture; the tradition of reproduction of the self from the reflections of the other—the relation between organism and machine has been a border war. The stakes in the border war have been the territories of production, reproduction, and imagination. This chapter is an argument for pleasure in the confusion of boundaries and for responsibility in their construction. It is also an effort to contribute to socialist-feminist culture and theory in a postmodernist, non-naturalist mode and in the utopian tradition of imagining a world without gender, which is perhaps a world without genesis, but maybe also a world without end. The cyborg incarnation is outside salvation history. Nor does it mark time on an oedipal calendar, attempting to heal the terrible cleavages of gender in an oral symbiotic utopia or post-oedipal apocalypse. As Zoe Sofoulis argues in her unpublished manuscript on Jacques Lacan, Melanie Klein, and nuclear culture, *Lacklein*, the most terrible and perhaps the most promising monsters in cyborg worlds are embodied in non-oedipal narratives with a different logic of repression, which we need to understand for our survival.

The cyborg is a creature in a post-gender world; it has no truck with bisexuality, pre-oedipal symbiosis, unalienated labor, or other seductions to organic wholeness through a final appropriation of all the powers of the parts into a higher unity. In a sense, the cyborg has no origin story in the Western sense—a "final" irony since the cyborg is also the awful apocalyptic telos of the "West's" escalating dominations of abstract individuation, an ultimate self untied at last from all dependency, a man in space. An origin story in the "Western," humanist sense depends on the myth of original unity, fullness, bliss and terror, represented by the phallic mother from whom all humans must separate, the task of individual development and of history, the twin potent myths inscribed most powerfully for us in psychoanalysis and Marxism. Hilary Klein has argued that both Marxism and psychoanalysis, in their concepts of labor and of individuation and gender formation, depend on the plot of original unity out of which difference must be produced and enlisted in a drama of escalating domination of woman/nature. The cyborg skips the step of original unity, of identification with nature in the Western sense. This is its illegitimate promise that might lead to subversion of its teleology as star wars.

The cyborg is resolutely committed to partiality, irony, intimacy, and perversity. It is oppositional, utopian, and completely without innocence. No longer structured by the polarity of public and private, the cyborg defines a technological polis based partly on a revolution of social relations in the oikos, the household. Nature and culture are reworked; the one can no longer be the resource for appropriation or incorporation by the other. The relationships for forming wholes from parts, including those of polarity and hierarchical domination, are at issue in the cyborg world. Unlike the hopes of *Frankenstein's monster*, the cyborg does not expect its father to save it through a restoration of the garden; that is, through the fabrication of a heterosexual mate, through its completion in a finished whole, a city and cosmos. The cyborg does not dream of community on the model of the organic family, this time without the oedipal project. The cyborg would not recognize the Garden of Eden; it is not made of mud and cannot dream of returning to dust. Perhaps that is why I want to see if cyborgs can subvert the apocalypse of returning to nuclear dust in the manic compulsion to name the Enemy. Cyborgs are not reverent; they do not re-member the cosmos. They are wary of holism, but needy for connection—they seem to have a natural feel for united front politics, but without the vanguard party. The main trouble with cyborgs, of course, is that they are the illegitimate offspring of militarism and patriarchal capitalism, not to mention state socialism. But illegitimate offspring are often exceedingly unfaithful to their origins. Their fathers, after all, are inessential.

I will return to the science fiction of cyborgs at the end of this chapter, but now I want to signal three crucial boundary breakdowns that make the following political-fictional (polit- ical-scientific) analysis possible. By the late twentieth century in United States scientific culture, the boundary between human and animal is thoroughly breached. The last beach- heads of uniqueness have been polluted if not turned into amusement parks—language tool use, social behavior, mental events, nothing really convincingly settles the separation of human and animal. And many people no longer feel the need for such a separation; indeed, many branches of feminist culture affirm the pleasure of connection of human and other living creatures. Movements for animal rights are not irrational denials of human uniqueness; they are a clear-sighted recognition of connection across the discredited breach of nature and culture. Biology and evolutionary theory over the last two centuries have simultaneously produced modern organisms as objects of knowledge and reduced the line between humans and animals to a faint trace re-etched in ideological struggle or professional disputes between life and social science. Within this framework, teaching modern Christian creationism should be fought as a form of child abuse.

Biological-determinist ideology is only one position opened up in scientific culture for arguing the meanings of human animality. There is much room for radical political people to contest the meanings of the breached boundary. The cyborg appears in myth precisely where the boundary between human and animal is transgressed. Far from signaling a walling off of people from other living beings, cyborgs signal disturbingly and pleasurably tight coupling. Bestiality has a new status in this cycle of marriage exchange.

The second leaky distinction is between animal-human (organism) and machine. Pre-cybernetic machines could be haunted; there was always the specter of the ghost in the machine. This dualism structured the dialogue between materialism and idealism that was settled by a dialectical progeny, called spirit or history, according to taste. But basically machines were not self-moving, self-designing, autonomous. They could not achieve man's dream, only mock it. They were not man, an author to himself, but only a caricature of that masculinist reproductive dream. To think they were otherwise was paranoid. Now we are not so sure. Late twentieth-century machines have made thoroughly ambiguous the difference between natural and artificial, mind and body, self-developing and externally designed, and many other distinctions that used to apply to organisms and machines. Our machines are disturbingly lively, and we ourselves frighteningly inert.

Technological determination is only one ideological space opened up by the reconceptions of machine and organism as coded texts through which we engage in the play of writing and reading the world. "Textualization" of everything in poststructuralist, postmodernist theory has been damned by Marxists and socialist feminists for its utopian disregard for the lived relations of domination that ground the "play" of arbitrary reading. It is certainly true that postmodernist strategies, like my cyborg myth, subvert myriad organic wholes (for example, the poem, the primitive culture, the biological organism). In short, the certainty of what counts as nature—a source of insight and promise of innocence—is undermined, probably fatally. The transcendent authorization of interpretation is lost, and with it the ontology grounding "Western" epistemology. But the alternative is not cynicism or faithlessness, that is, some version of abstract existence, like the accounts of technological determinism destroying "man" by the "machine" or "meaningful political action" by the "text." Who cyborgs will be is a radical question; the answers are a matter of survival. Both chimpanzees and artefacts have politics, so why shouldn't we …?

The third distinction is a subset of the second: the boundary between physical and non-physical is very imprecise for us. Pop physics books on the consequences of quantum theory and the indeterminacy principle are a kind of popular scientific equivalent to Harlequin romances as a marker of radical change in American white heterosexuality: they get it wrong, but they are on the right subject. Modern machines are quintessentially microelectronic devices: they are everywhere and they are invisible. Modern machinery is an irreverent upstart god, mocking the Father's ubiquity and spirituality. The silicon chip is a surface for writing; it is etched in molecular scales disturbed only by atomic noise, the ultimate interference for nuclear scores. Writing, power, and technology are old partners in Western stories of the origin of civilization, but miniaturization has changed our experience of mechanism. Miniaturization has turned out to be about power; small is not so much beautiful as pre-eminently dangerous, as in cruise missiles. Contrast the TV sets of the 1950s or the news cameras of the 1970s with the TV wristbands or hand-sized video cameras now advertised. Our best machines are made of sunshine; they are all light and clean because they are nothing but signals, electromagnetic waves, a section of a spectrum, and these machines are eminently portable, mobile—a matter of immense human pain in Detroit and Singapore. People are nowhere near so fluid, being both material and opaque. Cyborgs are ether, quintessence.

The ubiquity and invisibility of cyborgs is precisely why these sunshine-belt machines are so deadly. They are as hard to see politically as materially. They are about consciousness—or its simulation. They are floating signifiers moving in pickup trucks across Europe, blocked more effectively by the witch-weavings of the displaced and so unnatural Greenham women, who read the cyborg webs of power so very well, than by the militant labor of older masculinist politics, whose natural constituency needs defense jobs. Ultimately the "hardest" science is about the realm of greatest boundary confusion, the realm of pure number, pure spirit, C3I, cryptography, and the preservation of potent secrets. The new machines are so clean and light. Their engineers are sun-worshippers mediating a new scientific revolution associated with the night dream of post-industrial society. The diseases evoked by these clean machines are "no more" than the minuscule coding changes of an antigen in the immune system, "no more" than the experience of stress. The nimble fingers of "Oriental" women, the old fascination of little Anglo-Saxon Victorian girls with doll's houses, women's enforced attention to the small take on quite new dimensions in this world. There might be a cyborg Alice taking account of these new dimensions. Ironically, it might be the unnatural cyborg women making chips in Asia and spiral dancing in Santa Rita jail whose constructed unities will guide effective oppositional strategies.

So my cyborg myth is about transgressed boundaries, potent fusions, and dangerous possibilities which progressive people might explore as one part of needed political work. One of my premises is that most American socialists and feminists see deepened dualisms of mind and body, animal and machine, idealism and materialism in the social practices, symbolic formulations, and physical artefacts associated with "high technology" and scientific culture. From *One-Dimensional Man* (Marcuse, 1964) to *The Death of Nature* (Merchant, 1980), the analytic resources developed by progressives have insisted on the necessary domination of technics and recalled us to an imagined organic body to integrate our resistance. Another of my premises is that the need for unity of people trying to resist world-wide intensification of domination has never been more acute. But a slightly perverse shift of perspective might better enable us to contest for meanings, as well as for other forms of power and pleasure in technologically mediated societies.

From one perspective, a cyborg world is about the final imposition of a grid of control on the planet, about the final abstraction embodied in a Star Wars apocalypse waged in the name of defence, about the final appropriation of women's bodies in a masculinist orgy of war. From another perspective, a cyborg world might be about lived social and bodily realities in which people are not afraid of their joint kinship with animals and machines, not afraid of permanently partial identities and contradictory standpoints. The political struggle is to see from both perspectives at once because each reveals both dominations and possibilities unimaginable from the other vantage point. Single vision produces worse illusions than double vision or many-headed monsters. Cyborg unities are monstrous and illegitimate; in our present political circumstances, we could hardly hope for more potent myths for resistance and recoupling. I like to imagine LAG, the Livermore Action Group, as a kind of cyborg society, dedicated to realistically convert- ing the laboratories that most fiercely embody and spew out the tools of technological apocalypse, and committed to building a political form that actually manages to hold together witches, engineers, elders, perverts, Christians, mothers, and Leninists long enough to disarm the state. Fission Impossible is the name of the affinity group in my town. (Affinity: related not by blood but by choice, the appeal of one chemical nuclear group for another, avidity.)

Fractured identities

It has become difficult to name one's feminism by a single adjective—or even to insist in every circumstance upon the noun. Consciousness of exclusion through naming is acute. Identities seem contradictory, partial, and strategic. With the hard-won recognition of their social and historical constitution, gender, race, and class cannot provide the basis for belief in "essential" unity. There is nothing about teeing "female" that naturally binds women. There is not even such a state as "being" female, itself a highly complex category constructed in contested sexual scientific discourses and other social practices. Gender, race, or class consciousness is an achievement forced on us by the terrible historical experience of the contradictory social realities of patriarchy, colonialism, and capitalism. And who counts as "us" in my own rhetoric? Which identities are available to ground such a potent political myth called "us," and what could motivate enlistment in this collectiv- ity? Painful fragmentation among feminists (not to mention among women) along every possible fault line has made the concept of woman elusive, an excuse for the matrix of women's dominations of each other. For me—and for many who share a similar historical location in white, professional middle-class, female, radical, North American, mid-adult bodies—the sources of a crisis in political identity are legion. The recent history for much of the US left and US feminism has been a response to this kind of crisis by endless split- ting and searches for a new essential unity. But there has also been a growing recognition of another response through coalition—affinity, not identity.

Chela Sandoval, from a consideration of specific historical moments in the formation of the new political voice called women of color, has theorized a hopeful model of political identity called "oppositional consciousness," born of the skills for reading webs of power by those refused stable membership in the social categories of race, sex, or class. "Women of color," a name contested at its origins by those whom it would incorporate, as well as a historical consciousness marking systematic breakdown of all the signs of

Man in "Western" traditions, constructs a kind of postmodernist identity out of otherness, difference, and specificity. This postmodernist identity is fully political, whatever might be said about other possible postmodernisms. Sandoval's oppositional consciousness is about contradictory locations and heterochronic calendars, not about relativisms and pluralisms.

Sandoval emphasizes the lack of any essential criterion for identifying who is a woman of color. She notes that the definition of the group has been by conscious appropriation of negation. For example, a Chicana or US black woman has not been able to speak as a woman or as a black person or as a Chicano. Thus, she was at the bottom of a cascade of negative identities, left out of even the privileged oppressed authorial categories called "women and blacks," who claimed to make the important revolutions. The category "woman" negated all non-white women; "black" negated all non-black people, as well as all black women. But there was also no "she," no singularity, but a sea of differences among US women who have affirmed their historical identity as US women of color. This identity marks out a self-consciously constructed space that cannot affirm the capacity to act on the basis of natural identification, but only on the basis of conscious coali-tion, of affinity, of political kinship. Unlike the "woman" of some streams of the white women's movement in the United States, there is no naturalization of the matrix, or at least this is what Sandoval argues is uniquely available through the power of oppositional consciousness.

Sandoval's argument has to be seen as one potent formulation for feminists out of the world-wide development of anti-colonialist discourse; that is to say, discourse dissolving the "West" and its highest product—the one who is not animal, barbarian, or woman; man, that is, the author of a cosmos called history. As orientalism is deconstructed politically and semiotically, the identities of the occident destabilize, including those of feminists. Sandoval argues that "women of color" have a chance to build an effective unity that does not replicate the imperializing, totalizing revolutionary subjects of previ-ous Marxisms and feminisms which had not faced the consequences of the disorderly polyphony emerging from decolonization. ...

Taxonomies of feminism produce epistemologies to police deviation from official women's experience. And of course, "women's culture," like women of color, is consciously created by mechanisms inducing affinity. The rituals of poetry, music, and certain forms of academic practice have been pre-eminent. The politics of race and culture in the US women's movements are intimately interwoven. The [challenge] ... is learning how to craft a poetic/political unity without relying on a logic of appropriation, incorporation, and taxonomic identification.

The theoretical and practical struggle against unity-through-domination or unity-through-incorporation ironically not only undermines the justifications for patriarchy, colonialism, humanism, positivism, essentialism, scientism, and other unlamented -isms, but all claims for an organic or natural standpoint. I think that radical and socialist/Marxist-feminisms have also undermined their/our own epistemological strategies and that this is a crucially valuable step in imagining possible unities. It remains to be seen whether all "epistemologies" as Western political people have known them fail us in the task to build effective affinities.

It is important to note that the effort to construct revolutionary standpoints, epistemologies as achievements of people committed to changing the world, has been part of the process showing the limits of identification. The acid tools of postmodernist theory and the constructive tools of ontological discourse about revolutionary subjects might be seen as ironic allies in dissolving Western selves in the interests of survival. We are excruciatingly conscious of what it means to have a historically constituted body. But with the loss of innocence in our origin, there is no expulsion from the Garden either. Our politics lose the indulgence of guilt with the naïveté of innocence. But what would another political myth for socialist-feminism look like? What kind of politics could embrace partial, contradictory, permanently unclosed constructions of personal and collective selves and still be faithful, effective—and, ironically, socialist-feminist?

I do not know of any other time in history when there was greater need for political unity to confront effectively the dominations of "race," "gender," "sexuality," "and "class." I also do not know of any other time when the kind of unity we might help build could have been possible. None of "us" have any longer the symbolic or material capability of dictating the shape of reality to any of "them." Or at least "we" cannot claim innocence from practicing such dominations. White women, including socialist feminists, discovered (that is, were forced kicking and screaming to notice) the non-innocence of the category "woman." That consciousness changes the geography of all previous categories; it denatures them as heat denatures a fragile protein. Cyborg feminists have to argue that "we" do not want any more natural matrix of unity and that no construction is whole. Innocence, and the corollary insistence on victimhood as the only ground for insight, has done enough damage. But the constructed revolutionary subject must give late-twentieth-century people pause as well. In the fraying of identities and in the reflexive strategies for constructing them, the possibility opens up for weaving something other than a shroud for the day after the apocalypse that so prophetically ends salvation history.

Both Marxist/socialist-feminisms and radical feminisms have simultaneously naturalized and denatured the category "woman" and consciousness of the social lives of "women." Perhaps a schematic caricature can highlight both kinds of moves. Marxian socialism is rooted in an analysis of wage labor which reveals class structure. The consequence of the wage relationship is systematic alienation, as the worker is dissociated from his (sic) product. Abstraction and illusion rule in knowledge, domination rules in practice. Labor is the pre-eminently privileged category enabling the Marxist to overcome illusion and find that point of view which is necessary for changing the world. Labor is the humanizing activity that makes man; labor is an ontological category permitting the knowledge of a subject, and so the knowledge of subjugation and alienation.

In faithful filiation, socialist-feminism advanced by allying itself with the basic analytic strategies of Marxism. The main achievement of both Marxist feminists and socialist feminists was to expand the category of labor to accommodate what (some) women did, even when the wage relation was subordinated to a more comprehensive view of labor under capitalist patriarchy. In particular, women's labor in the household and women's activity as mothers generally (that is, reproduction in the socialist-feminist sense), entered theory on the authority of analogy to the Marxian concept of labor. The unity of women here rests on an epistemology based on the ontological structure of "labor." Marxist/socialist-feminism does not "naturalize" unity; it is a possible achievement based on a possible standpoint rooted in social relations. The essentializing move is in the ontological structure of labor or of its analogue, women's activity. The inheritance of Marxian humanism, with its pre-eminently Western self, is the difficulty for me. The contribution from these formulations has been the emphasis on the daily responsibility of real women to build unities, rather than to naturalize them.

Catherine MacKinnon's version of radical feminism is itself a caricature of the appropriating, incorporating, totalizing tendencies of Western theories of identity grounding action. It is factually and politically wrong to assimilate all of the diverse "moments" or "conversations" in recent women's politics named radical feminism to MacKinnon's version. But the teleological logic of her theory shows how an epistemology and ontology—including their negations—erase or police difference. Only one of the effects of MacKinnon's theory is the rewriting of the history of the polymorphous field called radical feminism. The major effect is the production of a theory of experience, of women's identity, that is a kind of apocalypse for all revolutionary standpoints. That is, the totalization built into this tale of radical feminism achieves its end—the unity of women—by enforcing the experience of and testimony to radical non-being. As for the Marxist/socialist feminist, consciousness is an achievement, not a natural fact. And MacKinnon's theory eliminates some of the difficulties built into humanist revolutionary subjects, but at the cost of radical reductionism.

MacKinnon argues that feminism necessarily adopted a different analytical strategy from Marxism, looking first not at the structure of class, but at the structure of sex/gender and its generative relationship, men's constitution and appropriation of women sexually. Ironically, MacKinnon's "ontology" constructs a non-subject, a non-being. Another's desire, not the self's labor, is the origin of "woman." She therefore develops a theory of consciousness that enforces what can count as "women's" experience—anything that names sexual violation, indeed, sex itself as far as "women" can be concerned. Feminist practice is the construction of this form of consciousness; that is, the self-knowledge of a self-who-is-not.

Perversely, sexual appropriation in this feminism still has the epistemological status of labor; that is to say, the point from which an analysis able to contribute to changing the world must flow. But sexual objectification, not alienation, is the consequence of the structure of sex/gender. In the realm of knowledge, the result of sexual objectification is illusion and abstraction. However, a woman is not simply alienated from her product, but in a deep sense does not exist as a subject, or even potential subject, since she owes her existence as a woman to sexual appropriation. To be constituted by another's desire is not the same thing as to be alienated in the violent separation of the laborer from his product.

MacKinnon's radical theory of experience is totalizing in the extreme; it does not so much marginalize as obliterate the authority of any other women's political speech and action. It is a totalization producing what Western patriarchy itself never succeeded in doing—feminists' consciousness of the non-existence of women, except as products of men's desire. I think MacKinnon correctly argues that no Marxian version of identity can firmly ground women's unity. But in solving the problem of the contradictions of any Western revolutionary subject for feminist purposes, she develops an even more authoritarian doctrine of experience. If my complaint about socialist/Marxian standpoints is their unintended erasure of polyvocal, unassimilable, radical difference made visible in anti-colonial discourse and practice, MacKinnon's intentional erasure of all difference through the device of the "essential" non-existence of women is not reassuring.

In my taxonomy, which like any other taxonomy is a re-inscription of history, radical feminism can accommodate all the activities of women named by socialist feminists as forms of labor only if the activity can somehow be sexualized. Reproduction had different tones of meanings for the two tendencies, one rooted in labor, one in sex, both calling the consequences of domination and ignorance of social and personal reality "false consciousness."

Beyond either the difficulties or the contributions in the argument of any one author, neither Marxist nor radical feminist points of view have tended to embrace the status of a partial explanation; both were regularly constituted as totalities. Western explanation has demanded as much; how else could the "Western" author incorporate its others? Each tried to annex other forms of domination by expanding its basic categories through analogy, simple listing, or addition. Embarrassed silence about race among white radical and socialist feminists was one major, devastating political consequence. History and polyvocality disappear into political taxonomies that try to establish genealogies. There was no structural room for race (or for much else) in theory claiming to reveal the construction of the category woman and social group women as a unified or totalizable whole. The structure of my caricature looks like this:

Socialist Feminism—structure of class//wage labor//alienation

labor, by analogy reproduction, by extension sex, by addition race

Radical Feminism—structure of gender//sexual appropriation//objectification

sex, by analogy labor, by extension reproduction, by addition race

In another context, the French theorist, Julia Kristeva, claimed women appeared as a historical group after the Second World War, along with groups like youth. Her dates are doubtful; but we are now accustomed to remembering that as objects of knowledge and as historical actors, "race" did not always exist, "class" has a historical genesis, and "homosexuals" are quite junior. It is no accident that the symbolic system of the family of man—and so the essence of woman—breaks up at the same moment that networks of connection among people on the planet are unprecedentedly multiple, pregnant, and complex. "Advanced capitalism" is inadequate to convey the structure of this historical moment. In the "Western" sense, the end of man is at stake. It is no accident that woman disintegrates into women in our time. Perhaps socialist feminists were not substantially guilty of producing essentialist theory that suppressed women's particularity and contradictory interests. I think we have been, at least through unreflective participation in the logics, languages, and practices of white humanism and through searching for a single ground of domination to secure our revolutionary voice. Now we have less excuse. But in the consciousness of our failures, we risk lapsing into boundless difference and giving up on the confusing task of making partial, real connection. Some differences are playful; some are poles of world historical systems of domination. "Epistemology" is about knowing the difference.

The informatics of domination

In this attempt at an epistemological and political position, I would like to sketch a picture of possible unity, a picture indebted to socialist and feminist principles of design. The frame for my sketch is set by the extent and importance of rearrangements in world-wide social relations tied to science and technology. I argue for a politics rooted in claims about fundamental changes in the nature of class, race, and gender in an emerging system of world order analogous in its novelty and scope to that created by industrial capitalism; we are living through a movement from an organic, industrial society to a polymorphous, information system—from all work to all play, a deadly game. Simultaneously material and ideological, the dichotomies may be expressed in the following chart of transitions from the comfortable old hierarchical dominations to the scary new networks I have called the informatics of domination:

Representation	Simulation
Bourgeois novel, realism	Science fiction, postmodernism
Organism	Biotic Component
Depth, integrity	Surface, boundary
Heat	Noise
Biology as clinical practice	Biology as inscription
Physiology	Communications engineering
Small group	Subsystem
Perfection	Optimization
Eugenics	Population Control
Decadence, *Magic Mountain*	Obsolescence, *Future Shock*

Hygiene	Stress Management
Microbiology, tuberculosis	Immunology, AIDS
Organic division of labor	Ergonomics/cybernetics of labor
Functional specialization	Modular construction
Reproduction	Replication
Organic sex role specialization	Optimal genetic strategies
Biological determinism	Evolutionary inertia, constraints
Community ecology	Ecosystem
Racial chain of being	Neo-imperialism, United Nations humanism
Scientific management in home/factory	Global factory/Electronic cottage
Family/Market/Factory	Women in the Integrated Circuit
Family wage	Comparable worth
Public/Private	Cyborg citizenship
Nature/Culture	Fields of difference
Co-operation	Communications enhancemenet
Freud	Lacan
Sex	Genetic engineering
Labor	Robotics
Mind	Artificial Intelligence
Second World War	Star Wars
White Capitalist Patriarchy	Informatics of Domination

This list suggests several interesting things. First, the objects on the right-hand side cannot be coded as "natural," a realization that subverts naturalistic coding for the left-hand side as well. We cannot go back ideologically or materially. It's not just that "God" is dead; so is the "goddess." Or both are revivified in the worlds charged with microelectronic and biotechnological politics. In relation to objects like biotic components, one must not think in terms of essential properties, but in terms of design, boundary constraints, rates of flows, systems logics, costs of lowering constraints. Sexual reproduction is one kind of reproductive strategy among many, with costs and benefits as a function of the system environment. Ideologies of sexual reproduction can no longer reasonably call on notions of sex and sex role as organic aspects in natural objects like organisms and families. Such reasoning will be unmasked as irrational, and ironically corporate executives reading *Playboy* and anti-porn radical feminists will make strange bedfellows in jointly unmasking the irrationalism.

Likewise for race, ideologies about human diversity have to be formulated in terms of frequencies of parameters, like blood groups or intelligence scores. It is "irrational" to invoke concepts like primitive and civilized. For liberals and radicals, the search for integrated social systems gives way to a new practice called "experimental ethnography" in which an organic object dissipates in attention to the play of writing. At the level of ideology, we see translations of racism and colonialism into languages of development and under-development, rates and constraints of modernization. Any objects or persons can be reasonably thought of in terms of disassembly and reassembly; no "natural" architectures constrain system design. The financial districts in all the world's cities, as well as the export-processing and free-trade zones, proclaim this elementary fact of "late capitalism." The entire universe of objects that can be known scientifically must be formulated as problems in communications engineering (for the managers) or theories of the text (for those who would resist). Both are cyborg semiologies.

One should expect control strategies to concentrate on boundary conditions and interfaces, on rates of flow across boundaries—and not on the integrity of natural objects. "Integrity" or "sincerity" of the Western self gives way to decision procedures and expert systems. For example, control strategies applied to women's capacities to give birth to new human beings will be developed in the languages of population control and maximization of goal achievement for individual decision-makers. Control strategies will be formulated in terms of rates, costs of constraints, degrees of freedom. Human beings, like any other component or subsystem, must be localized in a system architecture whose basic modes of operation are probabilistic, statistical. No objects, spaces, or bodies are sacred in themselves; any component can be interfaced with any other if the proper standard, the proper code, can be constructed for processing signals in a common language. Exchange in this world transcends the universal translation effected by capitalist markets that Marx analyzed so well. The privileged pathology affecting all kinds of components in this universe is stress—communications breakdown. The cyborg is not subject to Foucault's biopolitics; the cyborg simulates politics, a much more potent field of operations.

This kind of analysis of scientific and cultural objects of knowledge which have appeared historically since the Second World War prepares us to notice some important inadequacies in feminist analysis which has proceeded as if the organic, hierarchical dualisms ordering discourse in "the West" since Aristotle still ruled. They have been cannibalized, or as Zoe Sofia (Sofoulis) might put it, they have been "techno-digested." The dichotomies between mind and body, animal and human, organism and machine, public and private, nature and culture, men and women, primitive and civilized are all in question ideologically. The actual situation of women is their integration/exploitation into a world system of production/reproduction and communication called the informatics of domination. The home, workplace, market, public arena, the body itself—all can be dispersed and interfaced in nearly infinite, polymorphous ways, with large consequences for women and others—consequences that themselves are very different for different people and which make potent oppositional international movements difficult to imagine and essential for survival. One important route for reconstructing socialist-feminist politics is through theory and practice addressed to the social relations of science and technology, including crucially the systems of myth and meanings structuring our imaginations. The cyborg is a kind of disassembled and reassembled, postmodern collective and personal self. This is the self feminists must code.

Communications technologies and biotechnologies are the crucial tools recrafting our bodies. These tools embody and enforce new social relations for women world-wide. Technologies and scientific discourses can be partially understood as formalizations, i.e., as frozen moments, of the fluid social interactions constituting them, but they should also be viewed as instruments for enforcing meanings. The boundary is permeable between tool and myth, instrument and concept, historical systems of social relations and historical anatomies of possible bodies, including objects of knowledge. Indeed, myth and tool mutually constitute each other.

Furthermore, communications sciences and modern biologies are constructed by a common move—the translation of the world into a problem of coding, a search for a common language in which all resistance to instrumental control disappears and all heterogeneity can be submitted to disassembly, reassembly, investment, and exchange.

In communications sciences, the translation of the world into a problem in coding can be illustrated by looking at cybernetic (feedback-controlled) systems theories applied to telephone technology, computer design, weapons deployment, or database construction and maintenance. In each case, solution to the key questions rests on a theory of language and control; the key operation is determining the rates, directions, and probabilities of flow of a quantity called information. The world is subdivided by boundaries differentially permeable to information. Information is just that kind of quantifiable element (unit, basis of unity) which allows universal translation, and so unhindered instrumental power (called effective communication). The biggest threat to such power is interruption of communication. Any system breakdown is a function of stress. The fundamentals of this technology can be condensed into the metaphor C3I, command-control-communication-intelligence, the military's symbol for its operations theory.

In modern biologies, the translation of the world into a problem in coding can be illustrated by molecular genetics, ecology, sociobiological evolutionary theory, and immunobiology. The organism has been translated into problems of genetic coding and read-out. Biotechnology, a writing technology, informs research broadly. In a sense, organisms have ceased to exist as objects of knowledge, giving way to biotic components, i.e., special kinds of information-processing devices. The analogous moves in ecology could be examined by probing the history and utility of the concept of the ecosystem. Immunobiology and associated medical practices are rich exemplars of the privilege of coding and recognition systems as objects of knowledge, as constructions of bodily reality for us. Biology here is a kind of cryptography. Research is necessarily a kind of intelligence activity. Ironies abound. A stressed system goes awry; its communication processes break down; it fails to recognize the difference between self and other. Human babies with baboon hearts evoke national ethical perplexity—for animal rights activists at least as much as for the guardians of human purity. In the US gay men and intravenous drug users are the "privileged" victims of an awful immune system disease that marks (inscribes on the body) confusion of boundaries and moral pollution.

But these excursions into communications sciences and biology have been at a rarefied level; there is a mundane, largely economic reality to support my claim that these sciences and technologies indicate fundamental transformations in the structure of the world for us. Communications technologies depend on electronics. Modern states, multinational corporations, military power, welfare state apparatuses, satellite systems, political processes, fabrication of our imaginations, labor-control systems, medical constructions of our bodies, commercial pornography, the international division of labor, and religious evangelism depend intimately upon electronics. Micro-electronics is the technical basis of simulacra; that is, of copies without originals.

Microelectronics mediates the translations of labor into robotics and word processing, sex into genetic engineering and reproductive technologies, and mind into artificial intelligence and decision procedures. The new biotechnologies concern more than human reproduction. Biology as a powerful engineering science for redesigning materials and processes has revolutionary implications for industry, perhaps most obvious today in areas of fermentation, agriculture, and energy. Communications sciences and biology are constructions of natural-technical objects of knowledge in which the difference between machine and organism is thoroughly blurred; mind, body, and tool are on very intimate terms. The "multinational" material organization of the production and reproduction of daily life and the symbolic organization of the production and reproduction of culture and imagination seem equally implicated. The boundary-maintaining images of base and superstructure, public and private, or material and ideal never seemed more feeble.

I have used Rachel Grossman's image of women in the integrated circuit to name the situation of women in a world so intimately restructured through the social relations of science and technology. I used the odd circumlocution, "the social relations of science and technology," to indicate that we are not dealing with a technological determinism, but with a historical system depending upon structured relations among people. But the phrase should also indicate that science and technology provide fresh sources of power, that we need fresh sources of analysis and political action. Some of the rearrangements of race, sex, and class rooted in high-tech-facilitated social relations can make socialist-feminism more relevant to effective progressive politics. ...

Women in the integrated circuit

Let me summarize the picture of women's historical locations in advanced industrial societies, as these positions have been restructured partly through the social relations of science and technology. If it was ever possible ideologically to characterize women's lives by the distinction of public and private domains—suggested by images of the division of working-class life into factory and home, of bourgeois life into market and home, and of gender existence into personal and political realms—it is now a totally misleading ideology, even to show how both terms of these dichotomies construct each other in practice and in theory. I prefer a network ideological image, suggesting the profusion of spaces and identities and the permeability of boundaries in the personal body and in the body politic. "Networking" is both a feminist practice and a multinational corporate strategy—weaving is for oppositional cyborgs. ...

I want to suggest the impact of the social relations mediated and enforced by the new technologies in order to help formulate needed analysis and practical work. However, there is no "place" for women in these networks, only geometries of difference and contradiction crucial to women's cyborg identities. If we learn how to read these webs of power and social life, we might learn new couplings, new coalitions. There is no way to read the following list from a standpoint of "identification," of a unitary self. The issue is dispersion. The task is to survive in the diaspora. ...

The only way to characterize the informatics of domination is as a massive intensification of insecurity and cultural impoverishment, with common failure of subsistence networks for the most vulnerable. Since much of this picture interweaves with the social relations of science and technology, the urgency of a socialist-feminist politics addressed to science and technology is plain. There is much now being done, and the grounds for political work are rich. For example, the efforts to develop forms of collective struggle for women in paid work, like SEIU's District 925, should be a high priority for all of us. These efforts are profoundly deaf to technical restructuring of labor processes and reformations of working classes. These efforts also are providing understanding of a more comprehens- ive kind of labor organization, involving community, sexuality, and family issues never privileged in the largely white male industrial unions.

The structural rearrangements related to the social relations of science and technology evoke strong ambivalence. But it is not necessary to be ultimately depressed by the implications of late twentieth-century women's relation to all aspects of work, culture, production of knowledge, sexuality, and reproduction. For excellent reasons, most Marxisms see domination best and have trouble understanding what can only look like false consciousness and people's complicity in their own domination in late capitalism. It is crucial to remember that what is lost, perhaps especially from women's points of view, is often virulent forms of oppression, nostalgically naturalized in the face of current violation. Ambivalence towards the disrupted unities mediated by high-tech culture requires not sorting consciousness into categories of "clear-sighted critique grounding a solid political epistemology" versus "manipulated false consciousness," but subtle understanding of emerging pleasures, experiences, and powers with serious potential for changing the rules of the game.

There are grounds for hope in the emerging bases for new kinds of unity across race, gender, and class, as these elementary units of socialist-feminist analysis themselves suffer protean transformations. Intensifications of hardship experienced world-wide in connection with the social relations of science and technology are severe. But what people are experiencing is not transparently clear, and we lack sufficiently subtle connections for collectively building effective theories of experience. Present efforts—Marxist, psycho-analytic, feminist, anthropological—to clarify even "our" experience are rudimentary. ...

The permanent partiality of feminist points of view has consequences for our expecta-tions of forms of political organization and participation. We do not need a totality in order to work well. The feminist dream of a common language, like all dreams for a perfectly true language, of perfectly faithful naming of experience, is a totalizing and imperialist one. In that sense, dialectics too is a dream language, longing to resolve contradiction. Perhaps, ironically, we can learn from our fusions with animals and machines how not to be Man, the embodiment of Western logos. From the point of view of pleasure in these potent and taboo fusions, made inevitable by the social relations of science and techno-logy, there might indeed be a feminist science.

Cyborgs: a myth of political identity

I want to conclude with a myth about identity and boundaries which might inform late twentieth-century political imaginations. I am indebted in this story to writers like Joanna Russ, Samuel R. Delany, John Varley, James Tiptree, Jr, Octavia Butler, Monique Wittig, and Vonda McIntyre. These are our story-tellers exploring what it means to be embod-ied in high-tech worlds. They are theorists for cyborgs. Exploring conceptions of bodily boundaries and social order, the anthropologist Mary Douglas should be credited with helping us to consciousness about how fundamental body imagery is to world view, and so to political language.

French feminists like Luce Irigaray and Monique Wittig, for all their differences, know how to write the body; how to weave eroticism, cosmology, and politics from imagery of embodiment, and especially for Wittig, from imagery of fragmentation and reconstitution of bodies.

American radical feminists like Susan Griffin, Audre Lorde, and Adrienne Rich have profoundly affected our political imaginations—and perhaps restricted too much what we allow as a friendly body and political language. They insist on the organic, opposing it to the technological. But their symbolic systems and the related positions of ecofeminism and feminist paganism, replete with organicisms, can only be understood in Sandoval's terms as oppositional ideologies fitting the late twentieth century. They would simply bewilder anyone not preoccupied with the machines and consciousness of late capit-alism. In that sense they are part of the cyborg world. But there are also great riches for feminists in explicitly embracing the possibilities inherent in the breakdown of clean distinctions between organism and machine and similar distinctions structuring the Western self. It is the simultaneity of breakdowns that cracks the matrices of domination and opens geometric possibilities. What might be learned from personal and political "technological" pollution? I look briefly at two overlapping groups of texts for their insight into the construction of a potentially helpful cyborg myth: constructions of women of color and monstrous selves in feminist science fiction.

Earlier I suggested that "women of color" might be understood as a cyborg identity, a potent subjectivity synthesized from fusions of outsider identities. ... There are material and cultural grids mapping this potential. Audre Lorde captures the tone in the title of her *Sister Outsider*. In my political myth, Sister Outsider is the offshore woman, whom US workers, female and feminized, are supposed to regard as the enemy preventing their solidarity, threatening their security. Onshore, inside the boundary of the United States, Sister Outsider is a potential amidst the races and ethnic identities of women manipulated for division, competition, and exploitation in the same industries. "Women of color" are the preferred labor force for the science-based industries, the real women for whom the world-wide sexual market, labor market, and politics of reproduction kaleidoscope into daily life. Young Korean women hired in the sex industry and in electronics assembly are recruited from high schools, educated for the integrated circuit. Literacy, especially in English, distinguishes the "cheap" female labor so attractive to the multinationals.

Contrary to orientalist stereotypes of the "oral primidtive," literacy is a special mark of women of color, acquired by US black women as well as men through a history of risking death to learn and to teach reading and writing. Writing has a special significance for all colonized groups. Writing has been crucial to the Western myth of the distinction between oral and written cultures, primitive and civilized mentalities, and more recently to the erosion of that distinction in "postmodernis"' theories attacking the phallogo-centrism of the West, with its worship of the monotheistic, phallic, authoritative, and singular work, the unique and perfect name. Contests for the meanings of writing are a major form of contemporary political struggle. Releasing the play of writing is deadly serious. The poetry and stories of US women of color are repeatedly about writing, about access to the power to signify; but this time that power must be neither phallic nor innocent. Cyborg writing must not be about the Fall, the imagination of a once-upon-a-time wholeness before language, before writing, before Man. Cyborg writing is about the power to survive, not on the basis of original innocence, but on the basis of seizing the tools to mark the world that marked them as other.

The tools are often stories, retold stories, versions that reverse and displace the hierarchical dualisms of naturalized identities. In retelling origin stories, cyborg authors subvert the central myths of origin of Western culture. We have all been colonized by those origin myths, with their longing for fulfillment in apocalypse. The phallogocentric origin stories most crucial for feminist cyborgs are built into the literal technologies—technologies that write the world, biotechnology and microelectronics—that have recently textualized our bodies as code problems on the grid of C3I. Feminist cyborg stories have the task of recoding communication and intelligence to subvert command and control.

Figuratively and literally, language politics pervade the struggles of women of color; and stories about language have a special power in the rich contemporary writing by US women of color. For example, retellings of the story of the indigenous woman Malinche, mother of the mestizo "bastard" race of the new world, master of languages, and mistress of Cortes, carry special meaning for Chicana constructions of identity. Cherrie Moraga in

Loving in the War Years explores the themes of identity when one never possessed the original language, never told the original story, never resided in the harmony of legitimate heterosexuality in the garden of culture, and so cannot base identity on a myth or a fall from innocence and right to natural names, mother's or father's. Moraga's writing, her superb literacy, is presented in her poetry as the same kind of violation as Malinche's mastery of the conqueror's language—a violation, an illegitimate production, that allows survival. Moraga's language is not "whole"; it is self-consciously spliced, a chimera of English and Spanish, both conqueror's languages. But it is this chimeric monster, without claim to an original language before violation, that crafts the erotic, competent, potent identities of women of color. Sister Outsider hints at the possibility of world survival not because of her innocence, but because of her ability to live on the boundaries, to write without the founding myth of original wholeness, with its inescapable apocalypse of final return to a deathly oneness that Man has imagined to be the innocent and all-powerful Mother, freed at the End from another spiral of appropriation by her son. Writing marks Moraga's body, affirms it as the body of a woman of color, against the possibility of passing into the unmarked category of the Anglo father or into the orientalist myth of "original illiteracy" of a mother that never was. Malinche was mother here, not Eve before eating the forbidden fruit. Writing affirms Sister Outsider, not the Woman-before-the-Fall-into-Writing needed by the phallogocentric Family of Man.

Writing is pre-eminently the technology of cyborgs, etched surfaces of the late twentieth century. Cyborg politics is the struggle for language and the struggle against perfect communication, against the one code that translates all meaning perfectly, the central dogma of phallogocentrism. That is why cyborg politics insist on noise and advocate pollution, rejoicing in the illegitimate fusions of animal and machine. These are the coup-lings which make Man and Woman so problematic, subverting the structure of desire, the force imagined to generate language and gender, and so subverting the structure and modes of reproduction of "Western" identity, of nature and culture, of mirror and eye, slave and master, body and mind. "We" did not originally choose to be cyborgs, but choice grounds a liberal politics and epistemology that imagines the reproduction of individuals before the wider replications of "texts."

From the perspective of cyborgs, freed of the need to ground politics in "our" privileged position of the oppression that incorporates all other dominations, the innocence of the merely violated, the ground of those closer to nature, we can see powerful possibilities. Feminisms and Marxisms have run aground on Western epistemological imperatives to construct a revolutionary subject from the perspective of a hierarchy of oppressions and/or a latent position of moral superiority, innocence, and greater closeness to nature. With no available original dream of a common language or original symbiosis promising protection from hostile "masculine" separation, but written into the play of a text that has no finally privileged reading or salvation history, to recognize "oneself" as fully implicated in the world, frees us of the need to root politics in identification, vanguard parties, purity, and mothering. Stripped of identity, the bastard race teaches about the power of the margins and the importance of a mother like Malinche. Women of color have transformed her from the evil mother of masculinist fear into the originally literate mother who teaches survival.

This is not just literary deconstruction, but liminal transformation. Every story that begins with original innocence and privileges the return to wholeness imagines the drama of life to be individuation, separation, the birth of the self, the tragedy of autonomy, the fall into writing, alienation; that is, war, tempered by imaginary respite in the bosom of the Other. These plots are ruled by a reproductive politics—rebirth without flaw, perfection, abstraction. In this plot women are imagined either better or worse off, but all agree they have less selfhood, weaker individuation, more fusion to the oral, to Mother, less at stake in masculine autonomy. But there is another route to having less at stake in masculine autonomy, a route that does not pass through Woman, Primitive, Zero, the Mirror Stage and its imaginary. It passes through women and other present-tense, illegitimate cyborgs, not of Woman born, who refuse the ideological resources of victimization so as to have a real life. These cyborgs are the people who refuse to disappear on cue, no matter how many times a "Western" commentator remarks on the sad passing of another primitive, another organic group done in by "Western" technology, by writing. These real-life cyborgs ... are actively rewriting the texts of their bodies and societies. Survival is the stakes in this play of readings.

To recapitulate, certain dualisms have been persistent in Western traditions; they have all been systemic to the logics and practices of domination of women, people of color, nature, workers, animals—in short, domination of all constituted as others, whose task is to mirror the self. Chief among these troubling dualisms are self/other, mind/body, culture/ nature, male/female, civilized/primitive, reality/appearance, whole/part, agent/resource, maker/made, active/passive, right/wrong, truth/illusion, total/partial, God/man. The self is the One who is not dominated, who knows that by the service of the other, the other is the one who holds the future, who knows that by the experience of domination, which gives the lie to the autonomy of the self. To be One is to be autonomous, to be powerful, to be God; but to be One is to be an illusion, and so to be involved in a dialectic of apocalypse with the other. Yet to be other is to be multiple, without clear boundary, frayed, insubstantial. One is too few, but two are too many.

High-tech culture challenges these dualisms in intriguing ways. It is not clear who makes and who is made in the relation between human and machine. It is not clear what is mind and what body in machines that resolve into coding practices. In so far as we know ourselves in both formal discourse (for example, biology) and in daily practice ..., we find ourselves to be cyborgs, hybrids, mosaics, chimeras. Biological organisms have become biotic systems, communications devices like others. There is no fundamental, ontological separation in our formal knowledge of machine and organism, of technical and organic. The replicant Rachel in the Ridley Scott film *Blade Runner* stands as the image of a cyborg culture's fear, love, and confusion.

One consequence is that our sense of connection to our tools is heightened. The trance state experienced by many computer users has become a staple of science-fiction film and cultural jokes. Perhaps paraplegics and other severely handicapped people can (and sometimes do) have the most intense experiences of complex hybridization with other communication devices. Anne McCaffrey's pre-feminist *The Ship Who Sang* (1969) explored the consciousness of a cyborg, hybrid of girl's brain and complex machinery, formed after the birth of a severely handicapped child. Gender, sexuality, embodiment, skill: all were reconstituted in the story. Why should our bodies end at the skin, or include at best other beings encapsulated by skin? From the seventeenth century till now, machines could be animated—given ghostly souls to make them speak or move or to account for their orderly development and mental capacities. Or organisms could be mechan-ized— reduced to body understood as resource of mind. These machine/organism relationships are obsolete, unnecessary. For us, in imagination and in other practice, machines can be prosthetic devices, intimate components, friendly selves. We don't need organic holism to give impermeable whole-ness, the total woman and her feminist variants (mutants?). Let me conclude this point by a very partial reading of the logic of the cyborg monsters of my second group of texts, feminist science fiction.

The cyborgs populating feminist science fiction make very problematic the statuses of man or woman, human, artefact, member of a race, individual entity, or body. Katie King clarifies how pleasure in reading these fictions is not largely based on identification. Students facing Joanna Russ for the first time, students who have learned to take modern-ist writers like James Joyce or Virginia Woolf without flinching, do not know what to make of *The Adventures of Alyx* or *The Female Man*, where characters refuse the reader's search for innocent wholeness while granting the wish for heroic quests, exuberant eroticism, and serious politics. *The Female Man* is the story of four versions of one genotype, all of whom meet, but even taken together do not make a whole, resolve the dilemmas of violent moral action, or remove the growing scandal of gender. The feminist science fiction of Samuel R. Delany, especially *Tales of Nevèrÿon*, mocks stories of origin by redoing the neolithic revolution, replaying the founding moves of Western civilization to subvert their plausibility. James Tiptree, Jr, an author whose fiction was regarded as particularly manly until her "true" gender was revealed, tells tales of reproduction based on non-mammalian technolo-gies like alternation of generations of male brood pouches and male nurturing. John Varley constructs a supreme cyborg in his arch-feminist exploration of Gaea, a mad goddess-planet-trickster-old woman-technological device on whose surface an extraordinary array of post-cyborg symbioses are spawned. Octavia Butler writes of an African sorceress pitting her powers of transformation against the genetic manipulations of her rival (*Wild Seed*), of time warps that bring a modern US black woman into slavery where her actions in relation to her white master-ancestor determine the possibility of her own birth (*Kindred*), and of the illegitimate insights into identity and community of an adopted cross-species child who came to know the enemy as self (*Survivor*). In *Dawn* (1987), the first installment of a series called *Xenogenesis*, Butler tells the story of Lilith Iyapo, whose personal name recalls Adam's first and repudiated wife and whose family name marks her status as the widow of the son of Nigerian immigrants to the US. A black woman and a mother whose child is dead, Lilith mediates the transformation of humanity through genetic exchange with extra-terrestrial lovers/rescuers/destroyers/genetic engineers, who reform earth's habitats after the nuclear holocaust and coerce surviving humans into intimate fusion with them. It is a novel that interrogates reproductive, linguistic, and nuclear politics in a mythic field structured by late twentieth-century race and gender.

Because it is particularly rich in boundary transgressions, Vonda McIntyre's *Superluminal* can close this truncated catalogue of promising and dangerous monsters who help redefine the pleasures and politics of embodiment and feminist writing. In a fiction where no character is "simply" human, human status is highly problematic. Orca, a genetically altered diver, can speak with killer whales and survive deep ocean conditions, but she longs to explore space as a pilot, necessitating bionic implants jeopardizing her kinship with the divers and cetaceans. Transformations are effected by virus vectors carrying a new developmental code, by transplant surgery, by implants of microelectronic devices, by analogue doubles, and other means. Laenea becomes a pilot by accepting a heart implant and a host of other alterations allowing survival in transit at speeds exceeding that of light. Radu Dracul survives a virus-caused plague in his outerworld planet to find himself with a time sense that changes the boundaries of spatial perception for the whole species. All the characters explore the limits of language; the dream of communicating experience; and the necessity of limitation, partiality, and intimacy even in this world of protean transformation and connection. *Superluminal* stands also for the defining contradictions of a cyborg world in another sense; it embodies textually the intersection of feminist theory and colonial discourse in the science fiction I have alluded to in this chapter. This is a conjunction with a long history that many "First World" feminists have tried to repress, including myself in my readings of *Superluminal* before being called to account by Zoe Sofoulis, whose different location in the world system's informatics of domination made her acutely alert to the imperialist moment of all science fiction cultures, including women's science fiction. From an Australian feminist sensitivity, Sofoulis remembered more readily McIntyre's role as writer of the adventures of Captain Kirk and Spock in TV's *Star Trek* series than her rewriting the romance in *Superluminal*.

Monsters have always defined the limits of community in Western imaginations. The Centaurs and Amazons of ancient Greece established the limits of the centered polis of the Greek male human by their disruption of marriage and boundary pollutions of the warrior with animality and woman. Unseparated twins and hermaphrodites were the confused human material in early modern France who grounded discourse on the natural and supernatural, medical and legal, portents and diseases—all crucial to establishing modern identity. The evolutionary and behavioral sciences of monkeys and apes have marked the multiple boundaries of late twentieth-century industrial identities. Cyborg monsters in feminist science fiction define quite different political possibilities and limits from those proposed by the mundane fiction of Man and Woman.

There are several consequences to taking seriously the imagery of cyborgs as other than our enemies. Our bodies, ourselves; bodies are maps of power and identity. Cyborgs are no exception. A cyborg body is not innocent; it was not born in a garden; it does not seek unitary identity and so generate antagonistic dualisms without end (or until the world ends); it takes irony for granted. One is too few, and two is only one possibility. Intense pleasure in skill, machine skill, ceases to be a sin, but an aspect of embodiment. The machine is not an it to be animated, worshipped, and dominated. The machine is us, our processes, an aspect of our embodiment. We can be responsible for machines; they do not dominate or threaten us. We are responsible for boundaries; we are they. Up till now (once upon a time), female embodiment seemed to be given, organic, necessary; and female embodiment seemed to mean skill in mothering and its metaphoric extensions. Only by being out of place could we take intense pleasure in machines, and then with excuses that this was organic activity after all, appropriate to females. Cyborgs might consider more seriously the partial, fluid, sometimes aspect of sex and sexual embodiment. Gender might not be global identity after all, even if it has profound historical breadth and depth.

The ideologically charged question of what counts as daily activity, as experience, can be approached by exploiting the cyborg image. Feminists have recently claimed that women are given to dailiness, that women more than men somehow sustain daily life, and so have a privileged epistemological position potentially. There is a compelling aspect to this claim, one that makes visible unvalued female activity and names it as the ground of life. But the ground of life? What about all the ignorance of women, all the exclusions and failures of knowledge and skill? What about men's access to daily competence, to knowing how to build things, to take them apart, to play? What about other embodiments? Cyborg gender is a local possibility taking a global vengeance. Race, gender, and capital require a cyborg theory of wholes and parts. There is no drive in cyborgs to produce total theory, but there is an intimate experience of boundaries, their construction and deconstruction. There is a myth system waiting to become a political language to ground one way of looking at science and technology and challenging the informatics of domination—in order to act potently.

One last image: organisms and organismic, holistic politics depend on metaphors of rebirth and invariably call on the resources of reproductive sex. I would suggest that cyborgs have more to do with regeneration and are suspicious of the reproductive matrix and of most birthing. For salamanders, regeneration after injury, such as the loss of a limb, involves regrowth of structure and restoration of function with the constant possibility of twinning or other odd topographical productions at the site of former injury. The regrown limb can be monstrous, duplicated, potent. We have all been injured, profoundly. We require regeneration, not rebirth, and the possibilities for our reconstitution include the utopian dream of the hope for a monstrous world without gender.

Cyborg imagery can help express two crucial arguments in this essay: first, the production of universal, totalizing theory is a major mistake that misses most of reality, probably always, but certainly now; and second, taking responsibility for the social relations of science and technology means refusing an anti-science metaphysics, a demonology of technology, and so means embracing the skillful task of reconstructing the boundaries of daily life, in partial connection with others, in communication with all of our parts. It is not just that science and technology are possible means of great human satisfaction, as well as a matrix of complex dominations. Cyborg imagery can suggest a way out of the maze of dualisms in which we have explained our bodies and our tools to ourselves. This is a dream not of a common language, but of a powerful infidel heteroglossia. It is an imagination of a feminist speaking in tongues to strike fear into the circuits of the supersavers of the new right. It means both building and destroying machines, identities, categories, relationships, space stories. Though both are bound in the spiral dance, I would rather be a cyborg than a goddess.

25

Virtual bodies and flickering signifiers[1]

N. Katherine Hayles

> We might regard patterning or predictability as the very essence and raison d'être of communication . . . communication is the creation of redundancy or patterning.
>
> —Gregory Bateson, *Steps to an Ecology of Mind*

In this last decade of the twentieth century, information circulates as the currency of the realm. Genetics, warfare, entertainment, communications, grain production, and financial markets number among the sectors of society revolutionized by the shift to an information paradigm. The shift has also profoundly affected contemporary fiction. If the effects on literature are not widely recognized, perhaps it is because they are at once pervasive and elusive. A book produced by typesetting may look very similar to one generated by a computerized program, but the technological processes involved in this transformation are not neutral. Different technologies of text production suggest different models of signification; changes in signification are linked with shifts in consumption; shifting patterns of consumption initiate new experiences of embodiment; and embodied experience interacts with codes of representation to generate new kinds of textual worlds.[2] In fact, each category—production, signification, consumption, bodily experience, and representation—is in constant feedback and feedforward loops with the others. Pull any thread in the skein, and the others prove to be entangled in it.

The clue that I want to pursue through these labyrinthine passages is provided by the following proposition: *even though information provides the basis for much of contemporary society, it is never present in itself.* The site where I will pick up this thread is the development of information theory in the years following World War II. In information-theoretic terms, information is conceptually distinct from the markers that embody it, for example, newsprint or electromagnetic waves. It is a pattern rather than a presence, defined by the probability distribution of the coding elements comprising the message. If information is pattern, then noninformation should be the absence of pattern, that is, randomness. This commonsense expectation ran into unexpected complications when certain developments within information theory implied that information could be equated with randomness as well as with pattern.[3] Identifying information with *both* pattern and randomness proved to be a powerful paradox, leading to the realization that in some instances, an infusion of noise into a system can cause it to reorganize at a higher level of complexity.[4] Within such a system, pattern and randomness are bound together in a complex dialectic that makes them not so much opposites as complements or supplements to each other. Each helps to define the other; each contributes to the flow of information through the system.

Were this dialectical relation only an aspect of the formal theory, its impact might well be limited to the problems of maximizing channel utility and minimizing noise that occupy electrical engineers. Through the development of information technologies, however, the interplay between pattern and randomness became a feature of everyday life. A common site where people are initiated into this dialectic is the cathode tube display. Working at the computer screen, I cannot read unaided the magnetic markers that physically embody the information within the computer, but I am acutely aware of the patterns of blinking lights that comprise the text in its screen format. When I discover that my computerized text has been garbled because I pressed the wrong function key, I experience firsthand the intrusion of randomness into pattern.

This knowledge, moreover, is not merely conceptual. It is also sensory and kinesthetic. As Friedrich Kittler has demonstrated in *Discourse Networks 1800/1900*, typewriters exist in a discourse network underlaid by the dialectic of presence and absence.[5] The keys on a manual typewriter are directly proportionate to the script they produce. One keystroke yields one letter, and striking the key harder produces a darker letter. The system lends itself to a model of signification that links signifier to signified in direct correspondence, for there is a one-to-one relation between the key and the letter it produces. By contrast, the connection between computer keys and text manipulation is nonproportional and electronic. Display brightness is unrelated to keystroke pressure, and striking a single key can effect massive changes in the entire text. Interacting with electronic images rather than a materially resistant text, I absorb through my fingers as well as my mind a model of signification in which no simple one-to-one correspondence exists between signifier and signified. I know kinesthetically as well as conceptually that the text can be manipulated in ways that would be impossible if it existed as a material object rather than a visual display. As I work with the text-as-image, I instantiate within my body the habitual patterns of movement that make pattern and randomness more real, more relevant, and more powerful than presence and absence.[6]

In societies enmeshed within information networks, as the United States and other first-world countries are, this example can be multiplied a thousandfold. Money is increasingly experienced as informational patterns stored in computer banks rather than the presence of cash; in surrogacy and *in vitro* fertilization cases, informational genetic patterns compete with physical presence for the right to determine the "legitimate" parent; automated factories are controlled by programs that constitute the physical realities of work assignments and production schedules as flows of information through the system;[7] criminals are tied to crime scenes through DNA patterns rather than eyewitness accounts verifying their presence; right of access to computer networks rather than physical possession of the data determines nine-tenths of computer law;[8] sexual relationships are pursued through the virtual spaces of computer networks rather than through meetings at which the participants are physically present.[9] The effect of these transformations is to create a highly heterogeneous and fissured space in which discursive formations based on pattern and randomness jostle and compete with formations based on presence and absence. Given the long tradition of dominance that presence and absence have enjoyed in the Western tradition, the surprise is not that formations based on them continue to exist but that they are being displaced so rapidly across such a wide range of cultural sites.

Critical theory has also been marked by this displacement. At the same time that absence was reconceptualized in poststructuralist theory so that it is not mere nothingness but a productive force seminal to discourse and psycholinguistics, so randomness was reconceptualized in scientific fields so that it is not mere gibberish but a productive force essential to the evolution of complex systems. The parallel suggests that the dialectic between absence and presence came clearly into focus because it was already being displaced as a cultural presupposition by randomness and pattern. Presence and absence were forced into visibility, so to speak, because they were already losing their constitutive power to form the ground for discourse, becoming instead discourse's subject. In this sense deconstruction is the child of an information age, formulating its theories from strata pushed upward by the emerging substrata beneath.

The displacement of presence/absence hints at how central pattern/randomness may be in informing contemporary ideas of language, narrative, and subjectivity. The new technologies of virtual reality illustrate the kind of phenomena that foreground pattern and randomness and make presence and absence seem irrelevant. Already an industry worth hundreds of millions, virtual reality puts the user's sensory system into a direct feedback loop with a computer.[10] In one version, the user wears a stereovision helmet and a body suit with sensors at joint positions. The user's movements are reproduced by a simulacrum on the computer screen called a puppet. When the user turns her head, the computer display changes in a corresponding fashion. At the same time, audiophones create a three-dimensional sound field. Kinesthetic sensations, such as G-loads for flight simulators, can be supplied by the body suit. The result is a multisensory interaction that creates the illusion the user is *inside* the computer. From my experience with the virtual reality simulations at the Human Interface Technology Laboratory and elsewhere, I can attest to the disorienting, exhilarating effect of feeling that subjectivity is dispersed throughout the cybernetic circuit. The user learns kinesthetically and proprioceptively in these systems that the boundaries of self are defined less by the skin than by the feedback loops connecting body and simulation in a techno-bio-integrated circuit.

Questions about presence and absence do not yield much leverage in this situation, for the puppet both is and is not present, just as the user both is and is not inside the screen. Instead, the focus shifts to questions about pattern and randomness. What transformations govern the connections between user and puppet? What parameters control the construction of the screen world? What patterns can the user discover through interaction with the system? Where do these patterns fade into randomness? What stimuli cannot be encoded within the system and therefore exist only as extraneous noise? When and how does this noise coalesce into pattern?

The example, taken from technology, illustrates concerns that are also appropriate to literary texts. It may seem strange to connect postmodern bodies with print rather than electronic media, but bodies and books share a crucially important characteristic not present in electronic media. Unlike radio and television, which receive and transmit signals but do not permanently store messages, books carry their information in their bodies. Like the human body, the book is a form of information transmission and storage that incorporates its encodings in a durable material substrate. Once encoding in the material base has taken place, it cannot easily be changed. Print and proteins in this sense have more in common with each other than with any magnetic or electronic encodings, which can be erased and rewritten simply by changing the magnetic polarities. The metaphors of books, alphabets, and printing, pervasive in the discourse of genetics, are constituted through and by this similarity of corporeal encoding.

The entanglement of signal and materiality in bodies and books confers on them a parallel doubleness. Just as the human body is understood in molecular biology as simultaneously a physical structure and an expression of genetic information, so the literary corpus is at once a physical object and a space of representation, a body and a message. Because they have bodies, books and people have something to lose if they are regarded solely as informational patterns, namely the resistant materiality that has traditionally marked the experience of reading no less than it has marked the experience of living as embodied creatures. From this affinity emerge complex feedback loops between contemporary literature, the technologies that produce it, and the embodied readers who produce and are produced by books and technologies. The result is a network of changes that are moving in complex syncopation with one another. Changes in bodies as they are represented within literary texts have deep connections with changes in textual bodies as they are encoded within information media, and both stand in complex relation to changes in the construction of human bodies as they interface with information technologies. The term I use to designate this network of relations is informatics. Following Donna Haraway, I take informatics to mean the technologies of information as well as the biological, social, linguistic, and cultural changes that initiate, accompany, and complicate their development.[11]

I am now in a position to state my thesis explicitly. The contemporary pressure toward dematerialization, understood as an epistemic shift toward pattern/randomness and away from presence/absence, affects human and textual bodies on two levels at

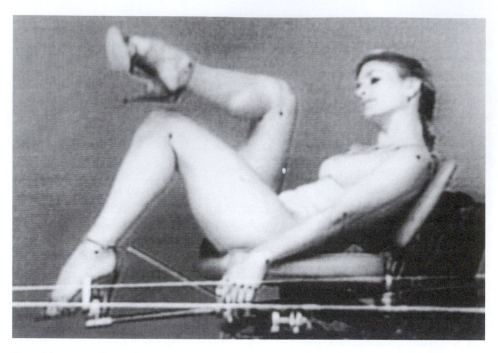

One of the most difficult problems in current computer animation is modeling human motion. It is much easier to simulate a flying corporate logo, for example, than to create a simulation of realistic human movement. As a highly articulated and nonlinear system, the body has yet to yield its secrets fully to computer algorithms. To solve the problem, Robert Abel and his associates marked position points on a human model's body and filmed her while she went through a series of exactly choreographed motions. They then analyzed the film using a computer, creating a data base that provided the basis for the female robot simulation. The juxtaposition of the materially present human model (left) with the simulacrum of the female robot from the computer-animated sequence "Brilliance" (right) illustrates the transformations that take place as the body is translated from a material substrate into pure information. The sequence shows the female robot manipulating objects on a dining table with a facility that is possible only because they have lost their materiality, as she herself has also. (Used with permission from Robert Abel, President of Synapse Technologies, Inc.)

once, as a change in the body (the material substrate) and a change in the message (the codes of representation). To explore these transformations, I want to untangle and then entangle again the networks connecting technological modes of production to the objects produced and consumed, embodied experience to literary representation. The connectivity between these parts and ports is, as they say in the computer industry, massively parallel and highly interdigitated. My narrative will therefore weave back and forth between the represented worlds of contemporary fictions, models of signification implicit in word processing, embodied experience as it is constructed by interactions with information technologies, and the technologies themselves.

The next thread I will pull from this tangled skein concerns the models of signification suggested and instantiated by information technologies. Information technologies do more than change modes of text production, storage, and dissemination. They fundamentally alter the relation of signified to signifier. Carrying the instabilities implicit

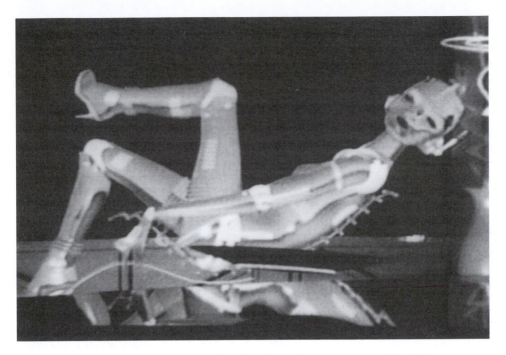

Also of interest are the transformations that allowed this illustration to appear in a print text. The images were published on a video laser disk entitled "Computer Dreams: Volume 1" (Voyager Company, Los Angeles CA, 1989). Lacking state-of-the-art equipment that would transfer the image directly from the laser disk to computer diskette to computerized typesetting (a series of exchanges that eliminates print text altogether), October requested that the illustrations be submitted as negatives. Because UCLA also lacks the state-of-the-art equipment that could interface an internal camera directly with the computer code, the video capture was done by taking long-exposure photographs of frames on a high-resolution monitor. Such hybrid splices are typical of this transition era. In a few months or weeks, the exchanges will be entirely electronic and the resistance of materiality (having to set up a camera on a tripod in a darkened room, for example) will diminish close to zero.

in Lacanian floating signifiers one step further, information technologies create what I will call *flickering signifiers*, characterized by their tendency toward unexpected metamorphoses, attenuations, and dispersions. Flickering signifiers signal an important shift in the plate tectonics of language. Much of contemporary fiction is directly influenced by information technologies; cyberpunk, for example, takes informatics as its central theme. Even narratives without this focus can hardly avoid the rippling effects of informatics, for the changing modes of signification affect the *codes* as well as the subjects of representation.

Signifying the processes of production

"Language is not a code," Lacan asserted, because he wished to deny any one-to-one correspondence between the signifier and the signified.[12] In word processing, however, language is a code. The relation between assembly and compiler languages is specified by a coding arrangement, as is the relation of the compiler language to the programming commands that the user manipulates. Through these multiple transformations some quantity is conserved, but it is not the mechanical energy implicit in a system of levers or the molecular energy of a thermodynamical system. Rather it is the informational structure that emerges from the interplay between pattern and randomness. The immateriality of the text, deriving from a translation of mechanical leverage into informational patterns, allows transformations to take place that would be unthinkable if matter or energy were the primary basis for the systemic exchanges. This textual fluidity, which the user learns in her body as she interacts with the system, implies that signifiers flicker rather than float.

To explain what I mean by flickering signifiers, I will find it useful briefly to review Lacan's notion of floating signifiers. Lacan, operating within a view of language that was primarily print-based rather than electronically mediated, focused not surprisingly on presence and absence as the dialectic of interest.[13] When he formulated the concept of floating signifiers, he drew on Saussure's idea that signifiers are defined by networks of relational differences between themselves rather than by their relation to signifieds. He complicated this picture by maintaining that signifieds do not exist in themselves, except insofar as they are produced by signifiers. He imagined them as an ungraspable flow floating beneath a network of signifiers that itself is constituted through continual slippages and displacements. Thus for him a doubly reinforced absence is at the core of signification—absence of signifieds as things-in-themselves as well as absence of stable correspondences between signifiers. The catastrophe in psycholinguistic development corresponding to this absence in signification is castration, the moment when the (male) subject symbolically confronts the realization that subjectivity, like language, is founded on absence.

How does this scenario change when floating signifiers give way to flickering signifiers? Foregrounding pattern and randomness, information technologies operate within a realm in which the signifier is opened to a rich internal play of difference. In informatics the signifier can no longer be understood as a single marker, for example an ink mark on a page. Rather it exists as a flexible chain of markers bound together by the arbitrary relations specified by the relevant codes. As I write these words on my computer, I see the lights on the video screen, but for the computer the relevant signifiers are magnetic tracks on disks. Intervening between what I see and what the computer reads are the machine code that correlates alphanumeric symbols with binary digits, the compiler language that correlates these symbols with higher-level instructions determining how the symbols are to be manipulated, the processing program that mediates between these instructions and the commands I give the computer, and so forth. A signifier on one level becomes a signified on the next higher level. Precisely because the relation between signifier and signified at each of these levels is arbitrary, it can be changed with a single global command. If I am producing ink marks by manipulating movable type, changing the font requires changing each line of type. By contrast, if I am producing flickering signifiers on a video screen, changing the font is as easy as giving the system a single command. The longer the chain of codes, the more radical the transformations that can be effected. Acting as linguistic levers, the coding chains impart astonishing power to even very small changes.

Such leverage is possible because the constant reproduced through multiple coding layers is a pattern rather than a presence. Pattern can be recognized through redundancy or repetition of elements. If there is only repetition, however, no new information is imparted; the intermixture of randomness rescues pattern from sterility. If there is only randomness, the result is gibberish rather than communication. Information is produced by a complex dance between predictability and unpredictability, repetition and variation. We have seen that the possibilities for mutation are enhanced and heightened by long coding chains. We can now understand mutation in more fundamental terms. Mutation is crucial because it names the bifurcation point at which the interplay between pattern and randomness causes the system to evolve in a new direction.[14] Mutation implies both the replication of pattern—the morphological standard against which it can be measured and understood as a mutation—and the interjection of randomness—the variations that mark it as a deviation so decisive it can no longer be assimilated into the same.

Mutation is the catastrophe in the pattern/randomness dialectic analogous to castration in presence/absence. It marks the opening of pattern to randomness so extreme that the expectation of continuous replication can no longer be sustained. But as with castration, this only appears to be a disruption located at a specific moment. The randomness to which mutation testifies is always already interwoven into pattern. One way to understand this "always already" is through the probability function that mathematically defines information in Claude Shannon's classic equations in information theory.[15] Were randomness not always already immanent, we would be in the Newtonian world of strict causality rather than the information-theoretic realm of probability. More generally, randomness is involved because it is only against the background or possibility of nonpattern that pattern can emerge. Wherever pattern exists, randomness is implicit as the contrasting term that allows pattern to be understood as such. The crisis named by mutation is as wide-ranging and pervasive in its import within the pattern/randomness dialectic as castration is within the tradition of presence/absence, for it is the visible mark that testifies to the continuing interplay of the dialectical terms.

Shifting the emphasis from presence/absence to pattern/randomness suggests different choices for tutor texts. Rather than Freud's discussion of "fort/da" (a short passage whose replication in hundreds of commentaries would no doubt astonish its creator), theorists interested in pattern and randomness might point to something like David Cronenberg's film *The Fly*. At a certain point the protagonist's penis does fall off (he quaintly puts it in his medicine chest as a memento to times past), but the loss scarcely registers in the larger metamorphosis he is undergoing. The operative transition is not from male to female-as-castrated-male, but from human to something radically other than human. Flickering signification brings together language with a psychodynamics based on the symbolic moment when the human confronts the posthuman.

Metamorphisis in progress in David Cronenberg's The Fly.

I understand "human" and "posthuman" to be historically specific constructions that emerge from different configurations of embodiment, technology, and culture. A convenient point of reference for the human is the picture constructed by nineteenth-century American and British anthropologists of "man" as a tool-user.[16] Using tools may shape the body (some anthropologists made this argument), but the tool nevertheless is envisioned as an object, apart from the body, that can be picked up and put down at will. When the claim could not be sustained that man's unique nature was defined by tool use (because other animals were shown also to use tools), the focus shifted during the early twentieth century to man the tool-maker. Typical is Kenneth P. Oakley's 1949 *Man the Tool-Maker*, a magisterial work with the authority of the British Museum behind it.[17] Oakley, in charge of the Anthropological Section of the museum's Natural History division, wrote in his introduction, "Employment of tools appears to be [man's] chief biological characteristic, for considered functionally they are detachable extensions of the forelimb" (1). The kind of tool he envisioned was mechanical rather than informational; it goes *with* the hand, not *on* the head. Significantly, he imagined the tool to be at once "detachable" and an "extension," separate from yet partaking of the hand. If the placement and kind of tool marks his affinity with the epoch of the human, its construction as a prosthesis points forward to the posthuman.

Similar ambiguities informed the Macy Conference discussions taking place during the same period (1946–53), as participants wavered between a vision of man as a homeostatic, self-regulating mechanism whose boundaries were clearly delineated from the environment,[18] and a more threatening, reflexive vision of a man spliced into an informational circuit that could change him in unpredictable ways. By the 1960s, the consensus within cybernetics had shifted dramatically toward the reflexivity. By the 1980s, the inertial pull of homeostasis as a constitutive concept had largely given way to theories of self-organization that implied radical changes were possible within certain kinds of complex systems.[19] Through these discussions, the "posthuman" future of "humanity" began increasingly to be evoked. Examples range from Hans Moravec's invocation of a "postbiological" future in which human consciousness is downloaded into a computer, to the more sedate (and in part already realized) prospect of a symbiotic union between human and intelligent machine that Howard Rheingold calls "intelligence augmentation."[20] Although these visions differ in the degree and kind of interfaces they imagine, they concur that the posthuman implies a coupling so intense and multifaceted that it is no longer possible to distinguish meaningfully between the biological organism and the informational circuits in which it is enmeshed. Accompanying this change, I have argued, is a corresponding shift in how signification is understood and corporeally experienced. In contrast to Lacanian psycholinguistics, derived from the generative coupling of linguistics and sexuality, flickering signification is the progeny of the fascinating and troubling coupling of language and machine.

Information narratives and bodies of information

The shift from presence and absence to pattern and randomness is encoded into every aspect of contemporary literature, from the physical object that constitutes the text to such staples of literary interpretation as character, plot, author, and reader. The development is by no means even; some texts testify dramatically and explicitly to the shift, whereas others manifest it only indirectly. I will call the texts where the displacement is most apparent information narratives. Information narratives show in exaggerated form changes that are more subtly present in other texts as well. Whether in information narratives or contemporary fiction generally, the dynamic of displacement is crucial. One could focus on pattern in any era, but the peculiarity of pattern in these texts is its interpenetration with randomness and its implicit challenge to physicality. *Pattern tends to overwhelm presence*, marking a new kind of immateriality that does not depend on spirituality or even consciousness, only on information.

I begin my exploration with William Gibson's *Neuromancer* (1984), the novel that sparked the cyberpunk movement and motivated Autodesk, a software company, to launch a major initiative in developing virtual reality technology. Hard on the heels of *Neuromancer* came two more volumes, *Count Zero* (1986) and *Mona Lisa Overdrive* (1988). The *Neuromancer* trilogy gave a local habitation and a name to the disparate spaces of computer simulations, networks, and hypertext windows that prior to Gibson's intervention had been discussed as separate phenomena. Gibson's novels acted like seed crystals thrown into a supersaturated solution; the time was ripe for the technology known as cyberspace to precipitate into public consciousness. The narrator defines cyberspace as a "consensual illusion" accessed when a user "jacks into" a computer (51). Here the writer's imagination outstrips existing technologies, for Gibson imagines a direct neural link between the brain and computer through electrodes. Another version of this link is a socket implanted behind the ear that accepts computer chips, allowing direct neural access to computer memory. Network users collaborate in creating the richly textured landscape of cyberspace, a "graphic representation of data abstracted from the banks of every computer in the human system. Unthinkable complexity. Lines of light ranged in the nonspace of the mind, clusters and constellations of data. Like city lights, receding . . ." (51). Existing in the nonmaterial space of computer simulation, cyberspace defines a perimeter within which pattern is the essence of the reality, presence an optical illusion.

Like the landscapes they negotiate, the subjectivities who operate within cyberspace also become patterns rather than physical entities. Case, the computer cowboy who is the novel's protagonist, still has a physical presence, although he regards his body as so much "meat" that exists primarily to sustain his consciousness until the next time he can enter cyberspace. Others have completed the transition that Case's values imply. Dixie Flatline, a cowboy who encountered something in cyberspace that flattened his EEG, ceased to exist as a physical body and lives now as a personality construct within the computer, defined by the magnetic patterns that store his identity.

The contrast between the body's limitations and cyberspace's power highlights the advantages of pattern over presence. As long as the pattern endures, one has attained a kind of immortality. Such views are authorized by cultural conditions that make physicality seem a better state to be from than to inhabit. In a world despoiled by overdevelopment, overpopulation, and time-release environmental poisons, it is comforting to think that physical forms can recover their pristine purity by being reconstituted as informational patterns in a multidimensional computer space. A cyberspace body, like a cyberspace landscape, is immune to blight and corruption. It is no accident that the vaguely apocalyptic landscapes of films like *The Terminator*, *Blade Runner*, and *Hardware* occur in narratives focusing on cybernetic life-forms. The sense that the world is rapidly becoming uninhabitable by human beings is part of the impetus toward the displacement of presence by pattern.

These connections lie close to the surface in *Neuromancer.* "Get just wasted enough, find yourself in some desperate but strangely arbitrary kind of trouble, and it was possible to see Ninsei as a field of data, the way the matrix had once reminded him of proteins linking to distinguish cell specialities. Then you could throw yourself into a highspeed drift and skid, totally engaged but set apart from it all, and all around you the dance of biz, information interacting, data made flesh in the mazes of the black market . . ." (16). The metaphoric slippages between urban sprawl, computer matrix, and biological protein culminate in the final elliptical phrase, "data made flesh." Information is the putative origin, physicality the derivative manifestation. Body parts sold in black-market clinics, body neurochemistry manipulated by synthetic drugs, body of the world overlaid by urban sprawl testify to the precariousness of physical existence. If flesh is data incarnate, why not go back to the source and leave the perils of physicality behind?

The reasoning presupposes that subjectivity and computer programs have a common arena in which to interact. Historically, that arena was first defined in cybernetics by the creation of a conceptual framework that constituted humans, animals, and machines as information-processing devices receiving and transmitting signals to effect goal-directed behavior.[21] Gibson matches this technical achievement with two literary innovations that allow subjectivity, with its connotations of consciousness and self-awareness, to be articulated together with abstract data. The first is a subtle modification in point of view, abbreviated in the text as pov. More than an acronym, pov is a substantive noun that constitutes the character's subjectivity by serving as a positional marker substituting for his absent body.

In its usual Jamesian sense, point of view presumes the fiction of a person who observes the action from a particular angle and tells what he sees. In the preface to *The Portrait of a Lady*, James imagines a "house of fiction" with a "million windows" formed by "the need of the individual vision and by the pressure of the individual will."[22] At each "stands a figure with a pair of eyes, or at least with a field glass, which forms, again and again, for observation, a unique instrument, insuring to the person making use of it an impression distinct from every other" (46). For James the observer is an embodied creature, and the specificity of his location determines what he can see as he looks out on a scene that itself is physically specific. When an omniscient viewpoint is used, the limitations of the narrator's corporeality begin to fall away, but the suggestion of embodiment lingers in the idea of focus, the "scene" created by the eye's movement.

Even for James, vision is not unmediated technologically. Significantly, he hovers between eye and field glass as the receptor constituting vision. Cyberspace represents a quantum leap forward into the technological construction of vision. Instead of an embodied consciousness looking through the window at a scene, consciousness moves *through* the screen to become the pov, leaving behind the body as an unoccupied shell. In cyberspace point of view does not emanate from the character; rather, the pov literally *is* the character. If a pov is annihilated, the character disappears with it, ceasing to exist as a consciousness in and out of cyberspace. The realistic fiction of a narrator who observes but does not create is thus unmasked in cyberspace. The effect is not primarily metafictional, however, but in a literal sense metaphysical, above and beyond physicality. The crucial difference between the Jamesian point of view and cyberspace pov is that the former implies physical presence, whereas the latter does not.

Gibson's technique recalls Robbe-Grillet's novels, which were among the first information narratives to exploit the formal consequences of combining subjectivity with data. In Robbe-Grillet, however, the effect of interfacing narrative voice with objective description was paradoxically to heighten the narrator's subjectivity, for certain objects, like the jalousied windows or the centipede in *Jealousy*, are inventoried with obsessive interest, indicating a mind-set that is anything but objective. In Gibson, the space in which subjectivity moves lacks this personalized stamp. Cyberspace is the domain of post-modern collectivity, constituted as the resultant of millions of vectors representing the diverse and often conflicting interests of human and artificial intelligences linked together through computer networks.

To make this space work as a level playing field on which humans and computers can meet on equal terms, Gibson introduces his second innovation. Cyberspace is created by transforming a data matrix into a landscape in which narratives can happen. In mathematics matrix is a technical term denoting data that have been arranged into an n-dimensional array. Expressed in this form, data seem as far removed from the fascina-tions of story as random number tables are from the *National Inquirer.* Because the array is already conceptualized in spatial terms, however, it is a small step to imagining it as a three-dimensional landscape. Narrative becomes possible when this spatiality is given a temporal dimension by the pov's movement through it. The pov is *located* in space, but it *exists* in time. Through the track it weaves, the desires, repressions, and obsessions of subjectivity can be expressed. The genius of *Neuromancer* lies in its explicit recognition that the categories Kant considered fundamental to human experience, space and time, can be used as a conjunction to join awareness with data. Reduced to a point, the pov is abstracted into a purely temporal entity with no spatial extension; metaphorized into an interactive space, the datascape is narrativized by the pov's movement through it. Data are thus humanized, and subjectivity computerized, allowing them to join in a symbiotic union whose result is narrative.

Such innovations carry the implications of informatics beyond the textual surface into the signifying processes that constitute theme and character. I suspect that Gibson's novels have been so influential not only because they present a vision of the posthu-man future that is already upon us—in this they are no more prescient than many other science fiction novels—but also because they embody within their techniques the assumptions expressed explicitly in the novels' themes. This kind of move is possible or inevitable when the cultural conditions authorizing the assumptions are pervasive enough so that the posthuman is experienced as an everyday lived reality as well as an intellectual proposition.

In *The Condition of Postmodernity*, David Harvey characterizes the economic aspects of the shift to an informatted society as a transition from a Fordist regime to a regime of flexible accumulation.[23] As Harvey, along with many others, has pointed out, in late capit-alism durable goods yield pride of place to information.[24] A significant difference between information and durable goods is replicability. Information is not a conserved quantity. If I give you information, you have it, and I do, too. With information, the constraining factor separating the haves from the have-nots is not so much possession as access. The shift of emphasis from ownership to access is another manifestation of the under-lying transition from presence/absence to pattern/randomness. Presence precedes and makes possible the idea of possession, for one can possess something only if it already exists. By contrast, access implies pattern recognition, whether the access is to a piece of land (recognized as such through the boundary pattern defining that land as different from adjoining parcels), confidential information (constituted as confidential through the comparison of its informational patterns with less secure documents), or a bank vault (associated with knowing the correct pattern of tumbler combinations). In general, access differs from possession because it tracks patterns rather than presences. When someone breaks into a computer system, it is not her physical presence that is detected but the informational traces her entry has created.[25]

When the emphasis falls on access rather than ownership, the private/public distinction that was so important in the formation of the novel is radically reconfigured. Whereas possession implies the existence of private life based on physical exclusion or inclusion, access implies the existence of credentialing practices that use patterns rather than presences to distinguish between those who do and do not have the right to enter. Moreover, entering is itself constituted as access to data rather than a change in physical location. In DeLillo's *White Noise* (1985), for example, the Gladney's home, traditionally the private space of family life, is penetrated by noise and radiation of all wavelengths—microwave, radio, television. The penetration signals that private spaces, and the private thoughts they engender and figure, are less a concern than the interplay between codes and the articulation of individual subjectivity with data. Jack Gladney's death is prefigured for him as a pattern of pulsing stars around a computerized data display, and it is surely no accident that Babette, his wife, objects to the idea that a man sexually "enters" a woman. The phrases she prefers emphasize by contrast the idea of access.

Although the Gladney family still operates as a social unit (albeit with the geographical dispersion endemic to postmodern life), their conversations are punctuated by random bits of information emanating from the radio and TV. The punctuation points toward a mutation in subjectivity that comes from joining the focused attention of traditional novelistic consciousness with the digitized randomness of miscellaneous bits. The mutation reaches incarnation in Willie Mink, whose brain has become so addled by a designer drug that his consciousness is finally indistinguishable from the white noise that surrounds him. Through a different route than that used by Gibson, DeLillo arrives at a similar destination: a vision of subjectivity constituted through the interplay of pattern and randomness rather than presence and absence.

The bodies of texts are also implicated in these changes. The displacement of presence by pattern thins the tissue of textuality, making it a semipermeable membrane that allows awareness of the text as an informational pattern to infuse into the space of representation. When the fiction of presence gives way to the recognition of pattern, passages are opened between the text-as-object and representations within the text that are characteristically postmodern. Consider the play between text as physical object and information flow in Calvino's *If on a winter's night a traveler* (1981). The text's awareness of its own physicality is painfully apparent in the anxiety it manifests toward keeping the literary corpus intact.

Within the space of representation, texts are subjected to birth defects, maimed and torn apart, lost and stolen, and, last but hardly least, pulverized when the wrong computer key is pushed and the stored words are randomized into miscellaneous bits.

The anxiety is transmitted to readers within the text, who keep pursuing parts of textual bodies only to lose them, as well as to readers outside the text, who must try to make sense of the radically discontinuous narrative. Only when the titles of the parts are perceived to form a sentence is the literary corpus reconstituted as a unity. Significantly, the recuperation is syntactical rather than physical. It does not arise from or imply an intact physical body. Rather, it emerges from the patterns—metaphorical, grammatical, narrative, thematic, and textual—that the parts together make. As the climactic scene in the library suggests, the reconstituted corpus is a body of information, emerging from the discourse community among which information circulates.

The correspondence between transformations in human and textual bodies can be seen as early as William Burroughs's *Naked Lunch* (1959), written in the decade that saw the institutionalization of cybernetics and the construction of the first large-scale electronic computer. The narrative metamorphizes nearly as often as bodies within it, suggesting by its cut-up method a textual corpus as artificial, heterogeneous, and cybernetic as they are.[26] Since the fissures that mark the text always fall *within* the units that comprise the textual body—within chapters, paragraphs, sentences, and even words—it becomes increasingly clear that they do not function to delineate the textual corpus. Rather, the body of the text is produced precisely by these fissures, which are not so much ruptures as productive dialectics bringing the narrative as a syntactic and chronological sequence into being.

Bodies within the text follow the same logic. Under the pressure of sex and addiction, bodies explode or mutate, protoplasm is sucked out of cocks or nostrils, plots are hatched to take over the planet or nearest life-form. Burroughs anticipates Jameson's claim that an information society is the purest form of capitalism.[27] When bodies are constituted as information, they can not only be sold but fundamentally reconstituted in response to market pressures. Junk instantiates the dynamics of informatics and makes clear its relation to late capitalism. Junk is the "ideal product" because the "junk merchant does not sell his product to the consumer, he sells the consumer to his product. He does not improve and simplify his merchandise. He degrades and simplifies the client" ("Introduction," xxxix). The junkie's body is a harbinger of the postmodern mutant, for it demonstrates how presence yields to patterns of assembly and disassembly created by the the flow of junk-as-information through points of amplification and resistance.

The characteristics of information narratives include, then, an emphasis on mutation and transformation as a central thematic for bodies within the text as well as for the bodies of texts. Subjectivity, already joined with information technologies through cybernetic circuits, is further integrated into the circuit by novelistic techniques that combine it with data. Access vies with possession as a structuring element, and data are narrativized to accommodate their integration with subjectivity. In general, materiality and immateriality are joined in a complex tension that is a source of exultation and strong anxiety. To understand the links between information narratives and other contemporary fictions that may not obviously fall into this category, let us turn now to consider the more general effects of informatics on narrative encodings.

Functionalities of narrative

The very word narrator implies a voice speaking, and a speaking voice implies a sense of presence. Derrida, announcing the advent of grammatology, focused on the gap that separates speaking from writing; such a change transforms the narrator from speaker to scribe, or more precisely an absence toward which the inscriptions point.[28] Informatics pushes this transformation further. As writing yields to flickering signifiers underwritten by binary digits, the narrator becomes not so much a scribe as a cyborg authorized to access the relevant codes.

To see how the function of the narrator changes, consider the seduction scene from "I Was an Infinitely Hot and Dense White Dot," one of the stories in Mark Leyner's *My Cousin, My Gastroenterologist*.[29] The narrator, "high on Sinutab" and driving "isotropically," so that any destination is equally probable, finds himself at a "squalid little dive" (6).

> I don't know . . . but there she is. I can't tell if she's a human or a fifth-generation gyne-morphic android and I don't care. I crack open an ampule of mating pheromone and let it waft across the bar, as I sip my drink, a methyl isocyanate on the rocks—methyl isocyanate is the substance which killed more than 2,000 people when it leaked in Bhopal, India, but thanks to my weight training, aerobic workouts, and a low-fat fiber-rich diet, the stuff has no effect on me. Sure enough she strolls over and occupies the stool next to mine. . . . My lips are now one angstrom unit from her lips . . . I begin to kiss her but she turns her head away. . . . I can't kiss you, we're monozygotic replicants—we share 100% of our genetic material. My head spins. You are the beautiful day, I exclaim, your breath is a zephyr of eucalyptus that does a pas de bourré across the Sea of Galilee. Thanks, she says, but we can't go back to my house and make love because monozygotic incest is forbidden by the elders. What if I said I could change all that. . . . What if I said that I had a miniature shotgun that blasts gene fragments into the cells of living organisms, altering their genetic matrices so that a monozygotic replicant would no longer be a monozygotic replicant and she could then make love to a muscleman without transgressing the incest taboo, I say, opening my shirt and exposing the device which I had stuck in the waistband of my black jeans. How'd you get that thing? she gasps, ogling its thick fiber-reinforced plastic barrel and the Uzi-Biotech logo embossed on the magazine which held two cartridges of gelated recombinant DNA. I got it for Christmas. . . . Do you have any last words before I scramble your chromosomes, I say, taking aim. Yes, she says, you first. (7)

Much of the passage's wit comes from the juxtaposition of folk wisdom and seduction clichés with high-tech language and ideas that makes them nonsensical. The narrator sips a chemical that killed thousands when it leaked into the environment, but he is immune to damage because he eats a low-fat diet. The narrator leans close to the woman/android to kiss her, but he has not yet made contact when he is an angstrom away, considerably less than the diameter of a hydrogen atom. The characters cannot make love because they are barred by incest taboos, being replicants from the same monozygote, which would make them identical twins but does not seem to prevent them from being opposite sexes. They are governed by kinship rules enforced by tribal elders, but they have access to genetic technologies that intervene in and disrupt evolutionary modes of descent. They think their problem can be solved by an Uzi-Biotech weapon that will scramble their chromosomes, but the narrator, at least, seems to expect their identities to survive intact.

Even within the confines of a short story no more than five pages long, this encounter is not preceded or followed by events that relate directly to it. Rather, the narrative leaps from scene to scene, which are linked by only the most tenuous and arbitrary threads. The incongruities make the narrative a kind of textual android created through patterns of assembly and disassembly. There is no natural body to this text, any more than there are natural bodies within the text. As the title intimates, identity merges with typography ("I was a . . . dot") and is further conflated with such high-tech reconstructions as computer simulations of gravitational collapse ("I was an infinitely hot and dense white dot"). Signifiers collapse like stellar bodies into an explosive materiality that approaches the critical point of nova, ready to blast outward into dissipating waves of flickering signification.

The explosive tensions between cultural codes that familiarize the action and neologistic splices that dislocate traditional expectations do more than structure the narrative. They also constitute the narrator, who exists less as a speaking voice endowed with a plausible psychology than as a series of fissures and dislocations that push toward a new kind of subjectivity. To understand the nature of this subjectivity, let us imagine a trajectory that arcs from storyteller to professional to some destination beyond. The shared community of values and presence that Walter Benjamin had in mind when he evoked the traditional storyteller whose words are woven into the rhythms of work echo faintly in allusions to the Song of Songs and tribal elders.[30] Overlaid on this is the professionalization that Lyotard wrote about in *The Postmodern Condition*, in which the authority to tell the story is constituted by possessing the appropriate credentials that qualify one as a member of a physically dispersed, electronically bound professional community.[31] This phase of the trajectory is signified in a number of ways. The narrator is driving "isotropically," indicating that physical location is no longer necessary or relevant to the production of the story. His authority derives not from his physical participation in a community but his possession of a high-tech language that includes pheromones, methyl isocyanate, and gelated recombinant DNA, not to mention the Uzi-Biotech phallus. This authority, too, is displaced even as it is created, for the incongruities reveal that the narrative and therefore the narrator are radically unstable, about to mutate into a scarcely conceivable form, signified in the story by the high-tech, identity-transforming orgasmic blast that never quite comes.

What is this form? Its physical manifestations vary, but the ability to manipulate complex codes is a constant. The looming transformation, already enacted through the passage's language, is into a subjectivity who derives his authority from possessing the correct codes. Countless scenarios exist in popular literature and culture where someone fools a computer into thinking he is an "authorized" person because he possesses or stumbles upon the codes that the computer recognizes as constituting authorization. Usually these scenarios imply that the person exists unchanged, taking on a spurious identity that allows him to move unrecognized within an informational system. There is, however, another way to read these narratives. Constituting identity through authorization codes changes the person who uses them into another kind of subjectivity, precisely one who exists and is recognized because he knows the codes. The surface deception is underlaid by a deeper truth. We become the codes we punch. The narrator is not a storyteller and not a professional authority, although these functions linger in the narrative as anachronistic allusions and wrenched referentiality. Rather, the narrator is a keyboarder, a hacker, a manipulator of codes.[32] Assuming that the text was at some phase in its existence digitized, in a literal sense he (it?) is these codes.

The construction of the narrator as a manipulator of codes obviously has important implications for the construction of the reader. The reader is similarly constituted through a layered archeology that moves from listener to reader to decoder. Because codes can be sent over fiber optics essentially instantaneously, there is no longer a shared, stable context that helps to anchor meaning and guide interpretation. Like reading, decoding takes place in a location arbitrarily far removed in space and time from the source text. In contrast to fixed type print, however, decoding implies that there is no original text—no first editions, no fair copies, no holographic manuscripts. There are only the flickering signifiers, whose transient patterns evoke and embody what G. W. S. Trow has called the context of no context, the suspicion that all contexts, like all texts, are electronically mediated constructions.[33] What binds the decoder to the system is not the stability of an interpretive community or the intense pleasure of physically possessing the book that all bibliophiles know. Rather, it is her construction as a cyborg, her recognition that her physicality is also data made flesh, another flickering signifier in a chain of signification that extends through many levels, from the DNA that in-formats her body to the binary code that is the computer's first language.

"Functionality" is a term used by virtual reality technologists to describe the communication modes that are active in a computer-human interface. If the user wears a data glove, for example, hand motions constitute one functionality. If the computer can respond to voice-activated commands, voice is another functionality. If it can sense body position, spatial location is yet another. Functionalities work in both directions; that is, they both describe the computer's capabilities and also indicate how the user's sensory-motor apparatus is being trained to accommodate the computer's responses. Working with a VR simulation, the user learns to move her hand in stylized gestures that the computer can accommodate. In the process, changes take place in the neural configuration of the user's brain, some of which can be long-lasting. The computer molds the human even as the human builds the computer.

When narrative functionalities change, a new kind of reader is produced by the text. The effects of flickering signification ripple outward because readers are trained to read through different functionalities, which can affect how they interpret any text, including texts written before computers were invented. Moreover, changes in narrative function-alities go deeper than structural or thematic characteristics of a specific genre, for they shift the modalities that are activated to produce the narrative. It is on this level that the subtle connections between information narratives and other kinds of contemporary fictions come into play.

Drawing on a context that included information technologies, Roland Barthes in *S/Z* brilliantly demonstrated the possibility of reading a text as a production of diverse codes.[34] Information narratives make that possibility an inevitability, for they often cannot be under-stood, even on a literal level, without referring to codes and their relation to information technologies. Flickering signification extends the productive force of codes beyond the text to include the signifying processes by which the technologies produce texts, as well as the interfaces that enmesh humans into integrated circuits. As the circuits connecting technology, text, and human expand and intensify, the point where quantitative incre-ments shade into qualitative transformation draws closer.

If my assessment that the dialectic of pattern/randomness is displacing presence/absence is correct, the implications extend beyond narrative into many cultural arenas. In my view, one of the most serious of these implications for the present cultural moment is a systematic devaluation of materiality and embodiment. I find this trend ironic, for changes in material conditions and embodied experience are precisely what give the shift its deep roots in everyday experience. In this essay I have been concerned not only to anatomize the shift and understand its implications for literature but also to suggest that it should be understood in the context of changing experiences of embodiment. If, on the one hand, embodiment implies that informatics is imprinted into body as well as mind, on the other, it also acts as a reservoir of materiality that resists the pressure toward dematerialization.

Implicit in nearly everything I have written here is the assumption that presence and pattern are opposites existing in antagonistic relation. The more emphasis that falls on one, the less the other is noticed and valued. Entirely different readings emerge when one entertains the possibility that pattern and presence are mutually enhancing and supportive. Paul Virilio has observed that one cannot ask whether information techno-logies should continue to be developed.[35] Given the market forces already at work, it is virtually (if I may use the word) certain that increasingly we will live, work, and play in environments that construct us as embodied virtualities.[36] I believe that our best hope to intervene constructively in this development is to put an interpretive spin on it that opens up the possibilities of seeing pattern and presence as complementary rather than antag-onistic. Information, like humanity, cannot exist apart from the embodiment that brings it into being as a material entity in the world; and embodiment is always instantiated, local, and specific. Embodiment can be destroyed but it cannot be replicated. Once the specific form constituting it is gone, no amount of massaging data will bring it back. This observation is as true of the planet as it is of an individual life-form. As we rush to explore the new vistas that cyberspace has made available for colonization, let us also remember the fragility of a material world that cannot be replaced.

Notes

1. I am indebted to Brooks Landon and Felicity Nussbaum for their helpful comments on this essay.
2. Among the studies that explore these connections are Jay Bolter, *Writing Space: The Computer, Hypertext, and the History of Writing* (Hillsdale, N.J.: Lawrence Erlbaum Associates, 1991); Michael Heim, *Electric Language: A Philosophical Study of Word Processing* (New Haven: Yale University Press, 1987); and Mark Poster, *The Mode of Information: Poststructuralism and Social Context* (Chicago: University of Chicago Press, 1990).
3. The paradox is discussed in N. Katherine Hayles, *Chaos Bound: Orderly Disorder in Contemporary Literature and Science* (Ithaca: Cornell University Press, 1990), pp. 31–60.
4. Self-organizing systems are discussed in Grégoire Nicolis and Ilya Prigogine, *Exploring Complexity: An Introduction* (New York: Freeman and Company, 1989); Roger Lewin, *Complexity: Life at the Edge of Chaos* (New York: Macmillan 1992); and M. Mitchell Waldrop, *Complexity: The Emerging Science at the Edge of Order and Chaos* (New York: Simon and Schuster, 1992).
5. Friedrich A. Kittler, *Discourse Networks 1800/1900*, trans. Michael Metteer and Chris Cullens (Stanford: Stanford University Press, 1990).
6. The implications of these conditions for postmodern embodiment are explored in N. Katherine Hayles, "The Materiality of Informatics," *Configurations: A Journal of Literature, Science, and Technology* 1 (Winter 1993), pp. 147–70.
7. In *The Age of the Smart Machine: The Future of Work and Power* (New York: Basic Books, 1988), Shoshana Zuboff explores through three case studies the changes in American workplaces as industries become informatted.
8. Computer law is discussed in Katie Hafner and John Markoff, *Cyberpunk: Outlaws and Hackers on the Computer Frontier* (New York: Simon and Schuster, 1991); also informative is Bruce Sterling, *The Hacker Crackdown: Law and Disorder on the Electronic Frontier* (New York: Bantam, 1992).
9. Sherry Turkel documents computer network romances in "Constructions and Reconstructions of the Self in Virtual Reality," a paper presented at the Third International Conference on Cyberspace (Austin, Texas, May 1993); Nicholson Baker's *Vox: A Novel* (New York: Random House, 1992) imaginatively explores the erotic potential for better living through telecommunications; and Howard Rheingold looks at the future of erotic encounters in cyberspace in "Teledildonics and Beyond," *Virtual Reality* (New York: Summit Books, 1991), pp. 345–77.
10. Howard Rheingold surveys the new virtual technologies in *Virtual Reality*. Also useful is Ken Pimentel and Kevin Teixeira, *Virtual Reality: Through the New Looking Glass* (New York: McGraw-Hill, 1993). Benjamin Woolley takes a skeptical approach toward claims for the new technology in *Virtual Worlds: A Journey in Hyped Hyperreality* (Oxford: Blackwell, 1992).

11. Donna Haraway, "Manifesto for Cyborgs: Science, Technology, and Socialist Feminism in the 1980s," *Socialist Review* 80 (1985), pp. 65–108; see also "The High Cost of Information in Post World War II Evolutionary Biology: Ergonomics, Semiotics, and the Sociobiology of Communications Systems," *Philosophical Forum* 8, no. 2–3 (1981–82), pp. 244–75.

12. Jacques Lacan, "Radiophonies," *Scilicet* 2/3 (1970), pp. 55, 68. For floating signifiers, see *Le Séminaire XX: Encore* (Paris: Seuil, 1975), pp. 22, 35.

13. Although presence and absence loom larger in Lacanian psycholinguistics than do pattern and randomness, Lacan was not uninterested in information theory. In the 1954–55 Seminar, he played with incorporating ideas from information theory and cybernetics into psychoanalysis. See especially "The Circuit" (pp. 77–90) and "Psychoanalysis and Cybernetics, or on the Nature of Language" (pp. 294–308) in *The Seminar of Jacques Lacan: Book II*, ed. Jacques-Alain Miller (New York: W. W. Norton and Co., 1991).

14. Several theorists of the postmodern have identified mutation as an important element of post-modernism, including Ihab Hassan in *The Postmodern Turn: Essays in Postmodern Theory and Culture* (Columbus: Ohio State University, 1987), p. 91, and Donna Haraway, "The Actors Are Cyborgs, Nature Is Coyote, and the Geography Is Elsewhere: Postscript to 'Cyborgs at Large,'" in *Technoculture*, ed. Constance Penley and Andrew Ross (Minneapolis: University of Minnesota Press, 1991), pp. 21–26.

15. Claude E. Shannon and Warren Weaver, *The Mathematical Theory of Communication* (Urbana: University of Illinois Press, 1949).

16. The gender encoding implicit in "man" (rather than human) is also reflected in the emphasis on tool usage as a defining characteristic, rather than, say, altruism or extended nurturance, traits traditionally encoded female.

17. Kenneth P. Oakley, *Man the Tool-Maker* (London: Trustees of the British Museum, 1949).

18. The term "homeostasis," or self-regulating stability through cybernetic corrective feedback, was introduced by physiologist Walter B. Cannon in "Organization for Physiological Homeostasis," *Physiological Reviews* 9 (1929), pp. 399–431. Cannon's work influenced Norbert Wiener, and homeostasis became an important concept in the initial phase of cybernetics from 1946–53.

19. Key figures in moving from homeostasis to self-organization were Heinz von Foerster, especially *Observing Systems* (Salinas, Calif.: Intersystems Publications, 1981) and Humberto R. Maturana and Francisco J. Varela, *Autopoiesis and Cognition: The Realization of the Living* (Dordrecht: Reidel, 1980).

20. Howard Rheingold, *Virtual Reality*, pp. 13–49; Hans Moravec, *Mind Children: The Future of Robot and Human Intelligence* (Cambridge: Harvard University Press, 1988), pp. 1–5, 116–22.

21. The seminal text is Norbert Wiener, *Cybernetics: Or Control and Communication in the Animal and the Machine* (Cambridge: MIT Press, 1948).

22. Henry James, *The Art of the Novel* (New York: Charles Scribner's Sons, 1937), p. 47.

23. David Harvey, *The Condition of Postmodernity: An Enquiry into the Origins of Cultural Change* (New York: Blackwell, 1989).

24. The material basis for informatics is meticulously documented in James Beniger, *The Control Revolution: Technological and Economic Origins of the Information Society* (Cambridge: Harvard University Press, 1986).

25. For an account of how tracks are detected, see *Cyberpunk*, pp. 35–40, 68–71.

26. David Porush discusses the genre of "cybernetic fiction," which he defines as fictions that resist the dehumanization that can be read into cybernetics, in *The Soft Machine: Cybernetic Fiction* (New York and London: Methuen, 1985); Burroughs's titular story is discussed on pp. 85–111. Robin Lydenberg has a fine exposition of Burroughs's style in *Word Cultures: Radical Theory and Practice in William Burroughs' Fiction* (Urbana: University of Illinois Press, 1987).

27. Fredric Jameson, *Postmodernism, or, the Cultural Logic of Late Capitalism* (Durham: Duke University Press, 1991).

28. Jacques Derrida, *Of Grammatology*, trans. Gayatri C. Spivak (Baltimore: Johns Hopkins University Press, 1976).

29. Mark Leyner, *My Cousin, My Gastroenterologist* (New York: Harmony Books, 1990).

30. Walter Benjamin, "The Storyteller," *Illuminations*, trans. Harry Zohn (New York: Schocken, 1969).

31. Jean-Francois Lyotard, *The Postmodern Condition: A Report on Knowledge*, trans. Geoff Bennington and Brian Massumi (Minneapolis: University of Minnesota Press, 1984).

32. It is significant in this regard that Andrew Ross calls for cultural critics to consider themselves hackers in "Hacking Away at the Counterculture," in *Technoculture*, pp. 107–34.

33. George W. S. Trow, *Within the Context of No Context* (Boston: Little Brown, 1978).

34. Roland Barthes, *S/Z*, trans. Richard Miller (New York: Hill and Wang, 1974).

35. Paul Virilio and Sylvère Lotringer, *Pure War*, trans. Mark Polizzotti (New York: Semiotext(e), 1983).

36. "Embodied virtuality" is Mark Weiser's phrase in "The Computer for the 21st Century," *Scientific American* 265 (September 1991), pp. 94–104. Weiser distinguishes between technologies that put the user into a simulation with the computer (virtual reality) and those that embed computers within already existing environments (embodied virtuality or ubiquitous computing). In virtual reality, the user's sensorium is redirected into functionalities compatible with the simulation; in embodied virtuality, the sensorium continues to function as it normally would but with an expanded range made possible through the environmentally embedded computers.

26

The coming technological singularity: How to survive in a post-human era

Vernor Vinge

What is the singularity?

The acceleration of technological progress has been the central feature of this century. I argue in this paper that we are on the edge of change comparable to the rise of human life on Earth. The precise cause of this change is the imminent creation by technology of entities with greater than human intelligence. There are several means by which science may achieve this breakthrough (and this is another reason for having confidence that the event will occur):

- There may be developed computers that are "awake" and superhumanly intelligent. (To date, there has been much controversy as to whether we can create human equivalence in a machine. But if the answer is "yes, we can," then there is little doubt that beings more intelligent can be constructed shortly thereafter.)

- Large computer networks (and their associated users) may "wake up" as a superhumanly intelligent entity.

- Computer/human interfaces may become so intimate that users may reasonably be considered superhumanly intelligent.

- Biological science may provide means to improve natural human intellect.

The first three possibilities depend in large part on improvements in computer hardware. Progress in computer hardware has followed an amazingly steady curve in the last few decades.[1] Based largely on this trend, I believe that the creation of greater than human intelligence will occur during the next thirty years. (Charles Platt[2] has pointed out that AI enthusiasts have been making claims like this for the last thirty years. Just so I'm not guilty of a relative-time ambiguity, let me more specific: I'll be surprised if this event occurs before 2005 or after 2030.)

What are the consequences of this event? When greater-than-human intelligence drives progress, that progress will be much more rapid. In fact, there seems no reason why progress itself would not involve the creation of still more intelligent entities — on a still-shorter time scale. The best analogy that I see is with the evolutionary past: Animals can adapt to problems and make inventions, but often no faster than natural selection can do its work — the world acts as its own simulator in the case of natural selection. We humans have the ability to internalize the world and conduct "what if's" in our heads; we can solve many problems thousands of times faster than natural selection. Now, by creating the means to execute those simulations at much higher speeds, we are entering a regime as radically different from our human past as we humans are from the lower animals.

From the human point of view this change will be a throwing away of all the previous rules, perhaps in the blink of an eye, an exponential runaway beyond any hope of control. Developments that before were thought might only happen in "a million years" (if ever) will likely happen in the next century. (In *Blood Music*,[3] Greg Bear paints a picture of the major changes happening in a matter of hours.)

I think it's fair to call this event a singularity ("the Singularity" for the purposes of this paper). It is a point where our old models must be discarded and a new reality rules. As we move closer to this point, it will loom vaster and vaster over human affairs till the notion becomes a commonplace. Yet when it finally happens it may still be a great surprise and a greater unknown. In the 1950s there were very few who saw it: Stan Ulam[4] paraphrased John von Neumann as saying:

One conversation centered on the ever accelerating progress of technology and changes in the mode of human life, which gives the appearance of approaching some essential singularity in the history of the race beyond which human affairs, as we know them, could not continue.

Von Neumann even uses the term singularity, though it appears he is thinking of normal progress, not the creation of superhuman intellect. (For me, the superhumanity is the essence of the Singularity. Without that we would get a glut of technical riches, never properly absorbed[5].)

In the 1960s there was recognition of some of the implications of superhuman intelligence. I. J. Good wrote[6]:

Let an ultraintelligent machine be defined as a machine that can far surpass all the intellectual activities of any any man however clever. Since the design of machines is one of these intellectual activities, an ultraintelligent machine could design even better machines; there would then unquestionably be an "intelligence explosion," and the intelligence of man would be left far behind. Thus the first ultraintelligent machine is the last invention that man need ever make, provided that the machine is docile enough to tell us how to keep it under control. . . . It is more probable than not that within the twentieth century, an ultraintelligent machine will be built and that it will be the last invention that man need make.

Good has captured the essence of the runaway, but does not pursue its most disturbing consequences. Any intelligent machine of the sort he describes would not be human-kind's "tool" — any more than humans are the tools of rabbits or robins or chimpanzees.

Through the '60s and '70s and '80s, recognition of the cataclysm spread.[7,8,9,10] Perhaps it was the science-fiction writers who felt the first concrete impact. After all, the "hard" science-fiction writers are the ones who try to write specific stories about all that technology may do for us. More and more, these writers felt an opaque wall across the future. Once, they could put such fantasies millions of years in the future.[11] Now they saw that their most diligent extrapolations resulted in the unknowable . . . soon. Once, galactic empires might have seemed a Post-Human domain. Now, sadly, even interplanetary ones are.

What about the '90s and the '00s and the '10s, as we slide toward the edge? How will the approach of the Singularity spread across the human world view? For a while yet, the general critics of machine sapience will have good press. After all, till we have hard-ware as powerful as a human brain it is probably foolish to think we'll be able to create human equivalent (or greater) intelligence. (There is the far-fetched possibility that we could make a human equivalent out of less powerful hardware, if we were willing to give up speed, if we were willing to settle for an artificial being who was literally slow.[12] But it's much more likely that devising the software will be a tricky process, involving lots of false starts and experimentation. If so, then the arrival of self-aware machines will not happen till after the development of hardware that is substantially more powerful than humans' natural equipment.)

But as time passes, we should see more symptoms. The dilemma felt by science fiction writers will be perceived in other creative endeavors. (I have heard thoughtful comic book writers worry about how to have spectacular effects when everything visible can be produced by the technologically commonplace.) We will see automation repla-cing higher and higher level jobs. We have tools right now (symbolic math programs, cad/cam) that release us from most low-level drudgery. Or put another way: The work that is truly productive is the domain of a steadily smaller and more elite fraction of humanity. In the coming of the Singularity, we are seeing the predictions of true technological unem-ployment finally come true.

Another symptom of progress toward the Singularity: ideas themselves should spread ever faster, and even the most radical will quickly become commonplace. When I began writing science fiction in the middle '60s, it seemed very easy to find ideas that took decades to percolate into the cultural consciousness; now the lead time seems more like eighteen months. (Of course, this could just be me losing my imagination as I get old, but I see the effect in others too.) Like the shock in a compressible flow, the Singularity moves closer as we accelerate through the critical speed.

And what of the arrival of the Singularity itself? What can be said of its actual appearance? Since it involves an intellectual runaway, it will probably occur faster than any technical revolution seen so far. The precipitating event will likely be unexpected — perhaps even to the researchers involved. ("But all our previous models were catatonic! We were just tweaking some parameters. . . .") If networking is widespread enough (into ubiquitous embedded systems), it may seem as if our artifacts as a whole had suddenly wakened.

And what happens a month or two (or a day or two) after that? I have only analogies to point to: The rise of humankind. We will be in the Post-Human era. And for all my rampant technological optimism, sometimes I think I'd be more comfortable if I were regarding these transcendental events from one thousand years remove . . . instead of twenty.

Can the singularity be avoided?

Well, maybe it won't happen at all: Sometimes I try to imagine the symptoms that we should expect to see if the Singularity is not to develop. There are the widely respected arguments of Penrose[13] and Searle[14] against the practicality of machine sapience. In August of 1992, Thinking Machines Corporation held a workshop to investigate the question "How We Will Build a Machine that Thinks."[15] As you might guess from the workshop's title, the participants were not especially supportive of the arguments against machine intelligence. In fact, there was general agreement that minds can exist on nonbiological substrates and that algorithms are of central importance to the existence of minds. However, there was much debate about the raw hardware power that is present in organic brains. A minority felt that the largest 1992 computers were within three orders of magnitude of the power of the human brain. The majority of the participants agreed with Moravec's estimate[16] that we are ten to forty years away from hardware parity. And yet there was another minority who pointed to "other sources,"[17, 18] and conjectured that the computational competence of single neurons may be far higher than generally believed. If so, our present computer hardware might be as much as ten orders of magnitude short of the equipment we carry around in our heads. If this is true (or for that matter, if the Penrose or Searle critique is valid), we might never see a Singularity. Instead, in the early '00s we would find our hardware performance curves beginning to level off — this because of our inability to automate the design work needed to support further hardware improvements. We'd end up with some very powerful hardware, but without the ability to push it further. Commercial digital signal processing might be awesome, giving an analog appearance even to digital operations, but nothing would ever "wake up" and there would never be the intellectual runaway which is the essence of the Singularity. It would likely be seen as a golden age . . . and it would also be an end of progress. This is very like the future predicted by Gunther Stent. In fact, on page 137 of *The Coming of the Golden Age*,[19] Stent explicitly cites the development of transhuman intelligence as a sufficient condition to break his projections.

But if the technological Singularity can happen, it will. Even if all the governments of the world were to understand the "threat" and be in deadly fear of it, progress toward the goal would continue. In fiction, there have been stories of laws passed forbidding the construction of "a machine in the likeness of the human mind."[20] In fact, the competitive advantage — economic, military, even artistic — of every advance in automation is so compelling that passing laws, or having customs, that forbid such things merely assures that someone else will get them first.

Eric Drexler[21] has provided spectacular insights about how far technical improvement may go. He agrees that superhuman intelligences will be available in the near future — and that such entities pose a threat to the human status quo. But Drexler argues that we can confine such transhuman devices so that their results can be examined and used safely. This is I. J. Good's ultraintelligent machine, with a dose of caution. I argue that confinement is intrinsically impractical. For the case of physical confinement: Imagine yourself locked in your home with only limited data access to the outside, to your masters. If those masters thought at a rate — say — one million times slower than you, there is little doubt that over a period of years (your time) you could come up with "helpful advice" that would incidentally set you free. (I call this "fast thinking" form of superintelligence "weak superhumanity". Such a "weakly superhuman" entity would probably burn out in a few weeks of outside time. "Strong superhumanity" would be more than cranking up the clock speed on a human-equivalent mind. It's hard to say precisely what "strong super-humanity" would be like, but the difference appears to be profound. Imagine running a dog mind at very high speed. Would a thousand years of doggy living add up to any human insight? (Now if the dog mind were cleverly rewired and then run at high speed, we might see something different. . . .) Many speculations about superintelligence seem to be based on the weakly superhuman model. I believe that our best guesses about the post-Singularity world can be obtained by thinking on the nature of strong superhumanity. I will return to this point later in the paper.)

Another approach to confinement is to build rules into the mind of the created super-human entity (for example, Asimov's Laws[22]). I think that any rules strict enough to be effective would also produce a device whose ability was clearly inferior to the unfettered versions (and so human competition would favor the development of the those more dangerous models). Still, the Asimov dream is a wonderful one: Imagine a willing slave, who has 1000 times your capabilities in every way. Imagine a creature who could satisfy your every safe wish (whatever that means) and still have 99.9% of its time free for other activities. There would be a new universe we never really understood, but filled with bene-volent gods (though one of my wishes might be to become one of them).

If the Singularity can not be prevented or confined, just how bad could the Post-Human era be? Well . . . pretty bad. The physical extinction of the human race is one possibility. (Or as Eric Drexler put it of nanotechnology: Given all that such technology can do, perhaps governments would simply decide that they no longer need citizens!). Yet physical extinction may not be the scariest possibility. Again, analogies: Think of the different ways we relate to animals. Some of the crude physical abuses are implausible, yet. . . . In a Post-Human world there would still be plenty of niches where human equivalent automation would be desirable: embedded systems in autonomous devices, self-aware daemons in the lower functioning of larger sentients. (A strongly superhuman intelligence would likely be a Society of Mind[23] with some very competent components.) Some of these human equivalents might be used for nothing more than digital signal processing. They would be more like whales than humans. Others might be very human-like, yet with a one-sidedness, a dedication that would put them in a mental hospital in our era. Though none of these creatures might be flesh-and-blood humans, they might be the closest things in the new enviroment to what we call human now. (I. J. Good had something to say about this, though at this late date the advice may be moot: Good[24] proposed a "Meta-Golden Rule", which might be paraphrased as "Treat your inferiors as you would be treated by your superiors." It's a wonderful, paradoxical idea (and most of my friends don't believe it) since the game-theoretic payoff is so hard to articulate. Yet if we were able to follow it, in some sense that might say something about the plausibility of such kindness in this universe.)

   I have argued above that we cannot prevent the Singularity, that its coming is an inevitable consequence of the humans' natural competitiveness and the possibilities inherent in technology. And yet . . . we are the initiators. Even the largest avalanche is triggered by small things. We have the freedom to establish initial conditions, make things happen in ways that are less inimical than others. Of course (as with starting avalanches), it may not be clear what the right guiding nudge really is.

Other paths to the singularity: Intelligence Amplification

When people speak of creating superhumanly intelligent beings, they are usually imagining an AI project. But as I noted at the beginning of this paper, there are other paths to superhumanity. Computer networks and human-computer interfaces seem more mundane than AI, and yet they could lead to the Singularity. I call this contrasting approach Intelligence Amplification (IA). IA is something that is proceeding very naturally, in most cases not even recognized by its developers for what it is. But every time our ability to access information and to communicate it to others is improved, in some sense we have achieved an increase over natural intelligence. Even now, the team of a PhD human and good computer workstation (even an off-net workstation!) could probably max any written intelligence test in existence.

   And it's very likely that IA is a much easier road to the achievement of superhumanity than pure AI. In humans, the hardest development problems have already been solved.

Building up from within ourselves ought to be easier than figuring out first what we really are and then building machines that are all of that. And there is at least conjectural precedent for this approach. Cairns-Smith[25] has speculated that biological life may have begun as an adjunct to still more primitive life based on crystalline growth. Lynn Margulis (in *Microcosmos*[26] and elsewhere) has made strong arguments that mutualism is a great driving force in evolution.

Note that I am not proposing that AI research be ignored or less funded. What goes on with AI will often have applications in IA, and vice versa. I am suggesting that we recognize that in network and interface research there is something as profound (and potential wild) as Artificial Intelligence. With that insight, we may see projects that are not as directly applicable as conventional interface and network design work, but which serve to advance us toward the Singularity along the IA path.

Here are some possible projects that take on special significance, given the IA point of view:

- Human/computer team automation: Take problems that are normally considered for purely machine solution (like hill-climbing problems), and design programs and inter-faces that take a advantage of humans' intuition and available computer hardware. Considering all the bizarreness of higher dimensional hill-climbing problems (and the neat algorithms that have been devised for their solution), there could be some very interesting displays and control tools provided to the human team member.

- Develop human/computer symbiosis in art: Combine the graphic generation capab-ility of modern machines and the esthetic sensibility of humans. Of course, there has been an enormous amount of research in designing computer aids for artists, as labor saving tools. I'm suggesting that we explicitly aim for a greater merging of compet-ence, that we explicitly recognize the cooperative approach that is possible. Karl Sims[27] has done wonderful work in this direction.

- Allow human/computer teams at chess tournaments. We already have programs that can play better than almost all humans. But how much work has been done on how this power could be used by a human, to get something even better? If such teams were allowed in at least some chess tournaments, it could have the positive effect on IA research that allowing computers in tournaments had for the corresponding niche in AI.

- Develop interfaces that allow computer and network access without requiring the human to be tied to one spot, sitting in front of a computer. (This is an aspect of IA that fits so well with known economic advantages that lots of effort is already being spent on it.)

- Develop more symmetrical decision support systems. A popular research/product area in recent years has been decision support systems. This is a form of IA, but may be too focussed on systems that are oracular. As much as the program giving the user information, there must be the idea of the user giving the program guidance.

- Use local area nets to make human teams that really work (ie, are more effective than their component members). This is generally the area of "groupware", already a very popular commercial pursuit. The change in viewpoint here would be to regard the group activity as a combination organism. In one sense, this suggestion might be regarded as the goal of inventing a "Rules of Order" for such combination operations. For instance, group focus might be more easily maintained than in classical meetings. Expertise of individual human members could be isolated from ego issues such that the contribution of different members is focussed on the team project. And of course shared data bases could be used much more conveniently than in conventional committee operations. (Note that this suggestion is aimed at team operations rather than political meetings. In a political setting, the automation described above would simply enforce the power of the persons making the rules!)

- Exploit the worldwide Internet as a combination human/ machine tool. Of all the items on the list, progress in this is proceeding the fastest and may run us into the Singularity before anything else. The power and influence of even the present-day Internet is vastly underestimated. For instance, I think our contemporary computer systems would break under the weight of their own complexity if it weren't for the edge that the USENET "group mind" gives the system administration and support people! The very anarchy of the worldwide net development is evidence of its potential. As connectivity and bandwidth and archive size and computer speed all increase, we are seeing something like Lynn Marguilis's vision[28] of the biosphere as data processor recapitulated, but at a million times greater speed and with millions of humanly intelligent agents (ourselves).

The above examples illustrate research that can be done within the context of contemporary computer science departments. There are other paradigms. For example, much of the work in Artificial Intelligence and neural nets would benefit from a closer connection with biological life. Instead of simply trying to model and understand biological life with computers, research could be directed toward the creation of composite systems that rely on biological life for guidance or for the providing features we don't understand well enough yet to implement in hardware. A long-time dream of science-fiction has been direct brain to computer interfaces.[29, 30] In fact, there is concrete work that can be done (and is being done) in this area:

- Limb prosthetics is a topic of direct commercial applicability. Nerve to silicon transducers can be made.[31] This is an exciting, near-term step toward direct communication.

- Direct links into brains seem feasible, if the bit rate is low: given human learning flexibility, the actual brain neuron targets might not have to be precisely selected. Even 100 bits per second would be of great use to stroke victims who would otherwise be confined to menu-driven interfaces.

- Plugging in to the optic trunk has the potential for bandwidths of 1 Mbit/second or so. But for this, we need to know the fine-scale architecture of vision, and we need to place an enormous web of electrodes with exquisite precision. If we want our high bandwidth connection to be in addition to what paths are already present in the brain, the problem becomes vastly more intractable. Just sticking a grid of high-bandwidth receivers into a brain certainly won't do it. But suppose that the high-bandwidth grid were present while the brain structure was actually setting up, as the embryo develops. That suggests:

- Animal embryo experiments. I wouldn't expect any IA success in the first years of such research, but giving developing brains access to complex simulated neural structures might be very interesting to the people who study how the embryonic brain develops. In the long run, such experiments might produce animals with additional sense paths and interesting intellectual abilities. Originally, I had hoped that this discussion of IA would yield some clearly safer approaches to the Singularity. (After all, IA allows our participation in a kind of transcendence.) Alas, looking back over these IA proposals, about all I am sure of is that they should be considered, that they may give us more options. But as for safety . . . well, some of the suggestions are a little scarey on their face. One of my informal reviewers pointed out that IA for individual humans creates a rather sinister elite. We humans have millions of years of evolutionary baggage that makes us regard competition in a deadly light. Much of that deadliness may not be necessary in today's world, one where losers take on the winners' tricks and are co-opted into the winners' enterprises. A creature that was built de novo might possibly be a much more benign entity than one with a kernel based on fang and talon. And even the egalitarian view of an Internet that wakes up along with all mankind can be viewed as a nightmare.[32]

The problem is not simply that the Singularity represents the passing of humankind from center stage, but that it contradicts our most deeply held notions of being. I think a closer look at the notion of strong superhumanity can show why that is.

Strong superhumanity and the best we can ask for

Suppose we could tailor the Singularity. Suppose we could attain our most extravagant hopes. What then would we ask for: That humans themselves would become their own successors, that whatever injustice occurs would be tempered by our knowledge of our roots. For those who remained unaltered, the goal would be benign treatment (perhaps even giving the stay-behinds the appearance of being masters of godlike slaves). It could be a golden age that also involved progress (overleaping Stent's barrier). Immortality (or at least a lifetime as long as we can make the universe survive[33, 34]) would be achievable. But in this brightest and kindest world, the philosophical problems themselves become intimidating. A mind that stays at the same capacity cannot live forever; after a few thousand years it would look more like a repeating tape loop than a person. (The most chilling picture I have seen of this is in Larry Niven's "The Ethics of Madness."[35]) To live indefinitely long, the mind itself must grow . . . and when it becomes great enough, and looks back . . . what fellow-feeling can it have with the soul that it was originally? Certainly the later being would be everything the original was, but so much vastly more. And so even for the individual, the Cairns-Smith or Lynn Margulis notion of new life growing incrementally out of the old must still be valid.

This "problem" about immortality comes up in much more direct ways. The notion of ego and self-awareness has been the bedrock of the hardheaded rationalism of the last few centuries. Yet now the notion of self-awareness is under attack from the Artificial Intelligence people ("self-awareness and other delusions"). Intelligence Amplification undercuts our concept of ego from another direction. The post-Singularity world will involve extremely high-bandwidth networking. A central feature of strongly superhuman entities will likely be their ability to communicate at variable bandwidths, including ones far higher than speech or written messages. What happens when pieces of ego can be copied and merged, when the size of a selfawareness can grow or shrink to fit the nature of the problems under consideration? These are essential features of strong superhumanity and the Singularity. Thinking about them, one begins to feel how essentially strange and different the Post-Human era will be — no matter how cleverly and benignly it is brought to be.

From one angle, the vision fits many of our happiest dreams: a time unending, where we can truly know one another and understand the deepest mysteries. From another angle, it's a lot like the worst- case scenario I imagined earlier in this paper.

Which is the valid viewpoint? In fact, I think the new era is simply too different to fit into the classical frame of good and evil. That frame is based on the idea of isolated, immutable minds connected by tenuous, low-bandwith links. But the post-Singularity world does fit with the larger tradition of change and cooperation that started long ago (perhaps even before the rise of biological life). I think there are notions of ethics that would apply in such an era. Research into IA and high-bandwidth communications should improve this understanding. I see just the glimmerings of this now.[36] There is Good's MetaGolden Rule; perhaps there are rules for distinguishing self from others on the basis of bandwidth of connection. And while mind and self will be vastly more labile than in the past, much of what we value (knowledge, memory, thought) need never be lost. I think Freeman Dyson has it right when he says[37]: "God is what mind becomes when it has passed beyond the scale of our comprehension."

[I wish to thank John Carroll of San Diego State University and Howard Davidson of Sun Microsystems for discussing the draft version of this paper with me.]

Notes

1. Moravec, Hans, *Mind Children*, Harvard University Press, 1988.
2. Platt, Charles, Private Communication.
3. Bear, Greg, "Blood Music", *Analog Science Fiction-Science Fact*, June, 1983. Expanded into the novel *Blood Music*, Morrow, 1985.

4. Ulam, S., Tribute to John von Neumann, *Bulletin of the American Mathematical Society*, vol 64, nr 3, part 2, May 1958, pp. 1-49.

5. See Stent, Gunther S., *The Coming of the Golden Age: A View of the End of Progress*, The Natural History Press, 1969.

6. Good, I. J., "Speculations Concerning the First Ultraintelligent Machine," in *Advances in Computers*, vol 6, Franz L. Alt and Morris Rubinoff, eds, pp. 31-88, 1965, Academic Press.

7. Vinge, Vernor, "Bookworm, Run!," *Analog*, March 1966, pp. 8-40. Reprinted in *True Names and Other Dangers*, Vernor Vinge, Baen Books, 1987.

8. Alfve'n, Hannes, writing as Olof Johanneson, *The End of Man?*, Award Books, 1969 earlier published as "The Tale of the Big Computer," Coward-McCann, translated from a book copyright 1966 Albert Bonniers Forlag AB with English translation copyright 1966 by Victor Gollancz, Ltd.

9. Vinge, Vernor, First Word, *Omni*, January 1983, p. 10.

10. Bear, Greg, "Blood Music," *Analog Science Fiction-Science Fact*, June, 1983. Expanded into the novel *Blood Music*, Morrow, 1985.

11. Stapledon, Olaf, *Star Maker*, Berkley Books, 1961 (originally published in 1937).

12. Vinge, Vernor, "True Names," *Binary Star Number 5*, Dell, 1981. Reprinted in *True Names and Other Dangers*, Vernor Vinge, Baen Books, 1987.

13. Penrose, Roger, *The Emperor's New Mind*, Oxford University Press, 1989.

14. Searle, John R., "Minds, Brains, and Programs," in *The Behavioral and Brain Sciences*, vol 3, Cambridge University Press, 1980. The essay is reprinted in *The Mind's I*, edited by Douglas R. Hofstadter and Daniel C. Dennett, Basic Books, 1981 (my source for this reference). This reprinting contains an excellent critique of the Searle essay.

15. Thearling, Kurt, "How We Will Build a Machine that Thinks," a workshop at Thinking Machines Corporation, August 24-26, 1992. Personal Communication.

16. Moravec, Hans, *Mind Children*, Harvard University Press, 1988.

17. Conrad, Michael *et al.*, "Towards an Artificial Brain," *BioSystems*, vol 23, 1989, pp. 175-218.

18. Rasmussen, S. *et al.*, "Computational Connectionism within Neurons: a Model of Cytoskeletal Automata Subserving Neural Networks," in *Emergent Computation*, Stephanie Forrest, ed., pp. 428-449, MIT Press, 1991.

19. Stent, Gunther S., *The Coming of the Golden Age: A View of the End of Progress*, The Natural History Press, 1969.

20. Herbert, Frank, *Dune*, Berkley Books, 1985. However, this novel was serialized in *Analog Science Fiction-Science Fact* in the 1960s.

21. Drexler, K. Eric, *Engines of Creation*, Anchor Press/Doubleday, 1986.

22. Asimov, Isaac, "Runaround," *Astounding Science Fiction*, March 1942, p. 94. Reprinted in *Robot Visions*, Isaac Asimov, ROC, 1990. Asimov describes the development of his robotics stories in this book.

23. Minsky, Marvin, *Society of Mind*, Simon and Schuster, 1985.

24. G. Harry Stine and Andrew Haley have also written about metalaw as it might relate to extra-terrestrials: G. Harry Stine, "How to Get along with Extraterrestrials . . . or Your Neighbor," *Analog Science Fact- Science Fiction*, February, 1980, pp. 39-47.

25. Cairns-Smith, A. G., *Seven Clues to the Origin of Life*, Cambridge University Press, 1985.

26. Margulis, Lynn and Dorion Sagan, *Microcosmos, Four Billion Years of Evolution from Our Microbial Ancestors*, Summit Books, 1986.

27. Sims, Karl, "Interactive Evolution of Dynamical Systems," Thinking Machines Corporation, Technical Report Series (published in *Toward a Practice of Autonomous Systems: Proceedings of the First European Conference on Artificial Life*, Paris, MIT Press, December 1991.

28. Margulis, Lynn and Dorion Sagan, *Microcosmos, Four Billion Years of Evolution from Our Microbial Ancestors*, Summit Books, 1986.

29. Anderson, Poul, "Kings Who Die," *If*, March 1962, pp. 8-36. Reprinted in *Seven Conquests*, Poul Anderson, MacMillan Co., 1969.

30. Vinge, Vernor, "Bookworm, Run!," *Analog*, March 1966, pp. 8-40. Reprinted in *True Names and Other Dangers*, Vernor Vinge, Baen Books, 1987.

31. Kovacs, G. T. A. *et al.,* "Regeneration Microelectrode Array for Peripheral Nerve Recording and Stimulation," *IEEE Transactions on Biomedical Engineering*, v 39, n 9, pp. 893-902.

32. Swanwick Michael, *Vacuum Flowers*, serialized in *Isaac Asimov's Science Fiction Magazine*, December 1986 - February 1987. Republished by Ace Books, 1988.

33. Dyson, Freeman, "Physics and Biology in an Open Universe," *Review of Modern Physics*, vol 51, 1979, pp. 447-460.

34. Barrow, John D. and Frank J. Tipler, *The Anthropic Cosmological Principle*, Oxford University Press, 1986.

35. Niven, Larry, "The Ethics of Madness," *If*, April 1967, pp. 82-108. Reprinted in *Neutron Star*, Larry Niven, Ballantine Books, 1968.

36. Vinge, Vernor, To Appear [:-)]

37. Dyson, Freeman, *Infinite in All Directions*, Harper & Row, 1988.

27

Aliens in the fourth dimension

Gwyneth Jones

When two worlds collide

The aliens can always speak English. This is one of those absurdities of pulp fiction and B movies, like saucer shaped spaceships and hairdryer machines that track your brain waves,[1] that might well come true—suppose the visitors avoid those disconcerting forms of long haul space travel, that whisk you across the galaxy and dump you in the concourse of Lime Street station before you have time to say "Non Smoking." If they come in slowly they'll spend the latter part of their journey travelling through a vast cloud of human broadcasting signals, which they'll easily pick up on the alien cabin tv. They'll have plenty of time to acquire a smattering of useful phrases. Or so the current received wisdom goes. By now it's not *completely* inevitable that they'll speak English, and with a United States accent, in the traditional manner. They might get hooked on Brazilian soap opera. But whatever formal, articulate language our visitors may use in real life, all the aliens we know so far speak human. They speak our human predicament, our history, our hopes and fears, our pride and shame. As long as we haven't met any actual no kidding intelligent extraterrestrials (and I would maintain that this is still the case, though I know opinions are divided) the aliens we imagine are always other humans in disguise: no more, no less. Whether or not hell is other people, it is certainly *other people* who arrive, in these fictions, to challenge our isolation: to be feared or worshipped, interrogated, annihilated, appeased. When the historical situation demands it science fiction writers demonise our enemies, the way the great Aryan court poet[2] who wrote the story of Prince Rama *demonised* the Dravidian menace, in India long ago. Or we can use imaginary aliens to assuage our guilt. I think it's not unlikely that our European ancestors invented the little people who live in the hills, cast spells and are "ill to cross"—who appear so often in traditional fiction north of the mediterranean and west of Moscow—to explain why their cousins the Neanderthals had mysteriously vanished from public life. I see the same thing happening today, as science fiction of the environmentally-conscious decades becomes littered with gentle, magical, colorful alien races who live at one with nature in happy non-hierarchical rainforest communities. Even the project of creating an *authentically incomprehensible* other intelligent species, which is sporadically attempted in science fiction, is inescapably a human story. Do we yet know of any other beings who can imagine, or could care less, what "incomprehensible" means?

More often than not, the aliens story involves an invasion. The strangers have arrived. They want our planet, and intend to wipe us out. We have arrived. The native aliens— poor ineffectual technologically incompetent creatures—had better get out of the way. The good guys will try to protect them: but territorial expansion, sometimes known as "progress," is an unstoppable force. This pleasant paradigm of intra-species relations obviously strikes a deep chord. We, in the community of science fiction writers and readers at least, do not expect to co-exist comfortably with *other people*. Which ever side is "ours," there is going to be trouble, there is going to be grief, when two worlds collide. And whatever language everyone is speaking, there is definitely going to be a break down in communications.

When I invented my alien invaders "The Aleutians" I was aware of the models that science fiction offered, and of the doubled purpose that they could serve. I wanted, like other writers before me, to tell a story about the colonisers and the colonised. The everlasting expansion of a successful population, first commandment on the Darwinian tablets of stone, makes this encounter "the supplanters and the natives," an enduring feature of human history. Colonial adventure has been a significant factor in the shaping of my own, European, twentieth-century culture. I wanted to think about this topic. I wanted to study the truly extraordinary imbalance in wealth, power, and *per capita* human comfort, from the south to the north, that came into being over three hundred years or so of European rule in Africa, Asia and the Indian subcontinent: an imbalance which did not exist when the Portuguese reached China, when the first British and French trading posts were established on the coasts of India; when European explorers arrived in the gold-empire cities of West Africa.[3] I also wanted—the other layer of the doubled purpose—to describe and examine the relationship between men and women. There are obvious parallels between my culture's colonial adventure and the battle of the sexes. Men come to this world helpless, like bewildered explorers. At first they all have to rely on the goodwill of the native ruler of the forked, walking piece of earth in which they find themselves. And then, both individually and on a global scale, they amass as if by magic a huge proportion of the earth's wealth, power and influence, while the overwhelming majority of those native rulers are doomed to suffer and drudge and starve in the most humiliating conditions. But why? I wondered. How did this come about? Why *do* most of the women get such a rough deal?

I felt that my historical model would be better for throwing up insights, mental experiments, refutable hypotheses about sexual politics, than popular "alien invasion" narratives based on United States cultural history. The possibilities of an outright *lebensraum* struggle between settlers and natives would soon be exhausted; while a situation involving any extreme division between master race and slave race would be too clear cut.[4] I needed something in a sense more innocent. A relationship that could

grow in intimacy and corruption: a trading partnership where neither party is more altru-
istic than the other, whichever manages to win the advantage. Most of all, I needed
something *slow*. I needed to see what would happen to my experiment over hundreds
of years: over generations, not decades. So, the Aleutians appeared: a feckless crew
of adventurers and dreamers, with only the shakiest of State backing, no aim beyond
seeing life and turning a quick profit; and no coherent long-term plans whatever.

Interview with the alien

Some stories about meeting the aliens are recruiting posters for the Darwinian army.
Explicitly, we're invited to cheer for the home team, or to enjoy the pleasurably sad
and moving defeat of the losers. Implicitly, we're reminded that every encounter with
"the other," down to office manoeuvring and love affairs, is a fight for territory: and the
weak must go to the wall. Some people invent aliens as a Utopian or satirical exercise, to show how a really well-designed intelligent species would live and function, and
how far the human model falls below this ideal. I confess to adopting elements from
both these approaches. But above all, I wanted my aliens to represent an alternative. I
wanted them to say to my readers *It ain't necessarily so*.[5] History is not inevitable, and
neither is sexual gender as we know it an inevitable part of being human. I didn't intend
my aliens to represent "women," exactly; or for the humans to be seen as "men" in
this context. Human women and men have their own story in the Aleutian books. But
I wanted to make the relationship *suggestive* of another way things could have turned
out. I planned to give my alien conquerors the characteristics, all the supposed deficiencies, that Europeans came to see in their subject races in darkest Africa and the mystic
East—"animal" nature, irrationality, intuition; mechanical incompetence, indifference to
time, helpless aversion to theory and measurement: and I planned to have them win
the territorial battle this time. It was no coincidence, for my purposes, that the same
list of qualities or deficiencies—a nature closer to the animal, intuitive communication
skills and all the rest of it—were and still are routinely awarded to *women,* the defeated
natives, supplanted rulers of men, in cultures north and south, west and east, white and
non-white, the human world over.[6]

    They had to be humanoid. I didn't want my readers to be able to distance them-
selves; or to struggle proudly towards empathy in spite of the tentacles. I didn't want
anyone to be able to think, *Why, they're just like us once you get past the face-lumps,*
the way we do when we get to know the tv alien goodies and baddies in *Babylon 5* or
Space Precinct 9. I needed them to be irreducibly weird and, *at the same time*, undeniably
people, the same as us. I believe this to be a fairly accurate approximation of the real-
world situation—between the Japanese and the Welsh, say, or between women and men:
or indeed between any individual human being and the next. Difference is real. It does
not go away. To express my contention—that irreducible difference, like genetic variation,

is conserved in the individual, not in race, nationality or reproductive function, I often awarded my Aleutians quirks of taste and opinion belonging to one uniquely different middle-aged, middle-class, leftish English woman. And I was entertained to find them hailed by US critics as "the most convincingly *alien* beings to grace science fiction in years." Now it can be told. . .

Since they had to be humanoid I made a virtue of the necessity, and had someone explain to my readers that all those ufologists can't be wrong. The human body plan is perfectly plausible, for sound scientific reasons. This would lead me into interesting territory later on. Whether or not it's true that other planets are likely to throw up creatures that look like us, I don't know. No one knows. But humanoid aliens certainly make life easier for the science fiction novelist. The control our physical embodiment has over our rational processes is so deep and strong that it's excruciating trying to write about intelligent plasma clouds, if you're in the least worried about verisimilitude. It's a trick, it can be done. But the moment your attention falters, your basic programming will restore the defaults of the pentadactyl limb, binocular vision and articulated spine. You'll find your plasma characters cracking hard nuts, grappling with sticky ideas, looking at each other in a funny way, scratching their heads, weaving plots and generally making a chimpanzees' tea-party of your chaste cosmic emanations.

They had to be humanoid and they had to be sexless. I wanted a society that knew nothing about the great divide which allows half the human race to regard the other half as utterly, transcendently, *different* on the grounds of reproductive function. I wanted complex and interesting people who managed to have lives fully as strange, distressing, satisfying, absorbing, productive as ours, without having any access to that central "us and themness" of human life. I realised before long that this plan created some aliens who had a very shaky idea, if any, of the concept "alien," especially as applied to another person. Which was a good joke: and like the cosmic standard body plan, it lead to interesting consequences. But that came later.

Once my roughly humanoid aliens reached earth, interrogation proceeded along traditional lines. I whisked them into my laboratory for intensive internal examination, with a prurient concentration on sex and toilet habits. In real life (I mean in the novel *White Queen*) the buccaneers resisted this proposal. They didn't know they were aliens, they thought they were merely strangers, and they didn't see why they had to be vivisected before they could have their tourist visas. The humans were too nervous to insist, but a maverick scientist secured a tissue sample. . . With this same tissue sample in my possession, I was able to establish that the Aleutians were hermaphrodites, to borrow a human term. (I considered parthenogenesis, with a few males every dozen or so generations, like greenfly. But this was what I finally came up with.) Each of them had the same reproductive tract. There was an external organ consisting of a fold or pouch in the lower abdomen, lined with mucous membrane, holding an appendage called "the claw." Beyond the porous inner wall of this pouch, known as "the cup," extended a reservoir of potential embryos—something like the lifetime supply of eggs in human ovaries, but these eggs didn't need to be fertilised. When one or other of the embryos was triggered into growth—not by any analogue of sexual intercourse but by an untraceable complex of environmental and emotional factors—the individual would become pregnant. The new baby, which would grow in the pouch like a marsupial infant until it was ready to emerge, would prove to be one of the three million or so genetically differentiated individuals in a reproductive group known as the "brood." (I should point out that I'm going to use the human word "gene" and related terms throughout, for the alien analogues to these structures.) These same three million *people,* each one a particular chemically defined bundle of traits and talents, would be born again and again. In Aleutia you wouldn't ask of a newborn baby, "Is it a boy or a girl?" You'd ask, "Who is it?" Maybe there'd be a little heelprick thing at the hospital, and then the midwife would tell you whether you'd given birth to someone famous, or someone you knew and didn't like, or someone you vaguely remembered having met at a party once, in another lifetime.

So much for reproduction, but I needed to account for evolution. How could my serial immortals, born-again hermaphrodites, have come to be? How could they continue to adapt to their environment? It was a major breakthrough when I discovered that the brood was held together by a living information network. Every Aleutian had a glandular system constantly generating mobile cell-complexes called "wanderers" which were shed through the pores of the skin, particularly in special areas like the mucous-coated inner walls of the "cup." Each wanderer was a chemical snapshot of the individual's current emotional state, their status, experience, their shifting place in the whole brood entity: a kind of tiny self. The Aleutians would pick and eat "wanderers" from each other's skin in a grooming process very like that which we observe in real-life apes, baboons, monkeys. To offer someone a "wanderer" would be a common social gesture: *"Hello, this is how I am—."* Once consumed, the snapshot information would be replicated and shuttled off to the reproductive tract, where it would be compared with the matching potential embryo, and the embryo updated: so that the chemical nature of the person who might be born was continually being affected by the same person's current life. It was a Lamarkian evolution, directly driven by environmental pressure, rather than by the feedback between environment and random mutation, but it looked to me as if it would work well enough. Nothing much would happen from life to life. But over evolutionary time the individual and the whole brood entity would be changing in phase: growing more complex, remembering and forgetting, opening up new pathways, closing down others. I noticed, when I was setting this up, that the *environment* to which my Aleutians were adapting was the rest of Aleutian society, at least as much as the outside world. But that's another story. . .

I had done away with sexual gender. But if I wanted a society that seemed fully developed to human readers, I couldn't do without passion. I had no wish to create a race of wistful Spocks, or chilly fragments of a hive-mind. The Aleutians must not be deficient in personhood. Luckily I realised that the wanderer system gave me the means to elaborate a whole world of social, emotional and physical intercourse. The Aleutians lived and breathed chemical information, the social exchange of wanderers was essential to their well-being. But they would also be drawn, by emotional attachment, infatuation, fellow feeling or even a need to dominate, to a more intense experience: where the lovers would get naked and *lie down* together, cups opened and fused lip to lip, claws entwined, information flooding from skin to skin, in an ecstasy of chemical communication. They would fall in love with another self the way we—supposedly—fall in love with difference. Romantic souls would always be searching for that special person, as near as possible the same genetic individual as themselves, with whom the mapping would be complete.

More revelations followed. The whole of Aleutian art and religion, I realised, sprang from the concept of the diverse, recurrent Self of the brood. Their whole education and history came from studying the records left behind by their previous selves. Their technology was based on tailored skin-secretions, essentially specialised kinds of wanderers. Their power to manipulate raw materials had grown not through conscious experiment or leaps of imagination, as ours is held to have developed, but by the placid, inchworm trial and error of molecular evolution. Arguably there was only one Aleutian species—if there had ever been more—since this process of *infecting* the physical world with self-similar chemical information had been going on for aeons. The entire Aleutian environment: buildings, roads, furniture, pets, beasts of burden, transport, was alive with the same life as themselves, the same self.

Once I'd started this machine going, it kept throwing up new ideas. I realised their society was in some ways extremely rigid. Any serial immortal might be born in any kind of social circumstances. But no one could take on a new adult role in society or even retrain for a new job except over millennia of lifetimes. An Aleutian couldn't *learn* to become a carpenter; or to be generous. You were either born with a chemically defined ability or it was not an option. Aleutians, being built on the same pattern as ourselves but with a highly conservative development programme, revert easily to a four-footed gait. This is good for scaring humans, who see *intelligent alien werewolves* leaping at them. The obligate cooks use bodily secretions to prepare food: a method quite acceptable in many human communities, where teeth and saliva replace motorised food mixers; and Aleutians use toilet pads to absorb the minor amount of waste produced by their highly processed diet. I made up this because I liked the image of the alien arriving and saying *"Quickly, take me somewhere I can buy some sanitary pads. . ."*; but then I noticed this was another aspect of the way they don't have a sense of the alien. They don't even go off by themselves to shit. Aleutians live in a soup of shared presence, they are the opposite of Cartesians. They have no horror of personal death (though they can fear it). But things that are intrinsically *not alive*—like electrons, photons, the image in a mirror or on a screen, they consider uncanny . . . I could go on, but I won't. We'd be here forever. I believe the elaboration, the proliferation of consequences, could be continued indefinitely. It all goes to show, if anyone needed another demonstration, how much complexity, and what a strange illusion of coherence within that complexity, can be generated from a few simple, arbitrary original conditions.

It's said that the work of science fiction is to make the strange familiar and the familiar strange. I often find that what we do is to take some persistent fiction of contemporary human life, and turn it into science. By the time I'd finished this phase of the interrogation my Aleutians had all the typical beliefs and traditions of one of those caste-ridden, feudal, tropical societies doomed to be swept away by the gadget-building bourgeois individualists from the north. They were animists. They believed in reincarnation. They had no hunger for progress, no use for measurement or theory, no obsession with the passage of time. They were, in short, the kind of people we often wish we could be, except we'd rather have jet transport and microwave pizza.[7] But in the Aleutians' case, everything worked: and their massively successful ambient-temperature biotechnology was exactly tailored—as if by a malignant deity—to blow the mechanisers away. They were on course to take over a world, although they didn't know it: not because they were sacred white-faced messengers from the Sun God or what have you, but because they were *not* weird. *By chance* they had arrived at the historical moment when that jaded mechanist paradigm was giving out, and they had the goods that everybody on earth was beginning to want. They could do things the locals could do themselves, they had skills the locals could well understand, and they were just that crucial half a move ahead of the game.

Speech and silence

I interrogated my aliens in the language of science, looking for differences that would work. Eventually I became uneasy about this process. If the Aleutians were in some sense "supposed to be women," it was disquieting to note that I'd treated them exactly the way male-gendered medicine has treated human women until very recently indeed—behaving as if their reproductive system was the only interesting thing about them. I approached Aleutian speech and language with more humility, deliberately trying to remove the division between experimenter and experiment. I had travelled, fairly widely. I had been an alien in many contexts. Not least as a girl among the boys. I had observed that though the color of my skin and the shape of my chest would always be intriguing, I could often be accepted and treated like a person, *as long as I made the right gestures.* Wherever you go there will be bus-fares, light switches, supermarkets, airports, taps, power sockets, street food, tv cartoons, music cassette players, advertising hoardings, motorway landscape. Watch what the locals do, and you'll soon adjust to the minor variations in the silent universal language.

One can look on the sameness of the global village as an artefact of cultural imperialism, another bitter legacy of White European rule in all its forms. But I felt that these narrative signs of a single human life, repeated the world over, must be connected to that animal-embodiment we all share, or they would not survive. I had invented new forms of difference, now I wanted to celebrate sameness. I made my Aleutians silent, like dumb animals, for many reasons, but first of all because I knew that I could pass for normal in foreign situations as long as I didn't speak. And I made human body-language intelligible to them, on the grounds that just as our *common humanity* makes and recognises the same patterns everywhere, the aliens' wordless natural language had been deeply shaped by the same pressures as have shaped the natural languages of life on earth. The whole biochemical spectrum is missing, from their point of view, because we have no wanderers, no intelligent secretions at all. But every human gesture that remains is as intelligible to them as another brood's dialect of the common tongue that everyone shares at home. To make sure of my point I raised and dismissed the possibility that they were time-travellers returning to their forgotten planet of origin; and the other possibility that they had grown, like us, from humanoid seed sown across the galaxy by some elder race. They were an absolutely, originally different evolution of life. But they were *the same* because life, wherever it arises in our middle dimensions, must be subject to the same constraints, and the more we learn about our development the more we see that the most universal pressures—time and gravity, quantum mechanics; the nature of certain chemical bonds—drive through biological complexity on every fractal scale, from the design of an opposable thumb to the link between the chemistry of emotion and a set of facial muscles. This sameness, subject to cultural variation but always reasserting itself, was shown chiefly in their ability to understand us.

In line with my model of Aleutians as "women," and "native peoples," it was right for them to be wary and rather contemptuous of spoken language. I wanted them to be silent like the processes of cell-biology, like social insects exchanging pheromone signals: and like larger animals conversing through grooming, nuzzling, eye-contact and gesture. I wanted the humans, convinced that the barrier between self and other was insurmountable except by magic, to be deeply alarmed by these seeming telepaths—the way characters in classic male-gendered science fiction are so absurdly impressed at an occult power they call *empathy*: whereby some superbeing or human freak can walk into a room and *actually sense* the way the other people there are feeling. (God give me strength: my cat can do that.) But I didn't want to do away with spoken language altogether. Words are separation. Words divide. That is the work they do. I know this because I've felt it happen: whenever I open my mouth and speak, having been accepted as perfectly normal until that moment, and prove by my parlous accent and toddler's vocabulary that I'm not French; or whenever I make a public, female-gendered statement in a male group. Everything else that we think we use language for, we can handle without what the Aleutians call "formal speeches." But for the Aleutians not to have this separation, this means of stepping out of the natural cycles, would have made them less than people. So I invented a special class of Aleutians, the "signifiers," who were obligate linguists the way other Aleutians were obligate food-processors or spaceship-builders. Of course they assimilated human articulate languages with dazzling speed. This is another of the space-fantasy clichés that I think has been unfairly derided. I wouldn't be able to do it. But then, nobody would sign up an obligate monophone such as myself on a trading mission to another planet, would they?

It also transpired that the aliens did have a kind of no-kidding alien-life-form telepathy for long distance contact: another proliferation of the wanderer system. But that's another story. And there was no problem with the mechanics of speech, by the way. I gave them teeth and tongues and larynxes more or less like ours: why not?

I had made the Aleutians into self-conscious intelligences who still manipulated their surroundings the way bacteria do it; or the simpler entities that spend their lives manufacturing and communicating inside our cells. In their use of all forms of language I elaborated on this conservatism. They were beings who had reached self-consciousness, and spoken language, without abandoning any of the chronological precursor communication media. All life on earth uses chemical communication; then comes gesture, and vocalization comes last. Humans have traded all the rest for words—so that we have to rediscover the meaning of our own non-verbal gestures, and the likely effect of the hormone laden scent-cells we shed, from self-help books full of printed text. To the Aleutians, by the way, this lack of control gives the impression that all humans have Tourette's Syndrome: we're continually babbling obscenities, shouting out tactless remarks, giving away secrets in the common tongue. I pictured my Aleutians like a troop of humanly intelligent baboons, gossiping with each other silently and perfectly efficiently, having subtle and complex chemical interactions: and just occasionally feeling the need to vocalise; a threat or boast or warning, a yell of "Look at me!" It only occurred to me later that I'd made the Aleutians very like feminist women in all this: creatures dead set on *having it all*, determined to be self-aware and articulate public people, without giving up their place in the natural world.

But inevitably, insidiously the "signifier" characters, the aliens with the speaking parts, became an élite. I had already realised that I had to "translate" the wordless dialogue of Aleutian silent language into words on the page. In this I was up against one of the walls of make-believe. Science fiction is full of these necessary absurdities: I accepted it with good grace, the same way as I'd accepted the human body-plan, and used some funny direct speech marks to show the difference between spoken and unspoken dialogue, which the copy-editor didn't like. But now I felt that the male-gendered mechanist-gadget world was sneaking back into power, with historical inevitability in its train, in the Trojan Horse of articulate language. I did everything I could to correct this. I began to point out the similarities between the Aleutian "silent" language, and our spoken word as it is used most of the time by most humans. I found myself listening to human conversations and noticing the gaps: the unfinished sentences, the misplaced words, the really startling high ratio of noise to signal. I realised that most of our use of language fulfils the same function as the grooming, the nuzzling, the skin to skin chemical exchange that other life-forms share, but which with us has become taboo except in privileged intimate relations. I further realised that everything humans "say" to each other, either in meaningful statements or in this constant dilute muttering of contact, is backed, just like Aleutian communication, by a vast reservoir of cultural and evolutionary experience. We too have our "soup of shared presence," out of which genuinely novel and separate formal announcements arise rarely—to be greeted, more often than not, with wariness and contempt.

Re-inventing the wheel is a commonplace hazard in science fiction. It makes a change to find one has re-invented post-structuralist psychology. I recognised, some time after the event, that in the Silence of Aleutia I had invented the unconscious in the version proposed by Lacan, the unspoken plenum of experience that is implicit in all human discourse. Then I understood that my "signifiers" represented not a ruling caste but the public face of Aleutia; and the Silent represented all those people who don't want to "speak out," who "just want to get on with their lives": the group to which most of us belong, most of the time. In Aleutia, as in human life, the "signifiers" may be prominent figures. But who is really in charge? The intelligentsia, or the silent majority? Which is the puppeteer? The fugitive, marginal latecomer, consciousness? Or the complex, clever, perfectly competent wordless animal within?

Convergent evolution

It's now several years since I started writing about the Aleutians, and nearly a decade since I first outlined the project. . . on a beach in Thailand, one warm August night in 1988. A lot of history has happened in that time, and much of it somehow affected the story. The 1989 revolutions in Europe made a great difference to *White Queen*. The war in the former Yugoslavia had a grim influence on the second episode, *North Wind*. The nature of our local low-intensity warfare in Northern Ireland has also had a part in shaping my fictional conflicts, while the third book, *Phoenix Café,* is bound to have a *fin de siècle* feel. I've read and shakily assimilated lots of popular science, and science itself has become more *popular,* so that concerns which were completely science-fictional and obscure when I began are now topics of general interest: and that's made a difference too. Even the battle of the sexes has changed ground, both in my mind and in the real world. I'm not sure how much, if any, of my original plan survived. But this is okay. I intended to let the books change over time. I wanted things that happened at first contact to be viewed later as legends that couldn't possibly be true. I wanted concerns that were vitally important in one book to have become totally irrelevant in the next. I wanted phlogiston and cold fusion in my science, failed revolutions and forgotten dreams in my politics. I thought that discontinuity would be more true to life than a three hundred years' chunk of soap-opera, (or so, it's difficult to say exactly how much time has passed, when the master race finds measurement boring) that ends with everybody still behaving the same as they did in episode one. It's true to the historical model too. I don't think anyone would deny that the European Empire builders had lost the plot, sometime long before that stroke of midnight in 1947, climactic moment in the great disengagement.

My son Gabriel tells me stories. Not surprisingly, given his environment, he tends to tell me science fiction stories. I'm delighted when he comes up with some motif or scenario that I recognise as a new variation on a familiar theme: and he's furious (like some adult storytellers I could mention) when I point out to him he's doing something that's been done countless times before. Always, already, what we say has been said before. A while ago he came up with an adventure where the characters kept being swept away into the Fourth Dimension, an experience that transformed them, partially and then permanently if they stayed too long, into horrible gargoyles. That was where I found the title of my paper. Sadly, I can't fault his argument. There's no getting away from it, the Fourth Dimension makes monsters of us all. My Aleutians, though, have managed to change the process around. Sometimes science fiction aliens represent not merely other people, but some future other people: some unexplored possibility for the human race. Maybe my Aleutians fit that description. But it has been a surprise even to me to see how *human* they have become, how much I've found myself writing about the human predicament, about the mysteries of self and consciousness. But that's the way it has to be, unless or until the great silence out there is broken. Until we meet.

Notes

1. Saucer shaped flying machines: Hypersonic flying saucers driven by microwaves are at present the goal of serious researchers in the US (reported in *New Scientist*, 2017, 17 February 1996). MRI imaging of brain activity, involving something oddly similar to those old sciffy hairdryers, is already reality.
2. Valmiki, writing in the third century BC, Christian chronology.
3. Mungo Park, travelling in Africa in the eighteenth century was staggered by the size of the cities he found, comparing urban conditions very favourably with those in Britain (Mungo Park, *Travels In The Interior of Africa*, 1799).
4. Although Octavia Butler's trilogy '*Xenogenesis*' develops a 'slavery' narrative of alien invasion of great complexity.
5. Pleasingly, for me, a quotation from a *Porgy and Bess* lyric (George Gershwin and Dubose Heyward, 1935) intended to be sung by a black American who finds refuge from cultural domination in this defiant thought.
6. Annie Coombes, *Re-inventing Africa* (London and New Haven: Yale University Press, 1994).
7. Joanna Russ in *The Female Man* (New York: Bantam, 1975) makes a similar observation about idyllic separatism.

28

Technofetishism and the uncanny desires of A.S.F.R. (alt.sex.fetish.robots)

Allison de Fren

The interfusion of technology and sexuality—particularly when it takes the form of an artificial woman—has been an explosive combination, dating back to Pandora, the first artificial woman in literature. Hesiod tells us that Pandora was molded from clay by Hephaestus and endowed with desirable attributes by all the gods, at the behest of Zeus, who wished to punish men for the gift of fire that Prometheus had given them after stealing its secret from the heavens. The stolen fire has inspired various interpretations, many of which suggest a form of human knowledge or *technics*; thus, the artificial woman was meant to void the progress made from Prometheus's gift. Although Pandora was a "wonder" to behold, she was "sheer guile" (described with the oxymoronic *kalòn kakòn* or "beautiful evil"), an irresistible and deceptive exterior masking a secret horror in the form of a box (or jar) containing sickness, toil, and sorrow. On the orders of Zeus, Hermes offered Pandora as a gift to Prometheus's more gullible brother Epimetheus, who was so entranced by her beauty that he forgot to heed Prometheus's warning to beware all gifts from the king of the gods. And so Pandora entered the human realm and, soon thereafter, incited by curiosity, she opened the box, releasing pain and suffering into the world.

While the Pandora myth is an early reflection of and on the intersection of *technics*, knowledge, and desire, its indictment of women has been its enduring legacy. As Laura Mulvey notes, Pandora is the first in a long history of femme-fatale androids—creatures in which "a beautiful surface that is appealing and charming to man masks either an 'interior' that is mechanical or an outside that is deceitful"; this "inside/outside topography" connotes "mystery" and is "only readable in death" (55). While she mentions the fabricated women in Villiers de l'Isle-Adam's novel *Tomorrow's Eve* (*L'Eve future*, 1886), E.T.A. Hoffmann's story "The Sandman" ("Der Sandmann," 1816), and Fritz Lang's film *Metropolis* (1927), one might extrapolate from such early examples to those female WMDs that were a common trope of twentieth-century sf media, typified by the

female-android-cum-nuclear-warhead in the 1991 film *Eve of Destruction* and the villain-
ous fembots who took on Jaime Sommers in the original *Bionic Woman* television series
(1976-78). They were brought to a parodic extreme by their "bikini machine" and "girl
bomb" counterparts in the *Dr. Goldfoot* (1965, 1966) and *Austin Powers* (1997, 2002)
films. Such creatures both literalize the notion of the sexual *bombshell* while seeming
to corroborate Andreas Huyssen's proposition that within European modernism female
sexuality and technology become analogues:

> As soon as the machine came to be perceived as a demonic, inexplicable threat and
> as harbinger of chaos and destruction—a view which typically characterizes many
> 19th-century reactions to the railroad to give but one major example —writers began to
> imagine the *Maschinenmensch* as woman. There are grounds to suspect that we are
> facing here a complex process of projection and displacement. The fears and perceptual
> anxieties emanating from ever more powerful machines are recast and reconstructed in
> terms of the male fear of female sexuality, reflecting, in the Freudian account, the male's
> castration anxiety. (70)

Mulvey attempts to recuperate the iconography of Pandora and her box from its misogyn-
ist legacy by framing it within the context of psychoanalytic feminist theory. In her essay
"Pandora's Box: Topographies of Curiosity," she employs Pandora's curious gaze as an
intervening agent in the closed circuit that she describes, in her influential 1975 article
"Visual Pleasure and Narrative Cinema," between the gaze of the cinematic spectator,
understood as both active and masculine, and the passive female image that serves
as its object. There is, Mulvey suggests, a self-reflexivity at work in the curious gaze (a
gaze often coded as female), a desire to know that is "associated with enclosed, secret,
and forbidden spaces" representative of female interiority. So when Pandora looks inside
the box, a hidden space that many have read as a synecdoche for female sexuality, she
is interrogating the site/sight of sexual difference that she herself represents. Thus, the
curious gaze as *epistemophilia* (the desire to know) serves as a challenge to fetishistic
scopophilia (the desire to see, but not to know) through which the female image is constituted as a sight or "surface that conceals":

> While curiosity is a compulsive desire to see and to know, to investigate something secret,
> fetishism is born out of a refusal to see, a refusal to accept the difference the female
> body represents for the male. These complex series of turns away, of covering over, not
> of the eyes but of understanding, of fixating on a substitute object to hold the gaze, leave
> the female body as an enigma and threat, condemned to return as a symbol of anxiety
> while simultaneously being transformed into its own screen in representation. (64)

While Mulvey draws a binary distinction between knowledge and desire in an attempt
to reclaim the "inside/outside topography" of the artificial female, other critics have
questioned the relevance of both topographical and corporeal binarisms, as well as the
epistemology of fetishism, in relation to both cyberbodies and the crisis of representation

within the postmodern imaginary. Thomas Foster, for example, reflecting on the sexy robots and gynoids of the Japanese artist, Hajime Sorayama (see Figure 1), asks whether their explicit foregrounding of both technology and sexuality is reducible to traditional ideas around fetishistic disavowal: "If anything, these images represent technology as the truth of sexuality, and this inversion of the modernist tradition Huyssen defines produces anxieties that cannot be entirely or safely framed by the fetishism the images evoke" (101).[1]

If such technofetishistic imagery undercuts the psychoanalytic model of fetishism, however, it is by pushing "the logic of fetishism to a point of crisis" (Foster 98), inspiring an ambivalence and confusion that has haunted technologically-mediated bodies ever since Donna Haraway first suggested their critical potential in her "Cyborg Manifesto" (1985). Although Haraway heralded the possibilities of both "cyborg writing" and "cyborg imagery" for offering "a way out of the maze of dualisms in which we have explained our bodies and our tools to ourselves" (181), many critics have noted the difficulty of realizing a simultaneously female and post-gendered body, particularly in the visual field.

Claudia Springer, for example, draws attention to the cyberbodies in film and cyber-punk sf, which "appear masculine or feminine to an exaggerated degree. We find giant pumped-up pectoral muscles on the males and enormous breasts on the females" (66). Similarly, Anne Balsamo comments on the extent to which gender remains one of the more resilient markers of difference in the portrayal of technologically enhanced bodies:

> As is often the case when seemingly stable boundaries are displaced by technological innovation (human/artificial, life/death, nature/culture), other boundaries are more vigil-antly guarded. Indeed, the gendered boundary between male and female is one border that remains heavily guarded despite new technologized ways to rewrite the physical body in the flesh. (9)

Although for Haraway "cyborg sex" conjures "the lovely replicative baroque of ferns and invertebrates (such nice organic prophylactics against heterosexism)" (150), its visual interpretation seems to align more readily with the cyborgian nightmare depicted in Shinya Tsukamoto's cyberpunk film *Tetsuo* (1989), in which a salaryman becomes perfor-ated from the inside out by rapidly advancing metallic probes, whose mutating offshoots converge into a gigantic power drill with which he impales his lover. While *Tetsuo* offers a hyperbolic (and humorous) example of the technofetishistic imaginary, it also under-scores an interpretive dilemma in relation to the technological displacement of bodies and sexualities in the visual field: are they to be understood as compensatory or stra-tegic? Do we read the metallic "member" as an avowal or a return of the repressed, phallocentrism or a commentary on phallocentrism? Foster notes similar confusion around Sorayama's robotic and cyborg bodies: "these images make it impossible to determine whether the sexy robot is a fetish object or a woman who has been fetishized" (102). Moreover, he points out that, even when the technological mediation of bodies

Figure 1 Gynoid by Hajime Sorayama.

destabilizes traditional categories of gender and sexuality, it is difficult to escape the feedback loop of castration anxiety since "fetishism paradoxically uses ambivalence and a blurring of gender or sexual categories to defend against the anxieties created by the breakdown of such categories" (82). The ability to maintain the kind of ironic stance encouraged by Haraway in relation to technofetishistic imagery, as Foster notes, thus "seems to depend on the assumption that this technology and its popular imaging will not or cannot be 'psychoanalytically framed'" (98).

Foster points to the work of E.L. McCallum as a potential starting point for approaching technofetishism outside of the Freudian model. McCallum proposes a reconsideration of the discourse around fetishism, which, she reminds us, came of age with modernism and, particularly, with the rise of sexology, as a means of marking sexual differences and making categorical distinctions between the normative and deviant. She notes that while fetishism, within its narrow definition as a fixation, seems to work in opposition to the crisis of representation within postmodernity, "[t]his view reflects the fact that fetishism itself has come to be fetishized" (xv)—that is, fixed in meaning in a way that offers little theoretical wiggle room. By thinking *through* the fetishistic relationship—in which pleasure is courted despite "ambivalence, indeterminacy, and contradiction"—rather than merely *about* the fetish object, McCallum suggests that, far from serving as a screen against *epistemophilia*, fetishism can provide an alternative epistemological model for exploring the connections between subjects and objects, desire and knowledge (xvi).

In this essay, I follow the lead of both Foster and McCallum in an attempt to think *through* the technofetishistic relationship with the machine woman, as well as *about* the visual representations of machine bodies that are an outgrowth of that relationship, using as a springboard a little-known community of technosexuals with whom I have had contact, on and off, for nearly a decade.[2] It was an act of Pandora-like curiosity that first led me to the community: spurred by the saying that "if you enter any object in a search engine followed by the word 'sex,' you will find people who fetishize that object," I typed "robot" and "sex" into a search engine and, sure enough, found websites created by groups of people who collectively fantasize about, among other things, robots (many of whom found one another in the same way that I found them). While some do refer to themselves as "technosexuals," many call the fetish itself A.S.F.R., an acronym for alt.sex.fetish.robots, the name of the now-defunct Usenet newsgroup where members originally congregated online. Although A.S.F.R. was made possible by the advent of virtual communities, its fetishistic interests have historical antecedents that were documented in the early literature of sexology. Against their classifications of similar fetishistic practices as variations of necrophilia, as well as subsequent Freudian interpretations, I will argue that A.S.F.R. is less *about* technology in general, or the artificial woman in particular, than it is a strategy of denaturalization that uses the trope of technological "programming" to underscore subjecthood. Like the trope of "hardwiring"—which Foster discusses as a signal within cyberpunk of the constitution of bodies and identities in relation to "preexisting systems of control and power, as figured" for example "by the invisible computer network of *Neuromancer's* cyberspace" (74)—"programming" serves as a metaphor for the biological and cultural matrices within which desire is articulated and pursued. "ASFRians" experience pleasure and agency through, in a sense, hacking the system, the visual indicators of which often take the form of a female android who has run amok—an image that, in Freudian terms, emblematizes male castration anxiety. A.S.F.R. thus complicates the binary relationship between fetishism and curiosity proposed by Mulvey, while corroborating Foster's claim that technofetishistic imagery has the potential to foreground "the problematic status of psychoanalytic categories and arguments within technocultural contexts" (95).

I argue that in its attempt to unmask the artificial body (through physical breakdown), the ASFRian gaze is less aligned to fetishistic *scopophilia*—the desire to see but not to know, which is generally read in relation to the cohesive male subject—than with the self-reflexive curiosity of Pandora, the desire to see beneath the seen. Indeed, it embodies the etymological essence of curiosity as *cura*, the Latin word for care, which vacillates between its usage as a noun (meaning anxiety or sorrow) and a verb (meaning to provide relief or ministration). Curiosity often involves looking at that which causes anxiety rather than pleasure, and thus it stems from an impulse different from the visual delectation of the beautiful image. St. Augustine pejoratively referred to it as "the eyes' urges" in his *Confessions*, explaining that while the beautiful inspires the body to delight in sensual pleasures, *curiositas* "experiments with their opposites, not submitting to the gross for its own sake, but from the drive to experience and know" (240). It is *curiositas* that compels human beings to look at those things that make them shudder, the ultimate example of which is, according to Augustine, the mutilated corpse:

> This is something [in terms of sensual pleasure] they do not want to see even in dreams, or if forced to look at it while awake, or if lured to the sight expecting something pretty. . . . It is for this perverse craving that unnatural things are put on in the theater. This also leads men to pry into the arcane elements of nature, which are beyond our scope—knowing them would serve no purpose, yet men make of that knowing its own purpose. (245)

Any act of looking that involves prying into things that are "beyond our scope" or "ken" raises the specter of the uncanny, a word that, according to Victoria Nelson, is etymologically rooted in "that which cannot be 'kenned' or known by the five senses" and that, by definition, is "beyond what is normal or expected" (17). In his essay "The Uncanny" (1919), Freud discusses the term's relevance for psychoanalysis, using as a primary example Hoffmann's story "The Sandman," in which, significantly, a man falls in love with a mechanical woman. Freud, however, dismisses the relevance of the android female in order to prove that the origin of uncanniness lies beyond what he calls "the pleasure principle." The fetishistic use of the uncanny android body by ASFRians raises questions about Freud's analysis that have relevance for the critical understanding of artificial bodies in popular culture both past and present. In order to pursue these questions, I draw analogies between the uncanny artificial bodies at the heart of ASFRian fantasy and those fetishized by the Surrealists, in particular the disarticulated dolls of German artist Hans Bellmer, as well as those within the current technosphere as exemplified by Mamoru Oshii's cyberpunk anime *Ghost in the Shell 2: Innocence* (2004), which was deeply influenced by Bellmer's work.

Alt.sex.fetish.robots

The originary myth of the group A.S.F.R. is that it was started as a joke. The Usenet site, however, began to attract a loyal following of participants, primarily men, who had a secret attraction to the mechanical and the robotic. Many of them had believed that they were alone in their sexual preferences, and the site provided a sense of relief and community, a place to share their interests and compare notes with others, as well as a definitive name for the ill-defined feelings that they had been harboring in isolation. Although the acronym privileges robots, A.S.F.R. is, in fact, a blanket designation for a range of different fetishes, which includes sexual attraction to mannequins, dolls, and sculpture, as well as to real people acting like mannequins, puppets, dolls, or robots, being hypnotized, turned into statues, or immobilized or frozen in a variety of ways. While all of these fetishes were explored on the original newsgroup, many of their fans later splintered off and founded websites geared to their specific interests. They do, however, still consider themselves to be "ASFRian" and acknowledge their point of common interest: the thematic of programmatic control—whether imagined as hypnotism, magic, a puppet-master, or artificial intelligence—of a human object. When taken in this sense alone, A.S.F.R. strikes the imagination as a technological elaboration of standard BDSM (bondage-domination-sado-masochism) fantasies, in which one person dominates another for sexual pleasure. ASFRians are, in fact, sensitive to (and some might even agree with) this interpretation of their fetish, as well as the perception that it represents the reification of normative gender ideals (for when many first hear about the fetish—myself included—they imagine that, for ASFRians, desire is contingent on replacing a human subject with a vacant Stepford Wife or Husband, who mindlessly fulfills the orders of its master, both sexual and domestic). Indeed, it is this common assumption about their fetish that, according to ASFRians, necessitates its obscurity and keeps its members highly closeted in comparison to fetishists like the Furries and the Plushies (those who eroticize anthropomorphic and stuffed animals and animal costumes, respectively), who hold dozens of public conventions each year throughout the world. ASFRians are so concerned about the accusation of sadism or misogyny that they have coined a mantra or tagline, oft repeated on their websites: "ASFR is not about the objectification of women, it's about the feminization of objects."[3]

Aside from raising obvious questions about the extent to which the feminization of objects can be extricated from the objectification of women, the mantra does not so much clarify the fetish as strategically redirect it from the living to the nonliving. In so doing, it raises the specter of necrophilia, which is the lens through which the sexualization of artificial humans has been viewed since the establishment of sexology as a field of study, when "sexual pathologies" were first documented and catalogued. Although mention is made in Krafft-Ebing's landmark *Psychopathia Sexualis* (1886) of a "paraphilia" involving statues, including a reported incident of a gardener attempting to fornicate with a replica of the Venus de Milo (525), Iwan Bloch explores the preference for the artificial at greater length in *The Sexual Life of Our Time In Its Relation to Modern Civilization* (1928). In a chapter dedicated to sexual perversity, he highlights two variations of necrophilia, the first being "Venus Statuaria," the desire to have sexual intercourse with statues or other representations of human beings, a passion that he states can seize some merely by walking through a museum. The second,

"Pygmalionism," is the desire to enact the animation of an inanimate statue, usually by having real women stand atop pedestals pretending to be statues and then gradually come to life. Such a request was, Bloch suggests, common in Parisian brothels at the turn of the century.[4] Connected to the desire for statues is, according to Bloch, the use of new technologies to construct anatomically-correct human models for explicitly sexual ends:

> There exist true Vaucansons in this province of pornographic technology, clever mechanics who, from rubber and other plastic materials, prepare entire male or female bodies, which, as *hommes* or *dames de voyage*, subserve fornicatory purposes. More especially are the genital organs represented in a manner true to nature. Even the secretion of Bartholin's glands is imitated, by means of a "pneumatic tube" filled with oil. Similarly, by means of fluid and suitable apparatus, the ejaculation of the semen is imitated. Such artificial human beings are actually offered for sale in the catalogue of certain manufacturers of "Parisian rubber articles." (648)

While in the case of "Venus Statuaria" Bloch makes a distinction between those who become sexually aroused by statues *because* they are artificial and those merely responding to a naked human body *despite* its artificiality (the latter of whom he suggests comprise the bulk of the documented cases), in general he tends to collapse distinctions between the various desires that circulate around the inanimate and to suggest that they are all equally perverse. Moreover, he treats such tendencies as a separate topic from fetishism, a category that he reserves for those who invest sexual energy in a part of the human body at the expense of the whole.[5]

Writing in the 1970s, A. Scobie and A.J.W. Taylor draw a greater distinction between "agalmatophilia" or the love of statues and Pygmalionism, the desire to bring a statue *to life* (49), while Murray White, whose article appeared three years after their study, dismisses agalmatophilia entirely, stating that a negligible number of cases has been cited over the course of two thousand years, none of which are verifiable. Moreover, he attributes the interest in the phenomenon to the "insatiable preoccupation with deviant nosology" of sexologists in the late-nineteenth and early-twentieth centuries (248), many of whom, in their own fetishistic zeal, failed to make the distinction between fantasy and reality:

> Agalmatophilia has been sparingly treated as a pornographic fantasy, but there is very little evidence supporting its status as a behavioral perversion. Early scientific researchers of sexual behavior appear to have sometimes confused fantasy (the process of imagining objects or events in terms of imagery) with perversion (sexual behavior which differs widely from normal standards and which is typically prohibited by law). (249)

The constellation of artificial love schematized by Bloch has, however, been revived by Patricia Pulham, who suggests that the current popularity of life-sized silicone lovedolls, such as the Realdoll, indicates that with the help of new technologies, "agalmatophiliacs are alive and well, even if their objects of desire seem somewhat dead" (13).[6] Drawing on Meghan Laslocky's interviews with Realdoll owners documented in her 2005 *Salon.com* article "Just Like a Woman," Pulham compares the lovers of silicone dolls with both Pygmalion and Lord Ewald in Villiers de l'Isle Adam's *Tomorrow's Eve*, and she suggests that while some men attempt to enliven their dolls through a variety of techniques, including heating the silicone skin before engaging in physical contact, the resonances between their desires and necrophilia are "difficult to ignore" (14).[7]

Her views are, in fact, echoed in the first film to use a Realdoll as a character, *Love Object* (2003). A horror film that was, according to writer-director Robert Parigi, inspired by the visual similarity between Realdolls and the dead bodies that he had witnessed on a visit to the morgue, *Love Object* centers on a shy office worker who has a silicone lovedoll made in the image of a female coworker (named Lisa Bellmer, a reference to the dolls of Hans Bellmer, discussed below) on whom he has a crush.[8] At first it appears that the doll will serve as a successful transitional object to real women (a role that a Realdoll will later fulfill in the 2007 film *Lars and the Real Girl*); as he wines, dines, and otherwise engages his doll in a typical courting ritual, he gains an experiential confidence that enables him to relax around and ultimately start dating the woman on whom she has been modeled. The film suggests, however, that whatever pathology enabled him to invest life in a dead thing has a life of its own that requires an empty vessel for its fulfillment; and, since he disposed of the doll after he started to date the woman, he attempts to de-animate the woman through plastination in the story's horrifying climax.[9]

While there are clearly areas of overlap in the various desires around artificial bodies, the ongoing development of technologies for meeting such desires, as well as for the anonymous sharing of preferences within networked communities (the specificities of which tend to evolve in relation to one another), has made it somewhat easier to chart their distinctions. My own interviews with the buyers of life-sized silicone lovedolls and with ASFRians, and perusal of their respective websites, have led me to believe that, in general, they are two distinct groups.[10] Moreover, while "death" in general, and the "death drive" in particular, are of relevance to their proclivities (as I will discuss below), necrophilia is too reductive and misleading a term for understanding the broad spectrum of behavior associated with either.[11] Considering ASFRians in and of themselves, it is somewhat difficult to generalize (other than the fact that, with a small number of exceptions, they are predominantly male). As one member of the message board Fembot Central wrote in answer to one of my queries:

> the characteristics that any one of us "fetishizes" is always different—and often to a large degree—from anyone else's. But also, the psychological undertones and the way we integrate this into our lives is entirely individual. The common ground is pretty small. In the broadest sense, I suspect that each of us here can agree with the broad definition, "I am attracted to things that look like people but aren't." And that each of us will further want to qualify that assertion in some way that we feel is important. (online communication, 17 June 2009)[12]

Although meaning does vary from one individual to another, the group makes a distinction between two (somewhat oppositional) tendencies, the first indicating the desire for a robot that is entirely artificial ("built") and the second devoted to the metamorphosis between the human and the robotic ("transformation"). Nevertheless, there are certain kinds of images and erotic practices that appeal to both groups and that appear repeatedly in relation to the fetish. For example, scenarios in which a real person is acting the part of a robot would likely be of interest to both groups, albeit for different reasons. Indeed, the majority of the ASFRians that I interviewed described their earliest fetishistic experiences as occurring while watching actors and actresses playing robots on such sf television shows as *The Twilight Zone* (1959-64), *Outer Limits* (1963-65), and *Star Trek* (1966-69). Moreover, the primary indicators of mechanicity on such shows, which include silver and gold costuming and mechanical behavioral mannerisms like robotic speech, stilted movement, and repetitive motion, often enacted within moments of transition (such as when a robot is booted up, shut down, or programmed) are equally exciting to both groups. A large part of ASFRian activity revolves around the recreation in private of both the costuming and performances of these actor robots, giving the fetish a kind of do-it-yourself quality on which Katherine Gates comments in her book *Deviant Desires*. Gates places A.S.F.R. alongside slash fandom as a group that appropriates sf effects in homemade productions to their own erotic ends; ASFRians often write their own stories, create their own pictures, and construct their own robot costumes using shiny materials like latex, PVC, and Lycra to which they attach toys that "blink, bobble, and glow" in order to create the illusion of circuitry (229).

The emphasis on mechanicity complicates the relationship between ASFRian fantasy and the reality of artificial companions that achieve human verisimilitude; in fact, the state of tension and liminality—whether between the robotic and human or between control and loss of control, appearance and interior, motion and stasis—seems to have greater relevance to the fetish than the robot per se. As Gates notes, unmasking is a key aspect of the fetish, and many of the most exciting fantasies involve the sudden revelation of artificiality either through robotic malfunction (in which a human/robot gets caught in a repeat loop) or disassembly (in which a panel opens or a part is removed to reveal the circuitry beneath the semblance of humanity). While the latter is difficult to perform, ASFRians either search television and film for such moments (which they then list obsessively on their websites) or they produce disassembly images themselves in the manner of ASFRian artist Kishin, who either renders them from scratch in a 3D program or adds exposed circuitry to figures from erotic magazines using Photoshop, a practice that some call "rasterbation" (see Figure 2). When I asked Kishin what it was about such imagery that he most enjoyed, he replied, "It's something about the contrast between the cold hard steel and the circuits and the wiring and the smooth skin and the soft flesh." The "come shot" for Kishin occurs when a female robot reaches up "to remove the mask that *is* her face" because "it's like a revelation of who she really is" (personal communication, 24 July 2001).

But who is she really?

In his essay "Fetishism" (1927), Freud tells us that in all cases a fetish is "a substitute for the woman's (mother's) phallus, which the little boy once believed in and does not wish to forego" (205-206). It embodies an ambivalence, a double attitude towards female castration for which a compromise is struck by which the absent phallus is conjured elsewhere, a new point of erotic fixation that serves as both an acknowledgement and denial, "a sort of permanent memorial" that may manifest itself in a single part, like a foot, which the fetishist then worships, or a set of opposing attitudes that involve both hostility and reverence, such as "the Chinese custom of first mutilating a woman's foot and then revering it" (209).

The ASFRian fetish object is, however, less a "permanent memorial" than a vacillating sign; it is, to use Freud's analogy, like mutilating one foot while keeping the other whole,

Figure 2 Kishin: "Who She Really Is".

an ongoing reminder that a deformation has occurred. To the extent that it attempts to assuage the ambivalence around an absence via a displaced presence, it also repetitively restages the exchange between presence and absence at this alternate location, re-enacting the trauma by which it was, theoretically, constituted. In this sense, it smacks of the compulsion to repeat that Freud links to the "death instinct." Indeed, there is a distinct similarity between the hiding and revealing of the mechanical interior of the robot female in ASFRian fantasy and the compulsive throwing away and retrieving of the wooden reel by the child in the game *fort/da*, described by Freud in *Beyond the Pleasure Principle* (13-14).[13] There is, moreover, a correspondence between repetition compulsion and what is being revealed—the "who she really is" of ASFRian fantasy— that is bound up less in technology per se than in automatism, the revelation of a force (imagined as programming by ASFRians) beyond the rational mind or conscious will that controls behavior, and that is brought to the fore in moments of robotic unveiling or breakdown. Gates argues that the automatism at the heart of the fetish is a metaphor for sexuality itself: "the sense that we have no control over it; that we respond mechanically to stimuli; and that our sexual programming makes us helpless. Fetishes, especially, are a kind of hard-wired sexual subroutine" (228). In this sense, the erotics of automatism, as embraced by A.S.F.R., is a fetish whose object is, in part, a revelation of the compulsive mechanism of fetishism itself.

Read more generally, however, A.S.F.R. not only points to the slippage between the subject and object of fetishism, but also to the ways in which the circuit between them is wired with both biological and cultural contact points, the exposure of which is potentially denaturalizing (for the object) and self-revelatory (for the subject). For example, while many ASFRians are fascinated by the film *The Stepford Wives* (1975; remade 2004), for many its primary interest resides less in the idea of the perfect housewife than in those scenes in which the Wives break down or become caught in a repeat loop—scenes beneath which foreboding music plays and that are intended to evoke horror. These are moments of vertiginous rupture that offer a glimpse of the robotic programming beneath the ideal exterior of the Wives and that also throw into relief the cultural norms through which such ideals are constructed. Indeed, in the film, such scenes serve as feminist commentary on the extent to which real women (and men) have been socially programmed. A connection is also made in the original film between the domestic scripting of women and television advertising; many of the Stepford Wives speak as though they are actresses in commercials for household products.

It is, perhaps, of no small significance that ASFRians get particular pleasure out of those scenes in which normative gender roles, as shaped by media imagery and embodied by the female android, are short-circuited. Most of the ASFRians whom I interviewed came of age in the 1960s, 1970s, and 1980s, and while their fetish is a product of sf television shows, it is also a reaction to a historical and cultural moment in which mass consciousness was shaped by the centralizing force of media programming and advertising. Indeed, if the media in general, and television in particular, tend to codify normative social rules and behaviors, then science fiction stands out as a site where the normal rules are suspended and other worlds are imagined that, in many cases, serve as a critique of and an alternative to the conventions of our own world. Although one might apply the stereotype of the sf geek to many ASFRians, the shared attributes that stood out in the men I interviewed were a high degree of sensitivity and self-consciousness coupled with social awkwardness and difficulty reading social cues.[14] Puberty was, for these men, an unusually fraught time during which they felt both confused by and compelled to conform to the rules of social engagement and political correctness. Interestingly, many of the ASFRians I interviewed considered themselves to be feminists—after all, many had come of age at the height of second-wave feminism—but they expressed confusion about how to reconcile the way they were raised—i.e., "to respect women"—with their sexual impulses.

The female robot is, to some extent, a way out of the quandary: she represents the promise of a simplified playing field in which the rules of the game are programmed in advance, thus sidestepping gender politics and eliminating the anxiety of making social mistakes. Within that simplified playing field, however, ASFRians imagine endless concatenations of possible moves, the erotic loci of which are moments of tension and rupture between opposite states—the human and the artificial, control and loss of control, exterior and interior. Such rupture is, I would argue, both a metaphor for and a condensation of the eruptive effects of adolescent desire on the socially-regulated body; it is a re-enactment of the tension between biological and social programming, between the chaotic flux of inner experience and the unified and controlled self as mandated by the social order. Moreover, to the extent that it is an attempt at their reconciliation, it is through recourse to a third category, which has the potential to destabilize such dualisms as self and other, subject and object, and even male and female.

Technology, in this sense, signals both the desire for and identification with an Other, a slippage made particularly apparent in one of the media examples cited most often as relevant to the fetish, an episode from the first season of *The Twilight Zone* entitled "The Lonely" (1959). The story takes place in the year 2046 on a barren and desolate asteroid nine million miles from earth, which serves as solitary confinement for a convicted criminal named James A. Corry. When the episode opens, a supply ship, which makes occasional visits to the planet, is arriving, and the captain, who has taken pity on the isolated prisoner, has left behind a box that he instructs Corry not to open until after the ship has departed. When Corry does open it, he finds a lifelike female android named Alicia, programmed to keep him company. While at first he wants nothing to do with her, his need for companionship prevails and he starts to forget her mechanical nature and eventually falls in love with her. The next time the supply ship arrives, the captain informs Corry that he has been pardoned and can return home immediately. As the prisoner rushes excitedly towards the ship with his companion, however, the captain informs him that there is not enough room for the android. Corry argues with him, insisting that Alicia is not an android but a woman, *his* woman, but the captain stands firm and, in order to wake Corry up to reality, pulls out his gun and shoots Alicia in the face. In the final scene, the female android breaks down; her calls for Corry get slower and s-l-o-w-e-r as broken circuitry and loose wiring shoot off a few last sparks of life through the hole where her face had been (see Figure 3).

The narrative climax of "The Lonely" corresponds with the primary visual triggers of ASFRian desire—breakdown, disassembly, and unmasking. The android's exposed inner workings are, however, not so much a revelation as a remembering; Corry already knew that Alicia was a robot, and thus what lies behind her faceplate is integrally connected to the mechanism inside him that made him forget or, to put it in terms of the fetishistic relationship, that sustained his belief that she was a woman despite the knowledge that she was a robot. This visual reminder of his own psychic split is what Lacan calls the *objet petit a* or the *agalma* (by which he means a hidden yet alluring object that animates desire, but which is, notably, the Greek word for statue and the root of *agalmatophilia*). Lacan associates the *objet petit a* with the game *fort/da*, claiming that the spool on the string can best be understood not as a little mother, but as "a small part of the subject that detaches itself from him while still remaining his, still retained" (*Four* 62). Freud associates the return of the once familiar forgotten with the uncanny, an aesthetic term on which he elaborates psychoanalytically in reference to Hoffman's story "The Sandman," whose

Figure 3 *Twilight Zone*, "The Lonely" (1959).

climactic scene—in which the eyes of the mechanical woman, Olympia, are removed and she is revealed as an automaton—bears a distinct resemblance to the climax of "The Lonely." The uncanny is in this way a term and an experience of particular relevance to the "who she really is" of ASFRian fantasy.

The uncanny gynoid

Freud uses as a starting point for his psychoanalytical inquiry into the uncanny a study entitled "The Psychology of the Uncanny" by physician Ernst Anton Jentsch, published in 1906. For Jentsch, the uncanny is a function of *misoneism* (the fear of the new), in which the mind becomes disoriented in relation to a phenomenon that does not conform to one's established conceptual framework or "ideational sphere" (8). It is Jentsch who initially links the uncanny to the German word *unheimlich*, the opposite of that with which one is familiar, the "heimlich" (homely) or *heimisch* (native) in German, and who uses Hoffmann's story as a significant example of the uncanny since:

> Among all the psychical uncertainties that can become an original cause of the uncanny feeling, there is one in particular that is able to develop a fairly regular, powerful and very general effect: namely, doubt as to whether an apparently living being is animate and, conversely, doubt as to whether a lifeless object may not in fact be animate. (Jentsch 11)

Freud picks up where Jentsch leaves off but differs from Jentsch in his interpretation of the source of the uncanny. While for Jentsch the uncanny is rooted in uncertainty about something unknown, Freud insists that what makes this unknown thing frightening is the fact that it was once *known*, but has returned in an alienated form. While there is no more *Unheimlich* place than the female genitals—that "entrance to the former Heim of all human beings, to the place where everyone dwelt once upon a time in the beginning" (245)—this interpretation, interestingly, leads Freud away from the figure of the female automaton in Hoffmann's story and the emphasis placed on her in Jentsch's essay. According to Freud, the mystery surrounding Olympia is of less significance to the story's ability to elicit an uncanny sensation than the theme of the "Sandman," a mythological figure who steals the eyes of bad children while they are sleeping, and whose image haunts the protagonist, Nathanael, throughout the story. Uncanniness is based in the anxiety of losing one's sight, which is a substitute for the fear of castration and steeped in Oedipal drama. As Freud points out, Nathanael's anxiety about the Sandman (and losing his eyes) is intimately connected in the story with his father's death (his father dies mysteriously in the company of the frightening lawyer Coppelius, whom Nathanael associates with the Sandman). Moreover, there is a reoccurrence and doubling of characters; Nathanael's father is replaced by Spalanzani, the "father" of Olympia; the Sandman is Coppelius, who is also Coppola, the peddler who sells Nathanael the spyglass or "pocket perspective" through which he first sees Olympia. These doublings are linked to a theme of eyes: Coppola, whose name translates to *coppo* or "eye socket" in Italian, also made the eyes of Olympia, which he later steals back. All connect back, in a logically circular way, to Freud's overall premise that the uncanny effects of similar occurrences are related to repressed infantile sexuality.

Freud's marginalization of Olympia has been a point of great contestation, and many have argued that Olympia represents the repressed within Freud's theory of the uncanny. As Nicholas Royle puts it:

> Freud's reading of "The Sandman" is a violent attempt to reduce or eliminate the significance of Jentsch's work on the Uncanny, and in particular the importance of the figures of the doll and automaton for an understanding of the uncanny. It is also a violent attempt to reduce or eliminate the place and importance of women. . . . Freud failed to see that the question of woman is inextricably connected to Nathaniel's fear of castration. (41)[15]

An intentionality begins to take shape, however, when we consider that Freud is drawing our attention away from the visual ambiguity of Olympia's physicality towards the psychic register of the story's (imaginary) Sandman. Freud, in a sense, replaces vision with the symbolism of eyes, in this way moving within the etiology of hysteria, an illness that serves as the backdrop of Olympia's behavior and Nathanael's madness. Our first clue to the importance of hysteria in Freud's reading of the uncanny is his rationale for dismissing Olympia as a symbol of infantile sexuality. While Freud acknowledges that Olympia does evoke a sense of the uncanny, he suggests that it arises not from the return of the *repressed*, but from the return of the *surmounted*. The return of the repressed involves the revival of infantile complexes, or amputated aspects of oneself, which had been buried in the unconscious. The return of the surmounted involves discarded beliefs that are "primitive" or "animistic" in nature. When something happens that we cannot explain—for example, a coincidence of events, the manifestation of secret desires or thoughts, the animation of an inanimate body—it revives and brings into expression these old beliefs, raising doubts about our current material reality and creating a sense of the uncanny. Accordingly, the return of the surmounted tends to operate in the realm of reality more than fiction, where supernatural events are less unusual.

Olympia is, of course, fictional, but to the extent that her mechanical behavior strikes a supernatural chord, it evokes the real uncanniness of the hysterical body, whose paroxysmal and repetitive gestures seem animated by unseen forces. Jentsch draws an explicit association between the two, suggesting that while the automaton strikes some people more than others as uncanny, the uncanniness of a mental and nervous illness, such as epilepsy or hysteria, is nearly universal, since it renders the autonomous human subject mechanical or puppet-like:

> It is not unjustly that epilepsy is therefore spoken of as the *morbus sacer*, as an illness deriving not from the human world but from foreign and enigmatic spheres, for the epileptic attack of spasms reveals the human body to the viewer—the body under

normal conditions is so meaningful, expedient, and unitary, functioning according to the direction of his consciousness—as an immensely complicated and delicate mechanism. This is an important cause of the epileptic fit's ability to produce such a demonic effect on those who see it. (14)

It is because of its mechanical seizures, paradigmatically associated with grotesque body movements—such as spasms, convulsions, and catalepsy—that hysteria inspired varying interpretations about its animating force over the course of its history, reaching a low point in the late fifteenth century with the publication of the handbook for witch-hunters and Inquisitors, *Malleus Maleficarum* (1487), in which it was interpreted as a form of Satanic possession. Although the etiology of hysteria began to shift with the birth of modern medicine, the man who freed it, once and for all, from its association with animist superstition was the famous neurologist Jean-Martin Charcot (1825-1893), whose theatrical displays of hysteria at the Salpêtrière Hospital in Paris in the late nineteenth century became legendary and with whom Freud studied between 1885 and 1886.[16] There is, in fact, a significant parallel between Freud's redirection of our attention from the mechanical body of the female automaton in "The Sandman" and his shift in emphasis from the external symptoms of hysteria charted by Charcot to an exploration of internal psychic processes, a shift that directly paved the way for his development of psychoanalysis.

Charcot is, perhaps, most remembered as the man who not only tamed hysteria but also theatricalized it, transforming a cacophony of symptomatic gestures into a choreographed ballet whose movements could be anticipated and, as was often the case, provoked. His legacy includes both the unprecedented photographic document of hysterical symptoms, *Iconographie photographique de la Salpêtrière* (1876-77, 1878, 1879-80), and the famous Tuesday lessons in which he hypnotized patients, who then dutifully performed their symptoms before an audience of "literary men, artists, art critics, actors and politicians" (Schade 505). If, in fact, fetishism is grounded in condensing and fixing that which causes anxiety in a form that can be performed repeatedly for visual pleasure, then Charcot could be called hysteria's pornographer. As Freud would later state in his obituary for Charcot:

> He was not a reflective man, not a thinker: he had the nature of an artist—he was, as he himself said, a *visuel*, a man who sees. Here is what he himself told us about his method for working. He used to look again and again at the things he did not understand, to deepen his impression of them day by day, till suddenly an understanding of them dawned on him. In his mind's eye the apparent chaos presented by the continual repetition of the same symptoms then gave way to order. . . . He called this kind of intellectual work, in which he had no equal, "practicing nosography," and he took pride in it. He might be heard to say that the greatest satisfaction a man could have was *to see something new.* (qtd in de Marnaffe 92; emphasis added)[17]

Charcot's nosography, dedicated as it was to an unflinching vision that saw "something new," an intelligible order, within the unknown and visually chaotic, poses an answer not only to the indecipherability of hysterical symptoms, but to the uncanny as *misoneism* (the fear of the new) through which they are rendered demonic.

In domesticating and aestheticizing the unassimilable and frightening, Charcot produced the kind of theater through which the uncanny is rendered both pleasurable and cathartic; and this is precisely the role of the fictional uncanny, according to Ernst Jentsch, of which Hoffmann was a master:

> In life we do not like to expose ourselves to severe emotional blows, but in the theatre or while reading we gladly let ourselves be influenced in this way: we hereby experience certain powerful excitements which awake in us a strong feeling for life, without having to accept the consequences of the causes of the unpleasant moods if they were to have the opportunity to appear in corresponding form on their own account, so to speak. In physiological terms, the sensation of such excitements seems frequently to be bound up with artistic pleasure in a direct way. (12)

The theatrical framing of the uncanny, through which the spectator experiences dissimulation as pleasure, is related to the fetishistic pleasure that Nathanael experiences in his encounter with the female automaton, whose embodiment of both the human and artificial, the living and dead, strikes profound chords within him. In a similar manner to ASFRians, Nathanael is erotically drawn to those qualities in Olympia that others find inhuman: her stiff and measured gait and mechanical movements appear to him as ciphers of hidden meaning; her repetitive and vacuous utterances strike him as "genuine hieroglyphs of the inner world of Love and of the higher cognition of the intellectual life revealed in the intuition of the Eternal beyond the grave" (Hoffmann 207-208). Unlike ASFRians, however, he is driven mad by the revelation, at the end of the story, of the subjectivity that he has invested in the object of his love, a revelation that leads to his suicide. It is this madness, which Jentsch celebrates in Hoffmann's work, that Freud is interested in extracting from the visual and the aesthetic in his theorization of the uncanny. Freud is, in a sense, attempting to isolate that which leads to Nathanael's death rather than the mediated experience of death enjoyed by the viewer (or reader).

Moreover, Freud's insistence that we ignore the automaton in our attempt to understand the causes of the uncanny is, I would suggest, related to the extent to which Charcot's visual approach to hysteria occluded the real causes of the ailment. Although Charcot was able to find meaning in visual disorder, he discounted that which was most meaningful—what his patients were saying—as delirious banter. Freud, however, subsequent to his studies with Charcot, began in his private practice to listen for the psychological content of what his patients were saying, ultimately concluding that their hysterical symptoms were the result of sexually-based trauma that was repressed, displaced from the lower body regions, and somatically converted into motor activity.[18] And in lieu of hypnosis, which Charcot had so theatrically induced in his patients before a crowd of onlookers, he prescribed "the talking cure" through which access was gained to the analysand's "private theatre" only within the context of the psychoanalytic relationship.[19]

Aside from its larger implications in the development of the field of psychoanalysis, this core insight about the etiology of hysteria serves as the backdrop for Freud's interpretation of the uncanny as the return of repressed infantile sexuality and his insistence that we turn our attention away from the visual signs of Olympia's ambiguous nature, suggestive of supernatural influences, towards the symbolic register of Nathanael's castration anxiety, enacted through a narrative doubling in the form of the Sandman.

Unlike Jentsch, who is interested in the aesthetics of the uncanny and how something frightening in real life can be rendered pleasurable within art and literature, Freud is interested in linking the uncanny to a psychological drive that overrides the pursuit of pleasure. He will call this the "death instinct" in *Beyond the Pleasure Principle* (1920), a book that served as the impetus for his essay "On the Uncanny" (1919)—the latter was written between drafts of the former and published the year before—as well as a reworking of his theory of the drives. Early in the book, he states that while the enjoyment derived from "painful experiences" in the theater or art hints at that which he is addressing, they "are of no use for *our* purposes, since they presuppose the existence and dominance of the pleasure principle; they give no evidence of the operation of tendencies *beyond* the pleasure principle, that is, of tendencies more primitive than it and independent of it" (17; emphases in original). In elaborating on the compulsion to repeat at the heart of the death drive, Freud once again passes over the mechanical body of hysteria and uses as an example the traumatic dreams of soldiers returned from battle (with whom he had direct experience following World War I). Freud concludes that the repetitive war dreams of the soldiers were attempts at preparing for and mastering retrospectively traumas that, at the time they were experienced, had caught them by surprise, or of developing after the fact the shielding "anxiety whose omission was the cause of the traumatic neurosis": "They thus afford us a view of a function of the mental apparatus which, though it does not contradict the pleasure principle, is nevertheless independent of it and seems to be more primitive than the purpose of gaining pleasure and avoiding unpleasure" (37).

To extrapolate from this to Freud's interpretation of Hoffmann's story: the uncanny as a repetition compulsion that overrides the pleasure principle is better represented by the imaginary Sandman, who inspires revulsion and fear in Nathanael in every form in which he is repeated, than by Olympia, whose mechanical movements, however much they hint at the "death instinct" lurking beneath Eros, are marked by a vacillation between life and death, beauty and its shadow, that is experienced by Nathanael (and the reader) as both compelling and pleasurable.

Mad love

Freud's occlusion of the female body, as well as his denial of erotic pleasure, in relation to the "compulsion to repeat" is thrown into sharp relief in a strange anecdote in his essay "On the Uncanny" when he discusses an experience he had of unintentionally and repeatedly returning to the red-light district of a small Italian town that he was visiting, whose streets were unknown to him:

> I found myself in a quarter of whose character I could not long remain in doubt. Nothing but painted women were to be seen at the windows of the small houses, and I hastened to leave the narrow street at the next turning. But after having wandered about for a time without enquiring my way, I suddenly found myself back in the same street, where my presence was now beginning to excite attention. I hurried away once more, only to arrive by another *détour* at the same place yet a third time. Now, however, a feeling overcame me which I can only describe as uncanny, and I was glad enough to find myself back at the piazza I had left a short while before. . . . (237)

While Freud hints at the psychic origin of this "unintended reoccurrence of the same situation," he quickly moves on, ignoring the erotic significance of the "painted women" in the compulsion that repeatedly brought him back into their company. To the extent that the "painted lady" is repressed (both in this anecdote and in Freud's theorization of the uncanny) in order to stress the "death instinct" over the sexual drives, she will, however, return with a vengeance in the works of Surrealism, an artistic and cultural movement that came of age with psychoanalysis and that compulsively explored the link between Eros and Thanatos, often in the form of artificial women and imagery that invoked the disarticulations of hysteria. Indeed, Freud's experience in the Italian town was virtually recreated in 1938 at the height of the movement at the International Exposition of Surrealism held in Paris, which featured a network of dimly lit streets populated by mannequins, each outfitted by a different artist (with objects ranging from a bird cage to a fisherman's net), an uncanny red-light district through which visitors were initially asked to find their way in the dark with a flashlight (Belton 111).

Although Freud attempted to close a Pandora's Box by diverting attention away from the mechanical body, whether automaton or hysteric, he opened another in his "discovery" of the automatic psychic processes behind the compulsion to repeat. Just as the body of the automaton/hysteric was losing her meaning—for she had been emptied of demonic intrigue by Charcot and visual intrigue by the practice of psychoanalysis—she was once again invested with an invisible force (the repressed unconscious), inspiring a generation of artists and writers to make her a site/sight of psychic and erotic exploration. André Breton, the founder of the Surrealist movement, famously called hysteria "the greatest poetic discovery of the nineteenth century" (Breton and Aragon 61), for in its manifestations of psychic automatism he saw not symptoms of pathology but liberation, a means of expressing an inner psychic reality that was superior to external reality. Breton was first exposed to hysteria and the techniques of dream interpretation and free association during World War I, as a medical student interning in a series of neuropsychiatric clinics (under two former assistants of Charcot, Raoul Leroy and Joseph Babinski) that offered treatment to soldiers who had returned from battle. In the same symptoms of "post-traumatic stress" that had inspired Freud's theory of the death drive, Breton detected a psychic (sur)reality, and in those same techniques used to address the shock of war on the psyche and shepherd it back to normalcy, he intuited a system for shocking the mind out of its normative conditioning and tapping into its imaginative potential.[20] While Breton's poetic interpretation and creative use of psychoanalytic theory put Surrealism at odds with Freud, as well as the French School of Psychiatry as represented by Pierre Janet, Breton credited Freud with bringing back to light "the most important aspect of intellectual life" ("Exquisite Corpse" 66) and grounded Surrealist practice in the "psychic automatism" of Janet.[21]

The "official" definition of Surrealism offered by Breton in 1924, in the movement's first manifesto, was as follows:

> SURREALISM, n. Psychic automatism in its pure state, by which one proposes to express—verbally, by means of the written word, or in any other manner—the actual functioning of thought. Dictated by thought, in the absence of any control exercised by reason, exempt from any aesthetic or moral concern. ("Manifesto" 26)

The Surrealists experimented with psychic automatism through a variety of collaborative writing and drawing games whose goal was to bypass the mind and tap into the inner psyche, and the results of which were often nonsensical phrases or imagistic disarticulations that reproduced the illogic of dreams and the physical disjuncture of hysteria (viewed as analogues by the Surrealists). A favorite was called *The Exquisite Corpse*, played by a group of people on a piece of paper. The first person would compose part of a sentence or drawing, fold over the paper so that his contribution would be concealed from the next person, who would add onto it, until all were finished and the paper was unfolded. The resulting figures—disjointed hybrids that merged inanimate objects with parts of animals, as well as female and male body parts, conjoined or mutated beyond recognition—were extolled by Breton for their "total negation of the ridiculous activity of imitation of physical characteristics," as well as for carrying "anthropomorphism to its climax" ("Exquisite Corpse" 95).

Reminiscent of the ASFRian "feminization of objects," the anthropomorphism enacted by the *Exquisite Corpse* was one of a series of Surrealist interests—including dolls, mannequins, and the conjunction of the human and the mechanical—that dovetail with ASFRian proclivities, to which Breton gave the name "convulsive beauty." At the end of *Nadja* (the last line of which is, "Beauty will be CONVULSIVE or will not be at all" [160]), Breton links convulsive beauty to the trauma of a railway accident—which (like war trauma) Freud discusses in relation to the compulsion to repeat in *Beyond the Pleasure Principle*—resulting in a jolt, shock, or "short circuit" that *derails* the rational mind. In *L'Amour Fou* (Mad Love, 1937), he elaborates on the concept (and the train analogy), suggesting that the perfect illustration would be "a photograph of a very handsome locomotive after it had been abandoned for many years to the delirium of a virgin forest," for "there can be beauty—convulsive beauty—only at the price of the affirmation of the reciprocal relationship that joins an object in movement to the same object in repose" ("Mad Love" 162). Breton's erotic and liberatory interpretation of the trauma associated with the railroad thus offers an alternative reading of the machine woman of modernism about which Huyssen writes.

The artist who took the disarticulated figure of convulsive beauty even further than the Surrealists, who was perhaps most responsible for the Surrealist fascination with mannequins, and whose work intersects most blatantly with ASFRian proclivities, is the German artist Hans Bellmer (1902-1975), best known for his photographed *poupées* or dolls.[22] Bellmer drew an explicit connection between his dolls and the uncanny, stating that a large part of their inspiration was his attendance at Max Reinhardt's 1932 production of the Offenbach opera "Tales of Hoffmann," in which the story of Coppelia/Olympia from the "The Sandman" is recreated in the first act. He began work on his first doll shortly thereafter, building its frame from wood brooms and metal rods

jointed with nuts and bolts and filled out with flax fiber covered with plaster of paris. Throughout the doll's construction, he took photographs, ten of which were included in a small book that he published with his own money called *Die Puppe* (The Doll, 1934), preceded by a short introductory text entitled "Memories of a Doll Theme." In the winter of 1934-35, eighteen photographs appeared in a two-page spread in the Surrealist journal *Minotaure* under the title "Variations sur le montage d'un mineure articulée," launching his relationship with the surrealist movement (see Figure 4). In the images from the book and journal, the doll appears like a mannequin-wannabe caught in an ongoing state of arrested development between wholeness and dissolution, adulthood and adolescence, her sad, partial figure splayed on a bed or leaning against a wall and often posed against a backdrop of chiffon or delicate lace. Bellmer had wanted to allude to the internal or psychic nature of the doll's form through a kind of peep show embedded in her stomach. Activated by a button on the left nipple, it was to display in succession six miniature panoramas attached to a wooden disc, each of which made visible "suppressed girlish thoughts" (qtd. in Lichtenstein 174).

Although the peep-show was never implemented, Bellmer's desire to produce a figure capable of articulating an inner psychic reality was more fully realized through a second doll, completed in 1935. Inspiration came in the form of a pair of sixteenth-century wooden figures, each about eight inches tall, that he and Lotte Pritzel discovered in the Kaiser-Friedrich Museum in Berlin.[23] Used by artists as aids to study human proportions and movement (similar to the wooden figures that artists still use today), they could be manipulated to a high degree, since every body part, from limbs to neck and torso, was assembled around carefully crafted ball joints. Using them as a guide, Bellmer produced wooden ball joints around which he arranged a new set of interchangeable and multiplied limbs and breasts. Unlike the first doll, the second was less a construction than what Rosalind Krauss has called "construction *as* dismemberment" (86; emphasis in original), an endlessly transformable configuration of discombobulated body parts, which Bellmer

Figure 4 Bellmer's work in *Minotaure 6* (Winter 1934-35).

photographed in more naturalistic settings. Some of the more provocative images involve two sets of legs attached to the same torso, from which the upper body and head are missing. The uncanny doubling of limbs that are often contorted or flailing conveys both the disarticulation and the convulsive visuality of hysteria, by which Bellmer, like many Surrealists, was fascinated.

Bellmer elaborates on the connection between these dolls and hysteria in his *Little Anatomy of the Physical Unconscious, or The Anatomy of the Image* (1957), which serves as a theoretical and poetic counterpart to his work. The book translates the Freudian interpretation of hysteria as the physical migration of displaced psychic trauma into a theory of desire, particularly as expressed and transformed through the kinds of physical distortions made possible by the image. In a lengthy passage worth quoting for the way in which it eroticizes the shock associated with the uncanny, Bellmer suggests that

> desire takes its point of departure, when concerning the intensity of its images, not from a perceptive whole but from details. If a naked hand unexpectedly emerges from a pair of pants in place of a foot, it is provocative of quite another degree of reality and—like an embarrassing stain on the edge of one's underwear—infinitely more powerful than an entirely visible woman; it hardly matters, for the moment, whether this efficacy can be attributed to the surprise of discovering a deceptive aspect of desire, anticipated souvenirs, or even some reference to dark knowledge. The main thing to retain from the

monstrous dictionary of analogies/antagonisms, which constitute the dictionary of the
image, is that any given detail, such as a leg, is perceptible, accessible to memory, and
available (in short is REAL), only if desire does not fatally take it for a leg. *The object
identical to itself remains devoid of reality.* (31; emphasis added)

The conception expressed by Bellmer of a "REAL" that is invoked by a surprising and
embarrassing "stain" in the field of vision would be rearticulated as the Gaze by Jacques
Lacan in his 1964 Seminar, in which he applies to psychoanalysis the insights of, among
other surrealists, Breton in *Mad Love*. Lacan makes a critical distinction between the eye
of conscious perception and the Gaze that lies outside of consciousness, the former
associated with what he calls the *automaton* ("the insistence of signs, by which we see
ourselves governed by the pleasure principle") and the latter the *tuché* (the "encounter
with the real," repeated "as if by chance," which lies beyond the *automaton* [*Four* 53-54]).
While these terms, which Lacan deploys in order to articulate "the function of the real
in repetition" (54), are elaborations of that which lies within and beyond the pleasure
principle, unlike Freud, who steers us away from representational practices, Lacan is
interested in tracing the *tuché* or Gaze within the visual field, which he, like Bellmer, aligns
with "the stain": "The function of the stain and of the gaze is both that which governs the
gaze most secretly and that which always escapes from the grasp of that form of vision
that is satisfied with itself in imagining itself as consciousness" (*Four* 74). The "stain" is
thus that which visually undermines the *automaton* or Ideal-*I* constituted through what
Lacan calls the "mirror stage," a psychic turning point when the infant, who has yet to
gain full mastery of its body, identifies its "self" within a mirror for the first time. The exter-
iorized double, through which the infant appears whole, integrated, and individual, will
become the misplaced site of "self"-identification, whose Gestalt opposes the heterogeneous flux of the body, launching

the *I*'s mental permanence, at the same time as it prefigures its alienating destination.
This gestalt is also replete with the correspondences that unite the *I* with the statue onto
which man projects himself, the phantoms that dominate him, and the automaton with
which the world of his own making tends to achieve fruition in an ambiguous relation.
("Mirror" 5)

Bellmer's dolls reverse the process by which the *automaton* of the "mirror stage" is
constructed by disturbing the image with surprising "details," as well as through an
uncanny doubling that invokes the "fragmented body"—retained after the "mirror
phase," according to Lacan, in dreams and "the lines of 'fragilization' that define the
hysteric's phantasmatic anatomy, which is manifested in schizoid and spasmodic symptoms" (6-7). This gesture of derealization is exemplified by one of Bellmer's photographs
(see Figure 5) in which the ball-jointed doll, appearing as two sets of legs inversed and
attached to the same torso, each outfitted like a young girl in Mary Janes and bobby
socks, lies sprawled in front of a mirror, one set of legs braced against the wall and mirror,

Figure 5 "The Mirror Stage".

the other seemingly in the midst of kicking as if in a temper tantrum or hysterical fit. Visible in the mirror against which the doll is leaning is an amorphous jumble of parts, which has no correspondence to the body it is reflecting. Played out within the conflicted doubling of the doll and its disjointed reflection is an attempt at acknowledging the split upon which the subject is constituted. Like the robotic interior that ruptures the human exterior within ASFRian fantasy, the mirrored or doubled image within Bellmerian anatomy does not serve as a reconstruction so much as an unmasking, a sign (experienced "as if by chance") of the Real that lies beyond the *automaton*. It is for this reason that, as Rosalind Krauss suggests, Bellmer's dolls complicate the Freudian model of fetishism, in which an artificial monument is erected in place of a natural absence:

> Surrealist photography does not admit of the natural, as opposed to the cultural or made. And so all of what it looks at is seen as if already, and always, constructed, through a strange transposition of this thing into a different register. We see the object by means of an act of displacement, defined through a gesture of substitution. The object, "straight" or manipulated, is always manipulated, and thus always appears as a fetish. (69)

Hal Foster, on the other hand, suggests that Bellmer's dolls appeal to something more than fetishism and beyond the pleasure principle. As he notes, unlike the Freudian fetish object, they do not disguise sexual difference but explore it obsessively, and they do not hide the effects of their own production, as in the Marxist account of fetishism, but flaunt it repetitively. "Moreover, the notion of a 'dictionary of analogues-antagonisms' does not imply a fixing of desire (as in the Freudian account of fetishism); rather its shifting drives the many recombinations of the dolls" (103).

Bellmer's attempt to map the convolutions of the psyche and the rhizomatic work-ings of desire, free from outside control, complicates any understanding of the dolls as autonomous. Nevertheless, like Surrealism itself, Bellmer has been subject to a great deal of criticism for his blatant and seemingly sadistic manipulation of the female figure.[24] To such critiques, Foster responds that a distinction should be made between sadism and the representation of sadism: Bellmer's dolls "go beyond (or is it inside?) sadistic mastery to the point where the masculine subject confronts his greatest fear: his own fragmentation, disintegration, and dissolution. And yet this is also his greatest wish" (109). Moreover, both Foster and Therese Lichenstein insist that Bellmer's dolls should be read through the sociopolitical context in which they were created. Bellmer's first doll was constructed in 1933, the year that the Nazis came to power in Germany. At the time, Bellmer owned an advertising and design agency. He closed down shop, however, fearful of inadvertently creating work that would in some way benefit the government, and devoted himself entirely to art that, according to Lichtenstein, was produced, in large part, as a protest against the cult of the perfect body within fascism, as well as the more general appearance of a mechanized, spectacularized, and "feminized" mass culture (13). Against these idealized and stereotyped bodies, Bellmer pits a convulsively mutating figure that breaches the boundaries of physical beauty and unity policed by the Nazis, while also embodying the psychological tensions and displacements experienced under the social constraints of fascism. Bellmer suggests in his *Little Anatomy* that, as in hysteria, the greater the repression, the more convoluted the expression, and thus the dolls not only represent the promiscuity or "flow" of desire, but also the psychic distor-tions of a desire caught between inner longing and external forces. As he says elsewhere, "The origin of that part of my work that scandalizes is the fact that for me the world is a scandal" (qtd. in Jelenski n.p.). There is, then, both self-reflexivity and social critique at work in Bellmer's dolls; indeed, he seems to pose an unflinching self-reflexivity *as* a form of social critique.

In short, Bellmer's dolls were intended, as I have argued about ASFRian fantasy, as a desublimatory assault on the normative, stable, and cohesive subject, and in particular on the psychic armoring of the fascist body by which fragmentary, fluid, and chaotic drives were repressed, abjected, and mapped onto the Other, represented in the case of the Nazis by women, Jews, homosexuals, and Communists.[25] They speak not to the aesthetic gaze, in which the sexual drives are sublimated through the object of beauty, but to the curious gaze of Pandora, who opens the box and experiences the uncanny vertigo of her own true nature (as does Nathanael when the automaton is revealed as not just a mechan-ical object, but an extension of the mechanical compulsions of his own psyche).

Eye robot

Although Bellmer's dolls were a product of their time, created in dialogue with the cult of the perfect body within fascism and the hysterical body within Surrealism, they anticipate the dislocation of bodies and identities, as well as the interpretive dilemmas they inspire, within current technocultural contexts. Indeed, the extent to which cyberbodies are, like those of hysteria, displaced (by prosthetic implants and extensions), dispersed (by communications technologies), and subject to forces outside the will of their owners, is one of the central concerns of cyberpunk. Moreover, like Bellmer's disarticulated dolls, when such technologically decentered figures cross into gendered and eroticized zones, they often inspire conflicting claims of containment and liberation, as well as conflicting reactions between alienation and desire. The connection between the two is made explicit in Mamoru Oshii's *Ghost in the Shell 2: Innocence*, which uses Bellmer's dolls as a central visual thematic to underscore the uncanniness of embodiment and desire when mediated through technology.

The sequel to *Ghost in the Shell* (*Kôkaku kidôtai*, 1995) and similarly adapted from the manga by Masamune Shirow, *Ghost in the Shell 2* explores at greater length not only the kinds of questions posed by the first film about mind, matter, and spirit in the information age, but also the aesthetic and ethical concerns raised by the encounter with artificial bodies. The second film, in fact, seems to address directly the critical reception of the first film, particularly concerning the central protagonist, Major Motoko Kusanagi, a female cyborg. The first film takes place in the year 2029; Kusanagi is a special agent whose bodily parts are entirely artificial—except for her original brain tissue, which is encased within a titanium skull—and owned by her employer, the government security force Section Nine. Both cybernetically enhanced and contained, posthuman and sexualized, Kusanagi has inspired comparisons to Haraway's cyborg in her embodiment of both "the liberating and the dehumanizing power of technology," as well as critiques of her seemingly ambivalent suspension "between a progressive and a reactionary politics of technology or gender" (Bolton 730). Carl Silvio, for example, casts her as a posthuman update of Pandora, suggesting a deceptive split between her appearance and reality; while she poses as a radical cyborg, she ultimately reinforces traditional gender roles, exhibiting a duplicity of which a great deal of cyborg culture is guilty: "There is thus what might be called an element of seduction at work, whereby information technology often presents itself to us as potentially liberating when in fact our actual interactions with it often reinforce conventional social structures of domination" (55).

If Silvio's critique seems to echo those of Bellmer's dolls in its concern for the status of the culturally and physically situated female body in the face of its disarticulated counterparts, other critics have, in a manner similar to Bellmer's defenders, pointed out that such a critique ignores the distinction between representations of embodiment and actual bodies. Christopher Bolton, for example, draws from the long tradition of puppetry in

Japan in order to illustrate the ways that artificial bodies (especially when represented within anime) are marked by an added layer of performativity that inflects their meaning, and he suggests that to ignore the performative aspect of these bodies is to miss their critical potential:

> Concerned with linking anime to a real-world context in which flesh-and-blood bodies are threatened with genuine objectification and violence, this approach treats fictional cyborgs on more or less the same plane as living human subjects. But treating Kusanagi as a living subject clearly misses the ways in which her body will always fall inside quotation marks; she is a virtual or performed subject that is both unreal and more than real from the start. (737)

Bolton's reminder of the puppet's artifice is a leitmotif in *Ghost in the Shell 2*, a film that explores the confusion between the human and the artificial, as well as the real and the virtual, in relation to a central question posed, significantly, by a character named and fashioned after Donna Haraway: "Why are humans so obsessed with recreating themselves?" In the film, the character Haraway is a coroner, who appears in a lab surrounded by android parts, including bodies hanging from hooks and a vat of artificial eyes. Although one might be tempted to compare her appearance to that of the real Donna Haraway, when the scene comes to a close, she lifts up a faceplate to reveal, behind her eyes, a technological viewing apparatus implanted in her skull. Echoing the scene in "The Sandman" when Olympia's eyes are removed, it is one of many reminders in the film that we are in the zone of the visual uncanny, where the boundary between human and machine, as well as between perception and reality, is unstable. Indeed, Oshii has explicitly stated the importance of the concept of the uncanny for understanding his film, which displays, in particular, an "obsession with the uncanniness of *ningyō* (literally, 'human-shaped figures') in the form of dolls, puppets, automata, androids, and cyborgs" (Brown 222). Moreover, *Ghost in the Shell 2*, like Hoffmann's story, interrogates the uncanny in the realm of desire through the figure of the female android.

   The film opens three years after the close of the story in the first *Ghost in the Shell*. A prototype of a new gynoid model, the Hadaly 2052 (manufactured by the corporation Locus Solus specifically for sexual purposes), is running amok, and there have been a string of incidents in which Hadaly gynoids kill their owners and, shortly thereafter, self-destruct.[26] The film follows the investigation by Section Nine, this time led by the cyborg Batou, the second in command under Kusanagi in the first film, and his "mostly-human" partner, Togusa. It opens with a chase scene in which Batou follows the trail of a Hadaly who has just killed her owner and two police officers. Batou corners the wayward gynoid in an alleyway and, just as he is about to shoot her, she cries "Help Me!" and proceeds to self-destruct, ripping open her own chest to expose her inner mechanism and then ejecting her metallic skull like a jack-in-the box (see Figure 6). This scene is more than suggestive of the kind of unmasking central to both ASFRian and Bellmerian fantasy; as Steven Brown notes, it was inspired by an illustration by Bellmer entitled *Rose ouverte*

Figure 6 Exploding Gynoid in *Ghost in the Shell 2*.

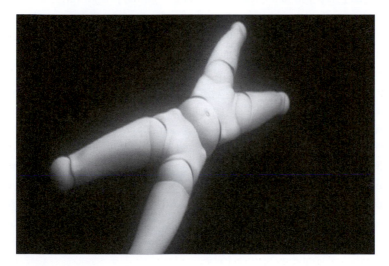

Figure 7 Ball-jointed doll in *GIS2* opening.

la nuit (Rose opened at night, 1934), in which a young girl rips open her own skin to reveal her inner organs (see Brown 239). The reference to Bellmer becomes more explicit in the opening credits that follow, in which title cards are interspersed with a series of sequences depicting the manufacture of a Hadaly-type gynoid, whose ball-jointed limbs move into place within a watery environment, accompanied by the sound of clicking gears. As a pair of legs without a torso floats into view, it seems to undergo binary fission, doubling before our eyes into a nearly exact replica of Hans Bellmer's ball-jointed doll, before separating into two identical gynoids (see Figure 7). The reference to Bellmer is reinforced yet again later in the film, when Batou finds a significant clue to the mystery of the malfunctioning gynoids in a representation of the Japanese reissue of Bellmer's book "The Doll" (published in 1995) that he discovers at a crime scene. An inspector has been murdered by yakuza affiliated with Locus Solus. The clue, slipped into the pages of Bellmer's book, is a holographic image of a young girl, whom Batou will eventually discover to be only one of many children abducted by the yakuza for Locus Solus for the purpose of "ghost dubbing"—extracting their ghosts to ensoul the Hadaly gynoids and make them more desirable. The children's bodies are kept suspended within mechanical cocoons. This turn of events not only echoes the narrative of Villiers's *Tomorrow's Eve*, in which the android Hadaly (the citational source for the Hadaly androids in the film) is ensouled by a living woman in a catatonic trance, it offers an inversion of the climactic scene within Hoffmann's tale: instead of the woman being revealed as an android, the android is unmasked to reveal the human beneath the mechanical exterior of the doll.

Although the resolution to the murder mystery is conventional in the sense that the villains are stopped and the young girls are saved, the ethical landscape of the film is less clear. When the little girl from the holographic portrait is freed, she explains to Batou that the inspector was killed for overwriting the ethics code programmed into the gynoids, which prevented them from harming humans or themselves, the rationale being that if they malfunctioned violently, it would help to draw attention to the children's plight. "But what about the victims?" Batou asks, to which she reacts with a tearful outburst, "I didn't want to become a doll!" Kusanagi, whose ghost appears in the film only in this final scene in the form of one of the Bellmerian Hadaly bodies (which she has temporarily inhabited to help Batou), responds to the little girl's lament: "If the dolls could speak, no doubt they'd scream: I didn't want to become human." There is, so the film seems to suggest, an equal injustice committed in forcing humanity upon the doll (whether visually, narratively, or critically), as there is in making human girls doll-like. Indeed, the film not only "remediates Bellmer's dolls" (Brown 223), it also rearticulates his aesthetic conviction (quoted above) that "the object identical to itself remains devoid of reality." This point is emphasized through a variety of strategies, both narrative and formal, for defamiliarizing or rendering uncanny the characters in the drama in ways that remind us repeatedly that they are not who or what they appear to be.

One strategy of defamiliarization, which Oshii borrows from French New Wave director Jean-Luc Godard, is citationality. The dialogue throughout the film is interspersed with quotations of other authors—meditations on the relationship between mind and body, as well as between dolls and humans, drawn from such diverse sources as René Descartes, Heinrich von Kleist, Villiers de l'Isle Adam, Julien Offray de La Mettrie, John Milton, and the Old Testament. This technique adds a critical dimension to the film by drawing attention to the history of ideas that informs its inquiry into the human and the artificial. In this way, the characters speak both *for* themselves and *within* a network of cultural and historical relations of which the viewer is made continually aware. Characters are also disrupted from within the diegesis through e-brain hacking. There are numerous instances in the film in which, as Brown puts it, "one character literally or metaphorically 'pulls the strings' of another" (224) by hacking into his cyberbrin (implanted cybernetic components that allow the brain to interface directly with information networks) in order to exert control or to implant false realities or memories.[27] A third strategy, of particular relevance to the discussion in this essay, is the kind of unmasking so critical to ASFRian desire and fantasy. The Bellmerian disassembly of the gynoid at the beginning of the film, which sets the murder investigation in motion, will return in an uncanny sequence towards the end, when Batou and Togusa enter the mansion of the hacker Kim. In the middle of interrogating a grotesque, puppet-like figure whose e-brain Kim controls (raising the question of whether or not Kim is still alive), Togusa's e-brain is hacked in such a way that the scene that we have just watched is repeated three times. In the first repetition, the puppet figure that Kim inhabits is now a doppelgänger of Togusa, who quotes freely from Jentsch's essay on the uncanny relationship between dolls and humans. The (seemingly) real Togusa watches in confusion when, suddenly, Batou turns mechanically towards him and his interior metallic skull ejects out of his head in the exact same manner as that of the wayward gynoid at the beginning of the film. This sequence of events sets off the second repetition: this time, the puppet that Kim inhabits resembles Batou, and the sequence ends with Togusa's chest exploding to reveal an artificial interior. It is only in the third repetition that Togusa is freed from the virtual feedback loop in which he has been caught.

This sequence, which employs all three techniques mentioned above, renders uncanny not only the characters in the film—both partly human and nonhuman, the investigators and the investigated—but also the film itself. Its kaleidoscopic repetition of events is confusing (particularly since Togusa is visible, so that the cinematic viewer is outside his point of view while being inside his hallucination) until we realize, along with Togusa, that an intervening force is at work. It also, as Brown notes, points to larger questions about "what it means to be human in a posthuman world and how we are to relate to all the *ningyō* (dolls, puppets, automata, and androids) that inhabit the world with us" (234). To the extent that answers are offered in the film, they are partially inscribed by its representational approach to the bodies that populate its posthuman landscape.

In conjunction with the above strategies of defamiliarization, Oshii adopts a style of animation that combines 2D and 3D rendering, which reinforces the critical distance between representation and reality, human and humanoid. The more lifelike the character, the more simply rendered and the more likely that it is a hand-drawn cell animation, whereas less animate objects are often computer-rendered in 3D. The contrast is made particularly apparent in a scene of an outdoor puppet festival, based on the annual Dajia Matsu Festival in Taiwan (see Oshii and Yamada 195), in which the larger-than-life, mechanical puppets are virtually realistic, while the living humans who move within and around them are both simply animated and partially obscured. The animation style of the film conforms to the aesthetic tenets of *bukimi no tani* or "The Uncanny Valley," a theory first articulated in a 1970 paper on robot design by Masahiro Mori, the man considered the father of Japanese industrial robots, but increasingly applied to computer-generated effects within animation and gaming.[28] Inspired by Jentsch's essay on the uncanny, Mori suggests that as anthropomorphic creations become increasingly human, they create greater expectations of human movement, behavior, and appearance, and when those expectations are not met, they produce a creepy or uncanny feeling. His ideas are illustrated in a graph, which charts the degree of realism or humanness achieved (both in terms of motion and appearance) and the resultant sensation evoked (see Figure 8). At one end of the graph are toys and puppets, while at the other end is perfect verisimilitude, both ends of which, according to Mori, inspire various degrees of pleasure. The graph dips dramatically into the unpleasurable uncanny valley between these two points, where one finds prosthetics and, at the lowest point on the graph, the moving corpse or zombie (see Mori).

Like Jentsch's theory of the uncanny, Mori's "Uncanny Valley" assumes the emotional investment and pleasure of humans in the nonhuman, offering an aesthetic program for enhancing that pleasure through a dedicated artificiality rather than a simulation of humanness. In so doing, Mori's views echo traditional Japanese aesthetics as influenced by Buddhism (Mori discusses the relationship between Buddhism and robotics in his 1974 book *The Buddha in the Robot*)—which tend to emphasize evocation over description, achieved via the interplay of opposite states, such as light and shadow or sound and silence. Thus they help to forge a bridge between current forms of technological embodiment and Japan's historical legacy of dolls and puppets.[29] Indeed, the current prototypes for Japanese humanoid companions, which tend to have a distinctly anti-realistic toy or puppet-like appearance, are often viewed as descendents of *karakuri ningyō*, autonomous mechanical or clockwork dolls that were popularized during the Edo period in Japan, which could perform a variety of tasks and entertainments, and whose goal "was not realism but charm" (Hornyak 25).

One of the most popular *karakuri* was a childlike *chahakobi ningyō* or "tea-serving" doll, which is recreated in the uncanny mansion sequence of *Ghost in the Shell 2*. A small puppet-like figure, the tea-serving doll would travel across the room with a teacup on a

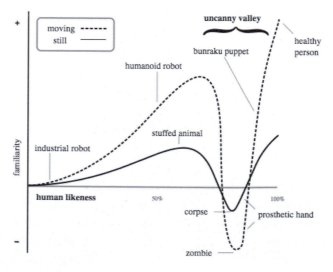

Figure 8 The Uncanny Valley.

small serving tray and, after the cup was taken, it would wait for its return to the tray, after which it would turn and travel in the opposite direction (see figure 9). The doll's ability to "perform the quintessential act of Japanese hospitality—serving green tea" (Hornyak 21) reflects Japanese cultural attitudes towards mechanical humans, including robotic humanoid companions, which are, as Hornyak notes, "social machines" designed primarily for "communication with human beings" (21).[30] The subtle and abstract motion achieved by this "robot from the Edo period" has informed everything from bunraku puppet theater to the cyberbodies of anime, all of which use an economy of expression to achieve a maximum emotional impact, reinforcing the idea, expressed by Mori's theory, that the deepest chords of humanity are better struck through an intended artifice rather than through realism.

Ghost in the Shell 2 recreates the legacy of Japanese *ningyō*, including dolls, puppets, and automated mechanisms (*karakuri*), and reminds us of their relevance to the cyber- bodies of the current technosphere. To the extent that we either desire or revile such bodies, it is, so the film suggests, because we have compromised their "innocence" with our own projections of humanity. In repeatedly shattering our illusions through its various strategies of unmasking, the film illustrates the affective power of nonhuman bodies recognized for what they are—both "real and unreal, simultaneously more and less than human" (Bolton 745)—and it demonstrates the possibilities for recuperating an increasingly lost humanity in relation to such bodies. For example, while the character Batou is a visually static, largely artificial being, his relationships with his basset hound, Gabriel, and Motoko Kusanagi form the emotional center of the film.[31] Like Haraway,

Figure 9 A "tea-serving" karakuri automaton, circa 1800 (British Museum).

whose *Companion Species Manifesto* on dog-human relationships echoes her "Cyborg Manifesto" in its concern for "an ethics and politics committed to the flourishing of significant otherness" (*Companion* 3), the film uses the relational interplay among a cyborg, a dog, and a networked ghost to gesture towards an ethical and emotional reciprocity outside of anthrocentrism. It is in the service of the relationship between Batou and Kusanagi, in particular, that, according to Oshii and Misaki Yamada (who wrote the novelized prequel to the film), the narrative structure of the "murder mystery" is used:

> The reason that Batou goes into enemy territory isn't because he really wants to rescue someone, nor is it really because he wants to solve the case. He just wants to meet his angel, Motoko. It doesn't really matter whether their relationship is a conventional romance or not. You see their love might seem cold to humans, but what is between them is no longer human, and now very innocent. (193-94)

Batou is, perhaps, a figure not so different from the socially-alienated ASFRian, who chases the path of the exploding fembot in order to release the human imprisoned beneath her ideal facade. As in A.S.F.R., it is neither the body of the doll nor of the human that is important in Batou's quest, but the interface between the two, where the ghost of his desire enters the picture. Illusions of humanity are shattered, and the film invites us, as spectators, to find something of ourselves within an increasingly posthuman, technofetishistic landscape.

Notes

1. Gynoids are humanoid robots that are gendered female. Sorayama borrows the term from sf writers Gwyneth Jones and Richard Calder to describe his cyborg (part female/part machine) pin-ups. His "Sexy Robots," while also presented in cheesecake poses, are entirely metallic figures.
2. In 2001, I made a documentary short about the group, which can be viewed at: http://www.ifilm.com/ifilmdetail/2408202.
3. While the mantra suggests a male heterosexual bias, a notable portion of the community is homosexual. All of the members with whom I communicated, however, are heterosexual males, so my descriptions should be considered most representative of their proclivities.
4. Consult Wood for a further discussion of this phenomenon (138-39).
5. For a general comparison between Freud's views on fetishism and those of Krafft-Ebing and Bloch, see McCallum (48-54).
6. For an overview of the companies manufacturing life-sized silicone lovedolls in the US, as well as their attempts at animating them robotically, see my article "Future Sex."
7. For a reading of the artificial female in Villiers's novel as *memento mori* rather than as object of necrophilic desire, see my "Anatomical Gaze in *Tomorrow's Eve*."
8. This accounting of Parigi's intentions in the film is based on two interviews that I conducted with him in 2004.
9. Plastination is a process through which the fluids of the body are replaced by a plastic resin that preserves specimens in perpetuity. The technique was invented and patented by the

controversial anatomist Dr. Gunther von Hagens, who is best known for the traveling exhibition of dissected cadavers called *Body Worlds* (originally *Köerperwelten*). The climax of *Love Object* echoes that of the 1954 classic *House of Wax*, wherein the mad Professor Henry Jarrod (Vincent Price) seeks to transform a captive young woman into a waxen replica of his beloved mannequin Marie Antoinette, which was destroyed in a fire.

10. For those ASFRians who do own Realdolls, the appeal is often a partner with whom they can enact a robotic fantasy, which may involve adding circuits and wires to the doll's silicone exterior.

11. For many ASFRians, the appeal of the artificial woman has, in fact, less to do with a love of the dead than what one ASFRian described to me as "the dream that goes on forever"—i.e., the fantasy of eternal life and beauty.

12. The exchange is archived on the Fembot Central website at: http://www.fembotcentral.com/viewtopic.php?t=7764.

13. Freud describes a game invented by his infant grandson for managing anxiety around the absence of his mother, which involves throwing away and retrieving a spool attached to a string while repeating *"Fort!"* and *"Da!"* (Gone! and There!).

14. It occurred to me more than once that A.S.F.R. might be related to a mild form of Asperger Syndrome. I was not surprised when I read a passage in Katherine Gates's book in which she explains the appeal of the android Data on *Star Trek: The Next Generation* (1987-94) for a female ASFRian whom she interviewed. Gates refers to the autistic slaughterhouse designer, Temple Grandin, who also "feels close to him [Data] in his clumsy efforts to perform like a human and in his urge to sort out the mystifyingly inconsistent rules of human social behavior" (Gates 228). Laslocky makes a similar supposition about the doll owners whom she interviewed. Data, claims Gates, has gotten more erotic mail than any other *Star Trek* character, Spock coming in second.

15. For further critiques of Freud along these lines, see Cixous and Kofman.

16. Derived from the word "saltpeter," Hospice de la Salpêtrière was established by Louis XIV on the site of what had been a gunpowder factory. Less a hospital than a holding pen, it originally housed mostly indigent and insane women whom the Sun King wanted cleared off the streets of Paris; it incorporated a women's prison for prostitutes at the end of the seventeenth century; and it became the largest asylum in Europe between the seventeenth and eighteenth centuries. The humanitarian and medical reform of the hospital is associated with Philippe Pinel (1745-1826), who became its chief physician in 1795; a statue in his honor still stands outside the hospital today.

17. On Freud and Charcot, see also Didi-Huberman (26-27).

18. Freud would later revise his "seduction theory," concluding that hysterical symptoms were less dependent on a reality-based sexual trauma than on projected fantasies and repressed desire.

19. "Private theater" was a term used by Anna O. for describing her "daydreams," which she explored with her analyst Josef Breuer, who collaborated with Freud on *Studies on Hysteria* (1895). Anna O.'s case formed the basis for much of Freud's discussion in the first of his *Five Lectures on Psychoanalysis* (1909).

20. As Hal Foster notes, "whereas surrealism began with hypnotic sessions, psychoanalysis commenced with the abandonment of hypnosis" (2).

21. Following a paper published in the *Annales Medico-Psychologiques* in which psychiatrist Paul Abély condemned the attack on psychiatry (and the call for the murder of psychiatrists) in Breton's *Nadja* (1928), Janet took part in a discussion at the Société Médico-Psychologique in

which he decried the work of Surrealists as "above all confessions of men obsessed, and men who doubt." Both the paper and discussion are reprinted at the beginning of Breton's "Second Manifesto of Surrealism" as a kind of initiatory prompt for the declarations that follow (119-23; the Janet quotation is from 121). Janet's *L'Automatisme Psychologique* was published in 1893; on its links with Surrealism, see Foster (1-5, n8, n221). Breton's *Nadja*, with its diatribes against psychiatry, was reportedly inspired by the author's personal encounter with a former female patient of Janet's.

22. Bellmer is generally discussed in relation to the Sadeian materialism of Georges Bataille, who invited him to illustrate his *Story of the Eye* (*Histoire de l'oeil*) in 1945.

23. Lotte Pritzel (1887-1952) was a German artist best known for her wax dolls, which served as inspiration for Rainer Maria Rilke's essay, *"Puppen"* (Dolls, 1914). Pritzel's suggestion that Bellmer read Rilke's essay led him to explore his own obsession with dolls (see O'Reilly, par. 1).

24. See, in particular, Brink and Taylor.

25. For a theoretical analysis of fascist abjection that tallies with this discussion, consult Theweleit.

26. Locus Solus is a reference to the country estate of "a Jules Verne inventor-hero" named Martial Canterel (Ashberry 192) in the 1914 book of the same name by French poet, novelist, and playwright Raymond Roussel (1877-1933). Roussel, who received psychiatric treatment from Pierre Janet, used, in the construction of his novel, a writing method that was based on homonymic puns, which was intended to help him tap into his unconscious. Such techniques made him greatly admired by the Surrealists. The novel, which follows a group tour of Locus Solus, describes, through an increasingly involved series of vignettes, the mechanical wonders and "inventions of ever-increasing complexity and strangeness" showcased by the eccentric inventor for his guests (Ashberry 199).

27. For a more extensive discussion of both citationality and e-brain hacking in the film, see Brown.

28. See, for example, Bode, as well as Butler and Joschko.

29. Jun'ichirō Tanizaki explains traditional Japanese aesthetics in the following way: "There is an old song that says 'the brushwood we gather—stack it together, it makes a hut, pull it apart, a field once more.' Such is our way of thinking—we find beauty not in the thing itself but in the patterns of shadows, the light and the darkness, that one thing against another creates" (29-30).

30. In 2003, when I attended Robodex in Yokohama, at the time the world's only humanoid robot exposition, there was an exhibit devoted to the tea-serving karakuri.

31. Gabriel was fashioned after Oshii's dog of the same name, who was brought into a recording studio so that she could also become the "voice" of her animated counterpart (Oshii and Yamada 191).

Works cited

Ashberry, John. "Postscript: On Raymond Roussel." *Death and the Labyrinth: The World of Raymond Roussel.* Michel Foucault. 1986. Trans. Charles Ruas. New York: Continuum, 2007. 189-203.

Augustine. *Confessions.* 397-98 CE. Trans. Garry Willis. New York: Penguin, 2006.

Balsamo, Anne. *Technologies of the Gendered Body: Reading Cyborg Women.* Durham, NC: Duke UP, 1997.

Bellmer, Hans. *Little Anatomy of the Physical Unconscious or The Anatomy of the Image*. Trans. Jon Graham. Waterbury Center, VT: Dominion, 2004.

—. "Variations sur le montage d'un mineure articulée." *Minotaure* 6 (Winter 1934-35): 30-31.

Belton, Robert. *The Beribboned Bomb: The Image of Woman in Male Surrealist Art*. Calgary: U of Calgary P, 1995.

Bloch, Iwan. *The Sexual Life of Our Time In Its Relation to Modern Civilization*. New York: Allied, 1928.

Bode, Lisa. "From Shadow Citizens to Teflon Stars: Reception of the Transfiguring Effects of New Moving Image Technologies." *Animation* 1.2 (Nov. 2006): 173-89.

Bolton, Christopher. "From Wooden Cyborgs to Celluloid Souls: Mechanical Bodies in Anime and Japanese Puppet Theater." *Positions* 10.3 (Winter 2002): 729-71.

Breton, André. "Exquisite Corpse." 1948. *Surrealism*. Ed. and trans. Patrick Waldberg. New York: McGraw-Hill, 1971. 93-96.

—. "Mad Love." 1937. *What is Surrealism? Selected Writings*. Ed. and trans. Franklin Rosemont. New York: Monad, 1978. 160-68.

—. "Manifesto of Surrealism." 1924. *Manifestoes of Surrealism*. Trans. Richard Seaver and Helen R. Lane. Ann Arbor: U of Michigan P, 1971. 1-48.

—. *Nadja*. 1928. Trans. Richard Howard. New York: Grove, 1960.

—. "Second Manifesto of Surrealism." 1930. *Manifestoes of Surrealism*. Trans. Richard Seaver and Helen R. Lane. Ann Arbor: U of Michigan P, 1971. 117-94.

—, and Louis Aragon. "The Quinquagenary of Hysteria (1878-1928)." 1928. *Surrealism*. Ed. and trans. Patrick Waldberg. New York: McGraw-Hill, 1971. 61-62.

Brink, Andrew. "Hans Bellmer's Sacrificial Dolls." *Desire and Avoidance in Art: Pablo Picasso, Hans Bellmer, Balthus, and Joseph Cornell*. New York: Peter Lang, 2007. 77-104.

Brown, Steven T. "Machinic Desires: Hans Bellmer's Dolls and the Technological Uncanny in *Ghost in the Shell 2: Innocence*." *Mechademia 3: Limits of the Human*. Ed. Frenchy Lunning. Minneapolis: U of Minnesota P, 2008. 222-53.

Butler, Matthew, and Lucie Joschko. "Final Fantasy or the Incredibles: Ultra-realistic Animation, Aesthetic Engagement and the Uncanny Valley." *Animation Studies: A Peer-Reviewed Online Journal for Animation Theory and History* 3. 16 July 2009. 21 Aug. 2009. http://journal.animationstudies.org/category/animated-dialogues/matthew-butler-lucie-joschko-final-fantasy-or-the-incredibles/.

Cixous, Hélène. "Fiction and Its Phantoms: A Reading of Freud's *Das Unheimliche* (The 'Uncanny')." Trans. Robert Dennomé. *New Literary History* 7.3 (Spring 1976): 525-48.

de Fren, Allison. "The Anatomical Gaze in *Tomorrow's Eve*." *SFS* 36.2 (July 2009): 235-65.

—. "Future Sex: The Evolution of Erotic Robotics." *Res* 5.3 (May-June 2002): 62-64.

de Marneffe, Daphne. "Looking and Listening: The Construction of Clinical Knowledge in Charcot and Freud." *Signs* 17.1 (Autumn 1991): 71-111.

Didi-Huberman, Georges. *Invention of Hysteria: Charcot and the Photographic Iconography of the Salpêtrière*. Trans. Alisa Hartz. Cambridge, MA: MIT, 2003.

Foster, Hal. *Compulsive Beauty*. Cambridge, MA: MIT, 1997.

Foster, Thomas. *The Souls of Cyberfolk: Posthumanism as Vernacular Theory*. Minneapolis: U of Minnesota P, 2005.

Freud, Sigmund. *Beyond the Pleasure Principle*. 1920. Trans. James Strachey. New York: Norton, 1961.

—. "Fetishism." 1927. *Sexuality and the Psychology of Love.* Trans. Joan Rivière. New York: Simon
    & Schuster, 1963. 204-209.

—. "The Uncanny." 1919. *The Standard Edition of the Complete Psychological Works of Sigmund
    Freud.* Vol. XVII. Trans. James Strachey. London: Hogarth, 1955. 219-52.

Gates, Katherine. *Deviant Desires: Incredibly Strange Sex.* New York: Juno, 2000.

Ghost in the Shell. Dir. Mamoru Oshii. Bandai Visual/Kodansha/Manga Video/Production I.G., 1995.

Ghost in the Shell 2: Innocence. Dir. Mamoru Oshii. Bandai Visual/Go Fish Pictures, 2004.

Haraway, Donna. *The Companion Species Manifesto: Dogs, People, and Significant Otherness.*
    Chicago: Prickly Paradigm, 2003.

—. "A Cyborg Manifesto: Science, Technology, and Socialist-Feminism in the Late Twentieth
    Century." 1985. *Simians, Cyborgs, and Women: The Reinvention of Nature.* New York:
    Routledge, 1991. 149-82.

Hoffmann, E.T.A. "The Sandman." 1916. *The Best Tales of Hoffmann.* Ed. E.F. Bleiler. New York:
    Dover, 1967. 183-214.

Hornyak, Timothy N. *Loving the Machine: The Art and Science of Japanese Robots.* Tokyo:
    Kodansha, 2006.

Huyssen, Andreas. "The Vamp and the Machine: Fritz Lang's *Metropolis." After the Great Divide:
    Modernism, Mass Culture, Postmodernism.* Bloomington: Indiana UP, 1986. 65-81.

Jelenski, Constantin. "Introduction." *Hans Bellmer.* Ed. Alex Grall. New York: St. Martin's, 1966. n.p.

Jentsch, Ernst. "On the Psychology of the Uncanny." 1906. Trans. Roy Sellars. *Angelaki* 2.1 (1996):
    7-16.

Kofman, Sarah. "The Double is/and the Devil: The Uncanniness of *The Sandman* (*Der
    Sandmann*)." 1977. *Freud and Fiction.* Trans Sarah Wykes. Boston: Northeastern UP, 1991.
    119-62.

Krafft-Ebing, Richard von. *Psychopathia Sexualis: A Medico-Forensic Study.* 1886. Trans. and
    adapted F.J. Rebman. New York: Rebman, 1922.

Krauss, Rosalind. "Corpus Delicti." *October* 33 (Summer 1985): 31-72.

Lacan, Jacques. *The Four Fundamental Concepts of Psychoanalysis: The Seminar of Jacques
    Lacan, Book X.* Trans. Alan Sheridan. Ed. Jacques-Alain Miller. New York: Norton, 1973.

—. "The Mirror Stage as Formative of the *I* Function, as Revealed in Psychoanalytic Experience."
    1936. *Écrits: A Selection.* Trans. Bruce Fink. New York: Norton, 1977. 3-9.

Lars and the Real Girl. Dir. Craig Gillespie. Sidney Kimmel Entertainment, 2007.

Laslocky, Meghan. "Just Like a Woman." *Salon.com.* 11 Oct. 2005. 21 Aug. 2009. http://dir.salon.
    com/mwt/feature/2005/10/11/real_dolls/index.html.

Lichtenstein, Therese. *Behind Closed Doors: The Art of Hans Bellmer.* Berkeley: U of California P,
    2001.

"The Lonely." *The Twilight Zone.* Columbia Broadcasting System. 13 Nov. 1959.

Love Object. Dir. Robert Parigi. Base 12 Productions, 2003.

McCallum, E.L. *Object Lessons: How To Do Things With Fetishism.* Albany: SUNY, 1999.

Mori, Masahiro. "The Uncanny Valley." Trans. Karl F. MacDorman and Takashi Minato. *Energy*
    7.4 (1970): 33-35. 21 Aug. 2009. http://www.androidscience.com/theuncannyvalley/proceed-
    ings2005/uncanny valley.html.

Mulvey, Laura. "Pandora's Box: Topographies of Curiosity." *Fetishism and Curiosity.* Bloomington:
    Indiana UP, 1996. 53-64.

Nelson, Victoria. *The Secret Life Of Puppets*. Cambridge, MA: Harvard UP, 2001.

O'Reilly, Sally. "Hans Bellmer and Pierre Klosowski." *Frieze* 103 (Nov.-Dec. 2006). 21 Aug. 2009. http://www.frieze.com/issue/review/hans_bellmer_and_pierre_klossowski/.

Oshii, Mamoru, and Masaki Yamada. "Afterward: Masaki Yamada and Mamoru Oshii on *Innocence*." *After the Long Goodbye: Ghost in the Shell 2: Innocence*. Vol. 1. Trans. Yugi Oniki and Carl Gustav Horn. San Francisco: VIZ Media, 2004. 185-96.

Pulham, Patricia. "The Eroticism of Artificial Flesh in Villiers de L'Isle Adam's *L'Eve Future*." *Interdisciplinary Studies in the Long Nineteenth Century* 7 (2008). 21 Aug. 2009. http://www.19.bbk.ac.uk/issue7/papers/pulham_sexdolls.pdf.

Royle, Nicholas, *The Uncanny: An Introduction*. Manchester, UK: Manchester UP, 2003.

Schade, Sigrid. "Charcot and the Spectacle of the Hysterical Body." *Art History* 18.4 (Dec. 1995): 499-517.

Scobie, A., and A.J.W. Taylor. "Perversions Ancient and Modern: Agalmatophilia, The Statue Syndrome." *Journal of the History of Behavioral Sciences* 11.1 (Jan. 1975): 49-54.

Silvio, Carl. "Refiguring the Radical Cyborg in Mamoru Oshii's *Ghost in the Shell*." *SFS* 26.1 (March 1999): 54-72.

Springer, Claudia. *Electronic Eros: Bodies and Desire in the Postindustrial Age*. Austin: U of Texas P, 1996.

The Stepford Wives. Dir. Brian Forbes. Palomar/Columbia Pictures, 1975.

Tanizaki, Jun'ichirō. *In Praise of Shadows*. Trans. Thomas J. Harper and Edward G. Seidensticker. New Haven, CT: Leete's Island, 1977.

Taylor, Sue. *Hans Bellmer: The Anatomy of Desire*. Cambridge, MA: MIT, 2000.

Theweleit, Klaus. *Male Fantasies, Vol 1: Women, Floods, Bodies, History*. 1979. Trans. Chris Turner, Stephen Conway, and Erica Carter. Minneapolis: U of Minnesota P, 1987.

White, Murray J. "The Statue Syndrome: Perversion? Fantasy? Anecdote?" *The Journal of Sex Research* 14.4 (Nov. 1978): 246-49.

Wood, Gaby. *Edison's Eve: A Magical History of the Quest for Mechanical Life*. New York: Knopf, 2002.

29

Animal alterity: Science fiction and human-animal studies

Sherryl Vint

The project of bringing together science fiction[1] (sf) and research in the emerging field of human–animal studies (HAS) might at first seem counterintuitive; indeed, when I spoke of my interest in researching animals in sf, a number of colleagues assured me that there probably were not that many. Although this book, by providing an overview of the many ways in which animals are present in sf, shows the degree to which such a conclusion is wrong, it is nonetheless not an unreasonable one for many readers of the genre to have reached. One does not tend to think of animals as *belonging* in sf for a number of reasons related both to the genre and to the assumptions that we make about animals and their place in Western cultural life. Animals, once central to human quotidian life, have steadily disappeared from human experience with the rise of modernity, whose processes of industrialization, urbanization and commodification have affected animal lives as much as human ones. Twenty-first-century society is no less dependent upon animal products than was the seventeenth (although many of the specific products may have changed, such as the replacement of animals used for transportation or the rise of animals used for biomedical research); yet a crucial difference between our use of animals and that of earlier cultural moments is that the use of animals in contemporary society is increasingly invisible: they are hidden away in laboratories and factory farms; slaughtered at mass disassembly plants and transformed into sanitized packages of meat; visible in mediated forms on Animal Planet or National Geographic television, but purged from city geographies. It is then not surprising that readers do not intuitively associate sf, "the literature of technologically saturated societies" (Luckhurst 3), with the presence of animals.

Yet there are many reasons to connect sf and HAS. Both are interested in foundational questions about the nature of human existence and sociality. Both are concerned with the construction of alterity and what it means for subjects to be thus positioned as outsiders. Both take seriously the question of what it means to communicate with a being whose embodied, communicative, emotional and cultural life—perhaps even physical environment—is radically different from our own. One of the premises of this study, then, is that sf and HAS have much to offer one another: sf has a long history of thinking about alterity, subjectivity and the limits of the human which is precisely the terrain explored by much

HAS, while HAS offers new and innovative ways to think about sf's own engagement with such issues, situating it within a material history in which we have always-already been living with "alien" beings. Additionally, sf's interest in thinking through the social consequences of developments in science and technology intersects usefully with key questions being worked out in HAS in an era of genetic transformation of animal species into "products" more suitable for human consumption, "factories" to produce useful chemicals or "models" to study disease. A central concern of HAS—and of this text—is the extent of our ethical duty to nonhumans with whom we share the planet, and both HAS and sf have much to say on this topic. Finally, in the past thirty years our discursive and material relationships with animals have changed radically, resulting in, on the one hand, what Derrida has called "*unprecedented* proportions of . . . subjection of the animal" (*The Animal* 25), and on the other increasing knowledge of animal cognition, communication skill and tool use, all of which reveal the tenuous nature of the firm and singular boundary between human and animal existence.[2]

Sf contains many animals and a plethora of perspectives on the nature of animal existence, and is an excellent tool for thinking through the implications of these cultural changes. The texts explored in the following chapters have no single perspective on the question of animals and their place in our social world, but rather demonstrate the range of ways humans have thought about this issue, sometimes challenging conventional wisdom and advocating a position of sympathy for the animal, and at other times embodying cultural anxieties about potential erosion of the human–animal boundary, a line which has been used to secure notions of human subjectivity since at least Plato. Sometimes the animals seem incidental to a text and their presence offers us a window on their ubiquity in laboratory life, such as the farcical "The Feline Light and Power Company Is Organized," by Jacque Morgan, which depicts an attempt to produce cheap power through the static electricity generated by "a plurality of cats" (320) trapped in a room. Similarly "The Hungry Guinea Pig," by Miles J. Breur, is more interested in the details of the massive military assault necessary to destroy a giant guinea pig that has escaped from the pineal gland research lab than it is in the animal's experience, even though the guinea pig is described as causing destruction through panic and fright, not malice. W. Alexander's "The Dog's Sixth Sense" does not even include the entire animal in the story, but instead focuses on the detective who becomes telepathic when he is given dog's rather than pig's eyes in his transplant surgery because he gains with the dog's eyes its ability to read human thoughts. Although this story is premised on the observation that dogs seem better attuned to human communication than do pigs (which might lead one to knowledge of dogs' cognitive skills), the story is not interested in exploring the ethics of sacrificing such creatures for their organs (the intelligence of pigs, the usual donors, is even further removed from the story's view).

More often, though, sf stories include animals because they are interested in what animals experience and in how our social relations with them might be transformed. Clare Winger Harris's *The Miracle of the Lily* (1928), for example, ironically draws attention to the world we make through an ethic of "man" as "master of the world with apparently none to dispute his right" (49); domination is taken to such an extreme in a war against insects for control of crops that humans destroy "every living bit of greenery, so that in all the world there was no food for the insect pests" (49). Often stories explore the perspective of reversing the human–animal hierarchy, such as F. Pragnell's "The Essence of Life" (1933). Humans are taken to visit a cat-eyed Jovian society by its pets, human-like beings who do not resent their subservient status but rather love their masters, who "are very humane and gentle, and have made poverty and want unknown amongst us" (443). The visitors offer "armies and guns" to help the human-like pets escape subservience, which is rejected as "obscene and traitorous" and as evidence that the Masters were right that on Earth "we shall find a race of men, lustful for power for its own sake, always ready to quarrel for the sake of quarreling" (443). The humans are there, it transpires, to be interviewed so that the Jovians might decide whether humans should be exterminated for the safety of the solar system, or whether "by careful selective breeding and developing, and above all, by the help of the Essence of Life, they might develop into quite unobjectionable and even pleasant creatures, like the domesticated men of Jupiter" (443). At times writers are even more directly polemical in their use of sf premises to question the treatment of actual animals in contemporary society. In an afterword to *Slave Ship* (1957), a novel about military use of animals to run unshielded nuclear weapons vehicles, Frederick Pohl draws his readers' attention to existing research on animal language, then rejects the idea that humans can be defined as exclusive tool users or exclusive language users; instead, he suggests, "Perhaps there is room for a third definition of Man, not much better than the other two, but very likely not much worse: 'Man, the snobbish animal . . . who clings to evolution's ladder one rung higher than the brutes beneath and saws away, saws away at the ladder beneath in an attempt to sever the connections between himself and the soulless, speechless, brainless Beast . . . that does not, in fact, exist" (147, ellipses in original).

Grant Morrison's *We3* (2005) similarly explores the potential for sf to query the ethics of using animals within military applications, embedding his tale of cyborg, weaponized animals within larger discourses of the human–animal boundary which structure twenty-first-century life. A graphic novel of three chapters, *We3* begins each with a "missing pet" poster of one of its animal protagonists: the dog Bandit who becomes 1; the cat, Tinker, or 2; and the rabbit, Pirate, later 3. These posters draw our attention to the widely disparate ways animals are integrated into human society. The posters show the animals in middle-class, domestic comfort, part of the home and family. The text indicates that these are individualized animals, named, known and loved by their owners: Bandit is "friendly and approachable," Tinker's individual markings are described in detail in text whose i's are dotted with hearts, and Pirate "likes lettuce and carrots." These posters are in stark contrast to the rest of the text in which we see the animals on their last mission, encased within armor and able to talk via implants in their heads. They are to be decommissioned, that is, killed, as their model is now obsolete. A sympathetic trainer enables their escape from the lab, and much of the rest of the book is about their attempts to find home which they define as "RUN NO MORE." The contrast between pet animals (part of human social networks) and numbered lab animals (instrumentalized and turned into things) is made all the more poignant by I's continual anxiety about whether he is "GUD DOG" and especially by his evident desire to help the humans he encounters, even though they are trying to kill him. In the end, he reclaims his name and sheds the armor, concluding that it "IS COAT NOT 'BANDIT'" that is bad. While Pirate is killed, Bandit and Tinker, purged of their cyborg enhancements, find a metaphorical home with a homeless man who recognizes that they are not dangerous but merely outcasts like him. This draws our attention to the relationship between ways of marginalizing and exploiting animals and the ways in which the discourse of species is used to animalize and marginalize some humans.

As Morrison's tale makes clear, one of the things sf can do is convey some sense of the animal's experience, in this case through the *novum* of technology which enables the animal to talk. Morrison's use of all caps, phonetic spelling and numerals (for example, 2 for the word "to" as well as for Tinker's new name) visually conveys animals' liminal category in human culture: they are similar but not identical to us, caught up within human language and other semiotic systems but not native speakers, precariously positioned along the axis of the binary pair nature/culture. And yet literary representations of animals are precisely that, *representations*, filtered through human consciousness and language. Must such representations be rejected, then, as necessarily false or at the very least limited, able to tell us only what we think of animal life and nothing about actual animal experience?

J.M. Coetzee explores the issue of animal experience and literary representation in *The Lives of Animals* (1999), the printed version of his Tanner Lectures on Human Values, and further in *Elizabeth Costello* (2003). In the Tanner Lectures, Coetzee constructs a story around the character of Elizabeth Costello, a novelist also called upon to give public lectures; the bulk of the text comprises the two lectures she delivers on animal rights, one called "The Philosophers and the Animals" and the other "The Poets and the Animals"; the expanded novel, *Elizabeth Costello*, includes this material and further background to Costello's life and her struggles to understand the role of literature in ethical and intellectual life. Whether or not literature can convey some truth of animal existence, and in so doing enable its readers to perceive them as fellow beings and thereby to heal the instrumentalized and damaging relationship that Western culture has with animal life, is one of Costello's central concerns. Coetzee's own investments are more difficult to ascertain as Costello's viewpoint is both expounded and challenged throughout the text, but at root they are interested in the same issue: the power of literature to shape subjectivity and all that flows from it. Costello refers to this as our capacity for sympathetic imagination.

Costello argues that the tradition of philosophy has failed to enquire about animal life and instead has used animals as a foil against which to define the distinct features of the human, a position very similar to that taken by Derrida in his posthumously published *The Animal That Therefore I Am* (2008). Derrida, too, divides human conceptions of the animal into two camps: philosophers "who have no doubt seen, observed, analyzed, reflected on the animal, but who have never been *seen seen* by the animal" and thus "have taken no account of the fact that what they call 'animal' could *look at* them, and *address* them from down there, from a wholly other origin" (13); and the poets "who admit to taking upon themselves the address that an animal addresses to them," but whose engagement with questions of animal–human relations is never from the point of view of "theoretical, philosophical, or juridical man, or even as citizen" (14). Derrida's point, ultimately, is that the entire discourse of philosophy and ethics must be reconceived if one conceptualizes the animal—as poetry does—as another subject who looks upon and addresses the human; such thinking, he says, is "what philosophy has, essentially, had to deprive itself of" (7).

Combining the poetic with the philosophical or juridical, then, will enable us to recognize the degree to which our entire philosophical tradition of subjectivity has been premised upon the separation of human from animal. Sf, more than any other literature, can defy this separation because its generic premises enable us to imagine the animal quite literally looking at and addressing us from a non-anthropocentric perspective, as in *We3*'s talking animals or the cat-like aliens of "The Essence of Life." Further, the ideal that sf should in some way reflect both the content of current scientific knowledge and the scientific technique of logical extrapolation—although of course never rigorously enforced in the genre—means that the genre's imaginings of animal being are inclined to incorporate knowledge gained from ethology (the scientific study of animal behavior) and thus to approximate what we know of animals' experiences of their worlds. Such an impulse is present even in early sf written before the development of such holistic methods of studying animal behavior.

For example, Edward Rementer's *The Space Bender* posits a society of intelligent beings evolved from cats rather than from primates, and speculates on the different cultural world that might emerge under such conditions. Careful to avoid anthropocentric hubris, the story's protagonist concludes,

> I could not decide if our system or theirs was better. The callous selfishness of King Tabi in regard to the welfare of his people was truly appalling, but, as he, himself, pithily remarked, is our paternalism altruistic or does it largely gratify a simian desire to poke our noses into some other fellow's business? (847)[3]

Thus sf offers a wider scope than does most literature for enabling animal agency to become part of the quotidian world, as well as space to attempt to grasp animals as beings in their own right rather than as beings defined through their place in human cultural systems. In addition to this specific concern with science, sf's long history of exploring questions of alterity and particularly of the boundary between human and other sentient beings—frequently explored through robot or AI characters—further positions it as uniquely suited to interrogating the human–animal boundary.

Why is it important that such ideas are explored through sf as a literature? Elizabeth Costello insists that it is only through the capacities cultivated by literature that we become able to be seen by the animal, to engage with it as a fellow being. She rejects the perspective of "behaviorists" who limit understanding to "a process of creating abstract models and then testing those models against reality. What nonsense. We understand by immersing ourselves and our intelligence in complexity" (Coetzee 108). Thus only the worldbuilding of fiction, something at which sf excels, is adequate for conveying the fullness of life before it has been contained within the reductive categories we use as shorthand to constrain the complexity of the world into units that can be grasped by rational thought. It is never entirely clear the degree to which Coetzee endorses Costello's position, but at the very least we can conclude that the question of whether literature enables us imaginatively to inhabit the animal's perspective is one that compels us to re-examine literary realism more broadly. This understanding of literature is similar to Derrida's suggestions that his entire work has been about the question of the animal's place in philosophical systems and notions of human subjectivity, that it "was destined in advance, and quite deliberately, to cross the frontiers of anthropocentrism, the limits of a language confined to human words and discourse" (*The Animal* 104). Derrida sees this as not necessarily a question of giving speech back to animals but "of acceding to a thinking, however fabulous and chimerical it might be, that thinks the absence of the name and of the word otherwise and as something other than a privation" (*The Animal* 48). Costello, writing in a more passionate idiom, puts it thus: "If I do not convince you, that is because my words, here, lack the power to bring home to you the wholeness, the unabstracted, unintellectual nature, of that animal being. That is why I urge you to read the poets who return the living, electric being to language" (Coetzee 111).

Erica Fudge points out that "a humanist arrogance lurks dangerously nearby" (*Pets* 46) the argument that human imaginative power is unlimited and might effectively capture an animal's perspective. In *Elizabeth Costello*, Coetzee positions this issue of the poet's access to animal experience within a broader series of deliberations which impel us toward the conclusion that, however imperfect, literature's ability to convey the experience of the animal being is no more or less problematic than any literary representation. Costello gains fame as a novelist for a book written from the perspective of Molly Bloom, one that counters the canonical representation of this woman's perspective as conveyed by a male writer. As one reader tells Costello, reading this book made her realize "that Molly didn't have to be limited in the way Joyce had made her to be, that she could equally well be an intelligent woman with an interest in music and a circle of friends of her own and a daughter with whom she shared confidences" (14). One might suggest that Costello was able to offer something of Molly's perspective that Joyce could not because, as a woman, she shares an embodied experience with Molly, unlike Joyce. While there is a degree of insight conveyed by this fact, at the same time Coetzee is careful to remind us that this is not the whole story either, first by a series of exchanges Costello has with an African writer which reveals the problems of becoming the voice of his "people" for a white audience, and second through Costello's insistence that "If I can think my way into the existence of a being who has never existed, then I can think my way into the existence of a bat or a chimpanzee or an oyster, any being with whom I share the substrate of life" (80). The embodied, vulnerable being that we share with animals is emphasized elsewhere by Costello and, it would seem, also by Coetzee, reminding us that humans, too, are animals, despite a long philosophical tradition, mostly strongly associated with Descartes and Heidegger (in different ways), that insists upon a separate kind of being for human subjects.[4]

Part of rethinking the human–animal boundary, then, is recognizing the embodied nature of human existence, that *Homo sapiens* is a creature of the same biological origin as the plethora of species we label "animal" and that we have greater or lesser degrees of kinship and common experience with them. Equally important, however, is recognizing that the beings we call "animals" are also inevitably caught up in human social systems and the language we use to create and give meaning to the world. On both a material level—what habitat remains, whether they spend their lives in captivity or "wild," and if "captive" whether as laboratory tools or pampered pets—and a discursive one—whether they are companions or pests, fellow beings or packaged meat, "noble" sign of a threatened wilderness or 'foreign" species invading a human-designated boundary of indigenous locale—animal lives are complexly interrelated with human culture. How we think about animals affects how we live with them, and how we live with them determines who they are, socially and biologically. Thus, in thinking about the ability of literature to convey new insight into animal being and potentially to reconfigure human–animal social relations, we must "acknowledge the limitations of our own perspective, but simultaneously accept that what we can achieve with those limitations is important and worthwhile" (Fudge, *Animal* 159). In so doing, it is essential that we remain cognisant of the fact that "our perception is based upon our limitations" and animal lives "exceed our abilities to think about them" (Fudge, *Animal* 160). In examining sf representations of animals, then, my focus will be twofold: on the one hand, such representations can provide insight into the way the discourse of species informs other ideologies at work, often opening the texts up to new meanings not evident when they are read without the insights of HAS; on the other, some sf texts themselves perform the work of HAS, striving to gesture beyond normative conceptions of animal and human being and thereby to glimpse, however imperfectly, something of their lives beyond the potentialities currently available to them in Western social relations.

Both Elizabeth Costello and Derrida are also interested in common vulnerability as one of the ways that humans and animals share embodied being. For Derrida, this critique is part of his deconstruction of the Cartesian *cogito* as model for human subjectivity, in a move in which Descartes

> abstract[s] from the "I am" his own living body, which, in a way, he objectivizes as a machine or corpse (these are his words); so much so that his "I am" can apprehend and present itself only from the perspective of this potential cadaverization, that is to say, from the perspective of an "I am mortal," or "already dead," or "destined to die," indeed "toward death." (*The Animal* 72)

Similarly, Costello argues,

> The knowledge we have is not abstract—"all human beings are mortal, I am a human being, therefore I am mortal"—but embodied. For a moment we *are* that knowledge. We live the impossible: we live beyond our death, look back on it, yet look back as only a dead self can. (Coetzee 77)

Thinking about alterity, ethics and literature through the perspective of HAS, then, has wider implications than merely a new way of thinking about animal being—although this too is an important site of ethical intervention for many working in the field. Thinking about our relationships with animals—social, conceptual, material—equally forces us to rethink our understanding of what it means to be human and the social world that we make based on such conceptions. In reconnecting with animals, we are also reconnecting with our embodied being, what might be thought of as our animal nature: this new way of conceptualizing human subjectivity and our relation with the rest of the living world thus has important affinities with scholarship on posthumanism.

In an essay that has become central to the discipline of HAS, "Why Look at Animals?," John Berger argues that industrial capitalism has radically transformed human's relationship with the natural world. When animals and humans look at one another, Berger suggests, it is across a gap of non-comprehension and thus when "man" is *"being seen by the animal, he is being seen as his surroundings are seen by him"*; that is, humans recognize that animals have a point of view regarding us, just as we see them as part of our surroundings. In pre-industrial times, Berger argues, humans acknowledged the mutuality of this gaze, grasping animals as both familiar and distinct, as having "a power . . . comparable with human power but never coinciding with it" (3). As animals were gradually removed from our day-to-day experience through urbanization, industrialism and other changes to the landscape wrought by capitalism which has eroded animal habitats and populations, we no longer encounter animals as fellow creatures who return our gaze. Instead, we see them in spaces that emphasise the radical disproportion in human–animal social relations: spaces such as zoos where animals are compelled to be visible in circumstances in which everything that would enable them to appear as fellow beings with their own perspective on the world and on us—freedom of movement, the opportunity to interact with other species, the habitat which is part of their lifeworld—has been stripped away. In such circumstances, humans are compelled to be like the philosophers critiqued by Derrida, able to look at the animal but not to be seen by it. Thus Berger concludes that the zoo is not a site of human–animal interaction, but rather "a monument to the impossibility of such encounters" (19).

For Berger, capitalism has irredeemably isolated man, who can no longer share an exchange of mutual looks with other species, whom he has marginalized or destroyed. Derrida begins his own reflections on philosophy and animals with an attempt to return to this site of exchange, reflecting upon the look of his cat, which he is careful to stress is *"this* irreplaceable living being" and not "the exemplar of a species called 'cat', even less so of an 'animal' genus or kingdom" (*The Animal* 9). To understand being from the point of view of mutual exchange of gazes, Derrida insists, one must take as axiomatic that the cat is fully as individuated, as much both part of her species and a being of "unsubsti- tutable singularity" (9) as is Derrida himself. He acknowledges that the cat "has its point of view regarding me. The point of view of the absolute other, and nothing will have ever given me more food for thinking through this absolute alterity" (11) than encounters which enable him not only to see his cat, but also to see himself being seen by the cat. Such encounters facilitate an ability to see "the abyssal limit of the human: the inhuman or the ahuman, the ends of man, that is to say, the bordercrossing from which vantage man dares to announce himself to himself, thereby calling himself by the name that he believes he gives himself" (12). In other words, thinking through the concept of "the animal" as well as through our relationships with material animals is indispensable for grasping what it means to be human, first because the concept "animal" has always been the ground for production of "the human," and second because in examining the real, material, complex existences of other species—as well as our own—we can also begin to see the ends of a certain historical concept of the human, as Foucault described in *The Order of Things*. But Derrida's critique is more radical yet, for he also incorporates knowledge of the observed capacities of animals instead of relying solely on philosophical abstractions, and comes to the conclusion that not only are humans not alone in possessing the capacities thereby deemed "proper" to humankind, but in fact for the most part humans do not achieve the qualities they ascribe to themselves with the name "human."

Derrida uses the human–animal boundary to ask questions about subjectivity that are very similar to those raised by critics such as N. Katherine Hayles under the rubric of posthumanism. Just as Hayles found in sf a tool for thinking through questions of embod- iment, subjectivity and ethics in concrete ways, so too might HAS turn to sf to explore the issues raised by Berger and Derrida. In sf we can once again find ourselves confronted by the gaze of "absolute alterity," an other who looks back at us from its own point of view and often one whom we must acknowledge as having power comparable if not identical to our own. The dialectic between similarity and difference that humans experience as we come face-to-face with animals is part of what Berger feels has been lost with industrial capitalism which has transformed them from fellow subjects into objects of consumption. This process has dramatically intensified in the past twenty-five years with genetic manip- ulation producing patented living beings that from one point of view cannot be regarded as other than objects. Animals modified for medical research, for pharming production, to survive the extremely restrictive conditions of factory farming without injury or for use in xenotransplantation research are patented creations of human culture that would not exist in nature and often cannot survive outside the artificially controlled conditions for which they are made.

Animals in sf can return to us a face-to-face encounter with another being whom we regard as a fellow subject. For example, Roger Zelazny's *Eye of Cat* (1982) is told in part from the point of view of a telepathic, polymorphic being called Cat. Cat has been imprisoned in a zoo by animal-trapper William Blackhorse Singer, who supplies the exotic zoos of this future with animals from many planets. Like most of the sf I will discuss, Zelazny's novel uses the tropes of sf in ways that simultaneously draw attention to our social relations with the "real" aliens with whom we share this planet (i.e., other species) and at the same time betrays in other ways some of the as-yet-unexamined assumptions about species and other difference that inform the human–animal boundary. The novel sets up a problematic equation, for example, between Cat as the last of his species (his planet has been destroyed since his capture) and Singer as the last Navajo, an authentic practitioner of the old ways who has made it into the twenty-first century through a combination of longevity treatments and the time-dilation effects of FTL travel. This parallel reinforces a colonialist history of seeing native peoples, like animals, as insufficiently possessing the land which then justifies its appropriation and also their treatment as less-than-fully-human subjects. Yet at the same time Zelazny interweaves traditional Navajo tales within his futuristic text, showing a respect for Navajo cultural traditions in the resemblance he demonstrates between them and sf as two ways of explaining the world through story. The Navajo tales also reveal the quite different way in which human–animal relations are conceptualized within native traditions, a mutual respect that resembles the ideal Berger describes.[5] Further, *Eye of Cat* both offers Cat as an exception to the normalized incarceration of animals in zoos—Singer apologizes and offers reparations once he works out that Cat is sentient and thus not "really" an animal—yet at the same times challenges our ability to know and judge sentience and thus to "correctly" make decisions about which beings might "ethically" be put in zoos. Further, news clips inserted in the text gesture toward a world in which significant changes have restructured the human–animal boundary in this future: dolphins are settling a lawsuit with a canning firm, and a composition by a humpback whale will premiere at the New York Philharmonic, but whooping crane populations will be culled. *Eye of Cat* complicates and makes multiple what we now take to be a simple binary division between all humans and all animals. Finally, the novel makes an effort to convey that Cat's consciousness is sentient but different from our own through sections of text expressing Cat's point of view that are fragmented streams of consciousness without clear word divisions, similar to ee cummings' poetry.

Eye of Cat successfully captures the dialectic of the human–animal relation that Berger feels has been lost with the rise of industrial capitalism that doomed humans to isolation in the universe. The emergence of sf during this same period might thus be understood as at least in part a desire to re-establish a world shared with other beings. Animals thus "haunt"[6] sf, always there in the shadows behind the alien or the android with whom we fantasize exchange. Another specter, anthropomorphism, also lingers about HAS and sf. Precisely how like or unlike us are animals, and what barriers does this pose to our ability to have an exchange across the border of alterity? This question has troubled animal-rights activists and defenders of anthropocentrism alike, and is one of the most contentious in the field of HAS. Although anthropocentrism has consistently been vilified since the rise of a culture of science, it nonetheless has proven impossible to stamp out, from the plethora of humanized animals in children's literature, to a consumer culture of pet ownership which interpellates them into such human practices as birthday celeb- rations and babysitting, and even to research such as Sue Savage-Rumbaugh's work on communication in primates that is attempting to establish a shared human-bonobo culture. As Derrida's interrogation of philosophy further points out, at issue in discus- sions of anthropocentrism is not merely whether or not it is acceptable to attribute some "human" characteristic—such as consciousness or language or emotion—to anim- als, but rather the more far-reaching question of the validity of the grounds upon which humans attribute certain capacities to themselves. Daston and Mitman credit the waning of anthropomorphic understandings of the world to the rise of the modern culture of science,[7] but further point out that "despite the official ban on anthropomorphism in science, thinking with animals permeated practice in the field and the lab" (8).

Thus, the "fallacy" of anthropomorphism is an alibi for human behavior. We construct animals as radically unlike ourselves in order to justify our behavior toward them: they do not feel pain but merely respond to stimuli as do automatons, says Descartes; they do not experience personal attachment and thus do not suffer when separated from their young, says the dairy industry; they have no capacity for consciousness and hence cannot experience boredom, say the factory farm and research industries. The challenge, then, is to pay attention to the actual lives of animals, to observe carefully the times at which it is appropriate to attribute to them motivations for behavior that are similar to our motivations for similar behavior, and times when their differences of embodiment, sens- ory organs and other capacities make such attributions unlikely.[8] Although there is a risk of what Frans de Waal has called anthropodenial in our refusal to see the ways in which fellow primates and fellow mammals in particular are similar to humans, at the same time we need to be careful that in the rush to embrace similarity we do not erase specificity.

If literature in general, and sf in particular, are to offer us something of the animal's experience and thus enable us to recover an encounter of mutual exchange of gazes, we must be attuned to resisting the two fallacies of too inclusive an anthropomorphism and too constant an anthropodenial. Beyond the rationale that anthropodenial provides for our continued exploitation of animals, resistance to anthropomorphism is also motiv- ated by a concern about the historical ways in which the discourse of species has been used similarly to exploit other humans animalized through this discourse, the two most significant historical examples being American enslavement of those of African descent and German extermination of Jews and others. Just as we must avoid extremes of both anthropomorphism and anthropodenial in trying to work through the place of animals in our ethical and social milieu, so too must we be sensitive to specificity in thinking through the similar, but not identical, exploitation of animalized humans and animals themselves. Often the desire to include animals within the circle of those to whom we owe an ethical duty is seen as a way of humanizing these animals, which seems then to imply a shadow double of animalizing some humans, particularly given that we live in a world in which many humans continue to be exploited and denigrated by others.[9]

Thomas Nagel's essay "What Is It Like to Be a Bat" (1974) has become a touchstone in HAS considerations of this problem. In contrast to Coetzee, who suggests that the literary imagination would enable us to capture something of an other's experience, Nagel cautions us to remember the difference between "what it would be like for *me* to behave as a bat behaves" (439) and what it would be like really to *be* in the way that a bat has being because, although bats have something in common with us, they are also differently embodied, have a different range of activity and a different sensory apparatus, which means that an encounter with them is essentially one with "a fundamentally *alien* form of life" (438). Nagel further stresses the serendipitous correspondence between the sf imagination and the sort of problematic he is developing by observing that "in contemplating the bats we are in much the same position that intelligent bats or Martians would occupy if they tried to form a conception of what it was like to be us" (440). The challenge of how to understand the alien, how to convey experience from a non-anthropocentric view, is similarly faced by sf. In *Archaeologies of the Future* (2005), Fredric Jameson connects this struggle to the difficulty of conceiving utopian possibility without allowing it to collapse into a necessarily reductive programme: how to achieve the delicate balance of enough familiarity such that the alien can be comprehensible to the human readers, but yet still incorporate enough alterity in the text such that the alien also pushes us to conceive of the world and ourselves otherwise. Even in sf's failure, then, to fully characterize the alien without reference to the human—a kind of anthropocentrism—Jameson finds a trace of hope, asking, "What, then, if the alien body were little more than a distorted expression of Utopian possibilities? If its otherness were unknowable because it signified a radical otherness latent in human history and human praxis, rather than the not-I of a physical nature?" (118).

There are parallels to literary representations of animals, all the more so when these representations are within the genre of sf and thus the limits of current human–animal relations can be transcended by imagining the world otherwise, a utopian desire for a world as it might appear had we not founded our subjectivity on the ideal of a radical separation of human from animal, and thus inherited many of the dualisms that structure Western thought: culture over nature, man over woman, colonizer over colonized, capital over labor. Nagel's insistence on the difference between *behaving* as a bat and *experiencing being* as one seems, on one level, to reestablish a radical separation between humans and animals—or at the very least a separation between the specific nature of being among all individual species. At the same time, however, he takes as axiomatic that at least some animals, like humans, do have conscious experience and thus can experience a mental state of being, a connection between human and animal denied by much of the philosophical tradition. Further, as Erica Fudge points out, Nagel "challenges humanist assumptions about the power of humans to construct and know the world . . . we can see that there are animals—many of them living in our homes—who share our world and who escape our understanding" (*Pets* 46), thus moving us closer toward the mutual exchange of gazes which Berger suggests once constructed less damaging human–animal social relations and prevented humans from feeling isolated as a species.

I want to suggest that sf literature is a particularly productive site for exercizing Costello's sympathetic imagination, striving to put ourselves in the place of the animal other and experience the world from an estranged point of view. Ralph Acampora advocates what he calls symphysis (common understanding based on shared embodied experience)— rather than sympathy (common understanding based on shared feelings)—as the basis for beginning to understand what it is like to be another species. He argues,

> to gain ontological access to the varied life-modes of different animals, one must enter environments not wholly of human making. This means beginning without making the assumption that there is just one world, permitting the possibility of other *Umwelten*— foreign, yet potentially familiar, forms of worldhood. Indeed, starting out this way may itself contribute to the revelation (or even constitution) of other animal worlds. (*Corporal Compassion* 12)

In contrast to Nagel, Acampora argues there is no need for thought experiments in being another species: "it will suffice 'merely' to arrive at some comprehension of what it means to *be-with* other individuals of different yet related species, because the experience of 'being-with' gives us all the mileage we need for tracking cross-species community" (*Corporal Compassion* 27).

This technique will no doubt seem very familiar to readers of sf. Much of the energy of the genre comes from the idea of "foreign, yet potentially familiar" worlds, from working through in detail how the world might be otherwise if some condition were changed. Examples include changing one's gender at will, as in the works of John Varley; humanity retreating from the material realm to civilizations within digital networks, as in Greg Egan's *Diaspora;* or having all necessary yet unfulfilling work done by non-sentient drones, as in Iain M. Banks's *Culture* series, or by genetically modified animal serfs, as in Cordwainer Smith's *Underpeople* stories. It is important, for two reasons, to look at the specificity of sf worldbuilding whose estranged perspective is that of an animal. First, animals have been the other of human identity at least since there has been recorded human history, and perhaps even before as is suggested by the animal subjects of the Lascaux cave paint- ings. Thus, remembering the specificity of this history of human-animal relations broadens our sense of sf's particular confrontation with alterity when this alterity is represented by an animal, connecting its motifs with a certain symbol of human history.[10] Second, it is important to remember that any alien animals or aliens who have animal-like qualities are both aliens *and* animals: we are currently in a time of ecological crisis and sf's animal representations are one of the places where we struggle to think our way through it. There is now general agreement[11] that we are living through a mass-extinction event, brought about by climate change (itself the result of human activity), the destruction of habitat by human industry and urbanization and the continued slaughter of animals for sport or food (a human practice that began causing animal extinctions as early as the period when Cro-Magnon replaced Neanderthal,[12] and has accelerated rapidly since 1500).[13] To understand how sf engages the history of animals in human social and intellectual

life, and more importantly how recent sf intervenes in the ongoing struggle to reconfigure human subjectivity, often in ways that transform our destructive relationship with the
rest of the natural world, it is important to remember that the alien and futuristic animals
in sf draw on this historical and material context. If our readings of such texts forget or
minimize their animal being—transforming them into analogues of robots or images of
technoscience or "just" aliens who might share some features with animals—then we
foreclose the texts' radically other utopian impulses. If we understand sf from the post-
WWII period to have been haunted by the specter of our own extinction through nuclear
annihilation, we can similarly see late twentieth and early twenty-first-century sf as shad-
owed by the impending threat of even more animal extinctions and perhaps the collapse
of our entire ecosystem.

From this perspective, we might understand our relationship with other species as an
expression of the current governance model of biopolitics, which Foucault has characterized as a change in the power of sovereignty: the old right to "take life or let live" is now
complemented and at the same time transformed by the new power "to make live and
to let die" (*Society* 241). This formulation is useful for understanding human sovereignty
over other species on the planet: some we make live in zoos or factory farms or specially
breed as laboratory tools and designer pets; others we let die through habitat erosion,
euthanasia of unwanted domestic animals or the exclusion of rodents from the US Animal
Welfare legislation (in order to control costs for pharmaceutical companies). Knowledge
about animals which takes them only as objects might be understood in Foucault's terms
as a disciplinary norm that is used to reinforce the species boundary through a policing
of what is "proper" to humankind alone and the construction of institutions and practices
that work not only to reinforce this boundary but further to prevent us from gaining any
knowledge of the animal as subject, knowledge which might challenge our investment in
this norm. HAS, then, might be understood as a subjugated knowledge that revisits and
interrogates this split, which has implications not only for our ability to see animals as
subjects but further for our ways of conceptualizing what it means to be human once this
ground of species difference has been destabilized. Akira Lippit points out:

> it is interesting to note that the invention of the idea of humanity, its appearance in the
> human sciences, was accompanied by an intensive investigation of the animal in those
> very sciences. At precisely the moment when the bond between humanity and animal
> came to be seen as broken, humanity became a subject and the animal its reflection. (19)

Interrogating the species boundary thus has important implications for ethics, not restricted to the question of our ethical duty to other species; rather it relates more broadly to
the philosophical foundations of ethical discourse as a whole, as well as to the political
implications of biopolitics, which thinkers such as Foucault, Agamben, and Hardt and
Negri have defined as a shift from governing humans as legal or civil subjects toward
governing the biological life of the species. One of the premises of this book is that
resistance to the biopolitical regime of neo-liberal capitalism requires acknowledging the

degree to which species difference has been foundational in structuring the liberal institutions that one might wish to contest. In this way, looking at HAS and sf is a continuation
of my earlier work on posthumanism and its critique of disembodied metaphysics of
subjectivity. A necessary supplement, in Derrida's sense, to this project of returning to a
sense of embodied subjectivity connected to the material world is an understanding of
humans as merely one species among many with whom we are in obligatory, symbiotic,
complex, contradictory and confusing exchange. This is a pressing political question of
our times, for as Rosi Braidotti observes in *Transpositions*:

> What "returns" with the return of Life and of "real bodies" at the end of postmodern-
> ism, under the impact of advanced technologies, is not only the others of the classical
> subject of modernity: woman/native/nature. What returns now is the "other" of the living
> body in its humanistic definition: the other face of *bios*, that is to say *zoe*, the generative
> vitality of non- or pre-human or animal life. Accordingly, we are witnessing a proliferation
> of discourses that take "Life" as a subject and not as the object of social and discursive
> practices. (37)

Foucault understands these shifts to create a specifically new form of war within the twentieth
century, one which is "the splitting of a single race into a superrace and a subrace" rather
than an understanding of racial difference and war as "a clash between two distinct races,"
one of which "came from elsewhere" (*Society* 61). Now, the discourse of power becomes

> the discourse of a battle that has to be waged not between races, but by a race that is
> portrayed as the one true race, the race that holds power and is entitled to define the
> norm, and against those who deviate from that norm, against whose who pose a threat
> to biological heritage. (*Society* 61)

In *The Open*, Agamben traces this split to the species boundary between man and animal,
suggesting that religious visions of everlasting peace imply not only harmony among
humans but also between humans and other species. Thus, the first biological split within
the species is that of humans from their animal being, leading Agamben to conclude
that "man . . . can be human only to the degree that he transcends and transforms
the anthropophorous [man-producing] animal which supports him, and only because,
through the action of negation, he is capable of mastering and eventually destroying his
own animality" (12). Agamben is here following the work of Heidegger, who insists upon
separating the Being of humans, the *Dasein*, from the being of other species, who live
but do not have being "as such." Heidegger defines humans as world-having in that their
Being is both part of the world and apart from it: humans "have" the world in the way of
standing apart from it, able to abstractly conceptualize it rather than be captivated by
materiality. Animals, in his view, are poor-in-world in that they are living and motile, able to
react to their environment, but not able to conceive of themselves as set apart, separate
from the world. A crucial part of Heidegger's distinction is the relationship to technology, which he describes as an "unconcealing" of nature: animals, in their captivated and
limited relationship to the world are closed off from the realm of technology.

Technology, however, is something that humans must master. It is a way of encountering the world as a possibility of tools and resources, a way of bringing forth, but at the same time technology is a way of revealing the world that shapes our understanding and limits our possibilities. Technology makes nature into a standing-reserve, and given their inability to access the realm of technology, animals become part of this standing reserve. Heidegger argues that "instrumentality is considered to be the fundamental characteristic of technology" (12), and modern technology poses a particular problem for Heidegger as it is "an ordered revealing" that "gathers man into ordering" (19). He refers to the "essence" of modern technology as "Enframing" and argues that it "starts man upon the way of that revealing through which the real everywhere, more or less distinctly, becomes standing-reserve" (24), a process so ubiquitous that humans are susceptible to being compelled to see the world in this way, thereby losing the world "as such" and being reduced to a captivated and limited relation to the world, that is, to animal being: "he comes to the very brink of a precipitous fall; that is, he comes to the point where he himself will have to be taken as standing-reserve" (27). Thus Enframing "conceals that revealing which, in the sense of *poiçsis*, lets what presences come forth into appearance," that is, it "not only conceals a former way of revealing, bringing-forth, but it conceals revealing itself" (27). Heidegger is thus continually concerned with finding ways of retaining the human's separation from animal being, in order to preserve what he sees as uniquely valuable about human Being, spirit and freedom.

Yet as Agamben makes clear, the task of separating human life from all other life is not easily achieved. As Judith Butler has suggested in another context regarding the "naturalness" of gender identity, the anxious and constant reiteration of "normal" performance betrays the lack of ontological grounding for difference. It must be continually reiterated to exist. Similarly, Agamben suggests that the difficulty in trying to separate anatomical or biological life (*zoe*) from consciousness or human life (*bios*) is that humans possess both; the gap between human and animal is always already internal to human existence. Thus, the real question of humanism is not to think of humans as a conjunction of body and soul; instead we need to "think of man as what results from the incongruity of these two elements, and investigate not the metaphysical mystery of conjunction, but rather the practical and political mystery of separation" (Agamben, *The Open* 16). Humanism thus becomes an "anthropological machine" (29) that attempts to define what is "proper" to humans, which proves precarious work since humans are neither properly divine nor fully animal, suspended between celestial and terrestrial states and forever at risk of degenerating into animal being. The discourse of speciesism in science, philosophy and culture is an expression of this machine's continual work to distinguish human from animal. Yet because this division between human and animal is always-already internal to humanity, there is constant risk. From the animal welfare perspective, we might be concerned about the ethical exclusion of at-least some animal species from the domain of ethics; one of Derrida's key arguments in his writing on this topic is the philosophical bankruptcy of the term "animal" to refer to a plethora of nonhuman species, the differences among which are often greater than the difference between humans and some species in this category. He argues that rather than defining a single boundary between human and animal, "it is rather a matter of taking into account a multiplicity of heterogeneous structures and limits: among nonhumans, and separate from nonhumans, there is an immense multiplicity of other living things that cannot in any way be homogenized, except by means of violence and wilful ignorance" (*The Animal* 48).

Yet there is a further risk, pertinent even to those who have no concern for animal welfare. As both Foucault and Agamben make clear, the human–animal division is both external and *internal* to human being, and thus the anthropological machine's work of including and excluding can—and has—put some *Homo sapiens* in the category "animal"; that is, the category of those who can be killed but not murdered because their lives and deaths are not included within the scope of our ethical discourse. Agamben argues that "In our culture, the decisive political conflict, which governs every other conflict, is that between the animality and the humanity of man. That is to say, in its origin Western politics is also biopolitics" (*The Open* 80). In addition to these questions of ethics, an important aspect of biopolitics is the degree to which life becomes managed as a calculation, a governance of people that sees them in terms of the statistical norms decided for the population, as Foucault makes clear in *Security, Territory and Population*. In *The Birth of Biopolitics*, Foucault elaborates this analysis and connects its particular mode of governance to neo-liberalism, which involves a shift toward competition as the primary image through which we understand social relations. Neo-liberalism involves a shift, also, in the object of governance such that price stability—rather than other aims such as full employment—becomes the goal, and further "the idea as not, given the state of things, how can we find the economic system that will be able to take account of the basic facts . . . [but rather] how can we modify these facts, this framework so that the market economy can come into play?" (*Birth* 141). In the realm of technoculture and biopolitics, one of the ways such a world has been materialized is through what Melinda Cooper calls the biotech revolution, "the result of a whole series of legislative and regulatory measures designed to relocate economic production at the genetic, microbial, and cellular level, so that life becomes, literally, annexed within capitalist processes of accumulation" (19). This shift means the extraction of surplus value is enacted on bodies on the biological level, resulting in the massive suffering of animals in locations such as factory farms, where they are reduced to machinic components of an industrial productive system whose ethos admits only efficiency as a value. From the point of view of Heidegger's argument concerning technology, however, we must also recognize that humans—conceived of as the population, the object of governance—have similarly become a standing-reserve of surplus value from the perspective of neo-liberalism.

Resisting such fates for humans and for animals requires a reconceptualization of subjectivity, and what Rosi Braidotti calls "future-oriented perspectives, which do not deny the traumas of the past but transform them into possibilities for the present. It is not the heavenly future at which we aim, but rather a more sustainable one, situated here and now" (268). Matthew Calarco argues that HAS's project of tracing the genealogy of the human–animal boundary across institutions, practices and discourses enables us to understand this distinction more fully in its various, contingent and specific manifest-ations, and also "help to uncover alternative ways of conceiving of human beings and animals that have been ignored, covered over, and distorted by dominant discourses" (140–141). This book participates in such a project, exploring what Teresa de Lauretis identified as sf's capacity to be "potentially creative of new forms of social imagination, creative in the sense of mapping out areas where cultural change *could* take place, of envisioning a different order of relationships between people and between people and things, a different conceptualization of social existence, inclusive of physical and material existence" (161). Each of the chapters explores the tension between, on the one hand, the gravitational pull of the sedimented weight of the species boundary and its attendant metaphysical and ethical boundary, which shapes the ways in which animals can and do appear in sf; and, on the other, the potentially subversive and new ways of conceiving species interrelations made possible by the genre's creative extrapolations, its ability to provide us with a future-oriented perspective that we might also achieve in the here and now. I have selected texts from across the spectrum of sf from early scientific romances and pulp magazine stories through golden-age novels to twenty-first-century works. Some of my examples are by authors who are well established within the sf tradition such as Frederik Pohl and Ursula K. Le Guin; others are authors from the early pulps who have since largely disappeared from academic considerations of the genre, but whose appearance in venues such as *Amazing Stories* signals the import-ance of animal themes to the emerging genre; and finally some texts, such as those by Karel Čapek and Kirsten Bakis, represent the more literary tradition within the genre and often find an audience outside its boundaries. Throughout I have organized my analysis of these works in terms of their thematic concerns, comparing and contrasting various ways animals serve to answer some of sf's questions about alterity, subjectivity and visions of another world. Thus texts from different historical and national contexts mingle in each chapter, serving to illustrate the richness of sf's engagement with the question of the animal.

Chapter 1 considers texts that foreground the problems of consumption as one of the demarcations of the human–animal boundary. The anxiety that accompanies visions of humans consumed by other beings speaks to the disquiet that haunts our relationship to animals as food. Further, these texts reveal the deep connection between the ethics of eating another and the metaphysics of subjectivity based on exclusion of the animal, which has significant consequences for our conception of the human as well.

Chapter 2 focuses on the difficulty of defining sentience in a nonhuman being, offering a model of becoming-other in the image of becoming-animal that promises to transcend the isolation of the human subject as defined through the human–animal boundary. The recognition of sentience in animal others thus promises a transforma-tion of human subjectivity that simultaneously enables a revolution in intersubjectivity, ultimately changing the relation of self/world. The experience of becoming-animal offers a glimpse of the utopian desire that Jameson suggests animates our imagining of alien bodies.

Chapter 3 turns to the question of language as one of the key criteria that has been used to differentiate human from animal being. Texts that narrate animal language and the experience of the world as perceived through this different semiotic filter, like the images of animal sentience, propose other ways of experiencing the world and thus work toward the sustainable-but-otherwise future that Braidotti desires. Sf's power to allow the animal to speak enables a powerful fantasy of communication with an alien other that might be realized in our material world.

Chapter 4 reflects on the various ways that discourses about gender and discourses about animality intersect, overlap and challenge one another. The parallel oppressions of women and animals suggest many sites for allied intervention and resistance to a biopolitical regime that constructs both as producers of surplus value. Sf animals in many of these texts offer a counter discourse of animal being that resists the hegemonic construction of "animal" by dominant anthropocentric discourse in a manner similar to feminist responses to patriarchy.

Chapter 5 similar explores the parallels between colonial discourse and the representations of animals. At root, both colonial racism and speciesism share a desire to accumulate wealth at the expense of excluded—because dehumanized—others, and thus struggles over resources and the status of labor unite them. Animals in sf texts who emerge as colonized others and exploited labor classes serve to dramatize the damaged relationship between humanity and the rest of the world that is the product of such discourses, and some offer visions of another way to structure our social relations.

Chapter 6 evaluates the uses of animal aliens in sf texts, considering them productive sites for thinking through sf's relationship with alterity and its desire to imagine a world of different subjects and different social relations. At times, alien animals serve only to reinforce a discourse of human exceptionalism, but other texts speak to a continuing desire to connect with another being whose subjectivity is unlike our own. In their staging of various ways that humans and animal aliens negotiate an ability to share the world—or refuse or fail to do so—these texts offer insight into the struggles we face in the twenty-first century as we come to recognize that humanity is part of a biosphere and in many ways dependent upon the existence of other beings.

Chapter 7 looks to the other common trope of incorporating animals into sf, reversing the position of humans and animals such that humans are treated by alien beings in ways similar to how we treat animals. Such texts resemble those discussed in the previous chapter in that they offer visions of how we might reconfigure our relationship with other species in the complex multispecies world in which we live but from which we have separated ourselves. Like texts discussed in earlier chapters, these reversal tales emphasize that transforming the relationship between humans and animals requires reconceptualizing what it means to be human, striving for an animal-oriented posthumanism.

Chapter 8 centers on the human-made animals that populate much of sf and increasingly parts of our material world as well. This chapter most fully explores the roots of sf as a genre linked to the rising culture of science and its values of technical rationality. The animals in laboratories and the spaces of biological manipulation that serve as the settings for such tales draw our attention to the links between the human–animal boundary and the biopolitical ethics of rational calculation that also informs the biopolitical governance of people as populations.

Finally, my conclusion looks to sf texts that offer lines of flight out of this configuration of human subjectivity based on the denial of the animal, and out of the damaged and damaging relationships to the world and other beings that it produces. I argue that closely considering the animals in sf offers promising ways in which we might reconceptualize human subjectivity, trying for a posthuman identity that addresses the pressing ecological problems of the twenty-first century. The conjunction of animals and sf produces other possible futures and envisions one of the longings that animates so much of the genre, a vision of communicating with a nonhuman species.

Notes

1. This project focuses on animals in sf, excluding texts that are explicitly fantasy or children's literature from its scope. At the same time, however, I recognize that the boundary between sf and other speculative literatures is permeable and continually in flux. I follow Roger Luckhurst in defining sf as "the literature of technologically saturated societies" (3) and thus dating its emergence to the late nineteenth century. Beyond finding this definition compelling. I also find it useful for positioning the relations between sf and HAS. The transformations wrought by the penetration of technological and scientific innovations into human lives during this period has been matched by equally radical transformation of both animal lives and the context in which human-animal social relations occur—or often no longer occur.

2. Regarding terminology, there is a considerable debate within the field of HAS regarding what language is appropriate to refer to humans collectively as distinct from nonhuman beings. Many people reject the terms "human" and "animal" as already ceding too much anthropocentrism and reinforcing a boundary whose deconstruction is precisely the point of much of this work. The distinction of human versus nonhuman is sometimes used, and occasionally I shall follow that usage when I am attempting to draw parallels between the discourse of speciesism and non-animal but similarly nonhuman others found in sf; although this terminology solves the problem of the conflation of widely disparate forms of life into the single category of "animal," thereby obfuscating differences among them, it still retains a special and set-apart space for humans which remains problematic. For the most part. I will use the terms "human" and "animal" while recognizing their limitations, as these terms connect to the history of human/animal separation in philosophy and history upon which I draw.

3. Interestingly, Gernsback felt it necessary to append an editorial note to this story which was published in the December 1928 issue of *Amazing Stories* suggesting that the author was having a bit of fun with speculations about a cat-race. Given Gernsback's insistence elsewhere—often in the absence of compelling evidence—of the plausibility of the "scientific"

premises of many of the stories he published, this anxiety about the non-centrality of *Homo sapiens* is intriguing.

4. See Calarco for an extensive overview and critique of this philosophical history.

5. For more on native ways of conceptualizing human/animal relations and sf uses of these ideas, see Dillon.

6. The phrase is Teresa Mangum's, who argues: "when empire and technology go terribly wrong, these dystopias unleash the truth about the violence and abuse animals often faced" (156–157). I agree with her analysis, but am also using the term in a broader way to encompass this and the other more positive ghostly presence of a desire to connect to being both like and unlike us.

7. James Serpell, building on Steven Mithen's argument that anthropo-morphism is a defining characteristic of *Homo sapiens*, points out that it has defined the sorts of social relations that modern humans have with other species: "By enabling our ancestors to attribute human thoughts, feelings, motivations, and beliefs to other species, [anthropomorphism] opened the door to the incorporation of some animals into the human social milieu, first as pets and ultimately as domestic dependents" (124).

8. A similar point can be made about genetic reasons for similar behavior that can be traced back to a common shared ancestor. Elliot Sober argues that although cladistic parsimony does not provide "a blanket justification for attributing human characteristics to nonhuman organisms" (95), nonetheless "parsimony does favor anthropomorphism over anthropodenial. *If two derived behaviors are homologous, then the hypothesis that they are produced by the same proximate mechanisms is more parsimonious than the hypothesis that they are produced by different proximate mechanisms*" (95–96).

9. See Luc Ferry's *The New Ecological Order* (1995) for an impassioned defence of humanism and a resistance of animal rights based on his belief that the "uniqueness" of humans must be protected to ensure the possibility of any ethics whatsoever. For an incisive critique of Ferry, see Cary Wolfe's *Animal Rites* (2003). For a more historical and less philosophical exploration of these issues, see Marjorie Spiegel's *The Dreaded Comparison* (1997). For a polemic from the opposite point of view from Ferry's, see Charles Patterson's *Eternal Treblinka* (2002).

10. For good overviews of some of the historically variable ways animals have figured in humans' material, intellectual and artistic lives, see Keith Thomas's *Man and the Natural World* (1984), Harriet Ritvo's *The Animal Estate* (1987), the collection *Companion Animals & Us* edited by Anthony Podberscek, Elizabeth Paul and James Serpell (2000), Erica Fudge's *Perceiving Animals* (2002), Linda Kalof's *Looking at Animals in Human History* (2007) and the Berg six-volume *Cultural History of Animals* series (2007).

11. See David Ulansey, "The Current Mass Extinction," <www.well.com/user/davidu/extinction. html>, for updated coverage of new research findings and news stories on this topic. Accessed December 5, 2008.

12. See De Vos 183.

13. See Simmons and Armstrong 12.

Works cited

Acampora, Ralph. *Corporal Compassion: Animal Ethics and Philosophy of the Body*. Pittsburgh, PA: University of Pittsburgh Press, 2006.

Agamben, Giorgio. *The Open: Man and Animal*. Translated by Kevin Attell. Stanford, CA: Stanford University Press, 2003.

Alexander, W. "The Dog's Sixth Sense." *Amazing Stories* (September 1952): 540-543.

Berger, John. "Why Look at Animals?" *About Looking*. New York: Pantheon, 1980. 1-26.

Braidotti, Rosi. *Transpositions: On Nomadic Ethics*. Cambridge: Polity, 2006.

Breur, Miles. "The Hungry Guinea Pig." *Amazing Stories* (January 1930): 926-935.

Calarco, Matthew. *Zoographies: The Question of the Animal from Heidegger to Derrida*. New York: Columbia University Press, 2008.

Coetzee, J.M. *Elizabeth Costello*. New York: Penguin, 2003.

Daston, Lorraine and Gregg Mitman. "Introduction." *Thinking with Animals: New Perspectives on Anthropomorphism*. Edited by Lorraine Daston and Gregg Mitman. New York: Columbia University Press, 2005. 1-14.

Derrida, Jacques, *The Animal that Therefore I Am*. New York: Fordham University Press, 2008.

De Vos, Ricardo. "Extinction Stories: Performing Absence(s)." *Knowing Animals*. Edited by Laurence Simmons and Philip Armstrong. Leiden: Brill, 2007. 183-195.

Dillon, Grace. "Totemic Human-Animal Relationships in Recent SF." *Extrapolation* 49.1 (2008): 70-96.

Ferry, Luc. *The New Ecological Order*. Translated by Carol Volk. Chicago, IL: University of Chicago Press, 1995.

Foucault, Michel. *The Birth of Biopolitics*. Translated by Graham Burchell. New York: Palgrave Macmillan, 2008.

—. *Security, Territory, Population*. Translated by Graham Burchell. New York: Palgrave Macmillan, 2007.

—. *Society Must Be Defended*. Translated by David Macey. New York: Picador, 2003.

Fudge, Erica. *Animal*. London: Reaktion, 2002.

—. *Perceiving Animals: Humans and Beasts in Early Modern English Culture*. Champaign: University of Illinois Press, 2002.

—. *Pets*. Stockfield: Acumen, 2008.

Harris, Clare Winger. "The Miracle of the Lily." *Amazing Stories* (April 1928): 48-55.

Heidegger, Martin. "The Question Concerning Technology." *The Question Concerning Technology and Other Essays*. Translated by William Lorett. New York: Harper Torchbooks, 1977. 3-35.

Jameson, Fredric. *Archaeologies of the Future: The Desire Called Utopia and Other Science Fictions*. London: Verso, 2005.

Kalof, Linda. *Looking at Animals in Human History*. London: Reaktion, 2007.

Lippt, Akira. *Electric Animal: Toward A Rhetoric of Wildlife*. Minneapolis: University of Minnesota Press, 2000.

Luckhurst, Roger. *Science Fiction*. Cambridge: Polity, 2005.

Mangun, Teresa. "Narrative Dominion or The Animals Write Back? Animal Genres in Literature and the Arts." *A Cultural History of Animals in the Age of Empire*. Edited by Kathleen Kete. Oxford: Berg, 2007. 153-173.

Morgan, Jacque. "The Feline Light and Power Company Is Organized." *Amazing Stories* (July 1926): 319-321, 383.

Morrison, Grant and Frank Quitely. *We3*. New York: DC Comics, 2005.

Nagel, Thomas. "What Is It Like to Be a Bat?" *Philosophical Review* 83.4 (1974): 435-450.

Patterson, Charles. *Eternal Treblinka: Our Treatment of Animals and the Holocaust*. New York: Lantern, 2002.

Podberscek, Anthony L., Elizabeth S. Paul and James A. Sperell. *Companion Animals & Us: Exploring the Relationships between People and Pets*. Cambridge: Cambridge University Press, 2000.

Pohl, Frederik. *Slave Ship*. New York: Ballantine, 1957.

Pragnell, F. "The Essence of Life." *Amazing Stories* (August/September 1933): 436-449, 455.

Rementer, Edward. "The Space Bender." *Amazing Stories* (December 1928): 838-850.

Ritvo, Harriet. *The Animal Estate: The English and Other Creatures in the Victorian Age*. Cambridge, MA: Harvard University Press, 1987.

Serpell, James A. "People in Disguise: Anthropomorphism and the Human-Pet Relationship." *Thinking with Animals: New Perspectives on Anthropomorphism*. Edited by Lorraine Daston and Gregg Mitman. New York: Columbia University Press, 2005. 121-136.

Simmons, Laurence and Philip Armstrong. "Introduction." *Knowing Animals*. Edited by Laurence Simmons and Philip Armstrong. Leiden: Brill, 2007. 1-26.

Sober, Eliot. "Comparative Psychology Meets Evolutionary Biology: Morgan's Canon and Cladistic Parsimony." *Thinking with Animals: New Perspectives on Anthropomorphism*. Edited by Lorraine Daston and Gregg Mitman. New York: Columbia University Press, 2005. 85-99.

Spiegel, Marjorie. *The Dreaded Comparison: Human and Animal Slavery*. 2nd revised edition. New York: Mirror, 1997.

Thomas, Keith. *Man and the Natural World: Changing Attitudes in England 1500-1800*. London: Allen Lane, 1983.

Wolfe, Cary. *Animal Rites: American Culture, the Discourse of Species, and Posthumanist Theory*. Chicago, IL: University of Chicago Press, 2003.

Zelazny, Roger. *Eye of Cat*. New York: Simon and Schuster, 1982.

Recommended further reading

Badmington, Neil. *Alien Chic: Posthumanism and the Other Within*. New York: Routledge, 2004.
    Considers how representations of aliens in SF and popular culture activate posthumanist fantasies, putting pressure on humanist ideologies and raising significant questions about selfhood and identity.

Balsamo, Anne. *Technologies of the Gendered Body: Reading Cyborg Women*. Durham, NC: Duke UP, 1996.
    A searching study of the implications of depictions of female cyborgs in SF and popular culture, focusing on particular intersections of embodiment and technoculture such as reproductive technologies and body modification practices.

Bukatman, Scott. *Terminal Identity: The Virtual Subject in Postmodern Science Fiction*. Durham, NC: Duke UP, 1993.
    A wide-ranging and penetrating analysis of how subjectivity and embodiment have been represented in contemporary SF, especially cyberpunk fiction and film, with its delirious visions of human-machine symbiosis.

Fernbach, Amanda. *Fantasies of Fetishism: From Decadence to the Posthuman*. Rutgers, NJ: Rutgers UP, 2002.
    Explores the implications of techno-fetishistic fantasies of self-transformation and the delirious sexualization of machines in SF and popular culture.

Hayles, N. Katherine. *How We Became Posthuman: Virtual Bodies in Cybernetics, Literature and Informatics*. Chicago: U of Chicago P, 1999.
    A pathbreaking study of how cybernetics discourse paved the way for posthuman constructions of the subject; offers incisive readings of SF by Philip K. Dick, William Gibson, Greg Bear, and others.

Latham, Rob. *Consuming Youth: Vampires, Cyborgs and the Culture of Consumption*. Chicago: U of Chicago P, 2002.
    Examines how contemporary popular culture, including SF and especially cyberpunk, mobilizes figures of nonhuman otherness to allegorize and critique ideologies of consumerism.

Milburn, Colin. *Nanovision: Engineering the Future*. Durham, NC: Duke UP, 2008.
    Explores how SF and popular-science discourses depict the biological and social implications of nanotechnology, including its challenge to conceptions of the embodied self and its proliferation of posthuman fantasies.

Raulerson, Joshua. *Singularities: Technoculture, Transhumanism, and Science Fiction in the 21st Century*. Liverpool: Liverpool UP, 2013.

A compelling study of "post-cyberpunk" SF that considers the implications of the technological Singularity for issues of embodiment and personhood, examining and critiquing both fictional and theoretical depictions of transhumanist and posthumanist futures.

Telotte, J. P. *Replications: A Robotic History of the Science Fiction Film*. Urbana: U of Illinois P, 1995.

Argues that the figure of the artificial person—robots, androids, cyborgs, and other "technological doubles"—is the central image of the SF film genre; offers probing readings of SF films, from *Metropolis* (1926) through *Total Recall* (1990), that depict this iconic figure.

Wolmark, Jenny, ed. *Cybersexualities: A Reader on Feminist Theory, Cyborgs and Cyberspace*. Edinburgh: Edinburgh UP, 1999.

A superlative anthology that gathers key readings on the relationship between cyborgs and the dynamics of gender and sexuality; three broad sections address "Technology, Embodiment and Cyberspace," "Cybersubjects: Cyborgs and Cyberpunks," and "Cyborg Futures."

Part 5

Race and the legacy
of colonialism

The first reading in this section, a 2003 essay by Istvan Csicsery-Ronay, argues that the emergence and consolidation of the SF genre during the nineteenth century was closely linked with the ideological dynamics of imperialism. Science fiction's central focus on technological "progress" was, Csicsery-Ronay claims, inextricable from the colonial enterprise of annexing and subjugating territory, a project that established technology as a governing force for both colonizer and colonized alike. Examining the growth of the genre within specific imperialist states, Csicsery-Ronay shows how distinct "national styles" of SF developed in synch with the realities of colonial expansion peculiar to each nation. At the same time, a general ideology of technological control—what Csicsery-Ronay, drawing on the theories of Michael Hardt and Anonio Negri, calls "Empire"—began to establish itself as the encompassing goal of the global colonial regime. This ideology also deeply informs SF, "which likewise rel[ies] on a cosmos governed by the laws and right of technoscience." The "imperial imagination" of classical SF—its fantasy of extending technocultural dominance outward to the stars—is thus essentially imbricated with imperialist agendas, but this does not mean that the genre cannot generate powerful and trenchant critiques of the implications and effects of technoscientific hegemony. Csicsery-Ronay's wide-ranging argument has seeded much subsequent SF criticism, which has deployed perspectives from the discourse of postcolonial studies to examine SF's undeniable debts to Empire.

The following selection by Kodwo Eshun brilliantly shows how SF can, despite its origins in colonialist histories, be used to arraign the logics of empire. Crafted as an imaginary report written by a team of African archaeologists in a future where African states (today still subject to neocolonial pressures) have combined into a self-governing federation, the essay makes a compelling case for the construction of "counterfutures" that can speak to those whose cultures have been disenfranchised or expropriated by the forces of imperialism. These counterfutures would operate as all SF does: not by attempting in some supposedly disinterested way to predict the coming future but by intervening into present-day politics in order to articulate alternatives. An eloquent defense of "Afrofuturism," the essay urges writers and other creative practitioners to sift through the genre's "audiovisions of extraterrestriality, futurology, and techno-science fictions" in search of expressive and ideological resources that can speak to peoples of the African Diaspora, in order to construct a technocultural imaginary out of a reclaimed tradition of black utopian thought. Though SF may have been forged in the crucible of colonialism, Afrofuturist artists can nonetheless use it to craft "powerful competing futures" that combat white European hegemony. As Eshun's discussion shows, one of the major contributions of Afrofuturism has been to open genre criticism to a broader range of cultural reference than the classic literary corpus, including centrally the work of visual artists and musicians who have used "extraterrestriality as a hyperbolic trope" to address Afro-Diasporic subjects seeking alternative, more just realities.[1]

The next essay, by Grace Dillon, offers an acute analysis of the work of a major Afrofuturist SF author, Nalo Hopkinson. According to Dillon, Hopkinson's SF and fantasy writings, emerging from native Caribbean mythology and the hybrid experiences of Creole peoples in the region, collectively articulate a powerful defense of "indigenous scientific literacies," expanding the parameters of what counts as authentic knowledge within the genre. By contrast with Western science, which constructs the natural world as humanity's other and opens it for technological management and exploitation, indigenous practices seek a more harmonious and sustainable relationship with the environment—a relationship based on a "sense of spiritual interconnectedness among humans, plants, and animals." In Hopkinson's SF, indigenous technological practices are evoked and celebrated in a way that fuses the concerns of Afro-Diasporic and Native American peoples, offering up nuanced and sophisticated explorations of alternative ecological systems.

Dillon's discussion links up with my essay on the theme of "Ecological Imperialism" within SF. I argue that SF's obsession with scenarios of alien invasion and catastrophe cannot be disentangled from colonialist assumptions and anxieties. Moreover, a significant number of these stories engage with concerns regarding the ongoing eco-apocalypse inaugurated by colonial expansion, wherein "alien biota" were transplanted into new environments with disastrous consequences. Looking closely at several works of New Wave SF informed by an ecological consciousness, I show that the genre is capable of developing critical alternatives to the Eurocentric hegemony over nature, including considerations of kinship with the nonhuman world, which Dillon also advocates.

The next selection, by Stephen Hong Sohn, expands the critical discourse on alternative futurisms within SF to consider the ways in which the genre has—and can—engage with Asian and Asian American peoples. On the one hand, there is little question that SF has historically trafficked in "yellow peril" fantasies, not just during the heyday of colonialism but in a lingering "techno-Orientalism" that remains legible in many contemporary texts. On the other hand, the thematic linking of Asians with aliens makes possible all manner of "imagined futures, alternative realities, and counterfactual narratives" that explore "racial tension and exclusion" in critical ways. Like Eshun, Sohn seeks to draw attention to cultural productions that not only confront the legacies of colonialist racism and ethnocentrism but also offer modes of extrapolation and speculation that escape the simple binary of the West and its "others."

Nalo Hopkinson's 2009 essay, "A Report from Planet Midnight," is at once a significant critical intervention into the discourse of race in SF and a brilliant work of performative Afrofuturism in its own right. Originally delivered as a speech at the 2008 International Conference on the *Fantastic* in the Arts, Hopkinson's piece uses the classic SF trope of "first contact" with alien others to explore the ways in which white authors, editors, and fans have sought, often with unfortunate results, to engage with issues of race and representation. Wearing a t-shirt reading "Speaker to White Folks," Hopkinson enacted a scenario of voodoo possession, in which her body was "ridden" by an extraterrestrial spirit trying to make sense of typically insensitive communications regarding race and ethnicity.[2] Many of the comments that she hilariously "translates" have to do with issues of racial stereotyping and the dynamics of intercultural appropriation. Yet at the same time as she exposes the lines of racial privilege and constraint that operate within the genre, she also makes clear that SF, with its rich and resonant ability to evoke alternative futures, can be a source for hope and solidarity.

The final essay in this section is Lysa Rivera's study of "borderlands SF" a work that explores the "experiences not only of alienation, displacement, and marginalization but also those of survival, resistance, and resilience" characteristic of subjects inhabiting the liminal geographic and ideological terrain separating the U.S. from Mexico. As Rivera shows, there has recently been a spate of artistic and cultural work by Latino futurists designed to address the fraught politics surrounding race, immigration, and cultural imperialism, especially in the wake of the North American Free Trade Agreement (NAFTA), which began implementation in 1994. With its construction of a frontier zone in which technosocial imperatives were given free rein, NAFTA reinvigorated debates about the dynamics of colonialism in a neoliberal era, spawning a series of speculative responses that use the resources of SF to "defamiliarize borderlands topographies, both social and political," in ways geared to provoke critical reflection and resistance. Like the other readings in this section, Rivera highlights ways in which colonialist imperatives lie at the very heart of the genre's engagement with the world with the key texts she analyzes showing that readers and viewers "can only apprehend and understand the future through their own colonial past."

Notes

1. The term "Afrofuturism" was coined in 1994 by Mark Dery in a piece included in his book *Flame Wars: The Discourse of Cyberculture* (Durham, NC: Duke UP, 1994) and developed in books by Eshun, Alondra Nelson, and Louis Chude-Sokei, among others. See "A Notebook on Afrofuturism," an excellent website with resources on the topic maintained by Howard

Ramsby II, which is available at: http://www.culturalfront.org/2012/04/notebook-on-afrofuturism.
html, as well as texts cited in the bibliography to this section.

2. Many of these comments are derived from a fraught online debate within the SF community that
has come to be known as "RaceFail '09." For a critical discussion, see (on top of Hopkinson's
speech) the entry on the topic on the Fanlore website at http://fanlore.org/wiki/RaceFail_%2709,
as well as the wealth of materials available on the Fanhistory website: http://www.fanhistory.
com/wiki/Race_Fail_2009.

30

Science fiction and empire

Istvan Csicsery-Ronay, Jr.

In this essay, I will make a preliminary attempt at cognitive mapping. I mean to look at sf as an expression of the political-cultural transformation that originated in European imperialism and was inspired by the ideal of a single global technological regime. I will make the claim that the conditions for the emergence of sf as a genre are made possible by three factors: the technological expansion that drove real imperialism, the need felt by national audiences for literary-cultural mediation as their societies were transformed from historical nations into hegemons, and the fantastic model of achieved technoscientific Empire.

A quick list of the nations that have produced most of the sf in the past century and a half shows a distinct pattern. The dominant sf nations are precisely those that attempted to expand beyond their national borders in imperialist projects: Britain, France, Germany, Soviet Russia, Japan, and the US.[1] The pattern is clear, but not simple. English and French sf took off when their imperial projects were at their heights, and have continued to thrive long after their colonies gained independence.[2] German sf was primarily a product of Weimar—that is, after the collapse of the short-lived German imperium.[3] Japanese sf—which is now one of the most influential of contemporary international styles—also produced relatively little before the end of World War II.[4] Soviet sf picked up a rich Russian tradition of satirical and mystical scientific fantasy and adapted it to its own revolutionary mysticism in the 1920s; after a long dormancy under Stalin, it revived again during the thaw of the 1960s, only to evaporate with the fall of Communism.[5] In the US, sf was a well-developed minor genre in the nineteenth century; it exploded in the 1920s and has continued its hegemony ever since. Whether this occurred during the collapse of imperialism as a world-historical project, or fully within a pax Americana that can stand as the American Empire, we will have to examine. Our answers may not only help us to interpret how the sf genre functions in twentieth-century cultural history, but also make us sensitive to its function as a mediator between national literary traditions and that chimerical beast, global technoculture.

To conduct this investigation, we must be clear about certain concepts that it is hard to be clear about. By sf, we should understand not an ideal category with a putative social or aesthetic logic, but what national audiences understand to be sf—which is less a class than a jelly that shifts around but doesn't lose its mass. Some core elements of the genre appear in every sf culture, and help to establish an international prototype for what audiences consider sf. But there are significant differences at the "margins" of the class.[6] We should also keep in mind that imperialist projects took different forms in different national cultures, depending on when they were embarked upon, the character of the home culture, and their material technological relations. I approach the matter as a complex evolution from imperialist projects that were expansions from nation-consolidat-ing modernizing projects—i.e., attaching territories to the nation-state with the naive belief that the metropole would not be changed—to the condition of global market capitalism that Michael Hardt and Antonio Negri, in their book *Empire* (2000), treat as postmodern empire. Sf, I will argue, has been driven by a desire for the imaginary transformation of imperialism into Empire, viewed not primarily in terms of political and economic contests among cartels and peoples, but as a technological regime that affects and ensures the global control system of de-nationalized communications. It is in this sense that Empire is the fantastic entelechy of imperialism, the ideal state that transcends the national competitions leading toward it.

For most commentators, imperialism is the ideological justification for attempts by a nation-state to extend its power over other, weaker territories, in competition with similar nation-states striving for the same goals. Hardt and Negri's concept of Empire, by contrast, is the more or less achieved regime of global capitalism. This regime fatally restricts the power of nation-states, and maintains itself through institutions of global governance and exchange, information technologies, and the de facto military domin-ance of the United States.

I am not concerned with whether Hardt and Negri's model accurately describes the real conditions of the global capitalist regime.[7] Its thesis is being put to the test at this very moment, as the US pursues a conquest that resembles classical imperialism at least as much as it does global conflict management. We will see in time whether it has irreparably disturbed the Pax Americana on which so much of Hardt and Negri's theory rests, or whether it has dramatically expanded the power of the American Empire to enforce "world peace." For my part, Hardt and Negri's notion is thin stuff upon which to base a critique of global capitalism. It is, however, immensely useful as a tool for understanding contemporary geopolitical mythology, as a cognitive map, in Jameson's terms, of the present. It manages to combine crucial ideas about globalization shared by multinational capitalism and Marxist critiques of imperialism; and by doing so it describes an imaginary world-picture in which fundamental historical transformations are concep-tualized and rationalized. As a political model, it has the flavor of sf—and thus joins other such political sf-myths as Haraway's cyborg, Baudrillard's simulacra, and Deleuze-Guattari's topologies.[8] As a world-model, it is simultaneously an ideological fiction and a way of experiencing the world. It is also what Peter Stockwell calls an architext: a complex cognitive metaphor onto which can be mapped readers' sense of reality and also the many different parts of the science-fictional megatext—the shared body of works and assumptions of the sf genre (204). In this sense, the idea of Empire is like that of utopia. Indeed, I will argue that the utopian architext is closely linked to the model of Empire. I will emphasize this in science fiction by treating real imperialism as the growing pains of imaginary Empire. I will treat Empire as the entelechy, the embedded goal, the conceptual fulfillment of imperialism.

SF and imperialism

The role of technology in propelling imperialist projects is often neglected.[9] And yet technological development was not only a precondition for the physical expansion of the imperialist countries but an immanent driving force. It led to changes of consciousness that facilitated the subjugation of less developed cultures, wove converging networks of technical administration, and established standards of "objective measurement" that led inevitably to myths of racial and national supremacy (Adas 145). It stands to reason that sf, a genre that extols and problematizes technology's effects, would emerge in those highly modernized societies where technology had become established as a system for dominating the environment and social life. Imperialist states were at the wavefront of technological development. Their projects had what Thomas P. Hughes calls "technological momentum" (111). The tools of exploration and coercion formed systems, as did the tools of administration and production in the colonies, and these systems gradually meshed. Colonial territories were treated as free zones, where new techniques and instruments could be tried out by companies and bureaucracies far from the constraints of conservative national populations. These innovations then fed back into the metropole, inviting more and more investment, technical elaboration, and new applications. The exponential growth of mechanical production and the production of mechanism continually widened the gaps between imperial agents and their subject peoples. Supremacy became a function of the technological regime (Adas 134).

There can be no doubt that without constantly accelerating technological innovation imperialism could not have had the force it did, or progressed so rapidly. Without steamships and gunboats, repeating rifles and machine guns, submarine cables, telegraph lines, and anti-malarial medicines, the power of imperial adventurers would have been greatly limited, and perhaps not even possible.[10] But imperial technology was not only a set of tools used for exploitation of the colonies. Imperial future shock blew back into the home country, consolidating a new idea of political power linked to technological momentum, essentially colonizing the homeland too, and at a speed that made all resistance futile. Each global technological success brought power and money to technological projects, creating a logrolling effect that drove irrational political and economic exploitation beyond its tolerances, in grandscale uncontrolled social experiments. It also fueled ever more focused and complex technological momentum—until social conflicts, both within and beyond the national borders, could only be seen as politically manageable through technological means. With imperialism, politics became technological.

Let us look at this proposition from the perspective of literary history. It is generally accepted that the novel was an instrument for establishing bourgeois national conscious- ness. In Benedict Anderson's well-known formulation, the novel was one of the tools for constructing the imaginary sense of national community in modernizing societies. The Marxist Georg Lukács, for his part, argued that the novel developed in every national culture in more or less the same way because modernization followed a single histor- ical trajectory. A society was either on the bus—indeed, like England and France, sitting behind the wheel—or off the bus and in the dust. The fact that novels were written in national vernaculars, relying on certain collective memories and myths, was irrelevant to Lukács. However, students of the Western novel can't ignore that novels were also projects of *national* consolidation and normalization. Novels were attempts to reconcile at least two great competing cultural desires: to preserve the specific knowledge of a soci- ety's present in its language and collective memory (what Balzac called "the archeology of the present"), and to ascend into the world community of modern players, to join the Club of Nations at the forefront of historical progress.

If the popularity of a literary genre is a sign of its power to mediate real social dilemmas through imaginary resolutions, what is sf's role? What and how does it mediate? Sf is generally set in marked contrast with the bourgeois realism of the novel. It has been linked to a variety of anti-realist, and so antibourgeois, literary forms (most frequently, pastoral, romance, and utopia). In the US, sf's most enthusiastic audiences were originally on the margins of the bourgeoisie: recent immigrants, working-class readers, and students of technical schools; for them the fantasies of physical mastery and engineering know-how offered an imaginary alternative source of social power to the norms of middle-class existence (Stockwell 99). In Weimar Germany, by contrast, sf was directed primarily to the middle class, but a class preoccupied with national resentment and revenge fantasies (Nagl 30-31). In both cases, the fantasies were quite similar to the ideologies of mastery that inspired the imperialist adventurers and colonists. Historians treat Cecil Rhodes's sublime statement of regret as the consummate expression of imperialist desire:

> The world is nearly all parceled out, and what there is left of it, is being divided up, conquered and colonized. To think of these stars that you see overhead at night, these vast worlds which we can never reach. I would annex the planets if I could; I often think of that. It makes me sad to see them so clear and yet so far. (qtd in Hardt and Negri 221)

To paraphrase Philip K. Dick's Palmer Eldritch: imperialism promises the stars; sf delivers.

I am not arguing that sf replaces bourgeois realism as the main mediating agent of late modernist national culture in the West. That would too great a claim. (Even so, some versions of that argument will make sense, if instead of sf we put forward a larger class of fantastic writing that incorporates sf's traditional devices and world-pictures, a version of slipstream writing in which bourgeois realism, the non-Western fantastic, visionary satire, and sf are blended.[11]) Aspiring technocratic audiences did not replace the bour- geois national publics wholesale. If sf took on some of the role of mediating between the national pasts and the late modern "future present," what role did national traditions have in the cultural work of sf?

Students of imperialism know from the work of Hannah Arendt and Edward Said that imperial expansion had a profound effect on culture in the home countries, even when the effect was hardly noticed at the time. Since most bourgeois nation-states had completed their political consolidation only recently, and their social consolidation not at all in many cases, their underlying conflicts were often still active and menacing. Imperialism attempted to resolve living domestic problems by exporting them beyond the borders of the Homeland. As these "offworld" colonial constituencies established themselves, they put great pressure on the metropoles to give up certain constraints that went with the nation-state, and to adjust to the "facts" of occupied territories: technological violence was justified by ideologies of supremacy (Arendt 136-38). The corrosive effect that this justification, and the reliance on technological violence, had on the most positive institutions and values of the nation-state is seen climactically in the attempt by the home powers to reproduce their offworld successes on the Old Earth of Europe in the First World War (Adas 365-66). At that point, the colliding would-be empires revealed that their technosystems had determined their identities more than their histories had. Their national traditions could not extend to the outer planets, mainly because the colonists themselves refused to accept the constraints placed on their liberty. For adventurers such as Rhodes, the national flag had been merely an asset in the work of imperial accumulation; for the home populations, it had represented the very reason for that accumulation. For imperialists, the twentieth-century's world wars proved merely that national identity is a volatile investment instrument; for national populations it catastrophically undermined the politics of reality itself.

Sf raises some very specific questions in this historical context. One is: are the differences in national traditions of sf due primarily to the desire to retain traditional cultural values historically established against the engine of technological expansion? Is this why we notice the significant differences of tone, of generic affiliation, of conventions of representation, that mark French sf from British, US from German, Japanese from Russian? If so, then sf may have much the same function that novelistic realism had in bourgeois national modernization: managing the abstract techno-political leap forward out of "domestic" culture, from a nation among nations to a global culture.

Another question is: has sf been a privileged thematic genre (perhaps in the way that film has been a privileged material medium) for expressing and representing the dialectics of this imperial process, because of its central fascination with technology? Has sf labored to manage the technological momentum inherent in imperialism, by infusing it with national cultural "dialects"—symbol systems, literary forms and formulas, artistic techniques, and discourse practices?

To study this genealogy, we will have to correlate at least three domains:

1. the character of the imperial moment—what difference did it make whether the expansion was a gradual and articulated process, as with the British and French; or intense, short, highly artificial, and self-reflective like the German and the Japanese;

or a smooth accession and aggrandizement of economic and military power, as in the case of the US?

2. the character of the techno-culture—was it widely diffused in social life, as in the US, Britain, and France, was it a foreign import as in Japan, was it associated with revolutionary mysticism as in Russia and the Soviet Union, was it an expression of romantic longing and resentment as in Germany? From the rear-view mirror of achieved Empire, what role did a given technoculture play: dominant agency, marginal late-coming, adversary counter-imperialism, or historical sublation?

3. finally, the character of the literary-cultural traditions that infused the fiction of sf. This is the zone of science fiction's literary unconscious. National literary or artistic forms may lead us to the traditions that distinguish the styles of different nations' sf. Clearly, sf is identifiable by the icons it uses: the spaceship, the alien, the robot, super-weapons, bio-monsters, and the more recent additions, wormholes, the net, the cyborg, and so on. It is not difficult to link these to colonialist and imperialist practices. They represent the power tools of imperial subjects, the transformations of the objects of domination, and the ambiguities of subjects who find themselves with split affinities. In these terms, sf's icons are abstract modern universals, free of any specific cultural associations. Yet when we view or read sf of different national styles, we feel marked differences. The same icons are cast in the mode of political and/or visionary fantasy in Soviet sf; scientific romance in British sf and its slapstick, dance-hall *Red Dwarf* inversions; as fanciful ironic surrealism in post-Verne French sf and its vertiginous inversion, the camp of *Métal Hurlant*; as supersaturated nationalist romanticism in German sf and its militant ecophile sf descendants; as catastrophism in Japanese sf and its hidden puppet-theatre traditions; and as galactic Edisonian problem-solving in US sf and its wired-beatnik bourgeois-bashing twin of tech noir. These are, of course, crude characterizations. National styles develop along with social life, and change constantly in response to influences, both domestic and foreign. There are also clear signs that these currents are converging, precisely because of the delight in diversity that Negri and Hardt consider characteristic of capitalist globalism.

SF and empire

If we look at sf's connection with technoscientific empire only from the perspective of historical imperialism, we will see an exoskeleton, the genre as the interface between the pressures of global capitalist evolution and national technoculture. To take a truly dialectical view, we also have to look at the internal space of the genre, its world-model, its assumptions of conceptual design through which it makes politics, society, ontology, and technology science-fictional. I believe that this imaginary world-model is technoscientific Empire—Empire that is managed, sustained, justified, but also riven by simultaneously interlocking and competing technologies of social control and material expansion. Sf artists construct stories about why this Empire is desired, how it is achieved, how it is managed, how it corrupts (for corrupt it must), how it declines and falls, how it deals with competing claims to imperial sovereignty, or how it is resisted. The history of sf reflects the changing positions of different national audiences as they imagine themselves in a developing world-system constructed out of technology's second nature.

To see this connection concretely, let us take a quick look at the qualities that Hardt and Negri attribute to Empire. Where imperialism is about unlimited growth, embodied in unlimited expansion (of capital, markets, and production), empire is also about the consolidation of the expansions of the past, and the irresistible attraction to imperial order. Its expansion is driven not by greed or national pride, but by the putatively superior ability of the imperial order to deliver peace and security.

Empire seeks to establish a single overdetermining power that is located not in a recognizable territory, but in an ideology of abstract right enforced by technologies of control. Its characteristic space is horizontal, expansive, and limitless; it exhausts and suspends historical time, pragmatically (i.e., cynically) taking up typological justifications from the past and the future as the occasion demands. Its goal is the management of global conflict, "world peace." Empire continually reproduces and revitalizes itself through the management of local crises, and indeed by the transformation of potentially global challenges into administrative conflicts. It eschews dialectics and transcendence (which are inherently destabilizing) in favor of constant intervention. It intervenes both in the social world and in the minds of private individuals, two spheres it fuses through pervasive communications technologies. Its physical space is limitless, open to perpetual expansion, and its social space is open to variety, hybridity, and relentless denaturing. Empire is the consummate replacement of nature by artifice. In its ontology, all existence is derived from a single, infinitely varied immanence—with rules that allow for infinite exceptions, but not repudiation.

Empire is the fusion of force and legitimacy. Since order is its driving value, its driving motive is enforcement. Its laws are not the laws of God, but of science. These are theorized globally, but they are enforced locally, as exceptions. Technology pervades Empire; it constructs a power grid through which it distributes its force and, by doing so, converts the line of communication into a power-cord. It rules, write Hardt and Negri, through the bomb, money, and ether (345). Its centers of power are the ganglia we know as global cities. To these, we can add Haraway's privileged sites of biopolitical virtuality: the gene, the fetus, and the lab—distributed interfaces where the essential conflicts of capitalism between social control and unbridled material expansion are ceaselessly engaged.

As an imaginary political domain, Empire is related to utopia. Utopia is an idealized image of the city-state—indeed, the nation-state—where internecine conflicts do not arise, since the ideal congruence of right and law is an ontological given. Utopias resolve inherent differences through the irresistible logic of their order. They are spatially circumscribed, and so they easily contain their people, reinforcing their self-identity. Their hegemony may extend past their city walls, but they are essentially insular. They do not expand, and so their stability depends on their strict adherence to natural laws of balance.

They are scientific and rational because their laws reflect a logic of stability inherent in natural reason.

The model of Empire is grounded in the history of real empires. Utopia is crafted from an abstract conjunction of community and natural harmony; Empire is energized by a more concrete relationship: the conjunction of might and right. Even in its most idealized form, Empire is a complex machine that distributes—and thereby produces—force. In utopias, force is occasionally rationalized as a way of protecting the balance between people and state, and insuring the inviolability of the enclave. In Empire, it is the vitaliz-ing condition of possibility. All the social and creative endeavors of imperial peoples are shot through with the institutional violence that makes them materially possible. Imperial violence is so powerful that it must expand; contained, its society would implode like a black hole.

Sf's debt to utopia is great; but it owes more to Empire. For sf's techno-science— which is the basis of its icons, energies, and imaginary historical conflicts—has little to do with utopia's institutionalized balancing acts and containment strategies. Technoscientific projects expand, mesh with others, and gain power from grand-scale conflicts that inspire new resolutions, which then evolve into new mechanisms. The expansion of tech-noscience is both internal (the logic of its technical applicability and improvement) and external (the logic of its universal application). An engine aspires to maximum relevance. Violently overcoming obstacles placed in its way by "nature" (which is nothing less that the world-as-given before imperial technologies go to work on it), technoscience charges all its claims to right and law with the irresistible expansion of its violence. The force is justified, however, in the name of peace and order.

Before armies and proconsuls, technoscientific Empire favors the adventurer, the Odyssean handyman far from home, whose desire for movement and conflict inspires his skill with tools. With each fight and each sociotechnical problem solved, the imper-ial handyman gains increased personal sovereignty and power. As Empire produces perpetual conflict on local levels that invite its intervention (a process Hardt and Negri call "omnicrisis" [189]), imperial fiction produces adventures in an immanent, lateral cosmos. Sf is most comfortable with such imperial adventure-worlds.

Even the classical genres to which sf is often traced (the pastoral, the romance, the utopian cityscape) originate in the imperial imagination (specifically from Alexandria, Byzantium, and Rome), as do their shadow-genres, the slave's narrative, the journey through hell, and the dark city. Utopias demand placement, position, definition; they are, as Louis Marin names them, games with spaces, real maps of imaginary territories. Empires are, by contrast, unbounded in space, and restless in time. Empire is a model of constant, managed transition: its worlds are perpetually at some point on the timeline of imperial evolution, from initial expansion, through incorporation, and then corruption, to decline and fall.

There is much more we could say about this rich political myth. But even this is enough to see how much this imaginary technoscientific Empire offers sf. The genre's favorite counterfactual operations and mechanisms are all made rational by imperial ontology. Time-machines, faster-than-light travel, galactic history, parallel universes, the restless reconstruction of relationships between the center and the periphery endlessly replayed in the relationship between Old Earth and the offworlds, aliens and cyborgs, space opera, utopia and dystopia—these motifs, like many others in sf, rely on a cosmos governed by the laws and right of technoscience, and yet are open to almost infinite variation. Sf is an endlessly productive engine of local crises in a highly tolerant universe from which it is impossible to depart.

Hardt and Negri's model of Empire has a distinctly science-fictional feel to it. Polybius, Machiavelli, and Spinoza may hover in the background, but the Empire of the contemporary resembles the familiar world of cyberpunk and tech noir.

> Empire appears in the form of a very high-tech machine: it is virtual, built to control the marginal event, and organized to dominate and when necessary intervene in the breakdowns of the system (in line with the most advanced technologies of robotic production). (39)

> The imperial order is formed not only on the basis of its powers of accumulation and global extension, but also on the basis of its capacity to develop itself more deeply, to be reborn, and to extend itself throughout the biopolitical latticework of world society. (41)

> The empire's institutional structure is like a software program that carries a virus along with it, so that it is continually modulating and corrupting the institutional forms around it. (197-98)

This is the imperial Sprawl, ruled not through decrees and armies (well, *mostly* not through armies) but through communication/control networks that distribute virtual power. This power is internalized by imperial citizens as surely as if they had chips embedded in their brains. In Empire, subjectivity is multicentered, produced through institutions that are terminally unstable, always breaking down. As the integrity of social institutions (such as schools, families, courts, and prisons) fragments, and the once-clear subject-positions associated with them weaken, the call for imperial comprehensiveness is strengthened, inaugurating a comprehensive ideology, a finely distributed pragmatic myth of networked, globally interlocking power. This is the twenty-minutes-into-the-future of Philip K. Dick, J.G. Ballard, William Gibson, Pat Cadigan, and Mamoru Oshii, where computerized communications operate 24/7, generating a mindscape of consuming subjects into which capitalist ideology feeds directly. It perpetually breaks down and reconstructs human consciousness, as in a Cadigan novel, into provisional target-identities to which the nostalgic, utopian dream of wholeness can be sold and resold perpetually in variant, sometimes mutually contradictory forms, and which can be hired to convey its fictions of sovereignty ever deeper into the self that once imagined it was itself sovereign. In this empire, there are infinite possibilities of projection, but only one reality.

> The most natural thing in the world is that the world appears to be politically united, that the market is global, and that power is organized throughout its universality. Imperial

politics articulates being in its global extension—a great sea that only the winds and the current move. The neutralization of the transcendental imagination is thus the first sense in which the political in the imperial domain is ontological. (354)

Since contemporary imperial power does not emanate from one center, but rather from the cyberspatial ganglia of postmodern metropoli, resistance manifests itself in the daily refusal on the part of "the multitude" to follow commands. For Hardt and Negri, revolution is neither possible nor desirable, since no class can act as the self-conscious agent of history. Freedom rests, as in Gibson's world, in finding one's own uses for things. In contrast with *sabotage,* the resistance strategy of national modernism, resistance under Empire consists of withdrawing consent, of *desertion* (212). Even the greatest rebels are refuseniks, choosing to withdraw, leaving behind them, like the fused AIs in *Neuromancer* (1984), a world in which "things are things" (270). Although this strategy hardly promises much as a way of landing blows against the empire, it is a dominant motif in the countercultural "Lost in Space" (or alternatively, "Lost in the Urban Labyrinth") subgenre. (Ironically, *Lost in Space* [tv series, 1965-68; film 1998] itself is as hysterically conservative as *Robinson Crusoe.*) Where the overtly imperial mode accepts the hierarchical network of administration—Starfleet commanders still representing the Federation—even mainstream popular works such as *Farscape* (1999-2003) and *Star Trek: Voyager* (1995-2001) try to establish a decentralized web of relationships in the uncharted territories, now just a wormhole away from the past (and the politics of empire).

This homology between Empire and sf extends to formal levels. The cinematic serial form, for example, is particularly well-suited for imperial sf. It permits an enormous variety of elements to be juxtaposed with only minimal motivation. In each episode, yet another cultural metaphor of spatial or temporal disruption is managed. This has been true from the earliest versions, such as *Flash Gordon*, to more recent ones—e.g., *Star Trek* and *Farscape.* The serial permits alien and local elements to be acknowledged, without threatening the order of things. The physically infinite expanse of space in such forms is generally controlled by forms of recursion and recapitulation—plot devices revealing that far-flung differences are related to the terrestrial metropole's perennial problems. At its most intellectual extremes, sf can even imagine that basic laws of nature are artificial, tools for the manifestation and communication of power—as, for instance, Stanislaw Lem's notion in "A New Cosmogony" of Great Cosmic Civilizations that change underlying cosmic laws in order to communicate with each other (and prevent human beings from ever threatening their hegemony).

Hardt and Negri's *Empire* is a creature of its time. Its model is the image of global capitalism that crystallized immediately after the first Gulf War. Their vision is essentially the liberal world-picture, slightly Marxified, of a post-Fordist international service economy attending the transformation of production by computers and robots. The authors have surprisingly little to say about technologies other than communication/control nets. For them, technology signifies control, the "imperial machine" (34). Their conception of historical imperialism, too, ignores the technological momentum that demolished the dams and breakwaters of the nation-states, and created the constantly mutating channels of global flows. From the perspective of sf, *Empire* belongs to a special subgenre—let's call it the sf of global management—with affinities not only to cyberpunk, but to Isaac Asimov's FOUNDATION novels (1951-53), James Blish's CITIES IN FLIGHT series (1955-1962), and *Star Trek*.

Sf's imperial imagination is more comprehensive than this. Since the basic conditions of sf are made possible by the hypothesis of the immanent ontology of technoscience, the genre sets out to imagine the effects of any technology that might affect the way we live now. This includes not only the near-future applications of already operative communication/control technologies, but technoscience that might radically transform the most basic aspects of physical reality, such as nanotech, faster-than-light space travel, genetic engineering, etc. The only restriction sf writers have historically set for themselves is that the powers in conflict must test technology as a basis for sovereignty. Sometimes the drama is explicit, as in overt imperial science fictions. In works as various as H.G. Wells's *The War of the Worlds* (1898), *The Day the Earth Stood Still* (1950), *Earth vs. the Flying Saucers* (1956), Frank Herbert's *Dune* (1965), Joe Haldeman's *The Forever War* (1974), *Star Wars* (1977), Orson Scott Card's *Ender's Game* (1985), Bruce Sterling's *Schismatrix* (1985), Dan Simmons's *Hyperion* (1990), Ursula K. Le Guin's HAINISH novels and Iain Banks's CULTURE novels, antagonistic technological regimes compete for dominance. Whatever their differences may be, however great the gulfs between them, they operate in the same social-ontological continuum, the most salient quality of which is the ability of sentient beings to construct technological cultures to manipulate and extend their power over the worlds in play.

In the human-against-nature varieties of sf descended from Verne, heroic protagonists use their know-how to cope with problems posed by hostile natural phenomena. They may be ultimately successful, as in most catastrophe films, or they may fall to the superior power of the physical universe, as in works like Arkaday and Boris Strugatsky's *Far Rainbow* (1963) and Sakyô Komatsu's *Japan Sinks* (1973). Whatever the outcomes, each contest is a local test case for the resilience and maturity of human technoscience as a species enterprise. Even in stories that take resolutely anti-technological stances, and where the technoscientific empire takes an Ozymandian fall, such as George R. Stewart's *Earth Abides* (1949), the terms of struggle are determined by technoscience. Technological culture's incapacity against the universe is the point of such parables.

To say that sf is a genre of empire does not mean that sf artists seek to serve the empire. Most serious writers of sf are skeptical of entrenched power, sometimes because of its tyranny, sometimes because it hobbles technological innovation. This is one reason why some Marxist critics consider the genre to be inherently critical, despite the fact that careful social analysis rarely plays a central role in sf narratives. Fredric Jameson, by contrast, has argued that sf thematizes (and indeed imitates) the way global capitalism prevents dialectical historical awareness from coming to revolutionary consciousness. Jameson traces the origin of sf in the West from Verne, whose works began to appear precisely at the point of transition from metropolitan modernism to imperialism (149). Jameson's terms are different from the ones under discussion here, but it may be a short step from his view to the one I am proposing. *Pace* Hardt and Negri, the technoscientific Empire that makes sf possible has much in common with Jameson's negative totality.

In the past fifty years, sf has come to occupy an important place in highly technologized cultures. In more and more areas, modernization wipes away pre-modern, and indeed pre-postmodern, hierarchical and transcendental world-views that obstruct market rationality and technological rationalization. Hypercapitalism labors to replace them with the "multicultural" coexistence of irresolvable, irreduceable, and intractable differences that must never develop into serious challenges to imperial sovereignty. The utopian ideal of universal right and law is replaced by the imperial practice of corruption—i.e., the constant violation of universality in the interest of power.

> Empire requires that all relations be accidental. Imperial power is founded on the rupture of every determinate ontology. Corruption is simply the sign of the absence of any ontology. In the ontological vacuum, corruption becomes necessary, objective. Imperial sovereignty thrives on the proliferating contradictions corruption gives rise to; it is stabilized by instabilities, by its impurities and admixtures; it is calmed by the panic and anxieties it continually engenders. Corruption names the perpetual process of alteration and metamorphosis, the anti-foundational foundation, the deontological mode of being. (Hardt and Negri 202)

Empire manages its populations by bombarding them with a multitude of subject positions, a multitude of hailings. Each one pretends to offer the prospect of unity, consummation, the fulfillment of wishes, yet each is comfortably corrupt. They reproduce the imperial process of establishing sovereignty (for the market, for law and order) by creating and managing crises in individual subjects. Mark Bould theorizes that modern fantastic fiction is inspired by the need to manage this relentless forced division and mutation of subjectivity through a strategy of paranoid self-construction.

But this psychic and aesthetic equivalent of deserting the Empire has limited force in sf. In its purist forms, sf ultimately places its trust in the problem-generating and problem-solving capacities of technology and the ontology of science. The more technoscientific hegemony is consolidated, the more contradictions it seeks out and strives to mediate in fiction. The most characteristic imperial fantastic forms may then be world-blends, in which the technoscientific ontology of sf is mixed with other kinds. This is a well-established element of the Japanese sf-anime idiom. In many of the major works of the genre—*Neon Genesis: Evangelion* (1996-97), *Serial Experiments: Lain* (1998), *Ghost in the Shell* (1995), *Galaxy Express* (1996)—non-realistic domains of power or styles of representation infiltrate realism, creating hybrid worlds. It is also characteristic of much French sf (whose influence on Japanese sf is considerable), for which scientistic plausibility is secondary compared with carnivalesque blending and philosophical metaphor. Many—perhaps most—important works of sf violate the strict rules of scientific plausibility and introduce heteronomic realities into their stories. Arguably, this signifies that the power to manage cultural differences is at least as important to sf as the cultivation of technoscience's mythology.

If my hypothesis is correct that the cognitive attraction of sf is closely linked to the imaginary world-model of Empire, many interesting projects may follow. It may help us to locate sf's place in the formation of a larger ideological mythology of modernization and capitalist globalization. It may help us to see how sf mediates between the cultures of nation-states and the imaginary coexistence of infinite variety in unbounded order. It may help us to see how specific national cultures undergo globalization; and how technology impinges on artistic culture not only as a set of tools, but as a mode of awareness. And perhaps most important, it may, by showing us the extent to which we imagine the world in imperial terms, begin to challenge us also to see the world differently.

Notes

1. The one significant exception to this pattern is the *Mitteleuropa* of Karel Čapek and Stanislaw Lem. A case might be made for the Austro-Hungarian Empire, the most northern city of which was Lem's Krakow.

2. For overviews of British sf, see Stableford, Griffiths, and Greenland. For French sf, see Lofficier, the more eccentric Gouanvic, Bozzetto, and the special issue of *SFS* on sf in France (16.3 [November 1989]). A serious book-length study of French sf as a whole has yet to appear in English.

3. For German sf, see Fischer, Fisher, and Nagl.

4. Regarding Japanese sf, Matthew is uninformative; see Napier on anime, and the *SFS* special issue on Japanese sf (29.3 [November 2002]).

5. On Soviet sf, see Heller, Griffiths, and Nudelman.

6. For a discussion of "prototype-effects" applied to sf, see Stockwell 6-7.

7. Critiques of *Empire* include: Kevin Michael, "The Non-Dialectical Marxism of Hardt and Negri," *Theory/Practice Newsletter* (April 2002) <www.newsandletters.org/Issues/2002/April/essay_apr02.htm>; Tom Lewis, "The Empire Strikes Out," *International Socialist Review* 24 (July-August 2002) <www.isreview.org/issues/24/empire_strikes_out.shtml>; Timothy Brenna, "The Empire's New Clothes," *Critical Inquiry* 29 (Winter 2003). 337-67; Louis Proyect, "Hardt-Negri's 'Empire': A Marxist Critique <www.columbia.edu/~lnp3/mydocs/modernism/hardt_negri.htm>; Gopal Balakrishnan, "Hardt and Negri's Empire," *New Left Review* 5 (Sept. - Oct. 2000) <www.newleftreview.net/NLR23909.shtml>; and Jon Beasley-Murray, "Lenin in America" <www.art.man.ac.uk/SPANISH/staff/Writings/empire.html>.

8. On Baudrillard and Haraway as sf writers, see Csicsery-Ronay, "The SF of Theory."

9. Adas and Headrick are exceptions.

10. See Headrick.

11. Brian McHale argues in *Postmodernist Fiction* that postmodernism replaces modernism's *epistemological dominant* (typified by detective fiction) with an *ontological dominant* (typified by sf). He elaborates on sf's privileges in *Constructing Postmodernism,* where he identifies cyberpunk as the quintessential postmodern genre. I have argued (in "An Elaborate Suggestion,"

my review of *Constructing Postmodernism*) that sf is not truly concerned with ontology, since the many worlds it admits are part of the single, albeit diverse and highly malleable, immanent world of scientific materialism. To the extent that there are significant world differences, sf posits that they were either created or discovered (and hence understood and appropriated) by technology. McHale's notion of postmodernism's ontological dominant is strengthened, however, if we take not sf, but the fantastic as the privileged genre of the age. Fantastic fiction and its various slipstream hybrids do not require any ontological decisions about the status of the imaginary worlds. (See my review of the Marxism and Fantasy issue of *Historical Materialism* in this issue.)

Works cited

Adas, Michael. *Machines as the Measure of Men: Science, Technology, and Ideologies of Western Dominance*. Ithaca, NY: U of Cornell P, 1989.

Anderson, Benedict. *Imagined Communities: Reflections on the Origins and Spread of Nationalism.* London: Verso, 1983.

Arendt, Hannah. *The Origins of Totalitarianism*. New York: Meridian Books, 1951.

Bould, Mark. "The Dreadful Credibility of Absurd Things: A Tendency in Fantasy Theory." *Historical Materialism* 10:4 (2002): 51-88.

Bozzetto, Roger. "Intercultural Interplay: Science Fiction in France and the United States (As Viewed from the French Shore)." *SFS* 17.1 (March 1990): 1-24.

Csicsery-Ronay, Istvan, Jr. "An Elaborate Suggestion." [Review of Brian McHale, *Constructing Postmodernism*.] *SFS* 20.3 (November 1993): 457-64.

—. "The SF of Theory: Baudrillard and Haraway." *SFS* 18.3 (November 1991): 387-404.

Fischer, William B. *The Empire Strikes Out: Kurd Lasswitz, Hans Dominik, and the Development of German Science Fiction*. Bowling Green, OH: Bowling Green State U Popular P, 1984.

Fisher, Peter S. *Fantasy and Politics: Visions of the Future in the Weimar Republic*. Madison: U Wisconsin P, 1991.

Gibson, William. *Neuromancer.* New York: Ace, 1984.

Gouanvic, Jean-Marc Gouanvic. *La science-fiction française au XXe siècle (1900-1968): Essai de socio-poétique d'un genre en émergence*. Amsterdam: Editions Rodolpi, 1994.

Greenland, Colin. *The Entropy Exhibition: Michael Moorcock and the British New Wave in Science Fiction*. London: Routledge, 1982.

Griffiths, John. *Three Tomorrows: American, British, and Soviet Science Fiction*. Totowa, NJ: Barnes & Noble, 1980.

Haraway, Donna. *Modest Witness@Second_Milennium.FemaleMan© _Meets_Onco-Mouse™*. New York: Routledge, 1997.

Hardt, Michael & Antonio Negri. *Empire*. Cambridge, MA: Harvard UP, 2000.

Headrick, Daniel R. *The Tools of Empire: Technology and European Imperialism in the Nineteenth Century.* New York: Oxford UP, 1981.

Heller, Leonid. *De la science-fiction soviétique: par dela le dogme, un univers*. Lausanne: L'Age d'Homme, 1979.

Hughes, Thomas P. "Technological Momentum." *Does Technology Drive History? The Dilemma of Technological Determinism*. Ed. Merritt Roe Smith and Leo Marx. Cambridge, MA: MIT, 1994. 101-13.

Jameson, Fredric. "Progress Versus Utopia; or, Can We Imagine the Future?" *SFS* 9.2 (July 1982): 147-58.

Lem, Stanislaw. "The New Cosmogony." *A Perfect Vacuum*. Trans. Michael Kandel New York: Harcourt, 1979. 197-229.

Lofficier, Jean-Marc and Randy Lofficier. *French Science Fiction, Fantasy, Horror and Pulp Fiction: A Guide to Cinema, Television, Radio, Animation, Comic Books and Literature from the Middle Ages to the Present*. Jefferson, NC: McFarland, 2000.

McHale, Brian. *Constructing Postmodernism*. London: Routledge, 1992.

—. *Postmodernist Fiction*. New York: Methuen, 1987.

Marin, Louis. *Utopics: The Semiological Play of Textual Spaces*. 1984. Trans. Robert A. Vollrath. New York: Prometheus, 1990.

Matthew, Robert. *Japanese Science Fiction: A View of a Changing Society*. London: Routledge, 1989.

Nagl, Manfred. "National Peculiarities in German Science Fiction: Science Fiction as a National and Topical Literature." *SFS* 8.1 (March 1981): 29-34.

Napier, Susan. *Anime from AKIRA to PRINCESSE MONONOKE*. New York: Palgrave, 2000.

Nudelman, Rafail. "Soviet Science Fiction and the Ideology of Soviet Society." *SFS* 16.1 (March 1989): 38-66.

Said, Edward. *Culture and Imperialism*. New York: Vintage, 1994.

Stableford, Brian. *Scientific Romance in Britain 1890-1950*. New York: St Martin's, 1985.

Stockwell, Peter. *The Poetics of Science Fiction*. Harlow, UK: Longmans, 2000.

31

Further considerations on Afrofuturism

Kodwo Eshun

Imagine a team of African archaeologists from the future—some silicon, some carbon, some wet, some dry—excavating a site, a museum from their past: a museum whose ruined documents and leaking discs are identifiable as belonging to our present, the early twenty-first century. Sifting patiently through the rubble, our archaeologists from the United States of Africa, the USAF, would be struck by how much Afrodiasporic subjectivity in the twentieth century constituted itself through the cultural project of recovery. In their Age of Total Recall, memory is never lost. Only the art of forgetting. Imagine them reconstructing the conceptual framework of our cultural moment from those fragments. What are the parameters of that moment, the edge of that framework?

The war of countermemory

In our time, the USAF archaeologists surmise, imperial racism has denied black subjects the right to belong to the enlightenment project, thus creating an urgent need to demonstrate a substantive historical presence. This desire has overdetermined Black Atlantic intellectual culture for several centuries.

To establish the historical character of black culture, to bring Africa and its subjects into history denied by Hegel et al., it has been necessary to assemble countermemories that contest the colonial archive, thereby situating the collective trauma of slavery as the founding moment of modernity.

The founding trauma

In an interview with critic Paul Gilroy in his 1991 anthology *Small Acts,* novelist Toni Morrison argued that the African subjects that experienced capture, theft, abduction, mutilation, and slavery were the first moderns. They underwent real conditions of existential homelessness, alienation, dislocation, and dehumanization that philosophers like Nietzsche would later define as quintessentially modern. Instead of civilizing African subjects, the forced dislocation and commodification that constituted the Middle Passage meant that modernity was rendered forever suspect.

Ongoing disputes over reparation indicate that these traumas continue to shape the contemporary era. It is never a matter of forgetting what it took so long to remember. Rather, the vigilance that is necessary to indict imperial modernity must be extended into the field of the future.

Futurism fatigue

Because the practice of countermemory defined itself as an ethical commitment to history, the dead, and the forgotten, the manufacture of conceptual tools that could analyze and assemble counterfutures was understood as an unethical dereliction of duty. Futurological analysis was looked upon with suspicion, wariness, and hostility. Such attitudes dominated the academy throughout the 1980s.

For African artists, there were good reasons for disenchantment with futurism. When Nkrumah was deposed in Ghana in 1966, it signalled the collapse of the first attempt to build the USAF. The combination of colonial revenge and popular discontent created sustained hostility towards the planned utopias of African socialism. For the rest of the century, African intellectuals adopted variations of the position that Homi Bhabha (1992) termed "melancholia in revolt." This fatigue with futurity carried through to Black Atlantic cultural activists, who, little by little, ceased to participate in the process of building futures.

> *Imagine the archaeologists as they use their emulators to scroll through the fragile files. In their time, it is a commonplace that the future is a chronopolitical terrain, a terrain as hostile and as treacherous as the past. As the archaeologists patiently sift the twenty-first-century archives, they are amazed by the impact this realization had on these forgotten beings. They are touched by the seriousness of those founding mothers and fathers of Afrofuturism, by the responsibility they showed towards the not-yet, towards becoming.*

Control through prediction

Fast forward to the early twenty-first century. A cultural moment when digitopian futures are routinely invoked to hide the present in all its unhappiness. In this context, inquiry into production of futures becomes fundamental, rather than trivial. The field of Afrofuturism does not seek to deny the tradition of countermemory. Rather, it aims to extend that tradition by reorienting the intercultural vectors of Black Atlantic temporality towards the proleptic as much as the retrospective.

It is clear that power now operates predictively as much as retrospectively. Capital continues to function through the dissimulation of the imperial archive, as it has done throughout the last century. Today, however, power also functions through the envisioning, management, and delivery of reliable futures.

In the colonial era of the early to middle twentieth century, avant-gardists from Walter Benjamin to Frantz Fanon revolted in the name of the future against a power structure that relied on control and representation of the historical archive. Today, the situation is reversed. The powerful employ futurists and draw power from the futures they endorse, thereby condemning the disempowered to live in the past. The present moment is stretching, slipping for some into yesterday, reaching for others into tomorrow.

SF capital

Power now deploys a mode the critic Mark Fisher (2000) calls *SF* (science fiction) *capital*. SF capital is the synergy, the positive feedback between future-oriented media and capital. The alliance between cybernetic futurism and "New Economy" theories argues that information is a direct generator of economic value. Information about the future therefore circulates as an increasingly important commodity.

It exists in mathematical formalizations such as computer simulations, economic projections, weather reports, futures trading, think-tank reports, consultancy papers— and through informal descriptions such as science-fiction cinema, science-fiction novels, sonic fictions, religious prophecy, and venture capital. Bridging the two are formal-informal hybrids, such as the global scenarios of the professional market futurist.

Looking back at the media generated by the computer boom of the 1990s, it is clear that the effect of the futures industry—defined here as the intersecting industries of technoscience, fictional media, technological projection, and market prediction—has been to fuel the desire for a technology boom. Given this context, it would be naïve to understand science fiction, located within the expanded field of the futures industry, as merely prediction into the far future, or as a utopian project for imagining alternative social realities.

Science fiction might better be understood, in Samuel R. Delany's statement, as offering "a significant distortion of the present" (*Last Angel of History* 1995). To be more precise, science fiction is neither forward-looking nor utopian. Rather, in William Gibson's phrase, science fiction is a means through which to preprogram the present (cited in Eshun 1998). Looking back at the genre, it becomes apparent that science fiction was never concerned with the future, but rather with engineering feedback between its preferred future and its becoming present.

Hollywood's 1990s love for sci-tech fictions, from *The Truman Show* to *The Matrix*, from *Men in Black* to *Minority Report*, can therefore be seen as product-placed visions of the reality-producing power of computer networks, which in turn contribute to an explosion in the technologies they hymn. As New Economy ideas take hold, virtual futures generate capital. A subtle oscillation between prediction and control is being engineered in which successful or powerful descriptions of the future have an increasing ability to draw us towards them, to command us to make them flesh.

The futures industry

Science fiction is now a research and development department within a futures industry that dreams of the prediction and control of tomorrow. Corporate business seeks to manage the unknown through decisions based on scenarios, while civil society responds to future shock through habits formatted by science fiction. Science fiction operates through the power of falsification, the drive to rewrite reality, and the will to deny plausibility, while the scenario operates through the control and prediction of plausible alternative tomorrows.

Both the science-fiction movie and the scenario are examples of cybernetic futurism that talks of things that haven't happened yet in the past tense. In this case, futurism has little to do with the Italian and Russian avant-gardes; rather, these approaches seek to model variation over time by oscillating between anticipation and determinism.

> *Imagine the All-African Archaeological Program sweeping the site with their chrono-meters. Again and again, they sift the ashes. Imagine the readouts on their portables, indicators pointing to the dangerously high levels of hostile projections. This area shows extreme density of dystopic forecasting, levels that, if accurate, would have rendered the archaeologists' own existence impossible. The AAAP knows better: such statistical delirium reveals the fervid wish dreams of the host market.*

Market dystopia

If global scenarios are descriptions that are primarily concerned with making futures safe for the market, then Afrofuturism's first priority is to recognize that Africa increasingly exists as the object of futurist projection. African social reality is overdetermined by intimidating global scenarios, doomsday economic projections, weather predictions, medical reports on AIDS, and life-expectancy forecasts, all of which predict decades of immiserization.

These powerful descriptions of the future demoralize us; they command us to bury our heads in our hands, to groan with sadness. Commissioned by multinationals and nongovernmental organizations (NGOs), these developmental futurisms function as the other side of the corporate utopias that make the future safe for industry. Here, we are seduced not by smiling faces staring brightly into a screen; rather, we are menaced by predatory futures that insist the next 50 years will be hostile.

Within an economy that runs on SF capital and market futurism, Africa is always the zone of the absolute dystopia. There is always a reliable trade in market projections for Africa's socioeconomic crises. Market dystopias aim to warn against predatory futures, but always do so in a discourse that aspires to unchallengeable certainty.

The museological turn

For contemporary African artists, understanding and intervening in the production and distribution of this dimension constitutes a chronopolitical act. It is possible to see one form that this chronopolitical intervention might take by looking at the work of contemporary African artists such as Georges Adeagbo and Meshac Gaba. In the tradition of Marcel Broodthaers and Fred Wilson, both artists have turned towards museological emulation, thus laying bare, manipulating, mocking, and critically affirming the contextualizing and historicizing framework of institutional knowledge.

Gaba's "Contemporary Art Museum" is "at once a criticism of the museological institution as conceived in developed countries, as well as the utopian formulation of a possible model for a nonexistent institution. This dual nature, critical and utopian, is related to the artist . . . founding a structure where there isn't one, without losing sight of the limitations of existing models that belong to a certain social and economic order based in the harsher realities of domination" (Gaba 2002).

Proleptic intervention

Taking its cue from this "dual nature" of the "critical and utopian," an Afrofuturist art project might work on the exposure and reframing of futurisms that act to forecast and fix African dystopia. For the contemporary African artist of 2005, these projections of relentless social disaster contain certain conceptual implications.

The African artist that researches this dimension will find a space for distinct kinds of anticipatory designs, projects of emulation, manipulation, parasitism. Interpellation into a bright corporate tomorrow by ads full of faces smiling at screens may become a bitter joke at the expense of multinational delusions. The artist might reassemble the predatory futures that insist the next 50 years will be ones of unmitigated despair.

Afrofuturism, then, is concerned with the possibilities for intervention within the dimension of the predictive, the projected, the proleptic, the envisioned, the virtual, the anticipatory and the future conditional.

This implies the analysis of three distinct but partially intersecting spheres: first, the world of mathematical simulations; second, the world of informal descriptions; and third, as Gilroy (2001) points out in *Between Camps*, the articulation of futures within the everyday forms of the mainstream of black vernacular expression. Having looked at the implications for African art through the first and the second dimensions, we now turn our attention to the third. To work with this material, Afrofuturism is obliged to approach the audiovisions of extraterrestriality, futurology, and technoscience fictions with patience and seriousness.

Imagine the archaeologists in their downtime. They sit round their liquid gel computers generating possible futures for real cities through World Scenarios, a video game that assembles alternative scenarios. Set in Lagos, with other options to follow, the game invites users to specify variables for transportation, energy consumption, waste disposal, residential, commercial, and industrial zoning. The game returns visions of what those choices will mean for life in 2240.

Black Atlantic sonic process

It is difficult to conceive of Afrofuturism without a place for sonic process in its vernacular, speculative, and syncopated modes. The daily lifeworld of black vernacular expression may be anathema to contemporary art practice. Nonetheless, these histories of futures passed must be positioned as a valuable resource.

> *Imagine that the artist Georges Adeagbo created an installation that uses the artwork of Parliament-Funkadelic albums from 1974-1980 to build a new myth cycle of politico-socio-racio-sexual fantasies from the cultural memory of this era. Imagine that the archaeologists from the future are now discovering fragments from that work, techno-fossils from tomorrow's yesterdays . . .*

Afrofuturism studies the appeals that black artists, musicians, critics, and writers have made to the future, in moments where any future was made difficult for them to imagine. In 1962, the bandleader and composer Duke Ellington wrote "The Race For Space" (Ellington 1993), a brief essay that attempted to press the future into the service of black liberation. By 1966, however, Martin Luther King, in his text "Where Do We Go From Here?" could argue that the gap between social and technological achievements was deep enough to call the very idea of social and economic progress into question (Gilroy 2001).

Afrophilia in excelsis

Between the demise of Black Power in the late 1960s and the emergence of a popular Pan-Africanism in the mid-1970s with Bob Marley, the Afrodiasporic musical imagination was characterised by an Afrophilia that invoked a liberationist idyll of African archaism with the idea of scientific African modernity, both held in an unstable but useful equilibrium.

This equilibrium was personified, in populist terms, by the Egyptological fantasias of Earth, Wind, and Fire. The oscillation between preindustrial Africa and scientific Africa, however, was established in the 1950s with Sun Ra, the composer and bandleader whose lifework constitutes a self-created cosmology.

The cosmogenetic moment

In 1995, the London-based group Black Audio Film Collective released *The Last Angel of History*, also known as *The Mothership Connection*, their essay film which remains the most elaborate exposition on the convergence of ideas that is Afrofuturism. Through the persona of a time-traveling nomadic figure known as the Data Thief, *The Last Angel of History* created a network of links between music, space, futurology, and diaspora. African sonic processes are here reconceived as telecommunication, as the distributed components of a code to a black secret technology that is the key to diasporic future. The notion of a black secret technology allows Afrofuturism to reach a point of speculative acceleration.

> *Imagine the archaeologists squinting at the cracked screen of the microvideo installation that shows the Data Thief trapped in the history vaults of West Africa . . .*

Black Audio director John Akomfrah and scriptwriter Edward George integrated a thesis from critic John Corbett's "Brothers from Another Planet," a 1993 essay whose title references John Sayles's 1983 science-fiction movie of an alien that takes on African American identity to escape his interstellar captors. Akomfrah and George take up in particular the oeuvres of Sun Ra and his group, the Arkestra; Lee Perry, reggae producer, composer, songwriter, and architech of dub reggae; and Parliament-Funkadelic funk producer George Clinton, three figures analyzed in terms of their use of the recording studio, the vinyl record, and the support of art work and record label as the vehicle for concept albums that sustain mythological, programmatic, and cosmological world pictures.

Corbett pointed to Ra's group, the Arkestra; Perry's 1970s recording studio, the Black Ark; and the *Mothership Connection*, Parliament's 1974-1981 album cycle to argue that "largely independent of one other, each is working with a shared set of mythological images and icons such as space iconography, the idea of extraterrestriality and the idea of space exploration."

Identification code unidentified

By the 1980s, the emergent digital technology of sequencers, samplers, synthesizers, and software applications began to scramble the ability to assign identity and thereby racialize music. Familiar processes of racial recognition were becoming unreliable. Listeners could no longer assume musicians were racially identical to their samples.

If racial identification became intermittent and obscure to the listener, for the musician, a dimension of heteronomy became available. The human-machine interface became both the condition and the subject of Afrofuturism. The cyborg fantasies of the Detroit techno producers, such as Juan Atkins and Derrick May, were used both to alienate themselves from sonic identity and to feel at home in alienation. Thelma Golden's notes towards the formulation of a twenty-first-century "post-black" aesthetic describe this cultural moment of studio-based sonic process more satisfactorily than it does gallery-based visual practice.

The implications of revisionism

Gilroy argues that the articulations sketched above tend to overlap with historical flashpoints. To analyse black popular futures in this way is to situate them as fallout from social movements and liberation movements, if not as direct parts of those movements. These moments may be historicized by politico-spiritual movements such as Black Christian Eschatology and Black Power, and postwar politico-esoteric traditions such as the Nation of Islam (NOI), Egyptology, Dogon cosmology, and the Stolen Legacy thesis.

The Nation of Islam's eschatology combined a racialized account of human origin with a catastrophic theory of time. Ogotomelli, the Dogon mystic, provided an astronomical knowledge of the "Sirius B" Dog Star, elaborated by French ethnographers Marcel Griaule and Germaine Dieterlen, that demonstrated a compensatory and superior African scientific knowledge.

Egyptology's desire to recover the lost glories of a preindustrial African past was animated by a utopian authoritarianism. Before Martin Bernal's *Black Athena* (1988), George G. M. James's *Stolen Legacy* (1989) simultaneously emphasised the white conspiracies that covered up the stolen legacy of African science, reversing Hegelian thought by insisting upon the original African civilization.

Afrofuturism is by no means naively celebratory. The reactionary Manichaenism of the Nation of Islam, the regressive compensation mechanisms of Egyptology, Dogonesque cosmology, and the totalizing reversals of Stolen Legacy–style Afrocentricity are immediately evident. By excavating the political moments of such vernacular futurologies, a lineage of competing worldviews that seek to reorient history comes into focus. In identifying the emergence and dissemination of belief systems, it becomes critical to analyze how, in Gilroy's words, "even as the movement that produced them fades, there remains a degree of temporal disturbance."

By creating temporal complications and anachronistic episodes that disturb the linear time of progress, these futurisms adjust the temporal logics that condemned black subjects to prehistory. Chronopolitically speaking, these revisionist historicities may be understood as a series of powerful competing futures that infiltrate the present at different rates.

Revisionist logic is shared by autodidact historians like Sun Ra and George G. M. James of *Stolen Legacy*, and contemporary intellectuals such as Toni Morrison, Greg Tate, and Paul D. Miller. Her argument that the African slaves that experienced capture, theft, abduction, and mutilation were the first moderns is important for positioning slavery at the heart of modernity. The cognitive and attitudinal shift demanded by her statement also yokes philosophy together with brutality, and binds cruelty to temporality. The effect is to force together separated systems of knowledge, so as to disabuse apparatuses of knowledge of their innocence.

Afrofuturism can be understood as an elaboration upon the implications of Morrison's revisionary thesis. In a 1991 interview with the writer Mark Sinker, cultural critic Greg Tate suggested that the bar between the signifier and the signified could be understood as standing for the Middle Passage that separated *signification* (meaning) from *sign* (letter). This analogy of racial terror with semiotic process spliced the world of historical trauma with the apparatus of structuralism. The two genealogies crossbred with a disquieting force that contaminated the latter and abstracted the former.

The uses of alienation

Afrofuturism does not stop at correcting the history of the future. Nor is it a simple matter of inserting more black actors into science-fiction narratives. These methods are only baby steps towards the more totalizing realization that, in Greg Tate's formulation, Afrodiasporic subjects live the estrangement that science-fiction writers envision. Black existence and science fiction are one and the same.

In *The Last Angel of History*, Tate argued that "The form itself, the conventions of the narrative in terms of the way it deals with subjectivity, focuses on someone who is at odds with the apparatus of power in society and whose profound experience is one of cultural dislocation, alienation and estrangement. Most science fiction tales dramatically deal with how the individual is going to contend with these alienating, dislocating societies and circumstances and that pretty much sums up the mass experiences of black people in the postslavery twentieth century."

At the century's start, Dubois termed the condition of structural and psychological alienation as *double consciousness*. The condition of alienation, understood in its most general sense, is a psychosocial inevitability that all Afrodiasporic art uses to its own advantage by creating contexts that encourage a process of disalienation. Afrofuturism's specificity lies in assembling conceptual approaches and countermemorial mediated practices in order to access triple consciousness, quadruple consciousness, previously inaccessible alienations.

> *Imagine that later, on that night, after the site is sealed off, ready for the next day, after the AAAP have all been disinfected, one of the archaeologists dreams of six turntables; the realization of the Invisible Man's dream of hearing Louis Armstrong's "What Did I Have to Do to Be So Black and Blue" multiplied to the power of 6.*

The extraterrestrial turn

Afrofuturism uses extraterrestriality as a hyperbolic trope to explore the historical terms, the everyday implications of forcibly imposed dislocation, and the constitution of Black Atlantic subjectivities: from slave to negro to colored to *evolué* to black to African to African American.

Extraterrestriality thereby becomes a point of transvaluation through which this variation over time, understood as forcible mutation, can become a resource for specu-lation. It should be understood not so much as escapism, but rather as an identification with the potentiality of space and distance within the high-pressure zone of perpetual racial hostility.

It is not that black subjectivities are waiting for science-fiction authors to articulate their lifeworlds. Rather, it is the reverse. The conventions of science fiction, marginalized within literature yet central to modern thought, can function as allegories for the systemic exper-ience of post-slavery black subjects in the twentieth century. Science fiction, as such, is recast in the light of Afrodiasporic history.

Afrofuturism therefore stages a series of enigmatic returns to the constitutive trauma of slavery in the light of science fiction. Isolating the enigmatic phrase "Apocalypse bin in effect" from the 1992 Public Enemy track "Welcome to the Terradome," Mark Sinker's 1992 essay "Loving the Alien" argued that this lyric could be interpreted to read that slavery functioned as an apocalypse experienced as equivalent to alien abduction: "The ships landed long ago: they already laid waste whole societies, abducted and genetically altered swathes of citizenry. . . . Africa and America—and so by extension Europe and Asia—are already in their various ways Alien Nation."

Temporal switchback

Afrofuturism approaches contemporary digital music as an intertext of recurring literary quotations that may be cited and used as statements capable of imaginatively reorder-ing chronology and fantasizing history. The lyrical statement is treated as a platform for historical speculation. Social reality and science fiction create feedback between each other within the same phrase. The alien encounters and interplanetary abductions people experienced as delusions in the Cold War present had already occurred in the past, for real.

All the symptoms specific to a close encounter had already occurred on a giant scale. The collective delusion of the close encounter is transplanted to the Middle Passage. The effect is not to question the reality of slavery, but to defamiliarize it through a temporal switchback that reroutes its implications through postwar social fiction, cultural fantasy, and modern science fiction, all of which begin to seem like elaborate ways of concealing and admitting trauma.

Black-Atlantean mythos

In 1997, this aesthetic of estrangement was pursued to its limit-point by Drexciya, the group of enigmatic producers, synthesists, and designers operating from Detroit. In the liner notes to their CD *The Quest*, Drexciya (1997) proposed a science-fictional retelling of

the Middle Passage. The "Drexciyans" are water-breathing, aquatically mutated descendants of "pregnant America-bound African slaves thrown overboard by the thousands
during labour for being sick and disruptive cargo."

> Could it be possible for humans to breathe underwater? A foetus in its mother's womb
> is certainly alive in an aquatic environment. Is it possible that they could have given birth
> at sea to babies that never needed air? Recent experiments have shown mice able to
> breathe liquid oxygen, a premature human infant saved from certain death by breathing
> liquid oxygen through its underdeveloped lungs. These facts combined with reported
> sightings of Gillmen and Swamp Monsters in the coastal swamps of the South Eastern
> United States make the slave trade theory startlingly feasible.

In treating Gilroy's *The Black Atlantic* (1993) as a science fiction which is then developed
through four-stage analysis of migration and mutation from Africa to America, Drexciya
have constructed a Black-Atlantean mythology that successfully speculates on the evolutionary code of black subjectivity. In turn, their project has inspired a series of paintings
by the contemporary African American abstract artist Ellen Gallagher, and responses in
the form of essays by the critics Ruth Mayer and Ben Williams.

Drexciya's project has recently extended itself into space. For their *Grava 4* CD,
released in 2002, the group contacted the International Star Registry in Switzerland to
purchase the rights to name a star. Having named and registered their star "Grava 4,"
a new installment within their ongoing sonic fiction is produced. In wrapping their speculative fiction around electronic compositions that then locate themselves around an
existing extraterrestrial space, Drexciya grant themselves the imperial right to nominate
and colonize interstellar space. The absurdity of buying and owning a distant star in no
way diminishes the contractual obligation of ownership that the group entered into. The
process of ratification therefore becomes the platform for an unexpected intervention: a
sono-fictional statement that fuses the metaphorical with the juridical, and the synthetic
with the cartographic. Contractual fact meets sonic fiction meets astronomical mapping in
a colonization of the contemporary audiovisual imagination in advance of military landing.

To conclude: Afrofuturism may be characterized as a program for recovering the
histories of counter-futures created in a century hostile to Afrodiasporic projection and as
a space within which the critical work of manufacturing tools capable of intervention within
the current political dispensation may be undertaken. The manufacture, migration, and
mutation of concepts and approaches within the fields of the theoretical and the fictional,
the digital and the sonic, the visual and the architectural exemplifies the expanded field
of Afrofuturism considered as a multimedia project distributed across the nodes, hubs,
rings, and stars of the Black Atlantic. As a tool kit developed for and by Afrodiasporic
intellectuals, the imperative to code, adopt, adapt, translate, misread, rework, and revision these concepts, under the conditions specified in this essay, is likely to persist in the
decades to come.

References

Bhabha, Homi. 1992. "Postcolonial Authority and Postmodern Guilt." In *Cultural Studies*, edited by Lawrence Grossberg, Cary Nelson, and Paula Treichler. New York: Routledge.

Bernal, Martin. 1988. *Black Athena: The Afroasiatic Roots of Classical Civilization*. Vol. 1, *The Fabrication of Ancient Greece, 1785–1985*. Piscataway, N.J.: Rutgers University Press.

Corbett, John. 1993. "Brothers from Another Planet." In *Extended Play: Sounding off from John Cage to Dr. Funkenstein*. Durham: Duke University Press, 1994.

Drexciya. 1997. Liner Notes. *The Quest*. Submerge SVE-8. Compact disk.

Ellington, Duke. 1993. "The Race for Space." In *The Duke Ellington Reader*, edited by Mark Tucker. New York: Oxford University Press.

Eshun, Kodwo. 1998. *More Brilliant Than the Sun: Adventures in Sonic Fiction*. London: Quartet Books.

Fisher, Mark. 2000. "SF Capital." *Themepark* magazine.

Gaba, Meshac. 2002. *Short Guide to Documenta XI*. Ostfildern, Germany: Hatje Cantz.

Gilroy, Paul. 1993. *The Black Atlantic: Modernity and Double-Consciousness*. Cambridge, Mass.: Harvard University Press.

—. 1994. "Living Memory: A Meeting with Toni Morrison." In *Small Acts: Thoughts on the Politics of Black Cultures*. London: Serpent's Tail.

—. 2001. *Between Camps*. Allen Lane.

James, George G. M. [1954] 1989. *Stolen Legacy: Greek Philosophy is Stolen Egyptian Philosophy*. Khalifahs Book Sellers. Reprint.

The Last Angel of History. 1995. Directed by John Akomfrah. London: Black Audio Film Collective, C4/ZDF.

Sinker, Mark. 1991. Interview with Mark Tate. Unpublished transcript, *Arena* magazine.

—. 1992. "Loving the Alien." *The Wire* 96 (June 1992).

32

Indigenous scientific literacies in Nalo Hopkinson's ceremonial worlds

Grace L. Dillon

In archeologies of the future, Frederic Jameson bridges the schism between science fiction and fantasy by recalling Claude Lévi-Strauss's discussion of "thinking Indians," specifically the Algonquin/Ojibwa, whose metaphorical totemic narratives display the allegorical mind necessary to navigate the imagined divide (61). Similarly, in the definitive book on Canadian sf and fantasy, David Ketterer points to native myth-making and Indian and Inuit peoples' folktales and legends as a major source of Canadian speculative literature, whose allegorical "consequential other worlds" emphasize spatial and temporal "otherness" reinforced by "the human other" and concentrate not only on alienation but also on the "recognition of constraints and respect for the powers of Evolution, History, and Nature" (166–167). Brian Attebery reconstructs aboriginality in sf as the indigenous Other becoming a part of the textual unconscious "always present but silenced and often transmuted into symbolic form" (387). He sees sf as a contact zone that "links [Aboriginal] traditional oral literatures with a high-tech or post-tech future" (402).

Whether or not we will remain satisfied with these categories, fantasy, sf, and speculative fiction often rely on so-called "cautionary tales" to depict dystopic worlds where the slavish embracing of advancing western technologies leads to environmental decay. And, increasingly, tellers of cautionary tales are juxtaposing the technologically compromised natural order with native and indigenous worldviews, as Attebery, Ketterer, and Jameson observe. Further refining distinctions, we sometimes include this emerging movement within the larger category of "postcolonial sf" because it reintroduces "indigenous" elements that fifteenth- through twenty-first-century colonization has marginalized.

Drawing on First Nation Ojibwa/Anishinaabe tradition invoked by Jameson, we might go further and characterize postcolonial sf's cautionary tales as "ceremonial worlds." Environmental philosopher Jim Cheney defines ceremonial worlds as "worlds or stories within which we live, the worlds—myths if you like—that have the power to orient us in life" ("Truth, Knowledge" 110). Cheney implicitly points to the primacy of storytelling in the transfer of indigenous knowledge, where story functions as ceremony to preserve tradition—specifically, proper custom and practice. Examples are manifold throughout Native American experience, but in maintaining focus on the Ojibwa/Anishinaabe, one might consider the compilations archived by Basil Johnston (*Ojibway Ceremonies; Ojibway Heritage*). Ojibwa stories tend to exercise an allegorical spirit while explaining the origins and usage of natural resources, such as the tale of "Mandamin" (corn). Many stories detail the habits of animals, who are considered to have spirits and equal "personhood" status with humans. The tale of the little girl and grandmother picking blueberries illustrates the use of story to pass down knowledge of medicine while also emphasizing the relationship among generations, as the older serves to instruct the younger. A little girl watches as a snake pursues a frog until the frog takes refuge in a grove of poison ivy; fittingly, though, she had not noticed the drama unfolding on her own but was directed to take notice of it by her grandmother:

> Once out of the poison ivy the little frog fairly flew over the ground bounding without pause until he came to another grove of plants. Within that grove of jewel weed, the little frog twisted and turned and writhed washing every part of himself. . . . From the conduct of the little frog the Anishnabeg learned the cure for poison ivy. (*Ojibway Heritage* 42)

Like these orally transmitted ceremonial worlds, Nalo Hopkinson's *Midnight Robber* (2000), the preceding *Brown Girl in the Ring* (1998), and the later *The Salt Roads* (2004) and *The New Moon's Arms* (2007), blend history and myth in a manner that heightens the natural extrapolative qualities of sf while offering complex plotlines that at first may resemble dystopic soothsaying, but that inevitably unfold junctures of hope. As meditations on indigenous contact with colonial power, the ceremonial worlds created in these novels cast the landscape as the "dreamwork" of imperialism where indigenous or diasporic aboriginal peoples engage colonizers in conflicted (sometimes ambivalent) negotiations that potentially evolve into positive exchanges of commodities and customs. Whereas head-hard, street-wise '80s cyberpunk engaged neoliberal globalization policies from the low-tech back alleys of first-world corporate city-states, Hopkinson's postcolonial ceremonial worlds contemplate "third world" and "fourth world" future-worlds that overcome the exported "technoscientism" of '90s globalization practices. This overcoming occurs by going back, way back, to tradition through the telling of story/ceremony, and by going forward, way forward, by mining the imagination to construct an ameliorated technology informed by indigenous tradition and practice.

A key element of Hopkinson's ceremonial worlds is what I call "indigenous scientific literacies." Indigenous scientific literacies are those practices used by indigenous native peoples to manipulate the natural environment in order to improve existence in areas including medicine, agriculture, and sustainability. The term stands in contrast to more invasive (and potentially destructive) western scientific method. And since indigenous scientific literacies are shaped by the diverse natural environments of the indigenous groups that use them, no single set of practices summarizes the possibilities. However, Charles C. Mann offers a useful review of practices for the Americas while establishing the continuity and sophistication of their sustainable approach to resource management:

> Until Columbus, Indians were a keystone species in most of the hemisphere. Annually burning undergrowth, clearing and replanting forests, building canals and raising fields, hunting bison and netting salmon, growing maize, manioc, and the Eastern Agricultural Complex, Native Americans had been managing their environment for thousands of years . . . they modified their landscapes in stable, supple, resilient ways. . . . But all of these efforts required close, continual oversight. (353)

M. Kat Anderson underscores the ideological differences between indigenous scientific literacies and western scientific method. Noting that "the first European explorers, American trappers, and Spanish missionaries entering California painted an image of the state as a wild Eden providing plentiful nourishment to native inhabitants without sweat or toil" (1) who played out a "hand-to-mouth existence" (2), Anderson establishes that the paradise discovered by colonial explorers was the outcome of "sophisticated and complex harvesting and management practices" (1). But more importantly, she focuses on the element of spirituality that lies at the root of indigenous resource management. Take, for example, her study of the word "wilderness":

> Interestingly, contemporary Indians often use the word "wilderness" as a negative label for land that has not been taken care of by humans for a long time, for example, where dense understory shrubbery or thickets of young trees block visibility and movement. A common sentiment among California Indians is that a hands-off approach to nature has promoted feral landscapes that are inhospitable to life. "The white man sure ruined this country," said James Rust, a Southern Sierra Miwok Elder. "It's turned back to wilderness" (pers. comm. 1989). California Indians believe that when humans are gone from an area long enough, they lose the practical knowledge about correct interaction, and the plants and animals retreat spiritually from the earth or hide from humans. When intimate interaction ceases, the continuity of knowledge, passed down through generations, is broken, and the land becomes "wilderness." (3–4)

The essence of indigenous scientific literacy, in contrast to western science, resides in this sense of spiritual interconnectedness among humans, plants, and animals. If the historic resource management of the Americas by indigenous peoples was for the most part successful, as Mann and Anderson argue, the reason is not because resources were so abundant that hard work and systematic thinking simply were not required, or that indigenous groups did not inflict environmental damage simply because they did not aspire to grand public projects. Instead, to echo Anderson's study of indigenous thinking, the concept of indigenous scientific literacy suggests that sustainability is about maintaining the spiritual welfare of natural resources rather than simply planning their exploitation efficiently so that humans do not run out of necessary commodities. Wilderness is not an undiscovered country renewing the possibility of new development; it is the loss of continuity with the land and the decay of generational memory.

By recapturing and sharing indigenous scientific literacies, Hopkinson's ceremonial worlds offer an alternative to Ulrich Beck's contemporary "risk society," whose defining features are public unease and skepticism over "distribution and management of hazards such as global warming that result from techno-economic development itself" (Demeritt 173). Indigenous scientific literacies in Hopkinson's ceremonial worlds offer indigenous technologies as pathways to sustainable existence.

Indigenous scientific literacies today

What economic and social aspects of western exploitation of indigenous scientific literacies are relevant to our discussion of postcolonial ceremonial worlds? Anthropologists, social scientists, scientists, and international lawyers connected to environmental science and interacting with transnational trade policies are mired in the potential for exploitation of biomedical and botanical indigenous resources. Much like their nineteenth-century counterparts in ethnography, twentieth- and twenty-first-century ethnobiologists engage indigenous cultures and territories to gain traditional knowledge of medicinal plants; natural insecticides and repellants; fertility-regulating drugs; edible plants; animal behavior; climatic and ecological seasonally; soils, forest, and savanna management; and skin and body treatments. Ethnobiologists must grapple not only with intellectual property rights but also with issues of what Frans de Waal's *cognitive altruism*, or altruism with the other's interests explicitly in mind, with "reciprocal altruism," a kind of system of repayment that de Waal characterizes as "a complex mechanism based on the remembrance of favors given and received," a system to be distinguished from simpler forms of cooperation (qtd. in Newmyer 77–79).

This reciprocity or gift-giving has been a facet of indigenous environmental ethics in stories re-told throughout time. For example, cross-fertilization of philosophy and anthropology that western social scientists label either "ethnometaphysics" or "cultural studies" is a mainstay in Ojibwa tradition. Original transcriptions, translations of Ojibwa narrative, and interpretive essays explore the intricacies of *pimadaziwin*—good health and long life—as an aboriginal scientific literacy (Callicott and Nelson 100–135). In literary studies and the social sciences, ecocriticism details ecological imperialisms and moves the social ecological perspective from a preoccupation with the merely pastoral or wilderness to places of hinterland that are no longer pristine: open-pit uranium mines on or near reservations, for example. Ecocritic Greg Garrard invites us "to take a hard look at the contested terrains where increasing numbers of poor and marginalized people are organizing around interrelated social and environmental problems, [where there is] no 'vanishing Indian' but ongoing struggles against improbable odds, in which no conclusions can be taken for granted" (123–131).

Traditional ecological knowledge (TEK) can be thought of as an intersection between researcher and indigenous knowledge, a collaboration rather than an appropriation. The hybrid nature has taken two paths. The neocolonial path models TEK as taxonomy: that is, as a set of categories and facts used to legitimize western management systems. The decolonial path posits TEK as a negotiated event and process. Because indigenous knowledge is embedded within a cultural context and "expressed through language, ceremony, artifacts, cosmology, and social relationships" (Paci and Krebs 269), it should not be wielded as a rational intellectual methodology aimed at discovering exploitable (and exhaustible) natural resources. Exploring the complex convergence of indigenous local knowledge and the interests of the academic community in their consideration of TEK, James Paci and Lisa Krebs ask: "Can TEK be a force for decolonization, of knowledge and power, or will it be appropriated and then serve only as an engine for neocolonization?" (263).

Notwithstanding these concerns, TEK is moving from the arena of social science to the "harder" sciences in practice and empirical content. Stephen Bocking traces the history of scientists' evolving perceptions of indigenous knowledge in northern Canada, where knowledge is often transmitted orally through story-form, and is complemented or mixed with the increasing emphasis on taxonomic classifications or behavioral information that can be readily understood in western scientific terms. Science, here, indicates "a complex amalgam of practical skills, technical devices, theory, and social strategies tied to its wider political, social, and institutional contexts" (236). The inspiration for this new academic inclination included a shift in biology towards mandating native input in wildlife management decisions. At the same time, native self-determination and land claims negotiations necessitated increased study of land use and harvesting practices.

Finally, Ruth Mathis and Terry Weik's *Indigenous Archeologies: Decolonizing Theory and Practice* represents a milestone in the developing relationship and counter-hegemonic practices between western science—whether in the garb of ethnographer, ethnobiologist, or anthropologist—and the aboriginal and indigenous subjects of its research. Mathis and Weik offer the "first volume in indigenous archeology that has more Indigenous than non-Indigenous authors" (9). It is dedicated to the indigenous peoples in seventy-two countries world-wide and re-defines archeology theory as "integrating material culture such as historical linguistics, poetry, music, dance, oral histories, and folklores" (10).

Of interest to the present analysis, Mathis and Weik argue for a broadening of African-American diaspora studies to include the social and political relationships between diasporic Africans, African Americans, and Native Americans, particularly within the context of evolving scientific research that redefines itself from the vantage point of indigenous and African diasporic scholars. Sven Ouzman expands the notion of indigenous knowledge ("held and developed by specific autochthonous people, usually long-term residents of a landscape") to work with an additional form of "embedded knowledge"—one that has been built by "a variety of people who have lived on a landscape;

some of whom may not be indigenous" but are almost identical, "akin to a storyteller and her apprentice" (209). Tradition, here, is posed as "those beliefs and practices that are consciously cast in opposition to colonialism, globalization, and the like" (217).

In counterpoising a monolithic indigenous view with a variety of international indigenous elements, Hopkinson takes a similar direction. Her novels, especially the tour de force *Midnight Robber*, cover transnational geographies from harsh bush and vast hinterlands to urban landscapes of decay, from contaminated Cayaba salt pits to transplanted cashew groves, while at the same time acknowledging the transferences that historically have occurred among African, Caribbean, and Amerindian indigenous and diasporic peoples. She derives material from the Anishinaabe/Ojibwa of First Nations Peoples in the northern United States and Canada, West African Yoruban and Caribbean Yoruban, Australian Aboriginals, the non-vanished Taino/Arawak, and Maroon communities, perhaps especially Jamaican Blue Mountain, John Crow, and Haitian locales. In personal terms, she aligns her own history with the Taino/Arawak, which she traces through her grandmothers' Maroon ancestry (Mohanraj 2; Rutledge 600). Her family traditions are supported by archeological research in the region. E. Kofi Agorsah comprehensively establishes Maroon-Amerindian fusions and suggests that the first Maroon settlements in the Caribbean were in fact earlier established by Spaniard-enslaved Arawak aborigines who escaped into the less accessible parts of Jamaica, such as the Blue Mountains (165–167). Archeological digs lead Agorsah to conclude that Arawaks were the first people in Nannytown and were gradually absorbed into later Maroon migrations (182). Underscoring obscured lines of ancestral transmission, contemporary indigenous organizations such as Trinidad's Santa Rosa Carib Community (SRCC) are in strong contact with northerly counterparts, such as Canada's Assembly of First Nations and Seminole communities, to begin exploring historical connections and to facilitate the cultural revival of the so-called "extinguished" Taino and Arawak and Caribbean Amerindians (see Forte).

Hinte songs, Maroon "break-aways," and oral traditions: The transmissions of indigenous scientific literacy

In *Midnight Robber* Hopkinson sets out to imagine "a world rooted in Caribbean culture and folklore, particularly the Trinidad carnival," in an effort to speculate "what paradigms for technology a society might develop without the all-pervasive influence of American technology" (Hopkinson, "Code Sliding" 1). The story focuses on Tan-Tan, "a little girl living on her home planet who gets yanked hither and yon between her parents as they carry on a hugely troubled relationship" (1). A runaway from this abusive situation, Tan-Tan becomes a folk hero reminiscent of the "midnight robber" of Trinidad Carnival fame. The midnight robber is "a powerful metaphor for exile and longing for home and strongly references the Caribbean history of the African slave trade" (1).

The worlds in *Midnight Robber*, especially New Half-Way Tree, express the nature of a deep time earthshaper story, reflecting the Algonquin tradition under the ostensible guise of a Maroon-embedded griot tale. For "woodland Indians" used to surviving the harshness of the bush and the fierceness of the hinterland, the animate and inanimate worlds, including humans (such as the Runners and settlers), other creatures (such as the douen), and the land itself, exist in a constantly negotiated set of reciprocal relationships. Managing and manipulating the ecosystem through controlled fires, selective harvesting of desirable species, and horticulture, indigenous communities deploy a flexible resource base and a diverse settlement strategy, one dubbed by Schaghticoke elder Trudie Lamb Richmond and anthropologist Russell Handsman as a "homelands model," or a site where individual and communal activities take place and where all relationships negotiated between humans and nonhumans within that territory occur over a long span of time (Bruchac 59–61). Algonquian stories and Maroon griot tales are "family stories" marked by the transmission of sophisticated knowledge.

In this landscape of memory, doing battle with superhuman elementals and "molding giant megafauna down to their present size" (Bruchac 61) are the tasks of earthshapers and transformers; fossils of megafauna extinct species, Pokumtuck giant beaver stories, and Great Lakes Anishinaabe transformers such as "Naanabozho" mirror New Half-Way Tree's huge dinosaur-like mako jumbies and the heroic nonhuman douen who defeat them in battle.

In Hopkinson's imagined world, the fantastical hinte, packbirds to the colonists but wives and beloved comrades to the male douen (who are deprived of flight unless partnered with hinte) sing nonsense songs and warbles that echo the more obviously scientific literacies of organic computer Granny Nanny, Nansi's Nanny song (*Midnight Robber* 173). Their prophetic urgency promotes interactions and negotiations with the colonizing "tallpeople" from the planet Toussaint, a compromise that the indigenous douen and hinte must accept if they expect to survive. On Toussaint, would-be colonists prepare for their journey to New Half-Way Tree by watching a computer-generated history lesson that projects the simulacra of the douen and other species indigenous to this new world as terrifying creatures that had to become "extinct to make it safe for people coming in on nation ships" (32–33). Simulated Toussaint history therefore prepared colonizers by illustrating the "naturalness" of douen, mako jumbie, and hinte extinction. Toussaint tallpeople think of the indigenous douen and hinte as non–human, categorizing them as species of fauna or flora. In this way the narrative asks its readers to consider the question: What constitutes "personhood" and which beings deserve that status?

Toussaint Runners, so-called for their occupation as pedicab runners, live in Headblind homes that are inaccessible to Granny Nanny's neural networked ears and eyes. Others view them as a 50-year-old Luddite sect that has reverted to "break-back" labor in order to survive without Nanny (*Midnight Robber* 4–12). Ironically, their preference for work in the fresh air and for homes that do not lock out other community members is mistaken for primitivist escapism. In fact, they actually are more technologically savvy than other inhabitants of the planet. One history nearly buried in oblivion is Nanny's own near-dismantling. It was the Runners who had saved her by tapping into her operating language, her argot, creole, and Nannysong, a fusion of computer language and protocols in Eleggua, Marryshow, and Calypsonian tongue, a song so complex it had been mistaken for "fuzzy logic" garble (50–52).

Herbal science is another measure of their knowledge. Maka, with "the massive chest and tree branch arms" of a Runner, carefully conducts scientific experiments on mice with woorari, a toxin later disseminated in battle. This weighing of scientific literacies of biological mutualism, distinguishing the biomedical usage of poisons, and understanding the balance of medicinal and toxic qualities of flora, is a pronounced characteristic of both the Runner society of Toussaint and the douen and hinte society of New Half-Way Tree. One of Chichibud's first lessons to Tan-Tan focuses on distinguishing between look-alike edible and poisonous plants, between, for instance, the water vine and the more dangerous jumbie dumb cane. Devil bush can poison and blister, but one who knows how to smoke it properly can acquire visions in which the plants "heal tallpeople and [they] see the voices of our own dreams" (98–99). Both the Runners who are exiled from Toussaint to New-Half Way Tree and the indigenous douen engage in what Carolyn Cooper calls "resistance science" in discussing griots and "break-aways," famous Maroon men and women, "walk-bouts" who were "slave piknis" and resorted to poisons in battle (109–112).

Indigenous and embedded knowledge of biological mutualism and the strong connection to Maroon societies grounded in *Midnight Robber* are even more transparent in *The Salt Roads*, a novel that portrays the interactions among diasporic African communities enslaved on a plantation and the Maroon freedom fighters who seek their liberation. Enslaved on the plantation owners' soil, Patrice makes his way to "the bush [that] the maroon runaways had made" (95). Going on a "marronage" is the "best way to get freedom in this wicked new world" (107), but he comes back to help his people in their struggle for freedom. Even the common-place rendering of the grinding out and eating of cassava takes on potency when noting that the cassava tuber, a crop often specific to Africa, but found also in the Caribbean, has high levels of cyanide and produces lethal effects if not properly processed. Understandably, the loss of indigenous knowledge of how to process the cassava has led contemporary scientists to wield agricultural biotechnology in an effort to eradicate its toxic effects (Makinde 120). Makandal, a powerful bokor who is "wise with herbs" (*Salt Roads* 107), comes up with a revolutionary plan: a spread of "physickes" slipped into the bakra's food, wine, and water through sharpened straws that are normally reserved for injecting remedies into the bloodstream (206). This narrative element reminds one that African communities had perfected the technology necessary to perform inoculations well before the usage was documented elsewhere (Brooks 157–161) but also conveys the ambiguity of a scientific literacy whose weapons "sometimes can slip and cut one's own people" (*Salt Roads* 201).

Brown Girl in the Ring depicts a pseudo-apocalyptic futuristic Toronto that has been abandoned by those wealthy enough to escape it; left without the comforts of western technologies, the remnants return to traditional indigenous farming and husbandry in order to survive. Grandmothers reclaim old memory and dispense "bush medicine" because federal, provincial, and city aid no longer exists. The state-influenced media blame the lack of civilized social services on the sovereignty efforts and land claims of the nearby Temi-Agami Anishinaabe Indians (*Brown Girl in the Ring* 11–13). The alternative urban Indian and diasporic Caribbean landscape imagined here depends for survival on adaptive fit and the oral transmission of knowledge to younger generations. Historical precedent is established particularly in the assiduous gathering and transmission of homemade medicines. "Among Caribbean people, bush medicine used to be something private, but living in the Burn changed all the rules" (14). The secrecy needed to ensure that those enslaved still acquired access to medical comforts is stripped under these fatalistic conditions. Secrecy is a means of survival; in the slavery days, one could get in trouble from the stories told (50). Ultimately, however, adaptive fit might not succeed. It is one thing to replace pharmaceutical products with homemade cures, but Mami's bush doctor herbs suffer and lose their potency over the course of Toronto's long, bitter winters, and healers can only speculate about dosages and possible side effects. Willowbark, for example, is a good painkiller, but too much quickly causes internal bleeding. Mami's daughter Ti-Jeanne desires the commercial drugs and views her mother's remedies as "old-time nonsense" (25–37).

The need for adaptation and the disharmony created by neocolonial globalization practices is one subject of Hopkinson's recent novel, *The New Moon's Arms*, whose plot revolves around the menopausal magic wielded by Calamity, a middle-aged but newly made "orphan" who discovers her ability to find lost things, suggesting a metaphoric take on the self-reflection that accompanies aging. The novel's setting (Calamity's home) evokes the theme of globalization: Cayaba island *is* hypercommodifed environmental-ism. Ecotourist enterprises intermingle signs such as "Welcome to Cayaba: Home of the Rare Seal Monk" with mermaid images "exotically brown but not too dark," expens-ive "boo-teeks," and a "Tourist Entrapment Zone" where imported reggae contends with the island's indigenous tumpa music and tourists put on their best Hollywood Jamaican accent (222–223). Hidden away from this zone are the struggles of the local salt farmers and fishermen. The US-based Gilmor Saline Company has operated a salt production factory on Cayaba since 1955, along with a second factory at Dolorosse, creating arti-ficial salt ponds next to the natural salt areas on the local coasts. The promise is extra waterbuses, a boosting of cell phone reception in the area, and increases in service on the ferry route (245). Oppositional leaders such as Caroline Sookdeo-Grant warn about accepting more financial aid from foreign multinationals when local fisherman already are in debt to the Fiscal Foundation for Worldwide Development: "The FFWD demands that we reduce trade restrictions as a condition of lending us money. This allows foreign multinationals [. . .] to grow unchecked [. . .] forcing small farmers out of business" (246). Independent salt farms, she further states, will go under, and farmers will be forced to seek minimum wage work in the Gilmor Saline factory (246). The recognition that the

FFWD along with China and other creditor banks will help Cayaba repay their past due loans, whose escalating interest charges already exceed $150 million, brings no comfort (273). The very real international globalization policies scrutinized here recall *Brown Girl in the Ring*, where the Ontario premier uses Anishinaabe nation-state sovereignty and land claims as a pretext for not funding inner-city needs (38–40), as do the intergalactic reshapings of *Midnight Robber*, where one questions how "humane" it is for "the Nation Worlds to exile their undesirables to a low tech world where they are stripped of the sixth sense that was Granny Nanny" (247).

"Lizards in trees feed me and teach me how to be invisible"

The Hopkinson canon strongly engages with a second component of Aboriginal scientific literacy: reciprocal altruism, a facet of learning and modeling sustainable behavior after, or along with, animal species. J. Baird Callicott and Michael Nelson's recent study is an exemplary form of scholarship that intertwines a philosophical and interdisciplinary analysis of what is sometimes referred to currently as the ethnometaphysics of Aboriginal thinking of animal-people and the scientific literacy to be gleaned from careful attentiveness to Ojibwa narratives. Animal-people form strong attachments to human-people in Hopkinson's stories; they range from douen/hinte as Lizard people/Packbirds to manicou rats to mermaids and mer-people to tree-frog creatures of the almond tree to monk seals. Notably, this form of ethnometaphysics can also be linked to Taino myths in a primordial world where rocks, plants, and animals can "speak" to each other, actors "can suffer transformations from one state (for example, "human") to another (for example, plants, rocks, or animals), usually after a specific behavorial act that changes their role" (Oliver 142). In some cases in Hopkinson's ceremonial worlds, the main characters may shape-shift into animals, such as Tan-Tan's metamorphosis into a manicou rat (*Midnight Robber* 74). Similarly, at the age of 53 Calamity finds herself to be a creature of the almond tree and very much "like a tree-frog" (*The New Moon's Arms* 105–106). But this is not mere simile. Calamity experiences many moments as a tree-frog throughout the novel, recalling Taino mythology that associates the feminine/women with water and that genders aquatic and semi-aquatic creatures, including frogs, as female (Oliver 153). And Makandal's ability to be a gaulin bird while speaking in human tongue to his friends or changing into a dog is described as the Yoruban "ouanga" or changing into other beasts (*Salt Roads* 111). Sometimes, in moments of deep distress, the need for this shapeshifting appears to produce more permanent effects. The dada-hair lady has the power to change humans' arms into flippers and their bodies into seals (*The New Moon's Arms* 317). Her gift is diaspora. The shackled peoples about to be marketed as slaves or cannibalized by the boss-men are thus transformed and dive into the sea where they can live freely as bahari (318).

The animal-people become strongly linked to selective methods of hunting, ones that sustain and balance the ecosystem, and to methods that preserve knowledge of migratory patterns and relocations. These features can include successful and sustainable hunting of animals, reciprocal gifts, right attitudes, genuine need, and the proper disposal of bones. In the Ojibwa tales, the animals are literally gifted with elements such as utensils, clothing, and body ornaments. Bones are respectfully returned to the element they are taken from while the animals, much like the douen and hinte in *Midnight Robber*, are understood to be "other-than-human-persons." Animals receive the genuine status of personhood in the traditional Ojibwa worldview; they are capable of reason, reciprocity, revenge, and even speech (Callicott and Nelson 112–119). In *Midnight Robber*, the bright-green-frilled douen or Lizard-people are "jokey-looking beasts" to the tallpeople, but through the experience of Tan-Tan, we come to respect their personhood. She is taught to survive in the bush by Chichibud, whose Taino name signifies honey, sweetness, medicine, and cure (Oliver 152). Through Chichibud's tutelage, Tan-Tan acquires the prowess necessary to kill a rolling calf, a fierce creature that only master hunters have the courage to confront (*Midnight Robber* 229). Tan-Tan's adventure with the fantastical rolling calf recalls the historical *cimaroon*, another Spanish naming of the Maroons and Arawaks. The Arawak-Maroon Amerindians became known as expert hog-hunters, not of tame pigs but of wild boars or "hogs of the wilderness" (Mackie 28–49). Moreover, Tan-Tan's suffering in the "The Tale of Dry Bones" incorporates the Taino/Arawak association of consuming of bones with the source of life itself and the power to create ordered life in the universe out of the deads' bones (Oliver 147–150). The impregnation or swallowing of bones recycles eventually into renewed life and hope for guilt-burdened Tan-Tan. Dry Bones swallows greedily the food that burdened Tan-Tan must bring him, gleefully stating: "You ain't go shake me loose until I suck out all your substance. Feed me, Tan-Tan" (*Midnight Robber* 201). But this "skin-and-bone man" in turn is swallowed by Master Johncrow, corbeau bird and buzzard (211) and Tan-Tan is free to journey out of Dead Duppy Town "where people go when life boof them, when hope left them and happiness cut she eye 'pon them and strut away" (198).

The fine line between analogy (such as colonists' analogizing of Amerindians and animals) and genuine animal-person cross-overs in these ceremonial worlds also separates rigorous "scientific" taxonomies. Monk-seals, phocids in the tropics that should not exist, "balanced on an evolutionary knife edge," are Cayaba seals, *Monarchus manachus*, Mediterranean monk seals that mysteriously appear in Caribbean waters (as witnessed in *The New Moon's Arms* 111–112). Evelyn cannot resist the challenge to imagine the scientific possibilities of actual mer-people. In adapting and living in the sea, one would need body fat to protect the body from cold, broad rib cages to make room for much larger lungs, hyper-developed lats and delts to help with swimming, relatively short limbs or arms, webbing between fingers and toes, and nictating membranes in the eyes (134–135).

Her description aptly fits a young child, Agway, whose appearance begs the question: Is this a human or an animal? But a stronger thread of mystery for Calamity is the relationship between her own parents. Her mother was in the habit of disappearing into the sea for a night or two at a time until on one occasion she did not return. Years later, Calamity discovers seal fur buried in the crevasse of a particularly twisted cashew tree and must question whether her mother had always been a seal or a mermaid who finally decided to go home. The interrelatedness of the evolutionary mutant monk seals, the appearance of mermaids and mer-people on shore, and the animal-human connections echo a theme of Ojibwa stories, "cross-species sexual intercourse" or human-animal marriage (a motif also found, of course, in folklore from many parts of the world). Notably, the sex is incidental. Strengthening of communal and societal bonds between animals and humans is the main reason for their marriages, which unite families, clans, tribes, and, at a royal level, nations. A human groom often takes an animal wife, clothed in fur as in *The New Moon's Arms* hybridization of human/monk seal (Ojibwa tradition often marries the human/beaver worlds). Reciprocity, respect for and proper treatment of the slain, giving goods as gifts, and exchanging horticultural and manufactured artifacts for flesh and fur ensures compliancy and happiness (Callicott and Nelson 119–121).

"Take one, give back two"

Consistently voiced throughout *Midnight Robber*, this mantra partially pertains to the restoration of a nation in danger of extermination. As in the reciprocal gift-giving exchange between animals and humans—or, more accurately, between nonhuman persons and humans—taking one and giving back two pertains to a replenishing of resources used on the trail or in the hinterland. Even the etiquette of sharing names forthrightly creates the courtesy of "trail debt" for the douen. Their world closely aligns with the Taino and Arawak Cosmos as Latin American archeologist José R. Oliver describes. Those of Taino and Arawak descent must learn how to steal, wrestle secrets through trial and error, and "learn how to make use of [cultivation, weaving, hunting, and fishing] for the benefit of mankind" (142–143). Taino tales such as the culture hero Deminán whose transgression (and yet eventual release of specific forms of knowledge of agriculture, fire and cooking) "lies in the act of stealing (food) from Yaya," both man and the supreme being or Creator (144 and 150) parallels the *Midnight Robber* Queen of the Taino griot fantastical tale of Tan-Tan and her father Antonio's exile to Kabo Tano's world. These tales establish the expectation that Tainos "upon reaching adulthood" must be able to prepare and harvest "their own *conuco* (garden plot)" (Oliver 150). Thus, traditional storytelling both encourages new generations to derive "sustenance from their own efforts" and gives them instructions about how to do so (150). Kabo Tano's eerie, surreal bush in "Tan-Tan Learns to Thief" consists of knotted up trees with twisted uproots, dangerously cold temperatures, the funny aroma of bones in the air, bark more purple than brown, and light coming through trees not yellow but red. A magic tree with cassava roots suggests the blurring into another dimension (*Midnight Robber* 76–82). Tan-Tan observes the manicou rat's tactics, uses a cutlass to steal Brother Rat's life and Brother Wild Pig's too. In the wattle and daub of huts, learning how to hunt and trap, she must also plant and leave portions of her hard labor to nourish the beasts of the land (89). These tactics restore this planet, Earth, which "was in a bad way":

> All she waters brown and foul. It ain't have no people living there, only dead fish floating on the surface of the oceans and rivers, stinking up the place. The land barren too; dry and parched. Tan-Tan and Antonio watch the sun hot up a patch of Earth so much it burst into flames. The air above Earth full with grey, oily smoke. The only thing growing was a thin, sharp grass that would cut up them feet if them not careful. The beasts of the Earth gaunt and hungry, for the grass wasn't giving them nourishment enough. (81–82)

Tan-Tan's wrenching decision to chop down the Kabo Tano tree, the source of all food, and her sharing and reciprocity, giving back two for one with the beasts of this planet, transform ruined earth into the land of the New Half-Way Tree (90). She must fight instincts that belie generosity (in a desperate time of survival, who has the will to share with others?), but her acquisition of a spirit of sharing quiets the chaos of the four dimensions of the Taino/Arawak world that were unbalanced by the arid and parched Earth.

Tests and struggles remain, however. The douen and hinte, like many Aboriginals, assume no one to be strangers but graciously lodge "guests" within the territory and typically assign them to a local family or clan for education. This thinking reflects many Native ways of articulating "communitism," as Jace Weaver terms it, indigenous community values with the exchange and movement of "diaspora (reservation, rural village, urban, tribal, pan-Indian, traditional, Christian)" (qtd. in Pulitano 73). It underpins First Nations sovereignty struggles, both intellectual and material, as voiced by leading Native scholars such as Elizabeth Cook-Lynn, Craig S. Womack, Gerald Vizenor, and Robert Warrior (Pulitano 59–70, 168–180). Those who give most generously and freely enjoy the strongest claims. In the branch of international law and treaty claims, the First Nations perspective simultaneously is both one of sharing and one of self-determination; it is the will, not the birthright, of Aboriginal peoples to ally with alien nations as a means of protecting Aboriginal values (Battiste and Semaganis 96–103). For example, the Tegami-Indians or Anishinaabe of *Brown Girl in the Ring* establish a shared territory of trust, promise, and protection; treaty federalism does not mean that the Aboriginal nation is a subject of the Crown remaining "alien" within its own land. Rather, it "walks side by side" with other established communities in the area. When the douen are thoughtlessly displaced by the Toussaint colonists who mistake them for monkeys or wasps, they must chop down their own daddy tree, their nation's sovereign home, and disappear further into the bush. Chichibud sums up douen relations with these colonists by wondering, "Maybe your people and mine not meant to walk together, oui" (283).

"Letting the sky into the bush"

The fourth component of indigenous scientific literacy concerns the aesthetics and experimentation of husbandry, grafting, and planting in ways that do not significantly alter the
landscape. To an outside eye, farmed areas can appear to be untouched forest or wild
ecoscapes (Posey 30). The migratory patterns of many tribes such as the Ojibwa included
the selective harvesting of wild rice grown on banks and cultivated in a manner that does not
fit euro-western conceptions of "farming." The US Dawes Act in the late nineteenth century
that sought to "civilize" Indians by giving them farming implements, a small plot of acre-
age, and a time-frame in which to demonstrate adequate production is one among many
miscues. This is the perspective the tallpeople have of the douen; they seamlessly merge
with their surroundings and somehow survive in the bush, but who could imagine that they
have the ability to plan, implement, and thrive on an indigenous agricultural strategy?

The open-minded youth of Tan-Tan creates a space for tutelage by Chichibud, who
relates the indigenous "art" of innovative grafting and husbandry. Ethnobotanists studying
indigenous use of plant resources have described many horticultural and gardening practices that preserve species diversity. "For example, indigenous horticulturalists exhibit a
keen interest in the location of rare and useful plants, replanting these when necessary. They
often intervene in pollination and succession, thereby protecting threatened species. . . .
They may also create anthropogenic islands of forests" (Mulder and Coppolillo 95).
Significantly, Chichibud has noted the settlers' disgust for a local parasitic fungus, and one
of his first interactions with Tan-Tan emphasizes the beauty of this tenacious plant, which
exists where nothing else catches, in places of rock lacking any soil (*Midnight Robber* 98).
Chichibud remarks on douen sovereignty that "Every douen nation have it own own daddy
tree" (179), the sacred spot that Papa Bois has given to the nation for food and shelter.
Its immensity is suggested automatically by the sheltering of so many douen and hinte
in its boughs and reminds one of the Ceiba or giant silk-cotton or kapok tree considered
sacred by the Taino, as well as by many African people who arrived later in the West Indies
(Highfield 162). Like a mangrove, fluorescent fungus becomes a guiding light in its cham-
bers, and the wasp-nest structure is carefully woven by the hinte's beaks. The douen graft
all kinds of plants onto the tree, relying on its root system for nurture. Any non-indigenous
invasive species introduced accidentally by the tallpeople's arrivals become for the douen
an experiment in adaptation and grafting (182–221). In times of crisis or a sudden need to
migrate, the remains of the daddytree are carried with the nation to preserve their state-
hood. When discovered (though not well-discerned), the douen destroy their home and
move away, "letting the sky into the bush" (274–277).

Ceremonial worlds

The metanarrative of all four novels replicates the aboriginal method of conveying
scientific literacy through storytelling rather than a rote set of instructional procedures,

a manual handbook, or a sharply demarcated taxonomic system. "Anansi" stories like these are adaptive stories, techno-trickster tales and narratives that chronicle the stratagems of the West African Yoruban spider, Anansi; of the great white hare and rabbit, the Ojibwa Anansi and Naanabozho; and of Brer Anansi, a "cunning little man who could become a spider" (*Midnight Robber* 31), part human, part animal-person, part immortal, and a Native, indigenous, and African diasporic metaphor for the intricately structured Web of Being.

Indigenous scientific knowledge is necessary for adaptive fit, the notion that we survive not by conquering the world but by recognizing ourselves as part of it and "seeking the proper road on which to walk" as Ojibwa colleague Dennis McPherson speaks of it (Cheney 118). In the ceremonial world, metaphors are literalized, and an allegorical spirit haunts taxonomic thinking. In such a world, scientific literacies stand out by slowing us down. In contrast to the accelerating effect of techno-driven western scientific method, the salt-making of the Maroon communities; the herb-cultivating of indigenous, Caribbean, and diasporic communities; and the husbandry of the douen and of the Cayaba islands people offer quiet meditations on the state of the Earth. In practice, her narratives maintain hope through the depiction of regeneration—specifically, of the younger generation's reawakening to cultural tradition, including scientific literacies. *Brown Girl in the Ring* depicts the reclamation of Toronto's inner city. *Midnight Robber* shows a new generation's reconnection with Granny Nanny with the birth of Tan-Tan's son Tubman, "the human bridge from slavery to freedom" (329). Attracted by local and global indigenous revival movements, Calamity's daughter joins the campaign against the salt farms. By illustrating the trajectory from indigenous primacy to global affliction, Hopkinson offers a holistic worldview in which scientific literacies happen every day.

Works cited

Agorsah, E. Kofi. "Archeology of Maroon Settlements in Jamaica." *Maroon Heritage: Archeological, Ethnographic, and Historical Perspectives.* Ed. E. Kofi Agorsah. Barbados: Canoe P and the U of West Indies, 1994. 163–187.

Anderson, M. Kat. *Tending the Wild: Native American Knowledge and the Management of California's Natural Resources.* Berkeley: U of California P, 2005.

Attebery, Brian. "Aboriginality in Science Fiction." *Science Fiction Studies* 32.3 (2005): 385–404.

Battiste, Marie, and Helen Semaganis. "First Thoughts on First Nations Citizenship Issues in Education." *Citizenship in Transformation in Canada.* Ed. Yvonne M. Hébert. Toronto: U of Toronto, 2002. 93–111.

Beier, J. Marshall. *International Relations in Uncommon Places: Indigeneity, Cosmology and the Limits of International Theory.* New York: Palgrave, 2005.

Bocking, Stephen. "Scientists and Evolving Perceptions of Indigenous Knowledge in Northern Canada." *Walking a Tightrope: Aboriginal People and Their Representations.* Ed. Ute Lischke and David T. McNab. Waterloo: Wilfred Laurier UP, 2005. 215–247.

Brooks, Joanna. *American Lazarus: Religion and the Rise of African-American and Native American Literatures.* Oxford: Oxford UP, 2003.

Bruchac, Margaret M. "Earthshapers and Placemakers: Algonkian Indian Stories and the Landscape." *Indigenous Archeologies: Decolonizing Theory and Practice*. Ed. Claire Smith and H. Martin Wobst. NewYork: Routledge, 2005. 56–80.

Callicott, J. Baird, and Michael P. Nelson. *American Indian Environmental Ethics: An Ojibwa Case Study*. Upper Saddle River: Pearson, 2004.

Cheney, Jim. "Truth, Knowledge, and the Wild World." *Ethics and the Environment* 10.2 (2005): 101–135.

Cooper, Carolyn. "'Resistance Science': Afrocentric Ideology in Vic Reid's Nanny Town." *Maroon Heritage: Archeological, Ethnographic, and Historical Perspectives*. Ed. E. Kofi Agorsah. Barbados: Canoe P and the U of West Indies, 1994. 109–118.

Demeritt, David. "Science, Social Constructivism, and Nature." *Social Nature: Theory, Practice, and Politics*. Ed. N. Castree. Malden: Blackwell, 2001. 173–19.

Forte, Maximilian C. "'We are not extinct': The Revival of Carib and Taino Identities, the Internet, and the Transformation of Off-line Indigenes into Online 'N-digenes.'" *Sincronía* (Spring 2002). <http://sincronia.cucsh.udg.mx/CyberIndigen.htm>

Garrard, Greg. *Ecocriticism*. New York: Routledge, 2004.

Highfield, Arnold R. "Some Observations on the Taino Language." *The Indigenous People of the Caribbean*. Ed. Samuel M. Wilson. Gainesville: UP Florida, 1997. 154–168.

Hopkinson, Nalo. *Brown Girl in the Ring*. New York: Warner, 1998.

—. "Code Sliding: About *Midnight Robber* and My Use of Creole in the Narrative." <http://nalohopkinson.com/writing/slide.html>

—. *Midnight Robber*. New York: Warner, 2000.

—. *The New Moon's Arms*. New York: Warner, 2007.

—. *Salt Roads*. New York: Warner, 2004.

Jameson, Frederic. *Archaeologies of the Future: The Desire Called Utopia and Other Science Fictions*. New York: Verso, 2005.

Johnston, Basil. *Ojibway Ceremonies*. Lincoln: U of Nebraska P, 1982.

—. *Ojibway Heritage*. Lincoln: U of Nebraska P, 1976.

Ketterer, David. *Canadian Science Fiction and Fantasy*. Bloomington: Indiana UP, 1992.

Lévi-Strauss, Claude. *Totemism*. Trans. Rodney Needham. 1963. Boston: Beacon, 2005.

Mackie, Erin. "Welcome the Outlaw: Pirates, Maroons, and Caribbean Countercultures." *Cultural Critique* 59 (2005): 24–62.

Makinde, Martin O. "Agricultural Biotechnology in African Countries." *Cross-Cultural Biotechnology*. Ed. Michael C. Brannigan. Lanham: Rowman, 2004. 119–124.

Mann, Charles C. *1491: New Revelations of the Americas Before Columbus*. 2005. New York: Vintage, 2006.

Mathis, Ruth, and Terry Weik. "Not just Black and White: African Americans Reclaiming the Indigenous Past." *Indigenous Archeologies: Decolonizing Theory and Practice*. Ed. Claire Smith and H. Martin Wobst. NewYork: Routledge, 2005. 281–297.

Mohanraj, Mary Anne. "Interview: Nalo Hopkinson." *Strange Horizon* 1 (Sept. 2000): 1–6. <http://web.strangehorizons.com/2000/20000901/NaloHopkinson_Interview.shtml>

Mulder, Monique Borgerhoff, and Peter Coppolillo. *Conservation Linking Ecology, Economics, and Culture*. Princeton: Princeton UP, 2005.

Newmyer, Stephen T. *Animals, Rights and Reason in Plutarch and Modern Ethics*. New York: Routledge, 2006.

Oliver, José R. "The Taino Cosmos." *The Indigenous People of the Caribbean.* Ed. Samuel M. Wilson. Gainesville: UP Florida, 1997. 140–153.

Ouzman, Sven. "Silencing and Sharing Southern African Indigenous and Embedded Knowledge." *Indigenous Archeologies: Decolonizing Theory and Practice.* Ed. Claire Smith and H. Martin Wobst. New York: Routledge, 2005. 208–225.

Paci, James C. D., and Lisa Krebs. "Local Knowledge as Traditional and Ecological Knowledge: Definition and Ownership." *Native Pathways: American Indian Culture and Economic Development in the Twentieth Century.* Ed. Brian Hosmer and Colleen O'Neill. Boulder: UP of Colorado, 2004. 263–282.

Posey, Darrell A. A *Darrell Posey Reader: Indigenous Knowledge and Ethics.* Ed. Kristina Plenderleith. NewYork: Routledge, 2004.

—. "Upsetting the Sacred Balance: Can the Study of Indigenous Knowledge Reflect Cosmic Connectedness?" *Participating in Development: Approaches to Indigenous Knowledge.* Ed. Paul Sillitoe, Alan Bicker, and Johan Pottier. New York: Routledge, 2002. 24–42.

Pulitano, Elvira. *Toward a Native American Critical Theory.* Lincoln: U of Nebraska P, 2003.

Rutledge, Gregory. "Speaking in Tongues: An Interview with Science Fiction Writer Nalo Hopkinson." *African American Review* 34:4 (1999): 598–601.

33

Biotic invasions: Ecological imperialism in new wave science fiction

Rob Latham

In an essay on H. G. Wells's *The War of the Worlds* (1898), Peter Fitting argues that tales of "first contact" within science fiction tend to recapitulate "the encounters of the European 'discovery' of the New World."[1] They are thus, whether consciously or not, conquest narratives, though "usually not characterized as [. . .] invasion[s]" because they are "written from the point of view of the invaders," who prefer euphemisms such as "exploration" to more aggressive or martial constructions of the encounter.[2] The accomplishment of Wells's novel, in Fitting's analysis, is to lay bare the power dynamics of this scenario by depicting a reversal of historical reality, with the imperial hub of late-Victorian London itself subjugated by "superior creatures who share none the less some of the characteristics of Earth's 'lower' species, a humiliation which is compounded by their apparent lack of interest in the humans as an intelligent species."[3] The irony of this switch of roles is not lost on Wells's narrator, who compares the fate of his fellow Londoners to those of the Tasmanians and even the dodoes, "entirely swept out of existence in a war of extermination waged by European immigrants."[4] Stephen Arata uses the term "reverse colonization" to describe this sort of story in which the centre of empire is besieged by fantastic creatures from its margins; as Brian Aldiss puts it, "Wells is saying, in effect, to his fellow English, 'Look, this is how it feels to be a primitive tribe, and to have a Western nation arriving to civilize you with Maxim guns!'."[5]

Taking this general argument one step further, John Rieder claims that all manner of disaster stories within SF "might profitably be considered as the obverse of the celebratory narratives of exploration and discovery [. . .] that formed the Official Story of colonialism."[6] The sense of helplessness—geographic, economic, military, and so on—reinforced by catastrophe scenarios lays bare the underlying anxieties of hegemonic power, its inherent contingency and vulnerability, notwithstanding the purported inevitability of Western "progress." Moreover, disaster stories, by inverting existing power relations and displacing them into fantastic or futuristic milieux, expose the workings of imperialist ideology, the expedient fantasies that underpin the colonial enterprise; for example, "although the colonizer knows very well that colonized people are humans like himself, he acts as if they were parodic, grotesque imitations of humans instead,"[7] who may conveniently be dispossessed of land, property, and even life. The catastrophe story brings this logic of dispossession home to roost, shattering the surface calm of imperial hegemony and thrusting the colonizers themselves into a sudden chaos of destruction and transform- ation such as they have typically visited upon others. Narratives of invasion in particular are "heavily and consistently overdetermined by [their] reference to colonialism," allow- ing a potentially critical engagement with "the ideology of progress and its concomitant constructions of agency and destiny,"[8] that is, the triumphalist enshrinement of white Westerners at the apex of historical development and the demotion of all others to what anthropologist Eric Wolf calls a "people without history."[9]

Of course, to interpret most invasion stories of SF's pulp era as critical of Western progress requires reading against the grain, since their evident message is the fearless- ness and ingenuity of Euro-American peoples when confronted by hostile forces. The magazine *Astounding Stories*, during its 1940s golden age, operated under a philosophy that Brian Stableford and David Pringle identify as "human chauvinism," by the terms of which "humanity was destined to get the better of any and all alien species."[10] Editor John Campbell saw the extraterrestrial expansion of the human race not only as a logical extra- polation of the exploratory impulse of Western civilization, but also explicitly as an outlet for martial aggression; as he remarked in a letter to A. E. van Vogt, when "other planets are opened to colonization [. . .] we'll have peace on earth—and war in heaven!."[11] One of the few tales of successful "foreign" invasion published during *Astounding*'s heyday was Robert Heinlein's *Sixth Column* (1941), where the invaders are not aliens from space but a Pan-Asiatic horde that occupies the United States, only to be undermined and eventually defeated by an underground scientific elite masquerading as a popular reli- gion; reverse colonization is thus foiled and the Westward trend of empire reaffirmed. *Sixth Column* is a forerunner of post-war tales of communist menace, such as Heinlein's own *The Puppet Masters* (1951), in which slug-like parasites seek to brainwash the US citizenry but ultimately prove no match for the native resourcefulness and righteous rage of humankind: "they made the mistake of tangling with the toughest, meanest, deadliest, most unrelenting—and ablest—form of life in this section of space, a critter that can be killed but can't be tamed."[12]

The cinema of the 1950s was filled with similar scenarios of sinister alien infiltration and dogged human resistance; essentially, they allegorized the US struggle with global communism and usually ended with the defeat of the invaders. Yet close readings of these stories reveal a strong undercurrent of unease beneath the bland surface confid- ence in American values. For example, in *Invaders from Mars* (1953), as I have argued in a previous essay, "the paranoia about alien invasion and takeover may merely serve to deflect anxieties about how seamlessly militarist power has inscribed itself into the suburban American landscape."[13] Similar disquiets can be perceived in films that depict literal communist attacks and occupations, such as *Invasion USA* (1952), which is, as Cyndy Hendershot has shown, as much about fears of US decadence and conformism as it is about Soviet perfidy.[14] In other words, even invasion stories that valorize human (that is, Western) cunning and bravery may be troubled by doubts regarding the susceptibility to external incursions, the lurking rot at the imperial core that permits such brazen raids from the periphery.

By contrast with American treatments of the theme, which were pugnacious in their refusal to succumb to invasion, post-war British disaster stories had a distinctly elegiac tone, a quality of wistful resignation in the face of imperial decline. As Roger Luckhurst points out, British tales of catastrophe had "always addressed disenchantment with the imperialist 'civilizing' mission," but 1950s versions, confronted with the ongoing collapse of the global empire, used the disaster plot as "a laboratory reconceiving English selfhood in response to traumatic depredations."[15] The popular novels of John Wyndham, such as *The Day of the Triffids* (1951) and *The Kraken Wakes* (1953), take refuge in pastoralist fantasy as Britain's cities are overrun by marauding invaders, the imperial hegemon shrinking to beleaguered individual (or small-communal) sanctuaries. Brian Aldiss has coined the term "cosy catastrophe" to describe these sorts of plot, a category in which some have also placed the early fiction of John Christopher, although here, as Aldiss says, "the catastrophe loses its cosiness and takes on an edge of terror."[16] In Christopher's *The Death of Grass* (1956) and *The World in Winter* (1962) there is no refuge from the crisis because the environment itself has grown hostile, stricken by a virus that kills off crops or the advent of a new Ice Age. The absence of an alien menace in these novels vitiates the possibility of heroic resistance, replacing it with an ethos of brute survivalism, whose long-term prospects are desperate and unpromising. The sense of imperial comeuppance is particularly strong in *World in Winter*, where Britons displaced by glacial expansion flee to Nigeria, only to be rudely treated by their former colonial subjects.

Christopher's novels welded the traditional British disaster story with an emergent trend of eco-catastrophe that gained strength during the 1960s. The master of this new genre was J. G. Ballard, whose quartet of novels—*The Wind from Nowhere* (1960), *The Drowned World* (1962), *The Drought* (1964), and *The Crystal World* (1966)—variously scoured the earth, inundated it, desiccated it, and (most curiously and perversely) immured it in a jewel-like crust. Throughout these works the author appears fundamentally uninterested either in explaining the disasters (only *The Drought* posits a human cause: widespread pollution of the oceans) or in depicting valiant efforts to fend off their ravages. Instead, the protagonists struggle towards a private accommodation with the cataclysms, a psychic attunement to their radical reorderings of the environment; as Luckhurst argues, "the transformation of landscape marks the termination of rationally motivated instrumental consciousness."[17] In other words, the very mindset that produced imperial hegemony—the confidence in reason, disciplined deployment of technoscience, and posture of mastery—has eroded, replaced by a deracinated fatalism and an almost mystical embrace of its own antiquation.

For Fredric Jameson, Ballard's scenarios of "world-dissolution" amount to little more than the exhausted "imagination of a dying class—the cancelled future of a vanished colonial and imperial destiny [that] seeks to intoxicate itself with images of death,"[18] Yet, while it is difficult to argue that Ballard's novels express a conscious politics—aside from the ironized libidinal commitments of a surrealism tinged with Freud—his influence over what came to be known as SF's "New Wave" helped foster an overtly anti-hegemonic strain of eco-disaster stories during the 1960s and early 1970s. The New Wave generally adopted an anti-technocratic bent that put it at odds with the technophilic optimism of Campbellian hard SF, openly questioning if not the core values of scientific inquiry, then the larger social processes to which they had been conjoined in the service of state and corporate power.[19] This critique of technocracy gradually aligned itself with other ideological programs seeking to reform or revolutionize social relations, such as feminism, ecological activism, and postcolonial struggles, adopting a counter-cultural militancy that rejected pulp SF's quasi-imperialist vision of white men conquering the stars in the name of Western progress. While Ballard might not have embraced this polemical thrust, his subversive disaster stories, with their stark irrationalism and pointed mockery of technoscientific ambitions, gave it a significant impetus as well as a potent model to follow.

Thomas M. Disch's 1965 novel *The Genocides* is definitely cast in the Ballardian mode, a positioning that drew the fire of critics opposed to the New Wave's ideological renovation of the field. Disch's novel, which depicts an earth transformed by faceless aliens into an agricultural colony in which humans are mere pests awaiting extermination, became something of a political hot potato within the genre. Responding to a laudatory review of the book by Judith Merril, the most prominent advocate for the New Wave among American commentators, Algis Budrys attacked the novel as "pretentious, inconsistent, and sophomoric," an insult to "the school of science fiction which takes hope in science and in Man."[20] Contrasting it with Heinlein's latest effort, *The Moon Is a Harsh Mistress* (1966), which depicts "strong personalities doing things about their situation," its hero a "practical man-of-all-work figure" who just keeps "plugging away," Budrys complains about Disch's "dumb, resigned victims" who simply wait passively to be destroyed.[21] Unlike the can-do heroism of Heinlein and his ilk, *The Genocides* is an "inertial" SF novel, modelled on the disaster stories of Ballard, wherein "characters who regard the physical universe as a mysterious and arbitrary place, and who would not dream of trying to understand its actual laws" putter about listlessly in a suicidal haze.[22] As David Hartwell comments, Budrys clearly could not imagine a successful work of SF in which scientific knowledge is not "*a priori* adequate to solve whatever problem the plot poses"—even, in this case, when vastly superior alien technologies have seeded and irretrievably transformed the entire surface of the planet.[23]

In a curious aside, Budrys considers the possibility that Disch is rejecting the "Engineers-Can-Do-Anything school" of pulp SF in favor of an older, more satirical and pessimistic tradition that extends back to H. G. Wells; and he goes on to forecast an imaginary critical-historical study championing Ballard for "having singlehandedly returned the field to its main stem" following the pulp era's arguably naive optimism.[24] Budrys's projected title for this volume, *Cartography of Chaos*, seems precisely to acknowledge the entropic dissolution of the scientific modes of missionary imperialism accomplished by the New Wave disaster story, although Budrys does not really develop the point. Another review of the novel, by Brian Aldiss, made a more concerted effort to link Disch with a strain of visionary pessimism in the field. Decrying the "facile optimism" of American pulp SF, with its fantasies of a prodigal nature effortlessly exploited by a sagacious "scientocracy," Aldiss praises *The Genocides* for providing "an unadulterated shot of pure bracing gloom."[25] The effect, despite Disch's American provenance, is "curiously English," portraying a "dwindling community" confronting an "unbeatable problem [. . .] as credible a menace as I ever came on."[26] Aldiss never quite explains why this scenario should be viewed as particularly English, but he doubtless had in mind the Wyndham—Ballard school of post-imperial melancholy, here transplanted to the United States.

And, indeed, that is the signal accomplishment of Disch's novel: to extrapolate the end-of-empire thematics of the post-war disaster story to a specifically American context. Certainly, by the mid- to late 1960s, revisionist historians and left-wing political commentators such as William Appleman Williams, David Horowitz, Gabriel Kolko, and Harry Magdoff had begun to critique US foreign policy during the Cold War as explicitly imperialist, driven by economic and military imperatives designed to enrich and expand the powers of a corporate elite.[27] While not suggesting that Disch was expressly aware of these thinkers, I do feel that his novel belongs within the general orbit of a New Wave critique of modern technocracy, scorning his country's nascent imperial aims with the same cold-eyed cynicism that Wells summoned to chasten his late-Victorian compatriots. Even more than Wells, Disch stresses the total indifference of the aliens to the monuments of human civilization, excrescent "artifacts" they are capable of wiping away as casually as a farmer uproots weeds; as one character bitterly muses:

> It wounded his pride to think that his race, his species was being defeated with such apparent ease. What was worse, what he could not endure was the suspicion that it all meant nothing, that the process of their annihilation was something quite mechanical: that mankind's destroyers were not, in other words, fighting a war but merely spraying the garden.[28]

Indeed, as this mundane metaphor suggests, Disch, in *The Genocides*, develops a powerful critique of what has subsequently come to be called by environmental historians and activists "ecological imperialism."

As the discipline of ecology was consolidated during the post-war period, and especially as the concept of ecosystem as a functional totality of life processes gained widespread currency,[29] evolutionary biologists began to study the implications of the introduction of foreign flora and fauna into existing environments. The classic study in the field is Charles S. Elton's *The Ecology of Invasions by Animals and Plants*, first published in 1958 and still in widespread use in biology classrooms.[30] Elton considers such significant "biotic invasions" as the spread of the Japanese beetle throughout the Northern US and the incursion of sea lampreys into the Great Lakes region, theorizing their competition for resources with native species, their unsettlement of and integration into food chains, and the ramifying consequences of genetic mixing through subsequent generations. In order to convey the dramatic quality of these "great historical convulsions," Elton occasionally has recourse to SF texts to furnish illuminating models or metaphors, from Professor Challenger's discovery of a "lost world" of primordial life in Arthur Conan Doyle's 1912 novel to the uncontrollable dissemination of escaped laboratory animals in H. G. Wells's 1905 *The Food of the Gods.*[31] As the latter example suggests, the study of biotic invasions cannot ignore the important role of human agency; as Elton comments, "One of the primary reasons for the spread and establishment of species has been quite simply the movement around the world by man of plants, especially those brought for crops or garden ornament or forestry."[32] He even addresses the history of colonial expansion, in a chapter considering the impact on the ecosystems of remote islands of Captain Cook's voyages during the late eighteenth century.[33]

During the 1970s and 80s environmental historians began to extrapolate some of the insights of ecosystems theory to explain the consequences of major migrations of human populations. William McNeill's *Plagues and Peoples* (1976), which examines the role of disease in shaping historical encounters between cultures, meticulously shows, in a chapter entitled "Transatlantic Exchanges," how the European conquest of the Americas was facilitated by the "biological vulnerability" of Amerindian groups to foreign pathogens, especially smallpox.[34] Rather than attributing the success of New World colonization to superior technology and culture alone, works such as McNeill's—and William Cronon's *Changes in the Land* (1983), which examines the environmental impact of the introduction of European livestock and agricultural practices in colonial New England[35]—anatomized the role, intended and unintended, of biotic transfers in conferring an advantage in the competition between native peoples and foreign invaders. As Alfred Crosby summarizes in his landmark work of synthesis *Ecological Imperialism* (1986), "the Europeans had to disassemble an existing ecosystem before they could have one that accorded with their needs," with the outcome at times resembling "a toy that has been played with too roughly by a thoughtless colossus."[36] In this new colonial history the influence of Christianity and gunpowder pales beside the proliferating synergy of microbes and weeds, deforestation and domestication. In Alan Taylor's words, "the remaking of the Americas was a team effort by a set of interdependent species led and partially managed (but never fully controlled) by European people."[37]

While Disch could certainly not have known this body of work when he wrote *The Genocides*, there is ample evidence that he was always deeply interested in ecological issues and in linking this concern with the developing New Wave critique of American technocracy. In 1971 Disch edited a major anthology of eco-catastrophe stories, *The Ruins of Earth* (1971), complaining in his introduction that "too often science fiction has given its implicit moral sanction" to wholesale transformations in the environment without concern for the consequences.[38] This introduction, entitled "On Saving the World," stands as one of the strongest statements of an ecological awareness within the New Wave assault on traditional SF:

> The very form of the so-called "hard-core" s-f saga, in which a single quasi-technological problem is presented and then solved, encourages [a] peculiar tunnel vision and singleness of focus that is the antithesis of an "ecological" consciousness in which cause-and-effect would be regarded as a web rather than as a single-strand chain. The heroes of these earlier tales often behave in ways uncannily reminiscent of psychotics' case histories: personal relationships (as between the crew members of a spaceship) can be chillingly lacking in affect. These human robots inhabited landscapes that mirrored their own alienation.[39]

SF, in short, had for too long been an uncritical cheerleader for the social engineering of nature emanating from a narrow technocratic mindset, and was only now beginning to shake free of this imperialistic delusion. Disch went on to celebrate the early novels of Ballard, especially *The Drought*, as prophetic visions of how a violated nature might take revenge on its heedless exploiters. Budrys was thus correct to infer in *The Genocides* a viewpoint inimical to "the school of science fiction which takes hope in science and in Man"—though instead of "hope," Disch would have said "the faith, usually unquestioning, in a future in which Technology provides, unstintingly and without visible difficulty, for man's needs."[40]

The Genocides is set in 1979, seven years after shadowy aliens have converted the planet into an agricultural preserve devoted to growing 600-foot trees with leaves "the size of billboards."[41] Pushing up through concrete, shouldering aside buildings, and growing at an incredible rate, the trees have destroyed the earth's cities and thoroughly colonized its rural areas. The story focuses on a group of farmers, located in northern Minnesota, who free up arable land by bleeding sap from the alien plants, which eventually kills them and thus conserves a tiny clearing amidst the planet-wide canopy. In this clearing they maintain a plot of corn, which in turn supports a small livestock population. Unfortunately, the aliens—"bored agribusinessmen," as Hartwell calls them, whose cultivation processes are entirely automated[42]—have finally taken notice of these human remnants, sending out flame-throwing drones "*adequate for the extermination of such mammalian life as they are likely to encounter*," as one of their inter-office memos blandly puts it (p. 49; italics in original). The drones incinerate the farm community, sending a handful of desperate survivors into the trees' hollow root system, where they subsist on the sugary fruit of the plants that grows underground. Murderous squabblings thin their ranks, which are further diminished by the arrival of mechanical harvesters that vacuum up the mature fruit. At the end, six ragged human scarecrows stagger across the scoured landscape, which has been burned clean by the harvesters, as the spores of "the second planting" begin to take root (p. 206).

Hartwell's reference to agribusiness is quite appropriate, since at one level the novel is a powerful critique of technoscientific methods for accelerating and amplifying natural processes of cultivation. This mechanized agriculture amounts to the systematic "rape of a planet" (p. 206), which has far-reaching consequences. A hybrid crop designed in alien labs, the trees are brilliantly efficient machines of growth, but their burgeoning comes at the expense of the overall ecology. Since they do not shed their leaves, no compost accumulates, so the topsoil rapidly withers to dust. Their greedy consumption of carbon dioxide is quickly cooling the planet, making the winters brutally severe. And their monopolization of resources has systematically killed off higher species: the "balance of nature had been so thoroughly upset that even animals one would not think threatened had joined the ever-mounting ranks of the extinct" (p. 26). An offhand allusion indicates the novel's critical perspective: as winter recedes and no birds emerge to herald the new season, the narrator grimly comments, "it was a silent spring" (p. 169), thus referencing Rachel Carson's classic 1962 critique of the deadly effects of agribusiness methods on the environment.[43] Unfortunately, human beings do not have the luxury of being absentee landlords of the planet, as Disch's aliens are, and so must suffer the long-term consequences of their ecological tinkering directly.

Disch's title, *The Genocides*, thus refers on one level to humanity's imminent self-extinction through ecological mismanagement, a snuffing out the narrator comments on at the end with Wellsian detachment:

> Nature is prodigal. Of a hundred seedlings only one or two would survive; of a hundred species, only one or two.
>
> Not, however, man. (p. 208)

On another level, the novel allegorizes the biotic invasion of the New World, which resulted in the wholesale destruction of native cultures and ways of life. Like the Europeans in America, the aliens reconfigure the existing ecosystem to satisfy their own needs, at first ignoring the original inhabitants and then, when their methods of cultivation come into competition, brutally eliminating them. Yet, as in the histories of ecological imperialism described above, the most effective genocidal technique by far is the environmental transformation wrought by the invaders, which literally makes indigenous modes of agriculture impossible. As William Cronon points out, "European perceptions of what constituted a proper use of the environment [. . .] reinforced what became a European ideology of conquest": whereas Amerindians generally favored mobile settlements and subsistence agriculture supplemented by hunting, the colonists preferred fixed habitats, organized animal husbandry, and surplus crop production for purposes of trade.[44] The latter system required widespread deforestation, which killed off deer populations on which the natives were dependent, and the cultivation of large tracts of land, now conceived as permanent property rather than an open bounty. Disch's novel shows the consequences of such an arrangement from the Amerindian perspective, as the humans are confronted by literally alien biota maintained by superior technology and policed by ruthless violence.

Disch's jaundiced view of European supremacy in the New World is underlined by the most viciously satirical scene in the book, a Thanksgiving Day celebration. Following the incineration of their cattle by the alien machines, the community has lost its main source of protein. To promote harmony among a population grown restive and contentious, the governing patriarch decides to proceed with the occasion, serving up sausages prepared from the bodies of a group of urban marauders the community has recently slain. "Necessity might have been some justification. There was ample precedent (the Donner party, the wreck of the *Medusa*)" (p. 78). But the patriarch's goal in enforcing this communal cannibalism is more sinister and jingoistic: to unite the group in a "complex bond," a "sacrament" that transmutes the squalid act into patriotic solidarity (p. 78). And so the others sit there, chewing desultorily, bickering with one another, and growing drunk on liquor fermented from the sap of the alien trees. As their resident scientist dryly comments, "Survival is a matter of ecology. [. . .] Ecology is the way the different plants and animals live together. That is to say—who eats whom" (p. 79). This pathetic remnant of European colonization, enjoying a hallowed holiday feast that sentimentally commemorates its triumph, is reduced to feeding on their erstwhile countrymen in order to survive. Reinforcing this sarcastic portrait of collapsed American hegemony, Disch dates the aliens' extermination order *4 July* 1979, with the projected completion of the project 2 February 1980—Groundhog Day, now the harbinger of an eternal winter for the human race (p. 11; my emphasis). Watching Duluth go up in flames kindled by the alien drones, one of the characters waves and snickers, "goodbye, Western Civilization" (p. 51).

While ecological extrapolation was not new to SF in 1965—indeed, Frank Herbert's *Dune*, serialized in *Analog* magazine during 1963–64, probably did more than any other single book to bring ecological awareness into the centre of the genre—Disch's *The Genocides* gave the topic a sharp polemical edge through its arraignment of traditional SF's complaisant scientism. Technoscientific development, in the novel, is not a cure-all for the problems posed, but is itself the problem: the faceless alien technocrats, armed with a battery of sophisticated machines, show a casual contempt not only for natural balance but for human life itself. The besieged community Disch portrays has as much chance against this monolithic apparatus as Third World farmers have against Western agribusiness enterprises; their small-scale agrarian revolt, pitched against the environmental monopoly of the trees, fails as miserably as, say, the Guatemalan revolution against the United Fruit Company in the 1950s. Disch's novel points the way towards more politicized engagements with ecological issues in SF, such as John Brunner's *Stand on Zanzibar* (1968) and *The Sheep Look Up* (1972); as Michael Stern observes of the latter novel, "the relation of the US to the rest of the earth's societies [. . .] takes the form of a total but undeclared ecological war"[45]—an invasion less of Western biota than of industrial pollution, resource extraction, and neocolonial "development" projects. During the early 1970s, the genre witnessed not only a handful of theme anthologies devoted to these issues—including, alongside Disch's *Ruins of Earth*, Rob Sauer's *Voyages: Scenarios for a Ship Called Earth* (1971), and Roger Elwood and Virginia Kidd's *Saving*

Worlds (1973)—but even fanzines with an environmentalist agenda, such as Susan Glicksohn's short-lived *Aspidistra*. In the balance of this essay, though, I shall focus on a second major New Wave text that specifically treats ecological imperialism in the terms outlined above: Ursula K. Le Guin's short novel *The Word for World is Forest* (1972).[46]

In many ways Le Guin's novel reads like an inversion of *The Genocides*: rather than the victims of biotic invasion, earth people are the invaders; and rather than seeding a host of trees, they lay waste to a vast forest on the planet Athshe. Le Guin quite calculatedly draws parallels between the exploration of space and the history of Western colonialism: despite the existence of "Ecological Protocols" governing interaction with alien biospheres, largely designed to keep other worlds from being reduced to the "desert of cement" bereft of animal life that the Earth itself has become,[47] the colonists on Athshe behave exactly like classic imperialists, renaming the planet "New Tahiti," conscripting its humanoid popula-tion into forced labor camps, and systematically extracting its riches, especially lumber. The tale's main villain, Captain Davidson, captures the mindset perfectly: contemptuous of the natives as lazy "creechies," yet lusting after their women, eager to command the landscape as proof of his manhood and cultural superiority, he can see in the endless vistas of trees only a "meaningless" expanse of wasted resources, rather than the richly meaningful cultural world it is for the native inhabitants. He has nothing but scorn for the "bleeding-heart" attitudes of the expedition's token ecologist and anthropologist, view-ing the situation in basically military terms: "you've got to play on the winning side or else you lose. And it's Man that wins, every time. The old Conquistador."[48] Whereas in Disch the motives of the alien invaders remain obscure, Le Guin provides, in Davidson, a scathing portrait of overweening racist machismo as the root impulse supporting projects of imperial domination. While the effect is perhaps to overly psychologize the colonial relationship, de-emphasizing crucial political-economic imperatives, her treatment does infuse a strong ecofeminist consciousness into the traditional invasion scenario.[49]

Still, the tale did have an essentially political origin; Le Guin has indicated that the military-ecological rape of Vietnam by US forces is what impelled her writing:

> it was becoming clear that the ethic which approved the defoliation of forests and the murder of noncombatants in the name of "peace" was only a corollary of the ethic which permits the despoliation of natural resources for private profit or the GNP, and the murder of the creatures of the Earth in the name of "man."[50]

Thus we see Davidson and his renegade band decimating creechie villages in classic counter-insurgency fashion, "dropping firejelly cans and watch[ing] them run around and burn,"[51] while the Athsheans adopt guerilla tactics as the only effective resistance. These blatant historical connections have led to complaints by some critics that the story is overly tendentious and moralizing.[52] Yet, as Ian Watson points out, the plot is broadly allegorical and can symbolize any number of instances of ecological imperialism, includ-ing "the genocide of the Guyaki Indians of Paraguay, or the genocide and deforestation along the Trans-Amazon Highway in Brazil, or even the general destruction of rain-forest habitats from Indonesia to Costa Rica."[53] William Cronon has shown how deforestation was a major factor in the reconfiguration of New World biota by European colonists: an ecological habitat to which the natives had adapted themselves was systematically culled to serve a new "mosaic" of settlement; and, like Captain Davidson and his comrades, the "colonists themselves understood what they were doing wholly in positive terms, not as 'deforestation,' but as 'the progress of cultivation'"[54]—even though the effects were often pernicious, ranging from topsoil erosion, to increased flooding, to the spread of marshes with their attendant diseases. The callous quality of the transformations wrought: by the colonists, their lack of concern for enduring consequences, in both the historical record and in Le Guin's story, suggests the heedless alien genocide depicted with such casual savagery in Disch's novel.

A key difference between Le Guin's work and Disch's, however, is that by the early 1970s a quite developed discourse regarding the effects of ecological devastation, and a growingly militant environmentalist movement, had risen up to assert the "rights" of nature and native peoples over against the needs of Western neocolonialism. Generally guided by an ethic of "responsibility" and governed by a concern for long-term "sustainability," this movement was propelled by a conviction that the ongoing exploitation of nature augured nothing short of a catastrophe for the planet—*Ecocide*, according to the title of a 1971 collection of essays.[55] The Club of Rome's best-selling study *The Limits to Growth*, published in the same year as Le Guin's novel, argued that current levels of resource depletion were likely to lead to major socioeconomic crises in the relatively near future. *The Word for World Is Forest* reflects these anxieties in its depiction of a home planet literally bereft of foliage, dependent on alien jungles to satisfy its appetite for "clean sawn planks, more prized on Earth than gold."[56]

In terms of the ethics of interaction with other species, positions ranged from John Passmore's view, in *Man's Responsibility for Nature* (1974), that human life is the basic standard of value in terms of which all potential violence against animals or plants must be gauged, to more radical arguments for the inalienable "rights" of nonhuman beings, such as Peter Singer's brief for *Animal Liberation* (1975).[57] An interesting text with relevance to Le Guin's story is legal scholar Christopher Stone's 1971 essay "Should Trees Have Standing?." Written as an intervention in a lawsuit pitting the Sierra Club against the Disney Corporation's efforts to build a resort in California's Sierra mountains, Stone's essay was groundbreaking in its attempt to define legal "'injury' not merely in human terms but with regard to nature. [. . .] Stone argued in all seriousness that trout and herons and cottonwood trees should be thought of as the injured parties in a water-pollution case," and not simply the people who might be deprived of clean water or the opportunity to enjoy a pristine landscape.[58] The impulse to protect trees in particular, not merely owing to their human uses but intrinsically for themselves, formed a significant impulse of the environmental movement, as the deployment of the term "green" as a political rallying cry suggests.[59] On the one hand, this impulse may merely express a sentimental romanticization of nature, one that has too readily led to the disparagement of environmentalists as "tree huggers" (an identification facilitated, for example, by the dedication to an anthology commemorating the first Earth Day celebration: "to the tree from which this book is made");[60] on the other hand, if pursued with intellectual rigor, such an attitude could lead to a conceptualization of "nature" not as an anthropocentric tool or an essentialist "other," but as a socially constructed reality with important dimensions of agency and autonomy.[61]

Le Guin's abiding humanism, however, makes it difficult for her to articulate an ethic of rights that does not inhere ultimately in human subjects. While the novel fudges the issue essentially by identifying the Athsheans with their habitat—like the forest, they are peaceful, close-knit, and actually green—the effect is to naturalize their culture and to see the violence committed against them as an environmental desecration. The forest *is* their world, as the title indicates, and alterations to it are alterations to them; by the end, they have, like the trees, learned violence and been scarred by the knowledge. They have been "changed, radically, from the *root*" by "an infection, a foreign plague."[62] The model of moral relation Le Guin finally defends is not surprising given the central bond in her celebrated novel *The Left Hand of Darkness* (1969)—a friendship, despite differences, between sentient humanoids. The novel's anthropologist-hero, Lyubov, is everything Captain Davidson is not: empathetic towards the Athsheans and comfortable in the enveloping forest, fondly protective of their mutual innocence and dignity.[63] Not only does this depiction bear a lingering noble-savage Romanticism,[64] but it leaves open the question of whether the denuding and strip-mining of an uninhabited planet would be ethically acceptable. If the forest were not *someone's* indigenous world, would it then be ripe for the picking? Can ecological imperialism only be committed against human subjects or their fictional surrogates?

Le Guin's attitude towards technoscience and its role in colonial conquest is also more ambivalent than in previous New Wave eco-catastrophes. Unlike Disch's *The Genocides*, in which advanced science is exclusively an agency of domination; and unlike eco-critics such as Lynn White, whose influential 1967 essay "The Historical Roots of our Ecological Crisis" indicts Europe's "superior technology" that permitted its "small, mutually hostile nations [to] spill out over all the rest of the world, conquering, looting, and colonizing";[65] Le Guin draws a distinction (a quite reasonable one in my view) between military-industrial technologies designed for violent purposes, whether warfare or resource extraction, and *communication* technologies, which allow for the exchange of ideas and information. In the novel, the arrival on the planet of an ansible—an interstellar radio that permits instantaneous messaging, despite the decades-long time-lag of space travel—is the mechanism that alerts the new League of Worlds to the violation of Ecological Protocols and leads to the termination of the colonial administration and the eventual economic quarantining of the planet. Similarly, in the present day, communications media such as the Internet have facilitated the worldwide dissemination of data about serious ecological problems, such as global warming,[66] and computer simulation software has been used to model ecosystem interactions, such as (to cite a relevant example) the growth and decline of forest areas.[67] Le Guin, to her credit, resists the assumption, common to some New Wave texts, that Western technoscience itself has been irreparably contaminated by its conscription for technocratic-imperialist ends.

In his environmental history of the twentieth century, J. R. McNeill summarizes recent biotic invasions and concludes with a prognostication: "In the twenty-first century, the pace of invasions is not likely to slacken, and new genetically engineered organisms may also occasionally achieve ecological release and fashion dramas of their own."[68] If they do, one can be certain that SF writers will be there to chronicle the results, and to craft powerful moral allegories out of them. While they will doubtless draw upon the compelling example of major New Wave precursors, it is likely that their treatments of the topic will cleave closer to Le Guin's ethical-political ambivalence than to Disch's neo-Wellsian despair.

Notes

1. Peter Fitting, "Estranged Invaders: *The War of the Worlds*," in *Learning from Other Worlds: Estrangement, Cognition, and the Politics of Science Fiction and Utopia*, ed. by Patrick Parrinder (Liverpool: Liverpool University Press, 2000), pp. 127–45 (p. 127).

2. Fitting, p. 130.

3. Fitting, p. 131.

4. H. G. Wells, *A Critical Edition of The War of the Worlds: H.G. Wells's Scientific Romance*, ed. by David Y. Hughes and Harry M. Geduld (Bloomington: Indiana University Press, 1993), p. 52.

5. Stephen D. Arata, "The Occidental Tourist: *Dracula* and the Anxiety of Reverse Colonization," *Victorian Studies*, 33.4 (1990), 621–45; Brian W. Aldiss, with David Wingrove, *Trillion Year Spree: The History of Science Fiction* (New York: Avon, 1988), pp. 120–21.

6. John Rieder, "Science Fiction, Colonialism, and the Plot of Invasion," *Extrapolation*, 46.3 (2005), 373–94 (p. 376).

7. Rieder, p. 376.

8. Rieder, p. 378.

9. Eric R. Wolf, *Europe and the People without History* (Berkeley: University of California Press, 1982).

10. Brian Stableford and David Pringle, "Invasion," in *The Encyclopedia of Science Fiction*, ed. by Peter Nicholls and John Clute (New York: St. Martin's, 1993), pp. 623–25 (p. 624).

11. John W. Campbell, Jr., Letter to A. E. van Vogt, 3 March 1945, in *The John W. Campbell Letters, Volume 1*, ed. by Perry A. Chapdelaine, Sr., Tony Chapdelaine, and George Hay (Franklin, TN: AC Projects, 1985), pp. 49–55 (p. 55).

12. Robert A. Heinlein, *The Puppet Masters*, rev. edn (New York: Del Rey, 1990), p. 338. For a reading of the novel as an allegory of Cold War conflicts see H. Bruce Franklin, *Robert A. Heinlein: America as Science Fiction* (New York: Oxford University Press, 1980), pp. 98–101.

13. Rob Latham, "Subterranean Suburbia: Underneath the Smalltown Myth in the Two Versions of *Invaders from Mars*," *Science Fiction Studies*, 22.2 (1995), 198–208 (p. 201). For a discussion of the 1956 film *Invasion of the Body Snatchers* that links it with Weils's and Heinlein's novels, see David Seed, "Alien Invasions by Body Snatchers and Related Creatures," in *Modern Gothic: A*

Reader, ed. by Victor Sage and Allen L. Smith (Manchester: Manchester University Press, 1996), pp. 152–70.

14. Cyndy Hendershot, "Anti-Communism and Ambivalence in *Red Planet Mars, Invasion USA*, and *The Beast of Yucca Flats*," *Science Fiction Studies*, 28.2 (2001), 246–60.

15. Roger Luckhurst, *Science Fiction* (Cambridge: Polity, 2005), pp, 131–32.

16. Aldliss, *Trillion Year Spree*, p. 255. For an alternative take on Wyndham's work, which defends him as a more subversive writer than Aldiss allows, see Rowland Wymer, "How 'Safe' is John Wyndham? A Closer Look at his Work, with Particular Reference to *The Cluysalids'*, *Foundation*," 55 (1992), 25–36.

17. Roger Luckhurst, *"The Angle Between Two Walls": The Fiction of J. G. Ballard* (Liverpool: Liverpool University Press, 1995), p. 53.

18. Fredric Jameson, "Progress Versus Utopia; or, Can We Imagine the Future?," *Science Fiction Studies*, 9.2 (1982), 147–58 (p. 152).

19. For an overview of the New Wave movement see my "The New Wave," in *A Companion to Science Fiction*, ed. by David Seed (Oxford: Blackwell, 2005), pp. 202–16. See also Luckhurst, *Science Fiction*, pp. 141–95.

20. Algis Budrys, "Galaxy Bookshelf," *Galaxy*, 25.2 (1966), 125–33 (p. 130).

21. Budrys, pp. 127, 130.

22. Budrys, p. 128.

23. David Hartwell, Introduction to Thomas M. Disch, *The Genocides* (Boston: Gregg, 1978), pp. v–xv (p. xiv).

24. Budrys, pp. 129, 131.

25. Brian W. Aldiss, "Book Fare," *SF Impulse*, 1,11 (1967), 51–54 (pp. 51–52).

26. Aldiss, "Book Fare," pp. 52–53.

27. See, e.g., William Appleman Williams, *The Tragedy of American Diplomacy*, rev. edn (New York: Delta, 1962); David Horowitz. *The Free World Colossus: A Critique of American Foreign Policy in the Cold War* (New York: Hill and Wang, 1965); Gabriel Kolko, *The Politics of War: The World and United States Foreign Policy, 1943–1945* (New York: Vintage, 1968); and Harry Magdoff, *The Age of Imperialism: The Economics of US Foreign Policy* (New York: Modern Reader, 1969).

28. Thomas M. Disch, *The Genocides* (New York: Pocket Books, 1979), p. 104.

29. See Frank B. Golley, *A History of the Ecosystem Concept in Ecology: More Than the Sum of the Parts* (New Haven, CT: Yale University Press, 1996).

30. Charles S. Elton, *The Ecology of Invasions by Animals and Plants* (London: Chapman & Hall, 1972).

31. Elton, pp. 31, 32, 109.

32. Elton, p. 51.

33. Elton, pp. 77–93.

34. William H. McNeill, *Plagues and Peoples* (Garden City, NY: Anchor, 1976), p. 177.

35. William Cronon, *Changes in the Land: Indians, Colonists, and the Ecology of New England* (New York: Hill and Wang, 1983).

36. Alfred W. Crosby, *Ecological Imperialism: The Biological Expansion of Europe, 900–1900* (Cambridge: Cambridge University Press, 1986), p. 279.

37. Alan Taylor, *American Colonies* (New York: Viking, 2001), p. 47.

38. Thomas M. Disch, "Introduction: On Saving the World," in *The Ruins of Earth: An Anthology of Stories of the Immediate Future*, ed. by Thomas M. Disch (New York: G. P. Putnam's, 1971), pp. 1–7 (p. 5).

39. Disch, "Introduction: On Saving the World," p. 5.

40. Disch, "Introduction," p. 5.

41. Disch, *The Genocides*, p. 5. (Further references to *The Genocides* are to the edition cited in note 28 above and will appear in the text.)

42. Hartwell, p. xiv.

43. The publication of *Silent Spring* is generally seen as the catalytic event that spawned the modern environmental movement: sec Victor B. Sheffer, *The Shaping of Environmentalism in America* (Seattle: University of Washington Press, 1991), pp. 119–21; and John McCormick, *The Global Environmental Movement*, 2nd edn (New York: John Wiley, 1995), pp. 65–67.

44. Cronon, *Changes in the Land*, p. 53.

45. Michael Stern, "From Technique to Critique: Knowledge and Human Interests in Brunner's *Stand on Zanzibar, The Jagged Orbit*, and *The Sheep Look Up*," *Science Fiction Studies*, 3.2 (1976), 112–30. See also Neal Bukeavich, "'Are We Adopting the Right Measures to Cope?': Ecocrisis in John Brunner's *Stand on Zanzibar*," *Science Fiction Studies*, 29.1 (2002), 53–70; and, for a review of ecological themes in post-1960s SF, Patrick D. Murphy, "The Non-Alibi of Alien Scapes: SF and Ecocriticism," in *Beyond Nature Writing; Expanding the Boundaries of Ecocriticism*, ed. by Karla Armbruster and Kathleen R. Wallace (Charlottesville: University Press of Virginia, 2001), pp. 263–78. A more general survey is Brian Stableford's "Science Fiction and Ecology," in *A Companion to Science Fiction*, ed. by Seed, pp. 127–41.

46. Ursula K. Le Guin, *The Word for World Is Forest*, in *Again, Dangerous Visions*, ed. by Harlan Ellison (Garden City, NY: Doubleday, 1972), pp. 32–117.

47. Le Guin, *The Word for World Is Forest*, p. 34.

48. Le Guin, *The Word for World Is Forest*, p. 35.

49. For a discussion of Le Guin's ecofeminism see Patrick D. Murphy, *Literature, Nature, Other: Ecofeminist Critiques* (Albany: SUNY Press, 1995), pp. 111–21.

50. Ursula K. Le Guin, "Introduction to *The Word for World Is Forest*," in Le Guin, *The Language of the Night: Essays on Fantasy and Science Fiction*, ed. by Susan Wood (New York: Perigee, 1979), pp. 149–54 (p. 151).

51. Le Guin, *The Word for World Is Forest*, p. 73.

52. Susan Wood complains that the author was "unfortunately [not] successful in avoiding the limitations of moral outrage at contemporary problems": see "Discovering Worlds: The Fiction of Ursula K. Le Guin," in *Ursula K. Le Guin; Modern Critical Views*, ed. by Harold Bloom (New York: Chelsea House, 1986), pp. 183–209 (pp. 186–87).

53. Ian Watson, "The Forest as Metaphor for Mind: *The Word for World Is Forest* and 'Vaster Than Empires and More Slow'," in *Ursula K. Le Guin*, ed. by Bloom, pp. 47–55 (p. 48).

54. Cronon, *Changes in the Land*, p. 124.

55. Clifton Fadiman and Jean White, *Ecocide—and Thoughts toward Survival* (Santa Barbara, CA: Center for the Study of Democratic Institutions, 1971). For a contemporaneous history see *From Conservation to Ecology: The Development of Environmental Concern*, ed. by Carroll Pursell (New York: Thomas Y. Growell, 1973).

56. Le Guin, *The Word for World Is Forest*, p. 35.

57. Although both these works were published after Le Guin's novel, the issues they treated were widely debated during the late 1960s and early 1970s. For an excellent overview of these debates see Roderick Frazier Nash, *The Rights of Nature: A History of Environmental Ethics* (Maclison: University of Wisconsin Press, 1989).

58. See Nash, p. 129. As Nash summarizes Stone's position: "Fines would be assessed and collected (by guardians) on behalf of these creatures and used to restore their habitat or create an alternative to the one destroyed."

59. On the emergence of Green activism see McCormick, pp. 203–24.

60. *Earth Day—The Beginning: A Guide for Survival*, ed. by the National Staff of Environmental Action (New York: Bantam, 1970), p. v. On the origins of Earth Day, see Sheffer, pp. 124–25.

61. For a critique of essentialist views of nature see Jeffrey C. Ellis, "On the Search for a Root Cause: Essentialist Tendencies in Environmental Discourse," in *Uncommon Ground: Rethinking the Human Place in Nature*, ed. by William Cronon (New York: Norton, 1995), pp. 256–68. Major theoretical/historical studies of nature as a social construction include Neil Evernden, *The Social Creation of Nature* (Baltimore, MD: Johns Hopkins University Press, 1992); and Carolyn Merchant, *Reinventing Eden: The Fate of Nature in Western Culture* (New York: Routledge, 2004).

62. Le Guin, *The Word for World Is Forest*, p. 86 (my emphasis).

63. On Lyubov and other similar figures in Le Guin's work see Karen Sinclair, "The Hero as Anthropologist," in *Ursula K. Le Guin: Voyager to Inner Lands and to Outer Space*, ed. by Joe De Bolt (Port Washington, NY: Kennikat, 1979), pp. 50–65.

64. On Romantic imagery in the novel, especially the anthropomorphizing evocation of the forest as "a metaphor for the landscape of consciousness," see Peter S. Alterman, "Ursula K. Le Guin: Damsel with a Dulcimer," in *Ursula K. Le Guin*, ed. by Joseph D. Olander and Martin Harry Greenberg (New York: Taplinger, 1979), pp. 64–76 (p. 65).

65. Lynn White, Jr., "The Historical Roots of our Ecological Crisis," in *Politics and Environment: A Reader in Ecological Crisis*, ed. by Walt Anderson (Pacific Palisades, CA: Goodyear, 1970), pp. 338–49 (p. 342). On the influence of White's essay see Nash, pp. 88–96.

66. See, e.g., Climate Ark's continuously updated website "Climate Change and Global Warming" at <http://www.climateark.org> [accessed 6 December, 2006].

67. See T. F. H. Allan, Joseph A. Tainter, and Thomas W. Hoekstra, *Supply-Side Sustainability* (New York: Columbia University Press, 2003), pp. 259–61.

68. J. R. McNeill, *Something New under the Sun: An Environmental History of the Twentieth-Century World* (New York: Norton, 2000), p. 262.

34

Alien/Asian: Imagining the racialized future

Stephen Hong Sohn

The Asian is no stranger to technology, science, or, for that matter, science fiction. Jack London's 1906 short story "The Unparalleled Invasion," for example, chronicles China's emergence as a world power coming out from the shadow of Japanese imperialism. In the story's 1976 setting, China threatens all modern civilizations due to its incredibly fecund citizens numbering in the hundreds of millions. To combat this reproductive menace, biological warfare is conveniently employed to annihilate the Chinese population. Sax Rohmer's infamous 1913 creation of Dr. Fu Manchu is another example. Fu Manchu twines the figure of the Asian intimately with the dark sciences, as he becomes known as the "devil doctor." Although set in London's Chinatown, Rohmer's Fu Manchu–centered series of novels nevertheless draws on the immigration anxieties that flourished in the United States at that time. The doctor's dark image was so popular, in fact, that Rohmer resurrected his infamous character time and again, his series becoming a bestseller.

While both London and Rohmer operated within early twentieth-century "yellow peril" fictions, their cultural representations did not emerge from a vacuum.[1] Sidney L. Gulick's foundational study, *The American Japanese Problem; a Study of the Racial Relations of the East and the West*, published in the same year as "The Unparalleled Invasion," explains that "Japan's amazing victory over Russia has raised doubts among white nations. The despised Asiatic, armed and drilled with Western weapons, is a power that must be reckoned with. In the not distant future Asia, armed, drilled, and united, will surpass in power, they aver, any single white people, and it is accordingly a peril to the rest of the world" (225). Here, Gulick refers to the 1905 conclusion of the Russo-Japanese War, which marked a sea change in international relations precisely because it was the first time an Asian nation had defeated a European power in modern warfare. However, Gulick's rhetorical descriptions illustrate how this historical event reoriented the way the West came

Author's Note: The original, longer version of this article appeared as an introduction to a special issue of *MELUS* on the topic of "Alien/Asian" (2008).

to see Japan, especially with respect to its potential destructive power. Certainly, this moment became embedded in the development of yellow peril discourse in the United States, as Asians regardless of their ethnic specificities became connected with territorial threat. For instance, continued tensions over Chinese immigrant laborers resulted in a series of U.S. federal exclusion acts throughout the late nineteenth century that further cemented the status of Asians as alien subjects, unfit for assimilation and integration. But the social context for Fu Manchu extended beyond U.S. borders, encompassing events in China: with the conclusion of the Manchu dynasty, Sun Yat-sen had begun a modernization campaign. According to Urmila Seshagiri, "Fu-Manchu and his hordes ... emblematize not only dynastic China's ideological opposition to the modern Christian West but also the emergent geopolitical ambitions of a post-1911 China determined to fashion itself as a nation unhindered by the imperial designs of Britain, Germany, France, Austria, Italy, Russia, or Japan" (170). From this perspective, both London's short story and Rohmer's book series draw from multiple anxieties over Asia as pollutive geography, military menace, and economic competitor. Both London and Rohmer imagine alternative temporalities in which the Asian is inextricably tied to science, the future, and technology.

Although yellow peril fictions and other such cultural forms first proliferated more than a century ago, the connection between the Asian and the alien remains a force to draw on to conceptualize racial tension and exclusion. Indeed, this relationship can be more strongly generated by pairing the terms as Alien/Asian. I employ the slash as a nod to the critical interventions offered by Laura Hyun Yi Kang and David Palumbo-Liu, who separately have argued that this punctuation mark functions in the term "Asian/American" to denote how Asia and America stand in an uneasy and unstable relationship with the other.[2] Deriving some inspiration, then, from the slash in the phrase Asian/American, the Alien/Asian emphasizes the need to consider the Asian/American through a diverse array of representational conventions that touch on and intersect with fantasy, speculative fiction, science fiction, and other similar genres. In its multiply inflected significations, the Alien/Asian stands as a convenient way to consider the range of methods by which the Asian/American is associated with social difference and fantastical fictional worlds. Indeed, the Alien/Asian can be the extraterrestrial being who seems to speak in a strange yet familiar accented English, the migrant subject tasked with creating innovative technology that can bend the rules of time and space, or the mystical figure who stands at the margins of a narrative providing sage advice to the central hero. In this respect, "Alien/Asian" does invoke conceptions of its homonymic counterparts, "alienation" and "alien nation," as well as sonically allied phrases such as "alien invasion" and "illegal aliens." Indeed, the notion of the Alien/Asian is concerned centrally with the racialized subject (and associated racialized entities and signifiers) as he or she appears in imagined futures, alternative realities, and counterfactual narratives. Asian Americans or figures of Asian descent often have played large parts in these speculative terrains and often conspicuously appear in tales of interplanetary travel and galactic exploration.

Examining the Alien/Asian allows us to consider the prospective thesis that cultural production continues to draw from, write against, challenge, negotiate, and problematize the yellow peril concept through speculative cultural productions. Traditionally, the yellow peril operates with an overtly racist representation predicated on the danger it represents to the West's economic and military primacy. Yet the spectrum that draws the Alien/Asian across the late nineteenth, twentieth, and twenty-first centuries demonstrates the dramatically divergent ways that writers have represented—and continue to represent—Asian/Americans and associated Eastern signifiers and cultures as dangerous, subversive, and tactical in visual, aural, and written texts that exceed the bounds of traditional realist narratives.

When viewed this way, it becomes apparent that the yellow peril continues to inform more modern cultural productions. For instance, the cyberpunk wave in the eighties and nineties that cast Asian nations, Japan in particular, as sites for projected futuristic anxieties operates within the same frame—that of the perceived threat the so-called East presents to the West. The most commonly cited cyberpunk texts that include these orientalized futures are William Gibson's *Neuromancer* (1984) and Ridley Scott's film *Blade Runner* (1982). The trend of orientalizing the future has continued through numerous major Hollywood films such as Luc Besson's *The Fifth Element* (1997), the Wachowski Brothers' *The Matrix* trilogy (1999, 2003, 2003), and Joss Whedon's *Serenity* (2005), and literary fictions such as Neal Stephenson's *Snow Crash* (1992), among other examples. These transformations of the earliest visions of cyberpunk suggest the continuing obsession of the East as a signifier of the future, technology, and other worlds.[3] Accordingly, Takayuki Tatsumi contends:

> [P]ostcyberpunk science fiction seems to have updated even the old future-war narratives.
>
> What is highly paradoxical, however, is that the more high-tech our society gets, the more atavistic our literature becomes. For us to recognize the extent to which the future-war literary heritage has unwittingly influenced the science fiction of the present, it is important to reconstrue the pre-Wellsian and post-Wellsian narratives that emerged at the turn of the century. (70)

Here, Tatsumi points back to the "future-war narratives" as characterized by London's "The Unparalleled Invasion" and reminds us how a stronger lineage must be drawn from yellow peril fictions to the contemporary representations of the Alien/Asian.

David Morley and Kevin Robins assert that cyberpunk representations embody a kind of techno-Orientalism. They specify that "[w]ithin the political and cultural unconscious of the West, Japan has come to exist as the figure of empty and dehumanised technological power. It represents the alienated and dystopian image of capitalist progress. This provokes both resentment and envy. The Japanese are unfeeling aliens; they are cyborgs and replicants" (170).[4] Morley and Robins suggest that this offshoot of Saidian Orientalism[5] manifests through ambivalence because it inspires both a desire to denigrate the unfeeling, automaton-like Alien/Asian and an envy that derives from the West's desire to regain primacy in the global economy. Christine Cornea places techno-Orientalism in a specific social context by explaining that

> at the time of *Blade Runner's* release certain Eastern economies were growing fast and countries like Japan and Korea were well known for their manufacture of computer components and other cutting-edge technologies. Prior to this, it might have been that these nations were understood as suppliers for the West, but over the course of the 1980s it became apparent that the so called "Tiger Economies" were growing fast and that they were moving from being the copiers/providers of Western-led technology to becoming the inventors/initiators of new technologies. (74)[6]

These Asian tiger economies, also known as the NICs (newly industrializing countries), required the United States to change its economic policies concerning Asia. In the process, terms such as "Asia-Pacific" and the "Pacific Rim" became ubiquitous. Reflecting on the rise of these economies in the 1980s, Miyohei Shinohara explains that "Japan ha[d] emerged as a big power economically, big enough to make the United States uneasy" (13) while Edson W. Spencer discusses how Japan was perceived during this period as an "economic predator" (153). Walden Bello and Shea Cunningham additionally recount:

> [B]y the early 1980s, US policy towards the NICs began to change. Triggering this

> transformation was that the increasing prosperity of the state-led economies was being achieved principally by running huge trade deficits with the US. This provoked the coming together of US industries threatened by NIC imports, resentful US corporations that felt excluded from growing NIC domestic markets. (447)

Given these international dynamics, the rise of techno-Orientalism reflects in part the anxieties that germinated in the Asia-Pacific in the 1980s.

In traditional Orientalism, the East is configured as backward, anti-progressive, and primitive. In this respect, techno-Orientalism might suggest an opposite conception of the East, one focused on future-based fictional worlds, except for the fact that the very inhuman qualities projected onto Asian bodies recall the yellow peril designations first levied on migrants and laborers. Even as these speculatively configured Alien/Asians conduct themselves with superb technological efficiency and capitalist expertise, their lack of affect resonates as an undeveloped or, worse still, a retrograde humanism. According to Toshiya Ueno, "Just as the discourse of Orientalism has functioned to build up the identity of the West, techno-Orientalism is set up for the West to preserve its identity in its imagination of the future. It can be defined as the orientalism of cybersociety and the information age, aimed at maintaining a stable identity in a technological environment" (94). Inasmuch as the techno-Orientalist peril destabilizes American exceptionalism in the global marketplace, Ueno clarifies how such cultural productions provide the means to stabilize the West as a terrain of technological war. In this conflict, the West maintains a moralistic superiority despite having lost its high-tech superiority to the East. Hence, the American subject emerges as an embattled but resistant fighter. "Faced with a 'Japanese future,' high tech Orientalism resurrects the frontier—in virtual form—in order to secure open space for America," writes Wendy Hui Kyong Chun. "As opposed to openly racist science fiction of the early to mid-twentieth century that featured the 'yellow peril,' cyberpunk fiction does not advocate white supremacy or resurrecting a strong United States of America. It rather offers representations of survivors, of savvy-navigators who can open closed spaces" ("Othering" 251). Chun reads the intricacies within high-tech Orientalist cultural productions as not simply exalting a superior United States, a perspective that has always been a hallmark of yellow peril fictions. London's short story and Rohmer's fictions ultimately uphold Western white supremacy at the expense of the Alien/Asian. However, techno-Orientalism, or what Chun calls high-tech Orientalism, troubles the viewpoint that the West can retain or recover a nostalgically configured purity, and posits instead the coherence of "open spaces" embodied through cyberspaces and the Internet. Chun points out that the failures of the West to retain its global economic positioning mean that the U.S. government and affiliated corporations are not to blame for problematic futures-capes. In this instance, a victorious narrative remains: the West, in the form of these "savvy navigators," can cast itself as the underdog challenger to aggressive Eastern economic growth, thereby cementing the West as the indisputable center for humanistic altruism.

The limits of specifically locating a Western-centric hegemony within techno-Orientalism become apparent when we consider Japanese approaches to cyberpunk. Jane Chi Hyun Park frames this issue elegantly by asking, "[W]hat happens to the gendered and racial-ized power dynamics of techno-Orientalism when the object becomes the subject, when Japan 'looks back' at the United States using the same ideological frame that has been used to render it 'other'?" (62). In a similar vein, Chun elucidates that techno-Orientalism is not unidirectional, citing the specific example of Japanese versions of cyberpunk in which one Asian ethnic group can potentially orientalize another. Anime films such as *Ghost in the Shell* (1995), for example, insist on the Japanese characters as signifiers of progress and displace "primitiveness" onto the Chinese culture (*Control* 196). The rubric that constructs Asia as a monolithic technological threat becomes fractured and redir-ected by techno-Orientalism's appropriation by Asian cultural producers, writers, and artists. Chun's critique of *Ghost in the Shell* demonstrates how high-tech Orientalism functions by locating a future dystopia in Hong Kong's urban metropolis, obscuring Japan's primacy in futuristic representations. Kumiko Sato further posits the import-ance of Japanese cyberpunk "as a new locus of the old Japanism with the pretentious look of advanced technology. The epistemological innovativeness that American cyber-punk carried in itself easily merged with this old mission of Japan's modernization . . ." (353). American cyberpunk is reappropriated to enable Japan to recover a terrain once considered lost and destroyed in the wake of World War II.[7]

Thus far, I have discussed American Orientalisms in which the desire to conceptu-alize the East through a technocratic framework within cultural production leads to a rearticulation and reemergence of the yellow peril. In response to these orientalized futures, Japanese cyberpunk and self-circumscribed techno-Orientalism employ genre conventions to consider different sociopolitical contexts and anxieties. Asian American cultural productions must also be considered as forming an important corollary to versions of cyberpunk and techno-Orientalist futures. This intervention is energized by Colleen Lye's provocative question placing American Orientalist studies[8] in conversation with Asian Americanist critique[9]:

> For critics of empire the concern is with American incorporations of Asia, while for Asian Americanists the concern is with Asian exclusion from U.S. civil society. Instead of using one as the political template for the other, how can we come to a better understanding of the nature of U.S. global power and the modernity of race relations by theorizing them in relation to each other? (1–2)

No question could be better suited to Asian Americanist approaches to the future, precisely because techno-Orientalism cannot be situated solely within American Orientalism or its counterpart that has emerged most forcefully through Japanese cyberpunk. A reading practice that attends to Asian American cultural producers offers more venues in which to engage techno-Orientalist cultural productions and how the future, technology, and associated issues can be imagined within fictional worlds. It is simplistic to call all Asian American cultural productions that invoke techno-Orientalist tropes oppositional, yet these works often operate from activist frameworks and illuminate obscured voices and histories.

Most critical conceptions of techno-Orientalism posit a binary between East and West, while eliding the possibility that other Orientalisms might exist concurrently within the United States. For instance, Perry Miyake's novel *21st Century Manzanar* (2002) imagines a future in which Japanese Americans are embroiled in the development of another World War. Derived from the cyberpunk social context of Japan as economic predator, the novel imagines that "World War III became the Economic War with Japan. If the economy went down the toilet, the terrorists would have won. If World War II was the battle to save Western Civilization from the Nazi party and the Japanese race, World War III—the Economic War—became the ultimate battle to save the very soul of America: its pocketbook" (13).[10] While techno-Orientalism clearly posits Asia as the geographical site of anxiety, Miyake's novel considers how Asian American subjects can be conflated with their Asian counterparts, thus creating the space to consider U.S. racial formation in the construction of East/West dynamics. Whether or not the premise of Miyake's novel is plausible, *21st Century Manzanar* investigates the continued preoccupation with the Alien/Asian as part of a futuristic world filled with tension and conflict.

The novel engages its speculative arc as individuals of Japanese ancestry are rounded up during ReVac (for "reevacuation"). Mirroring World War II, Japanese Americans are placed in internment camps, but the novel clarifies that such racial anxieties concerning the Alien/Asian do not appear out of a sociohistorical vacuum. At one point, a Japanese

American character states about her reevacuation to Manzanar, "At least in here, they don't have to worry about terrorists. No tall buildings to plow an airplane into. No crowded sporting events to bomb. If a group of overzealous patriots wanted to pull a drive-by, they'd have to drive a couple of hours into the desert" (30). This passage compares the Japanese American internment to the post–9/11 milieu and suggests a heightened awareness of larger-scale racial, ethnic, and religious tensions in the twenty-first century. The Japanese American internment experience grants the novel one way to enter into conversations about contemporary ethnic and racial politics. Even as the novel purports that the war on terror is "over," it also gives the sense that racial anxiety never dissipates; it only moves onto other bodies who are deemed a thread to nation-state integrity and security. In this new future, Japanese Americans are subjected to what is called "The Plan," in which all males are sterilized. In controlling the reproductive capacity of Japanese Americans, the nation-state deploys biopower as a way to subdue the oncoming generations, one ethnic "strain" of yellow peril having finally been eradicated.[11] We are reminded again of London's "The Unparalleled Invasion," as the reproductive menace of the Alien/Asian might be terminated. However, Miyake's *21st Century Manzanar* does not simply evoke the trope of the Asian American as the oppressed minority or radically resistant activist. Indeed, the murkiness of the plot shows how various Japanese American characters face the pressures of relocation, whether by passing for different Asian ethnicities, becoming docile internment camp residents, or working as informants for the relocation camp's director. Miyake's novel gestures to the ways in which those constructed as the Alien/Asian might find ways to harm and damage others rather than work together to eradicate systemic social inequality and prejudice.

Novels such as *21st Century Manzanar* move techno-Orientalism firmly back into America's national boundaries, locating the future within the geographical confines of the California deserts rather than over the Pacific and into the East. Within this geographical terrain, *21st Century Manzanar* also posits how the Alien/Asian is configured alongside other racial minorities and associated lineages. Some of the regular visitors to the Japanese American internment camps are local Native American tribe members. The novel's main character, David Takeda, thinks that "every time they came, he thought he saw someone he knew. Someone in the Tribe who looked Nisei" (136). David's perception of the physical similarities between Japanese Americans and indigenous characters acts as a harbinger for the novel's conclusion. A group of Navajo Indians ultimately enables Takeda and his family to escape from Manzanar, invoking the connected histories of the forced resettlement of both Native Americans and Japanese Americans. In this respect, even as there is a concerted effort to depict the Alien/Asian in what might be called a techno-Orientalist frame, Miyake's novel draws back into the past by linking racial groups within domestic geographies.[12] In particular, large sections of Japanese American internment camps existed on, overlapped with, or bordered Native American reservations. Such spatial proximities and intimacies become a constant reminder that marginalization necessarily twines together politically charged physical locations with undesirable racial subjects. *21st Century Manzanar* thus discloses an orientalized future, but also questions how Asian American spatial subjectivities are placed in a comparative scope. The novel leaves the now-fugitive Japanese Americans living on a tribal reservation, which has become a pan-Native location. As the narrator notes, "[David] had found refuge in a land of exile and discard that had been reclaimed by its original inhabitants" (381).

Another cultural production that examines other orientalized futures is the television episode "Detained," which first aired on April 24, 2002, as part of the *Star Trek: Enterprise* series (2001–2005). The episode revolves around the rescue of Captain Jonathan Archer (played by Scott Bakula) and Helmsman Travis Mayweather (played by Anthony Montgomery) from an unknown detention facility in which they awaken mysteriously. They are being held with a humanoid alien species known as the Suliban, who may or may not possess the ability to shapeshift. In their original form, their rough, rock-like skin exudes a lime green glow, while their eyes appear yellowish. The Cabal, members of a Suliban sect, are among the primary alien antagonists for the *Enterprise* crew in their travels. Thus, the crew's suspicion of their fellow Suliban inmates is not surprising. Archer and Mayweather are soon interrogated by Colonel Grat, a Tandaran, a different humanoid species similar to humans in physiology except for a distinct nasal bridge. Like the *Enterprise* crew, the Tandarans have suffered at the hands of the Cabal, and yet there are a number of Suliban still living in Tandaran territories. Under the auspices of protecting those Suliban who live in Tandaran boundaries, these Suliban are relocated to these holding facilities, but Archer and Mayweather learn that these Suliban are not part of the Cabal and are being held against their will in an internment camp. Indeed, what Archer and Mayweather discover is that not all Suliban are members of the Cabal. Befriending two of the prisoners, Archer makes the historically informed connection that the Suliban are being treated just like Japanese Americans living on the West Coast of the United States during World War II.

In and of itself, the analogic connection between the Japanese America internees and imprisoned aliens renders a striking parallel. One could make the case that the Suliban's skin color literalizes the yellow peril as an alien race, replete with yellowish skin and eyes. That is, the Suliban is the literalization of the metaphor: they are the Alien/Asian. Determined not to leave them behind, Archer and Mayweather enable the Sulibans' escape, even though it risks their chance of being rescued by the *Enterprise*. Like *21st Century Manzanar*, the politically progressive politics of the episode are more apparent in the relation to the post–9/11 milieu. Rick Berman, one of the co-executive producers of *Star Trek: Enterprise*, affirmed that the name "Suliban" drew inspiration from the Taliban; his decision to include references to the Taliban occurred after his visit to Afghanistan.[13] The violation of civil liberties after 9/11, especially for Arab Americans, Muslim Americans, South Asian Americans, or anyone suspected of potentially being a "terrorist," has generated numerous comparisons to the experiences of Japanese Americans after the attacks on Pearl Harbor.[14] Since this *Star Trek* episode was written four months prior to 9/11, the eerie prescience of Berman's vision serves as an indicator that part of science fiction's appeal is its ability to predict the future. Nevertheless, this episode cannot be considered only from an intergalactic, techno-Orientalist, transnational, or global lens because the dialogue refers to the Japanese American internment, comparing literalized alien abjection on another planet with a racially motivated and racist historical event that occurred within the domestic confines of the United States. Interestingly, one of the major *Enterprise* characters and regular cast members, Japanese American linguist and communications officer Hoshi Sato (played by Korean American actress Linda Park), takes no part in the major storyline related to the Suliban internees. While the character's ethnicity should not necessarily require her to function as an extension of the Suliban storyline, the narrative of liberation upholds the heroism of Captain Archer, as he is ultimately the one who mobilizes the Suliban to escape. Archer resists his own marginalized status and helps lead the Suliban detainees to their freedom. Although the Suliban leave the oppressive confines of the internment camp, the episode's conclusion remains focused on Archer, as he contemplates whether they will flourish now that they are not imprisoned.

One might therefore posit that the Japanese American internment narrative and the ensuing Suliban escape plan in "Detained" are other examples of the visually overdetermined symbolic potency of the white male hero, who signifies morality, value, and liberation. The Federation, in this case represented so gallantly by the square-jawed, handsome, and perennially plucky Archer, can be prevented from committing racially motivated mistakes again. History is invoked to promote the Federation's enlightenment and moral superiority. Hoshi Sato's marginalization from the storyline makes more evident the Federation's postracial politics in which its multicultural and racially integrated cast demonstrates how certain social inequalities have become a thing of the past. For all we know, Sato may not even identify with her ethnic or racial background in this apparently more integrated future. However, Sato's or, for that matter, Mayweather's role in "Detained" is minimized to the extent that heroism is embodied most effectively by Archer, the white male lead. Indeed, as Allen Kwan points out, Sato's and Mayweather's roles are marginal throughout the entire series, suggesting that the show's content must be illuminated from the dissonance created when comparing the show's speculative future with contemporary race politics (67). Racism's literal displacement onto the alien body consequently veils the ways in which the show operates to reproduce what David Golumbia has called "the white ideology of *Star Trek*" (87), in which minority cast members, while plentiful, do not receive as much screen time or as powerful positions within the Federation.[15]

My reading imagines a racialized future beyond the dualism that posits the West against the East and, even more specifically, destabilizes Asia as the primary site for projected future anxieties. *21st Century Manzanar* reminds us that Asian American cultural production provides important interventions into considering racialized futures, ones that intersect with other racial histories. Though I focus my analysis here on only a specific set of cultural productions, all Asian American cultural producers of speculative fiction remain woefully understudied. Miyake's novel is only one of a tremendous archive in which Asian American writers imagine a future centrally involving minorities whose racial differences still impact how the techno-Orientalist fictional worlds must be read. I am thinking here of Chang-rae Lee's *On Such a Full Sea*, Amitav Ghosh's *The Calcutta Chromosome*, Malinda Lo's *Adaptation* and follow-up *Inheritance*, Jacqueline Koyanagi's *Ascension*, Cathy Park Hong's *Dance Dance Revolution*, Peter Tieryas-Liu's *Bald New World*, Charles Yu's *How to Live Safely in a Science Fictional Universe*, Karen Bao's *Dove Arising* (part of a young adult fiction trilogy still to be completed),[16] Marie's Lu's *Legend* (and follow-ups *Prodigy* and *Champion*), Sangu Mandanna's *The Lost Girl*, as just a few of the notable recent publications that imagine the Alien/Asian occupying a tomorrow in which social inequality embeds racial relations, however allegorically or inconspicuously, within the fabric of the fictional world.

In the case of "Detained," the alien Suliban internees act as visual markers that suggest not only the past, through their connection to World War II–era Japanese Americans, but the present and future as well, in the way that their treatment ominously foreshadows the civil rights milieu following the terrorist attacks of 9/11. "Detained" is but one example of how the Alien/Asian continually reappears as a convenient racialized metaphor, deployed by cultural producers to explore and invoke the complicated asymmetries of social difference and oppression. Like all powerful and apt artistic metaphors, "Alien/ Asian" transforms in the ever-elastic boundaries of the fictional world but continues to impact how we understand the social dynamics of our everyday lived realities.

Acknowledgment

I would like to thank Gayle K. Sato, who provided late-stage revision suggestions.

Notes

1. A number of recent critical studies have emerged in relation to the figure of Fu Manchu. Chan traces a genealogy of Asian American male figures that have emerged in popular culture, specifically devoting his second chapter to an analysis of the "devil doctor." Seshagiri investigates the figure of Fu Manchu within a British context. Kim's third chapter draws out the emasculated Asian American teleology against which Frank Chin would write. For more recent scholarly considerations of Fu Manchu, see also Chen; Christensen; Kingsbury; and Ling.
2. See Kang; Palumbo-Liu.
3. Lisa Nakamura succinctly describes this Orientalist phenomenon within cyberpunk: "While the genre of cyberpunk fiction has since expanded and been reiterated many times, one things seems constant: when cyberpunk writers construct the future, it looks Asian—specifically, in many cases, Japanese" (62).
4. The term "techno-Orientalism" seems to have a twofold origination. While Morley and Robins were the first to define it in print, Nakamura cites Greta Ai-Yu Niu's paper presentation at Duke University in 1998 as her model for the definition. For other critical considerations of techno-Orientalism, see Bennett; Beynon; Pham; Roh, Huang, and Niu.
5. I use the term "Saidian Orientalism" to refer to the original conception of Orientalism as offered by Edward Said.

6. At the height of this unease between the United States and Asia in the mid 1980s, Kiyohiko Fukushima writes that "[t]rade tensions between the United States and Japan have recently reached the level at which they may endanger the most remarkable political achievement of the postwar era—the U.S.-Japanese political partnership" (22). But such economic growth was not limited to one country. Indeed, Saburo Okita recounts that "[t]he 1980s were a decade of growth for the Asia-Pacific countries as they steadily became more important in the world economy, their share of nominal world gross national product (GNP) increasing from 41 percent in 1980 to 52 percent in 1985" (26).

7. The route through which this recovery occurs, as Sato notes, appears through the proliferation of female cyborgs, a gendered phenomena that serves to trouble a feminist recovery of these hybrid figures who exist as protectors, shoring up the very instability at the core of Japanese identity.

8. See, e.g., Klein.

9. See, e.g., Lowe.

10. Perhaps problematically, Miyake states that "[u]nlike September 11, this enemy was imme-diately identifiable; the same economic foe, the same arch-enemy of the United States since December 7, 1941—Japan" (13). In this respect, the novel seems to posit that there was no visual racialization that occurred due to the events of September 11, which seems reductive. At the same time, the polemic here underscores the deterritorialized nature of terrorism itself—that it would not simply be linked to one country, or even one global region, as terrorist cells prolifer-ate in numerous areas.

11. I employ the term as Foucault defines it.

12. In this respect, the novel is a prime example of what Prashad has defined as a polycultural historical approach.

13. This *TV Guide* interview was published in the May 5–11, 2002, issue.

14. For comparison of the treatment of Japanese Americans during World War II and Muslim Americans/Arab Americans following the attacks on 9/11, please see Ahmad (101, 105); Bayoumi (272); Howell and Shryock (450); and Naber (225–27).

15. Hurd argues that the *Star Trek* franchise "still tends to reify a particularly loaded image from nineteenth-century psychology and anthropology in the United States: The Tragic Mulatto" (23). Joyrich also investigates the development of female characters within the *Star Trek* franchise.

16. The second installment, *Dove Exiled*, is scheduled to be published by Viking Books for Young Readers in February 2016.

Works cited

Ahmad, Muneer. "Homeland Insecurities: Racial Violence the Day after September 11." *Social Text* 20.3 (2002): 101–15.

Bao, Karen *Dove Arising*. New York: Viking Books for Young Readers, 2015.

Bayoumi, Moustafa. "Racing Religion." *New Centennial Review* 6.2 (2006): 267–93.

Bello, Walden, and Shea Cunningham. "Trade Warfare and Regional Integration in the Pacific: The USA, Japan, and the Asian NICs." *Third World Quarterly* 15.3 (1994): 445–58.

Bennett, Eve. "Techno-butterfly: Orientalism Old and New in *Battlestar Galactica*." *Science Fiction Film and Television* 5.1 (2012): 23–46.

Berman, Rick, and Brannon Braga. "The Visionaries." *TV Guide* 5–11 May 2002: 46–48.

Beynon, Davi. "From Techno-cute to Superflat: Robots and Asian Architectural Futures." *Mechademia* 7 (2012): 129–48.

Chan, Jachinson. *Chinese American Masculinities: From Fu-Manchu to Bruce Lee*. New York: Routledge, 2001.

Chen, Tina. "Dissecting the 'Devil Doctor': Stereotypes and Sensationalism in Sax Rohmer's Fu Manchu." *Re/Collecting Early Asian America: Essays in Cultural History*. Ed. Josephine Lee, Imogene L. Lim, and Yuko Matsukawa. Philadelphia: Temple UP, 2002. 218–37.

Christensen, Peter. "The Political Appeal of Dr. Fu Manchu." *The Devil Himself: Villainy in Detective Fiction and Film*. Ed. Stacy Gillis and Philippa Gates. Westport: Greenwood, 2002. 81–89.

Chun, Wendy Hui Kyong. *Control and Freedom: Power and Paranoia in the Age of Fiber Optics*. Cambridge: MIT P, 2006.

—. "Othering Cyberspace." *The Visual Culture Reader*. Ed. Nicholas Mirzoeff. New York: Routledge, 1998. 243–54.

Cornea, Christine. "Techno-Orientalism and the Postmodern Subject." *Screen Methods: Comparative Readings in Film Studies*. Ed. Jacqueline Furby and Karen Randell. London: Wallflower P, 2005. 72–81.

"Detained." Writ. Gene Roddenberry. Perf. Scott Bakula, Jolene Blalock, John Billingsley, Dominic Keating, Anthony Montgomery, Linda Park, Connor Trinneer. *Enterprise*. UPN. KCOP, Los Angeles. 24 Apr. 2002.

Foucault, Michel. *The History of Sexuality: An Introduction*. New York: Vintage, 1990.

Fukushima, Kyohiko. "Japan's Real Trade Policy." *Foreign Policy* 59 (Summer 1985): 22–39.

Ghosh, Amitav. *The Calcutta Chromosome*. New York: Harper Perennial, 2001.

Golumbia, David. "Black and White World: Race, Ideology, and Utopia in Triton and Star Trek." *Cultural Critique* 32 (Winter 1995–1996): 75–95.

Gulick, Sidney L. *The American Japanese Problem; a Study of the Racial Relations of the East and the West*. New York: Scribner, 1914.

Hong, Cathy Park. *Dance Dance Revolution.* New York: W. W. Norton, 2007.

Howell, Sally, and Andrew Shryock. "Cracking Down on Diaspora: Arab Detroit and America's 'War on Terror.'" *Anthropological Quarterly* 76.3 (2003): 443–62.

Hurd, Denise Alessandria. "The Monster Inside: 19th Century Racial Constructs in the 24th Century Mythos of Star Trek." *Journal of Popular Culture* 31.1 (1997): 23–35.

Joyrich, Lynne. "Feminist *Enterprise*? Star Trek: The Next Generation and the Occupation of Femininity." *Cinema Journal* 35.2 (1996): 61–84.

Kang, Laura Hyun Yi. *Compositional Subjects: Enfiguring Asian/American Women*. Durham: Duke UP, 2002.

Kim, Daniel Y. *Writing Manhood in Black and Yellow: Ralph Ellison, Frank Chin, and the Literary Politics of Identity*. Stanford: Stanford UP, 2005.

Kingsbury, Karen. "Yellow Peril, Dark Hero: Fu Manchu and the 'Gothic Bedevilment' of Racist Intent." *The Gothic Other: Racial and Social Constructions in the Literary Imagination*. Ed. Ruth Bienstock Anolik and Douglas L. Howard. Jefferson: McFarland, 2004. 104–19.

Klein, Christina. *Cold War Orientalism: Asia in the Middlebrow Imagination, 1945–1961*. Berkeley: U of California P, 2003.

Koyanagi, Jacqueline. *Ascension*. Germantown: Masque, 2013.

Kwan, Allen. "Seeking New Civilization: Race Normativity in the *Star Trek* Franchise." *Bulletin of Science Technology Society* 27.1 (2007): 59–70.

Lee, Chang-rae. *On Such a Full Sea*. New York: Riverhead, 2014.

Ling, L. H. M. "The Monster Within: What Fu Manchu and Hannibal Lecter Can Tell Us about Terror and Desire in a Post–9/11 World." *Positions: East Asia Cultures Critique* 12.2 (2004): 377–400.

Lo, Malinda. *Adaptation*. New York: Little, Brown Books for Young Readers, 2012.

—. *Inheritance*. New York: Little, Brown Books for Young Readers, 2013.

London, Jack. *The Strength of the Strong*. New York: MacMillan, 1914.

Lowe, Lisa. *Immigrant Acts: On Asian American Cultural Politics*. Durham: Duke UP, 1996.

Lu, Marie. *Champion*. New York: G.P. Putnam's Sons for Young Readers, 2013.

—. *Legend*. New York: G.P. Putnam's Sons for Young Readers, 2010.

—. *Prodigy*. New York: G.P. Putnam's Sons for Young Readers, 2011.

Lye, Colleen. "Introduction: In Dialogue with Asian American Studies." *Representations* 99 (Summer 2007): 1–12.

Mandanna, Sangu. *The Lost Girl*. New York: Balzer + Bray, 2012.

Miyake, Perry. *21st Century Manzanar*. Los Angeles: Really Great Books, 2002.

Morley, David, and Kevin Robins. "Techno-Orientalism: Japan Panic." *Spaces of Identity: Global Media, Electronic Landscapes, and Cultural Boundaries*. New York: Routledge, 1995. 147–73.

Naber, Nadine C. "So Our History Doesn't Become Your Future: The Local and Global Politics of Coalition Building Post September 11th." *Journal of Asian American Studies* 5.3 (2002): 217–42.

Nakamura, Lisa. *Cybertypes: Race, Ethnicity, and Identity on the Internet*. New York: Routledge, 2002.

Niu, Greta Ai-Yu. "Techno-Orientalism, Cyborgology and Asian American Studies." Discipline and Deviance: Genders, Technologies, Machines Conference. Duke University, Durham. Oct. 1998. Presentation.

Okita, Saburo. "Japan's Role in Asia-Pacific Cooperation." *Annals of the American Academy of Political and Social Science* 513 (Jan. 1991): 25–37.

Palumbo-Liu, David. *Asian/Americans: Historical Crossings of a Racial Frontier*. Stanford: Stanford UP, 1999.

Park, Jane Chi Hyun. "Stylistic Crossings: Cyberpunk Impulses in Anime." *World Literature Today* 79.3/4 (2005): 60–63.

Pham, Minh-Ha T. "Paul Poiret's Magical Techno-Oriental Fashions (1911): Race, Clothing, and Virtuality in the Machine Age." *Configurations* 21.1 (2013): 1–26.

Prashad, Vijay. *Everybody was Kung-Fu Fighting: Afro-Asian Connections and the Myth of Cultural Purity*. Boston: Beacon, 2001.

Roh, David, Betsy Huang, and Greta A. Niu. *Techno-Orientalism: Imagining Asia in Speculative Fiction, History, and Media*. New Brunswick: Rutgers UP, 2015.

Rohmer, Sax. *The Insidious Dr. Fu-Manchu*. New York: A. L. Burt, 1913.

Said, Edward. *Orientalism*. New York: Penguin, 2003.

Sato, Kumiko. "How Information Technology Has (Not) Changed Feminism and Japanism: Cyberpunk in the Japanese Context." *Comparative Literature Studies* 41.3 (2004): 335–55.

Seshagiri, Urmila. "Modernity's (Yellow) Perils: Dr. Fu-Manchu and English Race Paranoia." *Cultural Critique* 62 (2006): 162–94.

Shinohara, Miyohei. "Japan as a World Economic Power." *Annals of the American Academy of Political and Social Science* 513 (1991): 12–24.

Spencer, Edson W. "Japan as Competitor." *Foreign Policy* 78 (1990): 153–71.

Tatsumi, Takayuki. *Full Metal Apache: Transactions between Cyberpunk Japan and Avant-Pop America*. Durham: Duke UP, 2006.

Tieryas-Liu, Peter. *Bald New World*. Winchester: Perfect Edge, 2014.

Ueno, Toshiya. "Japanimation: Techno-Orientalism, Media Tribes, and Rave Culture." *Aliens R Us: The Other in Science Fiction Cinema*. Ed. Ziauddin Sardar and Sean Cubitt. Sterling: Pluto, 2002. 94–110.

Yu, Charles. *How to Live Safely in a Science Fictional Universe*. New York: Pantheon, 2010.

35

Report from planet midnight

Nalo Hopkinson

In 2009 I was a Guest Author at the International Conference of the Fantastic in the Arts, which takes place each spring in Florida, USA. The conference theme that year was "Race in the Literature of the Fantastic." Other invited guests included Native American writer Owl Goingback, Chinese-American writer Laurence Yep, and Japanese science fiction scholar Takayuki Tatsumi. It was also the first year that more than a handful of the conference attendees were people of color.

I'd known since 2008 that I was going to be a Guest Author, and that I would have to speak to the conference theme during one the luncheons. And I'd been dreading it. Talking about difference and marginalization in active science fiction community is rarely easy.[1] Although some of us are people of color and some of us non-Western, the community is dominated by white, middle-class people from the more "developed" nations of the Western world. Many of us are of an egalitarian bent, at least in principle. We are an intelligent, opinionated, and outspoken bunch. Many of us are geeks. We know too much about too many things that other people don't care about. Many of us are socially awkward observers who often don't quite get the hang of mainstream status signalling vis-à-vis dress codes, slanguage, mating rituals, and material possessions. We are often ridiculed by people who do understand those complex codes. We have created an active, passionate community centred on our love for science fiction and fantasy and devoted to the principle that no one should be singled out for being "different."

But principled does not de facto mean politicized. In practice, people in our community who try to talk about marginalization are often seen as fomenting divisiveness. We become the problem. In this community, many of us will firmly call bullshit when we see it. But that doesn't mean that our analysis is always informed, rigorous, or honest. Many of us come from backgrounds of relative privilege that we don't perceive, and are ignorant of what daily life is like for those with less of that privilege (even keeping in mind that relative privilege is always contextual). Many of us don't think beyond simplistic analyses of power that ignore systemic power imbalances in order to lay the blame on the victim. Just as much as the mainstream world, we are hierarchical. We can be dazzled by fame. Some of us are the cool kids and some are not.

I'm told that when I originally gave this speech, some of the academics in the audience were offended that I used my time at the podium to discuss what they saw as an issue from the "fans" and therefore beneath them. In 2009, one of the most far-reaching, paradigm-shifting (I fervently hope) community debates was burning up communications networks right beneath their noses, and they were proud of having been ignorant of it, and indignant that I would lump them in with fans.

Active fannish community not only constitutes a significant and enthusiastic portion of our audience for science fiction and fantasy in all media, it is the community that organizes, for love of the genre, the many annual conventions throughout the SF/F world which bring together artists and audiences to celebrate, share, debate, and critique the narratives of social and technological evolution in science fiction and fantasy stories.

I love the science fiction community fiercely and I will call you to task if you ridicule it or dismiss it lightly. I have found friends, allies, and fellow travellers here, of many racial, class, and cultural backgrounds. I have found stories that entertained me, made me marvel, made me hopeful. But it is not a haven for the perfect meeting of like minds (thank heaven, because how dull would that be? Not to mention impossible). I speak not to belittle my community but to participate in it.

It is common for science fiction and fantasy writers, most of whom are white, to say that they don't write about people of color because they don't know anything about us; or don't know what it's like to live as a racialized person; or, perhaps more honestly, because they don't want to piss us off. It is common for science fiction and fantasy writers to say that they set their stories in imaginary worlds among imaginary beings because that allows them to deal with fraught issues such as power and marginalization divorced from the real-world effects of such issues. But there are also many writers who see it differently.

In 2009, white science fiction writer Elizabeth Bear published a blog post in which she challenged her fellow authors to include racialized and otherwise marginalized people in their stories. That post ignited an Internet firestorm of discussion and argument about race, racism, and representation in science fiction/fantasy literature and community. Fans, major editors and writers in the field, and emerging writers took part. Some people of color expressed their frustration, pain, and rage at the field's ongoing racism. Some white people engaged thoughtfully, with understanding and respect. But many others responded quite negatively. They were indignant that we dared express rage in rageful ways.[2] Some of them loudly denied the existence of racism in the field, in ways that demonstrated their lack of understanding of how systemic racism operates. For a time, some of them appeared to be policing the Internet posts of politicized black women writers in the genre and attempting to verbally intimidate, berate, and belittle us. A couple of the major editors in the field, perhaps understandably upset at how some of the rage was being expressed, made statements of the ilk that they would never again allow communication from any of those they considered guilty of offence.

Among the angry people of color were unpublished and barely published writers. Our field is quite small. There's only a handful of large professional houses. They currently only publish a handful of people of color. To their credit, many of them want to publish more of us. But from my perspective, when key representatives of one of the most powerful houses in our genre say that they never again want to hear from people who could be the future SF/F writers, editors, illustrators, and publicists of color, and who are the current SF/F readers of color, that's a pretty clear expression of both the power and the will to actively keep the genre as white as possible.

I do not believe I overstate. I do believe that is not how they meant it; they are well-meaning people. But that is how it would have been heard by those who have been implicitly and explicitly, through ignorance or wilfulness, largely rendered invisible for decades. When you're historically the one with the power relative to another, if you really want to correct the imbalance, you have to be willing to hear pent-up rage and not retaliate. You have to be willing to acknowledge your actions that make you complicit. You have to be willing to apologize and then take visible, effective steps towards righting the imbalance.[3]

Some of the editors who made that type of statement have since been taking a little extra effort to be seen to be supportive of people of color in the genre; but they have not, to my knowledge, acknowledged why they are doing so. And they have not, to my knowledge, acknowledged fault and apologized. You can't bring about reconciliation by doing little or nothing. You can't make change that way. So at some level, perhaps the will really isn't there. I know some of these editors and I respect the good books they've made happen. But at the moment I have no reason to trust them and I do not wish to be published by them.

I believe it was a clueful white person who coined the phrase "RaceFail '09" to signify the more vehemently recalcitrant white voices in the debate. A couple of those voices have adopted the nomenclature "failfandom" as a pejorative to denote people in the community, especially people of color, who unapologetically name the racism we perceive. RaceFail '09 generated thousands of Internet postings, links to many of which have been archived on the Web.[4]

So that is the context in which I attended ICFA in 2009. It took me a long time to get over being so scared and angry that I couldn't write my speech. I actually completed the bulk of it at the conference the day before, when I had a bolt of inspiration about an angle from which to tackle it. I decided to make the first half of my address somewhat performative. It is a culture-jamming of references from fantasy, science fiction, and linguistic and cultural references from the American and Caribbean parts of the African diaspora. I've footnoted some of them here. Because the first half of the speech was in effect a script, there were a few performance notes in it that I'd written to myself. These are between square brackets, in capitals. There is also an afterword about an exchange I had minutes after finishing my speech.

A reluctant ambassador from the planet of midnight

Good afternoon. I'd like to thank the International Association for the *Fantastic* in the Arts for dedicating this year's ICFA to the theme of race in the literature of the fantastic, and for inviting Mr. Tatsumi, Mr. Yep, me, and many others to address the topic.

The first thing I'd like to say is . . .

[BE LIGHT-HEADED, THEN BECOME THE HORSE[5]]
Uh—oh my. It worked. I'm here. [LOOK AT HANDS, THEN AT AUDIENCE]
Dear people, please don't be alarmed. I mean no harm. I really don't. I'm riding on the head of this horse only for a short time, I promise you. Please don't hurt me. This was an extreme measure. There seemed to be no other way to communicate directly with you.

I come from another planet. For decades now, we have been receiving broadcasts from your planet that seem to be intended for us. We are delighted, and honored, and also puzzled. We have teams of our best translators working to decipher your messages, and we cannot honestly tell whether they are gestures of friendship, or of aggression. As you might imagine, it's quite important for us to know which. If it is indeed friendship, we would be delighted to reciprocate. If of aggression, well, as one of our ethno-cultural groups might say, "Don't start none, there won't be none."

I should be very clear: I do not represent my whole planet. Neither do I represent my whole ethnocultural group. Or even all of the translators assigned to this project; try to get any two of us to agree to the same thing . . . There was vehement disagreement among us about whether I should attempt this dire method of direct communication. So, frankly, I snuck away when no one was looking.

[FIDDLE WITH CLOTHING]
My, this horse does dress most uncomfortably, doesn't she?

[TAKE TOP SHIRT OFF TO REVEAL T-SHIRT THAT READS "SPEAKER TO WHITE FOLKS"]

This? This is merely my name, dear friends. Or my title, if you will. I hope I may indeed call you friends. But to help ensure my safety, or at least to create a record of what happens this day, I am accompanied by my companion, Dances With White People, and his recording device. [INDICATE DAVID FINDLAY, WHO'S VIDEOTAPING[6]] Again, please don't be alarmed. It is not a weapon of any kind.

So. To the business at hand. It is my hope that if I repeat to you some of the most vexing phrases we've received from your peoples, that you might be able to clarify their meanings. I decided to address this conference because, as you might imagine, we, as a different race of beings than you are, are very interested in the stories you tell each other about interracial relations. We have had bad experiences with the collision of cultures. Some of them even between groups on our own planet. So I'm sure you can understand why we are concerned.

Our first sign that perhaps our responses to you were going awry was when we released this document into your world:

[SLIDE: ORIGINAL COVER OF NOVEL MIDNIGHT ROBBER ACCURATELY DEPICTING THE PROTAGONIST, WHO IS A BROWN-SKINNED LITTLE GIRL WITH BLACK AFRICAN FEATURES]

When one of the cultures of your world reconfigured it, this was the result:

[SLIDE: COVER OF ITALLAN TRANSLATION OF MIDNIGHT ROBBER (IL PLANETA DI MEZZANOTTE) SHOWING PROT-
AGONIST AS A BLUE-SKINNED YOUNG WOMAN WITH EUROPEAN FEATURES AND STRAIGHT HAIR, WEARING A BRA
TOP AND FRINGED MINISKIRT]

As far as our translators can tell, the title of this version can be rendered as *The Planet of Midnight,* which, according to your understanding, seems to be where the blue people live. We have noticed a preponderance of wistful references in your literature to magical people with blue skin.

[SLIDES: NIGHTCRAWLER; MYSTIQUE; THE BEAST (ALL FROM THE X-MEN); KALI; KRISHNA; DR. MANHATTAN;
PAPA SMURF; SMURFETTE; THE COOKIE MONSTER; ETC. BUT NONE OF THE BEINGS FROM AVATAR, CUZ I'M
ORNERY THAT WAY AND DON'T WANT TO INVOKE THAT PARTICULAR FARCE IN THIS SPACE TODAY. BESIDES, THE
CONNECTION SHOULD BE SELF-EVIDENT]

Since none of the images of real people from your world show such blue-skinned beings, we can only theorize about what these images symbolize or eulogize. Perhaps a race of yours that has gone extinct, or that has self-destructed. Perhaps it is a race that has gone into voluntary seclusion, maybe as an attempt at self-protection. The more pessimistic among us fear that this is a race being kept in isolation, for what horrendous planet-wide crime we shudder to imagine; or that it is a race of earlier sentient beings that you have exterminated. Whatever the truth of the matter, we're sure you realize why it is of extreme importance to us to learn whether imprisonment, extinction, and mythologizing are your only methods of dealing with interspecies conflict.

Here are some of the other communications with which we're having trouble:

You say: "I'm not racist."
Primary translation: "I can wade through feces without getting any of it on me."
Secondary translation: "My shit don't stink."

Our dilemma: To us, someone making this kind of delusional claim is in immediate need of the same healing treatments we offer to people who are convinced that they can fly. Such people are a danger to themselves and to others. And yet, the communications from your world are replete with this type of statement from people who do not seem to be under treatment of any kind, and few among you take any steps to limit the harm they do. We are forced to conclude that you must be as laissez-faire in your response to people who think they can fly. This can't possibly be true, can it? Few of us are willing to visit a planet where we would clearly have to dodge plummeting bodies with every step.
[FLINCH, LOOK UPWARDS]

You say: "This story is a universal one."
Translation: "This story is very specifically about us, and after all, we're the only ones who matter."

Our attempts at translating this one caused quite an argument in our ranks. Several feuds have started as a result, and one or two of them have gotten quite ugly. Because why would any sentient race say something that means its exact opposite? Well, one of our number did point out that we ourselves do occasionally display this regrettable habit. But that's an us thing; you wouldn't understand.

You say: "That thing that you made doesn't belong to you. It's universal."

Now, this one is complicated. To make any sense of it at all, we had to proceed from statements of the previous type, in which "universal" means, approximately, "we own it."

Therefore, our attempt at a primary translation is this: "I like that thing you made, so I'm going to claim it's mine. And I'm bigger than you, and nobody who counts really likes you anyway, so you can't stop me."
Secondary translation, for brevity: "I think yours is prettier, so I'm just going to help myself to it."

You say: "Ethnic."
Primary translation: "Those quaint and somewhat primitive people over there."
Secondary translation: "Unnatural, abnormal, or, disgusting, as in your term 'ethnic food.'"[7]

You must understand that on our planet, everyone has an ethnicity. With cultural mixing, some of us have more than one. To us, "ethnic" means "the cultures of everyone." Clearly we are missing something crucial, and "ethnic" is not the word you actually mean. We beg you to provide us with clarity.

You say: "God, you people are so exotic."
Primary translation: "I, by the power vested in me as a representative of a dominant culture that needs never question its certainty that it is the centre of the universe, hereby dub you 'the entertainment.'"
Secondary translation: "God, you people are so ethnic."
One of our translators offered a tertiary translation: "Just take this money already and pose with my kid so I can take a picture." But, between you and me, he's somewhat, um, argumentative at the best of times.

You say: "But I'm not the one who enslaved your people. That was my ancestors."
Primary translation: "I benefit from the inequities that were institutionalized before my birth, and I have no interest in doing anything to disrupt that comfortable state of affairs."
Secondary translation: "I feel really guilty about this stuff, but it's bigger than me. I'm powerless."
Tertiary translation (from you-know-who): "Suck it up, bitches."

You say: "I don't have any culture of my own; that's why I want yours."

Primary translation: "I am wilfully unaware of or repulsed by how ubiquitous my rich and powerful culture has made itself. I'd really rather hang out with you guys."
Secondary translation: "I'm bored! This stuff is hard!"

You say: "I don't see race."
Primary translation: "If I keep very quiet, maybe you wont see me and ask me to do any work."
Secondary translation: "I'm just a little black rain-cloud, hovering under the honey tree."[8]

You say: "Eventually this race stuff won't matter, because we'll all interbreed and become postracial."
Primary translation: "If I keep very quiet, maybe you won't see me and ask me to do any work. Plus you might have sex with me."
Secondary translation: "I don't want to do my homework!
This stuff is hard! I want some cookies! Are we there yet?"

You say: "My grandparents had a hard time too when they came to this country."
Primary translation: "Oh, shut up, already. Let's talk about me some more."
Secondary translation: "La-la-la, I can't hear you. That's because I don't see race."

You say: "But we can't do that! That would be affirmative action!"
Primary translation: "I don't want to do something that's proven to work, because then, well, it might work."

Oh, dear. The horse is coming back online. She's putting up quite the struggle. Feisty little filly, ain't she? So I'm going to have to take my leave of you, and before I could get my answers, too. I'm so sorry. You have my questions, though? You heard them? You can send the explanations out via the usual channels through which you've been sending us messages. I promise we'll hear the . . .

[BECOME NALO AGAIN]

Wow. What happened there? Never mind, probably just nerves. [TAKE OFF T-SHIRT. UNDER-NEATH IS A PLAIN BLACK DRESS, INDICATE T-SHIRT] Dunno where that ratty thing came from.

Anyway, every few years I come up with another statement about what fantasy and science fiction do. I don't discard my previous notions; I just add new ones for the consideration of myself and others. I don't consider them definitive or all-encompassing, and I consider them at best only partially descriptive. But I find them fun to contemplate. The other day, our roommate told us that he'd asked his grandmother what technological invention had revolutionized her life. He thought she'd say the television, but she replied, "No, that thing destroyed my social life."

She told him that in fact it was the refrigerator that had changed her life. She said it freed up hours of her days, creating leisure time that allowed her to go and see a movie occasionally, and to hang out with friends.

My roomie's story left me thinking about just how labor-intensive it is to maintain a single human life, never mind a family of humans. We are a lot of work; really, to have any quality of life, we are more work than we can manage by ourselves.

Time was, if you were rich, you had servants to do a lot of the drudge and administrative work for you. Hang on; that one hasn't changed.

If you weren't rich, you got together in communities and shared what labor you could, and you had children to help with the rest. And that one hasn't changed much, either.

And if you weren't the breeding kind, you found other ways to make yourself invaluable to the people in charge. I don't suppose I'm saying anything about this that is news to this crowd, so please bear with me while I build my argument.

So that's a really glossed-over version of how the balance of labor and power has traditionally tended to play out. But as disempowered groups in society become more empowered, they begin to be able to make more choices about where they are going to place their labor efforts.

We've made magic; we've created this near-intangible substance called "money" (it's almost more an idea than a substance, really) which you can use—if you have enough of it—to compel or persuade others to do some of your work for you.

In many countries of the world, women and men can now choose to have fewer children.

Sometimes, people are able to choose to do blue-collar work over relatively unskilled labor; can get the education that allows them to do white-collar work, or even end up in the highly skilled labor pool, the one in which you find doctors and lawyers. If you manage to boost yourself there, you can afford to hire people to do a lot of your drudge work for you.

But the necessity for somebody to do the hard labor to sustain human lives and communities hasn't gone away. One way we make sure that there are always people to do that work is by deliberately keeping portions of our populations disenfranchised so that they have little choice but drudge work.

We also create "labor-saving" devices. But as anyone who's ever used a computer knows, in many ways, those just create new forms of work.

We're always imagining new ways around the dilemma. So it seems to me that one of the things that fantasy and science fiction do is to imaginatively address the core problem of who does the work.

Science fiction looks at technological approaches to the problem, and at all the problems the solutions create. (You know, the discovery that a computer isn't exactly a labor-saving device. Or the question of what happens when our machines become so complex that they are in effect sentient beings able to demand rights.)

Fantasy looks at the idea of work. Instead of using technology, it uses magic. But both are labor-saving devices.

And both fantasy and science fiction wrestle with the current and historical class inequities we maintain in order to have people to do the work.

Especially in North America, class differences have historically become so entrenched that they are characterized as or conflated with cultural or racial differences.

And as someone brilliant has said, "Race doesn't exist, but it'll kill ya."

So one might say that, at a very deep level, one of the things that fantasy and science fiction do is to use mythmaking to examine and explore socioeconomically configured ethnoracial power imbalances.

That's why those of us who live in racialized bodies, and who love and read fantasy and science fiction because we relate so strongly to it, can get so bloody irritated at the level of sheer, wilful ignorance that members of the dominant community bring to the discourse about race and its real-life effects. The discussion is everywhere in the literature, but some of the people in this community can be so adamant about being blind to it, and so determined to derail, belittle, obstruct, and silence those of us for whom it can literally affect the quality of our lives!

I've known for quite some time now that I'd end up on this podium, speaking on race in the fantastic. That was challenging enough, being a person of color addressing a mostly white crowd in North America on the issue of race in anything. I was already anxious and exercised about the whole thing. But then, white people in this community instigated the disturbance in the Force that we're now calling RaceFail '09, and what was already loaded became outright trigger-happy.

I know that some of you already have your backs up because I just said that white people instigated it. So be it. I'm not going to get into defending that statement. I'm up here presumably because somebody in this organization thinks I know what I'm talking about. My point is that writing this speech has been no doddle. I've been composing it in my mind for over a year now, through apprehension and anxiety. When it came down to the actual writing of it, I had to take frequent rage breaks.

In the course of RaceFail '09, I have heard white people in the community who are angry at the anger displayed by people of color in the community; people who say that we don't deserve to be listened to if we can't be polite. I couldn't figure out why this statement felt wrongheaded to me, until I read a post by my colleague, writer Nora Jemisin, on RaceFail. She pointed out that discussions of race in this community have been happening, politely, for decades. And though there has been change, it has been minimal. When we people of color started to blow up, suddenly there were more of you paying attention. That's the thing. I've said that when you step on my foot once or twice,

I might politely ask you to get off it. But by the thousandth time you do it, the excuse of "I didn't see you there" starts to sound a hell of a lot like, "I don't care enough about you to pay attention."

The vehement response of people of color to RaceFail got more people paying attention, both white and of color. It showed us people of color that we do have a certain strength of numbers, that there are more of us than the one or two visibly of color people you'll usually see at a convention. People of color in this community have started publishing ventures together as a result of RaceFail. Some white people in the community began addressing the issue and began creating forums for discussion. Some of them held fast, even when they came under attack from all sides. A small handful of them had the guts to examine their own statements and actions, perceive where they had been racist, and admit it. Without saying that they were now afraid to go to conventions because of angry brown people (in my experience, the wrath of the white majority is much more danger-ous), without name-calling, baiting, or (black!)listing, and without deleting their whole blog right after posting an apology on it.

Some of you will recognize yourselves or friends of yours, or, hell, friends of mine in the actions I'm describing. It doesn't necessarily mean that I hate these people. Believe it or not, my default is towards friendliness. People make mistakes. People say things they haven't thought through. People do things they later regret. People hurt other people. People propagate systemic inequities because they don't understand or care how the system works. I know that I do all those things. I'm learning that it's what you do after you make the mistake that counts. The people who took their courage into their own hands and apologized probably discovered that they didn't die from it. In fact, maybe they felt a little better than before.

More positive change that came out of RaceFail: fans of color began daring to blog their experiences and their feelings about systemic racism in fantasy and science fiction (both in the literature and in the community) because they realized there was some backup. Fans of all stripes—and by that I mean "white people, too"—began challenging one another to read books by people of color and review and discuss them, and they are by heaven doing it. Can I just say that I love me some fandom? Fandom is not exempt from the kind of wrongheadedness that humans display every day. But when fans conspire to do a good thing, it is most well done indeed, with verve and enthusiasm.

The white fantasy and SF community has a culture of arrogance and entitlement that is infuriating. It became clear last year just how patronizing some of you could be, just how little you trusted us to have any insight into our own experience, an experience about which many of you are proud to say that you're blind. If I'd ask one thing of you, it'd be to demonstrate your own impulses to equity and fairness—I know they're there—by beginning from the assumption that people of color probably know whereof we speak on issues of race and racism.

It also became clear that many of the white people who are able to make that collegial leap of equality and respect are so mired in guilt and trying to take the fall for the rest of you that they are somewhat paralysed. That doesn't help either, and I'm not sure what the solution is. I think you could stand to talk amongst yourselves about that one.

One of the things I really wanted to say from this podium: people of color in this community, I love allyou. I love allyou can't done. I love how you stepped up to the plate in this past year; I kept feeling that love even when rage led to regrettable actions from some of you. I love how you looked out for each other; I love how you got energized. It's bloody terrifying to be up on this podium right now, but you give me the courage to keep going, and for that, I thank you. When RaceFail first began to happen, I was dismayed. I didn't think the Internet with its trolls and incendiaries was the place to have the discussion. I was wrong. Tempest Bradford, I was wrong, and I love you for holding strong, for keeping your sense of humor, and for speaking hard truths while being honest with and generous to pretty much everyone (by "everyone" I mean, "white folks, too").

There are so many names to be named of people who did the right thing through all this. I cannot name them all. Because I'll tell you, people, I tired. Oonuh, I tired to rass. I get seen as one of the go-to people when it comes to race in this community. I spent most of the last two years homeless and couch-surfing with my partner, recovering from illness and fighting a still ongoing struggle to get enough to eat from day to day. I simply didn't have the energy to take RaceFail on the way I wanted to. And when I began to hear from some of the more arrogantly obstructive white people in the community who were all of a sudden being friendly to me without acknowledging their actions and the reasons for their overtures, I saw red. Allyou think I just come off the banana boat or what? That is one of the oldest tricks in the book, and my mother didn't raise no stupid children. I am not your tame negress. I mean, I know I'm published by a mainstream house and have achieved some recognition. I know I'm in the house, people. But house negroes get a bad rap for being inherently complicit with Massa. There were and are freedom fighters among them, too. I know that a large part of the reason I'm up here has to do with the brave actions of people on the inside, of all colors, at the IAFA. And I thank you all profusely for it.

By the way, to the people in the community who have coined and are using the term "failfandom" to mock people of color who dare to call you on your racism, that's using derision, minimizing, and discrediting as tactics of suppressing dissent. And we see you coming a mile away.

Sure I'm angry. I also love this community and this genre to pieces. This literature and some of the people in this community have kept me alive; in these past four years, some-times literally so. That's why, as much as I can, I keep fighting for and with the community to be the best it can be, to live up to its own visions of worlds in which no one is shut out. I'm very, very happy to be here, and happy to have been offered a podium from which to talk to this group of people on this topic. Any space created in this community for people of color, and any space we can make for ourselves makes it possible for more of us to find it easier to be ourselves, to speak up; makes it easier to write, or possible to write at all. That is true when we do it for any disenfranchized group of people within the larger fantasy and science fiction community: women, disabled people, queer people, poor and working class people, chronically ill people, old people. I'd lay odds that everyone in this room experiences at least one of those disenfranchizements. Making room makes room for all of us. It makes the possibility for even more great writing in a field where we are already blessed with so much of it. How wonderful would that be? And come right down to it, the writing is why we are all here, nah true?

Afterword

A postscript, if I may; a few minutes after I gave this address, an audience member approached me privately and asked whether I was a Marxist. Surprised I asked him why he thought I might be. He said it was because I had "reduced" the lofty subject of art to a mere question of labor. (Paraphrasing mine.)

To him I'd like to say, Mister, I am an artist who supports herself on the strength of her art and her ability to keep producing it. You'd be hard put to convince any artist that art isn't work. And you can't convince me that there's no art to labor. You can't convince me that art and the labor that creates it can be easily teased apart and considered as separate objects, and you sure as hell can't convince me that the latter is somehow base and impoverished in comparison to the former.

And how sad is it that you apparently managed to ignore the main gist of my speech so profoundly that all you got from it were the few paragraphs I used to contextualize a much larger discussion of how fantasy and science fiction approach race?

Notes

1. By "(active) science fiction community" I mean the people who attend and organize science fiction and fantasy conventions, who identify as science fiction/fantasy fans, and who are conversant and current with much of the body of science fiction/fantasy literature, a genre of storytelling that can be found in text-based, time-based (films, television, etc.) and visual media.
2. You'll notice that my "we" shifts according to context. In other words, when I say "we," I don't always mean the same group of people. Think Venn diagram.
3. I'm not asking people to do anything I haven't done. I've wronged and probably will wrong enough people in my time that I've had ample opportunity to put myself through the process of apology, addressing/redressing and hopefully reconciliation. I know in my bones how badly it grates. But I also know that it works, and that the subsequent healing soothes away the grating feeling.
4. See Rydra Wong's LiveJournal blog at http://rydra-wong.live-journal.com/146697.html.
5. Papa Legba, ouvre baye pou mwen, Ago eh! In African-derived religions of the Caribbean, the "horse" is a believer who, during a ceremony of worship, voluntarily consents to being

temporarily inhabited by one of the deities. The worshipper then exhibits characteristics specific to that deity (sometimes in defiance of their own physical capabilities when not in trance state), and is said to have the deity riding on their head.

6. A video recording of the 2009 speech is available at the following address, courtesy of artist/writer David Findlay: http://nalo hopkinson.com/2010/05/30/reluctant_ambassador_planet_midnight.html.

7. Tip o' the nib to Sally Klages.

8. Tip o' the nib to Winnie the Pooh and to A.A. Milne.

36

Future histories and cyborg labor: Reading borderlands science fiction after NAFTA

Lysa Rivera

For decades, writers of the US/Mexico borderlands have mined the icons and language of science fiction to articulate experiences not only of alienation, displacement, and marginalization but also those of survival, resistance, and resilience.[1] During the rise of the Chicano Movement [*el movimiento*] in 1967, Chicano agitprop playwright Luis Valdez cleverly used the symbol of the "drone" to examine and mock Chicano/a stereotypes in California in his stage act *(acto)* "Los Vendidos" [The Sellouts]. In Oscar Zeta Acosta's hallucinatory self-portrait, *Autobiography of a Brown Buffalo* (1971), the brilliantly cynical "Oscar" aspires to write science fiction in a sudden fit of artistic rebellion during a creative-writing seminar. The post-*movimiento* 1990s saw a far more pronounced interest in science fiction—more specifically, the subgenre cyberpunk—in Chicano art and literature. Visual and performance artists Guillermo Gómez-Peña, Roberto Sifuentes, and Rubén Ortiz Torres, for instance, militated against anti-immigration racism in the Southland area by creating sf narratives of resistance and parody. Whereas Gomez-Peña's "ethno-cyborgs" dramatized the ways in which mass-media technologies simultaneously criminalize and police brown bodies (see *Dangerous* 45-57, 246-60), Ortiz Torres's 1997 video installation *Alien Toy* spliced Hollywood images of alien encounters with footage of alleged UFO sightings around the US/Mexico border to comment on the "bizarre resonance of the official misnomer 'illegal alien'" and the various ways the phrase "physically and ideologically patrol[s] US national borders" (Chavoya 157). In literature, Alejandro Morales's *Rag Doll Plagues* (1991) and Ernest Hogan's *High-Aztech* (1992)—both uncannily similar to Neal Stephenson's *Snow Crash* (1992)—depart from their Anglo counterparts by relocating the familiar cyberpunk cityscape to south of the border.

Chicana feminists Gloria Anzaldúa and Chela Sandoval have turned to science fiction as well to theorize Chicano/a subjectivity in the postmodern era. Whereas Anzaldúa describes *mestiza* subjectivity as "'alien' consciousness" that speaks to an otherworldly experience beyond the "confines of the 'normal'" (25), Sandoval argues that "colonized peoples of the Americas" possess a type of "cyborg consciousness," an oppositional consciousness that "can provide the guides for survival and resistance under First World transnational cultural conditions" (375). These examples point to the existence of an under-examined history of Chicano/a cultural practice that employs science-fictional metaphors to render experiences of marginalization visible and to imagine alternative scenarios that are at once critically informed and imaginative. They speak to what Catherine Ramirez has called the "concept of Chicanafuturism," a cultural practice that "questions the promises of science, technology, and humanism for Chicanas, Chicanos, and other people of color" and "reflects colonial and postcolonial histories of *indigenismo, mestizaje,* hegemony, and survival" in the Americas (187). Chicanafuturism has become so pervasive that John Morán González, in his forecast of "Chican@ literary studies" in the "next fifty years," has predicted that Chicano/a writers will continue to turn to science fiction to articulate their political and social concerns and to "outline the increasingly complicated relationship of Chican@s with digital technologies, corporate globalization, and the future of cyborg labor" (176).[2]

This essay wishes to extend these conversations by putting Chicano/a science fiction produced north of the border in conversation with science fiction from the other side [*el otro lado*]. Specifically, I look at Mexican writer Guillermo Lavín's short-story "Reaching the Shore" (1994), the sf films of US filmmaker Alex Rivera, and Rosaura Sanchez and Beatrice Pita's Chicanafuturistic novel *Lunar Braceros* (2009). Analyzing these texts together invites a transnational reading of science fiction from a specific geopolitical region (the US/Mexico border) and during a particular moment in contemporary history (the era of multinational capitalism). All three borderlands sf texts not only offer critical visions of globalization both today and in the near future but also insist on reading late capitalism as a troubling and enduring extension of colonial relations of power between the United States and Mexico.[3] In so doing, they speak to Masao Miyoshi's insistence that the new millennium is not an age of "*post*colonialism, but of intensified colonialism, even though it is under an unfamiliar guise" (734; emphasis in original)—that guise being, above all, neoliberal economic hegemony.

Borrowing from David Harvey, I understand neoliberal economic hegemony to refer to specific social and economic conditions, including "the commodification and privatization of land" and labor power, "the suppression of alternative (indigenous) forms of production and consumption," and "neocolonial and imperial processes of appropriation of assets (including natural resources)," all in the service of multinational corporate capitalism (159). Since the passage of the North American Free Trade Agreement (NAFTA), borderlands writers and visual artists have increasingly turned to the metaphors and motifs of science fiction to articulate concerns over the problems of the so-called "Fourth World," which ostensibly declares the utopian elimination of national borders but actually promotes the "multiplication of frontiers and the smashing apart of nations" and indigenous communities (Hayden 280). More specifically, these writers and artists enlist the dystopian motifs and sentiments of cyberpunk, a subgenre of sf that emerged in the 1980s as a speculative response to late capitalism and information technologies, to militate against global capitalism's starvation of the indigenous to fatten the capitalists, thereby suggesting a timely reconsideration of the subgenre's hallmark ethos to "live fast, die young, and leave a highly augmented corpse" (Foster xiv).

Speculative or not, borderlands labor narratives are always tales of migration and movement, departures and arrivals, of reaching and sometimes crossing the river's shore. Works such as Tómas Rivera's . . . And the Earth Did Not Devour Him (1971), Ernesto Galarza's Barrio Boy (1971), and Helena Marìa Viramontes's Under the Feet of Jesus (1996) wrestle with the physical and psychological experiences of displacement that attend the itinerant and often unstable lives of migrants whose labor makes possible the affordability of bourgeois US consumerism. Yet within these narratives, "movement" also signifies the process of collective engagement in social and political issues that have been central to shaping a distinct borderlands literary history. The emergence of borderlands narratives are, then, the formal result of very specific political and historical conditions: the annexation of northern Mexico, the subsequent and steady industrializ- ation of the borderlands, and within that, the creation of a vast working class, now the "long-suffering 'disposables' of neoliberalism" (Hayden 271). Ramon Saldívar's pion- eering work on Chicano narrative offers important insight into the relationship between borderlands history and Chicano/a literature specifically: "History," he argues, "cannot be conceived as the mere 'background' or 'context' for [Chicano] literature; rather, history turns out to be the decisive determinant of the form" itself (6). Just as the US annexation of northern Mexico in 1848 gave rise to a borderlands vernacular (the border ballad, specifically), so have contemporary neoliberal hegemonic conditions after NAFTA given rise to an increase in borderlands science fiction—which, as I will show, repeatedly interrogates iniquitous labor practices (as we will see, a type of "cyborg labor," to recall González) in this economically depressed region. Post-NAFTA borderlands science fiction, in other words, is the formal articulation of a specific historical narrative: namely the history of US/Mexico capitalist labor relations in the region and militant fights for an alternative framework.

Representatives of cultural communities not normally associated with this First World genre, borderlands sf writers defamiliarize borderlands topographies, both social and political, to provoke a prolonged and deeper consideration of the devastating human and environmental tolls of neoliberal economic hegemony, the communications techno- logies that accelerate it, and the impoverished border communities that are forced to live under its so-called invisible hands. In doing so, they demonstrate Carl Freedman's point, building on Darko Suvin, that "science fiction is determined by the dialectic between estrangement and cognition" (16). Here, "estrangement" refers to the construction of an "alternative fictional world that, by refusing to take our mundane environment for gran- ted, implicitly or explicitly performs an estranging critical interrogation of the latter" (17; emphasis in original). The critical edge of the genre is made possible by the process of cognition, which "enables the science-fictional text to account rationally for its imagined world and for the connections as well as the disconnections of the latter to our own empirical world" (17). By inviting readers to rationalize the eerily familiar futures confronting them, science fiction thus raises an incisive question: *what have we as a society done to get here*? What in our collective history and our current historical moment has caused this strange, troubling, and uncannily familiar future to take shape? Readers of borderlands science fiction confront not only near and distant futures, but also how the histories of US/Mexico colonial and neo-colonial relations of power have provided and continue to provide the material conditions for this future.

Particularly relevant to borderlands science fiction is the concept of the "future history," a phrase John W. Campbell, Jr. used to describe elaborately constructed temporal universes. Future history enables sf writers to situate their imaginary futures somewhere along a projected historical time line, one that often begins during or shortly after their real-life historical moment and extends into the future. More generally (that is, beyond Heinlein), the phrase "future history" is most meaningfully applied to texts "in which the processes of historical change are as important as the characters' stories" themselves (Sawyer 491). The telling of history has, in fact, been central to the development of a distinct Chicano/a literary tradition, which is itself the direct result of shared historical, social, and economic conditions specific to Chicano/a lived experiences (Saldívar 6; McKenna 10). What most interests me in this essay, then, is the possibility for social and political critique at the intersection of science fiction and borderlands fiction—the latter encompassing both Chicana/a border narratives *as well as* sf from northern Mexican [*fronterizo*] writers. Although nationally distinct, these authors speak for a shared psychic terrain: the US/Mexico borderlands, where the "Third World grates against the first and bleeds" (Anzaldúa 25). In all three texts, the "future" represents not so much a site of progress and humanistic harmony as a return to the colonial past. Without alternatives, these futures promise to repeat the worst of colonial histories along the US/Mexico border.

For an example of *fronterizo* sf that immediately responded to the success of NAFTA in 1994, one need look no further than Mexican writer Guillermo Lavín's 1994 short story "Reaching the Shore" [*Llegar a la orilla*], which originally appeared in *Frontera de espejos rotos* [Border of Broken Mirrors], an anthology of sf stories that diversely interrogate the "uncertain economy" of millennial capitalism along the US/Mexico border (Schwarz and Webb ii). With contributions from both US and Mexican sf writers, *Frontera de espejos rotos* literally offers a transnational sampling of borderlands science fiction. In their introduction, entitled "La búsqueda de un espejo fiel" [The Search for a Faithful Mirror], the editors—Don Webb of the US and Mauricio-José Schwarz of Mexico—frame the anthology as offering two perspectives on the same geopolitical terrain in order to give readers a more authentic and complete image of this politically volatile and complicated region. That the two editors never met in person but instead collaborated by email to complete the project suggests that its very production appropriates the information technologies and transnational social relations imagined in the stories themselves. The metaphor in the title is fitting as it underscores the optical rhetoric of a border aesthetic, which is marked by a type of "double vision" that is the result of "perceiving reality through two different interference patterns" (Hicks xxii). In this way, the border text is structurally similar to the holographic image, with both optics reflecting the collision of two "referential codes," namely the juxtaposed cultural matrices of the United States and Mexico (Hicks xxiv).

"Reaching the Shore" takes place in Reynosa, a border city in the Northern Mexican state of Tamaulipas. Like the sprawling "hyperborder" cities of Tijuana and Juárez, Reynosa has experienced relentless urbanization and offers hospitable (cheap and deregulated) real estate for hundreds of *maquiladoras*—large foreign-owned assembly factories that absorb indigenous labor from the nation's interior (see Romero 223). The story centers on eleven-year-old José Paul and his father Fragoso, the latter a middle-aged *maquiladora* worker who is literally working himself to death. The story begins on the "special afternoon" of Christmas Eve and narrates José Paul's desire for a new modern bicycle, clearly a symbol for social mobility: "with it he could journey far beyond the Rio Bravo" to the other, more economically prosperous side of the border (Lavín 234). It is not insignificant that the story takes place on Christmas Eve, a holiday characterized, especially in the United States, by mass consumption of commodities often manufactured on foreign soil.[4]

Although the story is set in the near future, it is steeped in labor history familiar to the US/Mexico borderlands. Its clear denunciation of Northern capitalism is even reminiscent of earlier American proletarian fiction that sought "to define and coalesce an oppositional group within the political and economic realm of American capitalism" (Schocket 65). This is most evident in the story's first sentence, which describes a *maquiladora* whistle "split[ting] the air exactly fifteen minutes before six p.m." (224). The whistle, likened to an authoritative "order from the team captain," spreads through the city "to tell some of the workers that their shift had ended" (224). Preceding any mention of humans in the story, the whistle becomes a metonym for US capitalism and its subordination of the human worker to the mechanical demands of the factory. Here, the living cogs-in-a-machine are all but dehumanized and the ominous factories personified. The shrill of the whistle literally confines and controls the daily lives of the *maquiladora* workers, whose shifts are compared to a "long jail sentence" (225). It echoes earlier proletarian literature from the borderlands, most notably Américo Paredes's "The Hammon and the Beans" (wr. 1939, pub. 1963) and Rudolfo Anaya's *Heart of Aztlán* (1976).[5] Both narratives were written during times of Chicano/a political dissent, Paredes's during the "Mexican American Era," when Mexican Americans began to interact heavily with the CPUSA (Communist Party of the United States) to address migrant labor exploitation, and Anaya's—whose protagonist Clémente Chavez is a thinly veiled reference to labor activist Cesar Chavez—at the end of the Chicano Movement itself. In both narratives, a whistle symbolizes US economic dominance over a racially subordinated working-class population. Paredes likens the whistle to authoritative power, "like some insistent elder person who was always there to tell you it was time [to work]" ("Hammon" 172). Similarly, the "shrill blast" of the Barelas *barrio* whistle in *Heart of Aztlán* not only signals looming

disaster but also dictates and structures the everyday lives of the *barrio* inhabitants
(25). Itself a type of whistle-blowing critique of NAFTA, Lavín's story, although set in an
imaginary future, echoes a long trajectory of labor history and the anticapitalist borderlands literature that has militated against that history. His future history is clear: this is
a story not only about the future of labor practices in a hyper-urbanized border city,
Reynosa; it is also a story about the deep colonial relations that have led—and continue
to lead—to this grim future.

Published in 1994, immediately following the ratification of NAFTA, the story's critical
target would have resonated in the minds of those who opposed the trade agreement and
understood it to be a rhetorical euphemism for what is essentially a new manifestation of
colonialism (to many, "neocolonialism") and the systemic exploitation of a vulnerable indigenous Mexican population. On the eve of NAFTA's signing, Mexican journalist Carlos
Monsiváis criticized the utopian stance of the PRI (Mexico's Institutional Revolutionary
Party), exemplified by Octavio Paz's reference to NAFTA as "a chance finally for [Mexico]
to be modern" (Fox 19). In his critique, Monsiváis argued that NAFTA proponents such
as Paz demonstrate too much optimism in the agreement and take "as a given that
the single act of the signature liquidates centuries of backwardness and scarcity" (20).
Monsiváis's articles spoke in fact for an overwhelming number of Mexicans—including
students, progressives, and independent farmers [*campesinos*]—who believed the
agreement promised neither progress nor economic harmony, but rather a new class
of dependent, underpaid workers for foreign-owned factories and agricultural corporations. Critics of the agreement foresaw what it eventually would become: a renewed
form of transnational capitalism that is realized in the exploitation and administration of
workers and consumers through a worldwide division of labor. As one character put it in
describing an "economic bloc" to young José, free trade is, in Mexico, "the cause of all
problems" (Lavín 227).

Lavín's laboring body is a cyborg body, the quintessential posthuman hybrid produced
at the intersection of technology and humanity. His cyborg, however, functions metaphorically to symbolize not only the dehumanization involved in turning a man into a
stoop laborer—a being into a *bracero*; it also comments on the invisibility of Mexican
or indigenous labor in this region, a topic I will elaborate upon in greater detail below.
Tracing the function of the cyborg body throughout the story reveals why this particular metaphor is so useful in articulating opposition to the impact of Northern economic
(and technological) hegemony on indigenous Mexicans. The transnational corporation
for which Fragoso works, a US "leisure company," mass produces a virtual-reality implant
device known as the "Dreamer," which Lavín describes as a "personalized bioconnecter"
that attaches to the base of the cranium and provides virtual fantasies of consumption
and recreation (229). The Dreamer, "the most modern and sophisticated North American
technology ever," affirms the lure of the modern, which Mexican pro-NAFTA rhetorical
campaigns often promised its skeptics. As someone fatally "hooked" on the idea of
"progress," Fragoso economically and physically depends on the Dreamer, which is

slowly destroying him and the *fronterizos* among whom he lives (227). Having taken on the role of a corporate guinea pig by volunteering to use his own body to test the quality of each computer chip, Fragoso, now a cyborg, certainly evokes a dehumanized image of the *maquiladora* laborer (227). Lavín here ascribes a critical valence to the cyborg meta-phor through two different uses of the idea of dependence: Fragoso is both addicted *and* attached to the computer chip, now clearly a symbol of US consumerism. We can read this cyborg body through two conceptual frames. First, the fact that the chip itself becomes a part of Fragoso's body by "attaching" to the base of his brain comments on the idea that *maquiladora* workers' bodies are mechanized, mere object-bodies that are almost one with the machines they financially depend upon and produce. Fragoso is also fatally *addicted* to the Dreamer and by extension the illusion of the American Dream. By attributing Fragoso's fatal addiction to a US consumer commodity, Lavín suggests that the narcotic epidemic in the borderlands region is symptomatic of the presence and influence of US neoliberal economic dominance and not some savage Mexican predis-position to drugs and crime.

Through Fragoso, Lavín recasts the futuristic cyborg as a colonized subject, one whose labor is extracted by US capitalism at the expense of Fragoso's very humanity. Lavín's colonized cyborg clearly departs from Donna Haraway's more utopian vision of the cyborg as that which can subvert the "informatics of domination," a new form of power that I read as decentralized transnational capitalism that has replaced "the comfortable old hierarchical dominations" under colonialism ("Cyborg Manifesto" 161). So problem-atic was Haraway's sweeping claim that we are all cyborgs that even she would revise it by being "more careful to point out that [cyborgs] are subject positions for people in certain regions of transnational systems of production" ("Cyborgs at Large" 12-13). One such region, I argue, is the hyper-urbanized border city of the late-twentieth century, where the imperatives of multinational capitalism and globalization have produced a new mechanized labor force that, vast as it is, remains largely invisible to the consumers who benefit most from its production. Though it might begin as science fiction, cyborg labor becomes—in the borderlands narrative—nothing more than a politically-charged symbol for real-life labor practices under late capitalism.

Lavín's Dreamer invokes present-day technologies of visual media and marketing, technologies that in fact pervade the rest of the story. As its name suggests, the machine is a virtual product of empire, facilitating private fantasies of consumption, dreams that in this case involve being able to escape the material conditions of factory life. Because it offers merely the illusion of actual product consumption, however, the Dreamer under-scores Fragoso's curious position of being both within and yet alienated from the global market. Uncritical notions of hybridity and borderland third-space identities are absent in Lavín's border narrative. In their place is an image of the borderlands as a site of proliferated borders and rigid socioeconomic hierarchies. Lavín's representation of the borderlands is one in which the colonial relations of power materialize in the very objects of this new consumer-society as they (the objects) reinforce national differences (US exports vs. "shitty imports"). Through this juxtaposition, Lavín is able to comment on the paradoxical coexistence of free-trade border porosity and the rigid maintenance of national boundaries within the borderlands communities themselves.[6]

"Reaching the Shore" clearly offers a timely critique of present-day capitalist hegemony in the era of free trade.[7] Yet although it cautiously peers into the future. it is deeply invested in re-telling the colonial history of the borderlands region as well. Early in the story, for instance, Lavín references Juan Cortina, the nineteenth-century Mexican rebel from Tamaulipas who led two influential raids against the Texas Rangers in 1859-61. An icon of the underclass along the Rio Grande, Cortina symbolized the revolutionary spirit of indigenous *fronterizos* by defending the land rights of the Mexican Texans (*tejanas*) after the annexation of Mexico in 1848. When Fragoso and other workers enter a "semi-deserted bar" just outside of the factory grounds,

> The cashier pointed a remote control at the wall and the sounds of the big-screen TV filled the air. The men turned toward it and protested with jeers, shouts, and threats, until the cashier changed the channel; they told him they were tired of watching Christmas movies . . . so the racket continued while the screen skipped from channel to channel. Judith's face and voice flooded the place with the ballad of Juan Cortina. (226)

Within the borderlands, this particular ballad (*corrido*) has been, and to some extent continues to be, the voice of indigenous strength and opposition. Conventionally a genre in which community is valued over individuality, the *corrido* evolves around what Americo Paredes calls "a Border man" who heroically confronts Anglo dominance (*With His Pistol* 34). Lavín's reference to "The Ballad of Juan Cortina" is thus historically significant: the "earliest Border *corrido* hero" known (Paredes, *With His Pistol* 140), Juan Cortina haunts the site of the *maquiladora,* suggesting a temporal collapse of the neocolonial present and the colonial past.

Merging nineteenth-century borderlands history with the twenty-first-century *maquiladora* industry, the latter functioning as "the heart of globalization's gulag" (Brennan 338), Lavín underscores the point that contemporary forms of dominance in the borderlands are in reality logical extensions of colonial domination and exploitation. In other words, although the narrative is set in the near future, its scope is decidedly historical as it retells the history of the "consumer-oriented economic order" that has dominated the political, cultural, and economic landscape of the borderlands region since the late nineteenth century (McCrossen 24). New transportation and information technologies, combined with a dramatic increase in foreign capitalist investment, transformed what once had been a land of scarcity into a "land of necessity," where the manufacturing of dreams and new consumer "needs" precedes the actual surplus production of goods, turning the once arid terrain into a space ripe for rabid consumption and cheap labor production. For Lavín, the narrative of neoliberal hegemonic control of the borderlands' natural and human environment is not limited to developments in the late-twentieth century. It stands instead as part of a deeper historical continuum and longstanding colonial relations between the north and south that Lavín's futuristic narrative both retells and contests by imagining new forms of "cyborg labor" that seem ominously doomed to repeat history without sustained political intervention (González 176).

The conflation of history and the future is perhaps most readily apparent in Lavín's treatment of geography and landscape. The built and natural environments of Reynosa belie a community that has been thoroughly devastated by rapid urbanization and the encroachment of foreign investment. This is the condition of the borderlands' "horizontal city," which Fernando Romero describes as a city that sprawls "outward" and is "engulfed by slums due to rapid rural-to-urban migration" (271). Yet this horizontal urban sprawl also comes with tremendous depth—namely, the lost and buried histories of colonial rule and exploitation that perpetually haunt Lavín's near future, which is also the reader's defamiliarized present. This future city's "once magnificent" river—the Rio Bravo that borders the US and Mexico—now looks more "like a dinosaur skeleton," barely alive with all of its flesh "deserted" (Lavín 228). The built city, at one time a living, thriving organism, is now a "scarred" city, one resembling, curiously, a "zigzag of arteries" (228). The built and natural borderlands landscape demands to be read as both futuristic and historical. Though depicted in the future, the landscape perpetually signifies a "once magnificent" past that, although extinct like a "dinosaur," remains present in the minds of the *fronterizos*. Recalling Anzaldúa's description of the border as an "open wound" [*una herida abierta*], Lavín returns readers to what Norma Klahn calls "the scene of the crime," the seat of colonial violence along the US/Mexico border, which in turn reinscribes the colonized territory as the site of past, present, and potentially future conflicts (119).

Three short years after the passage of NAFTA, US filmmaker Alex Rivera would continue to interrogate the dehumanizing effects of "cyborg labor" by recasting the issue in yet another science-fictionalized scenario. In his short film *Why Cybraceros?* (1997), Rivera splices archival footage from a 1940s promotional video produced by the California Grower's Association to endorse the guest-worker Bracero Program (1942-64), into a short science-fiction film called *Why Cybraceros?* Like the original (*Why Braceros?*), this fictional and speculative promotional video extols the value and convenience of cheap, disembodied Mexican labor. The term "cybraceros" refers to a *bracero* whose manual labor takes place in cyberspace, providing the US employer with efficient—and, more importantly, invisible—Mexican labor. As the eerily cheerful female voice narrating the video explains:

> Under the Cybracero program, American farm labor will be accomplished on American soil, but no Mexican workers will need to leave Mexico. Only the labor of Mexicans will cross the border; Mexican workers will no longer have to. Sound impossible? Using high speed internet connections. . ., American farms and Mexican laborers will be directly connected. These workers will then be able to remotely control robotic farm workers, known as Cybraceros, from their village in Mexico. . . . To the worker it's as simple as point and click to pick. For the American farmer, it's all the labor without the worker. . . . In Spanish, Cybracero means a worker who operates a computer with his arms and hands.

But in American lingo, Cybracero means a worker who poses no threat of becoming a citizen. And that means quality products at low financial and social costs to you, the American consumer.

Rivera uses the cyborg metaphor to riff on the historical figure of the *bracero,* described by Ernesto Galarza in the 1960s as "the prototype of the production man of the future," an "indentured alien" who represents "an almost perfect model of the economic man, an 'input factor' stripped of the political and social attributes that liberal democracy likes to ascribe to all human beings ideally" (16). In other words, drawing from science-fictional metaphors and images of cyborgs and cyberspace, Rivera is able to comment on the ways in which "real" labor practices in the US/Mexico borderlands region are quite literally exercises in dehumanization and exploitation. The word "cybraceros" alone signals the future of borderlands labor as a type of "cyborg labor" (dehumanized and invisible), as well as the history of migrant labor along the border, specifically the midcentury practices, that initiated the rapid industrialization of the borderlands.

Rivera elaborated his *cybracero* metaphor in his debut feature-length film, *Sleep Dealer* (2008), a cyberpunk dystopia that projects life in the urban US/Mexico borderlands into a nightmarish near future where most of Mexico's indigenous population, once in control of over 80% of the nation's natural resources, lives in abject poverty. Like Lavin, Rivera privileges a Northern Mexican site of production. More specifically, it is set in the sprawl-ing border metropolis of Tijuana, which the film posits as the "City of the Future" but which is also a defamiliarized version of contemporary conditions plaguing this and other hyper-industrialized urban zones in Northern Mexico. *Sleep Dealer* centers on Memo, a young Mexican from the rural interior (Santa Ana, a small town) who harbors dreams of migrating to the city in the north (Tijuana), where he believes an egalitarian global society awaits. Unlike his brother and father, who are rooted to their family's land, Memo thinks of Santa Ana as "a trap," from which he must (and eventually will) escape. He spends most of the first fifteen minutes of the film alone in his room tinkering with old radios and receivers in an attempt to make contact with those living in Tijuana, the city to the North that seems initially to promise freedom, progress, and prosperity. The portion of the film set in Santa Ana ends with the murder of Memo's father, who is accidentally mistaken for an "aqua-terrorist"—an eco-activist of the future, so to speak.

After his father's murder, Memo migrates north in search of work to support his strug-gling family, whose *milpa* (small, locally-owned farm) is no longer able to compete with the large agribusinesses that now run the Mexican trade economy. Memo quickly finds employment with Cybertek, one of the many "virtual reality sweatshops" that populate Tijuana (and, presumably, all of the Northern metropolises in Mexico). Cybertek is owned and operated by an anonymous (and ominous) multinational corporation that absorbs thousands of expendable Mexican laborers from the nation's rural interior. These virtual *maquiladoras* are nicknamed "sleep factories" by the workers because the physical work is so taxing that it eventually leads to blindness and, in some cases, death. To become a cybracero, Memo has several "nodes" surgically implanted into his body, an act that

Rivera humorously refers to as "node jobs" early in the film, thus drawing a haunting metaphorical parallel between the laboring body and the body exploited for sexual pleasure (sex trafficking comes to mind). These nodes enable Memo to reroute his physical movements to robots on the other side of the border. With his nodes, Memo can "connect [his] nervous system to the other system, the global economy," a direct reference to the film's larger political context: multinational capitalism's presence in the everyday lives of *fronterizo* workers whose very livelihood is problematically reliant upon—yet alienated by—the new global (multinational) economy.

It is not long before Memo realizes that the so-called city of the future is really nothing more than a throwback to the colonial past. It is, in other words, less a space of opportunity and innovation than it is an abject contact zone replete with vastly disparate racial and economic hierarchies, tensions, and unrest. Memo's dreams of progress and futurity—symbolized by his love of technology earlier in the film—come to a startling halt as he realizes that the "future" he imagines is not only economically and geographically inaccessible (the physical border is a highly militarized zone in the film), but problematically made possible by a dying indigenous working class—by people like his father. Motivated by the murder of his father, and by the social injustices that confront him daily, Memo decides to remain in the city and join forces with Luz, a politically progressive cyber-writer who also uses "nodes" to connect to virtual space, but does so solely for the purposes of exposing the injustices visited upon the vanishing indigenous Mexican communities. Essentially using cyberspace for political activism, Luz and Memo appropriate the very information technologies of the *maquiladoras* by rerouting their purpose, in order to militate against neoliberal economic hegemony and labor exploitation in the borderlands. They fight for the land rights of the indigenous *campesinos* who suffer most under globalization. The two activists confront the future by honoring those who came before them, represented by Memo's late father, those whose egalitarian land practices they desire to recover. As Memo puts it in the closing scene of the film, they choose to "fight for a future with a *past."* Here, once again, borderlands science fiction works to collapse the colonial past with the neoliberal present and, in Rivera's case, explicitly calls for a future modeled upon a history that has all but vanished under the demands of late capitalism.

The laborer who functions as nothing more than a cog in a machine, and whose laboring body remains invisible to those who benefit most from it, is a cyborg laborer who helps to ensure the order of things in the imaginary new world economy. So says the excellent film *Sleep Dealer.* One particular screenshot from the film speaks to this reading of the cyborg in *Sleep Dealer.* Captured from a scene in which viewers are finally taken inside one of Cybertek's factories, the image depicts a dark-skinned female "cybracero" fully equipped with the high-tech nodes that connect her labor to the global economic system (see Figure 36.1).

Recalling Fragoso's cyborg body, the image conveys an equally scathing critique of US consumerism's demand for invisible—and therefore easily disposable—forms of

This is the American Dream.

Figure 36.1 "Cybracero" from *Sleep Dealer* (Copyright permission courtesy of Alex Rivera)

intense physical labor. Moreover, Memo's voice-over narration injects a healthy dose of irony and cynicism by referring to cyborg labor as "the American Dream," prompting us to acknowledge the invisible (because disembodied) labor that makes consumerism afford-able for the American middle class: physical and embodied, but all the while invisible, indigenous labor. This is what cyborg labor looks like, and Rivera does not shy away from implicating US consumerism in helping to create and sustain it.

As we saw in Lavín's future history, Rivera's *Sleep Dealer* invites spectators to appre-hend and understand the future through their own colonial past: they are encouraged to decode this near-future dystopian scenario through the framework of a longstand-ing history of power struggles between northern capital and indigenous resistance to that power from within the US/Mexico borderlands region. Just as the nineteenth-century revolutionary spirit of Juan Cortina haunted Lavín's future dystopia, so too does Rivera weave suppressed colonial histories into his own dystopian borderlands narrative. This temporal interplay is especially pronounced in the film's depiction of the "Mayan Army of Water Liberation," a paramilitary band of eco-activists who represent the film's coun-ter-narrative to capitalist hegemony in the borderlands. In one telling moment, Rivera establishes an allusion to the 1994 EZLN uprisings that occurred in direct response to NAFTA (see Figure 36.2).[8]

Viewers of this image would be unable to interpret its iconic power without mentally referencing the 1994 EZLN anti-NAFTA uprisings. In an instant, then, Rivera is able to signify a futuristic image and a historical referent, commenting once again on the ways in which post-NAFTA borderlands dystopias are a type of "future history" that forces readers/spectators to read the future through the historical presence of the colonial past. Moreover, Rivera's reference to the EZLN gestures towards the possibility for coun-ter-discourse and indigenous resistance. Just as Rivera's film itself repurposes cinematic technologies to voice concerns over imperial power, so too did the EZLN—and the EMLA for that matter—appropriate new technologies (the internet communiqués) to do what so many classic dystopian characters have done. From Offred's secret cassette recordings

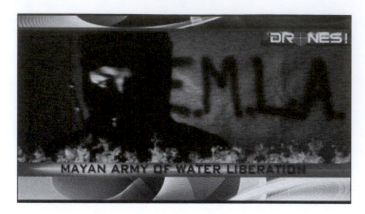

Figure 36.2 The EMLA as signifier for EZLN in *Sleep Dealer* (Copyright permission courtesy of Alex Rivera)

in Margaret Atwood's *The Handmaid's Tale* (1985) to Lauren Olamina's subversive Earthseed diaries in Octavia E. Butler's *Parable of the Sower* (1993), dystopian protagonists appropriate the oppressor's language (a veritable technology) to "recover the ability to draw on . . . alternative truths of the past and 'speak back' to hegemonic power" (Moylan 149).

Shortly after the release of *Sleep Dealer*, and perhaps influenced by the film, Chicana scholars Rosaura Sanchez and Beatrice Pita, along with visual artist Mario A. Chacon, published *Lunar Braceros: 2125-2148*, also set in the future (not necessarily near, but certainly not far) and centered on information technologies and fears of hegemonic global capitalism. *Lunar Braceros*—like Lavín's and Rivera's work before it—is also undeniably a border narrative. It too contains stories of migration, labor, and survival in the US/Mexico borderlands region. It too wrestles with issues related to indigenous labor and the white (or, more appropriately, Anglo) hegemonic power that extracts it. And it too insists on the importance of remembering colonial history in imagining the future. Put simply, *Lunar Braceros* imagines the future of labor exploitation along the borderlands while it simultaneously re-tells a deeper colonial history of the borderlands.

Narrated through a series of letters and emails, primarily between a mother (Lydia) and her son (Pedro), the novel centers on a small group of seven manual laborers—all people of color and primarily Chicano/a—who have been assigned grunt work on the moon. By the end of the twenty-first century, the moon has become an off-world landfill of sorts to store the Earth's surplus toxic waste, what Lydia tersely calls the "new spatial fix for capital" (59). Multinational corporations in high-tech, energy, and pharmaceutical industries developed these lunar sites to "stimulate capital investment," which in turn generated an ongoing need for techno-grunts, "low skill contract workers," including the "lowly lunar braceros" and "tecos" upon which the novel centers (15). Initially, the moon represents opportunity, a welcome respite from the drudgeries of twenty-first-century *barrio* life. Working under the assumption that their salaries would be wired back to Earth to help the struggling families they left behind, the crew of seven agree to a four-year lunar contract doing little more beyond manual (stoop) labor. As Lydia reasons to Pedro: "We could either be fucked up on Earth or fucked up on the Moon, and by that time, it didn't matter much. Same shit, different place" (19). Soon, the seven discover that the mining teams who arrived before them—whom, in fact, they were supposed to replace—were all summarily executed and their salaries never actually sent back to Earth. What ensues is a carefully planned escape back to Earth, where the seven "tecos" hope to work with the "World Human Rights Commission" to make "the massacre of miners and braceros . . . known to the world" (111). In ways similar to the borderlands labor narratives spotlighted above, the narrative trajectory of *Lunar Braceros* moves from acknowledgment (of labor exploitation) to resistance. It is a narrative of movement in both senses of the word: the movement of labor migration *and* the movement behind political activism.

As in so many cyberpunk near-future novels, traditional nation-states have given way to corporate hegemonic control. In fact, despite the novel's title, the majority of *Lunar Braceros* takes place on Earth and in "Cali-Texas," a "new nation state" that emerged in 2070 after "the end of the United States as it had been known till then" (11). Encompassing "the US, Canada and Mexico," all "autonomous regions but economically linked to and dependent on the hegemonic power" (12), it includes "several of the northern Mexican states" and "the former US Southwest states"—the borderlands projected into the future (6). Modern forms of state power have been replaced by transnational corporate power. The world is run by what Lydia calls the "New Imperial Order," a new form of global dominance that operates solely through multinational corporate and economic hegemony.[9] Made up of "ten dominant multinational consortia," the NIO, which was "pretty much calling all the shots," "controlled anything and everything that had to do with technology transfer, informatics and any kind of power generation, bio-fuel, nuclear or otherwise" (7, 23).

With its interest in information technologies and its critical assessment of multinational capitalism, *Lunar Braceros* adheres closely to the conventions of cyberpunk, but with one critical difference: the attention it places on *racialized* power and on labor practices in the near (dystopian) future. The vast majority of non-white US citizens live in what the novel refers to as "Reservations," public spaces created by the NIO to "keep the homeless and the unemployed off the streets" (13). As Lydia explains to Pedro, "the state created internal colonial sites" to contain and control a rapidly increasing "expendable, surplus population" (14). Once on "the Res," the multitude becomes little more than a "controlled laboratory labor force, like lab rats, a disciplinary society that was useful to the state" and that could be "used in a variety of areas as needed and determined by corporate interests managing the Reservations" (14-15). Sanchez and Pita here refer simultaneously to the colonial past (Native American conquest) while peering into and constructing what is essentially a neo-colonial future ("the Res").

In fact, as futuristic as the novel appears, it simply cannot be understood if extracted from its social and political contexts, specifically the historical practices of indigenous labor exploitation in the US/Mexico borderlands. As Lydia puts it, the lunar excavation sites "were turning out to be a recapitulation of Earth history" (59). They are even described as being modeled after "the ones they had carved out in the Arizona and Sonora desert" (6). To fully appreciate and understand the political critique at work in the novel, readers must thus be familiar with the history of US uranium extraction in the Arizona and Sonora deserts. Historical knowledge enables futuristic speculation as *Lunar Braceros*—like *Sleep Dealer* and "Reaching the Shore"—presents a "future with a past." Indeed, the very idea of a "lunar bracero" speaks simultaneously to the future of labor exploitation (lunar space travel) and the real histories of migrant labor under capitalism, specifically the Bracero Program initiated as part of the larger Border Industrialization Project in the mid-twentieth century.

Lunar Braceros is an enterprise in excavation on two different levels. First, the text's premise centers on mining and excavation expeditions on the moon. Second, and perhaps more interestingly, the text itself is a project in historical and cultural recovery as Lydia's letters and emails (and, by extension, Pita's and Sanchez's project) excavate borderlands histories, rendering the invisible hands of capitalism visible and available for criticism and scrutiny. Lydia is committed to cultural memory as she works against the government's project of "revising historical accounts not favorable to the Cali-Texas government" (38). By retelling her personal history to her son, a structure that constitutes the narrative trajectory of *Lunar Braceros*, Lydia provides "hope that one day what was being purged could be accessed and restored" (39). It is important to take into account, however, that this is a future that *must* remember the past—for the novel not only projects the timespan specified in the title (2125-2148), but, more crucially, the years leading up to that period (beginning with the year 2000). In other words, the majority of the novel is *about* its imaginary past: it is a *future history.* With topics ranging from developments in astronomy, physics, and, of course, transnational capitalism, Lydia's history lessons trace for her son Pedro not only the rise of global capitalist hegemony but also stories of resistance from the novel's past (our future). *Lunar Braceros*, although ostensibly set in the future, thus narrates centuries of colonial "history" (a future history, but a historical narrative nonetheless) while also commenting, quite explicitly, on the importance of historicizing more generally. As Lydia underscores in one of her diary entries about the importance of telling her story to her son (her history, that is): "Perhaps in the telling, in the writing, in the recollection of people, through memory, dialogues and scenes, it'll all make some sense to [Pedro], fragmented though it may be" (58).

With its trenchant critique of multinational capitalism and its attendant forms of labor and indigenous exploitation, borderlands science fiction produced after NAFTA represents, as I have suggested above, a critical incursion into classic cyberpunk, itself a politically charged sf subgenre that emerged in the 1980s, most notably with the publication of William Gibson's novel *Neuromancer* (1984), in direct response to multinational corporate capitalism and the computer technologies that facilitated it. The subgenre was immediately recognized as a quintessential literary reflection of the two "historic originalities" of late capitalism itself: "cybernetic technology" and "globalizing dynamics" (Jameson, *Archaeologies* 215). For Fredric Jameson, the primary conditions of postmodern life centered on issues of placelessness—more specifically, the postmodern subject's inability to locate, situate, and organize herself and her relations to others within the intricate webs of the new, highly networked world order. Anchorless, adrift, and disoriented, the First World postmodern subject is incapable of mapping her relative position inside multinational capitalism. For this reason, the postmodern subject needs a type of cartographic proficiency, an "aesthetic of cognitive mapping," which Jameson argues would "endow" it with a new "heightened sense of its place in the global system" (*Postmodernism* 54). Moreover, he cites cyberpunk as one possible aesthetic, going so far as to call it the "supreme *literary* expression, if not of postmodernism, then of late-capitalism itself" (*Postmodernism* 419n). While it is definitely worth noting that cyberpunk has also come under fire for privileging a white, masculinist, and imperialist cultural dominant, its predominant impulse was productive in questioning the ecological, economic, and existential implications of global multinational capitalism and its attendant information technologies.[10] As Tom Foster has argued, cyberpunk of the late-1980s and early 1990s affords a "distinct set of critical resources, an archive" that postmodern technoculture still very much requires (xviii).

In theorizing this marriage of borderlands literature and cyberpunk, it helps to turn to the critical work of Chicana feminist Chela Sandoval, who has convincingly argued for close affinities between the motifs of cyberpunk and the actual lived experiences of indigenous cultures of the Americas. Essentially revising Jameson's concept of postmodernism as a schizophrenic response to globalization and emergent information technologies, Sandoval argues that these apparently new First World anxieties over place and subjectivity actually find their prototypes in the experiences of colonized peoples. For Sandoval, the schizophrenic postmodern condition is not new; it is anchored in the history of "conquered and colonized Westerners" (33). The first-world subject, that is, inhabits a "psychic terrain" that is "historically-decentered": colonized subjects have learned to survive and negotiate for centuries (27). "Mere arms detached from intellect or political will," migrant laborers from the Bracero Program to the *maquiladora* phenomenon are little more than "tractable" bodies that, forced to migrate far from home, must constantly negotiate a sense of self and place in a rapidly changing urbanized society (Schmidt Camacho 63). Adapting to these neocolonial conditions, indigenous subjects have learned to develop what Sandoval refers to as "cyborg skills," oppositional and appropriative strategies that enable the colonized to contest, survive, and transform the experiences of cultural dislocation, labor exploitation, and diaspora (174-75). In the same way that Sandoval re-contextualizes the postmodern experience by locating it within the histories of Third World colonialism, so too do these borderlands sf texts embed the cognitive maps of cyberpunk within the lived experiences of millennial capitalism as they are endured by those most subject to its oppressive tendencies.

In retooling cyberpunk to write both within and against multinational capitalism and its ideological underpinnings, borderlands science fiction is a type of postcolonial literature that transforms dominant culture through appropriation. It exemplifies Nalo Hopkinson's definition of postcolonial sf as that which uses the "familiar memes of science fiction" to create "defended spaces where marginalized groups of people can discuss their own marginalization" (7-8). In similar fashion, these texts recast the dystopian cyberpunk gaze so that it focuses on the oppressive impacts of globalization from the perspective of indigenous communities along the borderlands. In doing this, they critically intervene in an sf sub-genre that has not always reflected the lived experiences of writers whose cultural histories have been intimately inscribed by the legacies of US imperialism and expansion. Borderlands sf practitioners such as Lavin, Rivera, and Sanchez and Pita demonstrate that cyberpunk need not be limited to serving as a mouthpiece for young white males with "biochips in their heads and chips on their shoulders" (Ross 138). As I have shown, these texts not only cast a critical light on the current and potential impacts of multinational capitalism, they also read these conditions as part of a history of indigenous exploitation, suggesting that what exists now and what looms ahead are to be viewed through the lens of deep colonial and racial memory. The persistence of the revolutionary past in Lavín's near-future Reynosa; the insistence on a "future with a past" in Rivera's *Sleep Dealer*; and, of course, the simultaneous reference to the history and potential future of US/Mexico labor practices in the terms "cybraceros" and "lunar braceros" attest equally to the ways in which borderlands science fiction embeds tales of futurity in deep-seated narratives of colonial history, labor exploitation, and racial violence, all of which continue to inform contemporary economic policy and labor practices within the region.

The presence and importance of historical recovery notwithstanding, these narratives invite their readers to speculate about the future as well. Borderlands sf writers refuse to foreclose on the possibility of change: the desire for new oppositional tactics that are simultaneously grounded in a revolutionary past—the desire, that is, for a "future with a past"—motivates these texts, which value cultural recovery but also underscore the vitality of speculation. In this way they mirror the cultural work of contemporary Afrofuturism, or African diasporic science fiction, which aims to "extend the tradition [of countermemory] by reorienting" readers "towards the proleptic as much as the retrospective" (Eshun 289).[11] For "power now operates predictively as much as retrospectively . . . through the envisioning, management, and delivery of reliable futures" (289). By participating directly in the construction and "management" of their future, borderlands sf writers not only articulate resistance to neoliberal forms of economic hegemony but also speak to the persistent validity of Darko Suvin's early observation that contemporary sf has "moved into the sphere of anthropological and cosmological thought, becoming a diagnosis, a warning, a call to understanding and action and—most important—a mapping of possible alternatives" (12). Such potent fusions are possible when the political punch of sf merges with the imperatives of borderlands fiction.

The works I have discussed function similarly to what Tom Moylan calls the "critical dystopia," a cousin of dystopia that rejects the latter's tendencies towards hopeless resignation by offering "a horizon of hope just beyond the page" (181). Moylan situates the emergence of critical dystopia in the "hard times of the 1980s and 1990s" when "betterment of humanity" was sacrificed to the "triumph of transnational capital and right-wing ideology" (184). Attuned to the difficulties of this time period, the critical dystopia articulated nightmare societies beleaguered by oppressive corporate-owned governments and harsh economic conditions, but it also exhibited a "scrappy utopian pessimism" with strong protagonists who endured the nightmare and sought altern-atives to it (147). Octavia Butler's PARABLE books (1993, 1998), for instance, imagine a post-apocalyptic Los Angeles decimated by a devastating war and rampant corporate greed, but it also sows seeds of hope, speculation, and optimism through the figure of Lauren Olamina, the strong black female protagonist whose dreams of space travel and an alternative social structure also inform the novel's vision of the future. In other words, the critical dystopia does not entirely abandon the future, even if that future appears bleak beyond imagining. The subgenre is apocalyptic, but it also imagines "alternative socio-political spaces that always already extrapolate from existing ones" and has the "formal potential to re-vision the world in ways that generate pleasurable, probing, and potentially subversive responses in its readers" (Moylan 43). As it pertains to border-lands science fiction, the critical dystopia is precisely the kind of "skeptically hopeful" work Subcomandante Marcos called for from post-NAFTA activists following the EZLN coup (Hayden 312).

This subversive potential of these borderlands narratives is visible in their open endings, which resist closure and invite a prolonged consideration of the shape of things to come. The futures of their imaginary societies depend entirely on the thoughts and actions of a new, younger generation of borderlands cultures, both Chicano/a and *fronterizo*. At the end of "Reaching the Shore," the young José Paul remains uncertain about whether he will succumb to his father's addiction to the Dreamer. "I really have to think it over," he says to himself at the story's conclusion, "I'll have to think it over" (234). The reader cannot help but hear Lavín himself demanding the same critical thinking of his post-NAFTA readers in 1994. In *Sleep Dealer,* one can reasonably assume that Memo and Luz—both intim-ately familiar with the cybernetic technologies that paradoxically oppress them—espouse (and perhaps eventually join) the anti-globalization EMLA, a not-so-subtle allusion to the Chiapas-based EZLN. Finally, the last entry in *Lunar Braceros* is written not by Lydia but by her eighteen-year-old son Pedro, for whom the entire narrative is in fact written. Pedro concludes the novel by announcing his readiness to join his parents' indigenous resist-ance movement, which, "inspired by the Zapatista Movement in Chiapas many years before" (85), represented a "rejection of everything that is hegemonic and dominated by capital relations" (25). Now a new member of the "Anarcho Maquis," Pedro voices the novel's oppositional discourse that, in the spirit of the critical dystopia, conveys a sense of cautious optimism tempered by historical awareness. As his mother puts it in one of her letters to him: "Its time for a new strategy . . . for something else . . . for a new version of the old urban guerrilla tactics" of the twenty-first century (116).

The past few years have witnessed an explosion of literary collections that have expanded the global sf archive by documenting decades of contributions by writers of color both within and beyond the so-called First World. Collections such as Nalo Hopkinson and Uppinder Mehan's *So Long Been Dreaming: Post-Colonial Science Fiction* (2004), Andrea Bell and Yolanda Molina-Gavilán's *Cosmos Latinos: An Anthology of Science Fiction from Latin America and Spain* (2004), and Sheree Thomas's two-volume anthology *Dark Matter* (2001, 2004) have drawn much deserved attention to the sf of Latin America and the African diaspora. In some cases, these collections invite new ways of reading texts not originally conceived of as speculative or science fiction, as evidenced by the inclusion of works by W.E.B. Du Bois, George Schuyler, and Amiri Baraka in *Dark Matter.* In other cases, they aim to spotlight a doubly underrepresented literary corpus—people of color *and* science fiction writers—to vocalize and legitimize culturally specific reactions to universal matters that are unique to sf, including not only technological innovation but also new forms of social relations that have emerged because of these innovations—including, in this case, troubling relations of power under the so-called New World Order. In an attempt to expand these new critical projects, I have examined the science fiction of the borderlands, which puts the defamiliarizing narrative strategies of the genre in the service of both revisiting colonial history and peering into the uncertain future of the US/Mexico border region. Writing about the future from the bottom up or from the margin to the center, is itself an act of agency and will, I believe, become increasingly more appealing to and visible within the broader Chicano/a literary community of the twenty-first century. After all, if the primary task of Chicano narrative is "to deflect, deform, and thus transform reality" by "opting for open over closed forms, for conflict over resolution and synthesis" (Saldívar 6), then it is clear why so many borderlands writers have been drawn to science fiction, a genre that renders the familiar strange and imagines alternatives to the political status quo.

Notes

1. For the purposes of this essay, the term "borderlands" refers specifically to the local communities and cultures, both rural and urban, that straddle, fuel, and shape the US/Mexico border. In this sense, I use the term somewhat capaciously to refer to both US citizens and Mexican nationals who, though linguistically, culturally, and racially heterogeneous, occupy the same physical, natural, and geopolitical space, a space unique to the most frequently crossed international border on the planet. To differentiate between Mexican nationals living on the border and Mexican-Americans in the US, I opt for the more eloquent *fronterizo* and Chicano/a, respectively. A "fronterizo" is a person who lives in the borderlands regions, including the southernmost regions of the US Southwest and the northern Mexican cities of Tijuana, Cuidad Juaréz, and Reynosa. Historically, the *fronterizo* regions were seen as extremely isolated communities, cut off from the densely populated urban centers of both Mexico and the United States.

2. One figure I have not included in this list is performer/writer Ricardo Dominguez, who has collaborated with filmmaker Alex Rivera, and who co-founded the Electronic Disturbance Theater,

a band of performance activists who use computer technologies to protest military dominance through non-violent acts of "cyber" activism.

3. Two important speculative borderlands novels—Leslie Marmon Silko's *Almanac of the Dead* (1991) and Alejandro Morales's *Rag Doll Plagues* (1992)—anticipate twenty-first century borderlands science fiction and, as such, warrant brief discussion. Although not pure science fiction (if there even is such a thing), both *Almanac* and *Plagues* combine history and speculation, narratives of the past and future, to rewrite the "alien invasion" of Mexico from the perspective of the colonized and to imagine oppositional tactics of resistance to neo-liberal economic hegemony (Silko 577). Spanning over 500 years of Anglo-European colonialism and indigenous resistance, both novels merge history with speculation; both articulate troubling connections between the colonial past, the neocolonial present, and the possible future awaiting both.

4. Lavín's depiction of Christmas Eve recalls the vignette "And All Through The House" in Tomás Rivera's classic borderlands novel, . . .*And the Earth Did Not Devour Him* (1971), which recounts a harrowing Christmas Eve story from the perspective of a poor migrant family for whom the sounds and sights of rampant consumerism bring nothing but dread, desire, and anxiety.

5. One also hears the whistle in the everyday life of Mazie, a young miner, in Tillie Olsen's *Yonnondio*, written in the 1930s but published in 1974, during *el movimiento*.

6. For an extremely insightful reading of the persistence of nationalisms in cyberpunk, a genre known for its transnational settings, see Foster's discussion of "franchise nationalisms" (203-28).

7. For an overview of Marxist ideological impulses in Latin American sf more generally, see Bell and Molina-Gavilán (13-15).

8. *Ejército Zapatista de Liberación Nacional*, EZLN [The Zapatista Army of National Liberation] is a revolutionary leftist group based in Chiapas, the southernmost state of Mexico. They are the non-violent voice of an anti-globalization movement that seeks to equalize and defend the human rights and land privileges of the indigenous populations of Mexico's interior.

9. Pita's and Sanchez's "NIO" recalls Guillermo Gómez-Peña's "Great Transition" in *Friendly Cannibals*, a 1997 cyberpunk novella that addresses, among other things, the disappearance of national borders after NAFTA.

10. For trenchant and convincing critiques of racial tension and anxiety in cyberpunk, see Ross (137-69) and Lowe (84-86).

11. As Catherine Ramirez has already pointed out, Chicanafuturism and Afrofuturism are indeed "fictive kin." This point is immediately brought to bear toward the end of *Lunar Braceros* during one of Lydia's many "history lessons." In it, she explains to Pedro the astronomical phenomenon known as "dark matter," energy that is "not directly visible," but knowable "because of its gravitational pull" (110). This reference is not insignificant or incidental: it is, I think, a very clear allusion to Sheree Thomas's *Dark Matter*, an anthology of African diasporic speculative fiction, published in 2000.

Works cited

Acosta, Oscar Zeta. *Autobiography of a Brown Buffalo*. 1971. New York: Vintage, 1989.
Anaya, Rudolfo. *Heart of Aztlán*. 1976. Albuquerque: U of New Mexico P, 1988.

Anzaldúa, Gloria. *Borderlands/La Frontera: The New Mestiza.* 1987. 3rd ed. San Francisco: Aunt Lute, 2007.

Bell, Andrea, and Yolanda Molina-Gavilán, eds. "Introduction." *Cosmos Latinos: An Anthology of Science Fiction from Latin America and Spain.* Middletown, CT: Wesleyan UP, 2003. 7-15.

Brennan, Timothy. "The Empire's New Clothes." *Critical Inquiry* 29.2 (2003): 337-67.

Chavoya, C. Ondine. "Customized Hybrids: The Art of Rubén Ortiz Torres and Lowriding in Southern California." *CR: The New Centennial Review* 4.2 (2004): 141-84.

Eshun, Kodwo. "Further Considerations on Afrofuturism." *CR: The New Centennial Review* 3.2 (2003): 287-302.

Foster, Thomas. *The Souls of Cyberfolk: Posthumanism as Vernacular Theory.* Minneapolis: U of Minnesota P, 2005.

Fox, Claire. *The Fence and the River: Cultural Politics at the U.S./Mexico Border.* Minneapolis: U of Minnesota P, 1999.

Freedman, Carl. *Critical Theory and Science Fiction.* Middletown, CT: Wesleyan, 2000.

Galarza, Ernesto. *Merchants of Labor: The Mexican Bracero Story, an Account of the Managed Migration of Mexican Farm Workers in California, 1942-1960.* New York: McNally and Loftin, 1972.

Gómez-Peña, Guillermo. *Dangerous Border Crossers: The Artist Talks Back.* New York: Routledge, 2000.

—. "Friendly Cannibals." San Francisco, CA: Artspace, 1997.

González, John Morán. "*Aztlán* @ Fifty: Chican@ Literary Studies for the Next Decade." *Aztlán.* 35.2 (2010): 173-76.

Haraway, Donna. "A Cyborg Manifesto: Science, Technology, and Socialist-Feminism in the Late Twentieth Century." 1985. *Simians, Cyborgs, and Women: The Reinvention of Nature.* New York: Routledge, 1991. 149-82.

—. "Cyborgs at Large: Interview with Donna Haraway." *Technoculture.* Eds. Constance Penley and Andrew Ross. Minneapolis: U of Minnesota P, 1991. 1-20.

Harvey, David. *A Brief History of Neoliberalism.* New York: Oxford, 2005.

Hayden, Tom, ed. *The Zapatista Reader.* New York: Thunder's Mouth/Nation, 2002.

Hicks, D. Emily. *Border Writing: The Multidimensional Text.* Minneapolis: U of Minnesota P, 1991.

Hogan, Ernest. *High Aztech.* New York: Tor, 1992.

Hopkinson, Nalo. "Introduction." *So Long Been Dreaming: Postcolonial Science Fiction and Fantasy.* Ed. Nalo Hopkinson and Uppinder Mehan. Vancouver: Arsenal, 2004.

Jameson, Fredric. *Archaeologies of the Future: The Desire Called Utopia and Other Science Fictions.* New York: Verso, 2005.

—. *Postmodernism, or the Cultural Logic of Late Capitalism.* Durham: Duke UP, 1990.

Klahn, Norma. "Literary (Re)Mappings." *Chicana Feminisms: A Critical Reader.* Ed. Gabriela F. Arredondo, Aída Hurtado, Norma Klahn, Olga Nájera-Ramírez, and Patricia Zavella. Durham, NC: Duke UP, 2003. 114-45.

Lavín, Guillermo. "Reaching the Shore." 1994. Trans. Rena Zuidema and Andrea Bell. *Cosmos Latinos: An Anthology of Science Fiction from Latin America and Spain.* Ed. Andrea Bell and Yolanda Molina-Gavílan. Middletown, CT: Wesleyan UP, 2003. 224-34.

Lowe, Lisa. *Immigrant Acts: On Asian American Cultural Politics.* Durham, NC: Duke UP, 1996.

McCrossen, Alexis. *Land of Necessity: Consumer Culture in the United States-Mexico Borderlands*. Durham, NC: Duke UP, 2009.

McKenna, Teresa. *Migrant Song: Politics and Process in Contemporary Chicano Literature*. Austin: U of Texas P, 1997.

Miyoshi, Masao. "A Borderless World? From Colonialism to Transnationalism and the Decline of the Nation-State." *Critical Inquiry* 19.4 (1993): 726-51.

Morales, Alejandro. *Rag Doll Plagues*. Houston, TX: Arté Publico, 1992.

Moylan, Tom. *Scraps of the Untainted Sky: Science Fiction, Utopia, Dystopia*. Boulder, CO: Westview, 2000.

Olsen, Tillie. *Yonnondio: From the Thirties*. Lincoln, NE: Bison, 1974.

Ortiz-Torres, Rubén. *Alien Toys*. Santa Monica: Smart Art, 1998.

Paredes, Américo. "The Hammon and the Beans." 1963. *Herencia: The Anthology of Hispanic Literature of the United States*. New York: Oxford UP, 2002. 172-76.

—. *With His Pistol in His Hands: A Border Ballad and Its Hero*. 1958. 11th ed. Austin: U of Texas P, 1998.

Ramirez, Catherine. "Afrofuturism/Chicanafuturism: Fictive Kin." *Aztlán: A Journal of Chicano Studies*. 30.1 (Spring 2008): 185-94.

Rivera, Tomás. . . .*And the Earth Did Not Devour Him*. 1971. Trans. Evangelina Vigil-Piñon. Monterey, CA: National Geographic/Hampton Brown, 2007.

Romero, Fernando. *Hyperborder: The Contemporary U.S./Mexico Border and Its Future*. New York: Princeton Architectural P, 2007.

Ross, Andrew. *Strange Weather: Culture, Science, and Technology in the Age of Limits*. London: Verso, 1991.

Saldívar, Ramon. *Chicano Narrative: Dialectics of Difference*. Madison: U of Wisconsin P, 1990.

Sanchez, Rosaura, and Beatrice Pita. *Lunar Braceros 2125-2148*. National City, CA: Calaca, 2009.

Sandoval, Chela. *Methodology of the Oppressed*. Minneapolis: U of Minnesota P, 2000.

Sawyer, Andy. "Future History." *The Routledge Companion to Science Fiction*. Ed. Mark Bould et al. New York: Routledge, 2009. 489-93.

Schmidt Camacho, Alicia. *Migrant Imaginaries: Latino Cultural Politics in the U.S.-Mexico Borderlands*. New York: New York UP, 2008.

Schocket, Eric. "Redefining American Proletarian Literature: Mexican Americans and the Challenge to the Tradition of Radical Dissent." *Journal of American and Comparative Culture* 24.1-2 (2001): 59-69.

Schwarz, Mauricio-José, and Don Webb. "La búsqueda de un espejo fiel." *Frontera de espejos rotos*. Ed. Mauricio-José Schwarz and Don Webb. Mexico City: Roca, 1994. i-iv.

Silko, Leslie Marmon. *Almanac of the Dead*. New York: Penguin, 1992.

Sleep Dealer. Dir. Alex Rivera. Likely Story/This Is That Productions, 2008.

Suvin, Darko. *Metamorphoses of Science Fiction: On the Poetics and History of a Literary Genre*. New Haven, CT: Yale UP, 1979.

Valdez, Luis. "Los Vendidos." 1967. *Luis Valdez Early Works: Actos, Bernabé and Pensamiento Serpentino*. Houston, TX: Arte Público, 1990. 40-52.

"Why Cybraceros? (a mock promotional film by Alex Rivera)." AltoArizona.com. 29 Apr. 2010. Online. 14 Aug. 2012.

Recommended further reading

Canavan, Gerry, and Kim Stanley Robinson, eds. *Green Planets: Ecology and Science Fiction*. Middletown, CT: Wesleyan UP, 2014.

A pathbreaking collection of essays that explores how SF deploys ecological theory and engages with environmental issues, including chapters on eco-catastrophes, green futures, and extraterrestrial ecologies.

Chude-Sokei, Louis. *The Sound of Culture: Diaspora and Black Technopoetics*. Middletown, CT: Wesleyan UP, 2016.

Examines the links among race, technology, and colonialism in popular literary and sonic cultures, especially figurations of Afro-Diasporic subjects and their relationship with machines.

Eshun, Kodwo. *More Brilliant Than the Sun: Adventures in Sonic Fiction*. London: Quartet, 1999.

A pioneering and creatively structured study of Afrofuturist theory and culture that probes the "possibility space" offered by SF and other popular forms for critiquing racialized histories and imagining alternative futures.

Foster, Thomas. *The Souls of Cyberfolk: Posthumanism as Vernacular Theory*. Minneapolis: U of Minnesota P, 2005.

Places race and ethnicity at the center of debates about posthumanism, in and outside the genre, showing how these debates have been unconsciously structured by racialized histories.

Kilgore, De Witt Douglas. *Astrofuturism: Science, Race, and Visions of Utopia in Space*. Philadelphia: U of Pennsylvania P, 2003.

Examines how race functions in the prognostication and promotion of space flight in both SF and popular science discourses; includes as a chapter a Pioneer Award–winning essay on the fiction of Vonda N. McIntyre.

Langer, Jessica. *Postcolonialism and Science Fiction*. New York: Palgrave Macmillan, 2011.

Explores the dialectic linking postcolonial theory and SF, exposing the imperialist fantasies that undergird much popular work while also showing how the genre enables articulations of decolonized futures.

Leonard, Elizabeth Anne, ed. *Into Darkness Peering: Race and Color in the Fantastic*. Westport, CT: Greenwood, 1997.

One of the earliest studies of race in fantastic literature and film, including SF; offers insightful chapters on the erasure of race in cyberpunk writing and on the "Africanist presence" in Ray Bradbury's and Philip K. Dick's fiction.

Otto, Eric C. *Green Speculations: Science Fiction and Transformative Environmentalism*. Columbus: Ohio State UP, 2012.

A study of "environmental SF" that shows how the genre has both powerfully warned against imminent ecological catastrophe while also offering transformative visions of sustainable futures.

Rieder, John. *Colonialism and the Emergence of Science Fiction*. Middletown, CT: Wesleyan UP, 2008.

Argues that the history of colonialism conditioned the emergence and consolidation of SF, including a number of the genre's classic themes, such as the imaginary voyage and encounters with "aliens," while at the same time making possible a critical popular discourse interrogating the myths of imperialism.

Roh, David S., Betsy Huang, and Greta A. Niu, eds. *Techno-Orientalism: Imagining Asia in Speculative Fiction, History and Media*. Rutgers, NJ: Rutgers UP, 2015.

A collection of essays (expanded from a 2008 special issue of the journal *MELUS*) that explores the ways in which Asians and Asian Americans have been depicted in SF and other popular technological discourses as, variously, mysterious, dangerous, robotic, and empowered.

List of contributors

Marc Angenot was senior editor of *Science Fiction Studies* from 1979–81. He has taught French literature and literary theory for many years at McGill University in Montreal, where he holds the James McGill Chair of Social Discourse. He is author of numerous books on philosophy, social theory, and utopian literature.

J. G. Ballard was one of the most important British authors of science fiction of the postwar period. His early work was associated with the New Wave movement, which sought to bring the genre into conversation with cutting-edge trends in contemporary art and modern literature. His major novels include *The Crystal World* (1966), *The Atrocity Exhibition* (1970), *Crash* (1973), and *Empire of the Sun* (1984). His nonfiction was gathered in *A User's Guide to the Millennium: Essays and Reviews* (1996).

Damien Broderick is a major Australian science fiction author, literary critic, and popular science writer. His SF novels include *The Dreaming Dragons* (1980) and *The Judas Mandala* (1982), and his fiction has won numerous major Australian Awards, including the Aurealis and the Ditmar. His critical study *Reading by Starlight: Postmodern Science Fiction* (1995) examines the relationship between the genre and contemporary experimental literature.

Istvan Csicsery-Ronay, Jr., a professor of English at DePauw University, has been a senior editor of *Science Fiction Studies* since 1992. He has written important essays on the work of Stanislaw Lem, Arkady and Boris Strugatsky, and the cyberpunk writers. His 2008 critical study *The Seven Beauties of Science Fiction* offers an important literary anatomy of the genre in terms of major aesthetic categories and modes.

Allison de Fren teaches in the Department of Art, History, and Visual Arts at Occidental College in Los Angeles. She has made numerous short films exploring links between contemporary technoculture and gender norms and values. Her 2009 essay on Villiers de l'Isle-Adam's *Tomorrow's Eve* won the Pioneer Award from the Science Fiction Research Association for best critical article of the year.

Samuel R. Delany is a celebrated American author of science fiction and fantasy literature, as well as an important literary theorist and cultural historian. Over the course of a five-decade career, he has won four Nebula and two Hugo Awards for such novels and stories as *The Einstein Intersection* (1967) and "Time Considered as a Helix of Semi-Precious Stones" (1969). His collections of essays include *The Jewel-Hinged Jaw*

(1977) and *Starboard Wine* (1988). In 1985, he received the Science Fiction Research Association's Pilgrim Award for lifetime contributions to SF scholarship.

Philip K. Dick was a major American science fiction writer whose most notable work chronicled the relationship between humans and artificial beings. His 1968 novel *Do Androids Dream of Electric Sheep?* was memorably filmed as *Blade Runner* (1982) by director Ridley Scott. Dick's essays and other nonfiction have been gathered in *The Shifting Realities of Philip K. Dick: Selected Literary and Philosophical Writings* (1996), edited by Lawrence Sutin.

Grace Dillon is a Professor of Indigenous Native Studies at Portland State University. She is the editor of *Walking the Clouds: An Anthology of Indigenous Science Fiction* (2012), the first collection of speculative writing by Native Americans. She has published widely in such journals as *Science Fiction Studies*, *Extrapolation*, *The Journal of Science Fiction Film and Television*, and *The Journal of the Fantastic in the Arts*.

Kodwo Eshun teaches in the Department of Visual Cultures at Goldsmiths College, University of London. He is a theorist of the cultures of the African Diaspora, including popular forms such as music and science fiction. His 1998 book *More Brilliant Than the Sun: Adventures in Sonic Fiction* offers a penetrating historical and aesthetic exploration of Afrofuturist art and culture.

Carl Freedman is the Russell B. Long Professor of English at Louisiana State University. His books on science fiction include *Critical Theory and Science Fiction* (2000) and *Art and Idea in the Novels of China Miéville* (2015), and he has edited collections of interviews with SF authors Isaac Asimov, Samuel R. Delany, and Ursula K. Le Guin. His essay on Stanley Kubrick's *2001: A Space Odyssey* won the 1999 Pioneer Award from the Science Fiction Research Association for best critical article of the year.

Hugo Gernsback was a major editor of science fiction pulp magazines, beginning with *Amazing Stories*, the first SF pulp, in 1926. He went on to edit *Wonder Stories* in the 1930s and *Science Fiction Plus* in the 1950s. He also wrote the SF novel *Ralph 124C 41+* (1911), which predicted a high-tech future dominated by transcontinental travel, television, video phones, and solar energy.

Donna Haraway is professor emerita in the History of Consciousness Program at the University of California, Santa Cruz. She is a theorist of feminist science studies and science fiction whose books include *Primate Visions: Gender, Race, and Nature in the World of Modern Science* (1989), *Simians, Cyborgs, and Women: The Reinvention of Nature* (1991), and *The Companion Species Manifesto: Dogs, People, and Significant Otherness* (2003). In 2011, she received the Science Fiction Research Association's Pilgrim Award for lifetime contributions to SF scholarship.

N. Katherine Hayles is a professor of literature at Duke University who writes on theories of science, electronic literacy, and science fiction. She is the author of *Chaos Bound: Orderly*

Disorder in Contemporary Literature and Science (1990), *How We Became Posthuman: Virtual Bodies in Cybernetics, Literature, and Informatics* (1999), and *How We Think: Digital Media and Contemporary Technogenesis* (2012). She received the Pilgrim Award for lifetime contributions to SF scholarship from the Science Fiction Research Association in 2013.

Robert A. Heinlein was one of the most celebrated science fiction authors of the twentieth century. He received the Hugo Award for best novel five times for works such as *Starship Troopers* (1959), *Stranger in a Strange Land* (1961), and *The Moon Is a Harsh Mistress* (1966). He was selected as an SF "Grand Master" by the Science Fiction Writers of America in 1974, and was posthumously inducted into the Science Fiction Hall of Fame in 1998.

Veronica Hollinger is professor emerita in the Cultural Studies Program at Trent University in Ontario. Her critical work focuses on science fiction in relation to feminist and postmodernist cultural theory. Since 1992, she has been a senior editor of *Science Fiction Studies* and has also coedited a series of anthologies, including *Edging into the Future: Science Fiction and Contemporary Cultural Transformation* (2002), *Queer Universes: Sexualities in Science Fiction* (2008), and *Parabolas of Science Fiction* (2013).

Nalo Hopkinson is a major Afro-Caribbean SF and fantasy author whose works include the novels *Brown Girl in the Ring* (1998), *Midnight Robber* (2000), and *Sister Mine* (2013), as well as the story collections *Skin Folk* (2001) and *Falling in Love with Hominids* (2015). She has edited several anthologies, including *Whispers from the Cotton Tree Root: Caribbean Fabulist Fiction* (2000). She teaches creative writing at the University of California, Riverside.

Fredric Jameson is Knut Schmidt-Nielsen Professor of Comparative Literature and Romance Studies and the director of the Center for Critical Theory at Duke University. His many critical works include studies of science fiction and utopian literature such as *The Seeds of Time* (1994) and *Archaeologies of the Future: The Desire Called Utopia and Other Science Fictions* (2005). He has received lifetime achievement awards for scholarship from the Science Fiction Research Association and the Modern Language Association.

Gwyneth Jones is a British author of feminist science fiction whose celebrated novels include *White Queen* (1991), *Bold as Love* (2001), and *Life* (2004). She has won numerous awards for her fiction, including the Arthur C. Clarke Award and the Philip K. Dick Award. Her critical writings on the genre have been gathered into the collections *Deconstructing the Starships: Science, Fiction, and Reality* (1999) and *Imagination/Space* (2009).

Rob Latham's critical work focuses on the intersections between science fiction and popular technoculture. For many years a senior editor of *Science Fiction Studies*, he is the author of *Consuming Youth: Vampires, Cyborgs, and the Culture of Consumption* (2002) and editor of *The Oxford Handbook of Science Fiction* (2014). In 2013, he received the Thomas. D. Clareson Award for Distinguished Service to the field from the Science Fiction Research Association.

Roger Luckhurst is professor of modern and contemporary literature in the English and Humanities Department of Birkbeck College, University of London. He is author of numerous books on science fiction, including a cultural history of the genre, *Science Fiction* (2005), as well as critical studies of zombies and mummies as cultural icons. His essay included in this volume won the Pioneer Award from the Science Fiction Research Association for best critical article of the year in 1995.

Judith Merril was a major science fiction author and editor. During the 1950s and 1960s, she edited the anthology *The Year's Best SF*, which included important annual summations of trends in the field. During the 1960s, she emerged as a significant proponent of the genre's "New Wave." Her scattered criticism of SF was gathered into *The Merril Theory of Lit'ry Criticism*, a 2016 volume edited by Ritch Calvin.

John B. Michel was one of the founding members of the science fiction fan group The Futurians in the early 1940s. A left-leaning association, the Futurians pushed the genre to mobilize its literary and cultural resources for social-utopian goals. Michel himself was a member of the Young Communist League and also of the Communist Party.

Wendy Pearson teaches in the Department of Women's Studies and Feminist Research at the University of Western Ontario. Her areas of scholarly concentration include science fiction, film studies, and queer theory, and she coedited the anthology *Queer Universes: Sexuality in Science Fiction* (2008). Her essay included in this volume won the Pioneer Award from the Science Fiction Research Association for best critical article of the year in 2000.

John Rieder is professor of English at the University of Hawai'i at Manoa. A senior editor of *Extrapolation* and a consulting editor of *Science Fiction Studies*, he is author of the pathbreaking study, *Colonialism and the Emergence of Science Fiction* (2008). His essay included in this volume won the Pioneer Award from the Science Fiction Research Association for best critical article of the year in 2011.

Lysa Rivera is associate professor of English at Western Washington University, where she teaches in the areas of Chicano/a and African American literature and culture. Her work has appeared in a wide range of journals, including *MELUS: Journal for the Study of Multiethnic Literature*, *Aztlán: Journal of Chicano Studies*, and *Science Fiction Studies*. Her essay included in this volume won the Pioneer Award from the Science Fiction Research Association for best critical article of the year in 2013.

Joanna Russ was a major science fiction author and critic, one of the founders of an overtly feminist SF. Her novels include *The Female Man* (1975) and *We Who Are About to . . .* (1977), and she won both the Nebula and the Hugo Awards for her short fiction. Her collected essays and reviews were published in 2007 as *The Country You Have Never Seen*. In 1988, she received the Science Fiction Research Association's Pilgrim Award for lifetime contributions to SF scholarship.

Mary Shelley, often cited as the founder of science fiction for her 1818 novel *Frankenstein*, was a major Gothic novelist, whose other science-fictional works include *The Last Man* (1826), a postapocalyptic fantasy. She was posthumously inducted into the Science Fiction Hall of Fame in 2004.

Stephen Hong Sohn is associate professor of English at the University of California, Riverside, where he specializes in Asian American literary and cultural studies. He is the author of *Racial Asymmetries* (2014) and editor of *Transnational Asian American Literature: Sites and Transits* (2006). In 2008, he coedited a special issue of *MELUS: Journal for the Study of Multiethnic Literature* on the theme of "Alien/Asian."

Susan Sontag was one of the most important cultural commentators of the twentieth century. Her collections of essays include *Against Interpretation* (1966) and *On Photography* (1977), which won the National Book Critics Circle Award. Her critical study *Illness as Metaphor* (1978) explored the implications of the cultural representation of disease.

Bruce Sterling is a science fiction writer and editor and a noted futurist. His novels include *Islands in the Net* (1988), which won the John W. Campbell Memorial Award, and *Distraction* (1999), which won the Arthur C. Clarke Award. During the 1980s, Sterling emerged as the major proponent of cyberpunk SF, editing the agenda-setting anthology *Mirrorshades* (1986).

Darko Suvin was, along with Richard D. Mullen, a founding editor of *Science Fiction Studies*. He is author of *Metamorphoses of Science Fiction: On the Poetics and History of a Literary Genre* (1979), *Victorian Science Fiction in the UK: The Discourses of Knowledge and of Power* (1983), and *Positions and Presuppositions in Science Fiction* (1988). In 1979, he received the Science Fiction Research Association's Pilgrim Award for lifetime contributions to SF scholarship.

Vernor Vinge, professor emeritus of mathematics at San Diego State University, is a major science fiction author and scientific theorist. He has won the Hugo Award for best novel three times, for *A Fire Upon the Deep* (1992), *A Deepness in the Sky* (1999), and *Rainbow's End* (2006). His scientific work centers on theorizations of Artificial Intelligence and its cultural import.

Sherryl Vint is professor of English at the University of California, Riverside, where she directs the Science Fiction and Technoculture Studies Program. A senior editor of *Science Fiction Studies*, she is author of *Bodies of Tomorrow: Technology, Subjectivity, Science Fiction* (2007), *Animal Alterity: Science Fiction and the Question of the Animal* (2010), and *Science Fiction: A Guide for the Perplexed* (2014). Her 2007 essay on Philip K. Dick's *Do Androids Dream of Electric Sheep?* won the Pioneer Award from the Science Fiction Research Association for best critical article of the year.

H. G. Wells was probably the most important British author of science fiction of all time. His many "scientific romances"—including *The Time Machine* (1895), *The Island of*

Dr. Moreau (1896), and *The War of the Worlds* (1898)—have been hugely influential in the field. A prolific author and activist, Wells was a founding member of PEN (Poets, Essayists, Novelists) International and served as the organization's president from 1932–35.

David Wittenberg is professor of English and Cinematic Arts at the University of Iowa, where he teaches literary theory, twentieth- and twenty-first-century literature, and science fiction. His 2013 book *Time Travel: The Popular Philosophy of Narrative* received the Science Fiction and Technoculture Studies prize for best scholarly monograph exploring links between technoscience and popular culture.

Lisa Yaszek is professor of literature, media, and communication at Georgia Tech University. A past president of the Science Fiction Research Association, she is the author of *Galactic Suburbia: Recovering Women's Science Fiction* (2008) and coeditor of *Sisters of Tomorrow: The First Women of Science Fiction* (2016). Her essay included in this volume won the Pioneer Award from the Science Fiction Research Association for best critical article of the year in 2005.

Index

NOTE: Page numbers in *italics* refer to pictures/photographs.